HISTORY OF
INTERIOR
ARCHITECTURE

HISTORY OF
INTERIOR
ARCHITECTURE

FURNITURE, DESIGN, AND GLOBAL CULTURE
SECOND EDITION

MARK HINCHMAN
University of Nebraska, Lincoln

FAIRCHILD BOOKS
NEW YORK • LONDON • OXFORD • NEW DELHI • SYDNEY

FAIRCHILD BOOKS
Bloomsbury Publishing Inc
1385 Broadway, New York, NY 10018, USA
50 Bedford Square, London, WC1B 3DP, UK
29 Earlsfort Terrace, Dublin 2, Ireland

BLOOMSBURY, FAIRCHILD BOOKS and the Fairchild Books logo are trademarks
of Bloomsbury Publishing Plc

First edition published 2009
This edition published 2024

Cover design by Louise Dugdale
Cover image: (front cover) Mediacolors/Construction Photography/Avalon/Getty Images); (back cover)
© Hugh Rooney/Alamy Stock Photo

A catalog record for this book is available from the Library of Congress.

ISBN: PB: 978-1-5013-8560-5

Typeset by Integra Software Services Pvt. Ltd.
Printed and bound in India

To find out more about our authors and books visit www.bloomsbury.com/fairchildbooks
and sign up for our newsletter.

Contents

Extended Table of Contents

Preface

A road makes for a powerful visual metaphor, beloved by artists, writers, and commencement speakers. The journey down a road centers on a perambulating individual, following a path, and with a corresponding progression of time and place. It might seem odd to start a book on interior architecture, design, and designed objects with a discussion of a road that runs parallel to a river, although a road, too, is a designed object in a social, political, economic, and cultural context.

A river is nature's pathway, cutting through the landscape in the journey from Point A to Point B, and rivers existed long before humans created their roadways. A consistent quality of rivers is that they rarely run a straight course. For precisely that reason, a meandering river can be a metaphor for the history of design that played out over millennia. Rivers run fast, they run dry, they overflow their banks; there are rapids, waterfalls, eddies, shallows, and depths; then there are sharp bends, loopy curves, and gentle changes in direction. Life follows a similar course. Consider the river as the billions of people over time and everything they have done, experienced, and produced. From the stone ages to the twenty-first century (the time period covered by this book), humanity has run a path, sometimes focused, more often disorganized, with exceptions and setbacks, revolutions, evolutions, and stability, the only constant being the relentless march of time forward.

Works diverse as *The Epic of Gilgamesh* (1200 BCE), Miguel de Cervantes' *Don Quixote* (1605), and Stephen Sondheim's *Into the Woods* (1987) explore characters moving along a path as a parable for the enlightenment that comes from a journey. A literal or literary path can be a metaphor for history, the collective journey that humanity has taken through time. It is an apt comparison for the journey through life, through college, or any educational or intellectual endeavor. It also serves as metaphor of what a reader encounters when embarking on the journey of reading this book, over the course of a semester or two.

Chronology

History of Interior Architecture employs the standard chronological sequence of many history books in the modern Western world, yet tweaks it to include artworks from across the globe, in all chapters.

Chapter 1 starts with caves and the Paleolithic and Neolithic periods. Chapters 2 and 3 present Egypt and Mesopotamia, then Greece and Rome, only from a global perspective, with attention to Nubia and Greek and Roman activities in North Africa and the Middle East. Time marches onward in Chapters, 4, 5, and 6, from Early Christian and Byzantine, to Romanesque and Islamic, and Gothic. Romanesque and Islamic are considered as two sides of a coin, with the Crusades, the religious expeditions of the twelfth and thirteenth centuries, as the mechanism by which Europe incorporated Islamic forms and the Islamic world incorporated European forms. Chapter 5 is therefore a look around the world in the year 1100.

Chapters 7, 8, and 9 are a look around the world in the year 1500. Chapter 7 examines some of the pre-Columbian American traditions. The year 1500 is significant because it falls within the period of the Spanish Conquest, when the American indigenous groups were violently incorporated into the Spanish colonial project. The circumstances for the year 1500 are happier in China, covered in Chapter 8. During the Ming dynasty, the development of classic hardwood furniture was at its height. In Europe, Italy was reinventing itself with the help of Renaissance artists, architects, and designers (Chapter 9).

Chapters 9, 10, and 11 present the logical sequence of Renaissance, baroque, and rococo, three periods in which artists were reacting to the artistic traditions they inherited. These periods are best understood when studied in succession.

Chapter 12 covers the same time period as the previous chapters, only it examines the artistic production of the British Isles. Chapter 13 looks at the phenomenon of colonialism around the world, including English colonialism, and therefore the United States.

One of the ways that design histories differ from art and architectural histories is that the time period from the eighteenth century to the present is more relevant, and therefore requires more scholarly attention. "Relevant" here means that unlike architecture and art, eighteenth- and nineteenth-century furniture types are still in production and still being specified. Antiques from those periods are not all in museums, but in people's homes and sold in auction houses. Chapters 14 through 20 address the nineteenth century and its various design permutations, starting with neoclassicism and ending with the movements that foreshadowed modernism.

Chapter 21 tackles twentieth-century modernism—not modernism as defined by the field of architectural history but as it relates to interior architecture and design. Chapters 22, 23, and 24 constitute a look around the world in the twentieth century. The principal difference between the first and second editions of this book is the increased attention to the twentieth and twenty-first centuries. They are covered in Chapters 21 through 27.

Regarding dates, the standard scenario is that the years of a person's life follow their name, for example, Émile-Jacques Ruhlmann (1879–1933). There are a few variations on the schema: Bernard Tschumi (b. 1944) gives the date of birth for a living person alive at the time of publication; George Hepplewhite (d. 1786) gives the year of death for a person whose birth year is unknown; Ahuitzotl (r. 1486–1503) gives the years of a ruler's reign. Many cultures only recorded their rulers' reigning years.

The focus on the twentieth and twenty-first centuries allows for attention to topics that are important to the field of interior design. Chapter 22 handles with greater detail the importance of decorators to the interior design profession. The number of designers covered in all the chapters has been increased from the first edition. Chapter 24 is a new chapter that addresses the phenomenon of the commercial interior. The reconceptualized Chapter 25 now increases the number of designers in two decades, the 1960s and 1970s, that are significant for design, and that deserve greater attention than being lumped into a general period that followed modernism. Chapter 26 tackles the thorny issue of postmodernism, in which interior architecture, decoration,

and designed objects were all important. Chapter 27 takes us up to date with what followed, chronologically and conceptually, with its look at deconstruction.

Objects of Scrutiny

On this journey down the path called history, what do we pick up and marvel at, and what do we leave lying in the gravel, buried in the sandbank, unexamined? This book mostly covers what previously was known as the history of interiors and decorative arts, fleshed-out with pertinent examples of art and architecture. To ensure that design is considered writ large, there are a few examples of urban design, landscape design, stage design, film sets, graphics, and fashion.

Histories of art and architecture are valuable references. In significant ways, the historians who worked in those arenas set the parameters for how furniture should be covered (Renaissance is followed by baroque, and so forth). For a long time, those who wrote about the objects that constitute the decorative arts—dishes, vases, candelabra, miniature portraits, salt-and-pepper shakers, beer steins, howdahs, hookahs, spittoons, braziers, commodes, mirrors, brooches, and cigarette cases—grudgingly accepted their second-class status behind their upscale cousins, art and architectural historians.

After the epoch of the *ancien régime* (eighteenth-century France), historians of design typically see their field as related to minimal state intervention, a move from seeing objects as instruments of state power to instruments of empowerment or even resistance. These new approaches often result in high-minded discussions rooted in everyday mundane objects. The objects one is surrounded by, and the personal articulation of interior space, can relate to concepts, constructions, or identity. And the construction of identity can be construed as a member of an ethnic group, a gender, a nation, a family, or an individual. This led to the conclusion that personal choice, regarding the material world, can become a site of protest. Design, rather than being the instrument of political power, as it was in the reign of Louis XIV, could become a field that mediates between politics and citizen. Design could support or resist the status quo and become the avant-garde. Looking at any American teenager's bedroom makes clear that personal design choice can be a sign of allegiance and a site of resistance.

The relevance of historical study to studio education remains open for debate. In periods directly concerned about history, including neoclassicism, nineteenth-century revivals, and more recently, postmodernism, the value of history to contemporary design was obvious. This was often accompanied by a renewed appreciation of hand-drawing and rendering techniques. In artistic movements related to modernism, the importance of history was less clear because the individuals involved sought to deny history's importance.

The institutional base for the design professions started in the eighteenth century with the importance of guilds, and the development of professional organizations and educational programs in the nineteenth century.

Recognition of the importance of designed objects, foremost furniture, started to change in the second half of the nineteenth century, when a trio of movements corralled the efforts of some well-meaning object crusaders. This group argued that the objects of daily life were worthy of design attention, and therefore also scholarly attention. Members of this group became active in the artistic movement Arts and Crafts, and also art nouveau, and the Vienna Secession (Chapters 16, 19, and 20).

Come the 1910s and 1920s, Bauhaus designers in Germany took on the task of rehabilitating the status of the common object; for them it was a call to arms, absolutely central to their design activities.

Along the way, Africans, Asians, and Native Americans joined the fracas, stating that the division between fine art and craftwork had never done justice to the objects they produced, and they were therefore all too happy to toss a limiting concept of "fine art" aside.

In the mid-twentieth century, Raymond Loewy was one of the innovators of the field now known as industrial design. He expanded the repertoire of what could be considered a designed object to include cigarette packages, buses, and rockets. He had little use for the category of the decorative arts and instead promoted a paradigm shift. Industrial design was a better category, to Loewy's mind, as it took the non-elitist approach, which began with Arts and Crafts, and gave it an American commercial application. Loewy's definition of designed objects included those made by people involved in traditional craftsmanship—artisans, potters, and basketmakers. But he was mostly concerned with commercial products produced by industrial processes.

Generalizing about how design history is taught, the emphasis is now on context. The practice of examining history with the framework of period styles has been largely (although not completely) abandoned by art history. There has been a general move away from object analysis and individual designers' biographies to an examination of social context. This is sometimes discussed as a thematic approach, to a method that looks at subjects and issues beyond style. In this work that entails, for example, the shift to a focus on the consumer, the importance of advertising, and the phenomenon of designing for the workplace (Chapter 24).

The 1960s saw a shift in the political realm that can be called the politics of inclusion, including the women's rights movement, the civil rights movement, and de-colonization. Under gender came women's studies, and an examination of the intersection of space and sexuality. More recently the plurality of gender is being explored. The design world quickly responded to these changes and this has resulted in a shift in how the history of design is taught (Chapter 25). How the history of design continues to engage with recent topics remains a lively work in progress.

Marcel Duchamp ran with the spirit of the 1960s, and provided a way for the design directions that were to follow. In his inimitable way, he created (or found) a class of objects that he termed ready-made art. He attached a bicycle wheel to a stool, called it a sculpture, and people have been scratching their heads ever since.

Recently, the academic side of interior architecture became a bridge between disciplines. Most historians of architectural interiors see their field as related to art and architectural history, and the decorative arts. The infusion of the field with interdisciplinary spirit has brought new perspectives to design historians. These come from material culture, crafts, archaeology, anthropology, and others. This opening allowed for new approaches, including feminist analysis and queer theory.

This ever-increasing list of what can be considered a designed object might lead one to think that anything is worthy of inclusion here, such as landscapes and the human body. Not so (for the most part). What is consistent is a steady focus on design. Pencils and toothbrushes are wonderful examples of designed objects whose utility has stood the test of time, but they have no place here. Cars are designed objects with a clear aesthetic bent. But that is a history better left for another place. Almost any object in the right context can pique the interest of archaeologists and anthropologists, but we focus here on the items that have made a contribution to the history of interior architecture, elite or modest, intentional or accidental.

The core of the book is formed around significant examples of interiors and the objects they contained. The legacy of the decorative arts is obvious, as there are lots of pieces of furniture. When examples from other arts, such as painting, fashion, or graphics, are used, it is usually to make a specific point that is particularly clear in that medium. In the rococo period, the topic of verisimilitude is addressed by looking at portraits, artworks that directly engage the issue of resemblance.

The book's title is *History of Interior Architecture: Furniture, Design, and Global Culture*. Global is meant in several ways: One is the sense of a worldwide look. The other regards context; this book considers examples of interior architecture as objects operating within a socio-cultural context. Thus, each chapter starts with an examination of architectural and design context, looking at the domestic sphere when possible. Furniture and interiors are considered in terms of their political, economic, historic, cultural, social, and personal meanings.

Global also refers to the various types of representation that convey information about interior architecture and designed objects. I have made an explicit attempt to include multiple representational techniques, from drawings to photographs to paintings to models, etc.

Regarding furniture, making the selections for furniture is not a simple process. This book mostly focuses on pieces made from wood and metal, but there were also pieces that could be called furniture that were made from bamboo and ceramics. The category of furniture might seem clear, but actually, categorization poses challenges. When crossing cultural lines, it is not always clear what is furniture and what is not. The boundaries vary, according to the purposes of the discussion. In cultures where tall chairs had a limited or non-existent role, should we instead look at mats and cushions? Isn't the topic, then, how people sit, so shouldn't we look at ways of sitting, even if they do not involve objects? Some of the chapters address these questions.

This book attempts to be fair to all cultures, yet also fit the need of its readers, and be reasonable when it comes to periods, cultures, and styles.

Minoan design is fascinating, but most designers do not need an encyclopedic knowledge of its details and major works—excepting possibly some stage designers. Reference books typically have a structure, and readers and students come to rely upon that structure. Yet in a cross-cultural endeavor such as this one, readers should expect that with every chapter, the rules change. Sometimes we know the names of artists, sometimes we do not. Sometimes we look at paintings to reinforce ideas that were also being explored in interiors, but not always. Sometimes precise dating is possible; sometimes the best we can do is guess at a century. This book has a major interest in furniture, yet when that is not a viable topic, the design field is explored through other art forms. The forms to be examined are also dictated by what is available.

With the objects selected here, I have a specific and explicit goal: to include the contributions of women, and of those across the globe who have been overlooked too often in histories such as this one. The exploration of non-Western design is achieved in two ways. There are entire chapters devoted to non-Western design on China, Africa, and pre-Columbian America. Chapters that cover material typically presented from a myopic Western perspective, Art Nouveau, Art Deco, and modernism, are here presented with examples from all continents. And whenever possible, I include the contributions of women, as designers, patrons, or the subject of artworks. I am telling the "master narrative" of design on the one hand; Egypt, Greece, and Rome are all here, yet I am also trying to overturn it by including those who have been ill served by standard histories.

Since the publication of the First Edition in 2009, interior design history has made great strides as an academic profession. To mention three examples of recent excellent scholarship: Fredie Floré and Cammie McAtee's *The Politics of Furniture* (2017); Andrea Wolk Roger's *The Radical Vision of Edward Burne-Jones* (2022); and Sarah Teasley's *Designing Modern Japan* (2022). Despite these stellar achievements, much remains to be done. Scholars have made gratifying progress on the design achievements in Asia and Latin America, but little progress has been made for serious books about design history in Africa. Major figures, such as Eleanor LeMaire and Barbara D'Arcy White, remain understudied.

There is no attempt to judge one time period or group as more advanced or artistically gifted than another. Chinese furniture, Chicago skyscrapers, Cambodian sculptures, Italian paintings, and African masks are all superior achievements. For certain times and places, the circumstances do not arise that allow for certain arts to flower: nomadic groups have little need or desire to create monumental architecture. Hence the Tuaregs of Mali employ their design skills crafting small and exquisite tea services, locks, and leather cushions.

One of the oddities of writing a book like this is that, while seeking to be comprehensive, it has to ignore and leave out many wonderful examples. It must be selective. Most of the examples are representative selections of major trends. But, to return to the road and river metaphor, there are also occasional side-trips, detours from the Autobahn, moments to linger along the riverbank and see what has washed ashore; that is, I've included judiciously selected examples of minor trends.

Styles

One of the ways historians attempt to tell the story of large swaths of history, thousands of years, is by noticing formal similarities between groups of artifacts, say paintings in Italy in the period 1400–1600, and calling them "Renaissance." Then they articulate the formal qualities those objects seem to share, the humanism, the idealization, and the shared inspiration of ancient Rome. So far so good.

Just when it seems that the problem of classification has been solved, two other problems take its place. Problem one: the historian, the art dealer, or the teacher is then in the position of defining what the era 1400–1600 in Italy was, effectively giving the requirements for membership in the club "Renaissance art." What then to do with oddballs such as Giordano Bruno, or other artistically active people active in the time period under discussion, who clearly don't fit the mold?

Problem two: the stylistic approach encourages the scholar to write about the era as though it were a person, to treat a time period as a biographical entity—as in "the rococo did such and such." Art historian of the eighteenth century, Matthew Craske, is vexed by the method of investing a style with an autobiographical identity, and then subjecting that creation to a "character assassination" (Craske 1997, p. 8). The criticism of this approach arises from those who logically point out that of course there was no

such thing as "the Ming period." Individual artists and artisans were working away, responding to their clients' needs, relying upon their training, responding to the tastes and mores of the time, and trying to make a living while producing the best works they could. No structure called "the Ming" dictated their every move.

Yet for certain periods, this lapse into personification is understandable and sometimes unavoidable. For the Gothic period, for example, little information exists on the thoughts of individuals involved; often we do not even know their names. Hence the tendency to write about "the Gothic" as a collective endeavor.

The concept of style is problematic for historians, and I do not pretend to put the issue to rest. In fact, the task of art and design historians is to endlessly debate questions such as the role of style and the importance of the individual in history. All I can do is articulate the pragmatic stance of this book, which freely employs stylistic nomenclature for the structure of chapters. There are admirable books that take pains to discuss eighteenth-century France without using the words rococo and neoclassical but this seems, to me, to cause as many problems as it solves. To study furniture without using stylistic monikers such as Louis XIV, Louis XV, and Louis XVI seems pointless, particularly when that is how many of those designed objects are known. Therefore, many major movements are discussed within the context of style and their major historical monuments; for example, it would seem ludicrous to discuss Hagia Sophia without making reference to Byzantine art. But I also want seek to give a sampling of the rich variety of things that defy categories.

Utilizing the vocabulary of styles need not lead to oversimplification. A healthy approach is to seek to understand how various communities use design vocabulary. These communities include designers, historians, people in sales, and the general public. Words do not have limiting and precise definitions. One motto is that the less precise the definition, the truer it can be.

Where most histories exemplify periods or movements with "perfect" examples (e.g., the Parthenon), I also include modest or imperfect examples (the Temple of Apollo at Bassae). Exceptions to the rule and slightly awkward pieces are valuable as one sees design in the process of being worked through, with the solution not yet at hand. This book therefore includes counter-movements and side measures. For example, Chapter 21 looks at classical modernism (the

Bauhaus and French modernism, Le Corbusier, etc.) and the conclusions offered are in keeping with what most researchers have to say. Yet the next two chapters (Chapters 22 and 23) complicate the issue and look at alternative design strategies.

As with many survey history books, this book tells the narrative of the history of architecture, interiors, and furniture over time, and looks at the history of changes and the meanings of why those changes came about. Where it is different than other history books is that it also looks at exceptions.

Meanings

The path metaphor also applies to the experience of reading a book. It takes time, the reader sees a lot along the way and arrives at a different place, a little tired, a little exhilarated, perhaps in need of a shower, thirsty, but no doubt with some new knowledge. The knowledge contained within this book's covers constitutes the core of what most people think an educated person involved in the design world should know. So other than looking at a parade of objects and designed spaces that aesthetically minded people should be familiar with, what is the purpose for delving so deeply into all this? The equally important goal is to understand the meanings that lie "behind" the art forms: the subtext of designed objects, or what these things *mean*.

Histories of objects, curiously, are always histories of people, so another way of looking at this book is that it is a history of designed spaces, and the people who created them and the people who lived in them. As Martindale writes, "Every major work of art is an expression of some aspect of the people and society that produced it" (Martindale 1967, p. 13). Buildings, rooms, and objects are cultural expressions of beliefs and values. The exterior and interior spaces we inhabit and the artifacts we use are mirrors of ourselves and how we experience the world around us. Designed spaces and objects also demonstrate our ability to change the world. As a form of communication, manipulated materials add shape and significance by providing a physical framework for events and rituals.

Design historian Clive Dilnot wrote two state-of-the-field essays in 1984 that are still current in many respects and frequently cited. He wrote: "The most significant aspect about design is that it is produced, received, and used within an emphatically social context. The social is not external to the activity, but internal to it and determining of its essential features" (Dilnot 1984b, p. 14). Designed places and objects reflect the world and also act upon it.

To engage in a scholarly inquiry into the disciplines of furniture and interior design is to embark on an adventure that requires breadth and depth. A broad investigation is required to develop penetrating critical abilities and concise analytical skills. The knowledge gleaned from searching outward from designed spaces and objects and across other disciplines permits, among other things, the precise identification of a context—its historical, institutional, and material dimensions. Designed projects sit at the interface between thinking and making, and incorporate knowledge of materials, artifacts, the processes that produce them, and the environments in which they are placed. This specialized knowledge is extracted by delving into the act of building as well, using the theories and methods of the social sciences, and the humanities. Scholarly research at the highest level yields skills, abilities, and knowledge required to interpret the past and shape the future.

Conclusion

The metaphor of a journey down a path has many applications. It relates to the unfolding of history over time, and the journey of a reader reading a book. I use the metaphor of two different paths, the river and the road, running parallel, to explain the aim of this book. One is the direct route, the other the meandering path. The former emphasizes the destination, and its chief attribute is clarity, the other the journey itself, characterized by richness and variety.

As for a reader embarking on a historical project, just as a road guides a traveler to a geographic destination, it can also guide a devotee to a spiritual destination. Here's another way to state this project's central focus: this book is about buildings, rooms, and the people and things in them. It glories in the properties and powers of interior architecture, pieces of furniture and other designed objects.

Sources

Craske, Matthew (1997). *Art in Europe: 1700–1830.* Oxford: Oxford University Press.

Dilnot, Clive (1984a). "The State of Design History, Part I: Mapping the Field." *Design Issues* 1, no. 1 (Spring): 4–23.

Dilnot, Clive (1984b). "The State of Design History, Part II: Problems and Possibilities." *Design Issues* 1, no. 2 (Autumn): 3–20.

Floré, Fredie and Cammie McAtee (2017). *The Politics of Furniture: Identity, Diplomacy and Persuasion.* Abingdon: Routledge.

Martindale, Andrew (1967). *Gothic Art: From the Twelfth to Fifteenth Centuries.* New York: Praeger.

Roger, Andrea Wolk (2022). *The Radical Vision of Edward Burne-Jones.* New Haven, CT: Yale University Press.

Teasley, Sarah (2022). *Designing Modern Japan.* Chicago: University of Chicago Press.

INSTRUCTOR AND STUDENT RESOURCES

History of Interior Architecture STUDiO:

We are pleased to offer an online resource to accompany the textbook—History of Interior Architecture STUDIO. The online STUDIO is specially developed to complement this book with rich media ancillaries that students can adapt to their visual learning styles to better master concepts and improve grades. Within the STUDIO, students will be able to:

- Study smarter with self-quizzes featuring scored results and personalized study tips
- Review concepts with flashcards of essential vocabulary

The History of Interior Architecture STUDIO can be accessed as follows:

SIGN IN

1. Go to https://www.bloomsburyonlineresources.com/fairchildbookstudios
2. Follow the instructions to enter your unique access code which is printed on the inside back cover of this book. The code is valid for one registration only.
3. Credentials to access the STUDIOs will be emailed once the code has been redeemed.

Having trouble registering or logging in? Be sure you have entered your access code, not your password when prompted.

STUDIO™ will be live within six to eight weeks of the book's publication date.

Instructor Resources

- The Instructor's Guide provides suggestions for planning the course and using the text in the classroom, including sample syllabi, in-class activities, and teaching ideas.
- PowerPoint® presentations include images from the book and provide a framework for lecture and discussion

Instructor's Resources may be accessed through https://www.bloomsburyonlineresources.com/fairchildbookstudios

Acknowledgments

Writing this book, and then rewriting it for the second edition, I often felt more like an orchestra conductor or director of a play. By that I mean that I was constantly relying on the efforts of many to produce these twenty-seven chapters with their accompaniment of five hundred illustrations. Others assisted me in multiple ways. This book relied on both primary and secondary materials. To the authors whose books are mentioned in each chapter's sources, I thank them for their valuable research. By necessity, this work summarizes a great deal of material. I encourage interested readers to consult the works whose richness this text only hints at. For years I have taught survey courses of architecture and interiors and have relied on the textbooks of William Curtis, Spiro Kostof, John Pile, and the triumvirate of Buie Harwood, Bridget May, and Curt Sherman. If I were to acknowledge every time my knowledge of a project has benefited from their insights, they would be cited on every page.

Producing the first edition of this book, there were hundreds who assisted me. To those who suggested a resource, read a draft, provided encouragement, acted as a sounding board, answered a question, raised an eyebrow, or otherwise pointed me in the right direction, I remain grateful. This time around, a smaller group helped me update and expand the material, and engage with contemporary design issues. This list includes Nnamdi Elleh, Koompong Noobanjong, Frank Ordia, Kendra Locklear Ordia, Andrew Peterson, and Amit Srivastava.

For earning and redeeming airline miles with me, thanks to Clyde Whitaker.

For years I have benefited from student research assistants funded by the University of Nebraska's UCARE program, under the capable direction of Laura Damuth and recently Kali Patterson. The students who assisted me on this edition are Caroline Goetz and Said Al Mahrouqi. An advantage of teaching in an architecture and design college is knowing students with sophisticated drawing and editing abilities, and I particularly thank Al Mundhir Al Mahrouqi and Jiang Chen. At the University of Nebraska, I thank my friends and colleagues in the Architecture and Interior Design programs, the Art History Department, and the History

Department. Interior Design Program Director Lindsey Ellsworth-Bahe and Interim Dean Sharon Kuska provided me with a semester's leave to focus on the manuscript.

New portions drew on research I conducted with my former student Elyssa Yoneda. While I relied heavily on secondary sources, living architects and designers occasionally provided information, including Jhane Barnes, Dale and Patricia Keller, Margaret McCurry, William Pulgram, Denise Scott Brown, and Margo Grant Walsh.

Outside peer reviewers provided insightful comments for the direction of this revised edition which improved the text immeasurably and constitute an act of intellectual generosity for which I am eternally grateful. They are: Susan Ray-Deggs, North Dakota State University; Isabelle Objaghian, Wake Technical Community College; Sheila Edwards, SCAD; Barbara Isherwood, Yorkville University, University of Toronto; Katherine Kennon, Bellmont University; and Yelena McLane, Florida State University.

A work of this scope is a testament to the vital role that libraries continue to play in disseminating knowledge. While online resources have expanded exponentially since 2009, I continue to be amazed at how much information is still only found on the printed page and often exceedingly difficult to find. At the University of Nebraska, Love Library, the Interlibrary Loan department literally delivered hundreds of books to my hands. Librarian Zach Eden admirably took on responding to my near daily requests for assistance, a role that had previously been handled by Kay Logan-Peters and Judy Winkler.

I relied on numerous reference works, including *The Dictionary of Art*, *Encyclopedia Britannica*, and the Getty Research Institute's online sources. The libraries of the Victoria and Albert Museum in London and the Thailand Creative and Design Center in Bangkok have proven invaluable.

For encouraging the project in its infancy, thanks to Olga Kontzias, Michelle Levy, and Joe Miranda at Fairchild Books. Joe Miranda has continued to play a vital role in this second edition, with his experience, calming presence, and big-picture vision. Emily Samulski played a vital role in getting this project started. The world of photographic sourcing is a generation past what it was in 2009. All the artwork had to be sourced anew, and for her herculean efforts, my gratitude to Edie Weinberg knows no bounds.

A book of this scope requires the eyes of many, including significantly the copy editor Katherine Carney. Emily Samulski at Fairchild Books took on the task of getting the project started. The design of a book about design is all important, and I thank Louise Dugdale for her work on the cover and page layouts.

A delightful occurrence since the first edition has been the creation of the History of Interiors Group (HIG) of the Society of Architectural Historians. Paula Lupkin, Anca Lasc, Karen White, and William Littman have helped more than they know with their scholarship and their comradery. Thank you to Grace Ong Yan for sharing her pioneering work on corporate interiors. For generously providing photographs, my thanks to Adeyemi Akande, Ethan Boerner, Jason Cote, Michael Freeman, Carl Matthews, and Brenton Rahn. Loretta Manuel provided interesting information about the hotel that graces the book's cover.

I am appreciative of the people who wrote after the publication of the first edition and offered additional insights. Their comments, and those of all the people mentioned above, have benefited this project, but minor errors in a project of this scope are inevitable and I take responsibility for them. Books about design are also books about people, and I am grateful for all those I have met, in person, via Zoom or through a letter or email, in writing this history.

Bloomsbury Publishing wishes to gratefully acknowledge and thank the editorial team involved in the publication of this book:

Senior Acquisitions Editor: Emily Samulski
Development Manager: Joseph Miranda
Assistant Editor: Maria Nunez
Art Development Editor: Edie Weinberg
In-House Designer: Louise Dugdale
Production Manager: Ken Bruce
Project Manager: Deborah Maloney

HISTORY OF
INTERIOR
ARCHITECTURE

Prehistory

2500000–9000 BCE	9000–2000 BCE	4000–1000 BCE
Paleolithic	Neolithic	Bronze Age

The oldest known artifact dates back two and a half million years, yet most of what we consider as art, architecture, and craftworks are more recent. The more recent the era, the more remains we have. It seems plausible that the earliest inhabitants made do with existing natural items that, with little modification, met their needs, such as sitting on stones and logs, and taking advantage of caves (Figure 1.0). A cave is a ready-made structure. Cave interiors had symbolic meaning and provided what is still considered the most basic, if limited, definition of architecture: providing shelter to protect inhabitants from the hazardous world of the outdoors.

Additionally, there is the variety of ways that the human figure has of sitting on the ground: kneeling, crossing the legs, and so on. What Stone Age preferences were, we do not know. The natural world was inescapable, and humans saw utility and meaning in nature. Some natural forms were benevolent, some menacing. The term Stone Age does not mean that inhabitants created everything out of stone. Stone being so difficult to work, it is more likely that there was considerable work with wood, hides, and reeds, almost nothing of which, from the earliest periods, remains.

This chapter addresses two stone ages, the **Paleolithic** and the **Neolithic**, and ends with the Bronze Age. Two and a half million years ago, people started making tools. One and a half million years ago, there was a humanoid species, *Homo ergaster*, who looked like modern beings, and *Homo ergaster* started creating hand axes. A hand ax is likely the first

Figure 1.0
(*Facing page*)
Three Peaks of Lavaredo, Sexten Dolomites, Italy.

3

example of a designed object (Figure 1.1). Many of the surviving ones come from Africa.

Looking at one prompts many questions. In attempting to craft a piece of stone into a useful implement, was something going on in the mind of the person doing the crafting that can be called design? It does not take long to deduce that the maker seems to be doing something above and beyond creating a useful object. Surely a jagged edge, with an asymmetrical line, would have served as well?

Looking at the hand ax raises questions about the person who made it. Had they previous experience with crafting these kinds of objects? Did they have a mental image of what they wanted the final product to look like? Was symmetry a goal? It seems as though the person crafting this wanted to create a symmetrical object, with the thought that a symmetrical object had a pleasing form.

We cannot know for certain what a person thought over a temporal distance of hundreds of thousands of years. Yet, just as it seems probable that the person who made this had experience making similar objects—that what lies in front of us is the product of practice and skill—we can make reasonable conjecture about the possible motivations of the maker.

This line of inquiry therefore involves the scientific discussion of the purpose of beauty. Randy Thornhill, a professor at the University of New Mexico, studies why people prefer symmetry when judging other people. Making a jump from Thornhill's thesis, from people to objects, we can conclude that Neolithic people responded well to symmetry in humans, and perhaps in objects as well. There is the probability that symmetrical objects were prized, such as whole seashells and perfect flowers. For prehistoric people, symmetrical bodies meant health. A humped back, a broken wrist, a droopy shoulder, a missing tooth—all were injuries that rendered the human figure asymmetrical. It is likely that the ancients admired beauty in humans and in objects, and that when they made objects they attempted to imbue the objects they crafted with their concept of beauty. A fastidious human, could eventually achieve symmetry, and therefore designed beauty, in an object.

This exercise, of understanding the mind of a historical person by way of the designed object they have left as their trace, is emblematic of what this book is about. It is tempting to think that we are hardwired in some respects the way that the ancients were. That is one of the pleasures of looking at historical materials, of making a connection across

Figure 1.1
Ironstone hand ax, *c.* 600000 BCE, South Africa.

epochs with people long gone, using objects as the vehicle of mental transport. But just as significantly, there are instances when this method fails, and we need contextual information to understand people temporally distant from us who, in many respects, seem very strange indeed.

Lascaux

The Paleolithic caves at Lascaux, 17000 BCE, date from before permanent architecture (Figure 1.2). Other caves in southern France and northern Spain are older and date from between 32000 and 10000 BCE. The population was sparse, with only approximately 5,000 people in the area that is today France.

Lascaux was not a site of habitation; it is likely that it was a location for ritual activity. Some 1,500 engravings and 600 painted animals and signs grace the site.

A mainstay of anthropological inquiry is the foundation myth: stories that explain the beginnings of a particular group. Myth, in this sense, is not the opposite of factual but the traditional telling of historical events of how a group came into being,

and which underpins their worldview. Foundation myths are frequently discussed in terms of ethnic groups or nationalities, such as the biblical tale of Adam and Eve. Foundation myths of the United States involve Captain John Smith and the pilgrims; these are examples of foundation myths involving people moving across a body of water to inhabit a new land.

Foundation myths satisfy the quest of those studying beginnings, including art historians interested in the earliest pieces of art, such as the female figure from Austria, the so-called Venus of Willendorf, and the cave paintings of Lascaux.

Many have sought, in interpreting Lascaux, to see in them a spiritual or ritual belief, a protoreligion. At the most basic level, what is clear is that

Figure 1.2
Shaft scene: man with bird and bison. Lascaux, France. 17000–15000 BCE.

the people represented animals because animals played significant roles in their lives.

Cave paintings constitute a decorative program, an ancient example of creating meaning in a space. Little of the cave was changed architecturally. In fact, one of the qualities of the caves is that the art responds to the existing configuration. The figures are representational, fairly accurate renditions of natural phenomena. Historians of art and design prefer the word "representational" to indicate art that resembles the object portrayed—this is, to distinguish it from the nineteenth-century art movement realism. There is a relationship between the caves and natural materials; of necessity, natural materials served as pigments.

Remains of grasses have been found in the soil in the caves, and Gregory Curtis has posited that the painters sat on grass pillows (Curtis 2006, p. 105). This is a beguiling hint of a whole material world, the world of things made from reeds, woods, and hides, of which we know next to nothing. Ladders and scaffolding must have been used to create the paintings, so the people who worked in Lascaux had woodworking abilities.

The images of Lascaux were seen exclusively by firelight. It is a worthwhile exercise to imagine the effect on people who had previously seen little; they were accustomed to the real world, not the represented world. French poet and critic Paul Valéry (1951) contrasted twentieth-century people with those of history. About modern man he wrote: "Your senses have to absorb without a day's respite as much of music, painting, drugs, strange drinks, shows, journeys, rapid changes of attitude and temperature, political and economic anxieties, as in the old days all mankind could absorb in the course of three hundred years" (Valéry 1951, p. 135). He was, by extension, also writing about people at the other end of the chronological scale. One of our suppositions is that those who saw and experienced few things in their lives were greatly impacted by them.

A frequent observation about twenty-first-century viewers is that people across the globe are bombarded with images. There was no Paleolithic equivalent. People had acute visual powers; their lives often depended on their sight, so when they looked, they looked with attention, focus, and interest. One effect of seeing painted images of bison, horses, and gazelles by flickering firelight is that they may have appeared to move.

Neolithic

Neolithic is a loose chronologic indicator, roughly 9000–2000 BCE, and it refers to the principal material used for construction and fashioning objects: stone. Stonehenge and Skara Brae are among the latest episodes of the European Neolithic story. **Lithic** means that buildings, and a number of objects, were crafted from stone. A Neolithic person had other materials on hand—hides, grasses, reeds, wood, sod, bone, and feathers among them, but few of those materials survive.

Menhirs and dolmens

Early Neolithic objects are **menhirs**, giant stones lifted upright and made into monuments (Figure 1.3). The result is a built form that has meaning by virtue of human intervention. A menhir is a directional focus, and it creates space by virtue of being a focal point. Yet the human handiwork does not reshape the objects; it changes their orientation. Menhirs come from across the globe, with a great many in the United Kingdom and France.

More benign climates—Mesopotamia, Anatolia, the Indus River Valley (Chapter 2 and following)—allowed for permanent or semipermanent settlements, where people could begin food production and animal husbandry, as opposed to hunting and gathering. A Neolithic legacy is, as Spiro Kostof terms it, "a fixed place under the sky" (Kostof 1995, p. 26). Fixity allowed for

Figure 1.3
Menhir, Carnac, France. *c.* 6500–4600 BCE.

the construction of furniture to accommodate a settled lifestyle and enhance the permanent home.

A later stage was to create monuments, to configure architectural entities to have specific meanings, and to arrange naturally occurring items—tree trunks, stones, and hides—to encourage certain social interactions.

Megalithic construction was a further step in the development of design. A way to create meaning was to pile stones on top of one another (Figure 1.4). Megalithic architecture is characterized by timbers stuck in the ground, stones assembled, and mud applied to the gaps.

A **dolmen** creates an interior space, relying on post-and-lintel construction. There was likely a furniture version of this process: a horizontal piece, stone or wood, on top of vertical supports, and which resulted in something like a bench. A dolmen was a predecessor to walls and a ceiling, made of vertical and horizontal elements, and structurally indicative of a frame construction.

Stonehenge

There are many henges in England and Scotland, of which Stonehenge, 3200–1600 BCE, is the most impressive (Castleden 1987, p. 53). A **henge** is a Neolithic monument in a circular form,

created with banks, ditches, and upright stones. Earthwork and timber construction preceded the stone construction phase of Stonehenge. The translation of the site into a construction made of permanent materials resulted in one of the most important examples of monumental European architecture.

Stonehenge was a place for ritual. It consists of two concentric circles, with their openings astrologically positioned according to the lunar and solar paths. Many of the stones weigh tons, and they were transported 18 miles. Stonehenge relies on **post-and-lintel**, or **trabeated**, construction (Figure 1.5), a structural system using (vertical) columns and (horizontal) **lintels**.

One step in this period was from nomadic to permanent settlements. Another was from single dwellings to multiple-unit housing. This constituted the beginning of civic life, and one of the earlier examples is in Scotland. Materials from Neolithic sites include spears, axes, pottery, and assorted personal items, including gold ornaments.

Skara Brae

Skara Brae is a small Neolithic village in Scotland dating to 3100–2500 BCE (Castleden 1987, p. 33). It is the residential complement to ritual centers

Figure 1.4
Pentre Ifan Dolmen, Pembrokeshire, Wales, 3500 BCE.

Figure 1.5
Inner megalithic
circle, Stonehenge,
Salisbury Plain,
England, 2250–
1600 BCE.

such as Stonehenge and Avebury. Curvilinear houses were built of stone, without mortar, in a group of six to ten structures. There are several examples of built-in furniture. Archaeologist Rodney Castleden (1987) writes: "The high quality of the interior finish of a Skara Brae house really has to be seen to be appreciated. The close-fitting **corbelled** masonry flows in soft curves round the walls. Small beehive cupboards are let into the thickness of the walls and tiny keeping-places like stoups were used for storing personal belongings" (p. 34).

The most prominent example of built-in furniture is a pair of large shelves, strategically located directly opposite the door (Figure 1.6). Castleden (1987) calls it a "dresser" (p. 34). The central hearth was midway between the low entrance and the dresser, whose scale and location suggest that it had a display purpose in addition to a functional purpose. Sleeping platforms lined the hearth; some structures at Skara Brae have benches. There was limited decoration on the walls.

Çatal Hüyük

Çatal Hüyük is a Middle Eastern Neolithic site in Anatolia (modern Turkey) dating to 6700–5650 BCE.

With a population of 5,000 to 7,000 people, it was the largest town in the region. The rectilinear houses were made of plastered mud brick. Although few trees grew in the area, houses were outfitted with wooden posts, beams, and ladders.

The houses had a central rectangular hearth; built-in platforms lined the perimeter and were used for sitting, sleeping, and working (Figure 1.7). Some of the platforms and posts were painted red. The walls were white plaster, painted with figures of humans, animals, or geometric shapes.

Houses had shrines, and there were also buildings used exclusively for ritual purposes. Their form and layout were similar to that of houses. The platforms in ritual buildings were used for the burial of human remains.

James Mellaart, the author of a book on the site, characterized the material culture of this early urban center: "At Çatal Hüyük it is clear that the crafts of the weaver and the wood-worker were much more highly esteemed than those of the potter or the bone-carver" (Mellaart 1967, p. 210).

Çatal Hüyük is chronologically a Neolithic site, although with little stone available, their stone-working activities were limited to crafting human figurines. Woven textiles and woven mats covered the floors and the adjacent platforms.

Figure 1.6
Skara Brae,
Scotland,
3200–2200 BCE.

Figure 1.7
Mud-brick house, with sleeping and sitting platforms, Çatal Hüyük,
Turkey, 6700–5650 BCE.

Tools were made from obsidian and other stones, and polished obsidian disks served as mirrors. Wooden bowls and coiled baskets existed in large quantities. Preceding the activities of the Bronze Age, artisans in Çatal Hüyük produced beads and pendants out of copper and lead (Mellaart 1967, p. 217).

The Bronze Age

The Bronze Age follows the Neolithic period. *The Encyclopedia Britannica* (2007) straightforwardly describes the Bronze Age as "the third phase in the development of material culture among the ancient peoples of Europe, Asia, and the Middle East" (p. 548). Looking across the globe, Europe was in the Neolithic period when the Middle East and Asia had entered the Bronze Age.

The term *Bronze Age* indicates that people were no longer primarily crafting buildings and objects out of stone, although stone was still used. They increasingly made objects out of metal for weapons, jewelry, and tools. In making material choices, availability was as important as technological progress or aesthetic decision. The Stone Age people of the British Isles continued to fashion items from stone because they had it in abundance.

Conclusion

Studying Paleolithic and Neolithic remains is not for everyone. While Stonehenge's grandeur impresses the hordes who visit it, most Stone Age remains are incomplete and small in scale. Recovering their meaning takes effort. The Irish and French countrysides are filled with dolmens and menhirs, carefully delineated with historic markers. Yet their untrampled grass indicates that they attract few visitors. Approached with patience, and with the imagination that those interested in design are blessed with, the earliest years of human design activity can be inspiring and evocative.

Having left the Stone Age, this book is not through with looking at buildings and things in stone. A means of crossing the line from temporary building to enduring monument was to build in stone. The Egyptians, Greeks, Khmer, Chinese, Aztec, and Inca perfected the practice.

For this scholarly endeavor, the Bronze Age has just begun. Chapter 2 starts with a region that, with little native stone, created buildings and civic centers on an unprecedented scale, using the humble brick. The first half of Chapter 3 completes the examination of the Bronze Age with the world that was ancient to ancient Greece, the civilizations of Minoan and Mycenaean Greece.

Sources

Aujoulat, Norbert (2005). *Lascaux: Movement, Space and Time*. New York: Abrams.

Castleden, Rodney (1987). *Stonehenge People: An Exploration of Life in Neolithic Britain, 4700–2000 B.C.E.* London: Routledge.

Curtis, Gregory (2006). *The Cave Painters*. New York: Anchor Books.

Encyclopaedia Britannica (2007). *The New Encyclopaedia Britannica*, vol. 2. Chicago.

Kostof, Spiro (1995). *A History of Architecture: Settings and Rituals*. New York: Oxford University Press.

Mellaart, James (1967). *Çatal Höyük: A Neolithic Town in Anatolia*. New York: McGraw Hill.

Mellaart, James (1978). *The Archaeology of Ancient Turkey*. London: Bodley Head.

Scranton, Laird (2006). *The Mystery of Scara Brae: Neolithic Scotland*. Rochester, VT: Inner Traditions.

Valéry, Paul (1951). *Reflections on the World Today*. London: Thames and Hudson.

Discussion and Review Questions

1. What is post-and-lintel construction? What is another name for it?
2. How many images, of any kind, do you see in a day, even if peripherally?
3. Think of examples of natural landscapes, untouched by humans, that come to have meanings not related to nature.
4. Think of landscape examples that have been modified by humans, but are not architecture; that is, landscapes that lie somewhere between nature and human artifact.
5. How is value added to a naturally occurring material?
6. What are the qualities of a naturally occurring material that cause them to be prized?
7. Are the Caves at Lascaux Paleolithic or Neolithic?
8. Name a Neolithic site.
9. Name a Bronze Age site.

Ancient Civilizations

5000–2000 BCE				911–612 BCE
Mesopotamia				**Neo-Assyrian Empire**
Sumer				

2650–2134 BCE	2040–1640 BCE	1570–1070 BCE	752–656 BCE
Egypt			**Nubia**
Old Kingdom	Middle Kingdom	New Kingdom	Twenty-Fifth Dynasty

In the ancient world of the Middle East, three civilizations stand out: Mesopotamia, Egypt, and Nubia. Interrelated yet individual entities, each was in contact with the others. Sometimes the nature of the contact was military, sometimes commercial, and there were cultural implications. These civilizations were not alike in either their importance then or what is known about them now. Egypt produced awe-inspiring monuments that have piqued the world's imagination for millennia. Mesopotamia, home to the world's first urban centers, saw strides in mathematics, writing, and astrology. Nubia, on the southernmost reaches of the Nile, is the least studied of the three. Also known as Kush, Nubia was the African civilization that continually influenced Egypt and that for a brief period ruled it. All three of these regions depended on rivers for their lifeblood: the Nile for Egypt and Nubia, the Tigris and Euphrates for Mesopotamia.

Figure 2.0
(*Facing page*)
Kiosk of Taharka,
Karnak Temple,
Luxor, Egypt,
c. 664 BCE.

Mesopotamia

Mesopotamia is a geographic designation that includes the fertile plain fed by the Tigris and Euphrates Rivers. Roughly contiguous with modern-day Iraq, it is generally believed that the region had something approaching agriculture in the period 8000 BCE. By 4000 BCE, a network of villages served one of the most productive grain-producing regions of the world. The granary of the Near East, it was cooler and greener than today. It is difficult to look at the ancient cultures in this region and not think of the present day, a region so troubled in the twentieth and twenty-first centuries.

Mesopotamia was a crossroads, with Anatolia to the north, Egypt and Nubia to the west, and Persia and the Indus River Valley to the east. Circa 3500 BCE, Mesopotamia and Egypt were strong competing economic forces with developed traditions of art and architecture. There is a vitality and ambition to their art. Creating representations of humans and animals, the ancient Middle Eastern people made great strides in furthering the endowment of matter with symbolic significance.

They were at the forefront of writing, mathematics, time, urban civilization, boat building, and astronomy. The people of the Tigris River Valley had the wheel and a system of standardized weights and record-keeping. Clay tablets preserve some of the earliest examples of writing. These tools formed part of a commercial and public archival system. The citizens of these cities had a capacity for organization that allowed them to develop the first urban centers. An active mercantile economy served a highly productive agrarian economy.

Initially, homes were made of mud, timber, and reeds. The standard building material of **Assyrian** structures, grand and modest, was a **mud brick**, so to build monumental architecture, and to differentiate royal quarters from less remarkable buildings, an elaborate taxonomy of applied finishes was utilized. Stone and wood were scarce and expensive and hence used sparingly.

Cities

Mesopotamian urban centers were the sites of ritual cult activities and functioned as the nucleus of organized agricultural and proto-industrial production. Mesopotamian construction workers built bridges, tunnels, moats, and walled cities with ceremonial gates. Glazed blue bricks used on exteriors highlighted the cities' entryways. These gates were prominent points, nodes where roadways originating in the countryside dove into the urban fabric. The urban thresholds signaled entrance, and they were a means of control. The walled cities themselves were defensive. The most famous example is the Ishtar Gate. These urban features are evident in a reconstruction drawing of Khorsabad (Figure 2.1).

Significant architectural monuments are the highlight of early periods, such as the White Temple at Warka, 3500–3000 BCE, and the **Ziggurat** at Ur, 2113–2006 BCE. Much of the extant sculpture, and our knowledge of furniture, dates from later periods. Mesopotamian cities were subjected to continual pressure and intrusion from outsiders. The period 746–609 BCE, the neo-Assyrian Empire, represents a return to power, and significant rulers include Ashurnasirpal (r. 884–859 BCE) and Ashurbanipal (r. 668–627 BCE). This period produced some of the finest sculptural **reliefs** and examples of Assyrian architecture. Ashurnasirpal's reign comes toward the end of 3,000 years of Mesopotamian prominence, yet it marks the beginning of the late Assyrian period.

Palaces

The plan of the Palace of Nimrud demonstrates that Assyrian palaces were conceptually additive. Individual rooms of the palace were not extraordinarily different from those of modest structures with regard to both size and materials. The largest spaces in the plan were exterior courtyards. What made the palace extraordinary was the quantity of rooms, in the hundreds, and the quality of the artwork. The length of available timbers dictated room width. Assyrian builders could expand a room longitudinally; hence the grandest room is the throne room. The complex had been called

Figure 2.1
Reconstruction of the citadel with palace and ziggurat, Khorsabad, Iraq, 721–705 BCE.

Calah, where Ashurnasirpal II built his palace; today it is called Nimrud.

While the overall complex is impressive in size, the principal rooms are surprisingly narrow. The reliance upon rooms that face a courtyard is a standard layout of residential architecture in a hot climate. With their use of local materials and construction methods, the palaces were extensions of vernacular traditions.

There were a variety of methods for signaling the importance of rooms and buildings. Mud brick walls could be skim-coated with an additional layer of mud or plaster. For building interiors, walls could be painted. Most exceptionally, important rooms were lined with reliefs carved into alabaster panels and massive three-dimensional sculptures marked the entrances, a technique increasingly important in the neo-Assyrian period.

Sculpture

The most famous artworks from these palaces are the colossal gateway figures that stood guard at entries. They dominate the reconstruction as they originally dominated the throne rooms. With human heads placed atop muscular winged lions and bulls, these imposing monolithic statues stood 15 feet (4.8 meters) tall. The sphinxes are initially experienced frontally, defining the entrance that they guard as a pair. They also function as directional devices. Carved on two adjacent sides (the front and one side), they encourage visitors to perambulate around them, to enter the room, and to turn the corner. The sculptures are impressive at a distance and up close. From far away, their size, form, and material impress. At close distance, it is the quantity and quality of the incised details that carefully delineate the contours of flesh and musculature. What makes them monumental is their size and material, but so too is the obvious point that their finely crafted details are the product of hundreds of hours of painstaking work. The Western and Asian penchant for flanking public buildings with recumbent lions has a precedent in the Assyrian palaces.

Reliefs

The sphinxes were but the largest element in an elaborate composition that covered the walls of the throne room. The sculptural program of a public room was a means of proclaiming the wealth of king and kingdom, and it served as a sophisticated means of visual communication that played to public audiences, both local and foreign. The state rooms of palaces featured decorative

programs that featured scenes of hunting, celebration, worship, processions of courtiers bearing tribute, natural landscapes, and scenes of military technology.

The vitality of the public spaces came from the processions of figures in horizontal motion. Most of the scenes involve movement, which makes the overall decoration dynamic. Chariots, horses, lions, rows of soldiers, penitents, and dignitaries are all represented in motion. Flowing rivers are populated with fish. Susanna Hare describes the reliefs as showing "figures in endless parade" (Hare and Porada 1946, p. 15). They appear as if pressed from a roller. The figures "repeated themselves along the walls in much the same way as the design of a Mesopotamian cylinder seal, rolled across clay" (Reade and Curtis 1995, p. 42). These linear compositions were carved in low relief, in comparison to the sphinxes.

While some scenes record natural landscapes or lines of dignitaries paying tribute, the overall theme is intimidation. The reliefs are at once beautiful and horrifying. They reassured the home audience, enforced a sense of decorum, and terrified non-Assyrians with their forthright expression of Assyrian might. J.E. Reade writes that this decorative program was designed "to impress, astonish, intimidate" (Reade and Curtis 1995, p. 40).

Ashurnasirpal's own words corroborate the unrelenting pictorial violence: "I captured the city; six hundred of their warriors I put to the sword; three thousand captives I burned with fire; I did not leave a single one among them alive" (Hare and Porada 1946, p. 12).

In addition to convincing its readers of Ashurnasirpal's might, the Standard Inscription of Ashurnasirpal II provides a list of materials that were prestigious: "A palace of cedar, cypress, juniper, boxwood, mulberry, pistachio-wood, and tamarisk, for my royal dwelling and for my lordly pleasure for all time I founded therein. Beasts of the mountain and of the seas of white limestone and alabaster I fashioned, and set them up in its gates, I adorned it, I made it glorious" (Hare and Porada 1946, p. 7).

Typical relief subjects related to warfare include scenes of siege, hunting, and battles with chariots. What they have in common is their horizontal composition. The scenes frequently juxtapose Assyrians with their neighbors, and these "foreigners" were readily recognized by anyone visiting the rooms, identified by their ethnically specific clothing. The Assyrians are consistently represented as militarily superior. They stand tall and erect, in perfect posture, while non-Assyrians are smaller in scale, broken, crumpled, and trampled upon by horses and chariots, their bodies ridden with arrows and spears. Megan Cifarelli writes, "These images, then, communicated highly organized and specific messages about the nature and goals of Assyrian power" (1998, p. 211). For Assyrians, the reliefs showed that in return for the considerable cost of maintaining a centralized government and their ruler's opulent lifestyle, there was the benefit of security and knowing that the king was in control.

For non-Assyrians, the decorative program was a dire warning of the consequences of confronting Assyrians. For citizen and visitor alike, these reliefs acted as a visual etiquette, a means of communicating to a nonliterate audience. Lines of polite dignitaries respectfully approach kings and priests, with both hands visible. This showed the proper way to act in the throne room; it also made clear the consequences of failing to heed this advice. Lest there be any doubt about the leader's might, the standard Inscription of Ashurnasirpal II (883–859 BCE) describes him as the king "who tramples on the neck of his foes" (Barnett 2009, p. 6).

To modern viewers this seems extreme; yet it is worth pointing out that across cultures, many government buildings show artworks that document historical scenes, and often these are scenes of battle. The passage of time has lessened the impact of viewing the carnage, but battles such as Carthage, Waterloo, and Iwo Jima were bloody in their day.

A fanciful reconstruction makes several points clear that the austere stone remains do not (Figure 2.2). Published in 1849, it is still useful as it demonstrates that the rooms, even if covered with stone reliefs, were **polychromatic**. Paint, used as outline and background, blended together elements of stone, plaster, wood, and mud, making them into a powerful decorative program.

Furniture

Assyrian furniture has not survived to the extent that Egyptian furniture has, but our knowledge of it comes from inscriptions and representations on reliefs. Ashurnasirpal's list of **booty** also provides valuable information about furniture; it includes "chairs of maple and boxwood, tables of ivory with **inlay**, silver, gold, lead, copper, iron."

The most famous relief with detailed views of furniture involves King Ashurbanipal and Queen Libbali-sharrat dining in a garden (Figure 2.3). This relief, dated to 645 BCE, is from their palace at Nineveh. Their suite of furniture is consistent with other representations of furniture. The Assyrian furniture was made of wood. The King reclines on a **couch**, while the Queen sits on a throne with a back; her feet rest on a footrest. There are two high tables. The King and Queen are dining in the fashion most often associated with Rome, in

Figure 2.2
Hall in an Assyrian palace, restored, Nineveh, Iraq, *c.* 705–681 BCE.

Figure 2.3
Garden
scene: King
Ashurbanipal and
Queen Libbali-
sharrat dining
on elaborate
furniture,
Nineveh, Iraq,
645 BCE.

which they lie recumbent, with food placed on tall tables that stand within arm's reach.

The Ashurbanipal relief shows the kind of furnishings known as the Assyrian Empire style. Chairs, beds, and tables rest on conical feet whose forms derive from either inverted pinecones or date **spathes**. Crossbars stabilize the pieces and are decorated with opposed **volutes**. Although not shown here, there were also backless thrones, some of which had lion's paw feet. Most pieces were made of wood, sometimes adorned with bronze plates. A stone table was found at Khorsabad.

The King and Queen dine outdoors, indicating that furniture used indoors was occasionally relocated for outdoor use. Servants or slaves fan them. On the King's couch, a bolster fits underneath the curved end. Similarly, a blanket or pad is thrown over the Queen's vertical backrest. The wood elements are carved and turned. The table has a tablecloth and stands on three legs (similar to the Greek and Roman trident table). This relief, sometimes called "The Garden Party," is a rare representation of a seemingly tranquil domestic scene that exceptionally also involves the Queen. Yet King Ashurbanipal remains his intrepid self. The head of one of his defeated enemies, Teumann, King of Elam, hangs from a tree.

The Assyrians developed a system of decoration in which sculpture and wall decoration in the public rooms of governmental buildings were meant to impress, intimidate, and instill a sense of decorum in visitors. Assyrian representation reveled in intricate detailing, of feathers, textiles, and foliage (Figure 2.4). A political and artistic center, Babylon was the last great Mesopotamian city, whose ruler was the equally renowned

Figure 2.4
Assyrian relief.

Nebuchadnezzar (605–562 BCE). The arrival of Alexander the Great signaled an end to Assyrian hegemony in the region and its absorption into the larger Greco-Roman world.

Egypt

Egyptian history has a parade of colorful characters and impressive monuments. Ancient Egyptians used a chronology based on dynasties and pharaohs, although modern historians selectively rely upon a simplified system that divides the period into the Old Kingdom, the Middle Kingdom, and the New Kingdom.

Egypt was centered on the Nile. A huge number of slaves and laborers worked in fields and crafted buildings of an unprecedented scale. Egyptians had a lot of stone, something that causes Egyptian monumental architecture to be different from Mesopotamian. Their monuments and artistic achievements were only possible because Egypt was a strong centralized power. Some two millennia before the establishment of the royal dynasties, *c.* 5200 BCE, Egyptians started practicing agriculture. They established villages where flint blades, grain storage pits, and animal bones were discovered. In Egypt, the knowledge of farming likely came from Mesopotamia via the Red Sea.

Monuments

The Old Kingdom

Egyptian religion was focused on death or, better, the afterlife, with architecture and material culture mediating between the ruling elite and gods, Earth, and heaven. The Old Kingdom, 2649–2150 BCE, is the age of the **pyramids**, when Zoser (2686–2613 BCE) built his famous pyramid at Saqqâra and when the great pyramids at Giza were built.

The earliest step in the progression of building pyramids was the Mortuary Complex of Zoser, located west of Memphis and north of Saqqâra. The architect who worked for Zoser was Imhotep. (No architects' names have survived from ancient Mesopotamia.) Their collaboration is a watershed moment in Egyptian history, as it involves the first monumental use of stone and monumentally

scaled columns. Stone columns from buildings that postdate Saqqâra were based on natural forms, such as bundles of reeds and open lotus blossoms (Figure 2.0).

This period is also important because the elite practiced the custom of entombing the dead, when the ruler's body was laid to eternal rest. Because of the practice of entombment along with items to serve in the afterlife, we have the oldest surviving pieces of furniture, including, miraculously, wooden furniture.

Because their attention was focused almost exclusively on monuments, tombs, cenotaphs, and temples, we know less about the daily life of Egyptians. Much of what we know about their daily life comes from the art and artifacts of tombs.

The sprawling **necropolis** at Saqqâra was not just for the pharaoh but also for members of the royal family and officials who shared in the use of a sumptuously prepared afterlife. Adjacent to the famous mortuary complex lies the entrance to a tomb that is unlike any other, the twin tomb of two male manicurists, Niankhkhnum and Khnumhotep (Figure 2.5). They were, as the tomb tells us, overseers of manicurists to the king. The paintings inside this otherwise unremarkable

Figure 2.5
Stone relief from the Tomb of Niankhkhnum and Khnumhotep, Saqqâra, Egypt, *c.* 2400 BCE.

tomb are unprecedented in Egyptian art because they show two men in what appears to be an embrace, a representation of a position that otherwise is only seen in male-female couples. Both Niankhkhnum and Khnumhotep were married and had children, who are also represented in the tomb, although smaller in scale. There are several representations of the two men throughout the tomb that show them intertwined, holding hands, or with Khnumhotep's hand on Niankhkhnum's shoulder. One interpretation is that they were a couple, with royal sanction.

Egyptian art was stylized, conventional, and conservative, meaning that changes came about slowly. Within an individual artist's lifetime, changes in style and technique were incremental. Artists worked within existing conventions; they were beholden to relying upon standard methods of representation. Regarding the human figure, the stylistics of Egyptian art show the body in a pose that no flesh-and-blood person can strike. The legs and feet, up to the hips and carefully delineated abdominal muscles, are shown in strict profile, while the upper chest and shoulders face the viewer. Each body part is shown in the way that shows it best. Thus, the full chest and broad shoulders face forward. The head, however, appears in almost perfect profile. The nose is in profile, but the eyes are shown frontally.

This beguiling image underscores the interpretation of history as an ongoing endeavor and that not all historians agree. Contemporary issues, such as race and gender, have an impact on what archaeologists and historians study. So while the precise meaning of the tomb of Khnumhotep and Niankhkhnum eludes us, we are not at a total impasse. Physical proximity in representation clearly represents physical proximity in life and some sort of emotional involvement that they wished to represent eternally.

An intermediate step in the development of the pyramids, which the pyramids of Giza are the highest expression of, was during the reign of the Pharaoh Snefru (2613–2589 BCE). He built several pyramids, among them the Bent Pyramid of Snefru in the town of Dahshur. It is noteworthy because it started out ambitiously, initially envisioned to be higher. Then, because of signs of structural failure in the course of construction, the angle of the pyramid was changed.

The most famous pyramids are those of Giza, made by Snefru's son. The pyramid named for him, Khufu (Cheops), is the biggest and was built first. The pyramid of Khafre (Chephren) followed.

Queen Hetepheres was Snefru's wife and Khufu's mother. Snefru reigned from 2575 to 2551 BCE. The oldest extant pieces of Egyptian furniture come from her tomb and its funerary furnishings (Figure 2.6). She was buried in a **mastaba** that is part of the layout of the Great Pyramid. A mastaba is an oblong tomb with sloped walls that covers a vault.

A draped pavilion protected Hetephere's furniture. Thin columns with capitals held up a framework from which lightweight textiles flowed. This shelter maximized air flow, while shielding its users from sunlight and pests.

The resemblance that Egyptian beds bear to modern beds is misleading. What looks like the headboard of Hetephere's bed is the footrest. A wooden framework supports a caned platform for the resting body. The wood has been gilded. A separate piece is the headrest. This is one of those items that underscore how very different the Egyptians were regarding conceptions of comfort. The legs have feet that all face the same direction.

Hetephere's armchair reveals the designer's reliance on geometry, cubic massing, and a grid. Seat, back, and armrests are all squares. The cubic composition contrasts with the armrest supports that represent three flowers, two of which languidly droop. In the conception of its form, this chair differs significantly from the pieces made some one thousand years later.

Middle Kingdom

During the Middle Kingdom (2030–1640 BCE), the hold of pyramids as the principal type of royal monument decreased, and the pharaohs turned their attention to building and outfitting the great **pylon** temples.

New Kingdom

Although some pyramids continued to be built during this period, 1550–1070 BCE, this is the classic age of Egyptian art and architecture, an age of prosperity and architectural achievement. The state machine was in full operation. In this period, Egypt controlled the southern region of Nubia.

Egypt was a political and cultural entity with an intricate and efficient organization and administration. This was the era of Thebes and Memphis. Two of the most significant works of architecture are the Mortuary Temple of Queen Hatshepsut, c. 1520 BCE, and the Temple of Amun-Re at Karnak, 1490 BCE. This period also featured some fascinating characters, such as Akhenaten, Hatshepsut, and Tutankhamen.

Figure 2.6
Canopy, bed and
armchair from the
Tomb of Queen
Hetepheres, Giza,
Egypt, 2575–2528
BCE.

Artistically, the reign of Akhenaten is significant because he introduced several new art
forms, including a unique style of portraiture. He
is responsible for having shifted Egyptian religious practices in the direction of monotheism, an
achievement that was reversed upon his death.

There was a zenith in the splendor of the
arts, particularly architecture, in the reign of
Ramesses II, who was the most active builder in
Egyptian history.

Tutankhamen

Tutankhamen was a minor sovereign who died
young and had few political accomplishments
to his credit. His greatest legacy is that he is the
only pharaoh whose royal tomb was discovered
intact. Discovered in 1922, it included a wealth
of furnishings. Among them was a remarkable
folding bed made of wood with rush matting for
support (Figure 2.7). Many Egyptian pieces, as
with Assyrian pieces, were collapsible, the obvious reason being that furniture pieces were used
in travel. The reason for the rush matting is that
it would "give," thereby providing comfort. The

Figure 2.7
Folding camping bed from the Tomb of Tutankhamun, Thebes,
Egypt, c. 1330 BCE.

bed has animal feet, facing in the same direction. Because it folds, this obviously indicates that it was moved. The Egyptian climate is ideal for preserving artifacts for long periods of time. This, in conjunction with the Egyptian penchant for entombing articles of daily life, means that there are an astonishing number of extant pieces of Egyptian wood furniture.

Noted Egyptologist Cyril Aldred (1984) writes that Egyptian art reflects a boxlike conception of the world. The Nile flows south to north, and the sun crosses it perpendicularly, thus putting Egypt into a grid. Egyptian art reflects an idealized view of nature. Ground plans and elevations often reflect a strict mathematical order based on a grid and the important right angle. Large drawings were created by a drawing being done in one scale then overlain with a grid, which was then transferred to a larger scale.

Pieces of furniture operate under two systems: the importance of the simple geometry, and a sensitivity to the shape of the human figure. In many reliefs, chairs are represented as cubes at a right angle, with **stretchers** occurring at either thirds or quarters.

A child's chair from Tutankhamen's tomb displays the characteristic Egyptian curved seat. The overall composition shows an initial reliance on a grid. The seat and legs form an approximate square. The legs are more or less straight. But then the seat and arms are curved. The back is a cube, lengthened into a rectangle with additional bands of decoration. This piece shows the high level of craft of Egyptian furniture makers. The curves employed in Egyptian furniture were complicated geometrically. The chair has carved legs. It is structurally stabilized with stretchers embellished with metal inlays. Its overall form is aesthetically pleasing but not over-the-top in its decoration. For its time period, it was comfortable.

While the chairs of Tutankhamen represent the highest level of craft of Egyptian furniture makers, it is possible to imagine that their forms were imitated in simpler pieces. In fact, representations of furniture on reliefs confirm this.

The full chest of drawers would not make its European debut until the Renaissance. Yet the drawer makes an unheralded appearance in ancient Egypt. A small chest on high legs from Tutankhamen's tomb sports a single drawer. Drawers were not the primary means of storage for either large-scale items or large quantities of items. A common motif that embellished furniture was the **ankh**, a looped cross that is a symbol of the regenerative quality of life.

Surviving images are important because they show furniture being made or in use (Figure 2.8). Drawings and carved reliefs also document the existence of modest pieces that have not survived, helping us learn about bygone lifestyles. A relief from Sobekhotep's tomb shows jewelry workers. They sit on two types of stool, one with curved legs and a seat, another with straight legs, reinforced with stretchers. They use tables, one with legs, another cubelike. This gives an idea of what straightforward stools were like, in which the sitters sit low to the ground; two of them perform their arts with outstretched legs.

A folding stool from Tutankhamen's tomb has duckbill supports, consistent with Egyptian artistic practices that make constant reference to the natural world. The seat curves in a manner characteristic of Egyptian furniture, an ancient version of **ergonomics**.

Stools were not only the purview of workers and slaves. Chairs with backs were exceptional, and many nobles are shown sitting on stools. The carpenter's simple stool is painted white, while the chair he is crafting has lion's feet and gilding.

In Egypt, artists introduced many conceptual approaches to working with materials that influenced later periods. One is that items are initially made in one material; for example, a bunch of reeds or grasses are bundled together and used as a support, such as a column. The form then takes hold in the imagination, and even when a different material is used, such as limestone, the form remains. The result is that Egyptian buildings make constant reference to the material world and organic materials. As with Mesopotamia, the existence of Egyptian art as an autonomous entity starts to unravel with the growing influence of Greece and Rome. A significant date for this is the ascendancy of Alexander the Great, 332 BCE.

Nubia

Nubia, the Mesopotamian kingdoms, and Egypt were coeval; they traded and intermittently fought with one another. Trade, politics, and military maneuvers were complicated mechanisms that resulted in cultural intermingling. Certainly, one of the interesting aspects of looking at historic styles and their development over time is to

Figure 2.8
Carpenter Making a Chair, Tomb of Rekhmire, Thebes, Egypt, 1479–1400 BCE. Wall painting, facsimile by Nina de Garis Davies.

understand why change comes about; one of the driving forces of artistic change is exposure to and influence by others.

Nubia is the land to the south of Egypt, below what Egyptians called Upper Egypt (upriver on the Nile). It occupied the area that today lies in Sudan and Ethiopia. Egypt itself is on the continent of Africa. Nubians remain a prominent ethnic group in Egypt today, and there are both white and black Nubians. Nubia is an African-influenced Egyptian culture, although also a melting pot of African indigenous, Egyptian, and later Roman influence.

Continual Egyptian incursions into Nubia, Libya, and northern Mesopotamia meant that the subjugated peoples took on Egyptian ways in architecture, religion, sculpture, and dress. The most valued of Nubia's natural resources were metals. Nubia helped satiate the Egyptian thirst for gold, and Egyptians relied upon Nubians for their knowledge of iron metallurgy. The land of Nubia, also known as Kush, was referred to by the Greeks and Romans as "Aethiopia," which means "land of burnt faces." For Greeks and Romans, Ethiopia did not mean the area that is today Ethiopia, or even Nubia, but was used to refer to the entire African continent. Around

3100 BCE, Nubia united into a central powerful kingdom.

Egypt, one of the most heavily researched areas of the ancient world, lies next door to one of the least. This is because Egyptian monuments are spectacular, and Egypt has had a political stability that the area of Sudan lacks. Uncovering the riches of Nubian architecture, interiors, and material culture is an ongoing endeavor.

The Twenty-fifth Dynasty

For most of its history, Nubia was ruled by Egypt. Nubians served in the Egyptian army and as slaves. Egyptian wall paintings and sculpture have many references to their southern neighbors.

The Twenty-fifth Dynasty sees a dramatic turn of events as Nubian pharaohs ruled Egypt. Piankhy (747–716 BCE) ushered in a period when control was centered on the Nubian capital. The height of Nubia's political and military strength was made possible by the demise of the Egyptian New Kingdom. Nubian control included lower Egypt and extended all the way to the Nile delta. Piankhy's reign was one component of the Kushite rule of Egypt, which occurred in 760–656 BCE, a period of less than one hundred years.

Nubian rulers made sure that Napata was architecturally worthy to rule Egypt. Beginning in 730 BCE, they built an Egyptian-style pylon temple, the Temple of Amun at Jebel Barkal. There are a significant number of other monuments and tombs in the area. Nubian pyramids are smaller in scale than their Egyptian counterparts and are characterized by a steep rake. In front of the steep pyramids is a pylon porch (Figure 2.9).

These tombs, with pyramidal form and pylon entrances carved in low relief, underscore the Egyptian influence on Nubian religion and artistic practices. Low-relief carving means the depth of the carving is shallow, placing the art form between sculpture and painting. Nubians worshiped Egyptian gods and built Egyptian-influenced temples and tombs.

Piankhy's successor, Shabaka, ruled from 716 to 701 BCE. He ruled from within Egypt, using Thebes as his capital. Part of Shabaka's foreign affairs included dealing with the Assyrians, and for this he turned to his nephew, Taharka. Taharka himself ruled Egypt, from 690 to 664 BCE, with his center of operations based in Memphis and Thebes. In 690 BCE, Taharka was crowned. Taharka did not ignore his Nubian homeland, and he added on to the temple of Jebel Barkal. His design influence is seen in multiple projects in Luxor (Figure 2.0). Taharka had continual battles with the Assyrians, who would ultimately be his downfall. He is generally considered to be one of Africa's greatest rulers, although Ashurbanipal defeated Taharka, who returned to Nubia for his final days.

Senkamanisken ruled from 643 to 623 BCE. He does not have the hallowed place in African history that Taharka does, although this is not obvious in a grand statue of him. The bodies of Nubian statues display a more robust physique

than their slimmer Egyptian counterparts. The statue of Senkamanisken shows him with broad shoulders and a muscular chest. The statue relies upon the Egyptian artistic approach to sculpture in the round.

Over the period of Nubian ancient history, there were three capitals: Kerma, Napata, and Meroë. In response to military pressure from the Assyrians, the Kushite rulers moved deeper into the African continent and established their final capital at Meroë. Meroë served as the Kushite capital following the Twenty-fifth Dynasty, when Nubia no longer ruled Egypt.

Because fewer excavations have been carried out in Nubia, it is difficult to construct a full picture of its material culture, including furniture. The Nubians, like the Egyptians, buried their nobles with furnishings to serve in the afterlife.

When making grand public gestures, such as temples, mortuary tombs, and sculpture of rulers, Nubians looked to Egypt for inspiration, yet to round out our picture of material culture, we should make note that more common objects continued to rely on local traditions, such as baskets, mats, simple pieces of furniture, and certainly ceramics.

Pottery began in Africa as early as the seventh millennium BCE. The Neolithic revolution was the period in which the tail end of the Neolithic period morphed into what we consider "history." This involved a move away from hunter-gatherers to agrarian life and included the introduction of pottery to Nubia. Anthropologist Nigel Barley writes that for the history of Africa, ceramics play an important role:

Pots are naturally used for the storage and cooking of liquids but have a much wider role than the Western saucepan and African clay is

Figure 2.9
Meroë pyramids with pylon entryways, which hold burial chambers for Kushite kings and queens, Nubia, Sudan, 592 BCE–350 CE.

Figure 2.10
Pottery from
Meroë, Nubia,
Sudan, *c.* 800
BCE–350 CE.

almost as versatile as plastic in the West. This
is clear from the way that pottery is often used
to produce skeuomorphs (representations of
objects usually made in one material executed
in another) so that pottery designs overlap
with those of wood, basketry and leather.

(1994, p. 69)

A piece of Nubian pottery combines geometric decoration with a naturalistic representation.
Such approaches are common in Nubian baskets
and textiles (Figure 2.10).

Nubian influence on Egypt occurred throughout Egyptian history and is not limited to the
Twenty-fifth Dynasty. Many have even posited
that Thutmose III's mother was Nubian.

Conclusion

Furniture from Egypt exists in quantity. Many of
the pieces are of high quality in terms of construction, materials, and decoration. The decorative
motifs of Egyptian furniture are consistent with
those that adorn other art forms, such as buildings and wall paintings. The latter also inform us
that most people sat on stools. Egyptian furniture

makers ingeniously combined two compositional
systems: a hard-edged grid and a curvilinear
anthropomorphism.

The Egyptians, like their neighbors to the
east, responded to the natural environment by
representing it and emulating it. The logic behind
taking a form such as a lotus blossom and carving
it in stone was not functional but spiritual and
aesthetic.

The legacy of the Mesopotamian civilizations includes large-scale cities, mathematics,
record-keeping, written laws, and the novel. A
feature of public buildings around the world also
derives from their use of sculpture as a complement to architecture. The important entryways of
Assyrian palaces were delineated with a pair of
animals carved in stone. These sentries marked
the entrance and guarded the public domain.

Nubia, next door to the all-powerful Egypt,
is an example of cultural intermingling. When
Nubian rulers were in power, they honored
Egyptian prowess by emulating her temples,
sculpture, religion, and dress. Yet Nubian art
forms also subtly affirm that Nubia was an entity
different from Egypt; it was African.

The legacies of these three regions include
stone columns, monumental sculpture, and the
use of fantastic animals in decorative programs.
Recovering the heritage of Nubia is an ongoing
project, in large part due to the interest of
twentieth- and twenty-first-century African
American scholars such as Harvard's Henry Louis
Gates (2001). Interest in ancient Nubia, Egypt,
and Mesopotamia is driven in large part by what
these civilizations mean to people today.

Sources

Assyria

Barnett, Richard David (2009). *The Balawat Gates of
Ashurnasirpal II.* London: British Museum Press.

Budge, Wallis, ed. (1914). *Assyrian Sculptures in the
British Museum.* London: British Museum.

Cifarelli, Megan (1998). "Gesture and Alterity in the Art
of Ashurnasirpal II of Assyria." *The Art Bulletin* 80
(June): 210–28.

Frahm, Eckart (2023). *Assyria: The Rise and Fall of the
World's First Empire.* New York: Basic Books.

Hare, Susanna and Edith Porada (1946). *The Great King:
King of Assyria: Assyrian Reliefs in the Metropolitan
Museum of Art.* Photographed by Charles Sheeler.
New York: Metropolitan Museum
of Art.

Reade, J.E. and J.E. Curtis (1995). *Art and Empire:
Treasures from Assyria in the British Museum.*
London: British Museum Press.

Egypt

Aldred, Cyril (1984). *The Egyptians*. London: Thames and Hudson.

Amenta, Alessia (2005). *The Treasures of Tutankhamen and the Egyptian Museum of Cairo*. Vercelli: White Star.

Badawy, Alexander (1966). *A History of Egyptian Architecture*. Berkeley: University of California Press.

Killen, Geoffrey (2017). *Ancient Egyptian Furniture*. Philadelphia: Oxbow Books.

Edwards, I.E.S. (1972). *The Treasures of Tutankhamun*. New York: Viking.

Smith, W.S. (1998). *The Art and Architecture of Ancient Egypt*. New Haven, CT: Yale University Press.

Svarth, Dan (1998). *Egyptian Furniture-Making in the Age of the Pharaohs*. Skarup: Skippershoved.

Nubia

Barley, Nigel (1994). *Smashing Pots: Works of Clay from Africa*. Washington, DC: Smithsonian Institution Press.

Gates, Henry Louis (2001). *Wonders of the African World*. New York: Knopf.

Discussion and Review Questions

1. What are some examples of forms created out of one material that are then crafted out of a new material?

2. How would you characterize the Egyptian approach to crafting monumental architecture?

3. How would you characterize the Mesopotamian approach to crafting monumental architecture?

Classical Civilizations

3

Greece	3000–1000 BCE	3000–1400 BCE	1600–1100 BCE	510–323 BCE	323–146 BCE
	Bronze Age	Minoan Period	Mycenean Civilization	Classical Period	Hellenistic

Rome		753 BCE	650–500 BCE	509–31 BCE	31 BCE–337 CE
		Founding of Rome	Etruscan Dominance	Roman Republic	Roman Empire

There are two principal theaters of Western classicism: Greece and Rome. Understanding them fully starts with looking at their predecessors, the Myceneans and the Minoans in Greece, and the Etruscans in Rome. These precursors to Western classical civilizations were contemporary with the Old, Middle, and New Kingdoms of Egypt. The Minoans established a color scheme of white, red and black that proved resilient and it reappears in Roman wall painting. From Greece, we have few remaining pieces of furniture, yet thanks to the indestructible vases, an entire corpus of furniture is known to us. We have a comprehensive knowledge of stools, chairs, couches, armchairs, thrones, and numerous table types. Roman secular interiors included concrete and vaulting and saw an astonishing amount of innovation in forming and furnishing interior architecture. In multiple artistic realms, there was a progression of development and improvement. Recognized standards of refinement had an extensive vocabulary, with words that we still use. But this should not blind us to the diversity of design approaches. There were ideals and the pull of perfection, but the exceptions were many. The classics are important for studying Western architecture and design as they form the basis of later periods, including the Renaissance, Neoclassicism, nineteenth-century revivals, and postmodernism. One can even argue that twentieth-century

Figure 3.0
(*Facing page*)
Apollodorus, The Pantheon, Rome, Italy, 113–125 CE.

modernism is best understood with a grounding in the classical arts. Each age pursues its own perspective on classicism. The historian Mary Beard said in a *New Yorker* interview: "history is always moving, because we're changing the questions and it's changing the answers."

Greece: Minoan and Mycenaean

The Mycenaeans and the Minoans were ancient to ancient Greece. The Mycenaeans inhabited mainland Greece, where they built **citadels** that capped mountaintops. The Minoans had a vibrant seafaring economy, centered on the island of Crete. For their urban centers, Minoans chose inland valleys, preferring to look at mountains from a distance.

Minoan Crete

Neolithic communities existed on Crete from about 6000 BCE, but the mature era of the Minoan period is dated to 2000–1400 BCE. As with Mycenaean towns, the most important structure was the palace and not a temple. Mount Ida is the tallest mountain on the rocky island of Crete, yet Minoan towns did not crown outcroppings of rock, but took advantage of plains. Minoan cities were not fortified; the island itself acted as a means of protection.

The major Minoan historical figures, on whom much of Greek mythology is based, include Minos, Daedalus, and Icarus. The civilization is named for King Minos, the monarch and builder of the largest palace, Knossos. It is worth remembering that in ancient Greece, the line between history and myth is blurry. Daedalus was an architect, inventor, and designer. He invented wings, and his son Icarus met an untimely death because he ignored his father's warnings not to fly too high. Icarus soared higher and higher, the sun melted the wax that bound the feathers together, and he fell to his death. His downfall is a metaphor for ambition and the perils of reaching too high. It is also a familiar familial story in which a son rebels against parental authority. Daedalus created the labyrinth, the prison that held the half-bull Minotaur. Theseus killed the creature but could only find his way in the labyrinth with the help of Ariadne and her thread.

Palace

The most important structure on Crete is the Palace of Knossos, and the story of the labyrinth likely derives from those who saw the palace's ruins as a confusing pile of rubble. The palace itself was constructed by an additive design process, its grandeur arising not from huge individual rooms but from the existence of hundreds of them. It is organized around a central courtyard. The palace looked inward toward the court; elaborate exterior façades are not a feature of Minoan architecture.

A central sequence of rooms includes a stairway and a throne room. The vertical connection is formed with broad flights of stairs, ceremonial because of their scale, symmetry, and prominent location. Important rooms were painted. The color palette relied heavily on white, red, and black—attractive colors because of the availability of natural pigments. Blues and greens were rare and reserved for important rooms.

The palace was the center of a town of some 40,000 inhabitants and had ceremonial, administrative, residential, and religious functions. There were rooms devoted to religious practices, but no separate temples. Houses, like the palace, were two or three stories high, with the ground floor devoted to storerooms; upper floors boasted windows.

The courtyard was an open place, the center of this proto-urban entity, and thus can be considered the predecessor to the **agora** and the **forum**. Most streets were paved. On the perimeter of the urban space stood buildings that were distinguished by the unique Minoan **cornice** and columns. The columns of Minoan architecture have a distinctive profile. From a large cushioned **capital** at the top they taper toward a narrow base. This profile follows the logic of structure, as the weight of the heavy entablature above is distributed to an increasingly narrow profile. (Frank Lloyd Wright appreciated the efficacy of the Minoan columns.) Minoan columns were a feature of exteriors and interiors alike.

The Minoans left behind a legacy in fired and glazed pottery. They made items out of metal, such as knives, and produced textiles. Crete is covered with oak, cypress, fir, and cedar, but few wooden products remain. There was little in the way of monumental sculpture.

The central ceremonial sequence of the palace contains a throne room and from it a rare example of Minoan furniture (Figure 3.1). The throne is made of alabaster and imitated a common chair type of wood or straw. This throne has no arms; the back is high and carved with the naturalistic forms that are a feature of the wall behind it. Alabaster benches lined the walls of the throne room and stood at

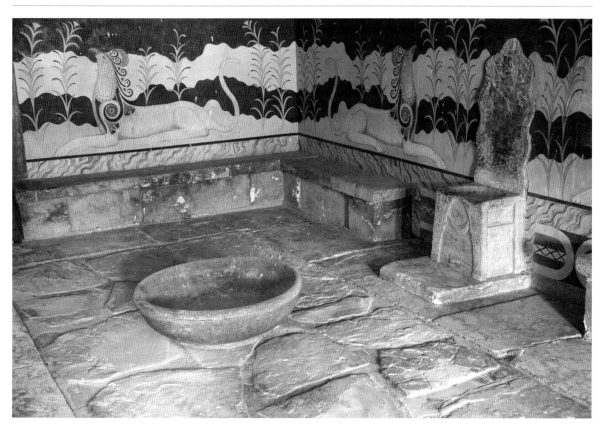

Figure 3.1
Throne of King
Minos, Palace of
Knossos, Crete,
Greece, late
fifteenth century
BCE.

the same height as the throne. Subsequent Greek furniture is made of wood, and it is probable that the Minoans had wooden furniture, of which this alabaster throne is the only trace. The word *throne* derives from the Greek *thronos.*

The important rooms of the palaces were richly decorated with wall paintings, including marine scenes and lively lines of men and women bearing offerings. One particularly grand fresco features a giant bull. At several points, the cornices of the palaces feature bull horns. Architectural historian Vincent Scully argued that Knossos is important for its siting in relation to the landscape. Subsequent Greek temples take their cue from Knossos. Scully ([1962] 1979) argues: "The mountain may have other characteristics of great sculptural force, such as rounded slopes, deep gullies, or a conical or pyramidal massing itself, but the double peaks or notched cleft seem essential to it. These features create a profile which is basically that of a pair of horns." According to Scully's interpretation, Minoans saw in the landscape the profile of the sacred bull and sited their cities accordingly.

Minoan history, and its age of grand building, came to an end around 1400 BCE, likely due to an earthquake or the exile or mass movement of people, setting the stage for the next episode in Greek history.

Mycenae

Mycenae is on mainland Greece and thus is the immediate forebear to classical Greece. Mycenae is the city for which the civilization itself is named. The history of Mycenae also features a beguiling cast of characters on whom countless myths were based, including Agamemnon, Cassandra, and Clytemnestra.

The simple **megaron** is the foundation of Mycenaean architecture. It is a U-shaped structure, with a porch that features two columns **in antis**, flanked by projecting side walls (Figure 3.2). A hearth stood at the center of the singular chamber.

In contrast to the Minoans, the mainland cities responded to the landscape in a direct way. These early cities, and thus the first chapter in the history of Greek architecture, date to approximately 1400 BCE. They chose to locate their fortified cities on mountaintops, thus starting a tradition that saw meaning in the landscape. This was a way of locating themselves in relationship to the cosmos. Walls were built of **cyclopean masonry**, big blocks of irregularly shaped stones. Gated openings in the walls sharply limited access.

Palaces were elaborations of the vestigial megaron; they were larger, and some were formed from agglomerations of this basic architectural unit.

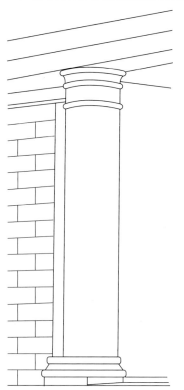

Figure 3.2
Columns in antis.

Tiryns sits on an outcropping of stone in the plain of Argos. The Argive plain is an agricultural area in the Peloponnese. It was occupied from the Bronze Age into the Mycenaean period, 1300–1400 BCE.

King Agamemnon dominates the list of important historical figures. He was married to Clytemnestra, and his children included Orestes, Electra, and Iphigeneia. He was the brother of Menelaus. Menelaus' wife was the beautiful Helen, and her preference for a man not her husband was the flashpoint that started the Trojan War. The tragic tribulations of Agamemnon's family, the House of Atreus, are central to Homer's *Iliad* and *Odyssey*. His family members' individual contributions to history were the focus of plays written by Aeschylus, Euripides, and Sophocles.

Rather than the palaces, a fantastic type of architecture exists outside of the citadel context. They were the beehive tombs. These deceptively simple structures hold subterranean **corbelled** domes; corbelling is a construction method in which each successive course projects past the lower course. A corbelled arch is structurally a forerunner to the rounded arch. The tombs were approached from a **dromos**, an elongated entryway with high retaining walls, also known as a **tholos**. In fashioning these structures, a hillside was selected and then partially excavated. After the dromos, the dome was built, half buried in

the ground; once the dome was completed, it was buried with earth. One of the best preserved is the so-called Treasury of Atreus (it was a tomb, not a treasury). A straightforward rectangular burial chamber lies off the rotunda.

The doorway is a classic **post-and-lintel** construction, flanked by Mycenaean columns. In the space above the lintel, a relieving triangle was left, which reduced the weight on top of the lintel and helped distribute the weight to the sides. Sometimes this panel was sculpted, thus starting the tradition of decoration that crowns doorways. A similar relieving triangle embellishes the main gate to Mycenae, the famous Lion Gate, the first piece of monumental sculpture in Greece. With its paired lions, it is reminiscent of Assyrian palaces. In the time period of the early Greeks, the Assyrians were prominent and formidable adversaries.

Mycenaean Greece has a direct relationship to classical Greece. It had a pantheon of gods, goddesses, and other mythical figures; these heroes and villains were the subjects of oral histories and represented in decorated pottery. Stories about the Trojan War were popular. The Greeks developed a graceful way of draping the body and an artistic strategy of developing forms in one material and transforming the shapes into stone. The end of the Bronze Age for the island of Crete and Mycenaean Greece marks the beginning of classical Greece.

Classical Greece

Temple development

The first Greek shrines followed the model of domestic architecture, the simple megaron. These modest structures hint at the riches that are to come. Mainland temples were also based on the megaron. What had been the hearth in a home became the statue of a deity in a temple.

The sources of Greek identity included the Greek language and the Gods, including Zeus, Hera, Apollo, and Athena. Greece, the birthplace of democracy, saw the rise of the city-state, the **polis**. These disparate elements all contributed to the Panhellenic community that was Greece. It was an urban culture whose citizens were beholden to a combination of local allegiances and also to a national Greek identity.

The development of the Greek temple was a way of forging a common identity, yet also an individual civic character that was based on the identification of a city with a god or goddess.

The Temple of Hera I, at Paestum, Italy, provides an example of a Greek temple plan. The central hall, the **cella** or naos, is flanked by two porches, the pronaos (at the entrance) and the episthodomos (at the rear). The plan shows several of the early steps in the process of crafting a monumental architecture. As with other early Greek temples, there were a number of spatial arrangements that are awkward compositionally and whose problems subsequent temple design would solve. First among these problems was the central row of columns. In the desire to have a larger building, but unsure of how to span an increased distance, Greek architects doubled the interior space with an intermediate row of columns. While this increased the size, it had the undesirable effect of creating a bifurcated interior. This layout was at odds with the building's function: to house a single statue.

William Dinsmoor wrote a standard text on Greek architecture, published in 1902. His *The Architecture of Ancient Greece* is still required reading. Writing about early temple design, he noted: "When a temple containing an inner row of columns had likewise a pronaos enclosed with *antae*, the inner row was usually recalled in the pronaos by a single post *in-antis*" (Dinsmoor [1902] 1975). That is, the odd layouts of early Greek temples were reflected in their façades.

The Temple of Apollo at Bassae represents a further development in which two rows of columns create a central nave with side aisles. From Pausanias, we know that Iktinos was the architect of the Temple of Apollo at Bassae. Pausanias referred to him as "contemporary of Perikles and architect of the Parthenon of Athens." Tzonis and Giannisi (2004) refer to Bassae as

having "a strange dual conservative-revolutionary identity." It had a new and unusual combination of **orders—Doric** outside, **Ionic** inside, and a single **Corinthian** column in the middle—which was perhaps the first column of its kind. Charles Robert Cockerell (1788–1863) visited Bassae in 1812 and created a famous drawing of the interior. It is an odd structure because the central nave leads to a single column and not a statue, and no statue or base has ever been found (Figure 3.3). The interior façade of the pronaos had three columns. The principal façade, accordingly, had nine columns. Eventually Greek architects reached a consensus that an even number of columns was ideal. Bassae, exceptionally, faces north and has a side entrance that faces east.

The optical refinements of Greek architecture involve defying strict geometries to improve the visual perception of a building. The Parthenon was the building that most fully employed the potential of optical refinements (Figure 3.4). The horizontal lines of the Parthenon are slightly convex; the temple platform, the **stylobate**, bulges in the middle. The resulting curvature had optical and functional effects. **Entasis** is the optical refinement of columns; it involves the outward swelling of the shaft. Additionally, the axes of column shafts were tilted slightly toward the center of the building.

Most famously, the location of **triglyphs** at the corners of the entablature was adjusted. Typically, triglyphs occurred along the centerline of a column, yet this would result in an awkward configuration at the building's corners; it seems logical that the entablature should end on a triglyph. At the Parthenon (and other temples), the corner column has the triglyph shifted off

Figure 3.3
Iktinos, Temple of Apollo at Bassae, 450 BCE.

Figure 3.4
Iktinos, Parthenon, Athens, Greece, 447–438 BCE.

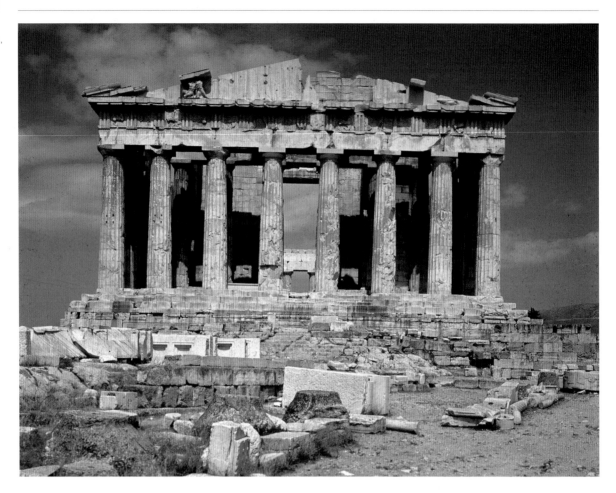

axis; the next triglyph is placed equidistant between the two columns, with the result that the spaces between the triglyphs, the **metopes**, vary. Yet this is imperceptible to the eye. The result of these manipulations is that while the actual building defies strict geometries, the perceived building is perfect. The detail of how a column meets the horizontal entablature remains influential to the present day (Figure 3.5).

We know little about Greek domestic architecture. One restoration of a house's section shows a courtyard surrounded by zones of construction (Figure 3.6). Greek houses were important, and epics and myths refer to them, but because they were made of mud bricks, they have largely disappeared from the archaeological record. The section of the so-called Maison de la Colline, a second-century BCE house in Delos, documents one of the few examples of Greek domestic architecture. It is speculative, as little more than the foundation remains, but foundations in conjunction with models of houses give some idea as to their three-dimensional projection. They were courtyard-centered houses, two-storied, with richly painted walls. A.W. Lawrence (1957) admits

Figure 3.5
Entablature.

Figure 3.6
Maison de la
Colline, Delos,
Greece, 176 BCE.
Building Section.

that the drawing is conjectural: "The restored section through a house at Delos, though unreliable in detail, must give a fair impression of late Hellenic decoration."

Poems extol the virtues of paintings, and there were important painters, but we have almost no information on Greek wall painting, as the organic materials of the pigments have not lasted. With the exception of a few remnants, almost no ancient Greek furniture has survived, yet we know an extensive amount about Greek furniture. How?

Material culture

When studying history, we, as twenty-first-century researchers, have no immediate access to the past. The past comes to us through oral, material, textual, and visual sources. Without sources, our knowledge of the past would be dim. For different time periods and places, the source materials vary greatly, and different source materials relay different types of information. A great deal about ancient Egypt is known because the society itself valued preserving items for eternity, and also because the climate is perfect for preservation. In sharp contrast, we have almost no information about Aztec or Khmer furniture; both were crafted largely out of wood and straw, and jungle environments are harsh on organic materials.

Some cultures created things out of durable materials, such as marble. Certain metals seem as if they would last, such as gold, yet although gold endures for a long time in the life of an individual, in historical terms it does not do well in terms of lasting for centuries.

History rarely bequeaths information on modest ways of living. To the extent that societies themselves set in motion the preservation process, as did the Egyptians, they rarely considered the objects of the lower and middling classes worthy of preservation. Which is why the subject of furniture in ancient Greece is such a delight. A wealth of information exists, not only about the objects but also their use.

The Greeks had an extensive pottery-making industry. They found utility in pottery in their daily lives, and they decorated their clay pots and vases with pictures. The material was inexpensive and durable. It was actually durable beyond their wildest dreams. Archaeologists love pottery because it is virtually indestructible. For almost all cultures, a great deal of valuable information is conveyed via the medium of pottery. Fired pottery can be thrown into a trash heap, and it will break, but the pieces can be pieced back together. The only way to destroy it is to grind it up.

Vase painting was a less exalted art form than wall painting. Whereas little to nothing is known about Greek wall painting, we have a comprehensive knowledge of vase paintings. Because many of the vases display furniture, we have a thorough knowledge of furniture. Though the information conveyed by this body of images is extensive, we need to realize that we are looking at representations of interiors and furniture and not the spaces and pieces themselves. It is certainly possible that pictorial conventions were at play that do not correspond to actual pieces of furniture.

For example, a drinking cup by the artist Onesimos shows the interior of a stable (Figure 3.7). The convention to indicate an interior is that an object, here a broom, hangs on the wall. Objects in vase paintings often look as though they are hanging in space. The other convention is that the ground plane, the floor, is visible at the bottom of the round "window" through which viewers are looking.

Some Greek vase paintings present versions of popular themes, such as the labors of Herakles. A scholar interested in them has hundreds of similar images to examine. Yet some wonderful vase paintings are one-offs, singular images whose interpretation remains elusive. There is no definitive authoritative interpretation of the African groom but some likely assertions. The fact that an African individual is represented is significant, underscoring that the Greek and African worlds were in communication. Many recent studies have explored the ancient concepts of race by looking at sources such as this. The Onesimos cup demonstrates that the world of images and objects contributes to constructions of racial and ethnic identity.

An achievement of Greek vase painting is the ability to capture a mood, a psychological moment that is complex, on the unforgiving medium of painted glaze on a spherical clay surface. Here, the horse appears ill at ease. The African character, not concerned, calms the horse with one confident hand on its back. One interpretation is that he holds a brush and that he is grooming the horse. He is possibly looking at the comb to see if any hairs are remaining; thus this image connects the human quality of diligence to this young man.

An example of the precise dating that is possible because of vase painting is the switch from black figure to red figure. Black figure refers to the method of painting black glaze on red clay. Details were then incised with a sharp instrument, revealing the red clay. Red figure is the opposite of black figure in both technique and result. The artists drew in outline, then painted the background black, leaving the figures red, a color that more closely approximated the human skin tone (red-figure artists left the red clay to indicate Greeks and Africans alike). *The Dictionary of Art* dates black figure to approximately 625 to 480 BCE, and red figure to 500 to 320 BCE (Turner 1996). White-ground has a light background, formed by applying a light slip of clay whitened with **kaolinite**.

A red-figure painting from 480 BCE shows a male youth sitting on a stool (Figure 3.8). It is an image that speaks across the ages, as it appears to show a student engaged in an activity that would be familiar today. He has, no doubt, just opened his laptop and is poised to check for Instagram updates. Obviously this is not true, but

Figure 3.7
Onesimos *The African Groom*, 480 BCE.

Figure 3.8
Douris, *The writing lesson: youth practicing calligraphy*, 480 BCE.

is therefore transportable. Leather connects the horizontal rails and forms the seat that in turn could support a cushion. The legs take the form of a gazelle's legs, each side facing in a different direction. The direction of the animal feet employs a different strategy from that of the Egyptians. On a Greek piece of furniture, the front and back face in different directions; on an Egyptian piece of furniture, all the feet are poised as if to march off in the same direction.

Klismos chair

The signature piece of Greek furniture is the **klismos** chair, presented on thousands of vase paintings. The klismos chair is a technically accomplished piece of furniture. When discussing Greek art, people often discuss its grace, its perfection, and its relation to human proportions—qualities that exist in the klismos chair. It is a rare example of a design that seems as though it could not be improved upon.

Greek architecture is anthropomorphic, with its proportions related to the human body. This is true of columns, the most obvious example being the **caryatids** of the Erechtheion, in which female bodies literally take the place of columns. The importance of the proportions of the human body also relates to Greek furniture. In fact, many of the names of a chair (as with a vase) rely upon parts of the body: feet, legs, arms, back, seat.

A red-figure painting from a krater held in Berlin is one of many that shows a klismos chair in profile. The klismos chair has splayed legs, and its seat is usually represented with caning or leather straps, sometimes with a cushion. The top rail of the chair back curves and conforms to the sitter's back, making it one of the earliest examples of the design of a piece of furniture related to the body's movement.

Reconstructions of the klismos chair successfully re-created how the chair was constructed out of wood. The chair has a central tapered splat that supports the curved back rail, aided by side vertical supports. The most problematic parts of the reconstruction were the splayed legs and lack of stabilizing stretchers. The chair, as crafted, is delicate and subject to structural failure at the legs. It is important to remember that we are looking at images of the furniture, not the pieces themselves. One possibility is that the mode of representing the furniture departed from actual construction techniques; perhaps the chairs had stretchers and the vase painters eliminated them from their paintings. Just as buildings are presented

this false familiarity is due to his engagement in an activity that relates human communication to the act of writing. He is practicing writing by using a stylus on an erasable wax table. The image conveys information about literacy and writing as they relate to a youth who craves communication.

He sits on a square stool that has upright legs. The seat is a frame, connected to the legs with dowels, and whose actual support is made from caning or leather straps. The comfort of such a stool is that the straps flex. We can interpolate that this modest stool was appropriate seating for young men who were studying.

Sculptural reliefs constitute another source for information about furniture. A **frieze** from the Parthenon shows multiple figures sitting on stools. Stools could be exalted as well as pedestrian.

Over the years, many have been interested to test the knowledge of furniture derived from vase paintings by attempting to construct them. One example is a common type of stool that folds and diagrammatically in vase paintings, it is possible that some of the actual details of the construction of the klismos chair are not conveyed.

In a red-figure vase painting on a **hydria** also from Berlin, three women engage in activities related to working and weaving wool. The klismos chair stands in profile. The dowel connections are visible and join the seat frame to the legs. The seat has no cushion.

A fifth-century **Attic** (from Athens) bell krater is one example in which a male figure sits on a klismos chair. An older man (he has a beard) is seated and touchingly tips a krater of liquid for a thirsty child. It is noteworthy that in these images the klismos chair has a visible backrest that the seated figures do not take advantage of. They do not lean back but sit upright, actively engage in playing an instrument or working wool.

Although both men and women use the klismos chair, in vase paintings it appears more frequently in activities that women engage in, such as dancing, weaving, and sewing.

In these images, the klismos chair is related to the arts of dancing and weaving. It is also witness to common daily activities, such as caring for children. These images suggest that the klismos chair was used in the context of conducting work. Showing a klismos chair in the context of dancing and weaving elevated those activities by relating them to an elegant piece of furniture. It is likely that common stools were most frequently used for daily activities.

Furnishing the symposium

Multiple images show people setting up furniture for a social engagement that will occur after the moment shown. One red-figure vase painting shows a satyr with a klismos slung over his shoulder. **Satyrs** were human figures with goat legs, ears, horns, and tail, and who were usually involved in mischief. The klismos chair dates to the late Archaic period, and its use was widespread in the classical period.

The Greeks had beds, made of wood, in a frame construction with attached legs. Like chairs, beds had either leather or cane strapping. A fifth-century red-figure vase painting shows a bed, couch, or settee, set up for the all-male, or mostly male, dining and drinking social engagement known as a **symposium**. In this painting, two men, one older, one younger, recline on a couch. They lean their arms on striped cushions. The younger man turns to speak with the older man. A three-legged table stands within arm's

reach (Figure 3.9). On another painting of two reclining men, the older gentleman is having his head held by the younger man so that when he vomits it will fall into a krater (another vase) and not soil the bedclothes.

A tradition that departs greatly from modern custom is how Greeks dined in formal situations, which was upright, in bed. Food and drink were placed on three-legged tables. The three-legged tables were round or rectangular. The couches were arranged to form a U-shape. When women are shown in the context of a symposium, they are typically either servers, entertainers, or prostitutes.

A vase painting from an **amphora** shows a young man carrying a klismos-type couch with a three-legged table attached to it. A klismos couch denotes a couch with the characteristic curved back of a klismos chair. The low backrest looks flat, but testament to the accuracy of the vase painter, he has correctly depicted the curved rail in profile. It is a wooden couch with attached legs. There was a method to attach the table to the couch. This youth is involved in setting up couches and tables for a social function. His nudity is a pictorial convention that elevates this daily activity to a higher artistic realm. Getting to the core of the matter, art historian Gloria Ferrari writes: "In the representation of manhood, the body takes center stage, naked because it is perfect" (2002, p. 162).

A limestone statuette also exists that shows a three-legged table slung over a male figure's shoulder. One reason for the three-legged rectangular version of a table was precisely that it could be carried over a man's shoulder.

A few actual table legs, such as those shown in front of the couches, remain. Some are marble and some are metal. In a reconstruction, metal legs are attached to a separately manufactured

Figure 3.9
Metal and wood trident table.

top. Table tops were either of stone or wood. The legs are fluted like columns and have lion's paws. The lion's feet on Greek furniture were likely an "Oriental" (Mesopotamian) influence. Furniture also existed with turned legs, another Eastern influence. The Greeks broadly referred to the Middle East as the East, or Orient, and this tradition lives on in modern institutions such as the Oriental Institute in Chicago; its collections are Middle Eastern, not Asian.

A common piece of furniture in paintings, as in life, was the modest chest. A chest portrayed in a red-figure **hydria** produced in Athens was crafted from planks. The front is a frame with an infill panel that has modest decoration. The chest has a flat top and attached legs. Chests are foremost useful storage devices, and they enter the narratives of vase paintings precisely because an object is held within them.

Another vase painting shows a lower chest with integral legs. A pattern decorates its side elevation (a pattern also found in textiles and architecture). A woman takes advantage of the low height and sits on the chest.

Chests are one of the most important furniture types. Because of their utility for holding things, they are found across the globe. A by-product of their design is that they provide a useful flat surface for sitting, dining, working, or sleeping. In the Greek realm, chests were gendered and metaphoric.

Art historian Gloria Ferrari writes about the representations of women and storage chests in vase paintings: "The footed chest is never far from the maiden. It sits on the ground, by her side, together with the wool basket" (2002, p.52). The use of the chest was not proscribed, but as an object that contains things, it was a space-enveloping piece of furniture. Smaller chests were related to women because they contained jewels, garments, and sewing equipment.

Just as women in vase paintings are shown cloaked and uncloaked, chests can be locked and they can be pried open. The supreme example of the chest as related to women, riches, and surprises is the story of Pandora's box.

Rome

Roman art and design, broadly defined, was inspired by Greece. The Romans were intimately familiar with Greek achievements in art, architecture, sculpture, and literature, and often compared their works to their cultural predecessors. The invention of Roman design is that it brilliantly operated within the stylistic parameters initially set by Greece, yet took it in new directions.

The Etruscans were the ancient people who preceded the Romans. The art and architecture of the southern half of the Italian peninsula show that southern Italians had direct experience with Greek culture and with Greek colonies.

The arch

Roman architecture was highly inventive, and much of the inventiveness was due to the discovery and use of the arch. Where Greek architecture was an architecture of the column and the post-and-lintel construction system, Roman architecture gloried in the arch. Other civilizations have had the arch and not really explored its possibilities, including Greece. When an arch is projected three-dimensionally, it becomes a **barrel vault** (Figure 3.10). When it is rotated around a single point, it becomes a dome. With the arch, the barrel vault, and the dome, the Romans had a whole new architectural vocabulary.

They also had a new material to accompany their explorations of form: concrete. Although Roman buildings often look as though built of stone, they were largely an architecture of bricks and concrete, faced with stone. Roman architects

Figure 3.10
Barrel vault.

saw the possibilities of the arch and concrete, and vaulting and use of the arch was widespread by the first century BCE.

Urban character

The Roman Empire adopted the grid for city planning in its military outposts. Yet the capital city, Rome itself, was irregular, responding to topography, important sites, and routes of trade. One oddity is that the best examples of Roman city planning are found in Rome's colonies.

The public infrastructure of Greece had been fairly limited. In a Greek city, there was never any doubt that the most important building was the temple. In Rome, new building types provided the public with amenities in addition to religious services. These included baths, theaters, amphitheaters, warehouses, and markets. Roman engineers also relied upon the arch to build aqueducts and bridges.

The Roman forum bears some similarities to the Greek **agora** and **stoa**, the Greek outdoor marketplace and public square, and the covered **portico** that delineated its perimeter. The Roman forum, an elongated rectangular space, was the civic and religious center. The Greek custom of public sculpture proceeds into the Roman period. There was a market, and a deceptively modest building type, the basilica, served as a combination stock exchange, general assembly room, and courtroom. And, of course, the most prominent structure was the center of religious ceremonies, the temple. Roman temples were similar to Greek temples to the extent that their primary function was the same—to house a cult statue.

Interiors

The Romans are broadly credited with a focus on interiors as carefully designed spaces. Greek temples, wonderful as they were, were figural objects meant to be viewed within the landscape. At close distance, it is clear that the Greek temple existed to house a statue. The development of temple interiors took a backseat to the development of the exteriors.

In Rome, even the forum was inward-looking, in comparison to civic developments that come after it. It was a conception of a public space as a single enclosed entity. The Roman forum did not lie at the end of a grand open roadway. Citizens and visitors experienced them by walking through the urban fabric. One happened upon the forum, passing through an entryway. The comparison is anachronistic, but as a process of experiencing

an urban space, it is more like the experience of arriving at the atrium in an American shopping mall, which comes as a bit of a surprise.

The Pantheon

Rome achieved its greatest geographic expanse during the reign of the long-lived emperor Hadrian. It included North Africa and the Middle East up to the tenuous border with Persia; Hadrian's famous wall in England constituted the western edge of the empire; and it included all of France and Spain. Hadrian was a prodigious builder, and his masterpiece is undoubtedly the Pantheon. An oddly self-effacing building, its **pediment** reads "M. Agrippa made me," although it was funded by Hadrian.

The temple faces north, with a standard temple front that gives no hint of the shape of the building behind it. The portico is made of monolithic, smoothly polished columns of Egyptian granite, with eight Corinthian capitals and a triangular pediment. Two additional rows of four columns make the porch a deep, ponderous entity.

The concrete dome is 4 feet (1.2 meters) thick at the top, swelling to 14 feet (4.3 meters) thick at the bottom. The dome contains one of the most magnificent spaces in the history of interiors (Figure 3.0). Surprisingly simple, it is a perfect half-dome, set upon a cylinder. It is 142 feet (43.3 meters) in height. It is one of the first examples of universal space, a giant column-free volume that does not house a myriad of functions; the primary purpose of its large volume is to impress. The hemisphere of the dome is divided into five tiers of **coffers**, lines that radiate outward from the center.

The drum is divided into two stories, delineated with the Corinthian order. The floor does not respond to the round dome that hovers above it, instead, it is a grid of squares made of granite, marble, and porphyry. A grid suggests that it is but a part of a larger pattern that extends far beyond this building. The interior, known as the **rotunda**, is richly ornamented, although the effect is still of simplicity.

A dome is subject to gravity. The round surface of the dome transfers the vertical forces and transforms them to lateral forces at the base; while the dome itself is subject to collapse, the greatest forces that need to be countered are at the base. The Pantheon counteracts the lateral forces of the dome with massive walls.

The building is superbly designed and required large amounts of labor and materials.

With a daring design, it is an architectural feat. It is, after all, called the Pantheon, the temple of *all* the gods. It seems cosmic, as though it has a universal meaning. Yet it was a Roman monument, built by Romans.

The lighting of the Pantheon is superb. It needs no artificial light. Natural light, from the **oculus**, is adequate on sunny days and creates a moody and dim atmosphere on cloudy days. The atmosphere changes under inclement weather; rain pours through the oculus, the raindrops refract the light, and a shimmering column of water connects the oculus to the floor.

Underscoring the geographic reach of the Roman Empire, Roman temples are also found in Baalbek, Lebanon; Pergamon, Turkey; and Thugga, Tunisia. It was the Emperor Hadrian who extended Rome into Africa. Part of his strategy to incorporate foreign lands into the empire was a grand building project that included establishing an architectural infrastructure in outposts. This was also a populist move to win people over.

L.P. Hartley grandly wrote: "The past is a foreign country: they do things differently there" (1953, p. 3). One of the pleasures of studying the past are those moments when one feels a human connection that traverses time. But there are instances when the past seems very strange. One example comes to us from the Roman African town of Thugga. As with all Roman towns, one of the grandest buildings was the bathhouse, and the Bath of the Cyclops in Thugga sported a very elegant privy (Figure 3.11).

The marble latrine seated twelve and shows a high level of craft with the unforgiving material of marble. They could have made this from wood, but for this location, it was made of a permanent material. The high level of technique also relates to the privy's connection to the city's plumbing. The privy was a social arena, and this is an example where contemporary practices depart from ancient ones. The Romans operated with a different concept of privacy.

Baths were grand buildings, and some of the largest in the empire. To finance the building of a public bathhouse was a way for leaders to show their populist leanings. The sequence of bathing rooms followed a standard procedure of **tepidarium**, **caldarium**, and **frigidarium**. A bather was first to slowly warm up; one then prepared for the hot bath. A final dousing of cool, fresh water completed the invigorating bathing process. Baths were separated for men and women. Grand baths also incorporated the Greek habit of an outdoor exercise area known as the **palaestra**.

Figure 3.11
Toilets, Baths of the Cyclops, Thugga, Tunisia, third century CE.

Domestic architecture

Up until the Roman period, little is known about domestic architecture and certainly little about how families of modest means lived. This situation changes dramatically with Rome, where the materials that document Roman domesticity are extensive. How? Our knowledge of Roman houses and their contents is largely due to one of history's greatest catastrophes, the eruption of Mount Vesuvius.

Pompeii lies 14 miles (22.5 kilometers) southwest of the modern city of Naples, at the foot of the volcanic Mount Vesuvius. Pompeii and the seaport of Herculaneum were destroyed by a massive eruption that occurred on August 24, 79 CE. A combination of lava and pumice blanketed the city to a depth of 9 feet (2.7 meters). A rain of ashes followed, for a total depth of 23 feet (7 meters). The deadly sludge fell so fast that humans and animals alike were trapped and buried alive.

Italian archaeologist Giuseppe Fiorelli developed a method of pouring plaster into the cavities formed in the volcanic ash where once there had been bodies that disintegrated.

The eruption preserved a large swath of the residential quarters, with the result that we know a great deal about Roman domestic architecture and interiors. The tragedy also gives history a precise date; all buildings and artifacts from Pompeii and Herculaneum date prior to the auspicious date of 79 CE.

The Roman house

The typical Roman house belonged to the larger category of Mediterranean courtyard-style houses (Figure 3.12). It followed a general approach to building that was suitable for the climates of the regions that surround the Mediterranean. A Roman house was similar to a Greek house in that both were centered on a courtyard. Openings connected rooms to the courtyard; openings to the street, were minimized.

The center of the house was the **atrium**, with an opening to the roof and a corresponding pool for collecting rainwater. Besides being a judicious way to collect and store rainwater, the atrium let in sunlight yet kept out the direct force of winds.

There was an idealized Roman house plan that grew out of an Italian house, the **domus**. ("Italian" here means the vernacular way of constructing houses on the peninsula.) This general layout, of a rectangular structure with an opening in the center, recalls the ancient Greek megaron.

A central room off the atrium held a small religious shrine. The principal room was the

Figure 3.12
Plan of the House of Marcus Lucretius Fronto, Pompeii, Italy, 79 CE.

tablinum where the head of the house received visitors and conducted the business of the household.

The house looked inwards and was regimented in its layout. From front to rear, street entrance to garden, there was a general progression of openings that become successively larger. Correspondingly, the area devoted to structure becomes smaller, so that a house progresses from architecture to garden.

From the Greeks, the Romans adopted the **peristyle**, the perimeter of columns that held up a covered colonnade. Running around three, if not four, sides of a rectangular space, the peristyle surrounded a space that usually centered on a fountain.

The Greeks painted their house walls, but these schemes became very elaborate for wealthy Romans. For both wall paintings and **mosaics**, skilled artists did the important work and apprentices did the prosaic infill work.

House exteriors did not receive the attention that interiors did; they were stuccoed and painted brick, with tiled hipped roofs. Over time, second stories became more common.

The desire and need for housing in Rome was great, and from ignominious beginnings, the Romans developed an apartment house, the **insula**. A domus housed extended families, servants, slaves, and tenants. Most single-family houses acted as multiple-family units. Not many modifications were necessary to turn the Roman house into an apartment house, hotel, or brothel. The insula also responded to the expanding Roman population.

Wealthy Romans developed another housing type, the villa, a sumptuous country house. In contrast to the inward focus of townhouses, villas had platforms, terraces, peristyles, and galleries that incorporated gardens and vistas.

Roman architecture was often symmetrically centered on an axis, and Roman architects increasingly relied upon the strategy of ending an axis on a curve, whereas the Greeks ended a prominent axis with a flat wall.

Hadrian's Villa in Tivoli is an extreme example of the other end of the scale of domestic architecture. It was a retreat for the emperor from Rome. The Empress Livy's rooms on the Palatine, the wife of the Emperor Augustus, were, in comparison, quite small.

Hadrian's Villa is an enigmatic design. Viewed in conjunction with the other major construction of Hadrian, the Pantheon, it is difficult to reconcile the two. One is his view of the cosmos, the world, and the place of the Roman Empire in administering it; the other is a private world that follows different rules. Some of its pavilions are highly inventive, almost baroque in the use of curves and countercurves.

Marguerite Yourcenar was a novelist, and her *Memoirs of Hadrian* was an imagined autobiography of the Emperor. It is highly regarded for its research and tone, and is often cited for its accuracy. Her approach is appropriate to a time period that saw little utility in separating history from myth. About the emperor's villa, she has Hadrian write: "The villa was the tomb of my travels, the last encampment of the nomad, the equivalent, though in marble, of the tents and pavilions of the princes of Asia" (Yourcenar [1951] 1963, p. 115). Yourcenar's scholarly musing is an explanation for the idiosyncratic nature of the design that follows no easily discernible plan. One theory is that the villa was a repository of his memories, and the various pavilions are architectural versions of his most cherished memories. This interpretation stems from Hadrian's Roman biographer, Spartianus, who wrote: "His villa at Tibur was marvelously constructed, and he actually gave to parts of it the names of provinces and places of the greatest renown" (1932, p. 378).

Art historian Indra Kagis McEwen writes:

Significantly enough, like the gradual accretions of memory itself, the Villa was not built all at once but was added to piece by piece over the period of years that spanned the period of its owner's reign. And although the pavilions in the linked sequence thus accrued over an Imperial lifetime are all discrete, with well-defined outlines, they ramble over the countryside in an overall assembly that has, like memory, no strict geometry.

(1994, p. 54)

Pompeii

Roman houses were richly decorated with wall paintings of a great variety. The painting was done directly on wet plaster. For a long time, Roman paintings were shoehorned into four designations. The usefulness of stylistic categories for Roman painting is disputed, but references to the four painting styles are frequent.

The first style, painted stucco, mimics other materials, such as marble and other stones. The French phrase "**Trompe l'oeil,**" literally "trick of the eye," refers precisely to this approach to wall decoration. *The Dictionary of Art* dates the first style to 300–100 BCE (Turner 1996). Because of the trove of wall paintings from Pompeii, they are virtually synonymous with the period 100 BCE to 100 CE.

The second style mimics architectural construction; thus, there are columns, entablatures, and arches (Figure 3.13). The color palette is similar to that of Minoans and Greeks. Red was the most popular color, in part because it was chemically stable and easy to produce. The color is known as "Pompeian red." The general composition had a **wainscot**, about waist high or lower, with the area above divided into panels, framed with painted architectural moldings. Second-style painting differs from first-style painting in that the illusionist painting is enhanced with perspective and shading. It is associated with the period 100 BCE to 20 BCE.

The third style shows an increasing amount of pictorial sophistication and the architecture represented is more fantastic; often it is unbuildable—that is, the frescoes show images of architecture that could never be (Figure 3.14). There are attenuated columns, garlands, birds, and vegetation. There are sometimes framed painted panels within the painted scenarios. Specific painters were responsible for these inset

pieces. The third style also includes landscapes. Green pigments were expensive and difficult to produce, hence the prevalence of reds, whites, and blacks. Republican Rome refers to a form of representative government in which there were patrician consuls. Augustus (63 BCE–14 CE) was the adopted son of Julius Caesar. He attempted to transform Rome and make it architecturally worthy of the empire. He claimed that he found a city of brick and turned it into a city of marble. The third style is related to the reigns of Augustus and his successor, Tiberius, the son of his wife Livia. The third style is mannerist, was popular in the period 20–50 CE, and often incorporates disembodied architectural features.

The styles are related to chronology, although there is also overlap. The fourth style is associated with the reign of Claudius (c. 40–79 CE). Wall paintings were representational and featured large scenes and panoramic vistas. They were full of figures, often in movement, and had foliage and other types of ornamentation. Fourth-style wall paintings often had painted paintings "hanging" as elements of their compositions. Many made overt references to theater sets, one example being the Emperor Nero's Golden House, 65–68 CE.

Figure 3.13
Architectural fresco, second style, from the tablinum of the House of Marcus Lucretius Fronto, Pompeii, Italy, 79 CE.

Figure 3.14
Fresco in the
third style,
triclinium, House
of the Tuscan
Colonnade,
Herculaneum,
Italy, first
century CE.

In addition to the retail spaces centered on the forum and urban markets, there were auxiliary retail spaces in residential areas. These were often perimeter rooms of houses that fronted the street and that were rented out. A food and wine shop has built-in **amphorae** (Figure 3.15). Pottery vessels were not just fine dinnerware, they were also industrial containers. **Tabernae** were essentially cafés or fast-food joints. Some public buildings, such as bathhouses, also had tabernae, or spaces for retail establishments, such as tailors. Part of the public infrastructure of Roman cities included raised sidewalks, paved streets, and stepping-stones.

Furniture

Roman furniture inherited Greek forms, and the general repertoire is the same: tables, beds, chairs, and stools. As a general rule, Roman furniture is more elaborate than Greek furniture.

The piece of furniture most associated with Rome is the couch. A couch, synonyms of which are bed and settee, is a horizontal surface for sitting or reclining, with arms at one or both ends. It was used at night for sleeping. It does not have a back. The Romans perfected the social art of dining while reclining. In fact, one Roman room takes its name, **triclinium**, from the standard dining configuration of three couches placed at right angles to one another. Sometimes the feet were made of ivory or metal, or wood covered with ivory. Cushions and blankets, placed on top of the couch, rendered it comfortable.

A bronze couch survives from the Villa Boscoreale, and a wood and ivory couch from the site has been reconstructed in the Metropolitan Museum of Art in New York. It features a **fulcrum**, a headpiece for leaning on, which was a Roman invention.

A variety of small tables served those who were reclining on couches. These include a small metal tripod table. Some tripods were folding armatures that when opened supported a top, wood or marble, that held food or drink. Often the legs were manufactured separately from the tops.

Seating

The Romans inherited the klismos chair, although it lost its central position and was only one of several seating options. The Roman **cathedra** chair is close to the klismos chair in its form. The stalwart X-frame stool continued to prove its usefulness in formal and informal settings. A noble version of the simple stool, the

Figure 3.15
Food and wine shop, Pompeii, Italy, 79 CE.

sella curulis, featured elaborate decoration. Marble thrones or stools were built-in and also used as freestanding pieces of furniture. The author of an early book on Roman furniture, Gisela Richter, wrote that chairs "with turned legs supply a vivid picture of the constant variations that were introduced on a central theme" (Richter 1966, p. 98). One of these, a chair from a Pompeian wall painting of a woman playing an instrument, has curved back rails, painted decoration, and elaborately turned legs.

Barrel-formed chairs and thrones were made of wood, wicker, and marble. A **barrel chair** is simply a chair with a rounded back (in plan). There are no remains of these wicker chairs, but Early Christian and Byzantine thrones resemble them in their form. In his classic work on Roman gold and silver, D.E. Strong (1966) informs us that wealthier houses had some pieces of silver furniture.

The Romans enjoyed the use of marble tables and benches. Trestle tables, with a marble slab supported by two pedestals, were often used in gardens, and were remarkably similar to garden furniture today manufactured out of concrete.

Conclusion

When we look at ancient Greece, we often find ourselves marveling at their products, their majestic temples, and their exquisite statues. Well-crafted vases delineated scenes of myth and life, and both played out in the world of things, including a vast repertoire of furniture. Roman history provides many distractions, from the violence of gladiatorial fights, the drudgery of military campaigns, the competence of engineering projects, and the epic destruction of Pompeii and Herculaneum. Rome took the art of monumental architecture in new directions, and Roman interiors developed an enhanced appreciation of luxury. The Greeks and Romans competed against each other culturally and aesthetically. It is only in retrospect that subsequent generations could view their artistic productions together as the model for the millennia that followed.

Sources

Beacham, Richard and Hugh Denard (2023). *Living Theatre in the Ancient Roman House*. Cambridge: Cambridge University Press.

Bell, Sinclair and Teresa Ramsby (2013). *Free at Last!: The Impact of Freed Slaves on the Roman Empire*. London: Bloomsbury.

Dinsmoor, William ([1902] 1975). *The Architecture of Ancient Greece*. London: B.T. Batsford.

Ferrari, Gloria (2002). *Figures of Speech: Men and Maidens in Ancient Greece*. Chicago: University of Chicago Press.

Hartley, Leslie Poles (1954). *The Go-Between*. Norfolk: Hamish Hamilton.

Lawrence, A.W. (1957). *Greek Architecture*. Baltimore, MD: Penguin .

McDonald, William and John Pinto (1995). *Hadrian's Villa and Its Legacy*. New Haven, CT: Yale University Press.

McEwen, Indra Kagis (1994). "Hadrian's Rhetoric II: Thesaurus Eloquentiae, the Villa at Tivoli." *Res* 25 (Spring): 51–60.

Richter, Gisela (1966). *The Furniture of the Greeks, Etruscans, and Romans*. London: Phaidon.

Robsjohn-Gibbings, T.H. and Carlton Pullin (1963). *Furniture of Classical Greece*. New York: Knopf.

Scully, Vincent ([1962] 1979). *The Earth, the Temple, and the Gods*. New Haven, CT: Yale University Press.

Spartianus (1932). *Historia Augusta*, trans. David Magie. Loeb Classical Library. London: Heinemann.

Strong, Donald Emrys (1966). *Greek & Roman Gold & Silver Plate*. Ithaca, NY: Cornell University Press.

Turner, Jane (1996). *The Dictionary of Art*. New York: Grove.

Tzonis, Alexander and Phoebe Giannisi (2004). *Classical Greek Architecture: The Construction of the Modern*. Paris: Flammarion.

Yourcenar, Marguerite ([1951] 1963). *Memoires of Hadrian*. New York: Farrar Strauss.

Vitruvius Pollo (1999). *De Architectura*. trans. Ingrid Rowland and Thomas Noble Howe. New York: Cambridge University Press.

Discussion and Review Questions

1. What are some examples of Greek design based on the human figure?

2. What are some examples of Greek design based on Egyptian or Mesopotamian art?

3. What are some examples of forms created out of one material that are then crafted out of a new material?

4. Describe the optical refinements of Greek temples?

5. What are the characteristics of a Roman house?

6. How does a Roman house respond to its climate? How is it sustainable (relies upon local materials, efficient in its use of energy and water)?

7. Compare a Plan of Hadrian's Villa to the Plan of Versailles. Using the plan as your evidence, what does each structure say about its owner? How is each one a different statement about the nation?

8. What are the similarities and differences between Greek and Roman architecture and design? Consider form, materials, and effect.

9. What is the Roman concept of monumental architecture? What is meant by Roman inventiveness?

Early Christian and Byzantine

330–800	330–1453
Early Christian	**Byzantine**

Edward Gibbon famously employed the phrase "fall of the Roman Empire" in the title of his book *Rise and Fall of the Roman Empire.* Its grandiloquence is appropriate for the end of one of the world's great empires. Yet it promotes a picture of complete collapse when life on the ground was less dramatic and more complicated. There were no immediate population shifts or definitive cataclysmic battles. People and stones did not go away.

Compared to the legacy of Greece and Rome, the works of the early Christians and the Byzantines are less easily grasped, because they lack the stylistic cohesiveness of the preceding periods. In fact, the word "Byzantine" is a synonym for opaque. This is due to most people's lack of familiarity with the materials. The two most important historical factors to remember when looking at Early Christian and Byzantine art are the decline of Rome and the rise of Christ.

Regarding form and style, considerable continuity links the Roman period and the Early Christian and Byzantine periods that followed it. This is true in dress, painting, sculpture, and furniture. Regarding architecture, the new religion, Christianity, inherited two architectural forms from the Romans: the straightforward **basilica** and the luxuriant, centrally planned domed space. Various camps developed, each promoting theirs as the most appropriate to house the services that honor Christ. Architects and clergy have been fighting over the issue

Figure 4.0
(*Facing page*)
Isidore of Miletus and Anthemius of Tralles, Hagia Sophia, Istanbul, Turkey, 532–537 CE.

47

of the appropriate architectural form for Christianity ever since.

In seeking to establish an architectural identity for the new religion, some saw the best prototype to be the practical meeting hall of the basilica form. Others, dazzled by the brilliance of Roman baths and mausoleums, created complicated forms that rotated around a single point, a profusion of domes and half-domes. Complications and idiosyncrasies abound. Those who worked with the more straightforward basilica often proceeded to make them as grand as possible. By adding a **transept**, the basilica became the **Latin cross**, the plan itself a representation of the cross on which Jesus was crucified.

Early Christian

Early Christian is a term that designates the art and architecture of the first Christian communities. It neither refers to a specific national polity, nor corresponds to a precise geography. When discussed in conjunction with the Byzantine Empire, which was a political and economic realm, Early Christian indicates Western Europe, or simply "the West," while Byzantine refers broadly to "the East." Early Christian churches appeared in parts of Europe, the Middle East, and North Africa.

The terms "Early Christian" and "Byzantine" are not synonymous but related. Some artifacts are purely Early Christian, others are mostly Byzantine; some on the Italian Peninsula are both.

The earliest buildings related to Christianity were not designed to house Christian services but were co-opted for that purpose. In the area, which is now modern Syria, for example, those who espoused the renegade religion held services in typical Mediterranean courtyard houses. The situation changed in 313 CE when the Emperor Constantine officially recognized Christianity as a religion of the empire. The Edict of Milan led to the first era of church building. And with the basilica, it had a form to take into the future.

Early Christian and Byzantine Churches

One way of understanding Early Christian and Byzantine churches is to consider, hypothetically, that Christianity was a client whose architect presented two philosophies of thought as to the new architecture. One side promotes the basilica, sober and straightforward, well suited to the function, a horizontal liturgical march to the **apse**. The alternative is the centrally planned church, with its symbolically resonant domes. Should Christianity not have a house of grandeur equal to the pagan temples, and the building, centrally planned, perhaps with multiple domes, be imposing and bold yet still serve a congregation? The Pantheon in Rome, one of the most moving interior spaces of all time, was the building to beat.

There is no direct evidence of architects and clergy discussing a particular commission and the appropriate form for it; hypothetically, those in the basilica camp promoted simplicity, and those in the centrally planned camp felt that Christianity deserved the grandest structure imaginable. It is an argument—simplicity versus grandeur—that survives to the present day. There were fusions, basilicas that attempt to be grand and vertical, and centrally planned churches whose designers do everything to impose a bilateral axis, apse, **sanctuary**, and space for an audience onto a centrally planned design.

Constantine

Constantine was one of the rulers who followed the Roman emperor Diocletian. He ruled the north from his capital at Trier, Germany. Christianity, needed to develop its own building and design culture. The monuments and art of the third century mostly follow Roman aesthetics and constitute the swan song of the Roman Empire. The final Roman monuments are grand indeed: the Baths of Caracalla in Rome, 212 CE; the Basilica of Maxentius, 307 CE; and Diocletian's Palace at Split, 305 CE.

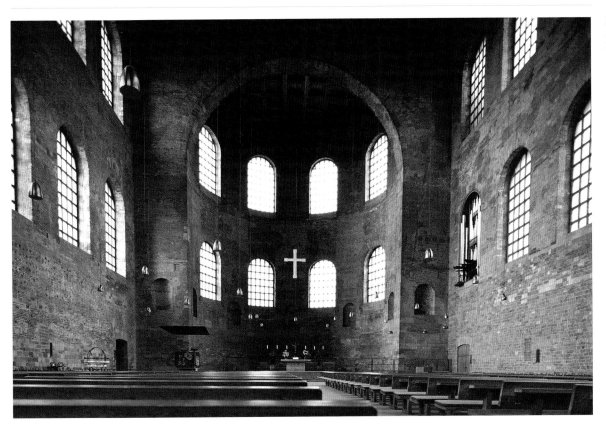

Figure 4.1
Apse of the
Basilica of
Constantine, Aula
Palatina, Trier,
Germany, fourth
century CE.

Part of Constantine's early fourth-century palace remains, the remarkable audience hall (Figure 4.1). While not built as a basilica in the religious sense, it is one of the purest examples of the basilica form. Its interior rivals that of the Pantheon. Trier is a large structure, important in its size yet reticent in its decoration. It is the epitome of restraint.

Its form could scarcely be simpler: a column-free rectangle with an apse at one end (Figure 4.2). It is an ancient forerunner to modern buildings that seek to explore the idea of universal space, that a simple well-designed program can result in a building that serves multiple functions. The Basilica at Trier is a straightforward shell that encloses a large space. Within a framework of simplicity, the plan does suggest certain uses. The rectangular area is the space for an audience (later, a congregation), the apse for a speaker, a statue, or an altar. The position of the apse at one end logically suggests an entryway at the other end.

Structurally the building breaks no new ground, although its size is impressive. It is a simple load-bearing construction that initially supported a timber roof. The exterior elevation is sober if odd; two rows of rounded windows suggest two floors, not a single interior space. The windows increase the amount of light. This early

Figure 4.2
Basilica with apse.

building starts the quest for a vertical expression in basilica shapes. The **piers** between the windows are expressed, while the **spandrels** underneath the windows are suppressed. Only the cornice suggests the classical roots of the basilica form. This prescient building looks forward to the nineteenth-century warehouse structures of Karl Friedrich Schinkel and Henry H. Richardson.

Early Christian churches

The fourth and fifth centuries saw Early Christian churches built throughout Europe, the Middle East, and North Africa. The Church of the Holy Sepulchre in Jerusalem, 328–336 CE, is a marvelously awkward structure that combines several forms, one of them a basilica, to house the congregation. Another famous Early Christian church is Old Saint Peter's, 333 CE (Old Saint Peter's was torn down for the present structure, built in the Renaissance). A huge basilica was built on the site where his modest tomb was part of a cemetery. The basilica itself was 275 feet (84 meters) long and 190 feet (58 meters) wide.

Italy

Sant'Apollinare in Classe, Ravenna, 535–538 CE, shows how Christian architects started with the basilica form and refined it to respond to a Christian service (Figure 4.3). In plan, Sant' Apollinare is an elongated rectangle with an apse at one end. The apse creates a focal point,

the perfect spot for an altar or a speaker, and eventually an image of Christ. Here, bread and wine were transubstantiated into the body and blood of Christ. Relying upon the model of Old Saint Peter's, side **aisles** flank the **nave** and allow visitors to proceed into the church without interrupting the service. What had been exterior walls at Trier became a screen of columns; a feature of Early Christian churches is that their builders felt free to avail themselves of the ready supply of Roman capitals and reuse them. In some churches, the **entablature** atop the columns was deep enough to walk on, a feature that became an actual **gallery** in future churches.

The addition of side aisles renders the building grander, and a row of columns separates the aisles from the nave. The side aisles have their own roof, which allows for a row of windows above the columns, known as a **clerestory**. This ingeniously allows outside light to enter the nave, and further emphasizes the building's verticality and the metaphor of light as a heavenly material. The straightforward timber roof echoed the pitch of classical temples.

In many Early Christian churches, as in Sant'Apollinare, a mosaic or fresco in the apse features a prominent story of the life of Christ.

Figure 4.3
Sant'Apollinare in Classe, Ravenna, Italy, 535–538 CE. View from nave toward apse.

Thus, the most architecturally significant part of the structure underscores the most important figure of the religion. The apse provides a backdrop for the altar, the sanctuary, the holiest part of the structure, and the point from which the priest addresses the congregation.

The term "Early Christian" is mostly used to describe buildings. There were also material artifacts, such as fashion, furniture, and household items from this period, although the fragmentary nature of the evidence tells us little. Early furniture and artifacts are typically classified as Byzantine.

The Byzantine Empire

There were three major Byzantine cities: Constantinople, Venice, and Ravenna. The Roman Emperor Constantine (280–337 CE) officially adopted Christianity and moved the capital to what had been Byzantium. The renamed Constantinople served as the capital and administrative center; Venice was a bustling center of trade. One of the most famous artistic links between Constantinople and Venice is that a statuary group of four horses that once ornamented Constantine's hippodrome was taken to Venice by Crusaders in 1204; it has since become a symbol of the city. The city of Ravenna served as the seat of the emperor's interests in the West, on the part of the Italian Peninsula still remaining in the empire. Ravenna, home to many Early Christian monuments, also houses many Byzantine artworks.

In Ravenna, San Vitale was built during the reign of the Emperor Justinian. Justinian (483–565 CE) was a master builder. San Vitale was an attempt to prove that a centrally planned church, if large enough, could hold a sizable congregation and outperform the basilica form symbolically. In the military and political sphere, Justinian attempted to return to the borders of the Roman Empire. San Vitale in Ravenna, in form and decoration, correspondingly attempts to restore the grandeur of Rome.

San Vitale is centrally planned, with a tall drum that supports a **cupola**. There is also an octagon. The sanctuary of San Vitale in Ravenna, the terminus of all processions, was dedicated in 547 CE.

A mosaic in San Vitale shows Christ receiving a model of the church. One of the most intriguing and evocative figures in history was Justinian's wife, the Empress Theodora, an actress praised (and decried) for her beauty and intelligence. A mosaic from San Vitale dates to around 547 CE and shows Theodora accompanied by her attendants. This is one of a pair of celebrated mosaics that flank the altar; the other shows Justinian himself, resplendent in purple, yet with the piety of a saint. Emperor and head of the Church, he offers the host, and Theodora carries the wine chalice. Near the hem of Theodora's gown, the three magi are depicted bearing gifts.

The mosaics of Justinian and Theodora are marvelous examples of political rulers who deftly treaded the thin line between aggrandizing themselves and presenting themselves as pious followers. Justinian never visited Ravenna, but the existence of a mosaic dedicated to him indicates that Ravenna was underscoring its allegiance to Constantinople.

Byzantine artists distanced themselves, artistically, from Roman artistic practices. A feature of Roman and Greek religions is that worshippers prayed to a statue. Many Christians sought to avoid charges of idolatry, the worship of idols, by staying away from statuary. This partially explains the lack of attention to statuary in-the-round in Byzantine art. Wall mosaics nicely played into the desire to have instructional motifs that were intelligible to their audience yet not repeat the sins of the Romans. Usually, the scenario was to have a representation of some important story from the life of Christ.

A wealthy Ravennate, Julianos Argentarios financed Sant'Apollinare in Classe. It contains a set of mosaics dedicated to the life of Christ. The theme is Christ's miracles, including curing the blind. Such images circulated widely in the Byzantine period via the medium of illuminated manuscripts. A mosaic from Sant'Apollinare is a most unusual rendering of the familiar Last Supper scene.

Christ and his disciples, dressed in Roman-looking robes, are shown dining in the Roman symposium fashion around a semicircular table. Christ is the dominant figure, gesturing as though orating (Figure 4.4). The mosaic showing Jesus and his disciples at the Last Supper reinforces how historical events are seen through the lens of the culture doing the telling. By the time of the Renaissance, the fashion of eating while reclining in bed was gone.

Byzantium

The Byzantine State constituted the longest political entity in Europe, lasting from 324 to 1453 CE. Unlike its immediate predecessor, the Roman Empire, it was Christian. Byzantium was the name used by Greeks and Romans; Byzantines

Figure 4.4
Last Supper, mosaic in Basilica of Sant'Apollinare Nuovo, Ravenna, Italy, sixth century CE.

referred to their state as the Roman Empire, as it was, effectively, a continuation of the Roman Empire. Culturally the heir to Greece and Rome, it followed the economic, legal, and administrative systems of Rome.

The word *Byzantine* itself, in modern parlance, is used to connote confusion, remoteness, and mystery. Actually, the Byzantine Empire was the model for many European medieval states, with its balancing of secular political leadership and religion.

Byzantine art is rich and evocative. It is Christian and humanist and continues to speak to the present day. Highlights of Byzantine art are mosaics, ivories, illuminated manuscripts,

and domed churches. Most liturgical manuscripts belonged to churches and monasteries, not private hands. Their illustrations, or **illuminations**, underscore the light they cast, metaphorically, on their subjects. Many of them look back to classical art but also provide invaluable information about Byzantine furniture and interiors. Both chronologically and stylistically, Byzantine art links the Greco-Roman tradition to the Renaissance.

The Byzantine Empire is the political entity that inherited the remnants of Rome. Byzantine cultural productions are characterized by their Eastern influences, and the Empire did thrive economically because of trade with the East. Geographically, the successor to the Roman

Empire, under the direction of Constantine, abandoned Rome. Not only did Constantine recognize Christianity, but he moved the capital city of the Holy Roman Empire to the shores of the Bosporus, to a city that he renamed. Byzantium was the Roman pagan city, Constantinople was the Byzantine Christian city, and Istanbul is the name of the Muslim city that now stands.

Constantine's city, Constantinople, dominates Byzantine art like no other. The Emperor took a politically insignificant city and made it the center of a rich empire. It became one of Europe's largest cities, with a population perhaps as high as 500,000. Constantine's ascendancy is paralleled by the descent of Rome, one of whose most notorious events was the Sack of Rome, when Visigoths and Vandals plundered the city on the Tiber.

The three periods of Byzantine art relate to the political structure of this new empire and its geographic reach. In the Early Byzantine phase, the state's borders followed the geographic outlines established by the Roman Empire. During this period, correspondingly, Byzantine art closely follows Roman traditions, although representing Christian themes and outlook.

The second phase, the Middle Byzantine period, increasingly exhibits Islamic influences. The Byzantine Empire lost its North African and Middle Eastern territories; various Italian states emerged that distanced themselves politically and culturally from Constantinople. The Byzantine Empire consolidated and retrenched to an area that is today Turkey, Greece, and the Balkans. This phase was medieval, coherent stylistically, and resolute in its obligation to Christianity. The use of ivory and enamel was prevalent in furniture and small precious objects.

In the Late Byzantine period, the last florescence, the empire had become a diminished polity, with Constantinople as its spiritual center and limited Greek territories.

Hagia Sophia

Constantine ruled from 306 to 327 CE. His son, Constantius II, in an auspicious move, dedicated a Christian Cathedral, an early Hagia Sophia, as part of a complex that included a public urban space, church, and palace. The Emperor Justinian ascended the throne in 527 CE. He and his architects turned their attention to the site first built on by Constantius. Richard Krautheimer, whose comprehensive work on Byzantine architecture is standard reading, wrote that "Byzantine architecture starts with Justinian"

(1996, p. 152). Justinian belongs to the ranks of the greatest patrons of architecture. What clearly rankled Justinian is that no Christian building rivaled the Pantheon. Working with two architects, Anthemius of Tralles and Isidorus of Miletus, Justinian erected Hagia Sophia, in Constantinople between 532 and 537 CE. Hagia Sophia was an updated manifestation of what the Romans knew how to do exceptionally well—make grand structures in brick and concrete.

The multidomed structure is the supreme symbol of Constantinople's ascendancy and constituted the Christian claim of the mantel of universal rule (Figures 4.0 and 4.5). In most respects, Hagia Sophia seeks to out-do the Pantheon. The beauty of the Pantheon lies in its simplicity and geometric purity: the Roman structure was a dome on a drum. Built on a massive scale, Hagia Sophia has a dome lifted onto four columns and connected to them with **pendentives**. The plan of Hagia Sophia merges the basilica with the centrally planned church by abutting the central dome with two half-domes. The assembly of domes rests on the four giant piers. The space between the inner dome sequence and the outside wall is a perimeter of colonnaded **arcades**. Some of the innovations associated with Hagia Sophia are its unusual capitals, vaults, colonnaded arcades, carefully constructed interior pavements, and mosaics. Hagia Sophia is the supreme architectural monument of the Byzantine Empire. A hybrid of a basilica and a multidomed and vaulted superstructure, it had a sanctuary located in an apse, a nave, and side aisles. Forty round windows enliven the base of the dome and constitute a new type of clerestory. Once the dome is lifted up on

Figure 4.5
Idealized section of Hagia Sophia.

columns, it is possible to have a bigger system of openings between spaces.

The central dome of Hagia Sophia rises to a height of 55 feet (16.8 meters) above the floor, the largest vaulted space of the ancient and medieval world. It is the supreme example of a Byzantine church. And although it was designed and built as a church, it became a model for Ottoman mosques as well (Mark and Ahmet 1992). Hagia Sophia is to the Byzantine Empire as the Pantheon was to Rome.

The exterior is impressive in its size, with waves of domes that lead to the central dome. Yet the achievement of Anthemius and Isidorus was the interior. Art historian Robert Nelson writes: "During the nine hundred years of the Byzantine Empire that stretched ahead, no structure would surpass the size and grandeur of Hagia Sophia" (2004, p. 1). One interpretation of the complicated design is that the building explores a series of visual attributes from opposite viewpoints. It was the tallest building of its day, expressing verticality, yet its central space also displays a strong hint of the horizontal. Blind arches balance the two half-domes, flat elevations that appear as two-dimensional representations of a half-dome. In plan, the half-domes appear as equals to the central dome, yet they are lower in the building's architectural hierarchy.

A capital from Hagia Sophia detail shows shallow carving, a hint of classical volutes, and a spread of vegetal motifs. A Byzantine capital often looks like a pillow, its bulbous form reflecting the physical demands to distribute the weight of a stone entablature onto a single column. A profusion of shallow decoration is a feature of Byzantine art.

Part of the Byzantine attitude toward art is explained by the desire to distance itself from the idolatry associated with Roman paganism. Byzantine artists needed to establish a new direction for a Christian art. A mosaic floor shows the influence of Roman floor design and the use of **tesserae** (Figure 4.6). Byzantine artists incorporated glass, semi-precious stones, and metals into their mosaics. In Roman times, the mosaics brought life to the floors; Byzantine artists moved them to vertical surfaces that were sometimes curved and increased their color and sparkle.

Furniture

The furniture realm involves the reuse of Roman forms, sometimes unchanged, although with an increasing amount of invention and adaptation. Regarding inherited forms, the X-frame stool survives with its useful form intact. Beds continue

Figure 4.6
Mosaic floor, Basilica of Ayia Trias, North Cyprus, sixth century CE.

as well. The most ubiquitous piece of furniture was the chest, which when outfitted with strong hinges and a lock, kept thieves at bay.

Throne of Maximian

The Throne of Maximian incorporates magnificent examples of ivory carving and is the high point of Byzantine furniture (Figure 4.7). Byzantinist David Talbot Rice (1903–1972) considered it an artistic link between Ravenna and the ivory-carving schools of Alexandria, Egypt. Made in 540 CE, ten of the panels show scenes from the life of Joseph. The story of Joseph was popular in Egypt. Other details also suggest an Egyptian provenance.

The panels on the front of the throne show a grand Saint John the Baptist and may have come from Constantinople. It is possible that the artists for these panels came from Alexandria and Constantinople and traveled, or that the ivory panels were transported as panels to Ravenna, where a talented craftsman assembled them. Some of the lesser panels were done by others. The nonfigurative carved panels were stock items used as connectors.

The chair's form is reminiscent of a barrel chair, a form whose beginnings lie with the Roman cathedra. The Throne of Maximian is carved on all sides, with a rounded back; this suggests that it was not placed against a wall. The prominent and elaborate panels face forward. The throne itself is similar to other works. Its exceptional nature derives from the expertise of the ivory carvers, working their exacting craft on an expensive material.

Maximian was archbishop from 545 to 553 CE. He sat in this chair with his feet on the ground and his back erect. The throne's back is not for leaning against. The sitter's hands and arms lie in dignified repose on the armrests, which is to say that the throne demanded a public posture of its sitter.

Boxes, chests, and caskets made of ivory constitute the biggest cache of Byzantine designed objects and display the height of ivory carving. Although few examples survive, there were also simple wooden pieces.

An illumination that shows the scribe Ezra at work features a table, chair, footstool, and bookcase (Figure 4.8). One of the primary functions

Figure 4.7
The Throne of Maximian, *c.* 540 CE.

Figure 4.8
The prophet and scribe Ezra at work in a medieval armorium, from the *Codex Amiatinus*, eighth century CE.

of monasteries was copying texts, and the first libraries were in monasteries. This image shows the process of creating copies, and an armoire that holds completed works. The image can be considered a tribute to the importance of the book.

Medieval furniture

While the Throne of Maximian shows the highest level of what Byzantine furniture makers and ivory carvers were capable of, to understand how most people interacted with furniture, we turn to other sources. Two undated medieval stools of uncertain provenance, demonstrate that most people's experience with furniture involved utilitarian pieces. It is inspiring that even when someone sought to craft a piece of furniture as straightforwardly as possible, whose only purpose is to provide a sturdy seat, there is variety in form, and a simple aesthetic result.

One three-legged stool is anthropomorphic with soft curves that respond to the human figure who sat on it, and whose fingers carried it from place to place (Figure 4.9). The integral handle indicates that this rough-and-ready stool was picked up, carried about, and set down. The method to render this stool rugged relies on neither hardware nor strengthened connections; it relies on the inherent strength of the material from which it is made. A monoxylous work, it is made from a single piece of material.

Another **monoxylous** stool cleverly takes advantages of tree branches to form its legs (Figure 4.10). The resulting form retains resemblance to the natural material from which it was created: a trunk with branches. The resulting piece resembles the three-legged stools that satyrs and other Greeks were fond of slinging over their shoulders, responding to yet another part of the human anatomy.

Conclusion

In the thousand years after the end of the Roman Empire, Christianity became more important over time. While Early Christian basilicas lean toward the solemn, the multidomed church was pompous and emotive. Paintings and mosaics were all important; relief carvings were shallow and focused on the surface. The heritage from Rome was artistic and technical.

Figure 4.9
Medieval stool with integral handle.

Figure 4.10
Medieval stool
that takes
advantage of
natural tree
growth for its
design.

Furniture followed a similar path in its journey from Rome to the Renaissance. Some forms existed virtually unchanged. Modest tables and chests continued to demonstrate utility. Some forms were adapted and made of new materials. Barrel chairs, which the Romans made in marble and straw, were covered with ivory. The habit of dining recumbent all but disappeared.

The Early Christian and Byzantine periods inherited Roman forms and put them to contemporary use. The artists of these periods developed vibrant traditions of art, architecture, and the decorative arts. Not stylistically cohesive, the works from the time after Rome's implosion and before its rebirth in the Renaissance are known for multiple qualities. The works are secular and sacred, tender and brash, solemn and dazzling. It is no doubt that the combination of qualities resulted in a collection of works that speak to individuals and appeal to many.

Sources

Etlin, Richard (2022). *The Cambridge Guide to the Architecture of Christianity*. Cambridge: Cambridge University Press.

Krautheimer, Richard (1996). *Early Christian and Byzantine Architecture*. New Haven, CT: Yale University Press.

Mark, Robert and Ahmet Çakmet (1992). *Hagia Sophia: From the Age of Justinian to the Present*. Cambridge: Cambridge University Press.

McClendon, Charles (2005). *Origins of Medieval Architecture*. New Haven, CT: Yale University Press.

Nelson, Robert (2004). *Hagia Sophia, 1850–1950: Holy Wisdom Modern Monument*. Chicago: University of Chicago Press.

Oxenstierna, Eric (1959). *Die Wikinger*. Stuttgart: W. Kohlhammer.

Pentcheva, Bissera (2018). *Hagia Sophia: Sound, Space and Spirit in Byzantium*. University Park: Pennsylvania State University Press.

Discussion and Review Questions

1. What were some of the important materials in Early Christian and Byzantine architecture?
2. How is Early Christian and Byzantine art a continuation of Roman artforms?
3. How does the Throne of Maximian make its seated figure look visually prominent?
4. How would a viewer of the Throne of Maximian respond to it?
5. What do you imagine the throne's relationship to its architectural setting to be?
6. How important was comfort to those crafting the throne?
7. Compare Hagia Sophia to the Pantheon, considering both similarities and differences.
8. Discuss the basilica form versus the centrally planned form. What does each plan suggest about its use? How is each appropriate, or inappropriate, for certain types of religious services?

5

Romanesque and Islamic

800–1150	750–1492	1000–1200	1502–1736	1525–1750
Romanesque	Islamic Spain	Seljuq Empire	Safavid Dynasty	Mughal era

There is no shortage of ways to understand the one thousand years between the Fall of Rome and the Renaissance, the style inspired by ancient classicism. One could ignore seemingly singular achievements, consider them the results of minor trends and proceed as quickly as possible to the Italian Renaissance. In belated deference to the craftsmen and artists who produced so many fine works during this period, whose economy of material teamed with a fearful spirituality, the term "the Dark Ages" has fallen into disgrace. Another now-discredited approach was to emphasize the unintelligibility of the artifacts of this period. Yet, when approached with patience, the study of the medieval period, and the focus of this chapter, Romanesque and Islamic design, yields considerable riches.

For many people, Romanesque is not a pale version of the more florid Gothic that followed, it is the style they revere most. Henry Hobson Richardson, one of the most important American architects of the nineteenth century, worked almost exclusively in a Romanesque revival style. A seminal figure of his time, he saw the Romanesque style as the best way to express the modern age. His work led to a building type as important in its era as the cathedral had been for France: the skyscraper.

Islamic design is an ongoing endeavor. **Mosques** continue to be built in traditional Islamic styles. Furniture and works of decorative art, from Africa to the Middle East to Asia, are still produced that lay claim to being called Islamic.

Figure 5.0
(*Facing page*)
Gayer-Anderson House, Cairo, Egypt. Original houses, sixteenth and seventeenth centuries, contemporary decoration, 1935–1942.

This chapter considers Romanesque and Islamic design as parallel tracks, with separate beginnings and locations, that become intertwined by military operations, those of the European crusades into the Middle East and Islamic expansion into Spain and France. As with all military operations, there were horrible consequences for many people, yet the cultural results of this blending are often stunning. This is a testament to the powers of artistic creation. The greatest achievements of the Romanesque and Islamic periods are not found in freestanding pieces of furniture but in majestic buildings and the rich design legacies that they bequeathed to subsequent generations.

Romanesque

Frankish control of Gaul (the Franks were a Germanic ethnic group) was a step toward establishing a stable order with a centralized authority, a political achievement not experienced since the collapse of the Roman Empire. Two early pieces of furniture are inextricably linked to their famous occupants. Dagobert I and Charlemagne are rare figures of authority in a period known for factions and feudalism. Few pieces of furniture survive from the period. These two exceptional chairs are best understood by considering a triad of strong ruler, unified government, and imposing chair. Transitional pieces between medieval and Romanesque, they exhibit features of both.

Two early chairs

Dagobert I (605–639 CE) was a ruler with an unusual achievement: he ruled over a united realm. He oversaw a period of prosperity, and he was a patron of the arts. The "throne" that made its appearance, really a chair, is made of metal (Figure 5.1).

The **X-frame chair** existed in Egypt, Greece, and the Byzantine Empire. The most obvious precedent to Dagobert's chair is the Roman *sella curulis*. It is a modest type of chair, here rendered regal. In the second quarter of the twelfth century, the Abbot Suger, an advisor to King Louis VI, significantly altered what was a folding bronze stool by adding on a side and back panels. Dagobert's chair was ecclesiastical and secular: it was an emperor's chair and it resembled the X-frame chairs favored by popes.

Folding chairs had proven useful for military campaigns and when noble households took up new quarters. This is a frontally oriented folding chair. When facing the chair, a user grasps the two arms, pulls them together, and it collapses in the middle.

Dagobert's chair exhibits the conflicting trends of the earliest years of the Romanesque period. Small in scale, its grandeur derives from the intricate details of its cast bronze and complicated mechanical operations. It is unquestionably majestic, yet portable. It presages both the imposing Gothic chair and the now ubiquitous director's chair. The sturdy lion's paws provided a stable seat in a changing landscape. Its survival

Figure 5.1
Dagobert's Throne, France, early seventh century; arms and back, 1125–1150.

stems from its unusual material, and it operates as a stand-in for the innumerable wood chairs that have not survived.

Charlemagne's throne is similarly famous because of the person who sat in it (Figure 5.2). This piece of furniture confers authority on its user by its height, its material, and the social circumstances of its use. Situated on a raised platform, it exhibits the increasing preoccupation with height, a primary means of conferring status and confirming authority. Charlemagne (742–814 CE) has a lofty place in history because of his success at creating a unified government. Planar in form, its shape stems from its grand material, marble sheets. Barely decorated, it blurs the lines between ecclesiastical and secular furniture. It has several features in common with a number of Byzantine bishops' thrones.

The status that a throne confers upon its user derives from its context, and Charlemagne's throne has a grand context. Two of the finest constructions that resulted from the reign of Charlemagne are the palace and church at Aix-la-Chapelle (today Aachen). The architect Odo of Metz, began work on them in 792 CE. Only the chapel remains. The chapel owes its centrally planned form to ancient Roman monuments and is one of the key structures of the **Carolingian** period.

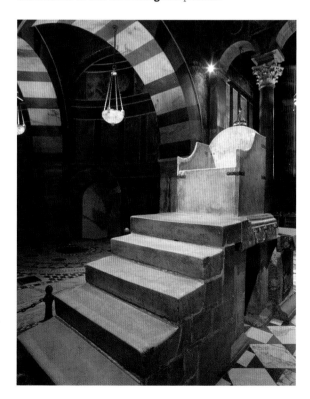

Figure 5.2
Charlemagne's throne, Palatine Chapel, Aachen, Germany, 792–805 CE.

With its location in Germany, it is one of the last direct links to the Roman presence in German lands. Yet the fact that French-speaking Charlemagne had his capital in Germany is also an early indication of the long periods in which French- and German-speaking people strove to form an alliance. The bicolored stonework is a dominant feature of the space and becomes one of the hallmarks of Romanesque architecture.

A time period and a style are associated with Charlemagne: Carolingian. In his eponymous style, one sees the beginnings of the forms that became known as Romanesque. Charlemagne ushered in an era of stability, grandeur, and consolidation. Following his death, political, military, and economic pressure from the north and south returned.

Cities

Many medieval cities were heavily fortified, and Aigues-Mortes, in the southern French region of Languedoc-Roussilon, is a fine example. Aigues-Mortes was the port of embarkation for the two Crusades of Louis IX. Medieval cities became individual strongholds. Inside the walls, **wattle-and-daub** and timber construction prevailed.

Although Aigues-Mortes followed a grid, a feature of many medieval towns was a narrow and winding street. One of the achievements of architectural historian Spiro Kostof's work is his examination of planned, and unplanned, medieval cities (Kostof 1995). The latter shared a characteristic with their Islamic cousins. Passageways in the Casbah had surprising dead-end streets and lacked an obvious logic. These quarters with their intimate scale provided charm and favored those familiar with their ins and outs. European medieval town planning, similarly, confused strangers, another example of the defensive posture of the medieval period. The defensiveness and xenophobia had cultural ramifications as well.

Other examples of extent medieval walls in Europe date to the eleventh century, and are found at Windsor Castle in the United Kingdom, and the town of Montagnana in Italy (Figure 5.3).

Churches

The twelfth-century Cathedral of Sainte Foy at Conques, France, is known for the masterfully carved decorative program of the façade. Romanesque façades offer a simple menu of options for a public who led a hard life. For the illiterate, the façade's reliefs, capitals, and **voussoirs** rendered the Bible's lessons visible. Acting

Figure 5.3
Windsor Castle,
Windsor, England,
eleventh century.

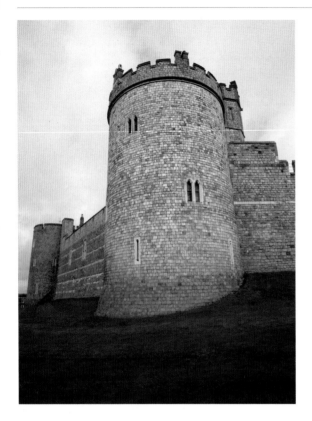

Figure 5.4
Tympanum,
Abbey church
Sainte Foy,
Conques, France,
1124–1135.

as a sign, the message is prosaic and immediate: going over the threshold and into the sanctuary of Sainte Foy was a step toward salvation. This is the spiritual direction represented by the central figure of Jesus. The tympanum, whose subject is the weighing of souls, makes clear the choices for parishioners and pilgrims alike. The alternative is hell, where a devil stands, all too eager to feed souls to a dragon (Figure 5.4).

Romanesque church plans are a development of Early Christian church plans, but they were also inspired by rediscoveries of antiquities. The buildings largely follow the form of the basilica, only their designers explored new means to fashion architectural monumentality (Figure 5.5). The most significant addition was the transept. Adding the transept provided a central focus on the altar and gave the building its shape. The building's interior became something to be walked around and experienced. And there was the considerable symbolic benefit that the plan of the church took on the shape of the crucifix.

A growing knowledge of architectural construction allowed for the addition of side aisles.

The addition of side aisles made the plan laterally expansive. A masonry barrel vault roof took the place of a wooden timber frame. On the longitudinal axis, the early Christian apse developed into a **choir** with an **ambulatory** (Figure 5.6). Viewed from the outside, the rounded mass of the rear elevation, made bulbous, plastic, and imposing, is known as the **chevet**. The prominent zone of the **narthex** corresponds in plan to the façade.

Saint Sernin in Toulouse (France) is a paradigmatic example of the heights that Romanesque ecclesiastical architecture could reach, literally and figuratively. The basilica shape was inherited; the nascent grandeur was new.

It is not incorrect to view the Romanesque cathedral as a predecessor to the Gothic cathedral, regarding chronology and form. It is misleading, however, to view it merely as a forerunner, or Gothic poorly done. Romanesque churches were significant achievements in their own right, at once majestic and sobering.

Saint Sernin's elevation is an honest projection of the building behind it. It was treated as a designed vertical surface, worthy of its own articulation, the foremost being the elaborate entryways and the giant oculus that is a forerunner to the Gothic stained-glass window.

Churches in the Romanesque period fall into three categories: urban pilgrimage sites, sprawling rural monasteries, and parish churches. Saint Sernin is an example of an urban pilgrimage church. Famous monasteries such as Cluny were important economic, political, religious, and cultural centers. Every village, no matter how small, felt the religious impulse.

Regarding scale and articulation of detail, a plan of a provincial church in Cézais, France, shows the other end of the spectrum. A minimal structure, it is not far removed from the humble basilica form of the Romans. Its primary gesture toward grandness is its apse. Hundreds of Romanesque parish churches dot the French countryside and visiting them is one of life's pleasures.

A goal of the crusades, not realized, was to put Christian monuments of the Holy Lands under European control.

Figure 5.5
Saint Sernin, Toulouse, France, 1080–1120. Plan detail of choir stalls and transept.

Figure 5.6
Romanesque ambulatory.

Houses

A Romanesque house in Cluny, 1159, is one of the few extant houses (Figure 5.7). It is a great material document of social history. The façade has a high level of craftsmanship. It indicates a separation of the commercial and residential functions. The smaller, private windows of the upper floor indicate the residential floor. The large opening on the ground floor clearly indicates the commercial space that lies behind it.

The façade corresponds to an exceedingly simple plan (Figure 5.8). This is a plan of another Romanesque house. The prominent room of the upper floor that fronts the street was a

Figure 5.7
Romanesque
house, Cluny,
France, 1159.

Figure 5.7
Romanesque
house, Cluny,
France, 1159.

Figure 5.8
Romanesque
house, Cluny,
France, 1159,
plan.

a premium. A feature of living in a Romanesque house was a lack of privacy. There is little doubt that commercial areas served double duty and that nighttime found workers sleeping there. The room was used for cooking, eating, entertaining, and, for countless numbers, sleeping at close quarters. And now, after considering these activities, we turn to the furnishings that help make them possible.

Furniture

Chests

In her study on medieval furniture, Penelope Eames demonstrates the centrality of the chest: "In an age in which mobility and security for household possessions were primary considerations, the adaptability of the chest in its various forms made it the most indispensable single article of furniture. The chest was, at one and the same time, a piece of furniture and an article of luggage" (1977, p. 108). A modest Romanesque chest is a practical response to real needs. Used for storage, transport, and other practical uses, most chests were made of sturdy and common woods. A British cupboard of the fifteenth century resembles its Romanesque ancestors in its straightforward **plank construction** and use of strap hinges (Figure 5.9).

A chest is one of the most basic types of furniture. A space-containing object, it provides storage for objects. The practical people of the Middle Ages took note that a piece designed for storage also resulted in a work surface. Chests had secondary functions, their horizontal surface occasionally called into use for sitting, working, dining, or sleeping.

Romanesque chests and cupboards were often of plank construction, meaning that they were constructed from milled lumber in a judicious manner. The construction method remains visible in the final product. The creators of many chests were joiners, with most of their professional experience in architecture.

Medieval chests often bear traces of their history as finished pieces. They spent long periods of time in places where their owners were concerned about cleanliness. The floors that supported chests were continually cleaned, and mops, dripping with oily soap, slapped thousands of times against the chest's feet, resulting in their darkening.

Footed chests were desirable because they raised the contents off the cold ground. Flat-lidded chests with feet were used for storage. For

general-purpose room. This confirms our knowledge about living spaces. There was an overall scarcity of resources, and rooms were not devoted to a single function.

Medieval cities were crowded, space was precious, and the linear footage on a street was at

Figure 5.9
Cupboard, fifteenth century. British.

to a surprising profusion of applied ornament, and the ornament arrives in the unexpected material of iron. Iron tracery is an applied means of decoration based on geometric designs, and figures of vegetation, animals, and exceptionally, human figures. This demonstrates a willingness to incorporate new materials that extended to decoration. In a time period known for restraint, when decorative motifs were created, they were often employed effusively.

The decoration gives the impression that it covers an entire object comprehensively. A series of horizontal lines binds the sides. On closer inspection, one sees that the pattern of lines responds to the chest, changing direction, running left, right, up, down, turning corners and recognizing the top and bottom. This wrought-iron strapping runs perpendicular to the boards, providing additional strength and reinforcement.

A prominent lock is a later modification. Attached rings facilitated transport. Both decorative and functional, the ironwork had several functions, as hinges, locks, and a means to bind and strengthen the oak planks. In the Romanesque period, furniture had to resist the unwanted intruder.

The word coffer, in French *coffre*, indicates where money and valuables were stored. The phrase "the coffers of the Pope" (or King or President), still in use today, indicates the place where money is stored or, even more abstractly, the treasury. Money, like nearly everything else in this period, was stored in chests.

Some chests emphasize furniture's debt to architecture, indicating that at least occasionally the same people created both. A **hutch** is a subset within the larger category of chests. It has uprights at its ends that form the legs. Again, when decoration was employed, it came full force. When iron tracery was not needed or could not be afforded, **chip carving** was another means to improve a chest's appearance. Hutch designs favored motifs accomplished with the skilled use of a compass, chisel, and block.

With certain pieces, a sure sign that a piece dates to the Romanesque period is the presence of the semicircular arch. The arches look exactly like the entryways of Romanesque churches, further emphasizing furniture's connection to architecture. With a walnut hutch, an arcade of **Romanesque arches** constitutes the body of the piece, lifted well into the air, spanning a considerable distance, an achievement in the world of furniture that is the equivalent of the Roman bridges and **aqueducts**.

private and commercial purposes, chests were the primary means of storage. Fairly large numbers survive, although not because they were deemed worthy of preservation. Because their *raison d'être* was storage, chests survived because their contents were considered valuable.

Chests with domed lids and flat bottoms were used for transport. They were indispensable when individuals prepared for travel and when noble households moved. The curved top expelled rainwater, and protruding feet were a liability when transporting a piece of furniture.

Eames argues convincingly that even a footed chest could have been used for transport if slipped into a **bahut**, the leather envelope that protected the piece of furniture. It also shielded protruding feet from damage

In some Romanesque pieces, the straightforwardness of the undecorated chest gives way

In French, the word used to denote Romanesque monuments, *roman*, is the same word that denotes ancient Roman monuments. Thus, the French term for this period emphasizes the continuity with ancient Rome, and the English term, Romanesque, emphasizes the differences. The builders of churches in Aquitaine attempted to emulate the grandeur of ancient Rome. Their knowledge of Rome was incomplete. Roman sites lay in ruins, with half-buried temples, and columns, capitals, and headless torsos strewn about. Books on Rome, or, for that matter, any subject, were rare. Many people were illiterate and had no access to libraries. Romanesque works were inspired by Rome, but the results were not encyclopedic copies.

Islam

Islamic design, like Romanesque, is centered on religion. Without Islam there is no Islamic design, and without Mohammed, there is no Islam. The story begins with the Prophet, Mohammed, who lived from 570–632 CE. An explanation for the success and spread of Islam into Africa, Europe, and Asia was its ability to incorporate local architectural and decorative trends. Thus, Islam developed a series of regional variations that are astonishing in their variety. In Mesopotamia, Persia, North Africa, Saharan Africa, Spain, and Anatolia, mosques were built that shared features: courtyard, **prayer hall**, **ablutions fountain**, and

qibla wall with **mihrab**. The decorative motifs of interior and exterior façades, columns, floors, and ceilings varied greatly from region to region.

Mosques

All mosques owe their form to the Prophet's farm in Medina and are in fact representations of it (Figure 5.10). The key elements can be seen in a re-creation of Mohammed's farm, the first mosque. Important features of all mosques are the perimeter wall, the covered hall of columns that becomes the prayer hall, and the courtyard, which acts as a forecourt to the prayer hall.

Middle East and North Africa

In Christian churches, a priest preaches to a congregation; hence the auditorium-like layout. In a mosque, the central activity is an individual praying, multiplied hundreds of times. The apse that signals the direction to Mecca is humanly scaled and significantly smaller than the apse of Christian churches. A large single space, therefore, is not a priority. The Great Mosque of Damascus, Syria, initially converted from a Roman temple, displays the repetitious, cellular quality of mosques (Figure 5.11). Although Muslim imams also preach, the central activity around which a mosque is designed remains that of an individual, on a carpet, facing Mecca and praying.

As Islam spread, it merged with local traditions. A comprehensive look at the broad topic of Islamic architecture, interiors, and furnishings requires volumes. This chapter, therefore,

Figure 5.10
Prophet Mohammed's farm, Medina, Saudi Arabia, 707–709. Axonometric.

Figure 5.11
Great Mosque of
Damascus, Syria,
705–711. Plan.

11. Damascus, Great Mosque, 706, plan

■ ROMAN

▨ UMAYYAD

modestly seeks to present what is meant when people refer to Islamic design, and provides a summary look at some of its forms and basic characteristics.

North Africa is blessed with an abundance of Roman ruins. Because of the drier climate, some of them are remarkably complete, and classical ruins grace Morocco, Tunisia, Libya, and Syria. Designers of Islamic mosques, like those of Romanesque churches, were often inspired to work within classical architectural languages. Sometimes they literally reused the ruins (Figure 5.12). The fusion of classical architecture with Islam is obvious in the interior of the Prayer Hall of the Great Mosque of Kairouan, one of the key Islamic monuments. From its classical capitals spring a field of Islamic arches. The **Islamic arch** is pointed like a Gothic arch, but it is distinctive because its semi-spherical shape exceeds 180 degrees, hence its other name, horseshoe arch. The pulpit from which the imam preaches is called a **minbar**, and they often incorporate Islamic arches (Figure 5.13). It is a hybrid of a stair, a chair, and a speaking platform.

Saharan and sub-Saharan Africa

In Africa, Islam worked within indigenous traditions. Craftsmen used local materials and relied

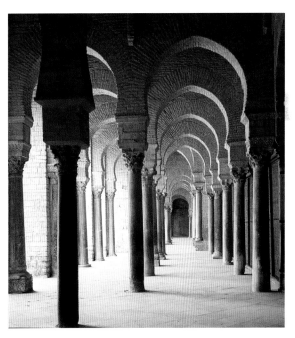

Figure 5.12
Great Mosque of Kairouan, Kairouan, Tunisia, 820–836. Gallery which precedes the prayer hall.

on local building methods. In the Sahara, all things come from and return to the earth. Art in the region frequently venerates the humble mudfish. Soil dredged from the bottom of the Niger River dyes mud cloth black or ochre. Saharan mosques, appropriately, are made of mud, or more accurately, sun-dried mud bricks

Figure 5.13
Minbar.

skim-coated with an outer layer of mud. The **toron** are the permanent pieces of scaffolding that give the buildings' exterior walls their distinctive look (Figure 5.14).

The toron are utilized during the annual resurfacing of the mosque, a communal activity. The archetypal Saharan mud mosque is the Great Mosque of Djenné.

Ottoman Empire

In regions of the Middle East under the Ottoman Empire, there occurs as audacious a case of cultural appropriation as the world has ever seen. Justinian's famed Christian temple, Hagia Sophia, was designed to outshine the pagan Pantheon. It was then converted to a mosque in the fifteenth century, and this church turned mosque became the prototype for hundreds of mosques that copy its domes, half-domes, clerestories, pendentives, and mosaics.

Persia

Persian mosques accomplished a form of architectural appropriation of a different sort. Isfahan (Iran) is a city filled with large-scale Islamic monuments. The buildings at Isfahan harken back to Assyrian and Babylonian palaces and thereby

Figure 5.14
Great Mosque of Djenné, Djenné, Mali, fourteenth century, restored 1905.

render Islam as the logical inheritor of those civilizations. This connection across millennia is achieved by a building material indigenous to the region: a brilliantly glazed blue brick. Isfahan had two important periods: it thrived under the Seljuq Turks (eleventh to twelfth century) and under the Persian Safavid dynasty (sixteenth to eighteenth century).

When comparing design motifs over time and geography, one of the more interesting occurrences is when decorative motifs travel and mutate. The process of transformation varies from culture to culture. Often in the process, the motif loses its function, but the form remains. A **skeuomorph** is an object of utility that becomes a decorative form.

One of the most interesting aspects of the structures of Isfahan, and indeed of all Islam, are the vertical architectural surfaces that resemble carpets. Fields of patterns rework motifs that originated in textiles. And carpets, analogously, often portray architectural details. Thus, there are walls that look like carpets and carpets that look like walls. A frequent motif of individual prayer rugs is a single Islamic arch indicating the direction to Mecca. Where walls resemble carpets, instead of staring at a flat vertical surface, a viewer stares at motifs that they associate with textiles. The type of decoration prevalent at Isfahan is what most people mean when they refer to Islamic decoration. It is geometric, nonrepresentational, and often formed by tiles or mosaics.

The Mughal Empire

Despite ample Persian riches, the **Mughals** of the East set the standard for Islamic luxury. In English, the word *mogul* means people who combine business savvy with an unparalleled sense of luxury. Of note in this corner of the Islamic world, today Pakistan and northwestern India, is that the most magnificent structures were not solely religious structures, but tombs and residential complexes.

A Muslim capital was established in the last years of the twelfth century, at Delhi, India, a significant milestone in Islam's eastward expansion. For more than three hundred years, five dynasties successively ruled from Delhi. The Delhi Sultanate is typically dated to the period 1200–1526 BCE. The first mosques in the Indian subcontinent were converted Indian temples or new buildings constructed from reassembled architectural fragments. A feature of these early mosques was the use of a decorative screen to separate the imam from the congregation. Buildings in Delhi, Agra, Fatehpur Sikri, and Lucknow established the foundation of Indo-Islamic architecture and design.

The following period is the era of the Mughal rulers, 1526–1707. Akbar (1556–1605) was a patron of the arts, and his reign the height of Mughal art. Art in this context means paintings, buildings, and illustrated texts. Akbar had the great Hindu epics, the *Ramayana* and the *Mahabharata*, lavishly illustrated. He built forts at Agra and Fatehpur Sikri that were fusions of indigenous forms and Islamic motifs.

Akbar's son, Jahangir (1605–1627), was an important patron. Like his father, and his son after him, he built mosques, mausoleums, forts, palaces, hunting lodges, and pavilions. In comparison to other regional Islamic traditions, it is significant that the Mughal building programs included secular building types.

While Akbar and Jahangir were active patrons, it was Jahangir's son, Shah Jahan (r. 1628–1658), who constructed the building that has a hallowed place in the world's imagination. Shah Jahan's wife was Mumtaz Mahal, and for her he built a monument of sandstone and white marble decorated with semiprecious stones. The Taj Mahal in Agra (India) is one of the most famous buildings in the world. In the widely reproduced photographic image of it, it stands perfectly symmetrical, its marble domes reflected in a pool. It is the touching monument that a grieving widower, Jahan, erected for his beloved wife.

Islamic interiors and furniture

Akbar and Shah Jahan were wealthy by any standard. A gouache owned by the Musée des Arts Asiatiques, Guimet in Paris shows two male figures on their knees. One has his knees together, the other sits cross-legged. Both sit on a raised platform. Sitting, kneeling, or lying on the ground in a warm climate is a perfectly adequate means of repose. Correspondingly, creative efforts focused on mats, carpets, and pillows. When chairs entered these realms, it was often the result of international exchange, and a matter of status and cultural identification rather than necessity. An eighteenth-century painting shows the Diwan Nawal Singh kneeling comfortably, surrounded by cushions (Figure 5.15).

In the area that was the Mughal Empire, many residential and administrative functions were carried out in structures that can be best described as pleasure pavilions. What these pavilions have in common with a mosque's prayer hall is that multiple columns support the roof. The structure is a **hypostyle hall**, formally linked to Egyptian hypostyle structures (see Chapter 2). The word that originates from these pavilions is **diwan**, or diwaniya, the root from which the modern English "divan" stems. Raised platforms formed the perimeter of these columned pavilions, and they were furnished with cushions, pillows, and carpets. This comfortable setting frequently served as the audience chamber for government officials, the place where business was conducted. And just as the word *coffer* came to mean treasury, so too *diwan* came to mean an office and its related finance, or a government's financial sector.

In photographs, Mughal pavilions today are portrayed as austere when they should be pictured in use. Assemblies of pillows, carpets, and tasseled cushions do not remain intact for centuries, so historical engravings are invaluable for re-creating this episode in the history of seating.

Saharan nomads carried leather pillows with them, a means of making some of the more modest comforts of the diwan transportable. Whether carried by camel or horse, a leather pillow made travel more comfortable. Also used for sitting on the ground around a fire, or when sleeping in a tent, leather was a favored water-resistant material of the medieval period.

As we have seen, there is a reason why, for this early period, Islamic furniture is practically an oxymoron. Many of the functions that were taken care of in the West by chairs and couches were accomplished with cushions, carpets, and other textiles. This is a cultural response to warm climates where it is less necessary to distance oneself from the ground.

As we have seen, a minbar is essential to outfitting a mosque. It is located immediately adjacent to the mihrab, the apse in the **qibla** wall (Figure 5.16). Usually made of wood and separate from the structure, some minbars are made of stone and built in. An elaborate minbar from the Great Mosque of Algiers even has wheels.

A number of Islamic prayer stools are intended for use when reading the Koran. Some are collapsible and portable. The position of the

Figure 5.15
Unknown, *Diwan Nawal Singh, Prime Minister of Datia, c.* 1750.

Figure 5.16
Qibla, Mosque Ibn Tulun, Cairo Egypt.

back piece is designed to keep the reader alert while studying.

It is a mistake to oversimplify Islam, both as a religion and as a system of decoration. A trend is not dogma—thus it is with the Islamic stance on representation. No hard-and-fast rule prohibits visual representations, though this is interpreted differently in different places and time periods. It is true that geometric designs, whether formed of carpet fibers or glazed bricks, constitute the majority of Islamic decoration. Sometimes these patterns suggest flowers and other botanical motifs. Animals are portrayed less frequently. An exceptional aspect of Persian and Mughal design is that human figures are represented. Geometric designs and vegetal motifs are the most frequent subjects of Islamic decoration.

In addition to the intriguing relationship between carpets and vertical architectural surfaces, there is a connection between residential architectural features and the human figure. In many areas of the Islamic world, in this case the historical trading center of Suakin (Sudan), houses were outfitted with a protruding bay window, or **roshan**. This hybrid space mediated between the public world of the street and the private world of the house. This created a space for women to observe city life yet be shielded from public visibility. In this sense, this architectural feature acted as does the veil; roshan is to the house as a veil is to the female body (Figure 5.17). Again, one should not confuse a widespread practice with dogma. Not all Islamic women are veiled; among the Tuareg of Mali, the men shield their faces from the public gaze.

Islamic Spain

Islamic designers of all sorts—architects, carpet weavers, and furniture craftsmen—were not shy about borrowing. In Islamic Spain the fullest fusion of Islamic and European models occurs, particularly when it comes to furniture. With Islamic Spain this chapter comes full circle; Romanesque becomes Islamic, and Islamic becomes Romanesque.

Jews, Christians, and Muslims thrived in Islamic Spain. Maria Rosa Menocal's *The Ornament of the World* (2002) is a well-written book that, in recovering a lost era, is at once general and specific. This section is indebted to her effort.

The story starts in Syria where the Umayyad dynasty, successors to Mohammed, ruled from Damascus. Damascus was an international place,

with its Greek, Aramaean, Hebrew, and Arabic histories. The Umayyads were violently overthrown by a rival dynasty, the Abbasids. Most of the Umayyads were murdered and their residences plundered. The Abassids subsequently moved the center of their operations to Baghdad. An Umayyad survivor, the tenacious Abd al-Rahman, headed to the Iberian Peninsula where he settled in Cordoba.

Al-Rahman and his followers created a brilliant European Islamic society that included a grand tradition of courtyard residences and rich furnishings. A descendant, Abd al-Rahman III, built Madinat al-Zahra, a hilltop structure that Menocal describes as the Versailles of Cordoba (Menocal 2002, p. 36). A rival faction of Berbers destroyed it in 1009, but its tradition of orange groves, palm trees, fountains and pools was to live on in two grander residential complexes.

Testament to the openness and multicultural quality of Islamic Spain comes from two cases in which the most important administrative position, vizier, analogous to prime minister, was held by a Jewish scholar. Hasdai Ibn Shaprut (915–975) and Samuel Ibn Nagrila (993–1056) served in the most important administrative position in Europe's Islamic caliphate.

Figure 5.17
Roshan, Gayer-Anderson House, Cairo, Egypt.

The comingling of languages, religions, and artistic traditions of every sort—in food, clothes, songs, houses, and chests—took place not only on the Iberian Peninsula, but also with increasing intensity far beyond the Pyrenees, into France. Several terms explicitly indicate the hybrid populations and the corresponding artistic productions. A "Mozarab" was a "wanna-be Arab," a Christian who took on Arabic manners. Similarly, "Mudejar" meant an Arab who lived in Christian areas of the city. "Moorish" refers generally to the late medieval hybrid artistic culture of Spain and North Africa.

The two most important buildings in Islamic Spain, one a mosque, one a sprawling residence, are associated with Cordoba and Granada, respectively. The Great Mosque of Cordoba was culturally complex from the start, with its recycled columns and capitals.

The prayer hall of the mosque incorporates both classical elements and **Moorish** arches. These arches employ the bicolored stone work, **ablaq**, that is a hallmark of Romanesque churches.

In the residential sphere, Ibn Ahmar built the Alhambra on the hills outside of Granada, 1250–1360. It consists of a series of pavilions and gardens, and the resulting ensemble is considered one of the two most important structures of Islamic Spain.

The centuries of the second millennium saw Islam, as the official religion, losing ground in Spain, yet the cultural effects lived on. The Castilian monarchs who ruled from Seville continued to build in the style started with the Alhambra. Their primary residence was the Alcazar, Arabic for palace. Mostly built by Peter the Cruel, starting in 1364, this house included Quranic inscriptions in the lush wall decorations made of plaster, paint, and ceramic tile. Their mosque turned cathedral is the largest Gothic church in Europe, yet its plan remains that of an Islamic prayer hall. The Giralda received a new top, yet retained its clear identity as a one-time **minaret**. And adjacent to the church is a courtyard with fountains and an orange grove, entered through a stately horseshoe-shaped arch.

Moorish furniture clearly shows the fusion of Western forms and Islamic decoration. A typical piece of furniture in sixteenth-century Spain is the **vargueño**. Initially a chest on a stand, it served well as a desk. With both a writing surface and storage, it is a predecessor to the French *secrétaire* and its importance in baroque Mexico is covered in Chapter 7. The carving is detailed, the decoration profuse. Moorish chairs, in many respects, resemble Italian and French chairs. Included in the group of Moorish seating is a folding chair, made of wood and leather, called **sillón frailero**. Highly decorated, they are a sign of the itinerant quality of the people during this time period.

Writing about this medieval culture of tolerance, Menocal states: "In its moments of great achievement, medieval culture positively thrived on holding at least two, and often many more, contrary ideas at the same time. This was the chapter of Europe's culture when Jews, Christians, and Muslims lived side by side and, despite their intractable differences and enduring hostilities, nourished a complex culture of tolerance" (2002, p. 11).

Conclusion

In the period when Rome became ancient, two religions sought to establish themselves as world players with major architectural monuments. The designers of Christian churches collectively pursued a strategy of refining a particular schema. The creators of Muslim mosques took the opposite approach and operated within a number of regional vocabularies.

The Christian and Muslim worlds alike experienced a shift from a civic order to religious power, and from cities to feudal families. Feudalism was a hereditary economic and political system. From fortified urban structures, to residences, to locked chests, the emphasis was on protection. There were also some remarkable coincidences. Both Europe and the Islamic world used leather as an industrial material, prized for its durability and ability to repel water. Two words from the world of furniture, *coffer* and *diwan*, curiously enough, came to act as stand-ins for a highly desirable commodity: money.

In many respects, the period from the Fall of Rome to the rebirth known as the Renaissance was a period of introspection, in which the delicately delineated illuminated manuscript took the place of the heroic statue in a public square. In the world of the arts, Islam and the West developed in ways that are the exact opposite of how they are perceived today. The West, as represented by Romanesque churches, was unflinching and austere. Islam, in the many variants of its mosques and palaces, became known worldwide for its sensuousness, because of the richness of surfaces, from silk to mosaics, and the complexity of its decorative patterns.

Sources

Romanesque

Conant, Kenneth (1959). *Carolingian and Romanesque Architecture: 800 to 1200*. Harmondsworth: Penguin.

Eames, Penelope (1977). *Furniture in England, France, and the Netherlands from the Twelfth to the Fifteenth Century*. London: Furniture History Society.

Mercer, Eric (1969). *Furniture 700–1700*. London: Weidenfeld & Nicolson.

Oursel, Raymond (1967). *Living Architecture: Romanesque*. London: Oldbourne.

Seidel, Linda (1981). *The Romanesque Facades of Aquitaine*. Chicago: University of Chicago Press.

Temple, Richard, ed. (1990). *Early Christian and Byzantine Art*. London: Element Books.

Islamic

Alloula, Malek (1986). *The Colonial Harem*. Minneapolis: University of Minnesota Press.

Blessing, Patricia (2022). *Architecture and Material Politics in the 15th-Century Ottoman Empire*. Cambridge: Cambridge University Press.

Darke, Diana (2020). *Stealing from the Saracens: How Islamic Architecture Shaped Europe*. London: Hurst.

Ettinghouse, Richard, et al. (1994). *Art and Architecture of Islam, 650–1250*. New Haven, CT: Yale University Press.

Greenlaw, Jean-Pierre (1995). *The Coral Buildings of Suakin*. London: Wiley.

Kostof, Spiro (1995). *A History of Architecture: Settings and Rituals*. Oxford: Oxford University Press.

Lewis, Bernard (1995). *The Middle East: A Brief History of the Last 2000 Years*. New York: Scribner's.

Menocal, Maria Rosa (2002). *The Ornament of the World: How Muslims, Jews, and Christians Created a Culture of Tolerance in Medieval Spain*. Boston: Little, Brown.

Michell, George (2007). *The Majesty of Mughal Decoration*. London: Thames and Hudson.

Sadan, Joseph (1985). "Furniture, Islamic." In *Dictionary of the Middle Ages*, edited by J.R. Strayer, vol. 5, pp. 313–16. New York: Scribner.

Discussion and Review Questions

1. In the nineteenth century, a significant number of architects professed their fondness for Romanesque churches. What is appealing about these buildings, if they are technologically less advanced than Gothic?

2. What are five vocabulary terms that refer to features of a church in plan?

3. What are some of the regional variations of Islamic architecture?

4. What are the standard features of a mosque? What is the corresponding vocabulary?

5. What are some of the variable features of a mosque that vary from place to place?

Gothic

800–1150		1140–1500	1150–1250		1230–1325
Romanesque and Norman		Gothic	Early and High Gothic		Rayonnant

By 1250, European design had changed dramatically and there existed what can be called the Gothic style. The building of French Gothic churches was a national surge of architectural expression. Gothic cathedrals of the Île de France are widely seen as one of the high points in the history of architecture. Initially associated with France, the effects quickly spread across Europe. Gothic architecture is important because it is an entire architectural system not derivative of the classical orders. Gothic furniture was closely allied with architecture in its forms and details. Over the course of the twelfth century, the interest in classical remains was spasmodic and in decline.

Gothic is the last style of the medieval period before the Renaissance. Gothic architecture and design become an entity in its own right, but it is also a bridge between Romanesque and Renaissance. One means of understanding Gothic is to examine it side by side with Romanesque; comparing arches, façades, and plans is a worthwhile endeavor. It is a mistake, however, to consider them as opposed. Gothic architecture grew out of Romanesque, and all the features for which Gothic architecture and design are known existed in the Romanesque period. It is a final florescence of the medieval period, but in some countries, most notably England, it marks the beginning of the Renaissance. For not the first time in art history, we employ a word that was initially meant derogatorily. *Gothic* was widely used in the sixteenth and seventeenth centuries to refer to art that was specifically not Italian and not

Figure 6.0
(*Facing page*)
North rose window, Chartres Cathedral, France, twelfth century, CE.

Renaissance. In the eighteenth century, the term became neutrally descriptive.

As with much of the medieval period, rarely do we have information about artists, architects, woodworkers, and masons. We also have little information about people's reactions to art. Religion was everything and there was a disdain for manual labor.

Civic Infrastructure

After the Roman urban-scaled endeavors, the return of European urbanism occurs in the Gothic period. Thus, the period known for one of the highlights of Western architecture is coincident with the reintroduction of urban design. The achievements in the realm of urban design in the Gothic period have not received the attention lavished on cathedrals. Many histories of urban design consider all medieval towns to be an example of laissez-faire capitalism, with irregular streets and squares (Figure 6.1). There were several types of medieval town plans, but San Gimignano, in Tuscany, serves our purposes here, for it illustrates what most people think of when they think of medieval towns. It grew up around trading routes that existed for centuries. Town squares were not designed to follow strict geometries but appear as a response to foot and vehicular traffic. Houses of irregular height and width line the square.

The Gothic period also sees a considerable number of new towns built, speculative real-estate ventures. Crisply rectilinear in plan, many of these towns had gates, defensive walls, and the central feature of medieval towns, the commercial street. Competition for space along this street was fierce, so structures had narrow façades and property lines extended backward. The Gothic period is known for its religious monuments. The achievements in urban design, however, are noteworthy. Over the course of the Gothic period, there was an increasing emphasis on civic government.

Beginning

Saint Denis is the patron saint of France because he was one of those responsible for converting Gauls to Christianity in the third century CE. The

Figure 6.1
View of medieval square and urban fabric, San Gimignano, Tuscany, Italy.

conversion process did not run smoothly, and after being tortured on a hot grill, Denis was decapitated. According to Catholic tradition, he picked up his head and walked north until he reached the area where the church that was dedicated to him still stands. In addition to being the burial ground of Saint Denis, the **abbey** church is the holding place for French kings. The abbey church of Saint Denis is one of the most importance places for the nation of France, French Christianity, and the history of architecture.

The royal abbey, founded in the fifth century, was rebuilt in the Carolingian and Romanesque periods. The Abbot Suger was the head of the monastery of Saint Denis from 1122 to 1151. The story of French Gothic typically begins with the Abbot and his abbey. Suger, famously, had the church remodeled, a move that set in place an architectural movement that redefined religious architecture. He is rightly considered the most important patron in the development of French Gothic.

Suger's started in 1137. He left intact the Carolingian and Romanesque hall and added on to it at the front and rear. To the front he added a new elevation, but it was his dazzling addition to the rear that was most impressive. He replaced the Carolingian apse, and his remodeling included an ambulatory and a new series of chapels (Figure 6.2). The design dispenses with the divisions between chapels, creating a continuous visual effect in which columns, walls, and ceiling are part of a continuous whole.

The term *chevet* refers to an elaboration of what had been the apse in the Early Christian basilica. An agglomeration of chapels and ambulatory, in Romanesque churches it is sculptural and bulbous; Gothic churches follow the model of Saint Denis, in which the chevet is an integral part of the plan. The chevet at Saint Denis includes three elements that constitute the foundation of Gothic architecture: **Gothic arches**, **rib vaults**, and **flying buttresses**.

Gothic architecture

Romanesque architecture relies upon a semispherical arch. The barrel vault is an extrusion of the arch into three dimensions. A Romanesque church is essentially a barrel vault lifted onto walls. The height of a Romanesque arch is based on its width; in combining spatial elements with different dimensions, such as a nave and side aisles, it is difficult to roof the system because each rises to a different height. Gothic architecture relies upon a pointed arch whose width can be manipulated.

When two barrel vaults intersect, the points of intersection are rib vaults. Gothic architects realized that the vault is an entity that transfers forces, and it can be an element of design. Rather than two intersecting cylinders, the Gothic system is akin to an umbrella and its multiple spokes.

The pointed arch came into existence after 1150. Whether Gothic or Islamic, the pointed arch is a design element struck from adjacent but separate circles. With less horizontal spread, it emphasizes the vertical. The genius of Gothic architecture can be found in one of its constituent details: the Gothic rib. To the Gothic mind, ribs and groin vaults were plastic design elements.

A masonry vault suspends heavy stones in the air, subject to the forces of gravity. As with all things in the earth's atmosphere, they are subject to the laws of physics. A barrel vault exerts tremendous lateral forces on the tops of walls, over time causing them to collapse outward. To counter this, walls are thick or strengthened with piers. Knowledge of how to do this was learned by trial and error. Many Romanesque churches failed structurally and were rebuilt. Visiting Romanesque churches, one often observes walls that had started to precariously peel away from

Figure 6.2
Saint Denis, ambulatory and choir, Paris, France, 1144.

the church, only to be propped back into place. Gothic architects took a necessity, structural reinforcement, and made it a virtue.

In Suger's remodeling of Saint Denis, all the characteristically Gothic features were put into place. Glass was used in new ways. Suger felt that expensive materials were appropriate for the buildings that housed the ritual of celebrating Mass. The results were highly admired and copied, and began a new era of church building.

Notre Dame de Paris

Romanesque and Gothic churches are the result of several hundred years of building and rebuilding, and one of the charms of visiting them is teasing out the parts that derive from each epoch. Many Romanesque churches have minor Gothic additions. Similarly, many Gothic churches were built on top of Romanesque or Carolingian structures, and almost all have nineteenth- and twentieth-century repairs and restorations. The lively façade of Saint Denis has a Romanesque band, a Gothic band, a **crenellated** cornice that recalls a feudal past, and significant modern restorations.

The Cathedral of Notre Dame de Paris (Our Lady of Paris) spectacularly sits on an island, Île de la Cité, in the center of Paris. It once had

Gallo-Roman, **Merovingian**, and Carolingian forebears, yet because its founder, Bishop Maurice de Sully, had those pulled down, it mostly dates to the end of the early Gothic period.

The façade of Notre Dame dates to the period 1200–1250 and belongs to the mature phase of early Gothic façade development (Figure 6.3). No longer an amalgam of elements, the result of an additive process, the façade of Notre Dame has become a canvas or field to be designed and manipulated. It no longer slavishly represents the cross section of the building behind it, as had Early Christian churches. The façade is a thick and heavy wall with windows cut into its depth. Horizontal elements predominate. All these features are held in common with its Romanesque predecessors. The front elevation contrasts greatly with the side and rear elevations, which emphasize vertical elements and have expansive windows—two architecture moves that dematerialize the wall as the principal architectural element.

The design of the Gothic church front elevation can be considered an elaboration of the Romanesque scheme. Most, such as Notre Dame, have two towers, three portals, arcading, voussoirs, round windows, and tympana.

Notre Dame's tripartite composition relates to the presence of the nave and side aisles, yet in the

Figure 6.3
Notre Dame, façade detail with tympana and archivolts, Paris, France, 1163–1250 CE.

façade, the three divisions are presented equally. The tripartite division of various parts of the Gothic architectural vocabulary, the **trefoil**, the nave with two side aisles, the three bays of the façade, all are consistent with a religious belief in the Christian Holy Trinity. From the baseline to the top of the cornice (below the towers), the front façade is a near-perfect square. The expression upward, so important in a Gothic church, in the elevation is relegated to several elements—the towers, the spires, and thc use of the pointed Gothic arch. The towers are half the height of the square. Vertically the façade is divided into thirds; horizontally each succeeding band is of a narrower width, which subtly gives the impression of greater height.

Portal

Centuries before scholars began discussing buildings as signs (semiotics) and relating architecture to advertising, Gothic sculptors lavished their attention on the portals to churches. The sculptural programs of Gothic cathedrals focus less on torture, evil, and doomsday scenarios (characteristic of Romanesque churches), and there is both secular and religious iconography. Gothic cathedrals and their frontal elevations acted like billboards. Their façades, and specifically the sculptural programs of the façades, related to an audience that was mostly illiterate in words but not in visual imagery. The sculptural and decorative programs of Gothic cathedrals announced to viewers, "Come, enter through these doors. Heavenly salvation awaits."

Interior elevation

Gothic architects gave considerable attention to the development of interior elevations, and one of the results of the ponderous front elevation is that visitors walk through a heavy wall that is foreboding in both scale and iconography. Once inside, a visitor met an architectural system focused on height and light. Considerable attention was paid to the lateral façades of the nave (standing in the middle of the church, looking at the side elevations). As Gothic churches grew more complex, the areas flanking the nave developed into a complicated assembly that comprised a side aisle, a gallery above it, yet another gallery above that, known as the **triforium**, and the clerestory above that. This was essentially an interior four-story elevation. The problem is that this configuration emphasized horizontal movement, physical and visual, and decreased the amount of space devoted to the clerestory. The clerestory is important

because it is the one element of the interior elevation that lets in light directly from the exterior to the nave. The side aisles have fenestration, but by the time the light reaches across the side aisles and galleries to the nave, it is greatly diffused.

Part of what highlights the sanctuary is that light reaches the apse unobstructed. Hence, despite all the attention to glass and light, many Gothic cathedrals are quite dark, and the light, as it is, has a diaphanous quality.

The solution to the "problem" of the side elevation at Notre Dame was to eliminate the triforium. This increased the depth of the clerestory and simplified, to great effect, the nave's interior elevations.

Flying buttress

Beginnings are important in history books. Many people see in Gothic architecture the first glimmers of several key precepts of modern architecture. The two most important are related: the distinction made between columns and walls as structural features or as space-defining (non-load-bearing) elements; and the development of an all-glass or nearly all-glass curtain wall. What made this possible—and one of the achievements of Gothic cathedrals—was the flying buttress (Figure 6.4).

Figure 6.4
Section of a Gothic cathedral flying buttress, twelfth to thirteenth century.

The buttress had a humble beginning, as a correction used to prop up a leaning wall. Stone or brick walls that support interior barrel vaults tend to splay outward at the top over time. Eventually, they topple over and the building structurally fails. A buttress, essentially an applied pier, holds the wall in place and helps it maintain stability. This led to the buttress being designed as an integral element from the start. Eventually, it was discovered that the buttress could be lightened to the smallest possible profile and separated from the wall, a step toward separating the wall from the structure.

The separation of the structure from the space-defining wall allowed architects to expand the area devoted to glass. Clerestories and stained-glass windows were not merely a means of letting in light. They delineated interior space in a new way and were central to the spiritual effect of a Gothic church.

Related to this is the development of a Gothic architectural detail, **tracery**. Tracery is not just a fussy decorative term. Two of the most common types of tracery, in architecture, interiors, and furniture, are **trefoil** and **quatrefoil**. Tracery involves a different approach to defining space and using materials. The architects of Romanesque churches considered walls to be solid elements conceptually, and windows were punched into them. When adding windows to a wall, there is a limit to how many and how wide they can be. If the windows are too numerous, the wall will fail. A consequence of the flying buttress is its ability to increase the expanse of glass while still supporting the roof. Yet glass cannot be produced in large pieces. The mullions between panes and sections of glass, instead of being remnants of a wall, are held together by the smallest of pieces possible, tracery—in stone or metal—whose only purpose was to hold the glass in place. Thus, the contemporary skyscraper million, or glass-to-glass pressure connections, lies with Gothic tracery.

A characteristic of tracery in furniture is that the material—stone, metal, or wood—is relatively unimportant. The goal is the decorative form. Tracery sections are as delicate as possible to emphasize the pattern they create.

Bourges and High Gothic

Major French Gothic churches were built at Chartres, Amiens, Rheims, and Bourges. Saint-Etienne at Bourges, begun shortly before 1200, is a remarkable example of **High Gothic** architecture (Figure 6.5). Like Notre Dame, it belongs to

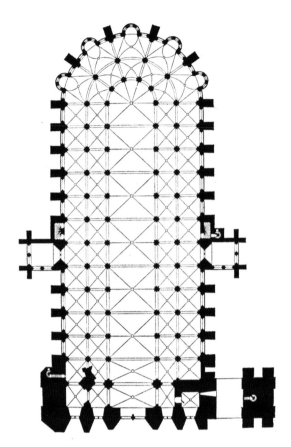

Figure 6.5
Bourges Cathedral, Bourges, France, 1195–1250 CE. Plan.

the tradition associated with Paris in which the church, viewed in plan, is a unified composition. The development of the Christian church had been additive, starting with the basilica form, which is a rectangle with a semicircular apse at one end. Over time, the layout became increasingly complicated, with the addition of a transept, narthex, side aisles, and chapels. One of the achievements of Gothic design was to consolidate these disparate elements as part of a unified plan.

Saint-Etienne at Bourges is 407 feet (124 meters) long and consists of a nave flanked by side aisles. The piers lie mostly on the exterior and the side aisles run seamlessly into the ambulatory. The unity and harmony of the nave are achieved by vaults that extend over two bays. The nave elegantly becomes the choir. More so than with any other Gothic cathedral, the expression of the transept is suppressed.

Sainte-Chapelle and Rayonnant

Louis IX reigned as king from 1226 to 1270. Known as one of the most pious and just kings, he was an important patron of architecture.

Canonized in 1297, he expressed his religious devotion by participating in a craze of the late medieval period—the acquisition of holy relics. Saint-Louis paid great sums of money for Jesus's crown of thorns, a nail and a wooden piece of the cross, fragments from the spear that pierced Jesus's torso, the vinegar-soaked sponge, and pieces of Jesus's robe and shroud. Sainte-Chapelle was the private royal chapel built to house these relics. The cost of obtaining the relics exceeded the construction costs.

Sainte-Chapelle is the best example of the **rayonnant** style (Figure 6.6). The distinguishing feature of rayonnant tracery is that lines radiate out from a single point. Unusual for a Gothic monument, the King's chapel is tiny. It has four small bays and a seven-sided apse. As it was a private chapel, there are no side aisles. Essentially a single room, continuous glass walls illuminate its interior. Three-quarters of the height of the walls is luxuriously devoted to stained glass. With an extensive system of flying buttresses, the building's structural support is external and separated from the walls. The walls, therefore, are space-defining elements with little structural function. Sainte-Chapelle is one of the most important monuments of Gothic glass. It is an impressive space, tall in section and devoted to color and light. One of the most important achievements of Gothic architecture is the separation of a building's structure from its space-defining walls and the development of nonstructural walls that are largely made of glass.

Wells Cathedral

Once the efforts of a group of architects and designers associated with a region achieves an across-the-board similarity, we have what historians refer to as a style. One feature of the development and dissemination of design styles is that they tend to appear in one region, then spread to another. It is conceivable that some architects and construction workers crossed the channel in both directions, and that the movement of workers was one of the mechanisms by which knowledge of the Gothic style was transmitted from France to England.

There is typically a time lag from region to region. For example, Gothic reigned in France in the period 1140–1230; elsewhere in Europe, it is associated with the period 1170–1250. Countries developed regional variations.

While all European countries were affected by the fashion to express devotion and economic success by erecting Gothic cathedrals, England made Gothic its own. One example is Wells Cathedral, whose construction began in 1174. A characteristic of English Gothic, evident at Lincoln Cathedral, is a profusion of surface ornamentation. Many vaults have extra ribs, taking a structural element and making it decorative. English Gothic churches have more elaborate patterns of vaults than seen elsewhere.

The emphasis on verticality is less pronounced. Wells was an abbey church, surrounded by a lawn. The interior elevations recall **Norman** Romanesque; the walls are thick and solid. Horizontal lines are continuous, while verticals are broken, the opposite scenario of French cathedrals. The most unusual features are the **strainer arches** at the transept, dating to 1338.

By the mid-thirteenth century, Gothic cathedrals were built throughout Europe. Germany joined the Gothic fray with the New Cathedral of

Figure 6.6
Pierre de Montreuil. Sainte-Chapelle, 1246–1248, Paris, France. Ceiling and glass side elevations.

Cologne in 1248. Spain embraced the Gothic style with major Gothic churches at Burgos (1222) and Toledo (1226).

A feature of Gothic outside of France (although also found in France) is an interest in column capitals formed with elaborate naturalistic foliages, such as those at Rheims. This became popular in England and Germany. This is significant because it underscores that the Gothic architect developed an entire architectural vocabulary independent of classic details. Deriving decorative motifs based on common plants was a way of personalizing the international the Gothic style and making it local. Foliate decorative patterns are also a feature of furniture and other designed objects.

Italian Gothic, like Italian Romanesque, fits oddly within the framework of European stylistic developments. There was considerable Italian resistance to Gothic architecture. For Italians, the Roman artifacts they dealt with were real and not imagined. Thus, Italians never lost sight of what actual Roman ruins looked like. Similarly, the Byzantine impulse was strongly felt, so one particular branch of Italian Gothic, Venetian Gothic, combines Gothic forms with Byzantine decoration.

The aspect of Gothic architecture most conducive to the Italian mentality was the façade. Freed from literally expressing the building's form, the Italian Gothic façade was precisely that—a false front that shaped the space in front of the church. The façades of Italian Gothic churches acted on the urban scale, and (thinking of the Pantheon) Italian architects, not surprisingly, were always interested in expressing the dome and making it visible from the exterior.

Interiors and Furniture

Interiors

When the most significant building interiors of an era are found in churches, it is clear that religious institutions had a great deal of power and money. Correspondingly, the greatest achievements and innovations are found in the building and outfitting of churches. Yet as we saw in our brief look at Gothic urban design, the period known for churches saw a decline in the power of the church and the ascendancy of secular institutions, such as hospitals, libraries, universities, and town halls.

There are few domestic structures from the Gothic period, and even fewer examples of modest Gothic houses. Paintings and illuminated manuscripts are an important source when examining the domestic world. Turning to the realm of interiors and furnishings, the most obvious observation is that Gothic furniture bears a remarkable continuity with Gothic architecture.

By the end of the Gothic period, designers had increasingly focused their attention on delineating the interiors of masonry buildings and increasing the amount of comfort. When working within masonry structures, there were two principal means of doing this: hanging tapestries and constructing paneling.

An early fifteenth-century French miniature shows Christin de Pisan offering her works, in the form of a book, to Isabel of Bavaria, and reveals details of a Gothic domestic interior (Figure 6.7). A barrel-vaulted roof caps a room made of masonry walls. Tie beams and vertical king posts act as tension rods stabilizing the arches of the roof structure. Tapestries hang on the walls. The bed has a canopy, or tester, and is draped for both warmth and privacy. This room, a bedroom, serves double duty as a sitting room during the day for a group of women.

Bars at the window let in air and light and prevent outsiders from gaining access. This is a straightforward indication of another aspect of secular life: the ever-present danger of burglaries, and hence the defensive nature of houses. Gothic domestic interiors of palaces, castles, and houses are at the tail end of the great period of fortified castles. The invention of gunpowder and other elements of warfare rendered the house-as-fort prototype obsolete.

Isabel of Bavaria sits on an X-frame chair, the others on small stools. The room is sparsely furnished; even for the nobility, pieces of furniture were exceptional and prized.

Another valuable aspect of this image is that it shows a preference for richness in color, material, and decoration, mostly achieved with textiles. Gothic buildings seem somber today, because the color of the statuary has worn off and current taste does not allow for stone statuary to be painted. The visual abundance in a Gothic interior was provided by the saturated colors of textiles.

A scene of a wedding banquet presents a view of furniture involved with ritual and daily life. Individual chairs were a rarity. The diners sit on benches behind draped trestle tables— no doubt hidden because of their inelegant construction. In some English great halls, a raised

Figure 6.7
Christin de Pisan
offers her works to
Isabel of Bavaria,
1410–1414 CE.
French miniature.

platform, or **dais**, distinguishes one end of the room. Other European countries also had the custom of outfitting a dining room with a dais. Being seated along one side of the table allows for servers, who were plentiful, to serve from the other side. Other guests similarly sit on one side of the table.

A tall cabinet serves as a sideboard. The sideboard acted as a staging area for servers and put the family's expensive serving pieces on display.

Carpentry

In a Gothic painting, a carpenter works with a plane. In front of his worktable stands the fruit of previous efforts, a partially constructed base cabinet. A woman unravels thread from a spindle. This image divides the labor force, with a man engaged with carpentry and a woman involved with weaving, underscoring the two primary means of articulating a Gothic interior, with carpentry and textiles.

A surefire way to identify a piece of furniture or carpentry as Gothic is the **linenfold** motif, usually featured in wood constructions. This frequently occurring motif is a shape achievable with planing and carving. It is also a testament to the value of linen, and textiles in general. Gothic painting and sculpture paid considerable attention to the folds of drapery, and the linenfold motif in furniture is related to conventions of drapery folds in sculpture.

In Gothic churches, wooden choir stalls and other interior partitions were often freestanding and self-supporting. Their design, in form and detail, is consistent with architectural Gothic (Figure 6.8). The most prestigious and innovative architectural projects were churches; hence, the finest and most highly paid carpentry jobs were found in outfitting them. It is therefore not surprising that this led to furniture production with strong visual ties to Gothic architecture. Many pieces of Gothic furniture are beholden

Figure 6.8
Canopied seat,
France, *c.* 1500.
Oak with storage
below.

to architecture and, in fact, are designed like miniature buildings, such as choirs, **buffets**, and display cabinets. While the vertical divisions between the individual seats are structurally expressive, most of the attention is devoted to decorative work. There are Gothic arches, crosses, **finials**, and quatrefoil tracery.

Regarding function, the choir stall is taller than necessary. The sitter's head would rest about three-quarters of the way up the backrest. The remainder of the choir stall exists for visual effect.

Tracery, initially carved in stone, is here carved out of wood. Tracery did not exist solely to support glass. Elements of tracery are intended to be decorative. The form is important, in stone, wood, or metal. Gothic tracery glories in curls, arches, and C- and S-curves. Expressing the nature of the material was unimportant.

Furniture

A Gothic chair looks as though a choir stall had been chopped off in slices and one piece turned into a chair. Up to this historical point in time, the late fifteenth century, important chairs, such as thrones, highlighted the status of the sitter by using elegant materials and time-consuming and exacting workmanship. The Gothic chair bestows status upon its sitter in a different fashion: by exaggerating its scale. From Gothic architecture, furniture designers inherited an emphasis on height. The Gothic chair renders the person sitting

in it high status and visual import by exaggerating their physical presence. The combination of seated person (resplendently dressed) and chair presents an eye-catching ensemble that relates Gothic architectural principles to the human body.

The stylized linenfold motif identifies a piece as a work of the Gothic period, as do the finials. In this chair, a storage unit supports the seat. Pieces of furniture were scarce in the Gothic period, and often had to take on several functions. A cushion could be added to provide a modicum of comfort. The rest of a chair emphasizes visual effect. A chair exacted a precise vertical posture of its sitter, with arms at a dignified position of rest.

Gothic chairs were rare. Most people sat on benches, chests, or stools, and these common seating types were less elaborate. Rather than being consistent with Gothic, their straightforward forms are a testament to their utility. The X-frame stool is remarkably consistent from ancient Rome to the twentieth century. X-frame stools of various kinds existed on all continents. Gothic X-frame stools take the typical form and dress it with Gothic detailing (Figure 6.9).

Just as the stylistic influences of Gothic architecture can be seen across Europe, the work of French carpenters also made its mark on European furniture. A coronation chair from Westminster Abbey in London is an exceptional piece of furniture for an exceptional function: the ceremony to crown the monarch (Figure 6.10). It represents how craftsmen combined the knowledge of furniture making with architectural detailing. It has a commanding presence

Figure 6.9
Folding X-frame stool, *c.* 1400.

Figure 6.10
Seigneurial chair, based
on a Coronation chair
from Westminster
Abbey, 1300 CE.

C H A I R,
Of Silver in the City of Barcelona.

Figure 6.11
Silver throne of
King Martin of
Aragon, Spain,
fourteenth
century.

in a room and is designed to receive the end of
an architectural axis. It is meant to be viewed
frontally.

The vertical expression is achieved by lifting
the seat itself atop two platforms. A triangular
backdrop frames the head. The lion feet underscore the regal nature of the piece, and the
polychrome decoration makes it a worthy focus of
those in the assembly room.

In the realm of decorative arts, the Gothic
period exhibits a love of small, precious things
made of exquisite materials. This is typically
evident in the production of finely crafted reliquar-
ies or chalices. When it was financially feasible,
the same attention was turned to furniture, and
a few exceptional pieces of metal furniture exist,
made of bronze or silver. The throne of King Martin
of Aragon shows architectural forms rendered
in silver (Figure 6.11). Its creator employed the
system of Gothic architectural detailing, which
had an international appeal. Although accom-
modations were made for the material, the
Gothic forms were applied with little regard for
the unique qualities of metal. The decorative
vocabulary remained unchanged. The emphasis
is on effect and not an "honest" expression of
materiality.

Its nonrepresentational decoration suggests
that by the seventeenth century, motifs associated
with Islamic Spain had spread around Europe.
Some artworks conform to the belief that Gothic,
Renaissance, and Islamic are distinct categories,
yet certain pieces display evidence of an overlap.

Conclusion

The Gothic period is the tail end of the Middle
Ages and the last period before the Renaissance.
The inspired period of building Gothic cathedrals
lasted some three hundred years.

The church played a central role as a religious, political, economic, and cultural entity.
Commissions for building and outfitting churches
involved large outlays of cash and resulted in most
of the high-end artwork. Yet the Gothic period saw
the growing importance of royal patronage. Power
was no longer the exclusive purview of monasteries. Gothic churches involved the input of nobles,
merchants, and artisans.

During the Gothic period, the necessity for
walled cities waned. Gothic domestic interiors are
more elaborate and comfortable than Romanesque
interiors. Yet the Gothic domestic realm is not the
equivalent of the religious realm.

Gothic furniture comes from and is an extension of Gothic architecture. The distinctive features of Gothic architecture constitute the distinctive features of Gothic furniture: pointed arches, tracery, finials, trefoils, and quatrefoils.

The interior spaces of churches were carefully delineated to affect the mood and spirit of the religious visitor. A visitor who entered a Gothic cathedral on a bright day noticed the difference between the bright outside and the dim inside. Before the pupils dilated, the visitor noticed the vertical orientation of the building and looked upward. Then, becoming accustomed to the light, the visitor noticed the existence of walls almost entirely of glass and brightly colored. There is a reason why Gothic cathedrals are known by the catchphrase "height and light."

Sources

Bony, Jean (1983). *French Gothic Architecture of the 12th and 13th Centuries*. Berkeley: University of California Press.

Bork, Robert (2016). *The Geometry of Creation: Architectural Drawing and the Dynamics of Gothic Design*. London: Routledge.

Branner, Robert (1961). *Gothic Architecture*. New York: G. Braziller.

Fitchen, John (1981). *The Construction of the Gothic Cathedral*. Chicago: University of Chicago Press.

Frankl, Paul (1962). *Gothic Architecture*. Harmondsworth: Penguin Books.

Mark, Robert (1982). *Experiments in Gothic Structure*. Cambridge, MA: MIT Press.

Martindale, Andrew (1967). *Gothic Art: From the Twelfth to Fifteenth Centuries*. New York: Praeger.

Scott, Robert (2011). *The Gothic Enterprise*. Oakland: University of California Press.

Simson, Otto Georg von (1956). *The Gothic Cathedral: The Origins of Gothic Architecture and the Medieval Concept of Order*. New York: Pantheon Books.

Wilson, Christopher (1990). *The Gothic Cathedral*. London: Thames and Hudson.

Discussion and Review Questions

1. What are the chief differences between Romanesque and Gothic?

2. What are the chief similarities between Romanesque and Gothic?

3. What are the elements of the Gothic design vocabulary that relate to the religious experience?

4. What are two technical achievements of the Gothic that predict modern developments?

5. How is Gothic furniture an extension of Gothic architecture?

6. How does a Gothic church seek to create a spiritual feeling in a viewer?

The Americas

Mexico	1500 BCE–200 CE		200 CE–900 CE		900 CE–1521 CE	
	Preclassic		Classic		Postclassic	

Peru	1800–900 BCE	900–200 BCE	200 BCE–600 CE	600–1000 CE	1000–1476 CE	1476–1534 CE
	Initial	Early Horizon	Early Intermediate	Middle Horizon	Late Intermediate	Late Horizon

This chapter represents a deficit and an attempt to address that deficit—namely, the role of indigenous American architecture and objects in a history of design. It is not a deficit in terms of high-quality objects for inclusion, but it is a deficit in the sense that these items have not traditionally taken a prominent role in design histories. There are many reasons for the lack of attention up until recent decades, and many reasons for righting the wrong.

But there are difficulties. For one, furniture as construed in the European way did not play a major role in **pre-Columbian** societies. Where there are hundreds of books on eighteenth-century English and French furniture, there is not a single book devoted to pre-Columbian furniture. The aesthetic impulse of many American groups presents itself in textiles, baskets, masks, headdresses, jewelry, sports equipment, and clay figurines—objects that standard design histories mostly ignore.

Architectural survey books have added pre-Columbian monuments to their canon. The task of architectural historians was easier: the temples, pyramids, and cities of Mexico, Guatemala, and Peru fit anyone's idea of great architecture. In addition, problematic for the history of interiors and furnishings, **Mesoamerican** architects focused their efforts on building exteriors and sculpture. And there is the problem of

Figure 7.0
(*Facing page*)
Juan O'Gorman, Central Library of National Autonomous University of Mexico, Mexico City, 1950. Mosaic with historic and contemporary themes based on Aztec murals.

preservation: most objects made of impermanent materials have disappeared. Although pre-Columbian arts receive less coverage in traditional architecture, art, and design histories, it is not for lack of scholarly materials. The task that this chapter tackles is deciding how to include these materials in a history of design that focuses on furniture and interiors.

Early History

In prehistoric periods, Europe, Asia, and Africa were connected. Shards of Chinese vases have been found in Africa; the Greeks and Romans knew and drew Africans; Europeans and Asians traveled and traded via the Silk Road, and on ocean voyages. Yet there was little knowledge of or contact between Asia, Africa, and Europe and the Americas. The inhabitants of the pre-Columbian Americas had no knowledge of the Old World—Europe.

Physical contact between Asia and the New World occurred around 30000 BCE, via the land bridge that connected Alaska and Asia. People of Asian ancestry crossed the Bering Strait and began the population of the Western Hemisphere. By 10000 BCE, people lived along the length and breadth of North and South America. They had stone points, fishing nets, sleeping mats, and pottery. Organized agriculture developed in some areas as early as 4000 BCE (Kostof 1995). By 1500 BCE, the range and depth of the production of objects constitute the beginning of an American vision regarding artistic expression.

The varieties of domestic architecture were innumerable, with some houses sunken into the earth, some tucked underneath cliffs, some made of ice, stone, bricks, reeds, wood, or leather. Over time, a mosaic of cultures stretched across the Americas down to Antarctica. The first Americans were hunter-gatherers, and some groups stayed that way. But major urban civilizations developed, the largest the world had ever seen.

For historians of architecture and design, the cultures that developed permanent ritual complexes are compelling, as they left significant historical remains. Some North American groups had earthworks, such as the Hopewell in the Ohio Valley. The Hopewell mounds were burial sites containing human remains and grave objects, including smoking pipes, pottery, and copper jewelry. In southern Illinois, Cahokia was a large city centered on giant mounds.

While the possible subjects of this chapter are many, it will focus on the buildings and objects of two areas that had major urban centers: Mexico and Peru.

Columbus's voyage to the Americas in 1492 set in motion a series of events that would lead to the downfall of the societies he found; hence the term "pre-Columbian." Two of the expeditions in Columbus's wake, Hernando Cortés's conquest of the Aztecs in 1521 (Mexico) and Pizarro's conquest of the Incas (Peru) in 1536, completed the process set in motion by Columbus, and the results of that encounter are addressed at the chapter's end.

When Columbus arrived, no national boundary lines separated the regions that are today the United States, Mexico, and Central America. "Mesoamerica" refers to the North American and Central American region. "Pre-Columbian" is a general term referring to any of the indigenous groups who predated the arrival of the Spanish-funded explorer.

The challenge in writing this chapter concerns not only what pre-Columbian artifacts we should look at, but also how we look at them. Art historian Esther Pasztory addresses the issue of Western viewers of pre-Columbian artifacts:

In order to reconstruct pre-Columbian aesthetics, one is forced to deal with the context as defined anthropologically. The most immediate issue is the function of art, which is said to be "utilitarian" in traditional societies and "free" in the modern West. While we can say that as an embodiment of value, status, taste, and intellect, art of all periods has a similar function, there is indeed a difference between implicit and explicit concepts of aesthetics.

(Pasztory 2005, p. 193)

Looking carefully at designed objects is the first step in reconstructing a pre-Columbian aesthetic.

Mexico

In the preclassic period, the major site was San Lorenzo and the artworks of the Olmecs, including the colossal heads. The classic period, covered in these pages, includes the major ethnic groups: Teotihuacán, the Toltecs, and the Maya. The post-classic includes the Aztecs, who were there at the time of the Spanish conquest. Several major urban centers dominated life in ancient Mexico; their most impressive structures were pyramids. It is easy to see the connection between earth mounds and pyramids, at once of the earth but reaching toward the sky.

Teotihuacán

100 BCE–750 CE

In scale and age, the most imposing ancient buildings in North America are found at Teotihuacán. They lie in the semi-arid Valley of Teotihuacán, north of Mexico City. Teotihuacán was a major ritual center, a center of agriculture, and a bustling marketplace. As architectural historian Spiro Kostof eloquently wrote: "Nothing can prepare us for the size, conviction, and majesty of Teotihuacán" (1995, p. 237). Their agricultural abilities were extensive enough to support the population. At its height, Teotihuacán had a population of 200,000, making it one of the largest cities in the world. The most spectacular buildings are two pyramids; they are surrounded by lower temples, platforms, and palaces and residential areas. The first age of inhabitation at Teotihuacán was in the period 100 BCE–200 CE, predating the Aztec capital, Tenochtitlan, by a thousand years.

Teotihuacán is built around a central axis. In one direction it trails off with no definitive formal conclusion; the other ends in the central ritual complex that includes the Pyramid of the Moon and the large Pyramid of the Sun (Figure 7.1). The Pyramid of the Sun is the largest pyramid in the Americas. Facing west, it is 705 feet (214.9 meters) square and 206 feet (62.8 meters) tall.

What the Pyramid of the Moon lacks in size, it makes up for with the precision of its construction. The Pyramid of the Moon marks the end of the central axis at Teotihuacán and faces south. The surrounding buildings, smaller platforms, temples, and palaces emphasize the horizontal orientation and relate to the broad expanse of the valley.

Pasztory wrote her dissertation on the murals at Teotihuacán and is the author of a highly regarded book on the ancient city (Pasztory 1976).

Figure 7.1
View of the Street of the Dead with Plaza of the Moon and Pyramid of the Sun, Teotihuacán, Mexico, fourth to eight century.

She considers the dominant aesthetic quality at Teotihuacán to be order and organization. The city was organized along an axis, with blocks laid out according to a grid. There was standardization of the city, its architecture and art.

In many ways, Teotihuacán was a forerunner to the Aztec Empire; it was ancient and mythical to the Aztecs. Like the Aztecs, the people of Teotihuacán spoke Nahuatl. There was a cult of warriors, warfare, and human sacrifice. But it was not exactly the same as the Aztecs.

Unlike other Mesoamerican sites, the major monuments of Teotihuacán were built at one time, and not in successive layers. The Pyramid of the Sun may sit over a sacred site. Like the Aztec, Teotihuacán temples honored the gods. The Teotihuacán and the Aztecs had a god in common, Quetzalcoatl, the feathered serpent. The identification of the serpent statues that exist in quantity at Teotihuacán with the Aztec god is under dispute. The Quetzal bird had long green tail feathers that the Mesoamericans incorporated into their dress.

The talud and the tablero

Architecture varies greatly across Mesoamerica, yet there are aspects of its development that are variations on a single compositional scheme, outlined here. A frequent composition had two parts: the **talud** was a base, frequently sloped, that acted as the physical and visual support for a raised panel, the **tablero** (Figure 7.2). This panel features a prominent flat frame and a sunken inset field.

Apartments

The so-called palaces (a more accurate term is apartments) reflect the horizontality of the landscape; they focus on a courtyard, with rooms that open off the central space.

The leaders of Teotihuacán, after the grand period of monument building, focused their efforts on the city's residential quarters. Teotihuacán's residents lived in these multifamily units. "Most of the population of Teotihuacán had lived in apartment compounds built on a grid plan" (Pasztory 1997, p. 33). Apartments had central patios with altars and a temple platform on one side of the court. The courtyard elevations are a different riff on the Teotihuacán style moldings—the talud and tablero—and utilize the same profile as the temples. The variation is that the base is two steps, followed by flat, square piers.

Figure 7.2
Palace of Quetzalpapaloti (Priests' Residence), courtyard, Teotihuacán, Mexico, fourth to eight century.

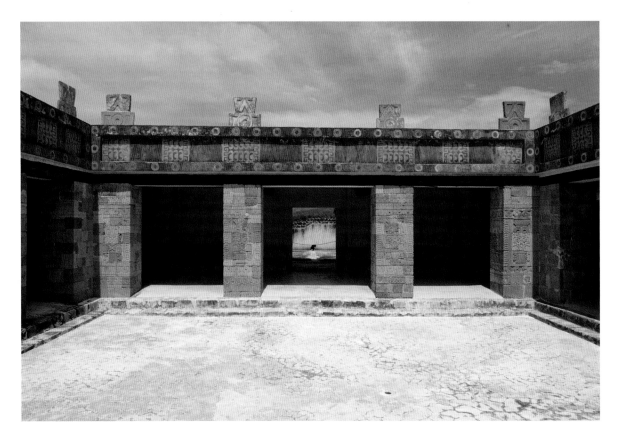

Artists

To create, maintain, and continue the artistic traditions of religious and domestic life required large numbers of masons, carvers, painters, and potters. The traditions of craft production were highly developed, and there were hundreds of workshops and thousands of artists. The markets of Teotihuacán sold the goods of artists and merchants, some of whom had traveled long distances.

The stone walls are similar to mural paintings. Many of the stones that constitute the buildings had originally been painted in vibrant colors, red being one of the most prominent. Yet a color scheme of red on red, with similar value and hue, emphasizes the compositional flatness. Pasztory broadly characterizes Teotihuacán art: "Lack of ostentation, simplicity, geometric form, and minimalism thus govern many Teotihuacán art forms" (1997, p. 159).

A high wall with a single entrance surrounded apartment complexes. The apartments, while pleasant, were not architecturally striking. They provided a high standard of living for a significant portion of the population. Some people were wealthy, others less so. It was not an egalitarian society, but collective. Pasztory sees the apartments as "representations and embodiments of civic wealth and power" (1997, p. 52). At

Teotihuacán, there were few representations of rulers. While less spectacular than the pyramids, the courtyard houses are worthy of attention for their skilled use of materials, stone, paint, and sunlight.

Zapotecs

The Valley of Oaxaca lies in southern Mexico and was inhabited by the Zapotec people from approximately 1500 BCE until the arrival of the Spanish.

Monte Albán

Monte Albán was the administrative center of the Zapotecs, centrally located in the Valley of Oaxaca. The grand plaza at Monte Albán sits on a level platform 985 feet (300.2 meters) by 656 feet (199.9 meters). The plaza is ringed by three conjoined temples and other structures, including a **ball court**. The period 200–700 CE was the height of the Zapotecs.

Ball courts, paraphernalia, and trophies

Ball courts were a prominent feature of many Mesoamerican cities (Figure 7.3). Ball courts and

Figure 7.3
Monte Albán, Ball Court, Zapotec, Mexico, 200–500 BCE. Plan.

the games played on them are noteworthy, both for their architecture and for the objects created for them, sports-related paraphernalia. A ball court from Monte Albán has two ranges of seats overlooking the central playing field. The sloped structures are reminiscent of pyramids, although they take the monumentality in a horizontal direction. These constructions, like pyramids, are compositions that involve shaping the landscape in addition to building on top of it. The playing field itself is characteristically I-shaped, a central field that opens up at each end.

In the Mesoamerican world, Mary Ellen Miller (2004) writes, ball games were played for some three thousand years. Later, this resulted in striking architectural works; most existing ball courts were built in the period 100–1519 CE. Outdoor ball courts were a prominent feature of the ceremonial centers of Mesoamerican cities. An I-shaped ball court stood directly in front of the Aztec twin pyramid in Tenochtitlan.

Mesoamerican people saw the ball game as a rich metaphor that reflected their place in the world and its relation to celestial movements of the sun, moon, and Venus. The courts themselves were sacred areas, liminal places "where man and god met" (Miller 2004, p. 23). They combined manipulated landscape with built architecture—the audience stands. Twentieth-century Mexican modernists were as impressed with the ball courts as with the flashier temples.

The category of ball game paraphernalia related to the games included hard rubber balls that fascinated the Spanish conquerors. The game itself is alternately described as relating to lacrosse, basketball, or jai alai; the goal was to get the ball through a vertical ring attached to the side of the court. Depending on the game, the ball was hit by hand or by a stick or paddle that was attached to the body. Murals and figurines of players inform us that players wore a U-shaped yoke around their waist.

Vertically oriented objects were attached to it, either the tall thin "**palma**" or the squatter "**hacha**." Their use is not exactly clear, which demonstrates the difficulty of interpreting objects without corroborating evidence. They may have been used to strike the ball. A variety of protective paddings, hand protectors, and knee pads were fashioned from soft, perishable materials.

Yet many yokes, palmas, and hachas were made of stone and carved. It is difficult to know if these are actual objects or commemorative versions of actual objects, trophies to commemorate a victory. In their creation of designed objects, the Mesoamericans of several areas had the habit of taking the form of simple, daily-use objects and making them into permanent form. In this transformation, the objects lost the ability to function in a mechanical or practical way, but gained the ability to function in a representative, commemorative, and emotive way. They were physical manifestations of prowess, vigor, and athletic ability.

Mitla

In the region surrounding Monte Albán, the Zapotec capital, there are numerous smaller villages and rural residences.

The courtyard interior of a palace from Mitla, a Zapotec site, is worthy of attention for the quality of its mosaics and carvings. Tourists in Mexico usually focus on the pyramids, yet the design of this interior space, open to the sky, reveals another kind of expertise. This is a carefully designed symmetrical space in which four low walls surround a courtyard; rooms open off this central space. The stone walls are faced with carefully dressed and carved stone, whose final delineation was turned over to the considerable talents of the stone carver. Everything emphasizes the horizontal: the low, broad openings, the broader lintels, and the rectangular panels that constitute the bulk of the façade.

These structures rely upon a façade profile that first appeared at Teotihuacán. Each panel has a broad, flat frame, and the frame emphasizes the field. There is a modestly sloped base. The talud supports two levels of framed panels that in turn support the uppermost, and most visually significant, tablero.

Considering the totality of the Zapotec courtyard, it functions as a testament to a stone carver's abilities and is illustrative of the social position of the artist. Within the tablero's border, the stone carvers and stone layers, it appears, were given free rein, each panel is a testament to the artist's expertise. There is a sense of one-upmanship, with each panel being a version of a previous panel's motifs yet rendered more complicated. There are patterns, repetitions, and small-scale changes from side to side, panel to panel. This appears to be an example of artistic bravado, each artist trying to outdo the next.

Yet the individuality of artistic expression has its limits. Each panel is subsumed as part of an overall composition; the prominent corner moldings overhang and frame the entire elevation. There was a mediation between the collective effort and the ability of artists to express themselves individually. They were all working on one project. The upper panel floats in a display of virtuosity in which common stone is made extravagant by the number of man-hours spent skillfully shaping it.

Maya

The Maya of the classic period are commonly dated to 300 to 900 CE. The Maya occupied the areas that today lie in Southern Mexico, the Yucatán Peninsula, and Guatemala. They had impressive urban centers whose dominant buildings were religious temples on top of pyramids. The Mayan pyramids are not as massive or as tall as the Pyramid of the Sun in Teotihuacán, but they are impressive for their steep slope. Mayan pyramids were platforms for temples and also contained burial places. There

is no indication that the Maya had extensive residential quarters of the city that consisted of apartment blocks made of durable materials, although the nobles and religious leaders lived in stone palaces.

Ancestors of the Maya continue to live in the region. Considerable visual evidence suggests that the temple structures on top of the pyramids bear a formal relationship to the classic Maya house (Figure 7.4). A temple, like a typical house, is a rectangular space of one to three rooms, approached laterally, with a central door in one of the long sides. There is a single range of rooms that may be interconnected.

Even the pitch of the stone temple roofs repeats the form of the thatched roofs of the Maya house.

Maya-Toltec

Chichén Itzá is a Toltec site, far to the south of the Toltec heartland around Tula, north of Teotihuacán. The reason for the existence of a Toltec city surrounded by Mayan sites remains

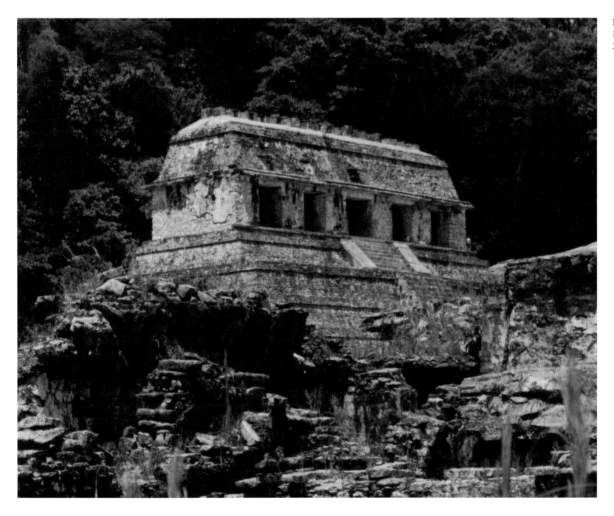

Figure 7.4
Palenque, Mexico, 250–290 CE.

unresolved. Its artifacts are therefore usually interpreted as benefiting from both traditions.

Architecture

The central pyramid at Chichén Itzá, now known as El Castillo, was a sacrificial temple related to the solar calendar (Figure 7.5).

The Temple of the Warriors is significant because it features a field of columns, which are no longer structural members, but stand-ins for human figures.

Designed objects

A designed object represented on numerous sculptural reliefs and wall paintings is a footed raised platform. Nobles or gods are shown kneeling on these low platforms and sometimes sitting on platforms. An altar is a version in stone of what was a common object.

Furniture

The jungles of the Yucatán Peninsula and Guatemala, in contrast to the more arid north, present terrible conditions for the preservation of artifacts, particularly anything made of biological materials, such as wood, leather, or textiles. The

Mesoamerican ritual centers were surrounded by bustling cities, their straw houses replete with items made of wood, reeds, grass, and leather, almost none of which survive. Today the pyramids sit in the middle of archaeological parks, a backdrop that gives little indication of what city life was like. Our knowledge of the life of the Maya is tilted in the direction of the elite, whose material culture is better preserved owing to their burial practices.

From the principal pyramid at Chichén Itzá comes one of the few extant examples of ancient Maya-Toltec furniture: the jaguar throne (Figure 7.6). It is a mid-height seat, neither as low as African or Asian examples, nor as high as European chairs. There are no backrest or arms. Its chief function is to provide visual impact, with little obvious attention to comfort. This was a seat for ceremonial and not casual use.

All continents had furniture-making traditions that were **zoomorphic**: They incorporated animal parts as elements of their overall form. With the jaguar throne, the identification of the throne is foremost as a jaguar; its identification as a seat is secondary. Mayan religious practices included rituals that involved wearing masks and costumes. Pasztory writes generally about cultures with masking traditions: "An impersonation is

Figure 7.5
Pyramid of Kukulcan, Chichén Itzá, Mexico, eleventh to thirteenth centuries.

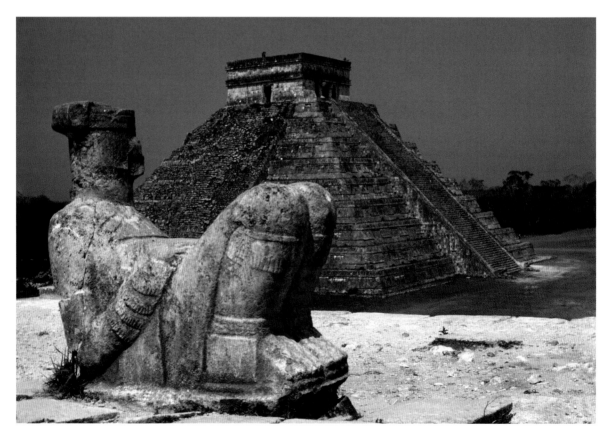

not just the mask but the whole costume, dance, music, and songs" (2005, p. 54). Herbert Cole similarly writes of the masked individual: "This *is* and *is not* a human being. So transformed, the being is saying: 'I am not myself.' Ambivalence and ambiguity exist in the presence of maskers" (1985, p. 20). A masking tradition involves humans who dress as spirits, and this included using animal skins and body parts to adorn and transform their human bodies. A logical interpretation of the seat whose primary identification is as an animal is to consider the aesthetics of the masking performance. This was an exceptional piece of furniture; the role that the chair plays was not merely to support a human figure. Considering the masking tradition encourages an interpretation in which the assembly of figure and chair is read as an impressive visual totality; jaguar, seat, and human figure became one. The throne had the role of visually transforming the seated human figure.

In the case of the jaguar throne, while it is possible that there were wooden benches of a similar configuration, the decoration of a jaguar's head was likely limited to ceremonial pieces. Compared to other cultures' use of animal legs for feet, it is also notable that the Mayan seat is laterally "walking" away. With its head turned and its teeth bared, the asymmetry adds to the dynamic impression the piece makes on a viewer, particularly when it supported a human in elaborate dress and makeup.

The seat is similar to the common **chacmool** sculptures found throughout the Toltec areas. A chacmool sculpture features a human figure who is lying down on his back, face up, legs and arms bent, with a shallow bowl balanced on his stomach. The vessel was used either for offerings, as a brazier, or as the location of animal sacrifices. Chacmool figures were widespread at Chichén Itzá.

Aztecs

The Aztecs were a cultural and political entity whose capital was Tenochtitlan (today Mexico City). For many, the Aztecs are synonymous with Mexico, although they were one of several ethnic groups. They spoke Nahuatl, and one of the Aztec groups was the Mexica.

Tenochtitlan was the Aztec capital city, the home of Montezuma. The center of the city was

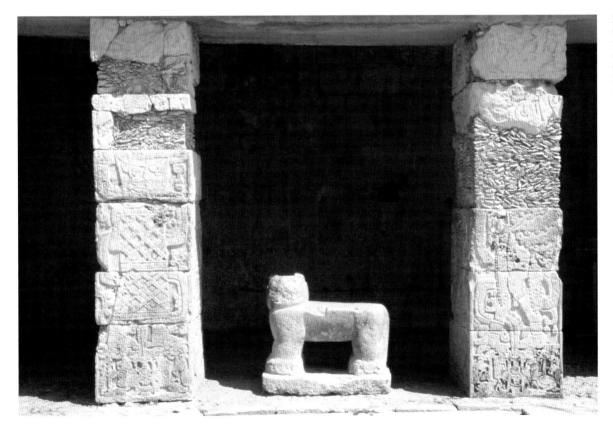

Figure 7.6
Carved jaguar throne, Temple of the Jaguars, Chichén Itzá, Mexico, 1000–1200 CE.

on an island in the middle of a lake; causeways connected the island to the shores. Founded in 1325, the city had grown considerably by 1487. At its center stood a great double pyramid, with a ball court in front of it (Figure 7.7). Hernán Cortés reported that the city had some 200,000 inhabitants.

The official religion of the state was polytheistic, and one of the significant deities was Huitzilopochtli. Huitzilopochtli was the sun god and war god, and he brought the Mexica people to the island in the middle of the lake that became Tenochtitlan. Along the way, he fought successfully in several battles; his cult was associated with military success.

The Templo Mayor is the central temple in Tenochtitlan's center. It is an unusual double temple that Huitzilopochtli shared with Tlaloc, the god of rain and god of agriculture. Statues of Tlaloc, large and small, exist in great number. For a place with no shortage of art, sculpture, reliefs, and murals, it is surprising that Huitzilopochtli's form and appearance are mostly unknown. He was rarely portrayed, and most of the images of

Huitzilopochtli were created post-conquest. One of the few, and most significant, representations of him comes from the backrest of a seat, the so-called Throne of Montezuma.

The Throne of Montezuma

Elizabeth Boone's writing on the image of the Aztec god Huitzilopochtli addresses Aztec religion and art, and in so doing provides an invaluable account, summarized here, of one of the most important pieces of Aztec furniture.

The object is called Teocalli, or alternately the Throne of Montezuma (Figure 7.8). It is important as a rare example of Aztec furniture, and it bears one of the few representations of Huitzilopochtli. It is a "blocky symbol-laden monolith that probably functioned as a throne" (Boone 1989, p. 15). The throne has the distinctive profile of an Aztec stepped pyramid, with a steep incline and a rectangular block on top of a base. The backrest of the throne has a rare presentation of Huitzilopochtli. Carved on the backrest is a composition centered on a sun disk with figures on each side. To the left is Huitzilopochtli in

Figure 7.7
Model of Tenochtitlan, Aztec capitol, fifteenth century, Mexico City, Museo Nacional De Antropología (Anthropology Museum).

Figure 7.8
Teocalli, Throne of Montezuma, Tenochtitlan, Mexico, 900–1521.

human form, identified by the hummingbird, and he is missing his left foot. He faces the figure who stands to the right, Montezuma. Understanding how god, ruler, image, and piece of furniture work together is crucial to interpreting this object.

Wrestling with the scenario of an important god who was visually absent, Boone examines the concepts of "teotl" and "teixiptla." The post-conquest Spanish translated "teotl" as god, saint, or devil. It was a "sacred and impersonal force or a concentration of power" (Boone 1989, p. 4). "Teixiptla" is referred to as an impersonator, substitute, image, incarnation, or actor—in other words, the physical representation. During performances and rituals, humans personified Huitzilopochtli. Thus, there was a god, a sacred power, who was without form or physical attributes until a variety of representations (including dressed humans) were created. A god was not a person, but a force or a natural phenomenon. Similarly, Tlaloc was lightning represented in human form.

The rare representations of Huitzilopochtli are therefore images of actors impersonating the god. One shows him standing in front of a steeply raked and stepped pyramid. He wears a headdress of quetzal feathers that spring from a metallic band, and he has a hummingbird attached to the back of his head. His face has

yellow and blue stripes, and his nose is turquoise. His body is painted blue, and he wears a blue cape and an apron of feathers. He carries a shield and spears; these are the identifying attributes of Huitzilopochtli, and the hummingbird is uniquely associated with him. He is sometimes represented missing his left foot, which is replaced with a serpent's head.

Boone writes that "the teotl can be defined—the 'god' as we think of him can be created—through the formulation of the teixiptla" (1989, p. 9). Carvings of Huitzilopochtli are of human impersonators of Huitzilopochtli. Cecelia Klein has proposed identities for the human figures represented on the throne. They are the ruler Ahuitzotl, dressed as Huitzilopochtli, and Montezuma, dressed as the Aztec god Tezcatlipoca. At the time of Montezuma's succession, Ahuitzotl was recently deceased. The throne's relief shows two rulers in the guise of gods.

The person who allegedly sat on this throne is Montezuma, who disastrously encountered Cortés. A more accurate transcription of his name, from Nahuatl into English, is Motecuhzoma Xocoyotzin, although his name is commonly spelled as Montezuma. And actually, the Montezuma who had the misfortune to rule when the Spanish arrived was Montezuma II.

Just how violent Aztec life was is a point of contention. There is no doubt that there was ritualized violence. Prisoners of war were sacrificed on the Templo Mayor, and many of the reliefs of Huitzilopochtli and other figures show them engaging in self-sacrifice through bloodletting. Blood was drawn by inserting bone awls into their ears. Additionally, prisoners of war were sacrificed, and Boone writes that "each war captive dispatched on the sacrificial stone before the shrine of Huitzilopochtli thus repeated symbolically the god's own victory over his adversaries" (1989, p. 2).

Pasztory reports that Ahuitzotl had 20,000 victims sacrificed (1983, p. 53). Understanding how ritualized violence functioned within a society is a complicated endeavor for those outside of that society. A partial explanation comes from military strategy: When on battlefields, soldiers from the losing side either have to be killed on the field, freed, imprisoned, or enslaved. The Mesoamericans choose not to slaughter their enemies on the battlefields, but to capture them alive, dispatching them later to honor their gods.

A throne is associated with a ruler and frequently is the place where the ritual of succession occurs. In other cultures, a throne often takes a common form of seating and aggrandizes it—for example, Byzantine. That does not appear to be the case with the Aztec throne. The form owes its shape to the pyramid on which it likely stood. "Bloodletting imagery associated with the Aztec Templo Mayor is part of the accession iconography of the Aztec rulers" (Boone 1989, p. 15). As a model of the building in which it functioned, this piece of furniture has an architectural design vocabulary.

As at other Mesoamerican sites, Tenochtitlan had large numbers of craftsmen—painters, stone carvers, metalworkers, furniture makers, and potters. A market-centered economy, correspondingly, had large numbers of merchants. Pasztory writes: "Wood was used for furniture, house posts, canoes, weapons, and tools, as well as for idols" (1983, p. 76). What they created and traded has mostly disappeared from the archaeological record.

Tlaloc, the other god of the temple complex, was the god of agriculture. This helps explain why anthropologists have frequently found objects that look like seats, yet it is not clear if they were seats, sacrificial altars, or grinding stones. The context of the Templo Mayor underscores that the confusion between seat, altar, and grinding stone is not arbitrary. In these arenas, agriculture by way of grinding corn, military success by way of sacrifice, and religion by way of an altar, were all brought together by an object that looks like a seat.

The talud-tablero architectural composition gets a particular riff in a room from the main temple, the Templo Mayor. Lining the perimeter of a room is a stone bench. Here, the talud has become a built-in seat, with the tablero on the (missing) wall behind. Archaeological work on rural residences in the area has confirmed that built-in benches were common.

Montezuma thought Cortés was the returning god Quetzalcoatl. It had been foreseen that the Quetzalcoatl would return as a bearded man who opposed human sacrifice. When Cortés arrived, Montezuma and his followers initially thought he was their god, a case of mistaken identity that resulted in the end of the Aztec Empire. Cortés communicated with the ruler by way of his female companion, La Malinche, who translated for him. The story of Montezuma's mistaking Cortés could be a fabrication. Both sides had reason to support this version of the encounter. For the Spanish, the story serves as justification for their destruction of the city and its temples. For the Aztecs, it presents the meeting as a predestined defeat, a fate that was out of their hands.

Central America

A feature of some Mesoamerican seats is that their exact use is not always clear, nor is it certain if they even were seats. The Isthmia region, including modern-day Costa Rica and Honduras, in the period 300–900 CE, produced a number of objects known as **metates**. These are stone-grinding platforms, made from porous volcanic rock, and some are found with their grinding stones, similar to rolling pins. Some bear traces of wear. Others do not. Initially, the favored form was a three-legged or tripod metate. Around 900 CE, there was a preference for four-legged grinding platforms. Some are elaborate, with caryatids supporting the platform. Practically, these were used for grinding grain into flour. Yet the same form served as an altar, possibly for animal sacrifice. These are also forms that suggest they served as seats. It is therefore possible that these pieces of furniture served multiple ritual functions. Elaborate ones were decorated with birds and monkey figures.

Peru

Human inhabitants have been in the Andean region that is today Peru since 9000 BCE. From the initial period, the people of Cupisnique culture, 1500–200 BCE, created a beautiful type of designed object. Anthracite mirrors were highly polished black disks that adequately reflected whatever faced them.

In the 1920s, an archaeological discovery took place in the southern Peruvian desert, Paracas. Paracas means "sand that falls like rain." The Paracas were active toward the end of the Early Horizon period, in the years 300 to 200 BCE. Archaeologists discovered four hundred funerary bundles that contained layer upon layer of textiles. Mummies were wrapped in fabrics and interred in baskets. Because they were protected by the dry climate, they survived two thousand years. Some of the oldest existing textiles come from Peru.

The Paracas wove cotton textiles embroidered with wool. They also painted and dyed textiles. The motifs included geometric shapes and abstracted animal forms.

In the Early Intermediate period, the Nazca, living on the plains of Nazca, created artworks unlike anything found elsewhere in the world. The giant geoglyphs are symbols using the earth itself as the artistic medium. They were created by removing a layer of the desert floor. The forms include precise straight lines and other geometric shapes, plants, animals, and insects, all at a colossal scale best appreciated from the air. The Nazca built adobe architecture and also developed traditions in textiles and ceramics.

From the Late Intermediate period, the Chimu are known for their delicate feather work. Feather panels and capes were made by painstakingly attaching feathers to a cotton backing (Figure 7.9). They were attached to form geometric patterns. As these delicate textiles were buried in tombs as in Paracas, they survive in a surprising number. In addition to using feathers to craft articles to adorn the human figure, panels were made that served as wall hangings, room dividers, or for outdoor celebrations.

Pre-Columbian scholar Nicholas Saunders (1999) terms feather work as belonging to an aesthetic of brilliance. He writes: "There is a wealth of evidence to suggest that indigenous Amerindians perceived their world as infused with a spiritual brilliance which manifested itself in natural phenomena—sun, moon, water, ice and rainbows; natural materials—minerals, feathers, pearls and shells, and artifacts made from such matter" (Saunders 1999, p. 245). The Chimu continued into the Late Horizon period and were an adversary of the Inca.

At their height, the Inca ruled the area that is today Peru, Bolivia, Chile, Ecuador, and northern Argentina. They spoke Quechua, and their capital, Cuzco, is located in the highlands of Peru.

Many types of structures became shrines, including buildings, sites, a terrace, a fountain, and occasionally a seat (Niles 1999, p. 54). After death, the departed were remembered by the locations where once they had slept, farmed, rested, dreamed, drank, or lived. A chair could represent the person who, in life, sat on it.

The Inca Empire is usually dated to 1438–1532 CE. The Inca are known for the precision of their stonemasonry. Giant blocks of stone were cut, or dressed, to fit tightly against one another without mortar. Carolyn Dean examines the relationship between the outcroppings and the masonry walls that sit on top of them and are supported by them. For years, the architectural journal *Progressive Architecture* had a regular feature titled "divine details"; the point was not only to highlight an impressive detail but also to show that good details themselves carry a project's concept and have meaning. Relying upon Dean's work, the goal here is to consider Machu Picchu and other mountain sites from a different approach, looking at the details of their construction as works that reveal their creators' intentions and worldviews.

The Inca used outcrops of rock as the foundation of the structures they built (Figure 7.10). The resulting form was a combination of nature and architecture. Dean offers the following rationale:

According to a Quechua story told in the Andes today, the ancient Inca of that area married Pachamama (Mother Earth) and produced human offspring. A trace of that union is still manifest in the ruins of Inca buildings in the form of rock outcrops— masses of bare rock protruding from the surface of the earth—that were integrated by Inka builders into masonry structures in the fifteenth and early sixteenth centuries

Figure 7.9
Feathered Panel, Peru, Far South Coast, Pampa Ocona, 600–900 CE. Papagayo macaw feathers knotted onto strings and stitched to cotton plain-weave cloth; camelid fiber plain-weave cloth upper tape.

Figure 7.10
The "Royal Tomb" beneath the Temple of the Sun at Machu Picchu shows a mixture of living rock, Inca walling, and Inca stone carving, Machu Picchu, Peru. Inca, pre-Columbian, detail.

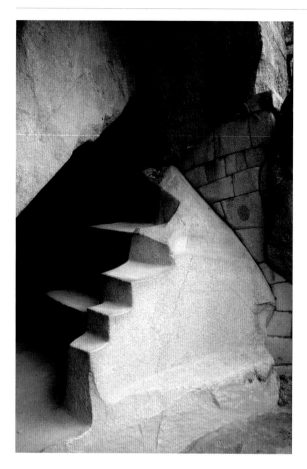

into the structures with precise joints. Because the blocks are not of regular size, it is believed that this was done by trial and error, meaning that the blocks had to be continually lifted into place and then extracted, or that precise models of each block were first made.

A stool from the Field Museum of Natural History in Chicago is also known as the Inca throne. It is made of wood and painted, and features a carved, round seat. Two jaguars, headed in opposite directions, support the seat. It was an important piece designed for the effect it would have on viewers, taking in an ensemble that included a clothed human figure.

The most famous of the Inca cities built on outcroppings is Machu Picchu, mid-fifteenth to early sixteenth century. Machu Picchu is the Incan settlement situated in the Andes north-west of Cuzco. Overlooked by the Spanish, it survived intact. The apex of its inhabitation was the sixteenth century. It was later abandoned and fell into disuse, its location known only by some locals.

Conquest

In an age of specialization, Jerod Diamond, author of *Guns, Germs, and Steel: The Fates of Human Societies*, continues to tell big stories in terms of chronological and geographic scope. He writes: "The biggest population shift of modern times has been the colonization of the New World by Europeans, and the resulting conquest, numerical reduction, or complete disappearance of most groups of Native Americans (American Indians)" (Diamond 1997, p. 67).

Mexico

The *Relaciones Geographicas* was the mapping project of Philip II of Spain. His administrators hired legions of Aztec artists to carry out the extensive project. The maps are representative of many things, including the desire of Spain to use mapmaking as a tool of consolidating its power. The maps are also representations of a *criollo*, or Creole, identity. They are examples of a new art form, with both Aztec and Spanish precedents. The churches and crosses are obviously due to the imposition of European Christianity, but the artist used Aztec symbols to indicate roads and rivers.

In Mexico, a generation after the conquest, the forced conversion was mostly complete;

throughout the Inka realm, an empire that eventually reached the greatest extent of any pre-Hispanic state in the Americas. By providing firm, petrous foundations for Inka structures, Mother Earth herself, called Pachamama by the Inka and other Quechua speakers, appears to have readily consented to, if not actually joined in, the interface between nature and art.

(Dean 2007, p. 502)

Inca architecture and urban planning are usually rectilinear; when they break the pattern it is to respond to the earth's naturalistic form (Dean 2007, p. 508). Dean outlines the laborious process of roughing out the great stones with hammers and chisels, using progressively finer tools. The process was time-consuming, although not technically difficult: a block was chiseled away, fitted into its eventual space, removed, then, using the word Dean prefers, "nibbled" away, then replaced, until a perfect shape was achieved. Some were quadrilateral, some polygonal.

The Inca ability with dressing stones is legendary. The blocks were individually cut to fit people had converted to Christianity and spoke Spanish.

Wheels, tiled roofs, horses, and other beasts of burden were commonplace (Kostof 1995, p. 442). Mass building followed mass destruction. New cities were built on top of the old, churches on top of temples. Mexico City was built on top of the ruins of Tenochtitlan. Teotihuacán, Palenque, and Chichén Itzá were saved from destruction because they had already been abandoned.

A chest from 1650 is a modest object to represent the conquest, but its ubiquity is equally telling. In the century after the destruction of the Aztecs, Mexican furniture makers were largely working within the stylistic parameters of Spanish craftsmen, although with a recognition of locality. The chest is made of Mexican woods, mahogany, with orangewood and rosewood veneers. It has iron hardware. It was likely made in Pueblo de los Angeles, an important center for furniture manufacturing, and was probably meant for travel.

Peru

Francisco Pizarro landed in Peru in 1527. He returned in 1532 with a small force. The Spanish *conquistador* met the Inca emperor Atahualpa in Cajamarca that year. Pizarro led 168 soldiers. Atahualpa being carried on a litter, sitting on a cushion on top of a stool, was in the middle of a giant tent city of 80,000 soldiers. Spanish witnesses report that among Atahualpa's minions, many carried furniture covered in gold and silver. Within minutes, Pizarro's men killed Atahualpa's attendants and imprisoned their emperor. How this happened is one of history's great stories. The Peruvians were divided. Those people recently incorporated against their will into the Inca Empire were all too happy to see its leader captured. And Atahualpa was politically weakened by a fratricidal war of succession. Technologically, the big point of Diamond's book is that the Spanish had steel swords, guns, and horses (Diamond 1997, p. 71).

At the height of their power, the Inca relied heavily on the symbolic use of objects seized in battle. Niles (1999) reports several methods of celebrating victory that involve objects, including turning the flayed skin of an enemy soldier into a drum, his teeth into a necklace, and drinking from a cup made of a victim's skull. Another means was physically trampling on the possessions of the vanquished: "In Inca military victories, the symbolic affirmation of victory and the granting of credit for the defeat were marked by the act of treading on captured enemies" (Niles 1999,

pp. 40–1). Booty is the category of objects seized in battle or siege. **Spolia** is the Roman term. The category of objects that became war monuments and trophies included exceptional pieces of furniture, such as a brass chair (p. 70). Niles writes: "It was the former custom of these Incas to bring back to Cuzco all the things they had seen that might cause admiration and wonder, so that the sight of these objects would enhance the fame of their deeds and would memorialize their accomplishments" (p. 70). An empty chair in this case was a sign of military victory and denigrated the person who no longer sat in it.

This was a lesson that the Spanish did not need to be taught. There is a long history of **iconoclasm**, the destruction of art, particularly in the name of promoting monotheistic Christianity, over a "pagan" polytheistic religion. In 1533, the Spaniards sacked the Incan capital Cuzco. They rebuilt it, following the street lines and reusing the Incan foundations for their own buildings. The Incan practice of trampling on the possessions of the defeated enemy got an ironic translation into architecture.

The Spanish city was built on top of the Inca ruins, so that there are several areas where Spanish buildings appear to grow from the carefully cut large Inca stones (Figure 7.11). One purpose of *spolia* was to commemorate victory

Figure 7.11
Wall of an Inca building in Calle Hatunrumioc (Hatunrumioc Street), Cuzco, Peru.

over an enemy. Another aspect was the belief that destruction ultimately results in regeneration.

Conclusion

The differences between the pre-Columbian societies and the modern world are striking. The prime example is ritualized sacrifice, an aesthetic performance in which the visual effect was paramount. In contrast, there was a Mesoamerican practice that is familiar to the modern age: ball games, complete with ball courts, souvenirs, trophies, and other sports-related paraphernalia. The Mesoamericans commemorated victory with stone mementos, whose forms, including knee pads and hand guards, were logical in a functional sense only when made from perishable, pliable materials. One cannot help but wonder what future civilizations will make of the quantity of bronze basketballs and footballs that fill today's trophy cases.

The massive and towering pyramids have lost none of their ability to impress. A means to connect earth and sky, in Mayan civilizations they also served as temple platforms. The temple structures atop the pyramids present a strategy of monumentalizing architecture: work with a common form, such as the typical Mayan domestic structure, and translate it into permanent materials. Pyramids were exceptional features of the first American cities, because the other structures, such as the courtyard houses of Teotihuacán, emphasized the horizontal, with their overall form, their expansive elevations, their squat openings, and their prominent door heads.

In North and South America, a brilliant material was used for the finest objects. Although feathers are still used today in ceremonial settings, they rarely appear in textiles that are meant to endure. It is amazing that so many works were produced using this exceedingly delicate material, and even more so that so many of them survive.

Few seats from the pre-Columbian era exist, but those that do are dynamic, with twisting, turning, and snarling animals. Looking at a throne alone is but half the picture; it was meant to be experienced as part of a performance that featured a brilliantly costumed ruler.

Pre-Columbian artistic communities were large and numerous. Building and maintaining

Figure 7.12
Vargueño.

the houses, temples, and ball courts, with all the corresponding objects, required large numbers of masons, stone carvers, potters, woodworkers, weavers, painters, and furniture makers. The Spanish conquest of the Americas was a rupture in all traditions. But artists continued to produce art, and their blending of Spanish and indigenous motifs, coerced and voluntary, started a new era of American designed objects, one of the most enduring of which is a traveling chest, the vargueño (Figure 7.12).

Sources

Aimi, Antonio (2019). *Aztecs, Mayas, Incas and the Cultures of Pre-Columbian America*. Milan: Silvana Editoriale.

Boone, Elizabeth (1989). "Incarnations of the Aztec Supernatural: The Image of Huitzilopochtli in Mexico and Europe." *Transactions of the American Philosophical Society* 79, no. 2: 1–107.

Cole, Herbert (1985). *I Am Not Myself: The Art of African Masquerade*. Los Angeles: Museum of Cultural History, the University of California.

Dean, Carolyn (2007). "The Inca Married the Earth: Integrated Outcrops and the Making of Place." *Art Bulletin* 89 (September): 502–18.

Diamond, Jared (1997). *Guns, Germs, and Steel: The Fates of Human Societies*. New York: Norton.

Klein, Cecelia (2002). "Not Like Us and All the Same: Pre-Columbian Art History and the Construction of the Nonwest." *Res*, no. 42 (Autumn): 131–38.

Kostof, Spiro (1995). *A History of Architecture: Settings and Rituals*. Oxford: Oxford University Press.

Kubler, George (1962). *The Art and Architecture of Ancient America*. Harmondsworth: Penguin.

Miller, Mary Ellen (1989). "The Ballgame." *Record of the Art Museum, Princeton University* 48, no. 2: 21–31.

Miller, Mary Ellen (2004). *Courtly Art of the Ancient Maya*. San Francisco: Fine Arts Museum of San Francisco.

Niles, Susan (1999). *The Shape of Inca History*. Iowa City: University of Iowa Press.

Pasztory, Esther (1976). *The Murals of Tepantitla, Teotihuacan*. New York: Garland.

Pasztory, Esther (1997). *Teotihuacan: An Experiment in Living*. Norman: University of Oklahoma Press.

Pasztory, Esther (2005). *Thinking with Things*. Austin: University of Texas Press.

Protzen, Jean-Pierre and Stella Nair (1997). "Who Taught the Inca Stonemasons Their Skills?" *Journal of the Society of Architectural Historians* 56, no. 2 (June): 146–67.

Saunders, Nicholas (1999). "Biographies of Brilliance: Pearls, Transformations of Matter and Being, c. AD 1492." *World Archaeology* 31, no. 2 (October): 243–57.

Schreffler, Michael (2020). *Cuzco: Incas, Spaniards and the Making of a Colonial City*. New Haven, CT: Yale University Press.

Young-Sanchez, Margaret (2003). *Pre-Columbian Art in the Denver Art Museum Collection*. Denver: Denver Art Museum.

Discussion and Review Questions

1. Think of examples, from any culture and time period, in which daily objects are commemorative and functionally useless when turned into a new material.

2. The topic of how violent the Aztec and Maya were is controversial. If today's world—and its cultural productions—were looked at by another civilization, would it be considered peaceful or violent?

3. Name some of the sites in Mexico.

4. What ethnic group was ruling the city that became Mexico City?

5. Name some of the ethnic groups in Peru that predated the arrival of the Spanish explorer Pizarro.

6. Name an unusual material that the Paracas made clothing and other textiles from.

7. What ethnic group was ruling the area that is now Peru when the Spanish arrived?

8

China, India, and Southeast Asia

	1600–1050 BCE	1050–256 BCE	221–206 BCE	206 BCE–220 CE	618–907 CE	1279–1368 CE	1368–1644 CE	1644–1912
China								
	Shang dynasty	Zhou dynasty	Qin dynasty	Han dynasty	Tang dynasty	Yuan dynasty	Ming dynasty	Qing dynasty

	802–1431
Cambodia	
	Angkor period

India and China play major roles in Asian history, both for their geographic heft and large populations. A difference between them is that in its early history, India was not a consolidated entity. India does, however, have the considerable distinction of having been the birthplace of Buddha. China is the world's longest continuous civilization, existing as a unified cultural and political entity for four thousand years without interruption. In the twenty-first century China has the world's second largest population, but even in its earlier periods it had a significantly large population.

Cambodia is one of Southeast Asia's smaller countries, but from the ninth to twelfth century, it produced extremely fine examples of monumental architecture and sculpture. The Hindu and Buddhist sculptures bear comparison to other representational sculptures, such as those of ancient Greece and medieval Benin. They are informative about seating postures, just as reliefs from the temples bear the only traces of historic Cambodian furniture.

Figure 8.0
(*Facing page*)
Tjong A Fie
Mansion, Medan,
Indonesia, 1900.
Gold-leaf screen
with mother of
pearl furniture.

Architecture and Sculpture

China

China plays a significant role in the fossil record of the earliest human habitations. A long and productive neolithic period left a variety of archaeological remains, including geometric pottery.

In the fourth millennium BCE, a series of settlements between the Yangzi River and the Yellow River were conducive to agriculture. Initially there were no major urban centers. Pottery sherds and the remains of a kiln date to this period.

One of the earliest Chinese capitals, a proto-urban center, Zhengzhou, relied on the waters of the Yellow River. With Zhengzhou starts the tradition of each dynasty building its own capital city. A wall surrounded the rectilinear-shaped enclosure that contained platforms upon which buildings stood.

Zhou dynasty rulers enforced the use of Chinese, thus creating a unified, linguistic geographical group. The Zhou had cast iron production and created two cities, Luoyang and Xian, that still exist today. The teacher and philosopher Confucius (551–479 BCE) belongs to the Zhou period.

The English term "China" comes from the Qin dynasty (also referred to as the Ch'in dynasty). Chinese people today refer to the country as "China" or "Zhong guo." The latter appeared in a Shang dynasty document, but it was a cultural and geographic term. It acquired a national meaning in the twentieth century.

From Stupa to Pagoda

Buddha is one of the names given to the teacher and enlightened one, also known as Gautama and Siddhartha. He lived in northern India and Nepal. The dates of his life are not certain, but one scenario puts the years of his time on Earth as 480–400 BCE. The religion that resulted from his teachings, Buddhism, celebrates the enlightenment and eventual passage of Buddha and his followers into nirvana.

Tracing Buddhism's effect on art, architecture, and material culture is an endeavor that includes considering the natural landscape, the body, the represented body, building, town planning and designed objects; all are interrelated to a diagrammatic pattern known as the **mandala**, a common feature of artworks and textile designs.

One of the vestigial means of finding meaning on Earth, proto architecture, occurred when indigenous people picked out distinguishing landscape features and in them saw meaning. Ayer's Rock in Australia, and Chimney Rock in the United States, are both examples of this. Sometimes the natural features are so extraordinary that it seems as though the landscapes themselves are a part of the selection process. Mountains and fantastic promontories stand out from their surroundings, a naturally occurring example of rarefied space.

India, Afghanistan, Thailand, and Tibet

The next step for human involvement in creating meaning in landscape is to shape the landscape and natural materials. One of the earliest shifts from seeing meaning in landscape to shaping landscape involves the burial places of Buddha's relics. He died at Kushinagar, his body was cremated, his remains buried, and the mound of earth that covered his remains became venerated. Over time, the mound of earth was faced with either bricks or stone, thereby rendered permanent and monumental, and evolved into a **stupa**. The Stupa at Sarnath, Darnek, in India, is a simple yet powerful creation that reveals the honest expression of facing a mound of earth.

The Stupa at Sanchi is a more elaborate composition that intertwines site, setting, and ritual. Buddhism was a religion of meditation, involving recitation in front of a stupa, sculpture, or images, and later a **pagoda**, that housed Buddhist relics. The ritual of visiting a stupa was to circumnavigate the mound clockwise. This was a processional homage and also a somatic activity that cleared the mind of extraneous thoughts. At Sanchi, gateways to the precinct stand at the four cardinal points. The gate at the front blocks direct access and prompts visitors to begin their meditative walk.

The practice of visiting a stupa relates to a diagram that tells how followers of Buddhism understand themselves, their place on Earth, and Earth's place in the cosmos. Over the course of centuries, stupas were built through the area that is now India and Nepal and gradually spread eastward. While early stupas were solid, structures with hollow domes followed. Stupas became elaborate and architectural practice increasingly emphasized the vertical. Sometimes a pole at the apex emphasizes the dome. One way of involving stupas with impermanent ritual was to attach a banner to the **chattri**, drawing attention to the highest point. Hanging a banner on a stupa was a further means of personalizing the experience. The banners that flew on stupas are some of the oldest surviving Asian textiles, today protected in museums.

An example of incorporating naturally occurring forms and rendering them elaborate occurs at the caves of Ajanta. There, the stupa sits within an interior space, yet the process of circumnavigating remains. A limit to the stupa as the sole element of Buddhist architecture is that there was no worship space. The caves of Ajanta provided a vocabulary and form for a larger space to house devotees and formed the basis of Buddhist temples with rectangular halls.

Some caves were utilized as they were; some are a combination of found configuration and elaborately carved-out architectural compositions. In the kingdom of Bamiyan, today Afghanistan, in the seventh century, two colossal statues, the tallest 165 feet (50.3 meters), were sculpted out of rock in giant niches. Over time, statues of Buddha were placed in front of the stupa, sometimes on top of the stupa, sometimes carved into the face of the stupa. Sometimes, the Buddha statue sits alone. This is full circle, where once the bodily remains of Buddha were represented by a mound of earth, there is now a statue that literally evokes his physiognomy. A temple at Sukhothai, Thailand dates to the thirteenth and fourteenth centuries and features a bell-shaped stupa (Figure 8.1).

A mandala is a design that features a circle circumscribed within a square, as did the rounded mound of the stupa. The circle is the heavenly realm and the connection of the Earth to the cosmos. The square represents the domain of

Figure 8.1
Wat Chana Songkhram, Sukhothai, Thailand, thirteenth to fifteenth century.

Figure 8.2
Tibetan Kalachakra mandala,
Nepal, contemporary.

humanity. This diagram is related to the layout of a variety of designed forms, including carpets, temples, and cities (Figure 8.2).

China

As Buddhism spread eastward into China in the Han dynasty, the religious practice and the buildings that supported it became **sinicized**—that is, rendered Chinese. Courtyard houses were donated and converted to temples, thereby merging established architectural forms with a new subculture. In the development of the stupa, the Chinese emphasis on vertical expression created a new type of Buddhist building: the pagoda.

The building of stupas spread into Thailand, Cambodia, and Indonesia, and they became more elaborate and more vertical. The vertical expression became the focus of Chinese design attention. The Chinese were familiar with the vertical construction of towers, made of timber or brick, so, consequently, the pagoda is a hybrid structure of the stupa and tower building technology.

One of the earliest Chinese monasteries to feature a pagoda is the Songyue Monastery on Mount Song, Henan. Its pagoda, which has twelve sides, dates to 523. The pagoda form became popular, and hundreds of them were built in China, Korea, and Japan (Figure 8.3). Like the stupa, the pagoda housed Buddhist relics. The pagoda at Songyue is the earliest extant pagoda in China. It is a prime example of the process

Figure 8.3
Idealized Chinese pagoda.

by which cultural influences from outside China merged with Chinese indigenous techniques. Having developed the technology, and custom, of creating watchtowers, the Chinese applied their knowledge to create a vertically oriented religious structure, the pagoda. Fu Xinian writes that by the late fifth and sixth centuries, Buddhist architecture had become Chinese architecture.

Qin Shi Huangdi is the emperor who unified China. The discovery of his tomb in the twentieth century is one of the greatest finds of Chinese archaeology. The cavernous complex has rammed-earth foundations and walls. It is populated by an army of 6,000 life-size terra-cotta warriors, accompanied by dogs and horses.

The Great Wall

As a visual icon in the modern world, the Great Wall is virtually synonymous with China. An architectural wonder and an engineering marvel, it is also an accomplished example of landscape utilization and manipulation.

Qin Shi Huangdi, founder of the Qin dynasty, declared himself emperor, consolidated power, and built 3,000 miles (4,828 kilometers) of the wall in the third century BCE. The wall's entire length is between 3,000 miles (4,828 kilometers) and 4,000 miles (6,437 kilometers). In photographs, the wall looks like a giant singular entity, unraveling over the northern Chinese mountainous landscape, but it is actually a defensive network and made of constituent parts. Initially made of rammed earth and rubble, its ramparts were strengthened over the years. It follows the ridgelines of mountains and hills.

There are two principal elements to the wall: the defensive walls themselves, topped with a roadway, and the watchtowers. Towers and walls were built in separate phases and were remodeled in separate phases, a building process that resulted in some odd intersections. The crenellated towers occur approximately every 100 yards (91.4 meters). In addition to arrows, the Chinese shot cannons.

The wall's purpose was to keep raiders at bay, and it is often considered a military failure. That view is tempered by the position that the Wall was one part of a broader foreign trade policy. Monumental in scale, it was not designed to be the monument it became, but to powerfully thwart the efforts of nighttime raiders. It is considered by many as a symbol of Chinese xenophobia, the most obvious expression of a desire to keep foreigners out. Traditionally, the Great Wall did not play the role of national symbol until the twentieth century, when, it became a symbol of Chinese nationalism.

Large stretches of the wall arose in the subsequent Han dynasty, although most of what is seen today was built in the Ming period. Other achievements during the Ming period include ceramics and furniture. Because of its immense scale, it is today considered a singular Chinese monument.

A new capital city built for the Han dynasty was Ch'ang-an (Figure 8.4). Noting that religious structures, such as temples and pagodas, were not major elements in the urban environment, Spiro Kostof (1995) writes: "Unlike their Indian neighbors, the Chinese had little sympathy for the mystical or the infinite. Theirs was basically a secular, intellectual order; unmoved by any need to search for some ultimate truth, they plotted their own precise, clear-cut place on earth." Chinese urban layouts share overall spatial principles with the layout of a stupa precinct—the reliance on the four cardinal directions, the placement of important structures in the center, and a walled rectilinear layout.

Cambodia

Cambodia is one of Asia's smaller countries, yet from the ninth to twelfth century, the small inland region produced magnificent works of urbanism, architecture, and sculpture. It is difficult to pinpoint the circumstances necessary to produce great art, though this likely includes political stability, central authority, and financial resources.

Figure 8.4
Chang'an urban plan, Tang dynasty, China, 618–907 CE.

These circumstances were present in the Mekong River valley, but nothing was affirmatively predictive of the wonders that would arise.

Helen Jessup articulates the circumstances aligning themselves in the Mekong River valley that allowed a political and economic entity to become a cultural one: "What is of interest in the study of art and architecture is the extent to which the consolidation and centralization of power resulted in the desire among the leaders to create symbols of material and spiritual power in permanent form" (Jessup 2004).

The region drew its wealth from agriculture, including rice cultivation made possible by fertile lands fed by the Mekong and the Tonlé Sap Rivers. The connection to river-faring international trade had cultural implications The great period of temple building, the Angkor period, started with the reign of Jayavarman II in 802 CE. The Angkor period is roughly contemporary with the Carolingian and Romanesque periods in Europe.

In terms of urban design, the cities built in the **Khmer** Empire are rectilinear and huge. The Khmer Empire was a dominant polity in the twelfth century in Southeast Asia. Khmer refers to the language and people, and Cambodia is the modern country. Khmer cities were larger than contemporary European medieval cities; all of ancient Rome would fit nicely within the borders of the Angkorian city, Angkor Thom.

Angkor Wat is the masterwork of the region, perfect in its architectonic expression and in the quality of its details (Figure 8.5). Suryavarman II (1113–1145) built the city that exceeded in scale and complexity the temples that preceded it.

The central temple complexes relate to the stupa and also to Mount Mehru, the mythological home of Hindu gods. The center is surrounded by a moat, which was part of a vast irrigation system and symbolically related to the cosmic ocean from which life began.

The moat of Angkor Wat is 623 feet (189.9 meters). The temple faces west, with entrances at the north, east, and south sides. What remains today is the religious complex that lay at the heart of an immense city. As a layout, the Khmer religious centers have points in common with the Indian stupa complexes; they are rectilinear, with a vertically dominant structure at the center and based on the cardinal directions. (Chinese cities follow this scheme as well, although a secular structure and not a religious structure, takes center stage.)

The main structure consists of five vertical towers, configured in a **quincunx** layout. They are in ascending height, with the highest in the center. Galleries line the perimeter. The windows are filled with vertical elements carved from stone. The forms clearly derive from wooden

Figure 8.5
Angkor Wat, Cambodia, 1100–1150 CE.

originals (Figure 8.6). Similarly, the roofs, made of stone, resemble clay tiles.

In the Cambodian historic cities, most of the secular buildings that surrounded the central complex were made of perishable materials, and therefore they have not survived. The stone galleries hint at the form of the wooden residential architecture. As for the climate being conducive to preserving artifacts, few places are as detrimental; Cambodia is hot, humid, and wet. This is the perfect condition to ensure that vegetal materials, wood and textiles, will perish. And, in fact, the Cambodian jungle even does an amazing job at eating into stone temples as well.

After Suryavarman, Jayavarman VII was Cambodia's most important patron. He reigned from 1181 to 1218, and he ruled over the largest swath of territory. His capital is Angkor Thom, or "Great City." Larger than Angkor Wat, its principal temple is the Bayon.

A statue of Jayavarman VII makes obvious that the Khmer were skilled in freestanding sculpture. For the history of furniture, statues from the era are significant for they demonstrate that accomplished societies can develop in which pieces of furniture play a small role and with many traditions of sitting. The sculptor's skill is exhibited in the naturalistic treatment of the torso, and the king is imbued with two qualities: he is powerful and humane. His power derives from his broad shoulders and strong chest. Being represented in a posture that clearly invites comparisons to Buddha is hardly a gesture of modesty, yet it does demonstrate the kings' authority as religious figures (Figure 8.7).

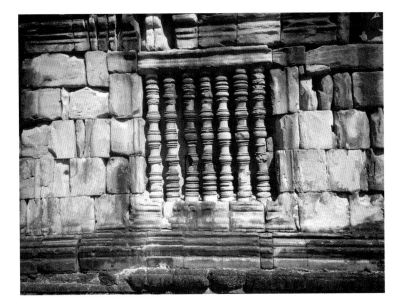

Figure 8.6
Bakong, Cambodia, 881 CE. Window detail.

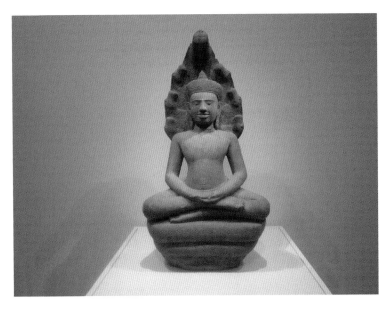

Figure 8.7
Buddha Enthroned on a Serpent (Naga), Cambodia/Thailand, 1201–1300.

These statues are appealing because they represent the figures as humble, benign, and spiritual.

The sculptural program of Jayavarman VII's temple, the Bayon at Angkor Thom, is unlike that found elsewhere; invaluably, many of the reliefs represent scenes from daily life. Some represent carefully delineated **howdahs**, the saddle and platform structure in which nobles sat when riding an elephant (Figure 8.8). One sculptural relief shows several people using a variety of chairs and tables, a rare representation of historic Khmer furniture. Another piece of furniture shown in several reliefs is a **palanquin**, a chair attached to horizontal poles and used for carrying someone about. A Cambodian nineteenth-century palanquin bears some relationship to pieces represented at Angkor Thom (Figure 8.9). The more recent palanquin is essentially a platform with a backrest. The rings underneath the platform are for the poles that are borne by carriers.

Chinese courtyard house

The history of building in Cambodia consists of a series of monumental works of religious architecture. Equally important in China is the development of a secular building type, the Chinese courtyard house. Chronologically, the earliest examples of Chinese houses postdate the temples of Angkor. Looking at historic Chinese architecture, several distinct types emerge. The accidental monument, the Great Wall, stands out because of its uniqueness. In contrast, hundreds of iterations of the pagoda form lend distinctive profiles to the Chinese landscape and play an important role in the practice of Buddhism. Regarding architecture, it is not always a series of individual monuments that are significant, but also the widespread use of the Chinese courtyard house, as a type, for buildings both modest and grand. The development of this dwelling type includes a modular system, which is what renders the house almost modern. The Chinese courtyard house is the essential unit of Chinese architecture, with its emphasis on symmetry, axiality, and rectilinearity. Incidentally, it shares these qualities with urban planning.

A few examples of Yuan dynasty houses remain, and additional information comes from paintings. From the Ming dynasty, numerous examples of houses exist. Most of the early pieces of furniture, discussed below, come from the Ming dynasty. Thirty-one courtyard houses stand in the village of Ding, and one was built in 1593. It has a central courtyard with ceramic seats and an entry at the southeast corner. This building, in the northern Shanxi Province, has a main building that stands separately from the buildings that house the side rooms. Winters are cold in Shanxi, so the courtyard is long on the north–south axis, to receive maximum sunlight. This modest house has a single courtyard.

Figure 8.8
Idealized Southeast Asian howdah.

Figure 8.9
Nineteenth-century palanquin, Cambodia.

In the system of the Chinese courtyard house, the unit of a courtyard and its central hall could be multiplied depending on the need and wealth of the owner. A drawing of a Qing dynasty courtyard house in Beijing delineates two courtyards (Figure 8.10). The entrance, as with the Ding house, is at the southeast corner, and the building is oriented on its north–south axis.

The first strip of buildings has a room for receiving guests, and vendors might proceed no farther into the house. A screen or wall blocks visual access and causes a visitor to enter the house on an oblique angle. The Chinese courtyard house looks inward, to the courtyard, with few openings. The courtyard house is the dominant type of residential building in China, and monumental Chinese architecture is based on it, including the Forbidden City and the Yonghe Palace in Beijing.

Across the first courtyard lies the main residential building with its central room. The interior of the house was separated from the raucous street life. In elaborate courtyard houses, the most private spaces sit farthest back from the front. Furnishings reflect the increasing level of privacy.

The central room, the Ming **jian**, is located in the center of the main hall. The entire main hall is raised on a platform. This was a house but also a social arena with rules of decorum that involved pieces of furniture—who sat where and with whom. There was a strict system of hierarchy. The final courtyard was for women, and the buildings behind it for servants.

Ideally, the Chinese courtyard house and temples and palaces based on it are oriented north–south. Initially earth and timber-frame constructions, the houses became more elaborate over time and came to include bronze fittings and ceramic roof tiles.

Yunnan Province is the south westernmost province in China and is known for its rugged landscape. Once part of the Silk Road, it developed an ethnically diverse population. In southern provinces such as Yunnan, the courtyard arrangement responded to climatic differences. Courtyard houses in the north were composed of freestanding pavilions set within the compound. Houses in the warmer south had smaller courtyards and their pavilions and halls were often contiguous, similar to Mediterranean courtyard houses.

Despite considerable demographic and economic changes in Qing China, the popularity of the courtyard house grew, and it proved to be a resilient form that responded to new conditions. A decline in timber resulted in the once all-wooden structures being built of timber, bricks, stone, stucco, and tile.

China was becoming more urban. The courtyard house as a prototype was remarkably strong. Even ethnic groups such as the Zhuang, who lived in houses on stilts, and the Li, who had boat-shaped houses, adopted features of the courtyard house. Urban areas saw the development of two- and three-story houses, and houses with shops in the front, the beginning of the ubiquitous Chinese shoplot. Until the second half of the twentieth

Figure 8.10
Courtyard house, Beijing, China, Qing dynasty (1644–1912).

century, the courtyard house was the dominant form for rural and urban residential architecture.

A reconstruction of a Ming room at the Metropolitan Museum of Art gives an idea of the planning principles that dictated the form of the central pavilion of a courtyard house (Figure 8.11). The pieces of furniture are Ming, and Chinese craftsmen built the room.

Chinese Classical Furniture

Many achievements date to the Ming dynasty, but for the history of designed objects, the Ming dynasty has a special place. Long esteemed for the high quality of its bronzes and porcelain, it plays an important role in the development of high-quality furniture.

In fact, most of what is now considered Chinese furniture, also known as Chinese classical furniture, traces its origins to the late Ming dynasty. Pieces from the subsequent Qing dynasty also fit into the category, and they continue forms whose profiles were set in the Ming period, the great age of Chinese furniture.

Some pieces of Ming furniture were similar to furniture that existed before the Ming period, although there is little knowledge of these pieces and few extant works. Classical Chinese furniture had its origins in the Song dynasty (960–1279), but it reached its highest expression in the Ming and Qing dynasties.

There were several categories of furniture: hardwood furniture, lacquered furniture, softwood furniture, and pieces made of other materials, such as porcelain, stone, and bamboo. Here we are mostly concerned with hardwood furniture.

Ming chairs came about as part of a general shift from a mat mode of sitting to a chair mode. In the former, people sat on the ground, on mats or rugs. In the latter, their bodies were elevated, and they sat on chairs with their legs pendant. This was exceptional in East Asia, where, as in other regions of the world, people sat low to the ground. The Cambodian statue of Jayavarman II demonstrates the spread of Buddhism, and that it is entirely possible to sit comfortably and have status without a chair. In fact, there are entire cultures that develop sophisticated systems of furnishing in which the chair plays no role.

Figure 8.11
Ming dynasty room (1368–1644), from Soochow, China, Metropolitan Museum of Art, New York, 1979.

Cambodia did not adopt tall chairs until the twentieth century.

The triumph of the chair

Initially, the Chinese, like other Asians, sat on the ground, on mats or on low platforms. People slept on mats. Corresponding to the mat mode of living, tables were low. During the period of the mat mode, furniture was limited.

Three major developments took place in Song dynasty China (960–1126). One, a framework and infill panel became the major structural system for furniture. Two, furniture became an important feature of interior layouts. Three, and most significant, the chair mode, or sitting on a tall chair, became the norm. The adoption of the chair mode of sitting had implications for all other pieces of furniture and architecture. The details of how this came about are somewhat murky. Xiao Hu states that people started to sit on high chairs in the period 200–500 CE. Art historian Craig Clunas posits that a key date for the change from mat sitting to chair sitting occurred around 1000 CE, which he refers to as the triumph of the chair.

The specific circumstances of the development of the high yoke-back chair are unclear, but several sources suggest Chinese exposure to "foreign" influence. This is a straightforward explanation: the early Chinese had contact with foreign chair-using people, they admired the pieces, and they copied them.

Why would tall chairs come about? Three reasons: function, comfort, and status. Sarah Handler writes that in the period of the mat mode of living, there were functional reasons why some people sat on high chairs; for example, women weavers needed to free their feet to operate trestles (Handler 2001). The comfort that chairs can provide derives from the desire to lift the human body off the ground and separate it from the cold. And there is status: in situations that involve a group of people, one or more individuals are to be singled out and afforded a higher rank. A tall chair aids in this process: it forces the sitter to sit upright, and it renders him or her more visible. Whether housing a deity, a noble, or a guest, a tall chair bestows status on its sitter.

Hardwood furniture

A note about chronology: furniture in this chapter is generally classified as classical Ming furniture. The first piece considered was initially owned by Gustav Ecke, one of the Europeans who brought attention to Chinese hardwood furniture in the

mid-twentieth century (Figure 8.12). It is an excellent example of a tall yoke-back chair, although its exact date is unknown. In some cases precise dates confirm that a piece comes from the Ming period. In other cases, as here, the piece is stylistically Ming although it chronologically belongs to a later period.

The yoke-back chair receives its name because of its distinctive curved top rail, with upturned ends that extend beyond the vertical supports. Textile runners were placed on top of the chair, folded over the top, and tied to the upturned top rail extensions. Silk or cotton chair runners were a way to update chairs and respond to seasonal changes.

The modern term "side chair" denotes a chair without arms. Side chairs were more common than armchairs and they predated armchairs. This chair has many of the features of a classic Ming chair. It is made of huali wood, a tropical hardwood.

The seat is a fixed frame. The advantage of a frame seat is that the infill panel can be changed. The existence of a series of holes in pieces suggests that the wooden frames once supported cane seats. For the seat frame, four pieces of wood are mitred at the corners—that is, cut and connected at 45-degree angles, with mortise (hole) and tenon (protrusion) connections. In early Ming

Figure 8.12
Yoke-back chair huali wood.

furniture, the tenons were visible. Over time, the methods for constructing the pieces became more sophisticated and tenons were concealed.

A curved **splat** dominates the backrest. The splat is the broad flat piece of wood that forms the centerpiece of the back and supports the top rail. It leans slightly backward, following the subtle profile of an S-curve. This allows the chair to "give" when a person sits in it. The chair also provides room for the broader expanse of the sitter's chest and shoulders, while its lower register approaches the body, corresponding to the slender area of the sitter's waist. This classic Chinese yoke-back chair is a forerunner of twentieth-century chairs in which designers respond to the human physiology.

Stretchers connect the four chair legs and stabilize the chair, a configuration known as a box-stretcher. The front stretcher has a surface to rest the feet on, recognizing that a sitter would likely use a stretcher close to the ground as a foot rest

A classical writer of the Ming period, Gao Ling, writing in 1591, referred to a broad armchair as a meditation chair (Handler 2001, p. 57). He stipulated that the chair should be half as wide again as the yoke-back chair. The name "meditation chair" prompts visions of repose and serenity, a stance reinforced by the restraint exhibited in the chair's form, materials, and lack of decoration. This name connects secular chairs to the spiritual realm. The vertical arm supports are frugally continuous with the front legs; similarly, the verticals of the seat back are continuations of the rear legs. The cross sections of all elements are rectangular. With its reliance on simple if not severe geometries, the chair has a modern aesthetic.

Huali wood is a tropical hardwood from Guangdong and Guangxi. Its color ranges from golden to reddish and orange tones. It has a close, dense, and heavy grain. Harder woods are difficult to work with, but the trade-off is that they are durable and resistant to pests. Many Chinese hardwood pieces were covered with a clear finish. Ming pieces did not rely on glue or metal nails.

In the distant past, huali wood grew in southern China. The deforestation of China has been going on for centuries, so even during Ming times the prized wood was imported. Most of the tropical hardwoods came from India and Indochina. Huali wood is usually translated as rosewood.

The fact that chairs exist in pairs makes reference to the symmetrical nature of the Chinese courtyard house. Furniture was moved, and many historical paintings show house furniture set up in a garden or on a terrace. But when placed in their proper locations, Chinese chairs lined up against a wall, and stood parallel to the wall. When the parallel configuration did not work, pieces of furniture stood at crisp right angles to one another. In public areas, they were arranged symmetrically. The placement of the furniture was an extension of the architectural layout of the Chinese courtyard house.

In modern Chinese, an important chair type is *guan mao shi yi*, or "official hat-shaped chairs," because the top rail resembles the profile of the winged hats of Ming officials. As with other yoke-back chairs, the rail extends beyond the vertical supports with its characteristic bend. The verticals of the chair back are continuous with the rear legs; they pass through the seat, a construction process that renders the chair sturdy.

A tall chair confers status upon its sitter. A chair with arms, in the company of chairs without arms, has higher status. Inviting a guest to sit down was, and is, a sign of politeness. People of a higher status sit in higher, grander chairs.

The move from the mat-mode to the chair-mode level of sitting had cultural and architectural repercussions. Beds, discussed below, also rose in height. The use of high chairs and beds affected other pieces of furniture. This resulted in taller rooms and higher tables.

Small tables had many uses, and generally, pieces of Chinese furniture were not limited to single uses. What in modern times is referred to as an occasional table is the adjunct to the tall yoke-back chair. This type of table, even though known as a wine table, could be used to display items, such as a single vase, and for dining. Historian Shixiang Wang divides tables into two categories: tables with set-in legs and tables with legs at the corners. The former, with inset legs, is an "an" type of table. The latter has legs at the corner, which Wang classifies as "zhuo." The English terminology for "an" and "zhuo" can be waistless, or inset, and waisted, or at the corner (Wang 1990, p. 19). The splayed legs and stretchers are circular in cross section. The apron (the piece hanging below the tabletop itself) curves downward and has a slot, into which the leg fits snugly, stabilizing the piece. Craftsmen also made similar stools, the difference being that the legs are shorter. Relatively simple pieces of furniture belong to the category George Kates calls "the general repertory of household furniture" (Kates 1948, p. xi).

The various iterations of the yoke-back chair represent one category of Chinese chairs. Another is the round-back armchair. Also known as horseshoe-back chairs, the signifying element is a continuous back and arm rail. The four vertical posts that support the arms are contiguous with the legs. Multiple joined pieces, however, come together to form the curved arm-and-back piece.

Lacquer, ceramic, and bamboo furniture

There is another category of furniture separate from hardwood pieces—pieces that were lacquered in either monochrome or polychrome.

Chinese furniture aficionado Sarah Handler writes: "The traditional folding armchair leads a double life: it folds away into transportable luggage and sets up with all the stability and grandeur needed to comfort an emperor. It is a protean object, momentarily beautiful and practical, but constructed for imminent metamorphosis. Through its long life it is an elegant vagabond" (2001, p. 60). It is likely that the fixed-frame, curved-back armchair derived from an older folding chair, which in turn derived from a simple folding chair that dates back to the second century CE. Folding chairs and stools were important and existed in hardwood and lacquer versions. Emperors, generals, and other nobles used folding chairs when traveling. As Chinese emperors undertook extended inspection tours, their entourage included folding chairs.

Many were made of huali wood. The horseshoe-shaped, curved-back rail is the piece that it has in common with other nonfolding round-back chairs. A curved splat and armrest support hold up the curved back-and-arm rail. The splat is divided into three panels and has a subtle S-curve (some chairs utilize a C-curved splat). Above the seat, this lively chair is all curves; below the seat, it is all straight lines. The front legs start at the base and extend to the rear, yet at the seat they curve powerfully upward and forward.

Such practical chairs were for travel and informal use. They also found formal uses inside. Lacquered, it is a prestige item. Similar chairs are shown in paintings in residential use—as a writing chair, for dining, and to offer to guests. As with other chairs, they could be covered with textiles or animal hides. Folding stools existed for quotidian purposes. An interesting side note is that Philip II of Spain possessed a folding Chinese chair.

Lacquer pieces were also known as palace pieces—the exceptional pieces owned by the wealthy. These grand pieces were elaborately decorated. Often called thrones, these were platforms with side and back panels. The apron that hangs below the sitting platform is continuous with the curved legs. A more elaborate type of chair leg than the horse hoof is the curving elephant trunk.

Such pieces are known as thrones, although the owner may have not been royal in the modern sense. A throne is a platform for sitting, in lotus or semilotus, or with one or both legs hanging down. Different time periods have been interested in different aspects of Chinese furniture. European aesthetes, from the initial stages of contact in the thirteenth century through the nineteenth century, were most interested in polychrome lacquer pieces, with highly elaborate forms, lively profiles, and profuse decoration. The prevailing attitude was that the more exotic, the better. Over time, Chinese furniture makers noticed that certain types were more appealing to foreign customers; they therefore started making pieces explicitly for the export market. It is not surprising that those who lived in Europe during periods that celebrated elaborate complex forms, such as the rococo and Victorian, preferred elaborate Chinese pieces. These consumers' conceptions of Chinese furniture were tainted by their own tastes. Chinese furniture makers responded to their market and made highly decorated pieces, whose new owners mistakenly concluded that such pieces were typical. Chinese furniture makers had always produced the simpler pieces, but they did not appeal to foreign buyers until the twentieth century. Then, the austere hardwood pieces found a willing audience in the West.

Another category of Chinese furniture consists of a material not used in Europe for furniture—ceramics. These durable seats were used in gardens and could serve as a seat or table. Sometimes these pieces had receptacles for hot coals. There was also an extensive production of bamboo furniture, which was less expensive and is not considered here.

Platforms

Boxlike platforms and platforms with legs existed. Just as small bronze boxes in the kitchen functioned as hot plates, so a large boxlike platform for sitting had the possibility of being warmed with toasty braziers. When a platform has had sides and back extensions added, it becomes a couch; the line between platform, couch, and bed is not always distinct.

Couches

Couches and beds are in fact raised platforms (Figure 8.13). As a general rule of thumb, couches were associated with males and canopied beds

Figure 8.13
Couch with back
and side panels,
China, late Ming
or early Qing
dynasty.

with women. This relates to their placement within the courtyard house. The gendering of bed and couch refers to their social use during the day. At night, both sexes used both platform types. Couches, like beds, were seen from the front, approached on axis, and symmetrically placed.

A Ming dynasty couch is waisted with a visual separation between frame and legs. Frequently, railings were added at a later date, and sometimes they remained removable. Often the back rail is higher. Those in the Ming period preferred platforms with four legs instead of boxlike platforms, which were popular in the Tang dynasty. The legs are thick and continuous with the **spandrel**, rendering this couch particularly sturdy.

Beds

These versatile and adaptable pieces of furniture accommodated many activities. All Chinese beds were used for sleeping at night and sitting during the day. They were intended for multiple people. Whereas chairs were for formal engagements, couches were for intimates.

A variety of accoutrements expanded the comfort and range of activities that took place on these platforms. Cushions and blankets, mats, bolsters, and armrests were added and taken away. If large enough, tables and trays with dishes of food could be placed on top of the platform; alternately, food and drinks could be placed on small auxiliary tables. Couches of this type appear in several woodblock illustrations from the late Ming dynasty.

Beds existed as early as the Han dynasty. When a platform was long enough for sleeping as

well as sitting, it became a bed. Deep platforms were double beds. The bed stood on axis in the center of a room. Some beds were large, virtually rooms within rooms. A canopied bed was the most important piece of furniture in a household. Some had full railings on three sides and partial railings on the front. As with couches, frequently the rear panel was higher.

Canopied beds had four or six posts. Beds with six posts required that the curtains hung inside the framework. The textiles were sometimes elaborate, making the brightly colored ensemble a figural element in the house. Hangings were cotton or silk, and people in warmer climates used the canopy for mosquito netting. As with couches, beds served as a social space during the day, sleeping quarters at night, and the place for romantic encounters.

Located in the rear of the house, the canopied bed was the realm of women. Beds dominated a woman's room and were sometimes a significant part of a woman's dowry. Incense could perfume the bed linens. At night the curtains were pulled, and the bed was completely enclosed.

Tables

The classic **zhuo table** is a table with legs at the corners. These tables served many purposes, from display to writing to serving food.

This type is also known as a **kang table**. Historically, a kang was a built-in platform of a northern Chinese house, a hollow brick form with a fire underneath. This heated surface was ideal for sleeping on wintry nights. Originally, kang tables were small tables placed on top of the platform. But the term came to be used for low

Figure 8.14
Couch with back panels and tray.

rectangular tables placed in front of couches or beds (Figure 8.14). A kang table is a forerunner of the Western coffee table.

The table depicted in Figure 8.15 is waisted and has horse-hoof feet. Tables, like chairs, require stretchers to stabilize them. Stretchers at the ground or even higher up can interfere with a person's legs or feet. The solution of waisted tables is that the stretcher becomes an integral part of the tabletop.

If well made, a horse-hoof shaped leg is crafted from a single piece of wood, rather than having a slice added on. The roster of creatures who lend their profiles to furniture designs in China includes elephants, horses, and the praying mantis.

The wine or occasional table, although well thought out in its detailing, belongs to the category of modest pieces of furniture. All the

constituent elements are visible as separate pieces, and there is no attempt to integrate them into an overall design.

Square tables were used for dining and playing games. The names for square tables relate to their overall size and the number of people they sat. There are thus four-immortals tables, six-immortals tables, and eight-immortals tables. The eight-immortals table sat two people on each side.

Chests

One of the characteristics of storage devices is that often they were made in two parts, with the possibility of the top and the bottom being used separately. They stored a variety of items, including carefully folded clothes. Clothes were not hung.

Conclusion

In early Asian history, India and China play important roles. A form initially associated with India and Buddha, the stupa, took hold across Southeast Asia. When combined by the Chinese with the structural technology to build watchtowers, the pagoda arose, which became an

Figure 8.15
Kang.

important architectural prototype and spread to Korea and Japan.

In the domestic realm, the Chinese courtyard house had a prominent role. When Chinese merchants emigrated throughout Asia, they brought the Chinese courtyard house with them. Equally influential were the objects created for the interiors of these houses, and the development of Ming-style furniture is one of the highlights in design history. In recent history, when other Asian countries started expanding their repertoire of furniture forms, they developed furniture pieces that exhibit an awareness of the forms developed in Ming China. A standout collection is found in the Tjong A Fie Mansion in Medan, Indonesia that dates to 1895 (Figure 8.0).

In China we are concerned with the contents of the domestic world, and indeed the houses themselves. In Cambodia, our attention is drawn to items connected to religion, such as the monumental temple complexes and statuary.

Sources

Clunas, Craig (1988). *Chinese Furniture*. London: Victoria and Albert Museum.

Ecke, Gustav (1944). *Chinese Domestic Furniture*. Rutland, VT: Charles E. Tuttle.

Handler, Sarah (2001). *Austere Luminosity of Chinese Classical Furniture*. Berkeley: University of California Press.

Jessup, Helen (2004). *Art and Architecture of Cambodia*. London: Thames and Hudson.

Kates, George (1948). *Chinese Household Furniture*. New York: Dover.

Kates, George (1952). *The Years That Were Fat*. Cambridge, MA: MIT Press.

Kostof, Spiro (1995). *A History of Architecture: Settings and Rituals. Oxford*: Oxford University Press.

Murthy, K. Krishna (1982). *Ancient Indian Furniture*. Delhi: Sundeep Prakashan.

Steinhardt, Nancy (2022). *The Borders of Chinese Architecture*. Cambridge, MA: Harvard University Press.

Wang, Shixiang (1990). *Connoisseurship of Chinese Furniture*. Hong Kong: Art Media Resources.

Zhang, Xiaoming (2011). *Chinese Furniture*. Cambridge: Cambridge University Press.

Discussion and Review Questions

1. Compare the Chinese house to the Roman courtyard house. What are the similarities and differences?

2. What were the regional differences of the Chinese courtyard house?

3. Look at a piece of furniture such as a chair. How does a piece of furniture suggest the kind of architecture in which it stood?

4. What were some of the ramifications of the adoption of sitting in tall chairs, with legs pendant?

5. What are some Asian-designed objects that involve sitting and yet, in the West, are not considered pieces of furniture?

Renaissance

1400–1500	1500–1520	1520–1600	1400–1500	1500–1600	1600–1700
Early Renaissance	High Renaissance	Late Renaissance	Quattrocento	Cinquecento	Seicento

The chronological and artistic period known as the Renaissance had many influences, but foremost it was, as its name implies, a historic revival. Renaissance literally means rebirth, and refers to the period, roughly 1400–1600, when artists, architects, and artisans looked to ancient Greece and Rome. As both an artistic and intellectual movement, validation was sought in classical art. The look to the antique encompassed most artistic realms, including painting and sculpture. For architecture, the most important building types were churches and private palaces.

God and religion, and fear of them, had been a unifying force of Gothic society. In the Renaissance, the unitary focus on God was joined by an interest in humanity, meaning increased attention on the individual and human secular institutions. Most art histories present the Renaissance in sharp contrast to the medieval period, or Gothic; these distinctions are less obvious in England. Some historians bristle at the presentation of the Renaissance as a departure from medieval traditions, or a rebirth of antiquity, and focus on the continuity that existed in many areas of life. This is especially true of the Italian Peninsula, where the knowledge of Roman ruins was a constant feature of medieval life.

Figure 9.0
(*Facing page*)
Unknown, Palazzo Davanzati, Room of the Parrots, Florence, Italy, *c.* 1350. Polychrome wooden ceiling.

The first works we now recognize as belonging to the Renaissance were in northern Italy, and the movement spread to other regions and became a continent-wide phenomenon. To some scholars, the shift from a God-centered concept of the world to a man- and individual-centered concept of the world constitutes the first step toward the modern age.

Innumerable scientific achievements impacted the arts. In sculpture and painting, there was an increased attention to the "reality" of the human form; in painting, art increasingly mimicked the processes of the human eye. This exhibited itself in architecture with the creation and widespread adoption of the **one-point perspective**. The one-point perspective is the drawing method of three-dimensional representation in which items are shortened as they proceed into the distance, often aided by a grid that disappeared into a vanishing point.

One of the many paradoxes that arise when studying the Renaissance is that its leaders constructed the foundation of modern civil and civic society by relying on the idea of the perfectibility of man in the years to come, yet they looked to the past. Unlike those involved in other revivals, Renaissance artists did not seek to re-create the past and were inventive in their use of classic forms. The ancient world served as a point of departure, but not a template.

For those who were not wealthy or politically connected, or who lived modestly in rural areas, the revolutionary changes wrought by Renaissance artists were less important. Interiors, particularly of churches, were more or less viewed from the lens of antiquity. Yet for furniture, no Renaissance cabinetmaker was lauded as were Michelangelo and Raphael.

The Renaissance was an artistic rebirth related to momentous political and medical events. By the end of the fifteenth century, most of Europe had recovered from the bubonic plague that had decimated the continent in the mid-fourteenth century. France had recovered from the Hundred Years' War and the Byzantine Empire gave way to the Ottoman Empire.

Europe beyond the Alps followed with rapt attention the goings-on in Italy. Whereas Italy enjoyed firsthand knowledge of the ancients, most of Europe knew it secondhand. Flemish, French, and German Renaissance architecture and design is the result of blending local vernacular traditions with imported Italian Renaissance forms.

Architecture

Germany

Dürer

Albrecht Dürer (1471–1528), the foremost German Renaissance painter, also contributed to the development of engraving. In 1495, Dürer established himself in Nuremberg. His house presents a different side of the Renaissance. It demonstrates that in certain areas of life and art, such as domestic architecture, interiors, and furnishings, there was a great deal of continuity from medieval traditions into the period known as the Renaissance.

Figure 9.1 shows a building that bridges the gap between medieval and Renaissance. Still standing, at first glance it looks medieval. It fronts directly onto the street and fills out its lot lines. The upper floors overhang the lower floors, and its most notable features are the exuberant timber-framing of the façades and the steeply pitched roof, the products of centuries of evolution. Yet it is a large and imposing house that stands out from its less illustrious neighbors. The interior features simple rooms, although all the walls have been plastered, their structure hidden. Its furnishings include classic Renaissance pieces, such as X-frame chairs and storage cabinets.

A stalwart of the Renaissance interior was the trestle table, reproductions of which were made faithfully into the nineteenth century (Figure 9.2).

Albrecht Dürer is an exception to the assertion that there is no such thing as a great northern Renaissance painter. Furniture pieces are important in configuring the interiors of this comfortable house. The interiors are not rigorously studied in their design but respond to the specific demands for a place to sleep, write, sit, and paint.

Italy

Palazzo Davanzati

An examination of the Renaissance typically begins with Florence, home to Brunelleschi, Donatello, and Masaccio. In the fifteenth century, the city's administration had evolved to a point where there was increased attention to buildings that served as a public infrastructure. This was a move away from absolute rule and gestures in the direction of democracy. The city and the buildings that composed it reflected the shift toward participatory government. The town hall of Florence, the Palazzo Vecchio; its public companion, the **Loggia** della Signoria; and the Baptistry were three public structures that rendered the city grander than its rivals, Pisa and Siena.

The sources for the Renaissance **palazzo** included traditional **Tuscan** farmhouses, the watchtowers for which San Gimignano was famous, as well as ancient prototypes. By the mid-fourteenth century, the townhouse, the palazzo, was becoming grander, more elegant, and civilized.

Revolutionary palaces

An analogous structure in Italy to Dürer's house is the Palazzo Davanzati, a transitional house

Figure 9.1
Unknown, Albrecht Dürer's House, Nuremburg, Germany, 1471–1528.

Figure 9.2
Reproduction of a Renaissance trestle table, Italy, nineteenth century. Walnut.

between the Middle Ages and the Renaissance (Figure 9.0). The Palazzo Davanzati, from the late fourteenth century, sports the first Renaissance interior. Its tall exterior hints of façade developments to come. Its façade is regularized and topped off with an open gallery. A **string course** delineates each floor. The ground floor is **rusticated** and houses shops. A deep cornice, vaguely classical-looking, crowns the top. The residential floors are above the ground floor; the most important is the first residential floor, the **piano nobile**. Subsequent floors decrease in height. This building mitigated the needs of one noble family and the general citizenry; it provided prestige and comfort for the family and lent an elegant façade to the street. Its interiors are at once rich and austere and include multiple iterations of the Renaissance staple, the Dante chair (Figure 9.3).

In Italy, the important social units were families, such as the Pazzi, the Medici, the Gonzaga, and the Pitti. The Palazzo Medici was another significant step in the development of the Renaissance palazzo. It is grand, symmetrical, and relied on classical forms and proportions for its considerable street presence.

Italy was not politically unified, so most of the cities acted as city-states, with the Vatican, in Rome, as a particularly significant player. Florence was a city of bankers and merchants, with ties to the agricultural life of the countryside.

Filippo Brunelleschi (1377–1446) is the most important figure of the early Renaissance. The Renaissance, as viewed from his architectural efforts, relied on the classical system in which all details are related to other details, and the entire building, by way of proportion. Brunelleschi is credited with having invented the one-point perspective. At San Lorenzo and the Foundling Hospital, he put arches on top of columns, something the Romans rarely did.

From 1420 to 1436, Brunelleschi was working on the Florence Cathedral. How to roof the cross of nave and transept? Renaissance architects wanted to do this with a dome. For the city's most important structure, he devised a double-shelled dome with Gothic vaulting and tension rings at the base that counteract the lateral forces. With this building, and the others that followed, Florentine architects were departing from international Gothic developments.

Leon Battista Alberti (1404–1472) was an architect and architectural theorist. He had a well-rounded education in the classics. His primary architectural treatise, the *Ten Books of Architecture* (1452), was a way of making the classic text of the Roman Vitruvius current. In the realm of urban design, he advocated that public spaces, like the buildings that fronted them, should be conceptualized and designed.

Urban design

Michelangelo

The Capitoline Hill is one of the seven hills of Rome. It provides a spectacular view of the Roman forum and also of medieval and Renaissance Rome; Saint Peter's can be glimpsed in the distance. Michelangelo famously redesigned it. Michelangelo never had a blank slate on which to work; all his projects grew out of existing projects started by others. And none was so daunting as the redesign of the Campidoglio, as it is known in Italian. His design process is a classic Renaissance design story in which there is a dramatic contrast between medieval urban and architectural traditions and those of the Renaissance. Through the genius of one architect, a new approach to urban space arose.

The project consisted of the Guild Hall, essentially a town hall with an adjacent palace for the senators at an awkward 80-degree angle to it. Michelangelo's solution was to reface the Guild Hall and move its tower to the center (Figure 9.4). He grafted a new façade onto the Palace of the Senators and mirrored it with a matching palace. The really ingenious move was to also place the new structure at 80 degrees, making a virtue

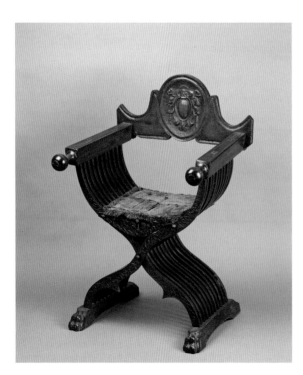

Figure 9.3
Dante chair, Italy, fifteenth to nineteenth century. Walnut, velvet and silk.

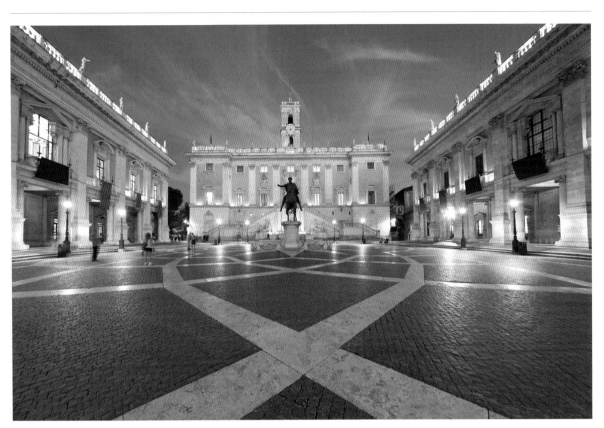

Figure 9.4
Michelangelo,
Campidoglio,
Rome, Italy,
1534–1538.

out of an oddity. For the center of the trapezoidal piazza, he devised a slightly raised oval, from which radiate curvilinear lines. Renaissance architects were well aware that a circular form had the benefit of accepting axes from varying angles. An imposing giant order of **pilasters** dominates the palace façades.

Renaissance Church design is a continuation of the Early Christian Church basilica form, as it survived through the Middle Ages, with some gestures toward the international Gothic style, and an increased desire to bring the Renaissance qualities of perfection of form, and idealization, into the ecclesiastical realm.

The Latin-cross plan had taken root and proved difficult to dislodge, as much as Renaissance architects tried. To the architectural mind, the perfectibility of form mirrored a spiritual awakening, although this proved a difficult sell to their clients, the Church. A rare example of a centrally planned church is Santa Maria della Consolazione in Todi. Many Renaissance architects tried their hand at crafting a centrally planned church—Michelangelo, Bramante, Leonardo da Vinci—so it is therefore difficult to know for certain who the designer of Todi was. The best example of a perfectly symmetrical geometry was likely designed under Bramante's

influence. It is similar to designs for centrally planned buildings by Leonardo da Vinci.

Some artworks are perfect examples of a particular artistic concept; they themselves appear as a manifestation of an artistic ideal. So it is with Santa Maria della Consolazione. Many Renaissance architects expressed a desire to see a project through that relied upon simple geometries, an artistic move in keeping with the overall desire to create a perfect solution. And a part of this was the necessity of achieving symmetry—often in contexts which made that difficult. The centrally planned church was difficult because it lacked an obvious entrance—and an obvious destination, the altar. Additionally, it did not indicate the location of a congregation.

The plan of Todi is relentless in its pursuit of symmetry (Figure 9.5). The entry is barely indicated by one apse that is made of line segments; the others are curved. Inside, all four interior elevations appear the same. Nothing mars the perfect interior, and the stairways are discreetly tucked into the poché of the walls. The plan gives no hint of the location of the altar, the priest, the congregation, and the principal entry.

Todi is not only bilaterally symmetrical (two halves of a composition are mirror images of each other), it is radially symmetrical around a central

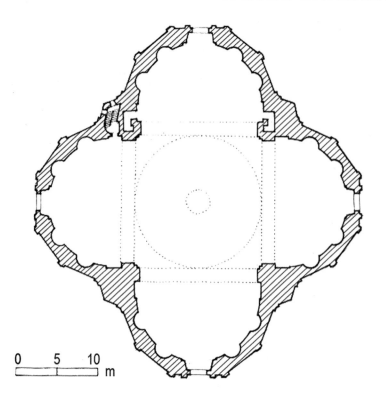

Figure 9.5
Multiple artists,
Santa Maria della
Consolazione,
Todi, Italy,
1494–1518. Plan.

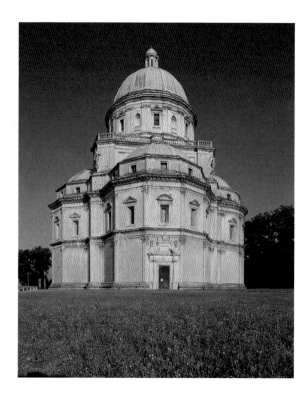

Figure 9.6
Multiple artists,
Santa Maria della
Consolazione,
Todi, Italy,
1494–1518.

point. The expression of the front façade and its correlate, the apse, is suppressed to the point of being inconsequential. All four elevations of Todi are almost exactly the same.

Todi's forms are simple: a square, a dome, and four half-domes. Yet the articulation of its façade ripples over four nearly identical elevations, compositionally bringing the pieces together (Figure 9.6). Its classical detailing is simple in design, inspired in its use. The building sits like a sculpture, upright in the landscape, a master-stroke of simplicity. This building stands today more as a statement about architecture than a response to the functional needs of a church. It is a remarkable event in the history of architecture when all the ostensible programmatic functions of a building are secondary to a relentless pursuit of the perfect form.

Da Vinci and Bramante

Santa Maria della Consolazione is the closest incarnation of the Renaissance architectural spirit. Collectively, the works of Raphael, Bramante, and Leonardo da Vinci present varied approaches— abstract, ideal, and pragmatic. The year 1500 was a benchmark of the High Renaissance. Leonardo da Vinci (1452–1519) was an architect, painter, and inventor. The painter of the *Mona Lisa,* 1503– 1506, he painted several fresco cycles throughout his life. The High Renaissance architect Donato Bramante (1444–1514) was one of those named as architect of Saint Peter's.

Some works are included in the Renaissance because they are transitions (Dürer's House) or important breakthroughs (the Campidoglio); studying them, one imagines the designer grappling with the problem at hand and arriving at a brilliant solution. Architectural developments, in addition to being inspired by classical form, are characterized by striving toward perfection, with perfection being defined as pure geometries and centrally planned buildings.

Interiors

Walls, floors, and ceilings

The standard composition of a Renaissance residential wall divided it into horizontal bands and fields. Starting at the intersection of wall and floor, a woodwork base made the initial transition from horizontal to vertical. Above the base was a

dado line (waist high or higher). This band encircled the room and visually supported the main field, which extended to the juncture of wall and ceiling. A cornice mediated the wall-to-ceiling transition and frequently featured a decorated frieze. The frieze was sometimes three-dimensional, more frequently painted. Most walls were plaster, painted, or featuring frescoes. Frescoes were representational or architectural.

The most expensive options for treating a wall included marble or wood paneling, but these were rare in houses. Walls that were not elaborately painted had wall hangings whose supporting hooks were at the bottom of the frieze. Wall hangings were made of leather or fabric, simple or embroidered and **gilded**. Elaborate tapestries with narrative scenes were the purview of the wealthiest homes. The ubiquity of textile wall hangings is indicated by the presence of walls that were painted or tiled to resemble hanging fabric, such as the Palazzo Davanzati.

Floors were most commonly made of wood. Fancier rooms had brick or tiled floors; marble floors in houses were rare, because of the weight. Some houses had Turkish carpets, although they were not common.

There were many famous commissions for replacing a simple timber ceiling with a grand one. Looking at these projects reveals the Renaissance approach toward the horizontal plane of the ceiling. The ceiling, like an elevation, became a field to be designed, yet it followed its own parameters. It was foremost considered a piece of architecture. In one type of construction, the **joists** running in one direction were visually dominant. These parallel timbers spanned the length of the room and literally supported the floor above. An alternate ceiling strategy emphasized the cross-beams as well, which turned the ceiling into a plane of rectangular panels. If the cross-beams' depth was emphasized, the ceiling became a waffle-grid of recesses, or coffers (not to be confused with storage chests of the same name). Some beams were carved with classical details; they were more frequently painted. There were also vaulted ceilings, an architectural element that some grand houses and **villas** shared with churches.

The first step of the architect working on a prominent ceiling commission was to construct a conceptual grid or framework that established the ceiling as an architectural entity, lent order to a blank upside-down horizontal plane, and divided it into smaller areas. Some spaces within the framework were turned over to painters, with the paintings being subordinate to the architectural system. Some plaster ceilings make a nonliteral gesture toward representing beams and joists. The real ones were covered up, then idealized and painted. They were classical in their detailing, although ancient ceilings did not look like the Renaissance ceilings that ostensibly paid them homage.

Michelangelo

Michelangelo famously took the plain plaster ceiling of the Sistine Chapel and painted it himself to look like architecture, a singular endeavor of heroic proportions (Figure 9.7). Part of his scheme was to wittingly make visual statements about the status of the arts of architecture and painting. Some figures step outside of their "assigned" panels.

The Renaissance approach to ceiling design was unlike that of the ancients, unlike that of the Middle Ages, and unlike that of the baroque period that followed it.

Inigo Jones

Inigo Jones is the central figure credited with introducing Italian Renaissance architecture to England. Banqueting House in London was one of the buildings that did this, and it still stands in

Figure 9.7
Michelangelo, Sistine Chapel, Rome, Italy, 1508–1512.

contrast to its neighbors. The rectilinear elements of the ceiling establish a grid. They appear as structural beams, reminiscent of timber ceilings, yet decorated and gilded to the hilt. They also can be read as an oblique reference to Roman coffered ceilings. Rubens did the celebrated paintings that are an integral part of the composition.

Gradually, over the period of some two hundred years known as the Renaissance, the approach to ceilings changes. The geometries become less rigid. In Carraci's ceiling for the Palazzo Farnese, Rome, the panels resemble picture frames and the scenes within them are given more visual importance. In many cases, the narrative scenes trump the architecture.

The study

In her book on the Italian Renaissance, art historian Dora Thornton addresses a single room type: the study. A study could be a small low-ceilinged area in a house's **mezzanine**, a monk's cellular room, or part of a bedchamber delineated with a wood partition made by a carpenter. Carpenters also constructed freestanding booths that served as private studies within the context of a larger space, such as a church.

Studies were outfitted with built-in desks and benches that were continuous with a raised platform. For those involved in trade, a study accessible to a house's visitors served as a place for meeting with vendors and discussing and signing contracts. For others, it was a place of solitude, for reflecting, reading, and writing.

As freestanding furnishings became more common, a desk or a simple trestle table served as the work surface. A movable bench, stool, or X-frame chair provided seating. A lectern was a shallow storage unit with a sloping top that acted as the writing surface. It sat on top of the desk or table, and its storage space held ink, paper, and other writing supplies. Travelers found lecterns particularly useful.

The objects that completed a study could include a small collection of contemporary artworks, antiquities, and exotic souvenirs. Pen knives, seals, spectacles, and magnifying glasses were common accessories. Some surprising objects found in a study included a mirror and a reading cushion to rest one's forearms against.

An important function of a study was to store and display books. Shelves were built in, recessed, or surface mounted. A freestanding piece of furniture, a **cabinet** with shelves and doors, was a secure way to secure valuable books. Thornton

writes that "The evolution of the cabinet as a piece of furniture was the single most important development in the history of the study in Renaissance Italy, for it demonstrated the importance of collecting as a form of interior decoration" (1997, p. 74). Cabinets and **chests** that held books, either in private homes, churches, or town halls, were the forerunners to libraries just as the study was the forerunner to the twentieth-century workstation.

Considering a single room type such as the study underscores the role that rooms and interior furnishings played in the development of ways of interacting with the world. Dora Thornton writes: "Reading, studying and thinking were considered by Renaissance writers to be free and pleasurable pursuits which gave shape and elegance to one's leisure, so that a study represented the ideal of making the pleasures of thinking and working continuous with the rest of one's existence" (1997, p. 2). The celebrated Renaissance focus on the individual was encouraged by a place whose objects were configured to encourage careful, informed thought.

Raphael

In the periods that followed the Renaissance, the interior became a completely designed space, with an integration of all the constituent elements. In the Renaissance, the full integration of interior design elements does occur in churches, less so in houses. In many respects, the Renaissance domestic interior remained, as it had been in the Middle Ages, a collection of disparate elements. By modern standards, a Renaissance interior was sparingly furnished.

Da Vinci and Michelangelo influenced the painter and architect Raphael (1483–1520). For Pope Julius II, he did a series of rooms in his Vatican apartments. These projects involved painting wall and ceiling frescoes. They are known as the **Stanze**, which means, simply, rooms. The most famous was the Stanza della Segnatura, which includes Raphael's painting *The School of Athens*.

Raphael's *stanze* in the Vatican was an inspired set of interiors that follows Renaissance principles. But the furnishings of the suite of rooms were not a part of the design, and in fact were at odds with it.

Palazzo interiors were the product of almost continual rebuilding and remodeling. Furniture and tapestries, therefore, played an important role in shaping the use and disposition of rooms.

Renaissance rooms typically had beamed ceilings and prominent fireplaces. The ensemble of fireplace, mantel, and overmantel was a favored site of elaborate decoration. Where Renaissance interiors depart from medieval practices is that there is an increasing tendency to mask the actual structure—ceiling, beams and joists, floorboards, walls of studs and lath—and present a unified plane to those in the room. These unified planes became blank canvases awaiting artistry.

Furniture

Two strands of Renaissance furniture stand out: one strand comprises pieces of furniture that are clearly derivative of Renaissance architecture; the other constitutes the continuation of medieval forms. The former is chiefly large cabinets and beds; the latter includes tables, chairs, and stools. Information on medieval Italian furniture is sparse, although we know that there were tables, chairs, stools, and chests. The invention in 1322 of the saw mill eased the production of furniture based on planks. Harold Eberlein, the author of an early twentieth-century work on Italian Renaissance interiors and furniture, emphasized a central duality to his subject matter: it was complex or simple. He wrote: "The Italian Renaissance interior was either richly ornate with all the wealth of polychrome treatment that could be applied to walls and ceiling … or else it was severely simple, and even austere with points of concentrated enrichment only where they would give the greatest emphasis" (Eberlein 1916, p. vii). High contrast characterized a Renaissance interior, regarding color and surface articulation. Individual pieces were sometimes elaborate, but the overall effect of simplicity was achieved with a judicious use of elaborate objects within a straightforwardly articulated space.

Large-scale architectural furniture

One category of designed objects includes large ponderous items that attract a viewer's attention. Eberlein explained, "Few rooms could stand many of the more ornate pieces of Renaissance cabinet work, whether polychrome or carved, and it was not intended they should. To have had more than a few would have been like trying to make an entire dinner on plum pudding" (Eberlein 1916, p. ix).

A feature of one class of Renaissance furniture pieces, including wardrobes and large chests, is that they are architectural, with a clear architectonic profile, and their detailing relies on the classical architectural vocabulary. Knowledge of Italian Renaissance architecture circulated around Europe via the printed book; hence, the invention of the mechanical printing press in Germany in 1439 impacted furniture design, as well. Furniture designers had access to a precise grammar of ornament, with classical capitals, **fluting**, **putti**, caryatids, and so on.

Cupboards and wardrobes

Many big Renaissance pieces of furniture resemble buildings. They have a base, multiple stories and columns, and an overhanging cornice. Meticulously designed, their elevations promote multiple readings. Sometimes they combine furniture detailing with architectural detailing. One particularly impressive piece shows doors opening to reveal an elaborate scene crafted out of veneers. The marquetry scene exploits the impression of depth with a false perspective.

The two two-storied pavilions can visually predominate, or the giant order of columns, a motif borrowed from Michelangelo's buildings on the Campidoglio, can be read as the visually dominant elements (Figure 9.8). The overall cabinet can look like it comprises two two-story pavilions set on a base; an alternate reading is of a three-story piece. The rows of lozenges, ovals, and rectangles can also be read to stand in for framing columns.

The local engagement with the imported Italian style is found in the infill panels: non-architectural motifs, a surfeit of marquetry and parquetry.

Edward Lucie-Smith writes that such pieces of furniture "are in every detail like miniature renaissance palaces—far more correctly classical than the buildings which were being erected simultaneously by German architects" (1979, p. 55). Printed pattern-books served as guides to making furniture. The list of architects whose careers were largely due to their publications includes Peter Flötner in Germany, Jacques Androuet du Cerceau I and Hugues Sambin in France, and Hans Vredeman de Vries and Theodore de Bry in the Netherlands.

The new style required a higher level of expertise in woodworking and resulted in a growing distinction worldwide among joiners, carpenters, and turners. Joiners did rough carpentry work;

Figure 9.8
Renaissance
Armoir (Fassadenschrank),
Nuremberg,
Germany, early
seventeenth
century.

a chest at the foot of the bed and benches at the sides. The benches had hinged lids that opened to reveal storage. Benches also provided seating, indicating that beds and bedrooms had a social function during the day. The custom of surrounding a bed with a chest and benches led to the construction of closed platforms that supported the mattress. Wider on three sides than the mattress, there was a space between the mattress and the platform's edge for guests to sit. Storage spaces lay underneath the guest's seat cushions (Thornton 1991, pp. 111–20).

The Renaissance bed differed significantly from the Roman bed. A bed's use for dining was long gone, and it was monumental in size, form, and decoration.

Chests and cassoni

In the fifteenth century, the chest remained one of the most important and numerous pieces of furniture. Over the course of the sixteenth century, its central role in a household's inventory of furnishings lessened. A storage device, it was also a means to transport items. The rounded top indicates the possibility that this piece was envisioned to stand outside; rounded tops evaded rainwater.

In less exalted households, a chest was frequently one of the few pieces of furniture and was called to serve many uses. A synonym is *coffer*. What distinguishes a coffer, sometimes, is that it was used to store money and valuable items; hence the phrase "the coffers of the pope," in which a piece of furniture is used as a stand-in for the papal treasury, or Chaucer's line from *The Canterbury Tales*, "Yet hadde he but litel gold in cofre" (1870, p. 12), in which a nearly empty coffer is a sign of poverty.

Within the domestic realm, the Italian **cassone** demonstrates how a piece of furniture did not just serve functional purposes but was a player in a familial, social, and ritual network (Figure 9.9). Many modern furniture traditions date back to this piece of furniture.

The Italian verb *accasàre* means to marry off, and a cassone, a large *cassa* (box or chest) is a piece of furniture that was part of the process. A cassone traditionally held items that were to serve a prospective bride in her marriage. As the bride decamped from her familial home to that of her husband's, the cassoni were carried through the streets, a public affirmation of the transference of property and wealth from one family to another, and a symbol that hereafter the young

carpenters were involved in house building, such as paneling and built-in pieces; and turners worked on smaller projects, such as pieces of furniture. One piece of evidence of this comes from the American continent, when on August 30, 1568, the City of Mexico issued separate ordinances for carpenters, sculptors, joiners, and makers of stringed instruments. By the end of the sixteenth century, it was possible to discuss national trends in furniture design and growing distinctions among the woodworking trades.

Beds

For those fortunate enough not to sleep on the floor, an essential item was a mattress, a textile bag stuffed with straw or feathers. A frame lifted the mattress off the floor, and there were multiple examples of the resulting space (between frame and floor) being used by a lower mattress and frame on wheels—a trundle bed.

More elaborate beds had tall headboards with an overhanging cornice. The visual dominance of a bed in a bedroom was furthered by the custom of surrounding it with auxiliary pieces of furniture,

Figure 9.9
Italian cassone.

lady's home was with her new family. This chest therefore had both a private and a public function. Once ensconced in its new home, the cassone often took its place at the foot of the marriage bed.

Art historian Cristelle Baskins wrote a book on cassoni. If the private study was mostly a male realm, Baskins states that "the cassone became a microcosm of the household, but also synecdochically, a figure for the wife herself" (1998, p. 2). The cassone, like the house, contained locked-up things that were watched over by women. These elegant chests might contain items of the bride's wardrobe, fine linens, purses, bags, scissors, gloves, and prayer books. The circulation and collection of these consumer goods was related to the wealth that stemmed from Renaissance trade. Symbolically, a cassone was related to its owner's reproductive contribution to her family and the social alliance and financial arrangement between two families. Cassoni were usually made

in pairs; commissioning them was an expensive endeavor reserved for wealthy families. Cassoni were most popular in the fifteenth century, and their manufacture and use declined in the sixteenth century, as did the importance of chests generally.

Elaborate cassoni featured painted or carved panels. These allegorical stories relate to courtship and marriage. Sometimes these allegories appear odd for modern viewers, such as the Rape of Daphne, but in their context, they underscored faithfulness within the bonds of marriage. These lavishly decorated chests were made in Italy in the fourteenth to sixteenth century; Florence was an important center of production for the cases and the painted panels. Commissioning and owning cassoni was initially an Italian practice, but over time some individuals continent-wide admired and purchased the carefully crafted storage units.

Cassapanche and credenzas

A **cassapanca** recognizes that chests were often used as seating (Figure 9.10). It is a piece designed for two purposes: storage and seating. Slightly higher than a chest, it is essentially a storage chest to which a back and arms have been added.

A **credenza** is a storage unit with a higher elevation than a chest. A credenza is a storage item, but its primary purpose is for the display of items. Some credenzas had stepped shelves to make even more precious objects visible. Credenzas were also initially associated with

Figure 9.10
Unknown,
Cassapanca, Italy,
c. 1500–c. 1600.
Walnut and pine.

Florence. The display of expensive objects publicly affirmed a family's status.

Renaissance palazzi did not have closets. Grand houses had storerooms on the upper floors, but on lower floors, cabinets or wardrobes held items. In many places of the world today, apartments do not have built-in closets and items of clothing continue to be stored in cabinets.

The approach seen with many furniture pieces is to accept a tried-and-true form and make it more valuable by covering its forms and surfaces with decoration. This presents the Renaissance solution to taking a common object and rendering it grand. This method takes a form known to be successful in workshops and farms, and decorates it to the hilt to render it acceptable for use in fine houses. This approach was seen to individual designed objects, and also the forms that make up the Renaissance interior, such as a coffered ceiling (Figure 9.11)

A chest, a cassapanca, a credenza, and a cabinet—each is of increasing height, and all are storage items. Drawers are used, yet entire chests of drawers were not common. While in no literal way does this constitute a forerunner of the twentieth-century office panel system, it does constitute a series of pieces of furniture, of increasing height, that were used to furnish a room, with a practical function and making a visual impact. The list of items that could be called upon to resolve the furnishing of a room had increased significantly from the medieval period.

Surface-forming furniture

Tables

A **trestle table** is a table whose horizontal surface is supported by a system of uprights at the ends and stabilizing cross-pieces. (Other types of tables are legged tables, plinth tables, and pedestal tables.) A **refectory table** has uprights that serve as end panels. The trestle table had a clear ancient Roman precedent, and trestle tables were widespread throughout the Italian Peninsula. They were frequently found in monasteries and convents, but were not limited to religious contexts. This table makes scant reference to Renaissance architecture. Its form presents an honest response to the need of supporting a horizontal work or dining surface. Two horizontal rails stabilize the panels. Such tables are translations into wood of Roman marble tables and benches that were used in gardens.

Renaissance furniture relied less on metal strapping and metal nails, as did medieval pieces, and more on wood pins and **dovetail joints**. Tables, if they had legs, generally had rails.

Seating

Unlike the other arts and the rare cabinet, furniture for sitting rarely took its inspiration from antique models. Those pieces that existed in ancient Rome were prevalent in the Renaissance not because they were rediscovered but because they never went away. There were three categories of seating: stools, benches, and chairs.

Stools

Sgabello literally means stool, although the term also denotes specifically Renaissance upper-class stools and small-scale chairs. For those at the lower end of the economic spectrum, the stool was the most common type of seating device. The most comprehensive book to date on Italian Renaissance interiors and furnishings is by Peter Thornton, the father of Dora Thornton. Much of the information about seating, other pieces, and Renaissance interiors presented here comes from his work.

The construction of a stool was simple; some were carved from solid pieces of wood, some from planks simply cut and assembled. The word stool is a misnomer as this category contains several elegant and elaborate pieces that provided seating in refined locations.

What all Italian Renaissance stools have in common is an ancestor in a common utilitarian seat, what Peter Thornton calls an "old-fashioned milking stool" (1991, p. 168). Simple stools consisted of a seat—round, octagonal, square, or rectangular—supported by three or four legs. Stools also existed with attached backs.

Figure 9.11
Coffered ceiling.

Another type of stool was the box stool, made from five boards (four sides and the seat) with the feet integral to the sides (Figure 9.12). The flat surfaces of a boxstool were rife for decoration. Some box stools were painted, carved, or inlaid with **intarsia**. Some stools featured a backboard, which blurs the line between chair and stool. Some stools were wide enough to seat two in close proximity, which blurs the line between stool and bench.

It is odd to name a chair sgabello, using a word that means stool, but the etymology reveals the history of design; a back was once upon a time added to a stool (Figure 9.13). The notches in the front and rear planks hint at legs.

Sgabelli were useful at social functions, in a public realm. They demanded no small amount of dexterity of the people who used them. An awkward move and together the seated person and chair would topple over. They were not intended for relaxing, but for a place of rest within the context of a public function. The small scale and delicacy of sgabelli contrast with the imposing cabinets and wardrobes.

Although cushions were used and limited upholstery on seats and arm rests appeared, no fully upholstered piece of furniture made an appearance in the Renaissance.

Furniture buyers did not purchase elegant chairs in large numbers; a collection of matching sgabelli in the Louvre is exceptional. Rooms that needed to accommodate many people did so with a variety of chair types, often combining armed chairs with sgabelli and benches.

When furnishing a room, a strict hierarchy of seating types reigned that mirrored the hierarchy of secular and religious life. The most elegant (and therefore of the highest status) type of chair was the armed **sedia**, followed by the X-frame chair, followed by a sgabello with a back, followed by a backless sgabello, and finally modest stools and benches. Stools were useful in homes of the wealthy and homes of the poor.

Benches

Benches, fixed (built-in), and freestanding, provided multiple seating. There were benches with and without backs. Most benches had hinged seats, providing access to storage below the seats. Thornton writes that most seating was provided by stools and benches until 1500, after which a variety of chair types became common (Thornton 1991, p. 174).

The X-frame chair

In the context of the Italian Renaissance, the X-frame chair seems to be yet another example of an ancient object rediscovered and embraced by fifteenth-century artisans. While it is true that there were ancient X-frame chairs, this is a case of an item whose continual utility is evidenced by the fact that it existed in ancient Rome, through the medieval period, through to the Renaissance.

A chair provides a horizontal surface for a human figure to sit upon at a decent height above

Figure 9.13
Sgabello, Italy,
c. 1560.

Figure 9.12
Box stool, Italy, 16th century.

the ground (at lower heights, it is then a stool). This makes the human figure appear important and separates it from the cold and damp of the ground. If the seated figure were a static (or "dead") load, the task of distributing the weight to the ground would be simple. Yet because the seated human figure fidgets, moving constantly from side to side, the chair as a designed object is subjected to lateral tensile forces as well as vertical compressive forces. Hence, a chair is complicated structurally and requires lateral bracing.

The continual appearance of the X-frame chair throughout history is testament to its ability to respond to the complicated forces of the seated figure. This is not an example of a simple solution; the construction of an X-frame is exacting and requires a skilled carpenter. It is an example of a form that endures over time because knowledge of how to build it becomes widespread. An X-frame chair was comfortable and transportable. Comfort here is a relative term, meaning comfort as opposed to sitting on a rock or log.

In fifteenth- and sixteenth-century Italian cities, even wealthy families owned few pieces of furniture, although many owned several homes. Prominent families typically owned a town house and a villa in the countryside (for example, the Palazzo Farnese in Rome and the Villa Farnese in Viterbo). Furniture was frequently moved from house to house; hence the foldable and transportable X-frame chair was a useful addition to a household. Pieces of furniture were also periodically moved within a house—for example, from public rooms to storerooms on upper stories. Another development over the two hundred years of the Renaissance is that families were less likely to move along with all their furnishings.

The Savonarola chair

The Dominican monk Girolamo Savonarola was a religious figure who fought the powerful Florentine Medici family. The Medici family fell in 1494 and were replaced as the rulers of Florence. Savonarola's reign was to be short-lived; he was executed in 1498.

He abhorred the excesses of the wealthy and powerful, and sought to lead the church down a simpler path. The church and its followers, he felt, should lead lives marked by self-discipline and self-denial. Restraint was one of the qualities that the arts sponsored by the state, the church, and the wealthy should reflect. The chair named after him, Savonarola, does precisely that (Figure 9.14).

Figure 9.14
Savonarola chair, c. 1500.

It is not an example of simplicity as a matter of economic necessity, but as a contemplated goal in itself. The austere lines of the chair reflect the religious attitude of **asceticism**. This chair raises what is a perennially recurring question among the religious: should art forms associated with a religion espouse virtues of simplicity, piety, discipline, and denial, or should they glorify God with grand impressive gestures?

Previously, we enumerated several functions of a chair: to raise the seated human figure off the ground, to provide a modicum of comfort, to avoid contact with damp and cold, and in some cases to be transportable. Added to this list is another function, a symbolic one: a chair should look like a chair. A challenge chair designers face is that their designs should be intelligible to those looking at them.

Dante chair

The starting point of the **Dante chair** is the X-frame chair, which had existed on the Italian Peninsula for some 1,500 years. This is not a new design, but a revised version of a tested form. Many Dante chairs take the form of a folding X-frame and elaborate on it, although they themselves do not always fold. Thus, the original derived out of the need to be transportable, but the form in itself became desirable and recognizable, outside of its ability to fold.

As with the heavily decorated sgabello, with the Dante chair, we observe the furniture designers working with a recognizable form and applying decoration to it. X-frame chairs of the Dante variety are synonymous with the Renaissance throughout Europe. Additionally, there were modest chairs that folded fore-and-aft—the X was visible on their side profiles.

The sedia

The standard Renaissance armchair is referred to with the Italian word that simply translates as "chair": the sedia (Figure 9.15). Sedia means chair, but it also indicates a Renaissance armchair. This type of chair is similar to some late Roman chairs that we know of from wall paintings. It is also important in that it starts what will be a long line of chairs. Most European seating from the time of the Renaissance onward is based on the sedia.

The sedia is a combination of a plank and **turned construction**. The legs of the chair are decorated by being rotated and carved during

Figure 9.15
Renaissance sedia, Italy, 16th century.

fabrication. The front legs stabilize the chair and continue through the seat to become the arm supports; similarly, the rear legs continue through the seat to form the backrest. Horizontal stretchers stabilize the chair against lateral forces. The front stretcher is raised. A seated human figure would likely want to raise his or her legs and possibly rest them on the front stretcher; this is made impossible on the sedia by the front rail's elevated position.

It is not fully upholstered, and thumbtacks hold down the leather that is attached over padding. They also form a part of the decoration. This chair's verticals and horizontals are all true. They are nearly vertical and horizontal, and connect at crisp right angles. There is some evidence that chairs of this type were imported from Spain and France (Thornton 1991, p. 186).

Conclusion

The knowledge of Renaissance forms circulated around Europe. Books were published and some pieces of furniture were exported. More importantly, craftsmen knowledgeable of Italian Renaissance techniques traveled and took their knowledge with them. Italian Renaissance decorative styles came to France first during the reigns of Charles VIII and Francis I. This was an outcome based upon French political and military incursions into Italy. Italian craftsmen traveled to France. A neighborhood developed in Paris that became known for furniture: the Faubourg Saint-Antoine.

England experienced continental Renaissance design at a remove from Italy; many of the furniture makers in England who produced Renaissance pieces were themselves Flemish. Throughout its design history, England is always more **eclectic** than the continent, but the reign of Henry VIII saw an interest in a particularly pure form of Renaissance art. Over the period of the two hundred years known as the Renaissance, there was a progression from simple and functional to decorated.

Renaissance furniture was more comfortable, and numerous, than medieval furniture. While not fully integrated into the design of interiors, some exceptional Renaissance pieces display the full virtuosity of carvers, sculptors, and gilders. Renaissance craftsmen established the essential roster of European furniture that would be further developed in the baroque and rococo periods.

Sources

Baskins, Cristelle (1998). *Cassone Painting*. Cambridge: Cambridge University Press.

Baskins, Cristelle, ed. (2005). *The Medieval Marriage Scene: Prudence, Passion, Policy*. Tempe: Arizona Center for Medieval and Renaissance Studies.

Boroli, Marcella (1985). *Il mobile del rinascimento*. Novara: Istituto Geographico De Agostini.

Chaucer, Geoffrey (1870). *The Canterbury Tales*. New York: D. Appleton.

Eberlein, Harold Donaldson (1916). *Interiors, Fireplaces, and Furniture of the Italian Renaissance*. New York: Paul Wenzel and Maurice Krakow.

Lucie-Smith, Edward (1979). *Furniture: A Concise History*. London: Thames and Hudson.

Mende, Matthias (1991). *The Dürer House in Nuremberg*. Nuremberg: Verlag Hans Carl Nürnberg.

Rowland, Ingrid (2001). *The Culture of the High Renaissance*. Cambridge: Cambridge University Press.

Teodori, Brunella (2018). *Palazzo Davanzati e Firenze*. Florence: EDIFIR.

Thornton, Dora (1997). *The Scholar in His Study: Ownership and Experience in Renaissance Italy*. New Haven, CT: Yale University Press.

Thornton, Peter (1991). *The Italian Renaissance Interior*. New York: Abrams.

Waddy, Patricia (1990). *Seventeenth-Century Roman Palaces: Use and Art of the Plan*. Cambridge, MA: MIT Press.

Discussion and Review Questions

1. Look at a Renaissance plan or façade. With the drawing as your evidence, explain how Renaissance designers designed. What was important to them? How does this differ from other design approaches, such as how people design today?

2. What was the attraction to centrally planned buildings? Why were they problematic for churches?

3. What are examples of forms, in furniture, art, or architecture, that were not reinventions but medieval holdovers?

4. How was the Renaissance a dramatic break from the medieval period?

5. Who are some of the major Renaissance architects and artists?

Baroque

1600–1720	1600–1700	1600–1700	1603–1649
Baroque	Seventeenth century	Seicento	Jacobean

The **baroque** period is known for its convergence of patronage and prodigious artistic talent. Two centers of increased wealth and the prestige they sought were significant: the Italian noble class and the French monarchy.

Art historians use the terms "seventeenth century" and "baroque" synonymously. Baroque, in common parlance, means elaborate. Often historians of art and design discuss the economic, religious, and political factors that lie behind the art—that is, they examine how the context was related to the artworks produced. This is true with baroque art. But, significantly, there is also the phenomenon of those active in the arts reacting to the stylistic traditions they inherited. What we have is a style that can be interpreted as reacting to another style. It is difficult to understand the genesis of baroque forms without first understanding the Renaissance. As happens when studying styles in progression, many of the elements that become the hallmark of baroque design are also present in late-Renaissance design; thus, a predecessor to the baroque are the late-Renaissance mannerist tendencies as seen in the work of Giulio Romano and Michelangelo.

As for the political and religious context, continual discord between Catholics and Protestants, throughout Europe, marred the seventeenth century. In France, the Edict of Nantes of 1598 sought to decisively put the religious wrangling to rest, yet failed to do so. Regarding economic power, the seventeenth century saw a shift in which the rivals for leadership in international trade were the Netherlands and Portugal. By the end

Figure 10.0
(*Facing page*)
Francesco Borromini, Palazzo Spada, Rome, Italy, 1632–1652. Forced perspective gallery.

of the century, the contest was between the Netherlands and England.

International contacts between Europe and the rest of the world had existed since the fifteenth century, but in the seventeenth century the effects were widespread. For furniture and the decorative arts, this resulted in new materials, such as tortoiseshell, ivory, brass, silver, and semiprecious stones. Increased trade in wood involved European timbers and also exotic hardwoods, foremost ebony.

The seventeenth century was an important time for interiors and furnishings, more important than the Renaissance had been. There was a move from heavy oak cupboards to lacquered cabinets. The desire for comfort increased, resulting in more heavily upholstered pieces of furniture.

Italy

Architecture

In Italy, the major baroque artistic figures were Francesco Borromini (1599–1667) and Gianlorenzo Bernini (1598–1680); they frequently competed against each other for the same projects. With projects that were geographically close, each tried to out-do the other.

Borromini

A church Borromini designed, San Carlo alle Quattro Fontane, dates to 1634. It is a seminal work of baroque architecture and is worthy of study in its façade, plan, and interior. It is also compelling as a work of urban design. It stands at the intersection of two streets, and each of the four buildings at the corners sports a fountain—hence the church's unusual name (Figure 10.1). The fountain is visible in the plan and to the extreme left of the façade.

Figure 10.1
Francesco Borromini, San Carlo alle Quattro Fontane, Rome, Italy, 1634. Plan.

The façade contains many of the elements that predominated in Italian Renaissance façades. In its detailing, the façade has classical elements—columns, pilasters, niches, bases, and Corinthian capitals. Yet the façade of San Carlo bends and breaks in ways no Roman temple ever did. The other aspect that represents a departure from Renaissance elevations is the depth of the façade. The cornices are deep and hang over the rest of the façade, at mid-height and at the top, casting the building in deep shadow. Compared to a Renaissance church elevation, it stands out from its context. The façade no longer expresses a central nave and side aisles. Instead, it reads as a baroque take on the idea of a church façade. Baroque architects frequently used the broken pediment. With its deep niches and scrolled gable, the façade expresses movement as does the interior.

Borromini was trained as a stone carver. Unlike his rival Bernini, he was an architect, not a painter and sculptor. The plan of San Carlo is startling: the geometric purity of the Renaissance is gone. Compared to Todi, geometric complexity and plasticity have replaced simplicity and solidity. There is nothing rectilinear in the plan; even the curves are complex. It relies on ovals and elliptical shapes. Half-domes hang over the altar and the side apses. San Carlo is a very small church with an astonishing amount of visual activity.

It bears comparison to the Renaissance church in Todi because it is not a version of the basilica/ Latin-cross plan, but a baroque version of a centrally planned church. The entrance is on one of the smaller sides. It vaguely resembles a **Greek cross**, with concave corners and concave apses at the entry, altar, and sides. Yet there is no individuation of parts; everything flows together.

Another tour de force of Borromini's planning abilities was Sant'Ivo, also in Rome. It was built in 1642–1662 as part of a complex by Giacomo della Porta for the University of Rome. It underscores that Borromini was interested in ovals, circles, and stars, but not the standard basilica form.

In the forced perspective gallery of his Palazzo Spada, Borromini displays a sense of humor (Figure 10.0). He uses the trick of forced perspective to fool a viewer into thinking that the gallery is larger than it is.

Bernini

Gianlorenzo Bernini (1598–1680) is the major figure of Italian baroque sculpture and architecture. Although Borromini at one point worked for Bernini, they were fierce rivals. Bernini was a sculptor before he turned to architecture. Bernini's sculpture *Apollo and Daphne* catches the mythological figures not in studied reflection, but caught up in the most emotional moment of the narrative from Ovid's *Metamorphoses* (Figure 10.2). Apollo is in hot pursuit of Daphne. The story is dramatic and involves one figure running, another fleeing. It is a trenchant moment filled with action and emotion. It portrays unbridled violence. She resists his attempts by turning into a tree. In addition, the sculpture is asymmetrical with no obvious front elevation. It encourages its viewers to walk around it. Bernini began as a sculptor, and many see in his architectural designs the mind of a sculptor at work.

Michelangelo's *David* also takes as its subject a narrative that involves two adversaries; yet Michelangelo's *David* barely hints at the most dramatic part of the story: David's slaying of Goliath. Emotion, in the Bernini sculpture, is explicit. Looking at baroque artworks helps explain that when people discuss interiors and

Figure 10.2
Gian Lorenzo Bernini, *Apollo and Daphne*, 1622–1625. Engraving 1884.

furnishings, they rely upon the same vocabulary, judging the works to be emotional, jubilant, or seductive.

In Bernini's time, the public space in front of Saint Peter's Basilica in Rome was a sorry lot. The Vatican Palace, to the north, was an asymmetrical mess on its exterior. To the south and east stood a smattering of irregular, undistinguished buildings, and the basilica itself was in the process of being remodeled. To complete the transformation of the Vatican, the square in front of the basilica begged for attention. The public space needed to hold thousands for special events, such as Easter when the Pope directly addresses the crowd. The new **piazza** needed to be huge, yet not overpower the cathedral.

Bernini's design for the Piazza San Pietro in 1667, the urban space in front of Saint Peter's, derives its perimeter lines from complex geometries and overlapping forms, yet it meshes with the Renaissance church with its classical detailing (Figure 10.3).

Bernini's composition has three parts. As an ensemble, it acted as a giant vestibule to the church, an outdoor room to prepare visitors for the act of visiting the church that housed the relics and tomb of Saint Peter. Most visitors, including pilgrims, approached Saint Peter's from the bridge over the Tiber River. The first element was a simple urban space, a forecourt (unbuilt in

Bernini's time and not realized until Mussolini's urban intervention in the twentieth century).

Then visitors reached the centerpiece of the design, the huge oval space wider than the church itself. The colonnades that form the perimeter of the oval piazza have columns that are slightly smaller than those of the giant order of Carlo Maderno's façade. There are four rows of unfluted, massive Tuscan columns. The piazza is self-contained in a way.

These outstretched arms express not the distress of Christ on the cross but the embrace of a motherly church. Completed with an Egyptian **obelisk** placed by Fontana, the piazza gave ordinary people an extraordinary experience.

A feature of many baroque artworks, paintings, buildings, and sculptures is that the works are not meant to be viewed from a single vantage point. Although there appears to be the single focal point of the obelisk, it is not the center of a circle but the focus of a shape derived from overlapping circles. The giant colonnade is resolutely classical in its details, baroque in its forms.

Finally, immediately in front of the church, low wings enclose a trapezoidal space. Eventual movement toward the church, up a broad flight of stairs, reinforces the baroque love of movement, and the dome disappears from view. Before entering the church, visitors have navigated their way through the piazza, moving laterally and vertically.

Figure 10.3
Gian Lorenzo Bernini, Piazza San Pietro, Rome, Italy, 1667.

Architectural historian Spiro Kostof (1995) writes: "Bernini absorbs us into a palpable world of devotion, ravishes our senses, persuades us through visual testimony instead of rational argument or abstracted passion. Architecture, painting, sculpture—all the arts and every device of theatrical illusion work together to sweep us into a realm of unashamed emotionalism" (p. 509). This is nowhere more true than with the Baldacchino, a Bernini design that highlights the altar of Saint Peter's (Figure 10.4).

Michelangelo and Bramante had been given the task of fashioning for Christianity a basilica in Western Europe that rivaled the Pantheon. Bernini created the public space in front and refashioned parts of the interior. Bernini is unquestionably to the baroque what Michelangelo was to the Renaissance.

Figure 10.4
Gian Lorenzo Bernini, *Baldacchino*, Saint Peter's, Rome, Italy, 1623–1634.

Residential interiors

Architectural historian Patricia Waddy writes that visitors to residential Italian interiors experienced continual movement, an experience that contrasted to the act of viewing a somber exterior. The architectural part of an interior ensemble acted as a stable framework—for people, furnishings, and therefore a variety of uses. Waddy writes:

The organization of the whole palace involves relationships of various sorts among the parts. There may be some underlying organizing armature, or each connection may be seen as an isolated incident. Axes of organization may or may not be the same as axes of vision or movement. Symmetry may be present with respect to a wall (a picture-like field) or with respect to a spatial axis. The three-dimensional organization of a palace may involve vertically continuous walls or other supports, or it may involve transformations from level to level. Interior order and exterior order may or may not coincide.

(1990, p. 68)

Examples of palaces that exhibit these features include the Palazzo Barberini and the Palazzo Borghese. Italian interior design features influenced building across Europe.

Central and Northern Europe

Baroque churches became a dominant feature in many towns, large and small, in Germany, Austria, and Switzerland.

Churches

In Germany, Dominikus Zimmermann designed a pilgrimage church, known as Die Wies, in Steingaden. The ceiling is painted to go away, as though the building opens to the sky. This introduces a new element into the art of interior decoration; Renaissance artists, under the right circumstances, also appreciated a good trick— false perspectives and the like. A standard part of the baroque architectural vocabulary is to paint elements to deliberately give a false impression. Thus, a painted ceiling pretends to be a window, or the sky itself. The ceiling at Die Wies is a rich composition of color, detail, and form.

German churches relate to Italian baroque churches because they rely on complex geometries, rich decorative schemes, and illusionistic painting to achieve effects. As a designed interior, there is an overall continuity; some wall elements flow seamlessly onto the ceiling. Details are part of a dynamically designed whole.

The spread of baroque design into central and northern Europe confirms that Gothic had lost its hold, and the supremacy of classical detailing reigned. In Vienna, Johann Bernhard Fischer von Erlach (1656–1723) was the designer of the Karlskirche, a major baroque monument. It encourages its visitors to look up at the dome, where a variety of figures and objects, freed from the weight of gravity, float around haphazardly. It is a painting with an illusionistic view upward into the skies and heaven. The plan is an oval. The overhanging cornice forms a distinctive break from the wall's surface.

The decoration of the walls is with restrained, gilded Corinthian pilasters, which, in addition to the streaming sunlight, draw attention to the visual complexity of the dome.

The association of baroque design with curves is correct. Yet there are also resolutely rectilinear examples of baroque architecture particularly outside of Italy, one of them being Fischer von Erlach's Schönbrunn Palace in Vienna. In such structures, one finds the essence of baroque design, the emotion, the restlessness, the movement, and the depth expressed in rectilinear projects. The palace itself is no flat block, but a figural object that recedes and progresses into space.

Gardens

Garden design was important in the baroque period. Landscape designers further developed an approach to landscape that started in the Renaissance and that used nature as a raw material. Baroque garden design also explored many of the design principles that Bernini developed for his urban design for the Vatican. The gardens of Schönbrunn extend off into the distance. They are an important presence and an integral part of the palace design. They appear to cut through a natural-looking forest, setting up a relationship between designed nature and natural nature. Just as many baroque objects are considered to proceed forward into space, baroque gardens aggressively march off into the distance, if not to infinity itself.

Neumann and Tiepolo

Johann Balthasar Neumann (1687–1753) was a German military engineer who became an accomplished architect with the encouragement of his chief patron, the Prince-Bishop of Würzburg. One of Neumann's largest works is the home of the Bishop, Das Residenz, built in 1735. It is a huge structure with a sober exterior, which gives little indication of the baroque and rococo delights that lie within it. This building and its interiors prove the fact that no precise line divides baroque and rococo art. In some circles, rococo is considered as a final, if delicate, version of baroque. There are many examples of baroque buildings that were refashioned with rococo interiors.

One of the finest baroque ceilings is the collaboration of the German architect Neumann and Italian painter and frescoist Giovanni Battista Tiepolo (1696–1770). They worked together on the stairwell, the Treppenhaus, of Das Residenz (Figure 10.5). Stairways were a natural focus of baroque designers, because their function involved both horizontal and vertical movement. This is the giant ceremonial staircase where guests, having left their carriages, mounted the stairs to reach the upper, principal floor.

Figure 10.5
Giovanni Battista Tiepolo and Johann Balthasar Neumann, Das Residence, Würzburg, Germany, 1720–1744.

Apollo is the central figure of the painted ceiling of the Treppenhaus. In one vignette of the composition, Tiepolo painted those who contributed to the project: the architect Neumann, the stucco decorator Antonio Bossi, Tiepolo himself, his son Giandomenico Tiepolo, and his painting assistant, Franz Ignaz Roth. Tiepolo also grandly included his client, the resident of Das Residenz, Prince-Bishop Karl Philipp von Greiffenklau. Known as the Apotheosis von Greiffenklau, it shows the Prince-Bishop accompanied by the allegorical figure of Fame, who leads him to Apollo (Pedrocco 2002, pp. 137–40).

Guests first climbed a single flight of stairs, then arrived at a landing, from which two more flights rose to meet the second floor. This means that the viewers of the painting were themselves in continual motion, viewing the painting from shifting vantage points.

Tiepolo was the most renowned painter of eighteenth-century Italy. Born in Venice, he was internationally successful, known for his less rigid approach to classicism. He was in Würzburg from 1750 to 1753, working with his sons and assistants.

In the Garden Hall, on the first floor and overlooking the palace's garden, an oval ring of columns stands within the room's perimeter. A gap between the columns and wall adds depth to the space. From them springs the rippled ceiling whose decorative stucco work spills out of the architectural framework. The painted ceiling features a landscape and sky and numerous figures. The ceiling is painted not to be there, with clouds and spectacular rays of light coming from many directions. Nature in this garden hall is beguiling and menacing.

The sun god is the subject of another room, the Kaisersaal, in the complex. There, Apollo is seen conducting Beatrice of Burgundy to the Genius of the German Nation (1751).

Neumann collaborated on the Kaisersaal with Tiepolo. It represents a lighter approach, predictive of the rococo fascination with less significant moments in time. Pink, blue, and gold dominate the color palette, signaling a trend that moves away from the saturated colors of early baroque design. The detail features a central oval frame, formed of both curved and straight elements, but certain figures from the painting defy the framing device and step out of and over the frame. Heavy elements miraculously float in midair, brusquely defying gravity. Certain elements recede back into space, while others spill forward toward the viewer. Neumann's and Tiepolo's works were dynamic and spatially complex, sometimes disturbingly so.

France

In France, the major baroque buildings were not churches but residences. Versailles is a residence of the state, a work of architecture with a charge to express the French national character. French architects worked with baroque fervor, not as an expression of religious sentiment but to express national power.

Louis XIV

One historical figure is particularly related to French baroque, and that is Louis XIV, both for how he lived and the art he patronized. Louis XIV consolidated the development of a French national style as part of a political program. Art and design were called into service of an absolute ruler. French artist Rigaud painted Louis XIV in 1702 (Figure 10.6). This is a portrait of political might: high-heeled shoes, flowing wig, heavy draperies, and gold are all signs of a leader at the height of

Figure 10.6
Hyacinthe Rigaud, *Portrait of Louis XIV*, 1701.

his powers. There is nothing effeminate about this man. The background is not parallel to the picture plane, and Louis addresses his viewers at an oblique direction. This is the portrait of one of Europe's most powerful monarchs, using everything at his control—dress, coiffeur—to make an impression. The drapery is heavy and peels back at several points to reveal ornate possessions. The colors include strong reds, blacks, and oranges.

The Louvre

Before Versailles became the center of the design world, considerable attention was paid to completing the eastern portion of the Louvre. In this project, the competing architectural approaches of Italy and France came head to head. Bernini's Louvre featured the geometry he was known for, a central oval and flanking curved wings, and a colossal order sitting on a tiered base. This project and two subsequent projects Bernini designed were rejected.

Louis XIV and his advisors decided on a restrained classical building, suggesting that the French conception of baroque architectural design depart from the Italian. The project that stands in Paris today is the result of Le Vau, Le Brun, and Claude Perrault. Its baroque features are the depth of its façade and its rhythmic use of paired columns.

French designers were aware of Italian achievements, yet they also furthered a local nationalistic agenda. Louis XIV had a director of building, Jean-Baptiste Colbert, who brought Gianlorenzo Bernini to Paris. French designers were important in establishing the reputation of France for crafting highly developed gardens, buildings, interiors, and furnishings.

Vaux

An early work, a seminal piece of French baroque architecture, was by the architect Louis Le Vau (1612–1670). Vaux-le-Vicomte, a country house or **chateau**, was designed for Louis XIV's finance minister, Nicolas Fouquet. A bulbous central mass protrudes from the building, aggressively asserting itself forward into space. It corresponds to the most important interior room, an oval **salon**. The chateau at Vaux is a forerunner to Versailles, where all the design elements were first experimented with.

As at Schönbrunn, the architecture is an integral part of the garden design. André Le Nôtre (1613–1700) designed Vaux's gardens, which established the guidelines for the French approach to palace garden design. The interiors survive intact and are a good example of interior design of the time of Louis XIV, prior to major construction at Versailles. The same trio of designers who worked at Vaux, Le Vau, Charles Lebrun, and Le Nôtre, worked at Versailles. Le Vau's purposely inconsistent use of the architectural orders in Vaux-le-Vicomte was something that the young Louis XIV admired.

When Louis XIV visited Vaux, he was impressed with its design but wary of its cost. Ensuing investigations led to the imprisonment of Fouquet, and the three designers set to work remodeling the royal residence at Versailles.

Versailles

Louis XIV considered himself the world's most powerful leader, and he sought an architectural backdrop that not only reflected that power but added to it. The siting of the seat of government away from Paris put all under his roof and under his control. Part of his power was the awe that those who visited Versailles felt at the richness of the architecture, the opulent interiors, the expensive furniture, and the clothing of the nobles.

At the core was the old chateau Louis XIII had built in 1624, a brick and stone structure. In the 1660s, Louis XIV had it enlarged by Le Vau, Le Nôtre, and others. In 1677, Louis XIV decided to move the court and the nation's administration to the former hunting lodge that lies some 12 miles (20 kilometers) southwest of Paris. Thirty-six thousand workers labored to create a place that eventually housed 100,000 people.

Versailles' growing opulence reflected the economic and political consolidation of the country. Versailles became the seat of the French government in 1682. It became the model that other European monarchies emulated, and also nobles in the French provinces. Versailles was the center of the design world.

The new palace needed to be furnished, so Louis XIV was also instrumental in promoting several manufacturing enterprises. He started a furniture manufactory, the Gobelins, to create furniture and tapestries for the royal palaces. Over the seventeenth century, the quantity of furniture found in a palace greatly increased.

Gardens

As at Vaux, André Le Nôtre was responsible for the garden design. Le Nôtre's signature move was to create a work of environmental greatness that included earthworks, pools and fountains, topiary, clipped hedges, and geometric flower beds. The axial relations of the garden and the building were one, an integrated whole that relied heavily on symmetry. The gardens impressed European nobles and every royal family did what they could to imitate them. Le Nôtre regularly used an open-ended perspective, which symbolized Louis XIV's ambitions for France. The iconography of the garden sculpture brazenly connected Louis XIV to Apollo the Sun God.

Baroque gardens represent a particular treatment of nature, where nature is an architectural material that can be used, cut up, or reconfigured to provide dramatic effects. Part of this effect were pools, canals, and extensive waterworks. The extent to which nature is tamed, and forced into submission by art, reflected French mastery over the elements and scientific achievements. The French attitude to nature, as espoused by landscape designers such as Le Nôtre, was antithetical to the English tradition. French baroque gardens continued trends that originated in the Italian Renaissance, yet on an unimagined scale. It is fair to describe the French baroque garden as an Italian Renaissance garden on steroids.

In the wake of Versailles, the designers of palaces around the world sought to emulate it, including the Nymphenburg in Munich, the Zwinger in Dresden, and Peter the Great's palaces in Saint Petersburg. L'Enfant's urban plan for Washington, DC, is formally related to Le Nôtre's garden designs.

Versailles was the most significant, and certainly the largest, if not the most artistically innovative project of baroque France. Louis Le Vau worked with the existing chateau that had already been enlarged. Le Vau refashioned its garden façade with a new structure that from the perspective of a visitor in the garden completely enveloped the original building and its entry court. Three blocks form the basis of Le Vau's design. The center block was set back with a terrace. The rhythm of "solid-recession-solid" invites nature into the building and subtly projects the building into nature.

The palace

Le Vau's work at Versailles had an Italianate flat roof with a balustrade instead of a steeped French roof (Figure 10.7). Le Vau's façades did not rely upon curves for their effect, but there was a real depth to them. The porticoes protruded and the window wells receded. The profusion of ornament around the windows was deeply carved and

Veuë du Chasteau de Versaille du côté du Parterre d'Eau

Fait par Perelle.

A Paris Chez N. Langlois, ruë s.^t Iacques a la Victoire. Avec Privilege du Roy.

Figure 10.7
André Le Nôtre, Louis Le Vau, and Jules Hardouin-Mansart, garden and palace, Versailles, France, 1662–1709. Engraving by Adam Perelle.

figural, the opposite of the flat early Renaissance surfaces. The statuary on the rooftop continue the lines of pilasters. Le Vau's first major project for Versailles consisted of simple cubical forms that were beautifully detailed. Its delicate composition did not last long.

After Le Vau's death, his position as principal architect at Versailles was taken by Jules Hardouin Mansart (1619–1690). Mansart's refashioning resulted in a dazzling interior space that marks the beginning of a rococo sensibility, yet some consider that his additions robbed the complex of the refinement it had reached under Le Vau's watch, particularly concerning the building's massing and its formal relationship to the garden.

Mansart tripled the length of the garden façade. He filled in the recessed central block and made it flush with the flanking blocks to build the centerpiece of his remodeling, the Galerie des Glaces. New wings to the north and south of Le Vau's building created a huge structure whose overall façade extended some 600 yards (550 meters).

Interiors

The consideration of Mansart's work at Versailles is more favorable from the perspective of its interiors and furnishings. Le Vau, Mansart, and Le Brun, a painter and architect who supervised many of the decorations, were responsible for a remarkable set of rooms that functioned as a central part of the French state apparatus. Their work included new apartments for the king and queen, a grand staircase, a suite of seven public rooms named after the planets, and the centerpiece, the Galerie des Glaces or Hall of Mirrors.

The apartments for the king and queen used stucco, gilding, and paint to create illusionistic scenes on the walls and ceilings. Marble covered the floors, and velvet served as wallcovering and upholstery. Le Brun and Le Vau collaborated on the Stairway of the Ambassadors, a deft composition that created illusionistic architecture by combining marble panels and paint. This vertical circulation element made a startling first impression on foreign dignitaries to the court.

The next step of the spatial and sensual experience of visiting Versailles included a suite of seven public rooms that similarly combined painted architecture, marble floors, and opulent furnishings.

The staircase and the salons were preparation for the culmination of a visit to Versailles: a long gallery overlooking the gardens, the Galerie des Glaces. Mansart filled in Le Vau's terrace to construct this gallery and two adjacent salons. Designwise it was conventional, yet it was built with an unprecedented scale and level of opulence.

It is a long gallery crowned with a barrel vault. Arched windows overlook the manicured gardens and are literally reflected by a wall of similarly arched mirrors framed with the same architectural details. Candelabra, freestanding and ceiling-hung, illuminated gilded capitals, illusionistic ceiling paintings, and a complete suite of silver furniture. The room is a negotiation between the use of a classical vocabulary and the desire for baroque dramatic effects. The space was further enlivened by its occupants, exquisitely dressed, powdered, bejeweled, perfumed, and coifed men and women.

Mirrors were costly. Poor families could not afford them, and wealthier families publicly announced their status with a single hallway mirror. To construct an entire room that used mirrors freely, as an unlimited architectural material, and then to fill that room with silver furniture, was an expression of wealth meant to impress and intimidate.

Under Louis XIV and the artists he employed, the arts were central to his political strategy. They were a means to centralize authority and create unity. They expressed the king's and the state's power to both domestic and European audiences. Louis XIV's involvement with art, architecture, and design is likely the most extensive control that a state has ever wielded over the arts. Legions of artists, gardeners, and craftsmen were all marshaled into serving the glory of France. British art historian Anthony Blunt felt that at Versailles, sometimes the parts are more impressive than the whole. He singled out the interiors and furnishings by Le Vau, Le Brun, and Mansart for praise.

"But if the principles are not original, the application of them is so brilliant as to produce quite new results. The scale, the richness of the materials, the delicacy of the detail, the ingenious relation of the three rooms to each other, all make of this suite something far more impressive than any earlier work" (Blunt 1999, p. 229). French baroque design did not follow in form the complex geometries of Bernini and Borromini.

In 1665, Bernini returned to Italy. The only project he completed in France was a bust of Louis XIV. Louis XIV and his artists gave the baroque style a secular twist, an aspect where it departed from the Italian baroque tradition. Most of the great French commissions were related to building and furnishing royal palaces. The result was that Versailles dominated France and France dominated Europe.

Furniture

The development of French baroque furniture had started when Henry IV (1553–1610), the first Bourbon king, set up furniture workshops in the Louvre. In furniture design, there was a shift from functional to decorative pieces. While seat furniture followed the models of the previous period, the multiplicity of furniture types expanded even further in subsequent periods. Furniture of the late sixteenth century increasingly complemented the interiors.

Under the administration of Louis XIV and Colbert, the Parisian furniture industry was organized into a system with three components: royal workshops, the guilds, and the neighborhood— the Faubourg Saint-Antoine. Colbert founded the Gobelins factory in 1667 under the direction of Charles Le Brun. Its charge was to provide furnishings, paintings, and tapestries for royal households. As a royal workshop, its furniture makers had apprentices and employed foreigners. The **Savonnerie** was the French carpet factory that became a royal workshop, also under Le Brun's leadership. The royal workshops of the Louvre produced various types of artworks and furnishings destined for royal palaces.

The guilds, predecessors to professional organizations and unions, were not allowed to hire foreigners. Auslander describes their operation as between free-trade and regulated manufacturing (Auslander 1996, p. 95).

The Faubourg Saint-Antoine is where most Parisian furniture makers set up shop who were not affiliated with royal workshops or the guild. They were not part of the apprentice system. The results of their efforts ranged from pedestrian to good.

A topic that concerns historians of design is the matter of style. Why do things look the way they do, and why do those parameters change over time? Looking at baroque furniture raises the issue of the evolution of styles. Considering first Renaissance furniture, then baroque, then later Regency, rococo, and neoclassical, each style appears to engender the next in an evolutionary way, and the reference to nature is explicit. Sherrill Whiton, one of the early historians of interior design and furniture, was emphasizing

precisely this point with a diagram that compares baroque, Regency, and rococo chair legs (Figure 10.8). The diagram treats the evolution of furniture scientifically: each succeeding leg became increasingly curved and light.

One of the finest books written on furniture takes as its subject the development of French furniture prior to the twentieth century. Its author, art historian, and one-time furniture maker Leora Auslander, is as adept at presenting a myriad of hard facts as she is with delivering nuanced interpretations. This chapter and the next rely heavily upon her efforts.

Women had a limited but significant role in the furniture industry. They did not typically work in the wood trades but did find employment as sanders, varnishers, and gilders. The art of upholstery, because it centered on textiles, was open to women.

The tasks that women were allowed to practice were not particularly creative but demanded a meticulous attention to detail (Auslander 1996, p. 131). Auslander mentions several instances in which a woman inherited a workshop from her husband. Sometimes she ran the shop after her husband's death. It was not uncommon for these masters' widows to marry journeymen furniture makers.

The **baroque armchair** is consistent with the aesthetics of other areas of baroque art, such as sculpture and architecture (Figure 10.9). The baroque armchair owes its overall form to the Renaissance sedia. The nature of the visual relationship between the two is that almost every element of the chair in the baroque version became more complicated in form, position, and decoration. The back, still straight across the top, is no longer upright but leans backward. The arms curve in both their vertical and horizontal expressions. The legs, contiguous with the arms, are straight yet richly carved and decorated. The stretchers are no longer straight rails, but form an

Figure 10.8
Typical French baroque, Regency, and rococo chair legs.

X- or I-shape, with pieces that have been turned, curved, and decorated. The amount of upholstery increased. In comparison to the Renaissance sedia, the chair is dynamic. It has the presence of a work of baroque sculpture; it leans back and protrudes forward into a room. Though solidly square and massive, it appears as if it could move.

A **Regency armchair**, in comparison to the standard baroque one, is decidedly lighter (Figure 10.10). Regency is the transitional style between baroque and rococo. The curves of the Regency chair are pronounced, and the elements are delicate, with smaller profiles. The back itself is curved and slightly tilts back. The legs have a pronounced curve to them. The X-shaped cross-stretcher is delicate and lightweight. Regency, also discussed in the next chapter, refers to the time when Louis XIV's successor, Louis XV, was too young to reign, so a regent led the country.

A baroque side chair has no arms, a curved back, severely raked rear legs, and straight although turned front legs, with the characteristic cross-stretcher. Generally speaking, sofas and chairs are lower to the ground than they were in the Renaissance. The back takes the form of a **bouchon**.

The Louis XIV **canapé**, a variety of sofa, has curved arms, and decorative carving frames the top and sides. The furniture associated with the Sun King, Louis XIV, inaugurates a system in France in which important pieces of furniture are labeled according to the reigning monarch. The most important styles of eighteenth-century France are, therefore, Louis XIV, Louis XV, and Louis XVI. A canapé is a descendant of the Roman couch or bed, to the extent that its user could recline while in the company of others. It is equally likely that the French sofa was a laterally expanded version of an armchair; they were decorated with all the design elements of chairs.

A gilded footstool was a handy piece of furniture. They typically had legs that were elaborately carved, while the stretchers twist and turn. Such pieces served as footstools, and also as seats, without armrests to encumber a voluminous gown.

The baroque **console** *c.* 1680 shown in Figure 10.11 is a furniture piece that stood in an entry hall, accompanied by a mirror and wall-mounted candlesticks. Separate pieces, and additional accessories, became an **ensemble**. Consoles were marble- or wood-topped side tables. The mirror, like the ceiling, opened up and visually (not literally) broke through the architectural framework. This was an example of designers integrating pieces of furniture and interiors in a way not done

Figure 10.9
Baroque armchair, 17th century.

Figure 10.10
Regency armchair, France, 1675–1700. Carved and gilded beech with wool and silk **Aubusson** upholstery.

previously. Pieces of furniture were no longer placed in isolation around a room.

The specialization of those involved in carpentry that started in the Renaissance continued.

Figure 10.11
Baroque console with ball feet and stretcher, 17th century.

The main distinction remained between those who worked on the carpentry of buildings and those who did furniture (Auslander 1996, pp. 77–85). Sawyers prepared lumber in the mill. Turners specialized in lathe work, producing legs, columns, and banisters. Sculptors specialized in carved panels, legs, and arms. *Menuisiers en bâtiment* did built-in cabinetry, staircases, doors, and moldings. They also created the chassis on which furniture makers crafted furniture. Carpenters who specialized in furniture created weight-bearing structures, including chairs, stools, and sofas.

Before the late seventeenth century, most of the wood carpenters used to make furniture was European. In the early eighteenth century, woods from Africa, the East and West Indies, and the Americas, were increasingly popular.

At the pinnacle of the hierarchical system of furniture makers was the **ébéniste**. This talented furniture maker did the finest work, and focused on pieces with large surfaces (desks and tables) and larger space-containing items (wardrobes). The name of the profession indicates that they were initially associated with veneers, such as ebony, but they were masters of all sorts of marquetry. They did not make chairs; they were designers, and much of their work involved coordinating the labor of others. These allied professionals included metal workers. Bronze hardware and mounts became increasingly visible parts of furniture designs. Bronzes had to be cast, chiseled, filed, and polished. After being attached by the ébeniste, the mounts were gilded by a gilder. Marble similarly had to be cut, polished, and mounted. In addition to upholstering chairs and sofas, upholsterers provided draperies, bed cloths, and wall fabrics.

Veneered furniture

Queen Marie de Médicis introduced the taste for ebony furniture. In France, the material lent its name to an exalted class of carpenters. The most prominent of the ébénistes was André-Charles Boulle (1642–1732). His workshop created a wide variety of pieces but was known for its elaborate **armoires** (Figure 10.12). Boulle was the most celebrated of Louis XIV's furniture makers. He worked for other members of the French royal family, other nobles, and Philip V of Spain. Boulle, his workshop, and his followers and imitators took polychrome wood **marquetry** to new levels. In addition to his celebrated furniture pieces, he did marquetry and **parquetry** floors, wainscoting, and paneling. Boulle and his assistants became as knowledgeable about metal as wood. His ormolu mounts, larger than most, were integrated elements of his designs. Ebony, pewter, brass, tortoiseshell, copper, mother-of-pearl, and colored foils were some of his favored materials. The subjects of his marquetry stemmed from classical mythology, but he also created popular scenes with secular references, such as *singerie.*

In crafting his furniture designs, he worked with inherited forms, but with his opulent decoration, he took those recognizable forms to a higher

Figure 10.12
André-Charles Boulle, Cabinet, Paris, France, 1700. Oak, Macassar ebony and Gabon ebony, fruitwood, burlwood, tortoiseshell, brass and ormulu.

level. His work is credited with popularizing three furniture types: the console, the bureau plat, and the bas d'armoire. Over the decades of his workshop's prominence, his pieces became lighter, more sculptural, and therefore more dynamic. His incorporation of the cabriole leg took his designs from the baroque period into regency. Spanning two centuries, Boulle's workshop was active for eighty years, first with Boulle, later with his sons, the most prominent of whom was Charles-Joseph Boulle (1688–1754). Boulle's influence is mostly seen in three stylistic periods—baroque, regency, and rococo—yet some neoclassical pieces were inspired by his methods. He is known for a body of work that is internally consistent. The term "**Boulle work**" came to indicate works in the style of Boulle and those done by his many imitators.

Boulle relied heavily on the use of **ormolu**, gilded bronze ornaments that were attached to furniture pieces. The process of gilding bronze involved heating mercury, which produced poisonous fumes detrimenta to the health of those working with it. The production of furniture for the wealthy involved the death of those making it; it was therefore emblematic of a style that catered to the needs of the rich at the expense of the lives of those who produced them.

Foreign influences on European furniture design increased over the course of the seventeenth century. From India came the habit of caning furniture. Travelers to China and Japan noticed with interest superior skill in lacquering. Lacquering in Europe was frequently referred to as **japanning**. John Stalker and George Parker wrote and published a book in 1688 titled *A Treatise of Japanning and Varnishing*. The topic of exoticism and Chinoiserie is covered in Chapter 11.

Pondering the existence of simple pieces of furniture within grand houses, Edward Lucie-Smith writes:

These small pieces represent an element of informality that had infiltrated what was still a very formal structure of living. Often they must have disrupted the grandiose decorative schemes of which the larger pieces of furniture in the same rooms formed an important part. One has a rather touching vision of people camping out amid their socially necessary but comfortable splendours, making themselves at home as best they could.

(1979, p. 87)

Furniture histories usually focus on more accomplished pieces, but the greatest number of pieces were ordinary, utilitarian furniture. Much of this is virtually dateless and without obvious national characteristics.

Certain pieces of furniture, because of their essential practicality and usefulness, began during this period to achieve definitive forms which they were to retain for many years. Skilled but unsophisticated country craftsmen, usually joiners rather than cabinetmakers, repeated the same designs again and again, without changing them much, because they had been found to be the best for a particular purpose. A good deal of furniture thus escaped from the influence of fashion and, however unconsciously, responded only to the principle of fitness for use.

(Lucie-Smith 1979, p. 91)

Because the industry was dependent on royal patronage and reputation, there was little advertising, although selling was important. **Marchands merciérs** were sellers, not producers, of furniture. They sold ready-made pieces, not at fixed prices, and sold on credit (Auslander 1996, p. 100). They increasingly functioned as taste masters, and in this capacity they served as early decorators. In addition to furniture, they sold clocks, mirrors, artworks, and porcelain. One of the most famous was Edmé-François Gersaint. The painter Antoine Watteau created a sign for him that became one of the most important works of eighteenth-century French painting.

The number of pieces of small furniture—such as tables, stands, stools—that were deployed in a room increased. The baroque style gradually lost some of its essential characteristics in the aftermath of Louis XIV. The subsequent Regency and Louis XVI styles, in the first half of the eighteenth century, took design in a different direction. During this period, there was a decline in royal patronage and an increase in private residential work. This shift worked in favor of the marchands merciérs and the unallied furniture makers of the Faubourg Saint-Antoine.

Conclusion

Baroque art, architecture, and design are related to the Renaissance, which, appropriately enough, also began in Italy. Yet Austria, Germany, France, and England themselves became major centers of baroque design. Like Renaissance design, baroque design was inspired by antiquity, but this was true of details more than overall forms. Baroque architects favored centrally planned churches and classical façades, but in new configurations.

Baroque forms arose from mathematically complicated geometries that involved overlapping shapes and multiple focal points. Forms, like color palettes and compositional strategies, were neither pure nor distinct. In discussing baroque artworks, most historians emphasize movement and emotion. The success at indicating movement is all the more significant in that buildings, paintings, sculptures, interiors, and furnishings rarely literally move. Yet one cannot describe baroque art without verbs. The works bend, break, melt, flow, retreat, advance, ravish—and above all, they twist, turn, and curve.

Bernini was the major baroque figure in Italy. The major figure in France was not himself a designer but the patron who marshaled their efforts, Louis XIV. He was responsible for rich decorative schemes and a national building program as ambitious as the world has ever seen. The works associated with Louis XIV, including interiors and furnishings, fostered the connection between design and national pride, wealth, and power.

Common baroque features included illusionistic painting, ceilings painted to open to the sky, and a focus on stairways, domes, and deep façades. Mirrors and veneered furniture were popular for their dazzling effects. From gardens to candlesticks, baroque designs were complex, plastic, and asymmetric. While clearly designed, the underlying order of a baroque artwork is not easily discernible. The baroque designed object was visually active, a remarkable feat because the activity was done by the viewer yet prompted by an incredibly complex object.

Sources

Auslander, Leora (1996). *Taste and Power: Furnishing Modern France*. Berkeley: University of California Press.

Ballon, Hilary (1999). *Louis Le Vau, Mazarin's College, Colbert's Revenge*. Princeton, NJ: Princeton University Press.

Blunt, Anthony (1999). *Art and Architecture in France, 1500–1700*. New Haven, CT: Yale University Press.

Gerbino, Anthony (2002). "The Library of François Blondel, 1618–1686." *Architectural History* 45: 289–324.

Kostof, Spiro (1995). *A History of Architecture: Settings and Rituals*. Oxford: Oxford University Press.

Lucie-Smith, Edward (1979). *Furniture: A Concise History*. London: Thames and Hudson.

Pedrocco, Filippo (2002). *Tiepolo: The Complete Paintings*. New York: Rizzoli.

Picon, Guillaume (2021). *Vaux-le-Vicomte: a Private Invitation*. Paris: Flammarion.

Waddy, Patricia (1990). *Seventeenth-Century Roman Palaces: Use and Art of the Plan*. Cambridge, MA: MIT Press.

Zanlungo, Claudia (2012). *The Story of Baroque Architecture*. New York: Prestel.

Discussion and Review Questions

1. Put a Renaissance artwork next to a baroque artwork—two portraits, two sculptures, two ceilings, or two armchairs. What are the significant differences between them?

2. What are the primary characteristics of a baroque artwork?

3. People generally describe baroque art as emotional. How do static objects create emotion? Give some examples.

4. A significant feature of baroque art is its dynamism; pieces seem to be moving. How do static objects simulate motion?

5. A development of the late twentieth century is the idea that gender is constructed and not innate—that is, different societies developed their own concepts about gender. How did seventeenth-century France define masculinity?

6. What was the baroque attitude toward nature, as evidenced by the gardens of Versailles?

7. List some of the materials used in the construction of Boulle works.

8. Do you think it is inevitable that an artistic period of simplicity is followed by one of complexity?

9. How do Regency pieces of furniture differ from baroque pieces?

10. What role did mirrors play in interiors?

Rococo

1643–1700	1700–1730	1730–1760	1760–1789
Baroque	Regency	Rococo	Neoclassical

The Enlightenment is a magnificent chapter in history in which the forces of many disciplines come together. The emphasis of the name of this intellectual movement, in three languages—Enlightenment, siècle des Lumières, Aufklarung—was on light. This seems right, as those active in science, philosophy, politics, and the arts focused on changing the status quo. The Enlightenment was the force that shined light on its subjects and saw them in a new way. After the Renaissance, many feel that it was the defining moment in the creation of a modern emancipated public, based on reason and thought, an alternative to monarchy and theocracy. With the assistance of Enlightenment thinkers, Europe recrafted democracy, promoted equality, promised individual liberty, and endeavored to build a secular state and moral code. The reliance on reason was central.

Enlightenment polemicists were idealists, and reality often failed to live up to promises. Just a few points: it was unquestionably Eurocentric, and some see it as an apology for colonialism. Equality was an ideal that excluded many, including women and nonwhites.

There was no direct artistic equivalent of the Enlightenment, and yet the artworks of the period were inevitably caught up in the desire to craft a new world. Artistic production of the eighteenth century was characterized by rapid stylistic change. Four distinguishable styles presented in succession: baroque, **Regency**, rococo, and neoclassical. This represents a modern trend of the speeding up of stylistic change.

Figure 11.0
(*Facing page*)
François de Cuvilliés, Amalienburg Palace Hunting Lodge, Munich, Germany, 1734–1739.

Rococo is the primary stylistic legacy of the mid-eighteenth century. It is inextricably associated with France, yet the artistic force was strongly felt in Austria, England, Germany, Italy, and elsewhere. It occurred during the reign of Louis XV and the early years of Louis XVI's reign. The style was most prevalent in the decorative arts, painting, sculpture, interiors, and fashion. Its formal qualities were often undetectable in architectural exteriors. Considered an elite art, its subject matter and visual impression was not ponderous but light.

This book has presented some marvelous pieces of furniture. Yet it has been constantly necessary to qualify that, for example, while the Renaissance saw great achievements in art and architecture, strides in interiors and furnishings were of a lesser degree. With the eighteenth century the importance of designed objects ascends. For the first time in this book, there is a period, the rococo, whose greatest achievements were in interiors and furnishings. According to many connoisseurs, eighteenth-century English and French furniture are among the finest objects ever crafted.

The word *rocaille*, in use in France in the eighteenth century, literally referred to "rock work." Its use to describe a range of artistic productions is a twentieth-century invention. Rococo is another example of a word now used to refer to a body of work, including a number of important furniture pieces, that was not used in that sense in its own time. When French citizens in the eighteenth century said "*rocaille*," they meant it as an insult.

From Baroque to Rococo: Regency

When Louis XIV died in 1715, the baroque died with him. Louis XV was a young boy and would not begin his reign until 1723. The period in which the country was ruled by a regent is known as Regency or régence (not to be confused with English regency). It was a transitional style between baroque and rococo. It is often difficult to distinguish the differences between rococo and French regency pieces if seen out of context, although when they are placed side by side, the differences are evident. Generally speaking, rococo curves are more pronounced, and the profiles are lighter than they were in regency pieces. Once he arrived on the throne, Louis XV reigned from 1723 to 1774.

Cressent

Charles Cressent (1685–1768) was one of the most successful and prolific French furniture designers. He is one of the relatively few cabinetmakers whose name is known. He started working during the reign of Louis XIV and became a leading cabinetmaker in the Regency period. Cressent specialized in fine marquetry work. Marquetry work involves creating scenes using pieces of veneer. Geometric marquetry is called parquetry. London born but French trained, Pierre Langlois was one of Cressent's contemporaries who did his part to bring rococo aesthetics to the English side of the English Channel (Figure 11.1).

Boulle and Boulle work

André-Charles Boulle (1642–1732) was Louis XIV's favorite cabinetmaker. His work moves into the regency and rococo periods. He made armoires, large-door cabinets that served the function of a closet, **commode**, and desk. Because he did not do seating, Boulle work pieces typically were lined up against a wall. An ébéniste, he worked with veneers and incorporated ivory, shell, brass, pewter, and silver. The tops were marble. The surfaces were painted, stained, sanded,

Figure 11.1
Pierre Langlois,
Commode,
Croome Court,
Worcestershire,
England, 1764.
Pine, oak,
satinwood,
kingwood,
mahogany, and
ormolu.

lacquered, varnished, and gilded. Boulle work was continued by his four sons and imitated by others. Although initially the term "Boulle work" indicated pieces by Boulle or his workshop, it came to denote objects that resembled his. Extraordinarily expensive, in twenty-first-century monetary terms, they would cost in the hundreds of thousands of dollars. Boulle work pieces are found in the baroque, rococo, and neoclassical eras. A two-drawer commode was made for Louis XIV in 1708 (Figure 11.2).

Ormolu mounts were decorative devices that protected the edges of veneered furniture. Veneered furniture is most likely to chip at its fragile edges, so Cressent and Boulle relied heavily on the use of ormolu mounts. As the process of gilding bronze endangered the workers engaged in the process, it is thus a detail of furniture in which workers produced objects for the very rich and paid with their lives. It is worthwhile to remember that regency and rococo design were associated with the rich, and that this is the century that was marching headlong toward the French Revolution. As early as 1750, there were protests against the extravagance of the rococo, and calls for artistic reform existed side by side with calls for political reform.

Rococo

Rococo is often used as a shortcut to describe the works of the *ancien régime*. The phrase refers to prerevolutionary France and its political system of absolute monarchy. Design criticism of the period initiated a trend that haunts the consideration of interiors and furnishings to the present day: that works that are decorative are decadent, frivolous, vapid, and less important than other types of art.

Figure 11.2
Rococo commode, France, eighteenth century. Original in Boulle work.

Historical background

Art historian Matthew Craske prioritizes the economic and social causes of stylistic change over the course of the eighteenth century. Unprecedented economic growth and the effects of urbanization contributed to the prevalence of rococo art. He writes: "A perplexing cocktail of positive and negative attitudes to urban growth arose concurrently not only in society at large but also in the minds of individuals" (Craske 1997, p. 12). The discussion of styles as discrete entities relates to the birth of a consumer culture. New means to advertise, market, and merchandise works arose. Also significant was the arrival of the public art museum; the first rooms of the Louvre Museum opened in 1793. Materials were available that had previously been rare or nonexistent, including tulip wood, zebra wood, and ebony.

Emphasizing effect over process

Art historian Marian Hobson articulated a way of considering the French arts, seeing in them a unity that extends from costume to theater to painting. Her point is that rococo artists, in many fields, had a similar approach to illusion, with the result being an emphasis on effect (Hobson 1982). Her concept is best grasped by first considering a painting. For example, an artist is in a room, brush and palette in hand. In front stands a canvas on an easel, on which he or she will paint. Posing in front is the subject, the live person. In summary, this idealized setup presents artist, artwork, and live person.

One way of broadly considering Western art, admittedly a simplification, is that artists sought to mimic optical process; when Italian Renaissance artist Raphael painted a portrait, he endeavored to make the artwork—the image he created on a canvas—resemble as closely as possible the live body (one example being his portrait of Baldassare Castiglione, painted in 1514–1515). A portraitist in eighteenth-century France, according to Hobson's thinking, took a different tack. For example, François Boucher (1703–1770) created his famous portrait of Madame de Pompadour in 1756. Boucher and Jean-Honoré Fragonard (1732–1806) were two of the most technically accomplished rococo artists. The emphasis of Boucher's work was no longer resemblance but the masterful tricks the artist could achieve on the canvas to render it as dazzling as possible. Boucher's apocryphal introduction to the influential court figure Madame de Pompadour resulted in numerous rococo masterpieces (Figure 11.3). In his famous portrait of her, effect on the canvas trumped verisimilitude. The attention to the artwork, over fidelity to the subject, had obvious implications

Figure 11.3
Edouard Gérard, *the Artist François Boucher presented to Mme de Pompadour*, Versailles, France, *c.* 1759. Engraving dates to 1861.

SALON DE 1861. — *Boucher présenté à madame de Pompadour, tableau de M. E. Gérard.*

for theater and opera, where performance was everything. The focus on operatic effect was demonstrated by the popularity of castrated opera singers, **castrati**, in Italy and France. Male sopranos took the leading roles, playing heroic figures. No one thought that Julius Caesar, a popular operatic role, was a soprano, but French audiences preferred having a male soprano, in a powdered wig and resplendently dressed, portray him. The emphasis was on the brilliance of the performance, the sustained high notes, and not the actor's resemblance to the historical figure.

Costume, makeup, and the art of wig-making followed suit. The towering wigs, the powder, the perfume—the goal was not to trick anybody into thinking that these attributes were real. In an introductory essay to an issue about the cultural meanings of hair, the art historian Angela Rosenthal writes: "In Europe, eighteenth-century individuals well-understood the potential of hair—be it powdered, dyed, curled, feathered, piled up to dizzying heights, or set into memorial jewelry—to communicate central cultural concerns" (2004, p. 8). Wigs were an artistic realm where wig-masters displayed their expertise; it was also a realm that explored conceptions of race, ethnicity, nationality, and gender.

Architecture and the French hôtel

Architecture, interiors, and furnishings are not representational arts. A set of interiors does not represent something else, whereas Boucher's portrait of Madame de Pompadour does represent something other than itself, the "real" de Pompadour. The interior arts were, however, consistent with the other arts to the degree that they also exploited the art of illusion and emphasized surface and effect.

Town mansions in Paris are known as *hôtels*; they were not an invention of the seventeenth century, although associated with it. Unlike Italian Renaissance *palazzi*, in which a large architectural block fills out the lot line, the hôtel has a strip of construction on the street, followed by a courtyard, which is in turn followed by the main body of the house. Architectural historian Michael Dennis (1986) sees in this building type the beginning of a suburban mentality. The first band is a screen that separates the house itself from street life. If space is permitting, there is a more private and green garden in the back. The house is an object within a garden and separated from the urban fabric. The courtyard was the *cour d'honneur*.

Considering the relationship of building to garden and the sumptuousness of a building's interiors, Spiro Kostof recognized the importance of this time period: "There is general agreement that something critical happened in the course of the eighteenth century to jar Western architecture loose from its moorings" (1995, p. 547).

Boffrand

Gabriel-Germaine Boffrand (1667–1754) was a pupil of Jules Hardouin Mansart, Louis XIV's chief architect. Boffrand's Hôtel Amelot, 1717, is a rare plan that looks rococo (Figure 11.4). That is because the oval courtyard dominates. The oval shape affects the other parts of the building, causing them to bend and adapt their walls to its curvilinear geometry. Yet the layout of the house remains that of a standard hôtel: The street façade is followed by a zone of service buildings. The body of the house straddles the space between courtyard and the garden.

In 1735, Boffrand designed an oval room that was inserted into the existing Hôtel de Soubise in Paris (Figure 11.5). Boffrand's remodeling of the Hôtel de Soubise is considered one of the earliest and most accomplished rococo interiors. The walls and ceiling were outfitted with white panels and a pale-blue, flattish-domed ceiling. Gilded cupids

Figure 11.4
Germain Boffrand, Hôtel Amelot de Gournay, Paris, France, 1713. Plan.

Figure 11.5
Germain Boffrand,
Hôtel de Soubise,
Paris, France,
1735–1740.

frolic in the room John Pile calls "an astonishing display of Rococo virtuosity" (2004, p. 177). Boffrand created an intimate space with imaginary pictorial realms.

Prior to this project, Boffrand was an unknown architect. Arguably the first work of rococo design, his widely admired rooms were considered modern in their time, as there was no classical detailing. They spawned legions of imitations.

Boffrand's room is oval in plan; its elevations are formed by a series of large rounded arches that alternate with smaller panels, also capped with rounded arches. A system is adhered to: the larger arches contain doors, mirrors, or windows. In classical architectural design, which Boffrand's room approximates in its composition, columns or piers supported the roof, with expanses of wall between them. The circular Temple of Vesta in Rome is the classical building closest in shape to the room at Soubise.

The smaller panels are vestiges of columns or piers, meaning that they would be structural elements, while the larger arches would be the intercolumnar spaces, or walls. Mirrors directly face the windows.

A large mirror can reflect a smaller oval panel. The mirror over the fireplace reflects a window, itself centered within an arched panel. The large panels are at various levels of transparency. They allow for literal entrance and egress, through doors, yet the doors are opaque. Some rounded arches sport windows that allow for visual or imagined egress, yet glass panes restrain a moving body. Some of the arches frame mirrors, which allow for virtual egress: Reflected bodies

look as though they are entering and leaving, yet it is an illusion. In rococo interior layouts, mirrors were often positioned to diagonally reflect mirrors in other rooms, resulting in an infinite blur of expanded space.

The Soubise interior wall elevations suppress the differences between pier and wall. Everything becomes an undulating surface, articulated with the same system of gilded panels and stucco decoration. Doors and piers alike (elements with different functions) receive the same decoration.

If the smaller panels are manipulated piers, the triangular forms above them are either pendentives, the structural elements that distribute a ceiling's weight to the walls, or oversized capitals. Yet in Boffrand's composition, the "structural" elements are painted canvases, the least structural material possible.

Even the use of paint was consistent with the emphasis on effect and illusion, and the disinterest in representing real objects and materials. Wood in a rococo interior was not a natural material whose inherent qualities were highlighted; it was a surface awaiting decoration. The application of white paint to woodwork and plaster alike rendered the materials unimportant.

Cuvilliés

Soubise deemphasizes structure by making piers and alternating panels of nearly equal visual weight. An equally accomplished room in Munich, Germany, takes the approach one step further. French rococo interior design had a strong influence throughout Europe, particularly in Germany and Austria. The existence of French rococo design in the Bavarian capital suggests two competing attitudes. One was the rise of a cosmopolitan culture. The Bavarian nobility wanted to operate on an international scale, and a clear signal of this was to embrace the latest trend in interior design. At the same time that rococo decorating represented an urban, international culture, outside of France it was also considered an example of French affectedness, kowtowing to luxury, and a danger to German artistic traditions.

François Cuvilliés (1695–1768) was a French architect of Flemish origin, active in Bavaria. His first royal post in Munich was as "court dwarf." A little person, his artistic aptitude was quickly recognized, and he was sent back to France to work under the supervision of French architect and designer Jacques-François Blondel (1704–1774). He returned to Germany, where he produced several modest but influential projects.

Credited with having introduced the French hôtel to Munich, he had the good fortune to be working within the parameters of French rococo at the height of its popularity.

His works were at once restrained and ornate. The Amalienburg is a small garden palace on the grounds of the larger Nymphenburg Palace in Munich, built in the years 1734 to 1739. It has a subdued exterior, and the corners of the room are rounded.

Like Soubise, the principal room is circular, has windows that open to the garden, and room upon room organized on axis (Figure 11.0). Stucco work, mirrors, a chandelier, and pieces of rococo furniture, stools and consoles, constitute an ensemble design that is light and airy.

In this application of the latest French style, nothing remotely resembles classical architecture, scarcely hinting at columns or pilasters. The decoration is applied, with no indication of the buildings' structure.

In designing the elevations, Cuvilliés expanded each rounded arch to be as wide as possible. The "structure" is reduced to the narrow vertical elements between them. Tellingly, the vertical lines do not fulfill a structural role. Instead of distributing weight to the floor, they turn into a decorative element: the mirror's frame. The rococo wall, in the designs of Boffrand and Cuvilliés, two of the biggest names in rococo design, became a surface to be lavishly articulated. All surface, it is the opposite of the post-and-lintel structure at Stonehenge. Several infill panels are filled with a decorative grid.

Details from Amalienburg highlight the predominance of asymmetry. Trees, vines, swags, and urns are nestled into a bevy of S- and C-curves. Even the silver grid is canted to respond to swags. A favorite device of rococo designers was the use of a grid. As Barbara Stafford writes, "The inlay, mesh, net, lattice, and grid: all pose the problem of fit" (2007, p. 136). Although custom-made for the project, the use of the grid suggests that it was a material, like wallpaper, that could be used at will and employed to solve the problem of an undecorated space. Allegorical figures are the only allusion to classicism. Some items lean into the distance; others break the frame and advance forward.

Cuvilliés also did the *Reichen Zimmer* (Ornate Rooms) at the Residenz in Munich, another inspired example of integrated decoration. In German rococo works, the designer acted autonomously, and actually had more control than with French commissions, resulting in a complete integration of architecture, furniture, and interior decoration. In his remodeling projects, he gave his German clients what they desired: the new-look *goût nouveau*.

Katie Scott is the author of a book on rococo interiors. She describes the goal of a rococo decorator, as articulated by Blondel, the mentor of Cuvilliés: "Interior decoration should, above all else, create a unified impression, analogous in this to the exterior treatment of the hôtel. Coordinated decorative schemes demonstrated both the architect's and the client's mastery and their control of the dominant cultural paradigm" (Scott 1995, p. 109).

The brothers Johann Michael and Johann Christian Hoppenhaupt crafted similarly integrated designs for rooms for Frederick the Great in Potsdam, outside of Berlin. The desire of German nobles to participate in the latest style was evidence of French supremacy in the decorative arts.

Rococo was an art movement associated with interiors, furnishings, the decorative arts, and graphics. It scarcely made an impact on urban design. This does not mean that no building was done on the urban or architectural scale, simply that those projects do not exhibit characteristics that can be defined as rococo. Many rococo interior designs were fitted into buildings whose exteriors were baroque or something else. Versailles, Schönbrunn in Vienna, and the Residenz in Würzburg are baroque palaces with extensive rococo interiors.

Louis XV furniture

The furniture production that started under Louis XIV continued under Louis XV. The number of Louis XV distinct furniture types was enormous, a departure from the Renaissance. When outfitting a room, patrons and their assistants—designers and merchants—could choose from a large selection of pieces. With a whole range of specific furniture types came a heightened sense of comfort, luxury, and decorum.

Fauteuil

A Louis XV armchair is an extremely elegant piece of furniture, an object in the history of design that perfectly meets its own design criteria (Figure 11.6). The aggressiveness of the baroque chair is gone. In contrast to baroque and regency chairs, the cross-stretchers have been eliminated. A Louis XV chair, also known as **Louis Quinze**, stands lightly on its legs. Yet it seems at rest because of the

Figure 11.6
Nicolas-Quinibert Foliot, Armchair, fauteuil à la reine, Beauvais, France, 1754–1756. Beech, gilding, wool, and silk.

Figure 11.7
Bergère or **marquise** chair, France, eighteenth century.

perfection of its proportions, lines, and silhouette. It is all curves. The back is lifted off the seat, the arms are curved, the legs are curved, and the back is curved. The curves are not segments of perfect circles but the result of a complicated geometry.

In the progression from the Renaissance sedia to this chair, furniture design became consistently lighter and more curvilinear. The **cabriole** leg, the vertical support with a gentle S-curve, was fully developed.

This armchair is known as a **fauteuil**, an armchair with upholstered seat, lifted back, and open padded arms. *Fauteuil* literally means armchair in French, but it commonly refers to Louis XV and Louis XVI chairs. Delicate cresting in the center completes the top rail. A seated person's arms rest on **manchettes**, small upholstered pads. The legs have carved knees that are formed of scrollwork, as are the feet. The back takes the shape of a **cartouche**.

Bergère

A more informal chair was the **bergère** (Figure 11.7). The bergère is a larger, commodious armchair, with enclosed back and arms. *Bergère* literally means farmer's wife, and the naming of the chair relies upon an idealized idea that a farmer's wife, after milking the cows, might rest for a moment in such a chair. Of course, this is nonsense. Chairs of this type were out of the price range of most farmers. A bergère had a separately upholstered seat cushion and a full backrest, and

the upholstery of the arms is continuous with the back. A profusion of curves in the legs, seat, and back hid the effect of its substantial weight-supporting structure.

A pet project of the queen is related to the bergère. Marie Antoinette's architect, Richard Mique, built for her a rustic house on the grounds of Versailles. The Hameau, or hamlet, was built in 1783. Modeled after a farmhouse, it was a retreat for the queen and her attendants, where they could escape from Versailles' spotlight, dress in simple clothes, and enjoy the pleasure of milking cows.

Furniture in mid-century was less likely to be moved about from house to house, a fact evident in the delicate leg profiles. Pieces were made in large numbers, so there are many examples of rooms being furnished with matching furniture, or furniture **en suite**. Art historian Mimi Hellman wrote an article in 1999 that addresses the importance of matching pieces of furniture: "Many of the basic elements of a well-appointed social space—couches and chairs, commodes and tables, tea sets and vases, decorative paintings—were designed as groups of objects that were either identical or closely coordinated in medium, color, style, or figurative motif" (1999, p. 130). The appeal of matched sets was evident when families reupholstered mismatched pieces—using a single textile. Some families combined Louis XV and Louis XVI pieces, blending them together with a monochromatic color scheme.

Performing objects

Furniture was not just a reflection of wealth but also a social player. The elite lived according to an elaborate system of etiquette that accommodated moments of formality and informality, and with pieces of furniture acting as social brokers. The social structure was rigid, but the more rigid the structure, the more intense the appeal of improvisation.

The **confidante** demonstrates how a piece of furniture was a player in social life (Figure 11.8). A large seating unit, it was usually positioned against a wall or in a niche. The confidante encourages sitters to sit close to one another yet be separated. Although they faced in different directions, the possibility existed of whispering to each other. The separating devices maintained decorum, but the sanctioned closeness allowed for a hushed intimacy. This was perfectly in keeping with themes addressed by artists, including Antoine Watteau (1684–1721), whose paintings highlight seemingly innocuous moments of conversation or casual activities like playing cards and blowing bubbles. The popularity of confidantes continued into the subsequent neoclassical period.

In another article by Hellman, she cleverly considers French furniture not as static objects but as agents. The art of leisure, as it related to furniture, looked easy, but, Hellman argues, it was actually difficult and learned. Furniture was at the heart of eighteenth-century French elite culture. They were important artistically and socially and played a pivotal role in the development of a French national identity.

The aesthetics of eighteenth-century French interiors are widely studied. All components of an interior—wall and ceiling treatments, draperies, and furnishings and fittings—were carefully considered. Hellman describes the delineation of interiors and furnishings as a two-part system, one part fixed, the other movable. The fixed part included the architectural envelope, the walls made of paneling or **boiserie**, fireplaces, and some pieces of furniture. For all practical purposes, heavy pieces were not moved, including consoles with marble tops. These pieces constituted the architectural backdrop, the stage set for the "actors," which includes furniture and people interacting with them. The second system involved the lightweight objects, dressing tables, music stands, coffee and chocolate services, and individual seat furniture—all objects that moved about (Hellman 1999, pp. 419–20).

Hellman argues that pieces of furniture acted on the people who used them, rather than the other way around. She writes:

Tables, chairs, and other decorative objects were social actors that both facilitated and, in a sense, monitored the leisure acts of privileged society. Through strategically designed aspects of form and function, furniture appeared to accommodate and flatter its users as they pursued such activities as reading, writing, conversing, eating, dressing, and game playing. Through the same design qualities, however, furniture also structured and delimited the behavior and appearance of individuals according to culturally specific codes of social conduct.

(Hellman 1999, p. 416)

Figure 11.8
After George Hepplewhite, settée or confidante, Brockenhurst Park, Hampshire, England, 1770–1780. Beechwood, gilding and silk moire.

That these obsessively designed interiors were comfortable, Hellman calls "a central mythology" of eighteenth-century French culture (Hellman 1999, p. 420). The French considered the achievement in interiors and furnishings to be uniquely French. While the artistic achievement is undisputed, the comfort, *commodité*, is another matter.

Genevieve Souchal's book from 1961 is an example of the mythology of the comfort and grace of eighteenth-century furniture that Hellman feels is misguided. On the opening page, Souchal writes: "Never, even during the Renaissance, had the art of living developed so high a degree of fastidiousness, and certainly comfort and elegance had never previously been so effectively allied" (1961, p. 7).

A **voyeuse**, or conversation chair, is an armchair whose upper back is padded as an armrest (Figure 11.9). The chair could be used for private in-house performances. One person was seated, while another stood behind, leaning on the backrest, ostensibly listening to the performers. This scenario was useful for those watching a card game.

François Boucher's painting of 1747 is titled *Are They Thinking About the Grape? (Pensent-ils*

au raisin?). It depicts an amorous pair; she feeds him a grape, and the barely hidden subtext is that they are thinking of something else. A voyeuse is the furniture equivalent to Boucher's painting. If a man were standing behind a seated woman and he leaned forward—allegedly interested in the performance—he was perfectly positioned to stare down the décolletage of her dress.

There is no doubt that the aesthetic and artistic transformation of France, begun by Louis XIV and consolidated by Louis XV and Louis XVI, was admired and emulated by all the European courts. The French cemented their place as the world authorities on artistic matters. But Hellman stresses that the apparent ease and comfort of eighteenth-century French furniture was just that, an appearance. Pieces of furniture could ease, or hinder, the desire to appear knowledgeable and graceful.

Beds and daybeds

Beds were important objects of the French state's political apparatus. Versailles was outfitted with state beds for the king and queen. The daily witnessing of the **levée**, watching the monarchs rise from their beds and start the day, was a reaffirmation that the country, which was synonymous with the royal family, was doing well.

The German-born American anthropologist Franz Boas (1858–1942) introduced into the popular realm the connection between culture and language, specifically looking at vocabulary elaboration. He noted that the Eskimos (Inuit) had innumerable words for snow. There is a question as to the accuracy of Boas's observation (the discrepancy rests on the Inuit use of prefixes and suffixes), yet the concept of vocabulary elaboration became mythologized. Boas's undisputed point was that snow was important to the Inuit. The Inuit were linguistically responding to their natural environment; the eighteenth-century French were building their own, literally, with their interiors and furnishings, and linguistically, with hundreds of words that refer to distinct furniture types.

In the private realm, a series of pieces allowed a person to recline while in the company of others. A **méridienne** provided a place for a person to relax, artfully arranged perpendicular to the viewing angle of visitors. This encouraged a sitter to be at ease in a social setting, yet it did not encourage total relaxation. **Chaise longue**, **settée**, canapé, **duchesse,** and **duchesse brisée** are some of the terms that refer to specific types of sofas and

Figure 11.9
Louis Magdeleine Pluvinet, side chair or voyeuse, France, 1785.

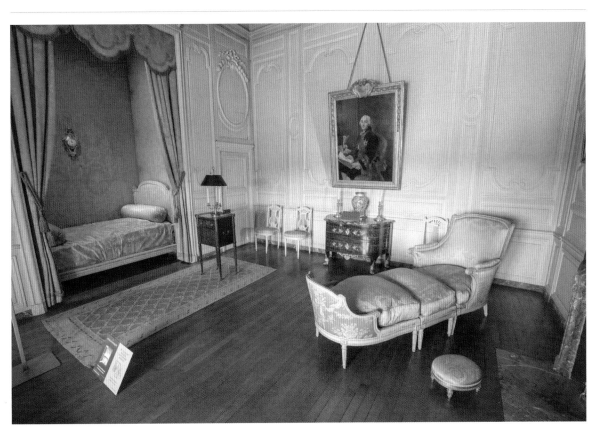

Figure 11.10
Louis Le Vau and
Charles Le Brun,
Vaux-le-Vicomte,
Maincy, France,
1661. Bedroom
with méridienne
or bergère en
gondole.

couches. A méridienne was an example of seat
furniture that no longer lined walls but occupied
a prominent place in the center of a room, as in a
bedroom of Vaux-le-Vicomte (Figure 11.10).

Flat surface and space-containing furniture

A **bureau** plat is today known as a table desk,
meaning that it has no **apron**, front panel, or
side drawers that rest on the floor (Figure 11.11).
A graceful piece of furniture, it looks like a table.
(This type was less popular with the English, who
preferred library desks, heavy-looking desks with
fronts that extended down to the floor.)

Another important category of rococo furniture was mechanical furniture (discussed later).
A high level of craftsmanship was exhibited in
exceedingly complex pieces. A roll-top desk,
bureau à cylinder, was a writing desk that
responded to the increasing need for storage.

There were numerous varieties of commodes,
a piece that provided storage and a surface to
display objects. A commode was the standard
chest of drawers. Taller chests were uncommon. A
commode typically had two, three, or four drawers; some had doors.

A console leaning against a wall is the epitome of a rococo furniture ensemble (Figure 11.12).

Figure 11.11
Joseph
Baumhauer,
table desk or
Bureau Plat, Paris,
France, 1770. Oak,
tulipwood, purple
wood, casuarina
wood, kingwood,
ormolu mount,
and leather.

The ensemble consisted of a mirror, hung in the
center of an architectural panel, a console placed
beneath it, and candles at its sides. A console
looks as though it is unstable, defying one of the
definitions of what a piece of furniture should be:
a freestanding piece of furniture. A console is half
a table, although reflected in a mirror it appears
to be a whole table. This is strange, as then the
"correct" table was an illusion, the "real" table
incomplete. There are curves everywhere, gilded
wood, ormolu mounts, and a stone top.

A **gueridon** was a small, ornate pedestal
table that often served as a stand for a candelabra. Candles were the primary source of light;

Figure 11.12
François Roumier, console, Versailles, France, eighteenth century.
Carved and gilded oak with verde antico marble.

hence candlesticks, candelabras, and wall brackets were numerous. Paired with a mirror, the ensemble of a reflecting mirror and a shiny candelabra in crystal or metal was an ideal source of flickering light.

Rococo pieces required the work of many trades. **Charpentiers**, carpenters, did rough carpentry. They were responsible for creating a chair's **chassis**, or framework of a chair. **Menuisiers** were artisans of more refined work; they made chairs, carved pieces, mirror frames, and console tables. These groups collaborated with those who specialized in marble, and finishers who did sanding, painting, varnishing, and lacquering. A gilder provided hardware, locks, drawer pulls, and mounts. They collaborated with another group, upholsterers.

As in the baroque period, ébénistes were the highest level of furniture makers, and they crafted veneered pieces. Their professional name stems from one of the veneers they worked with, ebony. Ébénistes also excelled at the complicated mechanical pieces that were the pride of a rococo household.

The father-and-son firm of Abraham Roentgen (1711–1793) and David Roentgen (1743–1807) operated out of a town close to Cologne, Germany. Their accomplished workshop sold pieces throughout Germany and France. David Roentgen sold several pieces to Marie Antoinette. Specific pieces were made for card-playing, writing, reading, working, sewing, and eating. English furniture makers also became adept at copying French pieces and brought the rococo style across the English Channel.

Some mechanical pieces were complicated, delicate, and technically complex. *Sprezzatura* is a musical term that refers to any art form in

which the final result makes the difficult process look easy. A dressing and writing table made by an accomplished ébénistes was as much a technical accomplishment as an aesthetic one Jean-François Oeben (1721–1763) was born in Germany, although active in France (Figure 11.13). Thinking of Hellman's work, an Oeben dressing table demanded that a user was knowledgeable about its operations, and also graceful to use it correctly and not appear clumsy.

Chinoiserie

Chinoiserie refers to Western imitations or evocations of Chinese or Asian art, a Western style inspired by China. These works were popular in the seventeenth, eighteenth, and nineteenth centuries. The pieces were often standard European shapes, such as consoles and commodes, decorated with Chinese motifs. A manual to assist those interested in Chinoiserie came when William Chambers published his *Designs for Chinese Buildings, Furniture, Dress, etc.,* in 1757.

Chinoiserie furniture pieces were not pieces of Chinese furniture but examples of European decorative pieces inspired by a fanciful idea of China. Exoticism and interest in foreign lands were prominent in art, opera, and the decorative arts. Chinese wallpapers, real and imitation, were popular.

Figure 11.13
Jean-François Oeben, Mechanical table for Mme. de Pompadour, France, 1761–1763. Oak, mahogany, kingwood, tulipwood, rosewood, holly, and ormolu.

Chinoiserie was the most prevalent of the foreign interests, but there were others. Those active in the decorative arts showed considerable interest in Turkey, India, and Persia. The minor trend of monkey motifs used in the decorative and graphic arts is known as **singerie**. Art historian and artist Elizabeth Liebman provocatively suggests that monkey pictures were anything but innocent: "The animals in these images do not wear the collar of the organ grinder's gentle companion; rather, they are masculine brutes, shackled at the pelvis in order to restrain the impulses of a body bereft of reason" (2003, p. 137).

If a piece of furniture was japanned, that meant that it was lacquered. Japanned pieces were popular in England, France, Germany, and the United States. A wooden two-drawer console from the United States makes visual reference to French rococo furniture, while finished to look Eastern (Figure 11.14). It has a marble top, veneered and lacquered sides, and ormolu mounts. Its pictorial composition, spread out over the five panels of its sides and front, vaguely resembles a Japanese screen. In addition, there was the fashion of purchasing Chinese and Japanese screens and taking them apart and using them for new pieces of furniture and in interior ensembles.

Maria Theresa (1717–1780) was the mother of Marie Antoinette and fifteen other children. She coped with her grief over the death of her husband by having his studio remodeled. The room of her palace in Vienna, Schönbrunn, was outfitted with lacquered Chinese panels that alternated with European-style paintings. Finished in 1772, it was called the "Vieux-Laque Zimmer" and became a popular place to show palace visitors. Michael Yonan (2004) discusses the specific meanings that the use of Chinoiserie could entail. About the room in Maria Theresa's royal residence, he writes that "the specific possibilities inherent to China brought it a greater prominence in her court imagery. Vienna's position as leader not of a monarchical state but of a multicultural, polyglot empire had a useful parallel in the mythical China" (Yonan 2004, p. 662). While Chinoiserie was often used in superficial ways ignorant of Chinese and Asian history, occasionally the political reasons that underlay its use were knowledgeable and complex.

Decorative arts and graphics

An offshoot of Chinoiserie was the popularity of resetting Chinese vases in French-made ormolu mounts (Smentek 2007). The favored vases were monochromatic porcelain jars. The preference for monochromes and single-color schemes was an extension of the interest in matched sets. The mounts include swirling bulrushes, finials, and multiple swirls. Europeans had imported Chinese vases for centuries, most famously the blue-and-white variety. The monochromes popular in France in the eighteenth century were made in China in the late 1600s or early 1700s. Few made it to Europe, and their scarcity increased their value. Many were produced for the domestic Chinese market. Creating monochromes was exacting work: the hard part was getting the color even, something less important in patterned work.

Resetting the vases involved a lot of work. One reason for the mounts is that they could hide chips or cracks. The process of cutting the vases was exacting, arduous, and occasionally hazardous. The mounts were commissioned by marchands merciérs, the sales force admired for their discerning taste. An artisan made a model in wax, wood, or terra-cotta, from which the bronze caster made the various parts. A **ciseleur** (chaser) did the filing and finishing of the raw bronze cast, and a **doreur** (gilder) gilded the bronze. The result of the effort is that the Chinese vases looked French.

Figure 11.14
Unknown, japanned dressing table, Boston, Massachusetts, United States, 1747. Lacquered maple, birch, and pine.

Rococo artists loved seashells. Real seashells were encrusted into the walls of garden grottoes, resulting in the rough-textured work called "rocaille." Some objects were created by fitting real shells with metal mounts. Artists were fond of drawing shells. Shells were made of a hard luminescent material. The resulting objects looked natural and effortless because they were natural. Shells, pearls, and mother-of-pearl were popular rococo materials. Shells had a connection to classicism as the ancients were similarly enamored of shells.

Rococo forms were popular in graphics because they represented the latest fashion and because they often included forms that could exist nowhere except on paper. Artist and designer Juste-Aurèle Meissonier (1695–1750) published hundreds of engravings showing wall panels, candlesticks, and furniture designs, often of fantastic and unbuildable shapes. Flowing curves predominate, the layouts were asymmetric, yet they appear designed. Many forms derived from shells and foliage. The graphic world of Meissonier was delicate, light, and florid.

Rococo graphic works exist in large numbers. They were frequently collected in pattern books, works that assembled examples of several designers, with the intention that they would be copied. The medium of two-dimensional representation was ideal, because it allowed the artistic imagination free rein, unfettered by practicality. It is difficult to imagine that Meissonier's multiple drawings of chairs, sofas, and mirrors could exist anywhere but on paper (Figure 11.15). Yet the carefully delineated frame could inspire a graphic artist.

Figure 11.15
Juste-Aurèle Meissonier, sofa for the Count de Bielenski, Grand Marshal of Poland, Warsaw, Poland, 1735.

Conclusion

The taste for rococo pieces survived into the early years of the reign of Louis XVI (1774–1779), although the pieces started to morph into forms associated with neoclassicism. One of the anomalies of France in the eighteenth century involves the association of styles with political movements. Although neoclassicism is generally associated with the Enlightenment, the French Revolution, and political reforms critical of the monarchy, its supporters included Louis XVI, Marie Antoinette, Madame de Pompadour, and Madame du Barry, the last two the king's official mistresses. Neoclassical artists positioned themselves in opposition to rococo, claiming that their creations were moral and not frivolous (see Chapter 14).

Rococo, a style aimed toward the very rich, also affected the tastes of the middle classes. Those in the middle and lower classes strongly felt the desire to emulate the nobility. Those on the lower rungs of the social ladder experienced rococo design primarily through simplified decorative arts objects, such as French **provincial** chairs.

Material objects always exist within a cultural context. Hellman stresses that "objects were agents that highlighted and enhanced the attributes of others in a social system" (Hellman 1999, p. 434). Her work stresses that comfortable-looking items were not necessarily easy to use. An equally important observation is that items that gave an appearance of effortlessness were often exceedingly difficult to craft.

The designs created during the reigns of Louis XIV, XV, and XVI are prime examples of art being produced in service to the state. Art did not merely reflect state power, it was a tool of its implementation. The relation of art to state unravels in the following chapters, with an increasing number of individuals who grab the artistic reins for their own purposes and explorations.

Rococo design was a continuation of artistic explorations that started in baroque Italy. The move away from classicism, the exploration of increasingly complicated geometries, and the preference for lighter profiles all reached their height in the rococo period. The period that followed rococo, neoclassicism, was a repudiation of the art and objects that are the subject of this chapter. Yet neoclassical furniture makers continued the attention to pleasing proportions and the high level of quality in construction.

Neoclassical designers sought to craft a style that was the opposite of rococo. With their attention to delicate, well-made forms, they joined their predecessors in continuing the tradition of fine furniture. The period 1716–1793, leading up to the French Revolution, was the golden age of French furniture.

Sources

Coffin, Sarah and Gail S. Davidson (2008). *Rococo: The Continuing Curve: 1730–2008*. New York: Assouline.

Craske, Matthew (1997). *Art in Europe: 1700–1830*. New York: Oxford University Press.

Dalloz, Fabienne (2021). *Le Tresor de Germain Boffrand*. La Valette du Var: Du Lau.

Dennis, Michael (1986). *Court and Garden: From the French Hôtel to the City of Modern Architecture*. Cambridge, MA: MIT Press.

Gallet, Michel and Jörg Garms (1986). *Germain Boffrand, 1667–1754*. Paris: Herscher.

Goodman, Dena and Kathryn Norberg, eds. (2007). *Furnishing the Eighteenth Century*. New York: Routledge.

Hellman, Mimi (1999). "Furniture, Sociability, and the Work of Leisure in Eighteenth Century France." *Eighteenth-Century Studies* 32, no. 4: 415–45.

Hobson, Marian (1982). *The Object of Art: the Theory of Illusion in Eighteenth-Century France*. New York: Cambridge University Press.

Koda, Harold and Andrew Bolton (2006). *Dangerous Liaisons: Fashion and Furniture in the Eighteenth Century*. New Haven, CT: Yale University Press.

Kostof, Spiro (1995). *A History of Architecture: Settings and Rituals*. Oxford: Oxford University Press.

Kraske, Matthew (1997). *Art in Europe, 1700–1830*. Oxford: Oxford University Press.

Levey, Michael (1966). *Rococo to Revolution*. New York: Praeger.

Liebman, Elizabeth (2003). "Unspeakable Passions: The Civil and Savage Lessons of Early Modern Animal Representations." In *Representing the Passions*, edited by Richard Meyer, pp. 137–62. Los Angeles: Getty Publications.

Pile, John (2004). *A History of Interior Design*. New York: Wiley.

Rosenblum, Robert (1967). *Transformations in Late Eighteenth Century Art*. Princeton, NJ: Princeton University Press.

Rosenthal, Angela (2004). "Raising Hair." *Eighteenth-Century Studies* 38, no. 1 (Fall): 1–16.

Scott, Katie (1995). *The Rococo Interior*. New Haven, CT: Yale University Press.

Souchal, Genevieve (1961). *French Eighteenth-Century Furniture*. New York: Putnam's.

Smentek, Kristel (2007). *Rococo Exotic: French Mounted Porcelains*. New York: Frick Collection.

Stafford, Barbara Maria (2007). *Echo Objects: The Cognitive Work of Images*. Chicago: University of Chicago Press.

Wilson, Gillian (2021). *French Rococo Ébénisterie in the J. Paul Getty Museum*. Santa Monica, CA: J. Paul Getty Museum.

Yonan, Michael (2004). "Veneers of Authority: Chinese Lacquers in Maria Theresa's Vienna." *Eighteenth-Century Studies* 37, no. 4 (Summer): 652–72.

Discussion and Review Questions

1. Name some specific types of furniture and their intended uses.
2. How did French furniture demand that its users be graceful?
3. How are Louis XV pieces different from Louis XIV?
4. How are Louis XVI pieces different from Louis XV?
5. What makes Louis XV pieces seem graceful?
6. What are the characteristics of rococo architecture?
7. How do rococo works, furniture, and architecture relate to baroque pieces?
8. What was modern about rococo design?
9. What similarities exist between rococo furniture design and painting?

England

1500–1558	1558–1603	1603–1625	1625–1649	1640–1660	1660–1689
Tudor	Elizabethan	Jacobean	Carolean	Cromwellian	Restoration

1689–1702	1702–1714	1714–1750	1750–1770	1770–1810
William and Mary	Queen Anne	Early Georgian	Middle Georgian	Late Georgian

A parade of enigmatic monarchs, including Mary Queen of Scots, Henry VIII, Elizabeth I, and James I, dominate English history. The history of decorative styles and furniture is, appropriately enough, named after the rulers. **Elizabethan** is named for Elizabeth I, **Jacobean** named for James I, and so forth. The system is widely used.

Confusing the nomenclature issue is that the English were well aware of continental developments, and figures such as Inigo Jones and Christopher Wren ensured that some of the finest examples of Renaissance and baroque architecture are found on the banks of the Thames. Design students thus find two systems at work, sometimes used concurrently. In some quarters, one hears about English Renaissance and English baroque; one also, more commonly, hears references to styles based on the rulers, such as Elizabethan and **Georgian**.

No hard-and-fast rule predominates, but generally, the continental terms of medieval, Renaissance, and neoclassical are used in conjunction with architecture, and the ruler-based names relate to furniture and the decorative arts. The English design nomenclature is also important for English colonies—for example, Australia, Canada, Kenya, New Zealand, South Africa, and the United States. These countries rely on the English system, although they make it their own, with modifications.

Figure 12.0
(*Facing page*)
Antonio Verrio and Jean Tijou, King's Staircase, Hampton Court Palace, Richmond upon Thames, England, 1700.

An exceptional quality of English art and design, throughout the ages, is that singular homegrown English inventions are few. English artists and designers worked marvelously with continental styles, such as classicism, Gothic, and Renaissance, adapting them to local needs and infusing them with local design motifs. The lack of categorical purity in no way indicates a lack of quality in art, architecture, interiors, and furniture. There was less internal design consistency than there was in France or Italy, yet seventeenth- and eighteenth-century English furniture is an unqualified high point in the history of designed objects.

Tudor

Little early medieval furniture exists, so the exploration of English furniture starts with the reigns of the **Tudor** monarchs. The list of significant Tudor monarchs includes Henry VII, Henry VIII, Edward VI, and Queen Mary.

For architecture, the word Tudor is associated with timber-frame construction (Figure 12.1). This type of **half-timber** construction, or wattle and daub, is found throughout much of Europe; in Germany called **fachwerk**, it is often found in typical medieval buildings, especially vernacular town buildings. But there is no neat correlation or distinction between Tudor and medieval. Tudor is chronologically the period in which Italian Renaissance forms started to appear. In Italy, the arrival of the Renaissance and its reinvented classicism was the death knell of medieval and Gothic forms. Across the Channel, the distinctions were less obvious.

Architectural historian Maurice Howard offers a counterpoint to the typical architectural history of the sixteenth and seventeenth centuries. Many works understandably focus on important churches and the official building and furnishing programs of Henry VIII. Another major center of English design history is the country house.

Figure 12.1
High Street, Lacock, Wiltshire, United Kingdom, medieval period. Tudor timber-frame houses.

Discussion of these stately manors often focuses on the degree to which designs were true to, or deviated from, continental fashions of classicism. Design innovations, however, were not only the result of new commissions. Howard suggests that:

far more importantly, there was a lot of making new from old materials: the flooring of halls open to the roof to create at least one more private space; the deployment of visible signs of luxury and comfort such as the fireplace (its stack often prominent for display purposes on the main façade of the house) and glazed windows; all these things customized old structures into modern dwellings.

(2007, p. 2)

The building legacy of England as it emerged from the medieval period includes innumerable informal structures that modestly line roads and face small town squares. These buildings were constantly being repaired and repainted. The elements of timber-frame buildings came from England's medieval past, and the honest architectural vocabulary proved flexible in responding to new functional demands.

The great hall and its furnishings

Mark Girouard's book from 1978, *Life in the English Country House*, is required reading for anyone interested in English domestic architecture. In his work, a work of architectural and social history, a medieval household is defined as several hundred people, with a noble and his family at the center. The most important architectural features of a medieval manor house or castle were a giant dining hall, called the **great hall**, its kitchen, and a chapel. The house was essentially a small village whose inhabitants ate communally; hence the need for a large dining space (Girouard 1978, p. 27). Female servants were responsible for cooking, cleaning, and setting up for meals.

At the end of the medieval period, the Elizabethan household inherited a means of dining in which a nobleman and his family ate in a large rectangular room, still referred to as the great hall. One end of the room had a raised platform, called the **dais**, on which the family ate. The other end of the room had a **screen**, a porous wall, sometimes of columns or arches. Initially, screens were made of wood and were removable. This created a passageway, behind the screen, that allowed servants and others to cross the room without disrupting the festivities.

The nobles ate on the dais, sitting behind a fabric-covered table, the table most likely being boards on trestles. Diners sat on one side of the narrow table and were served by attendants working on the other. Typically, only the sovereign or lord sat in a chair, with the others seated on stools and benches. The typical Tudor chair, the **settle chair**, was box shaped, similar in some respects to the Italian Renaissance sedia, as it had a straight back and arms.

Tables were removed after the meal. The continual setting up and dismantling of the dining furniture was a tradition that was to live on in **gate-leg tables**. This table with a folding top was a space saver. Unfolded, a leg shaped like a gate swung out and supported the top.

A palace inventory from 1547, near the end of Henry VIII's reign, indicates that a great deal of the royal furniture was imported. Henry VIII employed a vast retinue of artists, architects, and craftsmen who were Flemish, French, German, and Italian—one of the mechanisms by which continental styles traveled to the British Isles. Ralph Fastnedge writes that Flemish designers operating in England furthered "a florid Flemish interpretation of the Renaissance" (1955, p. 13).

Over time, the architectural entity of a country house became less feudal and castle-like and lost the features that made it resemble a village. By the Elizabethan era, the English country house became a single-family house, albeit with servants and the members of an extended family, the type of household associated with wealthy families today.

Elizabethan

The Elizabethan period (1558–1603) was an age of great wealth that resulted in an increase in furniture and fine furniture production. It was also a time in which England flexed her diplomatic and military muscles. A decisive moment was the defeat of the Spanish armada by the English in 1588. The Elizabethan period was characterized by significant cultural achievements, including the buildings of Inigo Jones and the plays of William Shakespeare.

Furniture

As new Renaissance construction techniques became prevalent in England, sophisticated

Elizabethan pieces increasingly relied on wood-on-wood connections, or mortise-and-tenon. The use of iron nails was associated with medieval, Romanesque, and Gothic furniture.

In furniture, as in architecture, the English were initially resistant to wholeheartedly embrace Renaissance models. The English Renaissance held on to Gothic forms for a longer time than did the rest of Europe, until 1550. Renaissance ideas flowed northward from Italy and France into Holland and Flanders, and finally to the British Isles. The result is that Flemish influences remained strong in England, and similarly, English influences appeared in Flanders.

Elizabethan furniture in many cases takes existing medieval forms and overlays them with a profusion of decoration and ornamental work.

Tables

By 1550, there were framed tables, meaning that the top was created with a frame with cut boards filling in the frame, as opposed to parallel board or plank construction. Some tables were of considerable size.

A signature piece of the Elizabethan period is the Elizabethan table, with its characteristic bulbous leg (Figure 12.2). The round **cup-and-cover** form was also known as a melon motif. Bulbous legs were a feature of beds, **sideboards**, and tables. This legged table had rails close to the ground. Elizabethan legs are often capped with classical Ionic capitals on top of the cup-and-cover, a hint of the tentative assimilation of classical and medieval forms.

The English had draw-top desks and sloped desks (the French preferred flat desks). Tables served occasional duty as desks. The height of the popularity of the bulbous leg lasted approximately

seventy-five years, although it later reappeared in numerous revivals.

Chairs and chests

Elizabethan X-frame chairs existed, as well as Gothic chairs and thrones. Another Elizabethan chair is the **Wainscot chair** (Figure 12.3). It bears similarities to its contemporary, the Italian Renaissance sedia. It is boxy, with turned legs and richly carved panels.

Its close-to-the-ground stretchers render it a sturdy piece of furniture, able to withstand the rigors of travel. When Elizabeth I traveled about the British Isles, she took a number of furnishings with her, including chests and wall hangings. Mark Girouard wrote:

A great household on the move was a familiar sight on medieval highways. It was also an impressive one. The number of people involved was unlikely to be less than one hundred, and could rise to well over five hundred in the case of a royal or semi-royal household. These numbers moved in three contingents of increasing size, probably spaced out several hours, or even days apart.

(1978, p. 14)

The English vocabulary makes a distinction between a chest, which has a flat top, meaning that it might be stacked, and a coffer, which has a round top to throw off the rain and to prevent other items from being piled on top of it. Chests remained important pieces of furniture; they were called into use for storage, as seating, as tables,

Figure 12.2 Unknown, Elizabethan/ Jacobean table with cup-and-cover motif legs and continuous stretcher, England, *c.* 1600–1650.

Figure 12.3 Unknown, Elizabethan-style Wainscot chair, Chester County, Pennsylvania, 1740–1780. Walnut.

and as beds. Chests were made from boards that remained visible. More elaborate chests were carved with tracery.

Beds

One of the most important furniture types of sixteenth-century England was the bed, and the grandest of Elizabethan beds is the Great Bed of Ware, 1590 (Figure 12.4). It has many of the signature characteristics of Elizabethan design—foremost its all-encompassing surface decoration.

Castles, churches, and dark-stained, heavy furniture give a false impression that Elizabethan life was somber. An installation in the Victorian and Albert Museum in London of the Great Bed of Ware presented it draped in full color. The medieval love of pageantry and bright color continued into the Elizabethan period in costumes and household textiles.

Beds were large, luxurious, and extravagant in a time period often known for scarcity. Houses were otherwise sparsely furnished. Beds were used as couches, for entertaining guests and friends during the day. Beds had a weight and consequence not seen on other pieces of furniture. Bed linens and draperies were expensive, and often finer than many pieces of furniture.

The Great Bed of Ware, like other Elizabethan beds, is architectural, with columns, arches, and a **tester** that looks like a cornice. A tester is the architectural canopy that caps off the bed. The bed's decoration is attributed to the Dutch

architect and painter Hans Vredeman de Vries (1527–1606). Vredeman de Vries was known more for his publications, pattern books filled with elaborate engravings, than his buildings. Pattern books were the medium by which continental design ideas and forms circulated. They were published with the intent that their designs would be copied. Some architects, like Vredeman de Vries, specialized in pattern books. The Great Bed of Ware, like Vredeman de Vries's other works, imagined and realized, has Dutch, Flemish, and Italian influences. In her book on dreams in the English Renaissance, Elizabethan historian Carole Levin informs us that "the expression of politicians getting into bed together was a common one then as now" (2008, p. 5). The heavy bed drapery provided warmth in the winter and also privacy, rendering the bed virtually a room within a room.

Architecture

Inigo Jones is commonly credited with having introduced Renaissance architecture to England. A feature of his work is that it relies heavily on Jones's admiration for the Italian Renaissance architect Andrea Palladio, and it constitutes a distancing from English architectural traditions.

The common understanding is that Jones and the Jacobean period he is associated with constitute the English Renaissance. An extension of this line of thinking is therefore that the preceding period, Elizabethan, is analogous to medieval.

Figure 12.4
Hans Vredeman de Vries, the Great Bed of Ware, Hertfordshire, England, 1590–1600.

That characterization is problematic. An examination of Elizabethan architecture demonstrates
that some English architects prior to Jones were
innovative and aware of continental trends,
although a feature of their work is that it relies
heavily on updating homegrown traditions rather
than importing new foreign ones.

The leading architect of the Elizabethan
period was Robert Smythson (1534–1614), and the
first Elizabethan great house is Longleat, begun in
1568. Smythson's training as a mason is evident in
his buildings, known for their blocky massing.

Another feature of his architectural interiors
was ornamental **strapwork**, a decorative design
formed of overlapping bands. His masterpiece is
unquestionably Wollaton Hall, 1580–1588, a fusion
of medieval and Renaissance forms, with an astonishing number of windows, a rigorously designed
symmetrical façade, and innovations in interior
planning that left the medieval castle far behind.

The plan of Wollaton reveals the multiple
features that Smythson skillfully incorporated into
the design. The Renaissance features include the
fact that the house is essentially symmetrical on
all four sides, a gesture to the Villa Rotunda that
Alice Friedman called "mirror-image symmetry"
(1989, p. 93). The great hall at Wollaton was still
a necessity in Smythson's time, yet it was not
a feature of the Italian houses he admired, nor
was it obvious how it could be incorporated into
a Renaissance plan. It was a large, asymmetrical, rectangular entity, with dissimilar ends,
approached off-axis and oriented perpendicularly
to the axis of approach.

Smythson rotated the great hall 90 degrees
from the central axis, although to arrive at it
actually required visitors to make three 90-degree
turns (Friedman 1989, p. 93). Friedman wrote:

Wollaton Hall and its occupants frequently
appear to be split between two different
worlds. In appearance, the house itself draws
on both Gothic and classical traditions, uniting
a trabeated surface of pilastered orders with a
centralized tower distinguished by its castle
like **bartizan** turrets. The plan brings together
traditional English sequences of rooms and
Palladian axial symmetry, but these two
very different planning strategies are never
integrated—the mazelike spaces of the hall,
screens passage, and service rooms on the
ground floor are a world apart from the open
and airy formal rooms above.

(1989, p. 9)

Smythson's other major country house was
Hardwick Hall (1591–1597). Gothic detailing overlays simple forms and a central rectangular block.
Its clever plan also incorporates an asymmetrical
hall. Smythson's residential designs at the end of
his life took a different turn. They were decidedly
more traditional, leaving Wollaton and Hardwick
Hall as his most innovative projects.

Jacobean

The Jacobean period corresponds to the reign
of James I. Roughly analogous to continental
baroque, it is also characterized by the continuation of Elizabethan forms. In fact, some
stylistically Elizabethan pieces continued to be
manufactured during the Jacobean period with
their forms unchanged. In general, compared to
Elizabethan, Jacobean is more elaborate in its
decoration and its profiles are visually lighter,
although exceptions abound.

James I (1566–1625) is the monarch for whom
the King James version of the Bible is named. He
was the son of Queen Mary.

Interiors

Plaster ceilings and paneling are features of
Jacobean interiors. What they have in common is
that both are an articulated surface set in front of
or below the physical structure. Timbered ceilings existed in the Jacobean period, but plaster
ceilings became more common. A plaster ceiling
with extensive strapwork is essentially a dropped
ceiling, hung beneath the beamed ceiling that it
hides. The physical structure of the ceiling is not
visible.

Paneling came into use in the early sixteenth
century and became prominent in the Jacobean
period; the Tudor habit of timber with plaster infill
was largely left behind in the construction of rich
people's houses. The increased reliance on paneling for vertical surfaces echoes the use of plaster
on ceilings (Figure 12.5). Paneling is a carefully
crafted surface that hides the structural wall
behind it. There were many names for those who
worked in wood, among them arkwright, smith,
cooper, and joiner. Work on paneling was one of a
joiner's areas of expertise.

At the end of the Jacobean period, there are
instances of paneling being painted white. James
Ayres has researched the varieties of painting

Figure 12.5
Unknown, early
Jacobean Oak
Room, 1603–1625.
Published in *The
Connoisseur*,
1912.

schemes used in historic British interiors. They include painting walls to look like tapestries and painting panels to imitate marble. Blackwork, which was inspired by the popularity of blackwork embroidery in textiles, featured elaborate patterns in black on a white background. In the eighteenth century, some patrons preferred murals, large-scale pictorial compositions, often landscapes, that covered entire wall surfaces (Ayres 2003, pp. 125–64).

Furniture

Jacobean furniture, still massive, was lighter than Elizabethan pieces. In many cases, it is impossible for the casual viewer to distinguish Elizabethan from Jacobean pieces. This is also because Elizabethan pieces continued to exist and were moved into Jacobean structures, and also because some furniture makers continued to make Elizabethan-style pieces. The use of cushions increased, and there were fully upholstered and partially upholstered pieces.

Chairs

Unassuming common tripod stools were hold-overs from the medieval period. Around 1500,

these simple seats were rendered elaborate with the addition of turned elements (Figure 12.6). Fastnedge described those covered with a profusion of decoration as "curious and rather monstrous" (1955, p. 24). They were indicative of a desire to rely upon turned pieces rather than chip

Figure 12.6
Unknown,
Jacobean high
chair with turning,
sixteenth century.

carving as the source of decoration. The technology of the lathe drove the design, evident in the piece's name: **turned chair**.

Upholstery was infrequent in the Elizabethan period. Some X-framed chairs were elaborately upholstered (Figure 12.7). The existence of an upholstered X-frame chair in Spain underscores the considerable political, economic, and cultural ties between England and Spain. The longstanding form of the X-frame chair was retained, yet the upholstered version was not collapsible. Chairs became increasingly elaborate, with tassels, fringes, and arched cresting.

In the Jacobean period, the **farthingale chair** was popular. A side chair with an upholstered seat, without arms and with a low back, it was useful for women wearing voluminous dresses. It was also called a "back chair." Some had front legs that protruded above the seat framing to hold the cushion in place. Historian of the decorative arts Peter Thornton wrote: "Although the farthingale chair was much used for relaxing in comfortable circumstances, it was the standard chair of its time and was also used for dining" (1978, p. 187).

Wainscot chairs continued to be produced, with slight differences between the Elizabethan and Jacobean versions. The Wainscot chair's top was surmounted by a crest. In the Jacobean period, the cresting was atop the side rails; in the

Elizabethan period, it lay between the side rails. The armrests sloped downward.

Walnut and beech became increasingly popular. A feature of many Jacobean pieces was twisting on the stretchers, also called **ball turning**. (Twisted stretchers, legs and columns were a feature of Italian baroque design.) Clients frequently purchased sets of two armchairs with six or more side chairs.

Because people kept their furniture and traditional-looking pieces (i.e., Elizabethan) continued to be made, many Elizabethan and Jacobean pieces look similar to the untrained eye. While the Jacobean period saw many innovations, some conservative pieces display an allegiance to previous forms.

Architecture

The most prominent architect of the Jacobean period was Inigo Jones, the figure credited with having introduced Italian High Renaissance into England; his work is often compared to that of the architect he admired and emulated, Andrea Palladio. Like the Italian Renaissance architect, Jones was a student of antiquity, and he brought several publications on Palladio back with him to England after his travels in Italy.

Jones's designs were consistent and rigorous forms of High Renaissance. He designed Queen's House at Greenwich (1616–1635) and Banqueting House (1619–1622). His work on Queen's House at Greenwich was an exercise in simplicity. Like Palladio, Jones was interested in the perfection of geometric shapes.

The rambling Whitehall Palace had originally been owned by a cardinal who was forced to relinquish it to Henry VIII. Its finest structure was also the only part to survive a fire in 1698, the exquisite Banqueting House. Contemporary drawings of Banqueting House, part of a larger complex intended to rival Versailles, show the sharp contrast between the medieval vernacular and the Renaissance England that Jones promoted. It is a single room with a double-story height— and with a single purpose, as its name suggests. Today the building is surrounded by a lot of grand buildings that vie for the viewer's attention, but in its day, its grand classical exterior, with Ionic and Corinthian orders, stood in sharp contrast to the context of timber-framed irregular buildings.

In multiple respects, Jacobean architecture was consistent with contemporary French architectural developments. In their embrace of luxury, styles across Europe in the late seventeenth

Figure 12.7
X-frame armchair,
Granada, Spain,
1480–1500.
Walnut and Elm.

and eighteenth centuries reflect the influence of Louis XIV.

Cromwellian and Restoration

Because the furniture classification system used in England is based on rulers, the Jacobean period is followed by **Carolean** (1625–1649), **Cromwellian** (1649–1660), and **Restoration** (1660–1689). Cromwellian refers to the figure of Oliver Cromwell (1649–1660), and his movement is known as the Puritan rebellion. Cromwell was the English statesman who led parliamentary forces in the English civil wars and played a central role in overthrowing Charles I. In his movement, the Puritans opposed the monarchy and sought to purify the Church of England of idolatrous (i.e., Roman Catholic) ways. The separation from Rome came in 1534, and a century later, the Puritans sought to further the division.

Cromwellian is not a distinct style, and it intermittently expresses the austerity promoted by its leading political figure. A Cromwellian side chair is a variation of the Jacobean farthingale chair (Figure 12.8).

The Puritan movement didn't long survive the loss of Cromwell, and a return of the monarchy came next, with the rulers Charles II and James II. The stylistic period related to their reigns is known as Restoration. Charles and James were contemporaries of the French king Louis XIV.

Figure 12.8
Unknown, Cromwellian or back stool, England, 1640–1660. Oak and leather.

They restored the English monarchy to power and, like most European royals, they wanted to emulate the French king, his palace, and its furnishings. English Restoration is known for its lavishness and its engagement with continental baroque movements. Restoration generally refers to baroque-looking forms and a return to the opulence associated with the monarchy that was frowned on by Cromwell. The persecution of the Puritans in this period was one of the factors that drove some people to emigrate to the North American colonies (Chapter 13).

In Restoration England, the **Mortlake Tapestry Works** was important, filling a role similar to that in France of the Gobelins tapestry. Furniture forms were inherited from previous eras rather than invented. Circa 1660, after the Restoration, oval and round tables became a feature of private rooms used exclusively for dining. Nobles favored eating in their private chambers, and the great age of communal dining in the great hall was over. Gate-legged tables and tables devoted to games were popular.

The recognition of continental developments reared its head in the growing use of glass and mirrors, most of which came from Venice. The fashion for glass-lined rooms was due to the fame of the Galerie des Glaces at Versailles. Paneled walls took the place of walls covered with tapestry hangings. Part of the need for ostentatious display was met by importing Chinese vases and Oriental rugs.

The Restoration court had an "Indian" taste for lacquered pieces and Oriental porcelains. Some furniture in China was made for European markets. Some pieces made in England were sent to China for lacquering, before European lacquerers figured out how to successfully emulate Chinese techniques.

The important architects of the day were John Vanbrugh and Nicholas Hawksmoore. Their classically detailed buildings are not always stylistically consistent with the furnishings they contained. The brief reign of Queen Caroline was not a stylistically unique period. For most people, the reigns that were accompanied by significant artistic developments are Jacobean, followed by **William and Mary** and **Queen Anne**.

The Great Fire of London in 1666 was a catastrophic event. It prompted a large amount of building and created a demand for a fresh infusion of furniture. The fire seemed to be the perfect opportunity to institute a baroque urban design, and Christopher Wren (1632–1723) created one, but it was not meant to be. Most of Wren's suggestions for the redesign of London were unrealized.

After the fire, fifty-one churches were built in the years leading up to 1700. Wren was in charge of the reconstruction of the city's religious infrastructure. Most of his churches were externally modest, with surprises to be found in their interiors. Wren produced a specifically English version of French and Italian design, sometimes described as baroque, yet more restrained and disciplined than elaborate Italian examples. One of the joys of visiting Wren's many London churches is to see the hand of one architect present in many buildings.

Wren traveled to Paris, where he met Bernini. He never traveled to Italy, but he was knowledgeable about Italian baroque through publications.

William and Mary

William and Mary was a style of furniture influenced by French and Dutch taste. A high-backed upholstered settee was part of the lavish furnishings of a house's public rooms. Such pieces were formally placed around a room's perimeter. A settee from Henry VIII's palace, Hampton Court has curves everywhere: in its back profile, in the outward curve of the wings, in the scrolled arms, and in the characteristic feature of William and Mary furniture, the perfectly curved cross-stretcher. A formal piece meant to impress, its shapes are simplified in comparison to the most elaborate baroque pieces.

The cross-stretchers also existed on tall chests, dressing tables, desks, tables, and chairs (Figures 12.9). Most have straight turned legs (like baroque pieces), but late William and Mary pieces have cabriole legs. Some pieces have ball feet, and others have the ball-and-claw foot. Dining room chairs had an open splat and a cresting rail, although the splat was moving toward the solid splat characteristic of the subsequent Queen Anne period (discussed later).

A dresser was essentially a chest of drawers set on top of a table, and some were manufactured in two parts that were later connected; hence its straightforward name: **chest on chest or chest on stand**. A chest on chest has relatively little carving, with the decoration relegated to the art of the turner. Other than a cornice, there is little overt classical detailing. These pieces were copied in English colonies, where the chest on chest was called a highboy.

Some William and Mary pieces were influenced by Boulle work, with a predilection toward

Figure 12.9
Unknown, William and Mary highboy, Massachusetts, United States, 1700–1720.

gilding and lacquering. A subset of William and Mary furniture was silver furniture, either gilded or, more rarely, solid silver. In England, France, Italy, and Spain, there were examples of solid silver furniture. Extraordinarily expensive, few survive.

For upholstered furniture, the printed calico **chintz** was popular. William and Mary pieces related to baroque design with their curves, yet they were simpler in profile, form, and decoration, and therefore predictive of the style to come, Queen Anne.

Queen Anne

The common use of the stylistic name "Queen Anne" is evidence of the occasionally arbitrary nature of artistic nomenclature. The historical Queen Anne herself was not an important monarch, nor was she particularly interested in or important for the arts, let alone furniture. (Nor does Queen Anne furniture relate to the nineteenth-century domestic architecture in the United States known as Queen Anne.)

Yet for many, a Queen Anne chair is unrivaled, on a par with the Ming armchair and the Louis XV fauteuil. What binds all three together, interestingly enough, is the cabriole leg. It follows a crisp curving line, practical, modest, and elegant. Queen Anne pieces were contemporary with the vigorous baroque architecture of John Vanbrugh, with which they had little in common.

Queen Anne pieces are known for their restraint and beautiful proportions. Fastnedge described them as "extremely graceful articles of furniture; they exhibit the rich taste of the period, with its sense of elaborate display" (1955, p. 82). By the time of Queen Anne, the ponderousness of Elizabethan and Jacobean furniture was a distant memory. A Queen Anne dressing table has no stretchers (Figure 12.10). Furniture was no longer made ruddy for travel. The pieces were almost modern in their simplicity of form and lack of decoration. The profiles were as thin as they could be.

There is no one-to-one correspondence between the continental style of baroque and English Queen Anne, but there is a stylistic relationship. Knowing that Queen Anne appeared at the same time as the late baroque period, one detects a growing appreciation of lightness, grace, and elegance. France was moving away from baroque forms to regency and rococo; England had Queen Anne.

A Queen Anne chair has the cabriole leg with an undecorated knee and slipper feet. The knee of a chair is just below the point where the leg meets the seat frame. The backrest has a solid central splat, in the shape of a vase. The back rail curves. The design's success is demonstrated by the fact that they are still manufactured (Figure 12.11).

In a different economic and artistic context of the Queen Anne period, the **Windsor chair** arose (Figure 12.12). Designed for modest circumstances, it was enormously successful. The Windsor chair has no stylistic relationship to other Queen Anne furnishings. The Windsor was a well-designed rural chair that proved to be a stalwart of modest houses. Endlessly copied, it did particularly well in the English colonies; there are many varieties of the Windsor chair. The original type was **bow-backed**, in which a bent hoop acts as the top rail; the **comb-back** variety has a straight top rail.

The other features of the Windsor chair are its saddle seat, turned legs, and stretchers. It was made as an armchair, a side chair, and as a settee. It is another example of a piece of furniture whose features stem from the widespread use of a lathe. Ayres informs us that another name for the Windsor chair is "**stick-back** seat" (2003, p. 171). He writes: "Although chairs of this type are now inseparably associated with the town of Windsor, stick-back chairs were in fact made in many parts of England as well as Scotland, Ireland, and Wales" (p. 172).

Making an individual Windsor chair was not an easy task. Because these chairs relied upon standardized forms made from common materials, they were popular throughout the British Isles. Soon after their introduction, they started appearing in English colonies worldwide.

Figure 12.10
Unknown, Queen Anne card dressing table, Newport, Rhode Island, 1740–1750.

Figure 12.11
Unknown, Queen Anne side chair, New York, 1750–1760. Walnut, maple, and pine.

Figure 12.12
Comb-back
Windsor armchair,
Great Britain,
c. 1770. Yew
and elm.

Figure 12.13
Georgian chest, England and the United States, late eighteenth century.

Georgian

Georgian is related to neoclassicism. A feature of English design is that whereas France and Germany experienced the significant design interlude of the rococo, which was not at all classical, classicism in England never went away. Georgian design was sometimes exceedingly plain, with nothing but the proportions and massing related to the classical tradition.

Supplies of mahogany from Hispaniola (Haiti) to England increased, with the result that mahogany is a common Georgian wood. It is a hard, close-grained tropical wood with a dark reddish color. Georgian pieces frequently had shell ornamentation on the knee, apron, or top. Chairs become lower, more square, and robust. The top rails were straight or bow-shaped. A Georgian dresser might terminate in a classical broken pediment. Some Georgian chests are characterized by their simplicity and loose adherence to classical proportions (Figure 12.13). Many leg types are found in Georgian pieces, curved and straight. An American Georgian **kneehole** desk demonstrates the popularity of Georgian furniture and architecture in English colonies. Alternating concave and convex shell carvings top the three vertical divisions. Another popular Georgian furniture piece intended for work was the drop-down desk (Figure 12.14). Additional Georgian pieces are discussed in Chapter 13.

Figure 12.14
Georgian drop-down desk, England, late eighteenth century.

In a book that argues for a reassessment of the **virtuoso**, or enlightened collector and knowledge seeker, art historian Craig Hanson traces the varying allegiances to England in the reigns of the three kings George. The German-born George I was not an enthusiastic supporter of London's arts scene, as his political and cultural ties were oriented toward Germany. George II, the last English king born in Germany, was better suited—temperamentally and linguistically—to attending to the English side of his international duties. His heir, George III, managed to be both nativist and internationalist, supporting English arts and keeping his eye on continental developments.

Hanson seeks to recuperate the reputation of the people, in many professions, who collected as a serious hobby in Georgian England. He proposes "a new framework for understanding the arts in the early modern period, a more malleable and far less tidy framework that stresses the virtuoso's fascination with objects in all their learned array" (Hanson 2008, p. 20).

People collected coins, cameos, prints, antiquities, fossils, shells, and dried insects. The growing number of objects people collected required more tables, desks, and bookcases for their sorting, storage, and display. Georgian furniture manufacturers were happy to meet the demand. The scholarly pursuit of collecting ushered in a period in which physical objects were seen by some as conveying information, constituting knowledge, and proving their owner's erudite sensibility. The historian of art and science Barbara Stafford writes that "crammed shelves and drawers, with their capricious jumps in logic and disconcerting omissions, resembled the apparent disorganization of talk" (1994, p. 238). Pieces of furniture were admired for their strong elegant profiles in an era that experienced an increase in both the quantity and quality of objects, found and designed.

Chippendale, Hepplewhite, and Sheraton

In the late eighteenth century, three furniture designers revolutionized the furniture industry with their designs, their publications, and their business practices. Before Chippendale, Hepplewhite, and Sheraton, most furniture makers worked by type and not by measured drawings.

Chippendale

Thomas Chippendale (1718–1779) was the son of a carpenter, and he became the head of an extensive business that made English furniture. His company also imported French furniture. In 1754, he published the *Gentleman and Cabinet Maker's Director*. Prior to Chippendale, although designers produced similar-looking pieces, most work was custom. His book standardized the product line, with the result that clients knew exactly what they were getting. His book was a first in that it documented almost every type of English household furniture.

He was a designer, an author, and a manufacturer. His production was vast: he produced or drew almost the entirety of English furniture. Among his many pieces, three principal strands stand out: Gothic (Figure 12.15); a restrained version of rococo (which was not particularly faithful to French rococo) (Figure 12.16); and his version of Chinoiserie (which was not particularly faithful to Chinese design). In contrast to previous periods and designers, Chippendale's work is characterized by its variety and breadth. He is also known for refashioning the furniture business. He responded to the market's desire for well-made, sturdy, and practical furniture. His reasonably priced pieces allowed middle-class clients to enjoy decorative pieces.

Figure 12.15
Gothic armchair, Thames Valley, England, late eighteenth century.

Figure 12.16
Thomas
Chippendale,
Ribband-back side
chair, London,
England, 1754.
Mahogany and
damask.

Figure 12.17
Samuel McIntire, Hepplewhite-style side chair, Salem,
Massachusetts, United States, 1794–1799. Mahogany, ebony, ash,
birch, and pine.

Despite the breadth of his firm's output, when most people think of a Chippendale chair, they are referring to the armchair with the **ribband**, belonging to his so-called rococo furniture.

When his son, Thomas Chippendale the younger (1749–1822), led the firm, neoclassical pieces became a prominent part of the product line. Chippendale's supremacy in the furniture business was as much due to his business acumen as his talent as a designer. Chippendale did not stamp his furniture, so pieces referred to as Chippendale can indicate designs by Chippendale, the work of his company, or the work of his legions of imitators. Chippendale's encyclopedic book facilitated the process of copying its author's designs and ensured that Chippendale imitations are found across the globe.

Hepplewhite

Although George Hepplewhite (d. 1786) was not as prolific as Chippendale, nor his line as broad, he also created a variety of designs. He published them in his *The Cabinet Maker and Upholsterer's Guide* (1788). Hepplewhite is known for delicate chairs whose backs take a shield or oval form (Figure 12.17). For his settee designs, he relied on the same characteristic shield form. His settees are literally based on multiplying the single unit of a chair. This was an innovation as it created the possibility of having multiple pieces of furniture with a similar look.

Sheraton

Thomas Sheraton (1751–1806) created pieces that were rectilinear, of a smaller scale, and with delicate refined profiles. His chairs are known for their straight legs and backs. His upholstered pieces were simple, with light padding. Although he also published a catalog of his work, *Cabinet Maker and Upholsterer's Drawing Book* (1791), Sheraton was more of a designer and less of a businessman.

Like Hepplewhite, Sheraton's designs were firmly attached to the international neoclassical aesthetic.

Prior to Chippendale, Hepplewhite, and Sheraton, most commissions were **bespoke**—clients ordered furniture in individually negotiated transactions whose details concerned style and price. With their publications, the three late eighteenth-century designers and authors revolutionized the furniture business with a standardized product line and ready-made objects. This opened up the possibility of furniture being produced in quantity, in advance, and warehoused, waiting for eventual sale. The nineteenth-century furniture business was indebted to the publications, practices, and products of Chippendale, Hepplewhite, and Sheraton.

Conclusion

Ayres's recent work makes a valuable contribution to the study of interiors because he examines more modest structures. He writes: "Above all, the carpets, curtains and wallpaper which today provide vehicles for color and pattern in the home were largely absent from the pre-industrial vernacular interior. Most people did without such comforts and embellishments or made do with painted carpets (floor clothes or painted boards) and stenciled walls (in place of patterned wallpaper)" (Ayres 2003, p. 209).

Yet English design is mostly known for its grand country houses and their furnishings. When looking at English design, one must keep one eye on the continent and one eye on the British Isles. Architecture is generally known as Renaissance, baroque, and so forth; furniture and the decorative arts as Elizabethan, Jacobean, and so forth. The dual nomenclature is appropriate because, more so than for any of the great European powers, there is less internal design consistency within English design movements. The variations are endless, exceptions to the rule many. Yet this is no indication of a lack of mastery, for English design brilliance abounds.

This chapter covers a long chronological stretch, from Tudor to Georgian, the medieval period to the beginning of the modern age, and from castle to country house. The eclipse of the medieval era was heralded in ways modest and grand: nails were eschewed in favor of elegant timber-on-timber connections, and a variety of new construction methods for floors, walls, and ceilings that hid the structurally honest, if crude, timber-frame construction. The age of Shakespeare was the age of Elizabeth I, a monarch whose dresses confirm her understanding of the importance of a dazzling appearance. For designed objects, the drift toward opulence frequently resulted in new takes on medieval forms. Triangular stools and the X-frame chair were overlain with great quantities of decoration. The somber interiors of churches and houses contrasted with the bright textiles associated with pageants and fairs.

The Elizabethan architect Robert Smythson displayed an astute ability to develop a uniquely English style of large country houses that grew out of English traditions. Yet his designs exhibit an awareness of French and Italian traditions.

Smythson, for his ability to synthesize, represents one type of English architectural achievement. Inigo Jones represents another; Jones's buildings show the architect's ability to develop original designs absolutely in keeping with Italian Renaissance traditions.

In the Jacobean period, to which Jones belonged, furniture stalwarts such as the X-frame chair and the farthingale chair continued to be useful. Yet there was a distancing from the primacy of structure, be it medieval or Gothic. Parquet floors lay on top of floor joists, plaster ceilings hung from rafters, paneled walls hid framing systems, and the extensive use of upholstery enveloped a chair's chassis. Christopher Wren continued the English architectural attitude toward continental developments initiated by Jones—to master the vocabulary, employ it skillfully but not slavishly copy it. The result is that Wren's works are classical and scarcely look baroque.

Whatever reticence English architects felt toward baroque design was not seen in the works of furniture designers. With silver furniture, mirrored walls, and curvilinear William and Mary pieces, England experienced the baroque period to the fullest extent—from the inside of buildings.

Queen Anne furniture is a highlight of the history of furniture owing to its technical and aesthetic perfection. It neither hides nor glorifies its structure, but exhibits an absolute understanding of it. A Queen Anne tea table has the lightness of French rococo without the decoration. An important oddity, for a place rife with exceptions, is the Windsor chair, known for its simplicity yet not all that easy to craft.

An important subtheme of this chapter is the transmission of design information. The efforts of Hans Vredeman de Vries prove the importance of the printed image; he was more influential for his published drawings, and the designs they inspired, than his own works. The key role of the printed design book came full circle in the late eighteenth century when a trio of designer-authors intuitively understood that their reputations would be based as much on those who copied their works as on their own creations. It is poetic justice that Chippendale, Hepplewhite, and Sheraton gave the world the means to copy their designs, for copying, adopting, adapting, and changing is something that English architects and designers had been doing masterfully for centuries.

Sources

Ayres, James (2003). *Domestic Interiors: The British Tradition 1500–1850*. New Haven, CT: Yale University Press.

Bowett, Adam and James Lomax (2021). *Thomas Chippendale*. Shirehampton: Shire Publications.

Boynton, L. (1971). "The Hardwick Hall Inventory of 1601." *Furniture History* 7: 1–40.

Dutton, Ralph (1948). *The English Interior: 1500–1900*. London: B.T. Batsford.

Fastnedge, Ralph (1955). *English Furniture Styles: From 1500–1830*. Harmondsworth: Penguin.

Friedman, Alice (1989). *House and Household in Elizabethan England: Wollaton Hall and the Willoughby Family*. Chicago: University of Chicago Press.

Girouard, Mark (1978). *Life in the English Country House: A Social and Architectural History*. New Haven, CT: Yale University Press.

Hanson, Craig Ashley (2008). *The English Virtuoso: Art, Medicine, and Antiquarianism in the Age of Empiricism*. Chicago: University of Chicago Press.

Howard, Maurice (2007). *The Building of Elizabethan and Jacobean England*. New Haven, CT: Yale University Press.

Jussel, Christian and William DeGregorio (2023). *English Furniture 1680–1760*. New Haven, CT: Yale University Press.

Levin, Carole (2008). *Dreaming the English Renaissance*. New York: Palgrave Macmillan.

Lloyd, Nathaniel (1975). *A History of the English House: From Primitive Times to the Victorian Period*. London: The Architectural Press.

Mercer, Eric (1969). *Furniture 700–1700*. New York: Meredith Press.

Stafford, Barbara (1994). *Artful Science: Enlightenment Entertainment and the Eclipse of Visual Education*. Cambridge, MA: MIT Press.

Thornton, Peter (1978). *Seventeenth-Century Interior Decoration in England, France, and Holland*. New Haven, CT: Yale University Press.

Discussion and Review Questions

1. What are the general characteristics of Tudor design?
2. What are the general characteristics of Elizabethan design? How do these forms represent power? What is the concept of elite design being employed in Elizabethan pieces?
3. How do Jacobean pieces differ from Elizabethan pieces?
4. What are the general characteristics of Georgian design?
5. What are the general characteristics of William and Mary design?
6. What are the general characteristics of Queen Anne design? How does Queen Anne design differ from Elizabethan?
7. What is an example of a rural chair, from the Queen Anne period, that has no identifiable Queen Anne characteristics?
8. Who are the three furniture designers and manufacturers of the late eighteenth century who revolutionized the furniture industry?

In The Colonies

13

Colonial is a curious word. On the one hand, it refers to a style of furniture, interiors, and architecture that evokes feelings of nostalgia and tradition in the United States. On the other hand, it refers to a political and economic system that is inherently repressive. Ultimately, these two meanings are related, with the former arising from the latter. Art historian Mimi Hellman bemoans the fact that historians who look at major cultural preoccupations, such as colonialism, imperialism, and nationalism, tend to ignore the world of objects (Hellman 1999, p. 2). This chapter responds to her call and explores the relationship between colonialism and colonial furnishings.

This approach represents a change from how "colonial" is traditionally covered in design histories. What follows forges a global perspective by looking at a variety of colonial experiences from around the world. The purpose is to relate today's international environment to historical developments.

An American dictionary definition from 1993 gives an old-fashioned view of the North American/English colonial phenomenon:

Colonial: 1. of, concerning, or pertaining to a colony or colonies. 2. of, concerning, or pertaining to colonialism; colonialistic. 3. pertaining to the 13 British colonies that became the United States of America, or to their period. 4. Ecol. forming a colony. 5. Architecture, Furniture. a. noting or pertaining to the styles of architecture, ornament, and furnishings of the British colonies in America in the seventeenth and eighteenth centuries, mainly adapted to local materials and demands from prevailing English styles. b. noting or pertaining to various imitations of the work of American colonial artisans.

(Random House, 1993)

Figure 13.0
(*Facing page*)
Arthur Benison
Hubback, Kuala
Lumpur Station,
Kuala Lumpur,
Malaysia, 1911.

In contrast, University of Chicago anthropologists John and Jean Comaroff (1991), provide a multifaceted definition of colonialism. A two-volume work lays out their lifework and presents, if not a definition of colonialism, a theoretical approach to its multiple iterations. In theorizing colonialism, they list several attributes of the worldwide colonial encounter. Colonialism was, first and foremost, a political and economic system that involved actual agents—that is, the people who conducted colonialism's business, including soldiers, missionaries, traders, bureaucrats, artists, and scientists. Colonialism, the Comaroffs (and countless others) argue, had as many effects on the metropole (London, Paris, Amsterdam, Lisbon) as on the periphery (India, West Africa, East Indies, Macao). Colonialism, as a governmental initiative and as an idea, stood on a foundation of binary oppositions: near and far, center and periphery, black and white, ruler and ruled, modern and tradition, art and craft, Christian and pagan, and so on. Yet the categories that colonialism thrived on were ruptured, compromised, blurred, and reinvented, because they were based all along on discontinuities and contradictions.

This chapter starts by juxtaposing these two different conceptual positions of colonialism—one that has been, in the traditional American context, the common one in relationship to furnishings and the decorative arts, and one that is based on the writings of anthropologists. These dueling definitions suggest new directions in conceptualizing colonialism, appropriate to the twenty-first

century, and that start seeing material objects as players in complex societal and political relationships. This new approach is historically significant and pertains to the present day, in which globalism and multiculturalism are important topics.

Colonialism was a political and economic system that had profound cultural implications. It was a governmental system in which one country controlled another and thereby expanded its sphere of influence. It was often brutal. Looking at colonial artifacts is a testament to the ability of those involved in the arts to create beautiful things often out of terrible circumstances. This includes architecture, decorative arts, interiors, and furnishings.

Different colonial experiences around the world played out differently. As for cultural productions, what is consistent is that colonialism was the process by which cultures intermingled. Terms such as *syncretism* and *hybridity* refer to the culture-making processes in which two or more cultures and their stylistic and craft traditions came together. This process was often highly inventive and veered off into unexpected directions, sometimes producing objects not found in either of the original contexts. One such example is Arthur Benison Hubback's Kuala Lumpur Train Station and its adjacent Administration Building in which he responded, curiously, to the Malaysian context by importing Mughal forms (Figure 13.0).

Stylistic change occurs when traditions travel from mother country to colony; this is sometimes admired, sometimes abhorred. Some see the resulting hybrid culture as an artistic achievement that mirrors the biological process of the mixing of races and ethnic groups. One of the features of many colonial developments is the colonial time lag—which posits that most colonial achievements occurred in the colonies at a later date than in Europe.

English Colonial

In the United States, *colonial* usually refers to English colonial, although significant portions of the Americas were colonized by the Dutch, French, and Spanish. (Around the world, there were Dutch, English, French, Portuguese, and Spanish colonies. Danes, Germans, and Russians played smaller colonial roles.) The word *colonial* in the United States now has a neutral tone, largely because of the close political relationship between the United States and the United Kingdom; the press regularly refers to it as a "special relationship." It is worth remembering that initially England was an avowed enemy of the United States, and France her greatest ally. Buildings and objects were created in recognizable styles, and part of what it meant to be American, English, French, democratic or royalist, was played out in the realm of aesthetics.

For the early periods in the United States, the following terms can be used: Jacobean, Cromwellian, William and Mary, Queen Anne, and Georgian. Colonial refers to the early days of the American colonial encounter, while Shaker, Pennsylvania "Dutch," and the works of Iowa's Amana colonies are stylistically, although not chronologically, related. *Federal* is the term that refers to the American version of neoclassicism.

United States

Although there were Europeans in the Americas from the time of the late fifteenth century, their lives were harsh. The terms Renaissance, baroque, and rococo are not used to refer to American colonial pieces. The works the early settlers produced were a response to limited resources rather than to stylistic influences, and had little in common with ornate European artworks, although they were produced at the same time.

With few exceptions, the earliest extant American pieces are from the seventeenth century. Known as **colonial** or **early American**, they are simple, hardy pieces that are ingenious responses to difficult living situations. Pieces of furniture were few and valuable. A table-chair is a chair that folds into a table and that boasts a small storage area under the seat. It exhibits an accomplished level of workmanship, made from milled lumber, with no parts stemming from a lathe. Table-chairs were particularly useful in taverns and inns. When a single piece of furniture has multiple functions, as seating, as storage, and as a horizontal surface, it is an indication that furniture was rare. Incidentally, this single piece of furniture responded to the three essential functions of furniture: space-enveloping (storage), supporting a human figure (seating), and providing a horizontal surface (for work or display).

A colonial Brewster chair looks to medieval England for its form, although its manufacture was assisted by a mechanical lathe (Figure 13.1).

Figure 13.1
American colonial Brewster chair, seventeenth century.

A large number of early pieces were made of pine, but also cherry, oak, and hickory. A feature of many colonial chests, including the famed **Hadley chest**, is that many were made from wide boards (Figure 13.2). The austerity of colonial life, from the houses to the ways of living, appealed to the **Puritans**. The Puritans originated with the Protestant English religious reform movement that opposed both Roman Catholicism and the Church of England. The persecution of the Puritans in England was one of the factors that contributed to the establishment of North American colonies, and various strains of New England Puritanism developed.

A Hadley chest, so named for the Hadley region of Massachusetts, is typically a chest on top of two drawers, with a flip top. Shallow relief carving, mostly floral decorations and biblical references, cover a surface that was further embellished with paint. The Hadley chest is a mediation between the desire to have simply crafted objects and the desire to embellish objects and make them beautiful.

Some pieces are found in English colonies that are called Jacobean or Cromwellian. American Jacobean sideboards are simplified versions of English sideboards.

In large part due to the arrival of skilled chair and cabinetmakers from England, Pennsylvania and New England had burgeoning furniture-manufacturing centers; by 1720, imports of English furniture had declined significantly.

In 1730, almost all American mirrors were imported; by 1740, many of them were locally produced. Virginia and Maryland were responsible for a large amount of the imports.

Figure 13.2
Chest, New England, United States, 1650–1700. Oak and pine.

In response to the growing capacity of Americans to produce their own furniture, in the late seventeenth and early eighteenth centuries, England sought to protect its export trade in manufactured items, including furniture. Laws were passed to force colonists to purchase English goods, thereby supporting the English furniture industry at the expense of the nascent American one. American imports of English furniture, chairs, cabinets, and upholstered pieces mostly went to wealthy homes. American producers and consumers resisted these laws.

The English ports of the American east coast stretched from New England to South Carolina. The colonies were increasingly selling to one another, and also abroad.

Furniture historian Edward Cooke writes: "Furniture making, like other Connecticut crafts of the late colonial and early national period, was not simply an economic task, a means to supplement an income or increase self-sufficiency. Rather it was an essential part of the region's mixed agricultural economy from the earliest settlements. Making chests, chairs, and tables was one facet of the agricultural cycle" (1996, p. 199).

William and Mary

Throughout the 1730s, many British-American towns were large and prosperous and had a variety of specialized craftsmen, some from England. Unlike those active in England, American cabinetmakers were not members of guilds; they were independent businessmen. The development of regional traits was largely due to their freedom to explore personal expression within the boundaries of a retail economy based on stylistic type and object.

By the early eighteenth century, the situation had changed from the early colonial period and furniture makers were working clearly within European stylistic conventions. The finer American William and Mary pieces are nearly indistinguishable from their European forebears. Many pieces have all the standard William and Mary features: the unique curved stretcher, the bun feet, and the **scalloped** apron (Figure 13.3). A William and Mary high chest of drawers relies on a combination of form and applied decoration—paint—to achieve its grandeur. Wentworth House in Portsmouth, New Hampshire, is filled with a number of William and Mary or American baroque pieces (Figure 13.4).

Queen Anne

Experts can distinguish English from American pieces although their task is made easier

Figure 13.3
Japanned William and Mary highboy, Boston, Massachusetts, 1710–1730. Maple, poplar, and pine.

because actual English pieces of furniture were rare in the American colonies. Because information was available in accurate, printed form, many pieces, such as tea tables and chairs, are high in quality and similar to English pieces. American Queen Anne pieces have characteristic features, such as slipper feet, cabriole legs, and other attributes that contribute to a graceful economy of line. Initially, some furniture makers who were trained in England immigrated. Those who felt that their employment options in Europe were stymied were attracted by the promise of a better life. Once in North America, they continued to produce the types of pieces they were familiar with.

Windsor chairs, the workhorses of English agriculture, proved to function well in modest American settings (Figure 13.5). Many forms of these chairs developed in the American colonial context. A Windsor settee in a colonial interior shows the chair form expanded laterally to become a settee. This is a piece at home in a rough-and-tumble environment. Windsor chairs also appeared in other English colonies, including South Africa, Australia, and New Zealand.

By 1810 to 1820, the United States was fully recovered from the Revolutionary War, whose crowning moment was the Declaration of

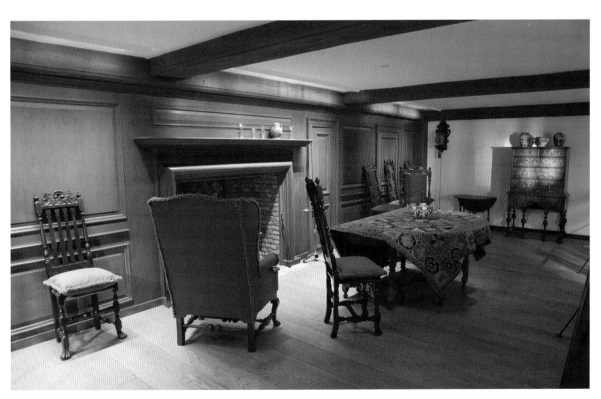

Figure 13.4
Wentworth House, Portsmouth, New Hampshire, 1695–1700. Room with wingchair, gate-leg table, and highboy.

Figure 13.5
English colonial
Windsor chair,
eighteenth
century.

Independence of 1776. The first decades of the nineteenth century saw the new country and its artisans ready to participate in the world's economy. Some Windsor pieces belie the humble circumstances of their intended context and are elaborate renditions of a modest furniture type. A Windsor settee has turned legs, spindle backs, and carved plank seats. Made with simple joinery techniques and repetition of parts, it is an early nonindustrial version of mass production. Windsor pieces were often painted.

Georgian

The cultural productions of the reigns of the English monarchs, George I, George II, and George III, are referred to as "Georgian." A simplified form of classicism, Georgian design is characterized by symmetry, restrained decoration, and heavy-looking forms.

Architecture

The English colonies use the same nomenclature for furniture and architectural styles; hence there is English Georgian and American Georgian. Although the term "Georgian" refers to the English kings, it is felicitous that the first American president was also named George. Around 1776 in the United States, when George Washington became president, was also the era

of American Georgian architecture and furniture. Georgian is a classical style.

In American Georgian buildings, the classical legacy of Georgian design is subtly apparent. A Georgian house in Trenton, New Jersey, has a classical cornice and is proportioned perfectly according to classical principles. Being made of local brick or wood places it in the local American context. Although no columns support its roof, with its proportions and fenestration, it is as though six columns were once there and have disappeared. Gadsby's Tavern in Alexandria, Virginia, has an intact interior that demonstrates that even less exalted structures often employed highly developed classical detailing (Figure 13.6).

Furniture

Many Georgian furniture pieces are staunch, resolute, and earnest. An American Georgian **highboy** has little obvious classical detailing. The legs firmly support the base and the cornice protrudes, giving the piece an architectural profile. The broad plinth supports a base unit on top of which sit four ranges of drawers. This is known as a chest on chest.

Another member of the Georgian furniture canon is the kneehole desk (Figure 13.7). The

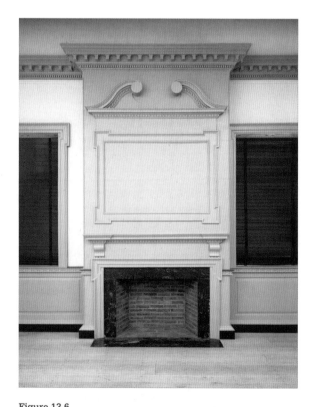

Figure 13.6
Gadsby's Taveran, ballroom fireplace detail, Alexandria, Virginia, 1792–1793.

Figure 13.7
John Townsend, kneehole desk, Newport, Rhode Island, 1765.
Mahogany, chestnut, and tulip poplar.

delicately scrolled brass **escutcheons**, in a
bat-wing shape, are neatly aligned and constitute
the bulk of the ornamentation. Scalloping, or carving in the form of a seashell, was popular because
it had a classical prototype. Scalloping was also
an impressive design that could be created easily
with a radius and a gouging tool. The former
could be as simple as a pencil and string or, later,
a protractor.

Dressing tables, also known as **lowboys**,
often accompanied high chests. The taller chests
held linens and apparel, while the dressing table
held personal items such as combs, ribbons,
jewelry, and cosmetics.

Georgian upholstered pieces share the same
weighty presence and substantial profile as highboys. They make their presence known in a room.
A **camelback sofa**, also known as a **humpback
sofa**, has a pronounced curve to its back, vaguely
reminiscent of baroque pediments, and stands
firmly on curved legs (Figure 13.8). The armrests
curve like classical scrolls. Yet the reference
to classicism is indirect. The Georgian sofa is
restrained in its decoration. Its sharply defined
profile gives it a clear, recognizable shape.

Georgian armchairs or wing chairs became
staples of the American furniture scene. By the
late eighteenth century, skilled cabinetmakers were active in Boston, Philadelphia, and
Charleston. They produced chairs with the same
curved back and scrolled arms as sofas, and
which were usually fully upholstered. They were
comfortable pieces for people of means, or for
people who wanted to imitate, at least for an
hour or two, the lifestyle of people of means. Wing
chairs were often paired in front of a fireplace,
responding to the symmetrical architecture with
their placement. Georgian furniture, as a group,
employs a range of details, but certainly a good
indication that a piece is Georgian is the characteristic ball-and-claw foot. Sometimes the knees of
armchairs also feature the Georgian scallop.

The wings themselves, purportedly to protect
the sitter from drafts, in practice were used to lean
against when napping. Sometimes they rolled
horizontally; sometimes they were curved and

Figure 13.8
Unknown,
camelback sofa,
Philadelphia,
Pennsylvania,
1760–1790.
Mahogany and
pine.

shaped in the vertical dimension as well. Some Georgian chairs and chests have slipper feet, and exceptionally, Georgian chairs have rear cabriole legs. Backswept rear legs support some Georgian wing chairs, a baroque touch. Sometimes thumb tacks held down the upholstery and by highlighting the edges further delineated the form.

The curvilinear **bombé** form demonstrates the high level of quality that American furniture makers achieved in the late eighteenth century and early nineteenth (Figure 13.9). It appeared in numerable pieces, tall and short, and demonstrates that Georgian is a broad category that addressed multiple functions. The bombé profile curves in two directions, is difficult to achieve, and is one of the most baroque-looking American pieces. With no classical detailing, it has curved legs and the characteristic swell in its profile. The bookcase stands solidly on the ground, a very different approach to a piece of furniture and its relationship to the ground plane than the Queen

Anne tea table. Georgian pieces share the quality of solidity with their architectural backdrop. Swelled or bombé chests were popular in Boston and Newport in the mid-eighteenth century, despite their cost.

Other colonial furniture

In contexts that required hardier pieces, **ladderback** and **banister-back** chairs were popular. They were sturdy, useful, and easy to produce and found use in Great Britain, the Americas, and Africa (Figures 13.10 and 13.11). With cane seating, they were relatively inexpensive. A ladderback chair is named for the horizontal rails of the backrest that resemble a ladder. Initially, it is probable that carpenters who produced ladders also utilized their skills making chairs. Alternately, it is possible that some chairs were made using leftover lumber. Banister-back chairs have a similar manufacturing history. Their backs

Figure 13.9
Bombé desk and bookcase, Boston, Massachusetts, 1765–1790. Mahogany and white pine.

Figure 13.10
Ladderback chair, Cape Coast, South Africa, nineteenth century.

Figure 13.11
Karen Blixen
House, dining
room with
banister-back
chairs, Nairobi,
Kenya, 1912.

are formed with vertical supports that resemble a stair railing and its vertical supports, the balusters. Sometimes the baluster form was made by turning on a lathe; sometimes it was cut out in profile from planks.

Shakers

Artworks are often connected to religion, with Chinese pagodas, Mayan temples, and Gothic cathedrals as obvious examples. The work of the **Shakers** in the United States adds a different wrinkle to the connection between design and spirituality. In the late eighteenth century, the predominant contextual note for furniture is that the United States was gradually moving from an era of privation to an era of wealth. Economic prosperity often was represented by the increased use of European styles. For the Shakers, design was a religious and moral statement about restraint and austerity. Journalist and author Adam Gopnik referred to the works of the Shakers as "so magically austere that they continue to astonish our eyes and our sense of form" (2006, pp. 162–68). Many of their pieces are breathtakingly beautiful and simple. (It is logical that twentieth-century modernists, who appreciated minimalism, admired Shaker pieces.) Shakers

shared property, and their communities were an early exploration of socialism. Shaker design reached its height around 1830.

The group's founder, Ann Lee, was from the North of England. In 1774, she and her husband immigrated to New York (Larkin 1995, p. 3). Lee and her followers saw a connection between chasteness, charity, organization, cleanliness, and some form of communal living. Her order had disciples who were eventually spread throughout New England in the late eighteenth century and the early nineteenth century. There were not many of them, approximately 5,000, but the enduring popularity of their artistic productions exceeds what is expected from a small community.

Shaker design is not the same as colonial design, although in many respects they are similar. Early colonial designers often created objects in an arena of scarcity. Their simple creations were the result of a lack of material resources and the time they could devote to crafting furniture. Shakers made a virtue of simplicity. Neither technologically nor stylistically innovative, they made ordinary pieces extraordinarily well. In some Shaker pieces, there is a connection to neoclassicism, to the extent that lines were simple, forms crisp, and edges hard. What came to be known as the Shaker style, in housing, dress, and furniture, was not different from that of other American creations, yet Shaker creations trod the fine line between the normal and the extraordinary. Author John Shea writes that "the Shakers' individuality and disdain of 'worldly superfluity' produced new techniques which made their furniture lighter, stronger, and more practical than that constructed by other craftsmen" (1971, p. 65). They were anti-worldly and anti-commercial, while also quite commercial; many of the items were specifically created for sale, initially for lower- to middle-class markets.

Shaker products are stylistically related to **Pennsylvania Dutch**, Quakers across the country, and Amish in Amana, Iowa (who eventually progressed from making pieces of furniture to refrigerators and microwaves).

Shaker design is surprisingly asymmetrical, a feature that departs significantly from contemporary neoclassical design. The ancient Greeks and their Renaissance imitators saw beauty in the proportions of the human body; they sought to imbue their objects with that beauty by relying upon human proportions. The Shaker creed rejected the idea that formed objects should reflect the human body; instead, they relied on repetition and the grid. Many pieces are arrhythmically broken up. Objects responded directly to the intended functions; Shaker products looked like useful objects that followed a functional and nonhuman law of design.

South Africa

South Africa is unique for a number of reasons and its artworks are examples of hybridity of a different sort. For one, the Dutch and the English in this area were competing interests. This is not unusual; different European parties fought for many colonies over the centuries. This can be a source of cultural richness, in addition to causing strife. What was unusual in South Africa is that the Dutch and the English interests remained as relative equals for much of the area's history. This is reflected in the nation's official languages, English and **Afrikaans**, a Dutch-based dialect. The indigenous context on the southern tip of the African continent was equally varied.

Significant European settlement started in Capetown with the Dutch merchant Jan van Riebeeck, who arrived in 1652. Van Riebeeck came with a party of eighty-two men and eight women. He either brought a lathe with him or one arrived shortly after his arrival, as many types of spindle (turned) chairs were in production as early as 1700.

South Africa has a rich heritage in the decorative arts, and one of them is furniture. The forms are clearly European, but the break from Europe happened early. A feature of some colonial arenas is that forms continue to live on in the colonies after they have expired or become less fashionable in the home country. African carpenters became familiar with European furniture types and the methods necessary to produce them. The integration and spread of European forms in South Africa was extensive, so that many indigenous practices virtually ceased to exist, from building to clothing. The extermination of local traditions and their replacement with hybrids or European ones was a tumultuous process.

The topic of European-style furniture in South Africa is well studied and documented. In contrast, there are no books devoted to English furniture in Kenya, Nigeria, and the Gold Coast (Ghana). While the situation in South Africa was in many respects unique, certain developments are probably indicative of continent-wide practices. These include the differences between city- and country-made furniture, the presence of actual European pieces on the coast and their absence in the countryside, and the effects of nineteenth-century transportation developments in challenging the first two. We can, by inference, consider them as indicative of furniture trends in other African regions as well.

Cape Country

South Africa, like much of Africa, saw little utility in and therefore ignored baroque and rococo design developments, including furniture. There are two principal categories of South African European furniture: Cape Coast furniture and Cape Country furniture. Author Mary Alexander Cook is one of the people who appreciates the latter for its combination of good design and simple decoration. Country furniture in South Africa can be called "Country," "Platteland," or simply "traditional furniture." About the relationship between country furniture and city furniture, she notes that the latter has more obvious ties to European styles. Country pieces, Cook (1980) writes, explore the same design trends, although mediated by the availability of materials and tools, and varying standards of training and apprenticeship.

Petrus Borcherds was born in 1786, and his memoir describes the dire living conditions of many South Africans of European descent: "The occupants, when in the Karoo, reside in small houses, or rather huts, consisting generally of but one room with a fire place and a small entrance hall, adjoining their sheep-folds (**kraals**), which are so situated that those inside the dwelling can easily protect all points by their muskets against rapacious animals or robbers" (Borcherds 1861, p. 52).

Many South African country houses were simply furnished with only a few chairs and small tables, such as tea tables. Often people slept on the floor, or on benches or mattresses. There was not always a bed or a dining room table.

The flagship of country furniture is the **Tulbagh chair**. It is unique to South Africa, as was its stylistic follower, the Tulbagh transitional chair (Figure 13.12). The lineage of these pieces starts with the English Queen Anne chair, although they are like it in another respect as well: the naming of the Tulbagh chair is similar to the naming of Queen Anne furniture; the name has stuck in the popular consciousness, with no logical explanation for it. There are two possible origins for the name of the Tulbagh chair: Tulbagh is a geographic designation, and there was a Governor Ryk Tulbagh. There is no evidence that Governor Tulbagh had anything to do with the chair's design, nor is it geographically limited to Tulbagh. The Tulbagh chair came about in the late seventeenth century, and its back resembles the vase-shaped central splat of the Queen Anne chair. Initially, the Tulbagh chair had a cane back. This was not a feature of the European Queen Anne chair, and therefore is one of the African chair's defining characteristics. Tulbagh chairs were not exact copies of European Queen Anne chairs—there is no cabriole leg. The Tulbagh chair has a box-stretcher, and the chairs range from ornate to simple. The Tulbagh transitional chair is made of wood, sometimes from a mixture of woods. The stalwart of the countryside, more elaborate versions stood on turned legs.

Its boxy frame resembles the Jacobean farthingale chair; chairs similar to the farthingale chair were also created in the Netherlands, and it is likely that the importation of this form to South Africa came from Dutch craftsmen.

The **transitional Tulbagh chair** drops the ornateness of the Tulbagh chair but maintains the sturdy box-stretchers. The legs, stretchers, and back were not turned. The squat legs are tapered and extend past the seat frame to form cushion knobs. Only the top rail is shaped; not a crest rail, it rests between the verticals.

In the eighteenth and nineteenth centuries, sets of chairs were rare; even if a household had ten to twelve chairs, they were mostly different. Tulbagh and transitional Tulbagh chairs were initially made of local woods, **yellowwood**, and **stinkwood**.

A specific type of transitional Tulbagh chair developed in the late eighteenth century. As they were made from the wood of lemon or orange citrus trees, they were called **Lemoenhout** chairs. Small and low, they have the same square proportions of the transitional chairs. They do not have a true box-stretcher, as the side stretchers were elevated. The seat side rails were also higher; this was because they were connected by a mortise-and-tenon, and the connections were stronger if they were not on the same level. Lemoenhout chairs were sanded literally by scrubbing them with sand; some were bleached and many were painted. Wired seats could be configured to incorporate patterns, such as spokes of a wheel. The pattern of the wiring was an area where the indigenous craftsmen innovated.

Despite an increase in furniture imports, seldom did imported furniture make it beyond Capetown into the countryside. Real Queen Anne chairs were seen only in the towns. Functionally,

Figure 13.12
Transitional Tulbagh chair, South Africa, eighteenth century. Lemoenhout.

aesthetically, and economically, there was little place for flamboyance. Initially, people in the countryside could not afford European furniture, so they relied upon indigenous furniture. Country furniture makers were usually active in other professions and could not devote all their time to crafting furniture. In addition to the higher cost of imported works, transport was difficult. Simply put, the coast and the African interior were two different cultural and economic worlds. The so-called Cape Country furniture, therefore, developed a distinct character and followed its own path of development. Country pieces used different woods and were created using simpler tools.

Over decades of change, the dynamics of furniture trade and production in South Africa varied. For one, the increase in imports of English furniture to Capetown came at the expense of locally made furniture. A general increase in trade included an increase in the quantity of timber shipped to Africa. Mahogany took a big share of the imported timber, with an important role for rosewood from Brazil, and ebony, satinwood, and zebra wood from the Netherlands East Indies. Although not immediately apparent, there is a relationship between the slave trade and the production of furniture. Slaving ships left Africa bound for Brazil, the United States, and the West Indies, all three of whom had copious supplies of timber. The ships had to return to Africa with their cargo holds filled, and timber was one of the New World products that sold well in Africa. So human cargo left in one direction, with the raw material of timber returning in the other direction. The result is that much African colonial furniture and architecture is made of North and South American timber. The growth in African timber imports coincided with a gradual depletion of African timber supplies.

Cape Coast

The initial creators of European-style furniture were Europeans, in the cities and in the countryside, and they hired Europeans, Africans, and Asians as their assistants. Many of the Asian assistants were Malaysian, called Malay or inaccurately Chinese. The presence of Malaysian furniture makers, operating in an environment in which the major interactions were between the Dutch, English, and indigenous African ethnic groups, represents the ethnic complexity of the colonial environment and the rich genealogy of the pieces they made.

Neoclassicism

Simplified versions of neoclassical pieces, however, were contemporary with the Tulbagh and Tulbagh transitional chairs. Neoclassicism in South Africa is another strand in the complicated ethnic web of South African furniture. South Africans were familiar with Dutch, English, and French variants of neoclassicism. From 1795 onward, many of the British who arrived brought neoclassical furniture with them. Eventually, neoclassicism made its mark on country furniture, especially in cupboards. A Cape County cupboard is Georgian in its detailing. Its form is rectilinear, resulting in a well-designed unyielding form, with a pediment and classically detailed feet and cornice (Figure 13.13).

Triangular pedimented cupboards were a feature of wealthier homes. Riversdale is a region in the Western Cape where craftsmen excelled at making them. The tapered legs shown in this cupboard are known as Riversdale block feet. They are identified as having three flutes, echoing classical triglyphs. The cornice overhangs. A defining feature of German neoclassical (and Biedermeier)

Figure 13.13
Split pediment Georgian cupboard, Cape Coast, South Africa, early nineteenth century.

pieces was a distinct contrast between cherry or mahogany (orange or reddish in color) and ebony or ebonized (black or near black) wood as accents. Riversdale pieces achieve the contrast by juxtaposing infill panels of yellowwood with dark stinkwood framing. Yellowwood trees are huge, growing to 150 feet (46 meters) in height. The dark-hued stinkwood is so named because it emits an unpleasant odor upon being felled that dissipates over time. Sometimes these cupboards were made with imported teak, although Africa also grows teak. Similarly, most ebony was imported, although it also grows in South Africa. The Riversdale cupboard has a visible closing strip. Cupboards and wardrobes were standard features of European households in South Africa, as chests of drawers or dressers were not common until the late nineteenth century. Metal escutcheons were rarely used in early colonial Africa.

A limited number of Indo-Portuguese chairs from Ceylon, Goa, and Bombay made their way to Capetown but not into the countryside. Wealthier urban families had Chinese and Japanese furniture, lacquered pieces, part of the fashion for Chinoiserie. Few survive. They arrived thanks to the routing of the ships of the Dutch East India Company.

The industrial revolution of the nineteenth century impacted the production of Cape Country furniture in a negative way. The arrival of railroads made it easier to import furniture made in South African cities and also European furniture. During the years of railroad construction, the number of roads from the coast to the interior increased, also facilitating transport of furniture to the interior. Locally made country furniture was therefore in decline.

Australia

The first fleet arrived at Sydney Cove in January 1788. John Earnshaw, a self-described amateur, wrote a book titled *Early Sydney Cabinetmakers*, which he published in 1971. It, and other books like it, does a good job of documenting the rich world of nineteenth-century furniture making in Australia. These books, however, are primarily interested in form and style and are written to promote the collecting of furniture. They do not consider their subject from a social perspective, as a body of cultural artifacts to be interpreted. For example, there is little information on the ethnic makeup of either creators or users of the furniture, and no consideration of the impact that European art forms had on indigenous arts. Indigenous Australians (of non-European background) are not even mentioned in passing. Nonetheless, Earnshaw's book provides the background for future scholars, and most of the information presented here benefited from his efforts.

Australia's history of European furniture differs from those of other English colonies, India, South Africa, and North America, because the starting date of the European presence is at the tail end of the eighteenth century. A feature of its colonial history is that it seems speeded up. Australian history bypasses any developments such as Elizabethan, Jacobean, baroque, and rococo.

In Earnshaw's telling, the 1790s were lean and hungry years, yet by 1800, furniture reflected a sense of stability. In the early years of the Australian settlement, before and after 1800, households were modest and furnishings consisted of chests, stools, tables, and beds. Convicts owned less. One of the unique characteristics of Britain's colonization of Australia is that it relied heavily on relocating prisoners, or convicts, to relieve pressure from Britain's prison population. The European population in 1800 was less than 5,000.

The first lathes on the island-continent were manual, spring-bow, or treadle-driven (operated by moving paddles with the feet). By 1810, New South Wales had a European population of 10,000, and Earnshaw surmises that the professional lines drawn between the activities of cabinetmakers, carpenters, and joiners were not distinct. Few English pieces arrived with the immigrants, so the production of European furniture was mostly by local furniture makers. Knowledge was passed down to the next generation through the apprentice system. Most workshops had only a few apprentices. Apprentices started working in their early teenage years, twelve hours a day, six days a week, with a contracted indenture of approximately seven years.

What gave early Australian colonial furniture its unique character was its material: Australian cedar wood. Red cedar wood grew plentifully on the eastern coast of Australia, providing materials for the local furniture industry. It was felled in sufficient quantity that by 1795 there were Australian cedar exports to India. The terms *cedar* and *mahogany* were frequently used interchangeably. Loggers almost completely depleted Australian cedar forests less than a hundred years after the arrival of the Europeans.

A butler's table has a removable tray that rests on top of a folding base. It likely originated in England in the eighteenth century, and soon after spread to English colonies worldwide (Figure 13.14). Simply made pieces met most people's needs.

Australian neoclassicism

Noris Ioannou describes a pine settee from the Barossa valley as vernacular Biedermeier. Once the economic success of Australia seemed inevitable, other ethnic groups, from Europe and Asia, immigrated to the island and brought their artistic traditions with them. In one settee, the classicism is barely discernible, and is limited to the klismos form of the backrest and the scrolled arms and feet. Some classical pieces included a cut-out tulip motif that provides a vernacular element, a German invention with no classical precedent.

As early as the first decade of the nineteenth century, some pieces were made in simplified versions of the global style of neoclassicism (Figure 13.15). Scrolled neoclassical armchairs made their way to Yangon, Burma, in the country's finest hotel, the Strand, and are evidence that some furniture operations produced high-quality work and maintained global standards. By 1840, powered woodworking machines in Australia and across Southeast Asia changed the way furniture was made. In some countries, there was an uneasy coexistence of Europeans and indigenous furniture makers. By 1840, there were first- and second-generation Australians of European descent and handmade furniture became a thing of the past.

In 1850, the European population stood at 260,000, and consequently both local production and furniture imports increased to meet demand. The mid-century saw the beginning of organized labor, and the furniture industry, like the country at large, sought to distance itself from its convict past by excluding convicts from the furniture trade. Two industries were largely responsible for the economic boom of the 1850s—gold mining and wool ranching. This economic activity brought about the existence of furniture middlemen and warehouses devoted to stockpiling furniture. Most furniture had been utilitarian before 1850, but Australians, from a distance, followed reports about the Great Exhibition of the Works of Industry of all Nations in London of 1851. Victorian pieces were imported and their arrival marked the decline in the appreciation, and therefore production, of both colonial and neoclassical works.

The decorative arts collection of the National Gallery of Victoria, in Melbourne, displays all the ambiguities of the Victorian age. Adding to the

Figure 13.14
Butler's table, Australia, nineteenth century.

Figure 13.15
Bookcase, Adelaide, Australia, 1875. Red cedar.

diversity of the Australian furniture scene, in the 1870s, Chinese furniture makers started to arrive. In 1890, Australia had seventy-two furniture workshops, nineteen of which were Chinese, and these nineteen workshops employed 386 Chinese workers. The importance of Chinese furniture workers in the history of Australian decorative arts is the subject of Peter Charles Gibson's book *Made in Chinatown: Chinese Australian Furniture Factories* (2022). Nineteenth-century Australia had a diverse workforce to produce the myriad Victorian styles that popular taste demanded.

India

Vasco de Gama's voyage of 1497 to 1498 delivered him to Calcutta in 1498, and he returned to Portugal to great acclaim in 1499. In the late fifteenth century, European trade with West Africa flourished, and Columbus sailed to the Americas. Indigenous Americans are called Indians because India was ostensibly Columbus's goal. The Italian explorer Marco Polo (1254–1324) was the first European to travel widely in Asia and to record his impressions. Polo's book, whose English title was *The Travels of Marco Polo*, brought discovery and foreign travel to a wide audience.

The Portuguese crown was attracted by the trade that expeditions to India promised to deliver. A fifteenth-century cliché provided a rhetorical answer to a query as to why the Portuguese were embarking on these costly and life-threatening endeavors: "We seek Christians and Spices." That is, the voyages were in the name of God and had an economic motive. Indian spices, small in volume, high in value, were ideal commercial items. The reasons for European expansion are not easily explained. In addition to economic, religious, and political motives, expeditions provided outlets for restless young men. Expeditions were attractive to the proverbial younger sons who did not benefit from the European inheritance system that favored firstborn males. Oceangoing voyages to East Asia acted as a release valve from social and economic pressures at home. Individuals caught up in the Portuguese colonial drive made little distinction between religion, economics, politics, and personal ambition.

A technological innovation made possible the extension of Europe's global reach. The caravel, developed in the 1440s, utilized the triangular sails that allowed sailors to tack against the wind. Before the Europeans' arrival, Arab traders had been trading up and down the East African seaboard, also known as the Swahili coast.

In the nineteenth century, India was primarily an English colony, and the vision of India as the jewel in the crown of the British Empire has stuck in the public consciousness. Yet in the earlier period, there were competing Dutch and Portuguese interests. The early Portuguese colonial experience was more cooperative and interactive than dominating. The goal was not territorial expansion but access to trade.

The influence and impact of the Portuguese on the whole of India, regarding authoritarian power and cultural productions, was relatively minor, with a few exceptions. The Portuguese and Dutch presence on the Indian coast resulted in some fantastic pieces of furniture—some of which stayed in India, some of which were shipped to England—that started appearing the world over.

India had a population in 1600 of some 150 million, with 100 million of those being in the Mughal Empire. The Mughal Empire was inland and not dependent upon coastal trade (Pearson 1987, p. 23). It was a different cultural and economic world from the coast.

The principal Portuguese trading center was the city of Goa. There was little European cultural impact outside of Goa. A characteristic of international trading centers such as Goa was a social mobility not found either in inland Indian areas or the European home countries.

Coastal India traded in cotton, indigo, pepper, cinnamon, intoxicants, wool, silks, and gold bullion. From China came silks and porcelain. Coastal Indian trade included ebony, slaves, ivory, beads, horses, pearls, carpets, dyes, opium, copper, rice, and rubies.

Hindu artists in India learned to do European-style portraiture, one step in the process of creating a multinational artistic world. Adding to the cultural mix, there were other Europeans—Italians, Germans, French, English, Flemings—and Africans. Few Portuguese women traveled to the Indian colonies; consequently, a significant mixed-race population arose.

Portuguese in India had been urban poor or peasants and were not rooted in Portuguese high culture. In sixteenth-century Portugal, chairs were unusual and were typically reserved for the head of the family. Portuguese sat on the floor, spoons were rare, and forks unknown.

Western-style seats did not traditionally exist in India, as people sat on the ground, on mats, cushions, or on drum seats made from a variety of materials. The Dutch, British, French, and Portuguese inhabitants of the early trading centers were the first to commission elevated seats from local carpenters, who were happy to oblige. These European forms were made out of "foreign" materials (non-European) and with "exotic" decoration. The resulting objects were interestingly exotic to both Indians and Europeans.

The standard chair was likely based on a Dutch original box chair—the same chair that inspired the Tulbagh chair. Initially, Dutch craftsmen oversaw Indian artisans and slaves who, in short order, took over their business. Because of their affiliation with the Dutch East India Company, these chairs were exported around the world, a few to Africa, many to the Netherlands, and some to England. The Dutch East India Company was founded in 1602 and remained an important economic and cultural force until its dissolution in 1799. Its charter was to protect and promote Dutch trade to India and to the islands of the Indian Ocean, including Indonesia. Initially a commercial venture, its activities had major political, military, and cultural implications.

The Coromandel Coast of India was another source of carved ebony furniture. It is the southeastern tip of India, on the Bay of Bengal. Ebony pieces were first made in India, and in Ceylon, **Batavia**, and the Dutch East Indies in the second half of the eighteenth century. Typical products were chairs, tables, beds, and chests. The common feature of this production is that they are covered with dense low-relief carving of foliage. They often have twisted stretchers and legs (Figure 13.16). Their backs are further embellished, sometimes with finials. The decoration has an affinity with carving traditions of southern India, drawn from Hindu mythology.

The Indian chairs that arrived in England caused mass confusion some hundred years after their arrival. Because of their dark appearance and profuse decoration, they were misidentified as English, from the Tudor, Elizabethan, or Jacobean periods.

Ivory work was made in Vizagapatam, Murshidabad, and Travancore, on the East Coast of India (Figure 13.17). These cities had traditionally been centers of Hindu ivory work, and they became known for producing ivory-veneered furniture. Some five-legged chairs were made to rotate and serve as barber chairs. Another explanation for the unusual form is that they were translations of round straw drum chairs. These five-legged chairs are exceptional examples of the inventiveness of Indian furniture. Indonesian furniture makers later copied them.

Figure 13.16
Unknown, ebony sidechair, Coromandel Coast, India, 1660–1680.

Figure 13.17
Burgomaster chair, Vishakhapatnam, India, 1760–1770. Haldu wood with ivory and caning.

Another branch of Indian furniture was influenced by the Muslim preference for geometric decoration (Figure 13.18). In this category seating was rare; most pieces were highly decorated Indo-Portuguese storage items.

Though it was not initially a center of locally made furniture, by the late eighteenth century, Bombay was producing furniture in quantities large enough to export to other parts of India and abroad. Bombay blackwood furniture was made from blackwood from the Malabar coast. The furniture of Bombay carvers is related to architectural work, especially the sort typical in Ahmedabad. Every visible surface was carved, a confluence of Indian tradition and Victorian taste. Flamboyant carving was central to the concept of quality. Bombay blackwood furniture was exhibited at the Great Exhibition of 1851. It gradually fell out of favor, because it was difficult to clean and aesthetically did not conform to the modernizing trends that characterize the tail end of the nineteenth century.

Spanish Colonial

European-style furniture was introduced to South and Central America in the sixteenth century, following the Spanish conquest. Initially, the items were imported; then they were made by local furniture makers. The pieces included X-frame chairs, chairs similar to the Renaissance sedia, trestle tables, beds, and chests.

Figure 13.18
Cabinet (Contador), Goa, India, late seventeenth century.

Latin America

The year 1500 marks an important time around the world. The Renaissance was flowering in Italy, the Ming dynasty was in full swing in China, and the Mughals were consolidating their power in the inland Indian region. The late fifteenth century also brought Europe into contact with South America, Asia, and Africa.

Hernán Cortés took the Aztec capital of Tenochtitlán, and the Spanish Hapsburg royal regime ruled New Spain for nearly two hundred years, 1521–1700. In 1535, the Spanish king Charles V installed a viceroy to represent the Spanish crown in New Spain (today Mexico). In Latin America, the Spanish sought to build and furnish in the styles they were familiar with, which resulted in a significant amount of baroque architecture, interiors, and furniture. Sometimes by intention, sometimes by necessity, the results were hybrids that incorporated indigenous techniques.

The official aesthetic of baroque New Spain centered on religious imagery, the building of churches, and the painting and sculpture they held. But the secular realm was equally important, with portraits of kings and viceroys, and secular objects including furniture. Art historian Michael Schreffler examines representation's role in the production of a visual and spatial order, with all its forms and symbols. In 1492, Antonion de Nebrija wrote that language always accompanies empire; Schreffler argues that there was also an official aesthetic that included paintings, interiors, and furnishings.

Some interpret the objects as proof of a growing Creole patriotism. Yet objects of royal propaganda were contested in the New World (North America) in ways that they were not in the Old World (Europe). The position they held regarding nationalism was tenuous. This dovetails with postcolonial theorizing on the inherent ambivalence of colonial objects that were part of a fractured counter discourse.

Plateresque or, in Spanish, Plateresco refers to the highly ornamented Spanish design of the sixteenth century. It is found in architecture, interiors, and furnishings. Related to baroque art, plateresque works frequently take Renaissance forms and embellish them with decoration, often Islamic motifs. This highly decorative style became prevalent in the Americas. **Mudéjar** refers to Islamic-influenced design in Spain, and it is used infrequently in reference to American works. A plateresque chair from Mexico has the form of a Renaissance chair, and it is opulent in its finishes, detailing, and applied decoration.

Charles II (r. 1665–1700) was the last Hapsburg king. While his life's work has been seen as a monarchy in decline, it can also be seen as a final expression of Spanish power in the Americas. **Churrigueresque** refers to late Spanish baroque design, in Spain and throughout Latin America of the seventeenth and eighteenth centuries. Named for three brothers from Barcelona, Spain, it is a continuation of the stylistic trend started in plateresque, only it is even more elaborate. The use of pattern in Churrigueresque allowed for furniture makers in the Americas to occasionally incorporate indigenous motifs.

French Colonial

France was a major colonial power whose ascendancy on the world stage coincided with the lessening of Dutch and Portuguese power. In addition to a large swath of North America, which resulted in the famous Louisiana Purchase of 1803, France had outposts on several Caribbean islands, including Guadeloupe, Martinique, and **Saint-Domingue** (today Haiti). France had substantial colonial holdings in Africa and Asia. In Africa, most of West Africa and parts of central Africa and the island of Madagascar were under French colonial control. In Asia, France had considerable presence on the eastern coast of India and, in Southeast Asia, controlled Vietnam, Cambodia, and Laos.

West Africa

The standards of design established by the French monarchy, from Louis XIV to Napoleon, baroque through neoclassical, had an enormous impact on monarchies around the world. Court taste also influenced design within France. People in the French provinces looked to the latest styles from Versailles and sought to emulate them—hence the term *provincial*. The word refers to pieces made simpler and for people of more modest means. Some nobles in the French countryside were able to afford fairly accurate versions of royal designs; for those of more modest means, simplified pieces were appealing. This included middle-class merchants, craftsmen, well-off farmers, and other successful professionals. This is the trickle-down

effect of design, in which the elite establish the standards of taste that the middle classes seek to emulate. While "provincial" implies a rural version, some people, then and now, preferred the simplified versions of regency and rococo designs. Many rococo designs are too elaborate in their appearance and difficult aesthetically to incorporate into a household.

French provincial furniture is more likely solid than veneered. Many chairs had rush seats and unattached cushions. French provincial pieces also made their way to the French colonies. In these new locations, they represented the home country, and they were elegant and sturdy.

Senegal, the westernmost part of the continent, was the center of France's West African interests. A mid-nineteenth-century watercolor was published in a book written by David Boilat, a mixed-race African priest. One of the book's ethnic portraits shows the interior of a home that belongs to the **habitants**, the name given to the mixed-race, or Creole, class that grew up in several West African coastal trading centers. Eighteenth-century prints show European-style homes, replete with a fireplaces, stone floors, windows, European artworks, and heavy draperies. The women of the habitant class were known as **signares**, a word of Portuguese derivation. In artworks, a signare is distinguished by her pointed headdresses; the headdress indicates that she did not carry items on her head. A famous depiction of a signare shows her sitting on a ladderback chair, an African woman, comfortably seated, and she is at home.

German Colonial

The German colonial initiative started late and never reached the scale of other European powers. Part of this was due to the late date of German unification, 1871. Germany had several colonies in sub-Saharan Africa, including Cameroon, Togo, Namibia, and Tanzania. Despite Germany's modest colonial holdings, an important colonial event occurred in Germany: the "Scramble for Africa." This phrase refers to the Berlin Conference of 1884–1885, in which European powers divided up Africa into spheres of European control.

Germany also had some Asian colonies, in New Guinea, Samoa, the Solomon Islands, and the Marshall Islands. Germany was stripped of all its colonies at the end of the First World War, in 1918.

Namibia

There are scenarios and features common to colonial situations, yet there are also distinctions in how the colonial relationship played out from place to place. The political effects range from relatively benign (English Hong Kong) to nefarious (Belgian Congo). Yet the cultural productions are always interesting.

A late nineteenth-century house in Namibia, formerly South West Africa, shows one attitude of those embedded in colonialism, which is to try to re-create the home country as much as possible, building structures that remind their inhabitants of home (Figure 13.19). In the cities of Lüderitz and Swakopmund, a feeling of nostalgia reigns, and there is little understanding of the local context in culture or climate. Germans built houses in a style that climatically made sense in the Bavarian Alps, but that made little sense in the deserts of South West Africa.

Conclusion

Across colonial contexts, the earliest designs, buildings, and furniture were an initial response to harsh conditions and limited resources; they constituted a fight for survival. The prosperity that later developed was reflected in the ability of furniture makers to interact with European styles. Yet some religious groups, the Shakers and the Puritans, retained the simplicity of the early objects and made aesthetic austerity a virtue.

Artistic traditions traveled by three principal means: furniture pieces that arrived with the colonists; trained furniture makers who emigrated, usually for economic reasons; and publications, such as those of Chippendale, Hepplewhite, and Sheraton, discussed in Chapter 12. The transmission of design information had implications other than design dissemination. The general characteristics of colonial design include the colonial time lag: artistic movements that originated in Europe took time to spread around the world; thus,

Figure 13.19
Heinrich Ziegler, Haus Eberlanz, Lüderitz, Namibia, 1909.

neoclassicism occurs at an earlier date in England than it does in Australia. An extension of the temporal delay is that some traditional forms lived on in colonies when their usefulness in the home country had expired, such as the resilient Tulbagh chair. African craftsmen kept alive a form associated with the sixteenth and seventeenth centuries in the Netherlands and England.

Colonial pieces were rarely exact copies of European originals. The transformation came about because of new materials: cedar in Australia, stinkwood in South Africa, and ebony in India. Colonial production was characterized by a freedom from rules—European artistic guilds had little control over colonial areas, where the demarcation between professions was less distinct. This resulted in another colonial characteristic: the freedom among furniture manufacturers to innovate.

The logistics of oceangoing and local transport had the result that those in international trading centers, such as Charleston, Capetown, Sydney, and Goa, had exposure to actual European items, while those in the countryside did not—and they therefore relied on local furniture makers. This resulted in differences between city and country furniture.

The nature of the interaction between colonizer and colonized varied from continent to continent. Africa and English North America saw little utility in baroque and rococo forms; Latin America, by force, did. The early presence of the Dutch and Portuguese in India and Africa was marked by cooperation (prompted by necessity as much as goodwill), resulting in some highly inventive pieces that combined European forms with Hindu decorative motifs. Sometimes colonialism resulted in cultural obliteration, as in Australia and the United States, where English styles were faithfully reproduced, with indigenous traditions having little impact on them.

Ethnic complexity is a feature of colonial furniture, and the plethora of words for mixed-race people—habitants, Creole, **coloured**, **mestiço**—is evidence of the fascination with racial and cultural mixing. Because Islamic motifs were prevalent in Spanish baroque forms, when those forms traveled to the Americas, the geometric patterns went as well, although the explicit relationship to Islam was lost.

In many countries, European art forms were a means by which colonial elites, of all races and ethnicities, expressed their status. Neoclassicism (Chapter 14) is likely the first international style. Curiously, even though it was itself a revival, for areas with no previous classical tradition, it was a means of expressing refinement, grandeur, and progress. Several inventions of the nineteenth century—railroads, industrial manufacturing processes, and steamships—were blunt tools whose effects reached all corners of the globe.

Sources

Baarsen, Reinier (1988). *Courts and Colonies: The William and Mary Style in Holland, England, and America*. New York: Cooper Hewitt Museum.

Baraitser, Michael and Anton Obholzer (2004). *Cape Antique Furniture*. Cape Town: Struik Publishers.

Borcherds, Petrus ([1861] 1963). *An Autobiographical Memoir*. Cape Town: Africana Connoisseurs Press.

Buttsworth, John (1987). *Australian Colonial Furniture*. Drummoyne, New South Wales: Colonial Living Press.

Comaroff, Jean and John Comaroff (1991). *Of Revelation and Revolution: Christianity, Colonialism, and Consciousness in South Africa*. Chicago: University of Chicago Press.

Cook, Mary Alexander (1975). *The Cape Kitchen: A Description of Its Position, Lay-Out, Fittings, and Utensils*. Stellenbosch: Stellenbosch Museum.

Cook, Mary Alexander (1980). *The Old Buildings of the Cape: A Survey and Description of Old Buildings in the Western Province*. Cape Town: Balkema.

Cooke, Edward (1996). *Making Furniture in Preindustrial America*. Baltimore, MD: Johns Hopkins University Press.

Craig, Clifford, Kevin Fahy, and E. Graeme Robertson (1972). *Early Colonial Furniture in New South Wales and Van Diemen's Land*. Melbourne: Georgian House.

Fahy, Kevin, Christina Simpson, and Andrew Simpson (1985). *Nineteenth Century Australian Furniture*. Sydney: David Ell Press.

Fairbanks, Jonathan and Elizabeth Bates (1981). *American Furniture: 1620 to the Present*. New York: Richard Marek.

Fehr, William (1963). *Treasures at the Castle of Good Hope*. Cape Town: Castle Art Collection.

Gibson, Peter Charles (2022). *Made in Chinatown: Chinese Australian Furniture Factories*. Sydney: Sydney University Press.

Gopnik, Adam (2006). "Shining Tree of Life." *The New Yorker* 82, no. 1: 162–68.

Hellman, Mimi (1999). "Furniture, Sociability, and the Work of Leisure in Eighteenth Century France." *Eighteenth-Century Studies* 32, no. 4: 415–45.

Ioannou, Noris (1995). *The Barossa Folk: Germanic Furniture and Craft Traditions in Australia*. Roseville East: Craftsman House.

Jaffer, Amin (2001). *Furniture from British India and Ceylon*. Salem, MA: Peabody Essex Museum.

Kenny, Peter, Michael K. Brown, Frances F. Bretter, and Matthew A. Thurlow (2011). *Duncan Phyfe: Master Cabinetmakers in New York*. New York: Metropolitan Museum of Art.

Kirk, John (2000). *American Furniture: Understanding Styles, Construction, and Quality*. New York: Abrams.

Larkin, David (1995). *The Essential Book of Shaker: Discovering the Design, Function, and Form*. New York: Rizzoli.

Pearson, M.N. (1987). *The Portuguese in India*. Cambridge: Cambridge University Press.

Peters, Walter (1981). *Baukunst in Südwestafrika: 1884–1914*. Windhoek: John Meinert.

Random House Unabridged Dictionary (1993). 2nd edition. New York: Random House.

Schreffler, Michael (2007). *The Art of Allegiance: Visual Culture and Imperial Power in Baroque New Spain*. University Park: Pennsylvania State University Press.

Shea, John (1971). *The American Shakers and Their Furniture*. New York: Van Nostrand Reinhold.

Shipway, Verna Cook, and Warren Shipway (1962). *Mexican Interiors*. New York: Architectural Book Publishing.

van Onselen, L.E. (1959). *Cape Antique Furniture*. Cape Town: Howard Timmins.

Veenendall, Jan (1985). *Furniture from Indonesia, Sri Lanka, and India during the Dutch Period*. Delft: Volkenkundig Museum Nusantara.

Discussion and Review Questions

1. What are the mechanisms by which styles travel around the world?
2. What are some of the causes for stylistic changes in the colonial era?
3. What are some of the general characteristics of artistic production in the colonial era?
4. What are some of the unique circumstances of specific colonial areas?
5. When is the last time you heard the word "colonial" used and what was the context?
6. Go to a local museum. How are the artifacts presented? What is emphasized in the presentation?
7. Think of one example of each of the following: an English colony, a French colony, a German colony, a Portuguese colony, and a Spanish colony. Talk about the regional differences in furniture and interior design.
8. Parts of the United States were, at one time, culturally if not politically English, Dutch, French, German, Russian, and Spanish. Name some of these areas.

Neoclassicism

1760–1789	1789	1789–1804	1804–1820	1830–1870	1780–1830
France					
Louis XVI	Goût Grec	French Revolution	Directoire	Empire	Restoration

1780–1830	1776	1810–1837	1815–1848	1772–1792	1810–1844
United States		**England**	**Germany**	**Sweden**	
Federal	American Revolution	Regency	Biedermeier	Gustavian	Karl Johan

Neoclassicism is a broad term for the artistic tradition whose artists reacted against rococo art by embracing simplicity and geometric purity. It was related to political reform and sought its inspiration in antiquity. *Neoclassical* describes several movements of the late eighteenth and nineteenth centuries. As with the Renaissance, it was a period whose artists looked to the ancient world for their grounding and sometimes did so with archaeological precision.

Any artistic movement grows out of the preceding period to some extent, even a revolutionary style based on rejecting the status quo. So it is with rococo and neoclassicism. Neoclassicism was the opposite, a rejection of everything rococo. But it also grew out of that period, so, not surprisingly, the earliest neoclassical works seem rococo in their expression, regarding the amount of decoration. Nonetheless, these were the pieces that started the process of artistic change.

For any period, it is worthwhile to consider cultural artifacts in political terms, but for no other period is this as true as for neoclassicism. It was a historical revival firmly connected to contemporary politics. Neoclassicism is associated with the age of reason, the Enlightenment, and the French and

Figure 14.0
(*Facing page*)
Karl Friedrich Schinkel and Ludwig Persius, Potsdam, Germany, 1830–1850.

American Revolutions. Its imprint was seen across Europe, with significant works in Sweden and Germany. Potsdam was the home of the Prussian royal family, and thus a period of inspired rococo interiors was followed by a flowering of neoclassical design, in architecture, interiors, and furniture (Figure 14.0).

France

The most important contextual note in France about neoclassicism is that a new way of creating art was related to a new way of governing the country. In the French political theater, the art–politics relationship is odd and rife with complications, discrepancies, and ambiguities. The art-equals-politics style that was considered as antithesis of the monarchy was born in the period of Louis XVI and Marie Antoinette. The style that came to signal the excesses of the monarchy and the aristocracy was first heavily supported by the monarchy. In the nineteenth century, after the Republican experiment of the **Directory**, the new emperor, Napoleon, took up neoclassicism with gusto. After him, so too did the restored Bourbon monarchy.

Louis XVI

The craze for all things rococo had ebbed by the mid-eighteenth century and was decidedly out of fashion by 1760. In its place came a new style that looked to antiquity, particularly ancient Greece. Known as *goût grec*, or Greek taste, the first neoclassical iteration occurred in the final decades of the French monarchy, or *ancien régime*.

The features of the new design approach included simpler materials, a lack of applied surface ornamentation, and a preference for symmetry and pure forms. Functionally, the Louis XVI neoclassical armchair, or fauteuil, played the same role in seating arrangements as had its predecessor, the Louis XV armchair. Yet aesthetically, the neoclassical Louis XVI is a departure from previous developments in French furniture. Most curves are gone. The legs are straight, and the back is square and only slightly off vertical. The detailing of scrolls and fluting is **classical**. What this piece shares with its rococo predecessor is the lightness of its profile. A Prussian Louis XVI chair shows how quickly the taste spread beyond France (Figure 14.1).

Many furniture designers worked within the neoclassical idiom, one of the more accomplished being Georges Jacob (1770–1841), who created several pieces for Louis XVI. His designs were weighty, broad, and sit close to the ground. Jacob, a politically astute man, managed to continue his career after the revolution. Other artists associated with the king and queen had to flee the country.

Later works reflected the changes in taste within the neoclassical idiom. The pieces became more austere, the lines straighter, the patterns simpler. A Louis XVI side chair (no arms) has a rounded seat. Its legs, seat, and backrest are elaborately carved, yet some pieces manage to convey simplicity. Exposed wood was left natural or monochromatically painted to look like gold. Monochromatic textiles were popular.

Directoire and Empire

The post-revolutionary style was known as **Directoire**. This was the Republican, representative government that had been the goal of the

Figure 14.1
Karl Friedrich Schinkel, armchair, Berlin, Germany, 1828.

revolutionaries. Directoire pieces continued the trends started in the reign of Louis XVI.

When Napoleon came to power in 1799, he co-opted the neoclassical style. He became emperor in 1804, and the style of his reign, and its imitators, is now known as **Empire**. The distinctions between Directoire and Empire were incremental. In both, the detailing was classical. The profiles were light. Rococo curves, complexity, and ambiguity were a thing of the past.

David, Juliette Récamier, and Napoleon

Charles Percier was commisioned, through one of his students, Louis Berthault, to refashion the interiors of the home of the banker M. Récamier. His young wife, Madame Récamier, was painted by the artist Jacques-Louis David (1748–1825). David's painting is important because of its integration of fashion and furnishings, and for the visual qualities of the painting itself. In the painting, Juliette Récamier reclines on a settee, which came to be known as a "**Récamier**." Luc de Nanteuil writes that the settee was made by the famed neoclassical furniture designer Georges Jacob (Nanteuil 1985, p. 132). Her feet are bare, which offended some people who thought it inappropriate for a formal and public portrait. She wears an empire gown, a close approximation of ancient dress, her hair curled like a Roman lady's. The fashion term *empire waist* originated in the Napoleonic Empire with dresses such as the one worn by Juliette Récamier. David's composition employs simplicity in several respects.

Just as many neoclassical artists were intrigued by the possibilities of simple geometries, David reduced his pictorial composition to the simplest possible elements: the horizontal and the vertical. The subtle dynamism of the painting, however, derives from Récamier's reclining figure. The curves of her body, her formal yet relaxed posture, and the draping of her gown contrast with the rigid X–Y axis established by the settee and lamp.

David was the most celebrated artist of his day, a fierce critic of the rococo style and a tireless proponent of neoclassicism and political reform. Juliette Récamier, as painted by David, is somber, serious, and intelligent. The moment captured is not psychologically complex, a singularity that Nanteuil notices in other aspects of the painting as well:

The décor is even more neutral than in David's other portraits. The vertical blends into the horizontal and the tones are in harmony, rather than in contrast. David tried to represent his model in that spirit of simplicity which attracted him to Greek art, and which inspired the fashions of the time. Juliette's long floating gown barely outlines her body and its folds fall softly to the foot of the stool.

Many neoclassical painters were successful— Vien, Mengs, Kauffmann—but Jacques-Louis David was able to fuse the taste of the day with a moral clarity and a fervent belief in artistic and political reform.

David turned his talents to representing the hero of the moment, Napoleon. The Italian neoclassical sculptor Canova did a larger-than-life sculpture of the leader that portrayed him as a Roman god. Napoleon was embarrassed by the overt heroicism of the nearly nude statue and stashed it away. David, in contrast, deftly worked with the Emperor's physiognomy and visage, yet never losing sight of his subject's heroic quality.

From throne to desk

David's portrait of Napoleon was his last painting of the Emperor. In portraiture of the time, it was fashionable for people to pose as classical heroes and heroines. In David's painting, modern history replaces antiquity as the supplier of heroes (Figure 14.2). David's portrait of Napoleon has clarity and dramatic intensity. Like his Bourbon predecessors, Napoleon was a patron of the arts, personally responsible for commissioning a great deal of neoclassical architecture, interiors, furnishings, paintings, sculpture, and fashion. Philippe Bordes writes: "Napoleon thoroughly believed that impressive pomp and splendor could be used to political advantage and that encouragement of the luxury trades had a favorable impact on the national economy" (2005, p. 65). Although the style of choice differed, Napoleon took a cue from Louis XIV with his belief that the arts were a political tool, for himself and for France.

In David's painting, the leader of the nation was working tirelessly for his citizens. It is an eerily calm view of a general. He is shown in his study at the Tuileries palace, which is completely outfitted with neoclassical furniture: a chair, desk, and clock. David was knowledgeable about neoclassical furniture (Nanteuil 1985, p. 146). The color palette, of furniture, costume, and painting, relies upon a restrained use of primary colors. The empire chair is red and gold, and the Emperor's uniform combines white, red, blue, and gold.

Figure 14.2
Jacques-Louis
David, *The
Emperor Napoleon
in His Study*, 1812.

architecture, with the support of the Emperor and his Empress. Publications of their work, including Percier's *Recueil des Arts décoratifs* (1801), made them well known in England and Germany.

One of the gems of their work was a redesign of the interiors of a chateau for Napoleon's wife, the Empress Josephine, the Château de Malmaison, 1801–1812. Percier and Fontaine draped the walls and ceilings of several rooms at Malmaison to look like a tent (Figure 14.3). The conceit, not totally convincing, is that this is a tent of a Roman commander, perhaps Marcus Aurelius, on a military campaign in foreign lands. Percier and Fontaine are considered the first interior designers in the modern sense in that they designed everything within sight. They were architects, yet they were less concerned with structure and more concerned with decorative effect. They designed the furniture, walls, ceilings, fireplace, lighting, and all accessories. Mario Praz was an Italian historian of the decorative arts whose writings are at once old-fashioned, perceptive, and forward-looking. About the first interior designers, he writes: "The line drawings of interior decorations by Percier and Fontaine combine the inspiration of classical antiquity with a Renaissance clarity" (Praz 1964, p. 185). Art historians of neoclassicism frequently reduce it in their discussion to a simple straight line.

Claude-Nicolas Ledoux (1736–1806) was a major French neoclassical architect, his chief commission being thirty-seven tollhouses. He was another of the politically astute architects who had royal commissions yet was able to stay in France after the revolution.

Furniture

A French empire trident table is one of the works whose creator sought to accurately re-create a classical piece (Figure 14.4). More of a reproduction than a reinvention, it resembles actual Greek and Roman three-legged tables. The Louis XVI penchant for gilding all wood surfaces gradually gave way to a preference for ebonized wood and natural wood. Some neoclassical artists of this period increased their efforts to be faithful to ancient models. The excavations at Herculaneum and Pompeii began in 1748, and this provided a fresh impetus for the craze for classical stylings. The ensuing publications provided accurate information about actual Roman artworks.

The last of the Napoleonic Wars included Napoleon's disastrous decision to invade Russia in 1812, the year of David's portrait. This marked

Napoleon had previously hired David to design uniforms for him.

Numerous paintings and engravings show the emperor on his throne, some by David, but David's painting of the Emperor in his study is significant because a desk has usurped the throne as the piece of furniture associated with the nation's ruler. Napoleon played the imperial card too, showing himself resplendently dressed and surrounded with all the trappings of empire. But David's canvas portrays him as the tireless worker. Hugh Honour writes: "The candles have burnt low, the clock shows that it is 4:13 in the morning and the Emperor stands by the writing table where he has been working on the legal code, with a volume of Plutarch at his feet" (1977, p. 179). Typical for David and other neoclassical painters, the background is parallel to the picture plane and the wall is also classically detailed.

Architecture and interiors

Charles Percier (1764–1838) and Pierre-François-Léonard Fontaine (1762–1853) met as students and became leading figures of interior design and

Figure 14.3
Charles Percier
and Pierre
François Fontaine,
Malmaison, Rueil,
France, 1800.

the beginning of his decline, and he was forced to abdicate in 1814. Napoleon tried to return to power, but in the Battle of Waterloo in 1815, he lost to an English-Prussian coalition. His fate was sealed and he spent the rest of his years in exile. The Empire style outlived the Emperor.

United States

During the period that neoclassicism was raging in Europe, Americans were no longer fighting the elements for survival but were fully able to engage with international design currents. Just as neoclassicism in France was related to democracy, so it was in the United States. Historian of the decorative arts Gerald Ward wrote: "Classicism permeated almost every aspect of life and thought in America. Its impact was felt in government, education, architecture, and dress, as well as furnishings, as citizens sought to emulate and recapture the virtues of the ancient Greeks and the Republic of Rome" (2006, p. 89).

With their nearly coincident revolutions, the United States and France were on parallel tracks politically and artistically. Famous American political figures such as Thomas Jefferson and

Figure 14.4
Empire tripod table, France, early nineteenth century.

Benjamin Franklin spent extended periods of time in France. Both countries overthrew their monarchs at approximately the same time—France deposed Louis XVI, the United States George III. There were parallel revolutions, in 1776 in the United States, and in 1789 in France. France and the United States, by the end of the eighteenth century and the beginning of the nineteenth, were great allies, and it was England that most Americans viewed with distrust and suspicion. France and the United States had a similar ideology in their desire to establish a representative government, and both found in neoclassicism the design that represented their political aspirations.

Benjamin Franklin (1706–1790) spent eight years in France, from 1776 to 1785. He was followed by Thomas Jefferson (1743–1826), a draftsman of the Declaration of Independence and the third American president. Jefferson was an important politician and is also known for his role in fostering the American version of neoclassicism. (Neoclassical buildings that resemble his works are sometimes referred to as **Jeffersonian**.) From 1784 to 1789, Jefferson served as ambassador to France, underscoring the strength of the Franco-American alliance. Few significant political achievements stem from Jefferson's time in Paris, but while there, he immersed himself in French art and architecture. He left shortly before the violence of the revolution began.

Jefferson designed a state capitol for Virginia, in Richmond, and the campus of the University of Virginia (1817–1826). His own house, Monticello (1796–1809), is formally related to two famous European classically inspired residences: the Italian Renaissance Villa Rotunda and its English eighteenth-century cousin, Chiswick House. But Monticello was also an inventive work of design.

It looks like a one-story building, but it actually has a second story of bedrooms and a lower service floor. An alcove bed borrows a configuration from Malmaison (Figure 14.5). It opened onto Jefferson's bedroom and his office.

Once the Declaration of Independence was signed in 1776, the United States was no longer officially a colony. American architects soon started taking the steps to establish the foundling profession. Benjamin Latrobe and Charles Bulfinch are considered the fathers of American architecture. Latrobe (1764–1820) was born in Britain but carried out his career in the United States. He knew Thomas Jefferson, who hired him to finish the United States Capitol. Latrobe's most accomplished work was for the Basilica of the Assumption of the Blessed Virgin Mary, in Baltimore in 1805. The dome of the basilica carefully replicates the dome of the Pantheon. Latrobe also designed a plausible copy of the klismos chair (Figure 14.6). Bulfinch (1763–1844) was the architect of the Massachusetts State Capitol (1795–1797). He had visited England, where he saw firsthand the work of the Adams brothers.

The visible similarities between European and American neoclassicism suggest that designers were reaching across the ocean and building a shared tradition. The father/son duo of Abraham and David Roentgen moved into a neoclassical

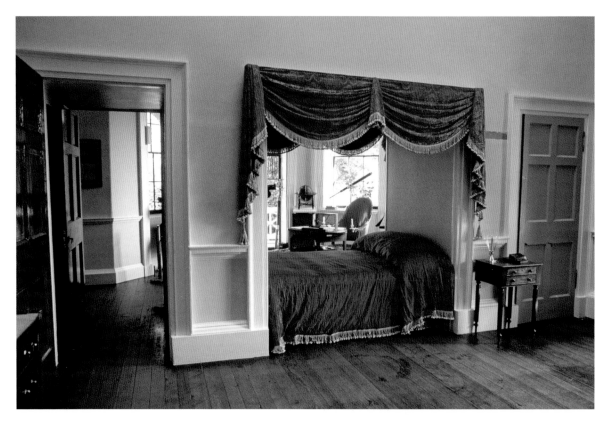

Figure 14.5
Thomas Jefferson, bedroom at Monticello, 1772.

Figure 14.6
Benjamin Henry Latrobe, neoclassical sidechair, Philadelphia, Pennsylvania, 1808. Poplar, oak, maple, and pine.

period with furniture that resembled American Sheraton pieces. American Georgian houses followed the parameters of English Georgian houses. They were symmetrical, with classical detailing in the cornices and the pediments, pilasters, and windows. Southern plantations also followed the model of English country houses, although they were less elaborate.

Federal

There were considerable numbers of pieces across the globe that were influenced by the neoclassical work of English furniture designers Sheraton, Hepplewhite, and Chippendale. In the United States, these pieces are called **Federal**, the American strand of neoclassicism. Black horsehair was a favored upholstery textile for neoclassical chairs. Publications played an important role in the international spread of neoclassicism and in providing accurate information about its forms and details. Robert Adams published engravings of his projects, and he, along with Thomas Hope and George Smith, published builder's guides. Knowledge of actual antiquity came from many sources, including Jean-François de Neufforge's *Receuil élémentaire d'architecture*. James Stuart

and Nicholas Revett traveled to Athens in 1751, and their publication of 1762, *The Antiquities of Athens*, provided much-needed information about Greek monuments. *The Society of London Cabinet-Makers' Book of Prices* (1788), provided technical information for producers, rather than consumers, of furniture (Clouston 1906, p. 131). English and French publications made their way to the United States and were largely responsible for the creation of American Empire. Jefferson himself collected many of these books in his library at Monticello.

A common American Empire settee has curved armrests and straight legs. The elements are ancient, but the form is nineteenth-century American (Figure 14.7).

Classical **lyres**, a musical instrument resembling a harp, and crowns of laurel leaves were favorite neoclassical motifs. Napoleon co-opted the **laurel wreath** as his personal insignia, a connection between his reign and France and the Roman Empire. The use of symbols was a significant feature of neoclassical furniture, with eagles being a favored American motif.

Daybeds were a favorite item of neoclassical designers, and they exist in great variety. This was, in part, due to David's iconic image of Juliette Récamier. A Lanniere bed has sphinxes, acanthus leaves, and a restrained use of gilding. Daybeds were used for napping or for reclining while in the company of others.

Samuel McIntire (1757–1811) was an American furniture maker whose father was a carpenter. Early in his career, he carved ship figureheads. He mostly made furniture according to the designs of others. He started out working in the colonial Georgian tradition and gradually developed a leaner style consistent with American Federal.

Duncan Phyfe (1768–1854) was the Scottish-born American cabinetmaker who is considered

Figure 14.7
Neoclassical settee, early nineteenth century.

Figure 14.8
Duncan Phyfe,
sofa, New York,
New York, 1810–
1820. Mahogany,
tulip wood, and
poplar.

one of the finest American furniture makers. In
1792, he moved to New York. He was a successful businessman, with many employees. He
was a major proponent of neoclassicism in the
United States, and he counted John Jacob Astor
among his clients. His signature piece was a
sofa or daybed, of which he designed innumerable variations (Figure 14.8). Neoclassical pieces
were configured differently as a part of furniture
arrangements. Praz notes: "Furniture was no
longer fused with wall decoration but regained an
independence that soon led to virtual isolation"
(1964, p. 160). Pieces were used as movable objects
in a room, and this would be characteristic of the
use of furniture throughout the nineteenth century.

Lambert Hitchcock (1795–1852) was another
successful furniture maker whose efforts made
neoclassicism part of the American design
mainstream. Neoclassicism, in contrast to rococo,
was not intended to be another elite style. In that
regard, Hitchcock, working out of Connecticut,
is mostly known for having created a chair made
out of wood with a common rush seat. His chairs
were painted black and then stenciled. Known as
Hitchcock chairs, they were popular with people
of modest means (Figure 14.9). Hitchcock chairs
are a ubiquitous part of the American furniture
vocabulary, all the while maintaining a striking
resemblance to the Greek klismos chair. A member
of the British royal family and himself a furniture
maker, David Linley, states, "In America the Greek
style was readily adopted as a means of embody-
ing the democratic principles of the new republic"
(1993, p. 54). Yet in England, neoclassicism was
related to an opulent resurgence of the monarchy.

Figure 14.9
Hitchcock chair, Hitchcocksville, Connecticut, United States,
1825–1828. Painted and stenciled maple.

England

Regency relates to the political structure in which a regent stands in for an underage heir to the throne. Theoretically, it can pertain to any regency. There were two significant furniture styles known as Regency: French Regency, which ushered in the rococo, and English Regency, which was related to neoclassicism.

English Regency is the English version of neoclassicism. Considerable stylistic similarities link French Directoire, American Federal, and English Regency, largely due to the international market for books on antiquities, architecture, and design.

Architecture and interiors

English Regency design is known as a restrained form of classicism, with occasional instances of uncharacteristic exoticism. Two projects by John Nash (1752–1835) exemplify this bifurcated aspect of regency design. One is Regent's Park and the other is the Royal Pavilion at Brighton. Nash's

Regent's Park is a grand urban gesture linked to capitalism; it was a neoclassical façade with unexceptional row houses behind it.

Lord Burlington (1694–1753) owned a substantial property in the outskirts of London. Burlington designed his own house, Chiswick House, in 1725. It is a building clearly modeled on Palladio's Villa Rotunda, with neoclassical interiors and furniture (Figure 14.10). Linley acknowledged Lord Burlington's role in setting the foundation for neoclassicism: "Palladianism, pioneered by Lord Burlington and his circle, ushered in a new era of design blending English practicality with the purest classical ideals" (1993, p. 43).

The central octagon acts as the figural and functional center of the project (Jefferson's Monticello also employs an octagon). Yet the house is no longer situated in a formal parklike setting, such as Versailles, but within an informal picturesque English garden. Romanticism was the cross-disciplinary movement that involved artists, poets, authors, and landscape designers. As it highlighted the capriciousness of nature and accidental forms, it was, in certain respects,

Figure 14.10
William Kent and Lord Burlington, Chiswick House, London, United Kingdom, 1725–1738.

a rejection of neoclassicism. Yet in the English context, such as Chiswick House's garden, a classically detailed house stood within a picturesque landscape, a setting that brought together two contrary movements. Another interpretation of Chiswick House is that it was a gesture to express English democratic freedoms. The Neopalladian house was a counteroffensive to the rococo, and the English garden was an alternative to the French formal garden. Certain commonalities aside, while they occasionally overlapped, Romanticism and neoclassicism are typically presented as distinct artistic entities.

The Adam brothers were Scotsmen who worked out of London. Robert Adam (1728–1792) was the chief designer, while James Adam (1730–1794) was the business partner. One focused on design, the other on commerce and practical matters.

The overall body of work of the Adams brothers contains rococo projects and neoclassical projects. The rococo projects stem from earlier in their career. Of their neoclassical work, one of their most accomplished was Syon House (Figure 14.11). Significantly, when designing the home for the Duke of Northumberland, Robert Adam referred to neoclassicism as the French style.

Their other neoclassical masterwork is Osterley Park, from the same time period, 1762–1769. Their designs often inventively combined several classical traditions. Much of their work was neoclassical, yet they were not directly copying the ancients but relating to it through the works of Renaissance architect Palladio. They also could be inventive with their use of the classical vocabulary, such as combining Ionic pilasters with a Doric entablature, or Ionic details with coffered ceilings. After experiments with dynamic shapes and deeply cut baroque and rococo carving, the Adam brothers later in their career created surfaces that were once again flat.

Furniture and graphics

A sideline of neoclassical artists was a renewed interest in Egyptian artifacts, and again there was a Napoleonic connection. Napoleon's expedition to Egypt in 1798 had cultural ramifications. The resulting publications, the 21-volume *Description d'Egypte*, made available detailed information about Egyptian antiquities. The desire was not necessarily to re-create Egyptian forms but to include Egyptian motifs in a neoclassical design, such as the use of Egyptian sphinx heads on a chair's front legs An Empire cylinder desk is supported by classical lyres (Figure 14.12). There were many strands of neoclassicism, including Greek, Roman, and Egyptian. Some artists took the desire to imitate the ancients to extremes. Pierre-François Hancarville did

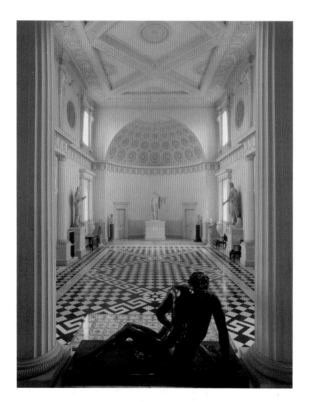

Figure 14.11
Robert Adam, Syon House Great Hall, Middlesex, England, 1760–1769. With Luigi Valadier's *Dying Gaul.*

Figure 14.12
Empire cylinder-front desk, 1810.

etchings in which he sought to faithfully re-create on paper the drawing techniques of red-figure Greek vases.

Germany

German history presents a complicated scenario, as early nineteenth-century Germany was not a unified country. German neoclassicism is commonly considered in light of Karl Friedrich Schinkel in Prussia and Leo von Klenze in Bavaria; both were talented architects and painters. Yet even Schinkel, the neoclassical architect *par excellence*, made a significant number of Gothic Revival designs. With his fanciful and accomplished designs for theater and opera, he experimented with Egyptian and Aztec forms.

Karl Friedrich Schinkel (1781–1841) designed the Altes Museum, a cubic mass that is a highly inventive project. A blocky form, it is not a re-creation of an actual classical building, for it is an abstraction of classicism. It uses a Greek temple's side elevation as a front elevation (Figure 14.13). Schinkel's patron was Friedrich Wilhelm III, for whom he designed singular public buildings—not urban complexes, nonetheless they were deftly suited to their urban environment.

One reason for singling out the Greeks for praise, as Schinkel did, is that they used columns structurally, whereas the Romans used them decoratively.

A corollary to Schinkel's interest in ancient Greece was the art critic Joachim Winckelmann, who passionately defended the supremacy of Greek art. Schinkel's inventive use of classicism with the Altes Museum demonstrates that those operating within neoclassical stylistics were not copying the past but working creatively with its vocabulary. And in architecture, neoclassical was often related to public buildings such as museums and libraries. Neoclassical interiors, by Schinkel and others, were light-years away from rococo extravagance.

Biedermeier

Biedermeier refers to a middle-class art whose geographic scope included Austria, the Czech lands, Germany, Denmark, and Poland. Its chronological benchmarks are the Congress of Vienna

Figure 14.13
Karl Friedrich Schinkel, Altes Museum, Berlin, Germany, 1825.

in 1815, which resolved the Napoleonic Wars, to the various European revolutions of 1848. The term "Biedermeier" was not used until the late nineteenth century, and, as with many stylistic terms, was initially a term of derision. "Bieder" means conventional, and "Maier" or "Meyer" is one of the commonest of German surnames, such as the names Jones or Smith in English.

Initially, German Biedermeier furniture was the rural version of neoclassical furniture. It was simple and restrained. Details were ebonized (stained to simulate ebony), such as columns and trim pieces. Gilding was limited. While it was a neoclassical offshoot, some very simple pieces show no classical detailing at all.

Unlike other manifestations of neoclassicism, Biedermeier was not particularly political. Biedermeier occurred when Romanticism was in full swing, such as the poetry of Byron. Biedermeier intersected with Romanticism in the field of landscape painting. Many Biedermeier paintings featured interior views. Indoors were comfortable, serene, and leisurely, and the outdoors were inviting and accessible.

Biedermeier furniture was most often made in red and blond woods, such as mahogany and cherry, but also ash and walnut, and a characteristic was an orange or reddish color. Many pieces are particularly sparse or simple, sometimes austere. Chairs are streamlined, elegantly functional. This is a style of furniture associated with the bourgeoisie and the provinces. Biedermeier is to neoclassical as French provincial is to rococo.

While initially created for a rural middle class, the pieces found fans, and customers, in the upper classes as well. On the occasion of an exhibition devoted to Biedermeier furniture, Hans Ottomeyer wrote: "Biedermeier is here interpreted not as a lowly product of bourgeois taste but rather as a highly cultivated and refined quest for simplicity and purity of form that has its roots in the late eighteenth century" (Ottomeyer, Schroder, and Winters 2006, p. 39).

Biedermeier storage units were mostly naturally finished wood, with columns, pilasters, and restrained use of metal. A Biedermeier sofa is an essay in simplicity. It is scarcely recognizable as classical, except for the curved ends and the outlines of the feet. Its design is abstract, relying on geometry, a clear finish, and a lack of ornamentation. Austrian Josef Danhauser started his career as a painter. Success eluded him until he turned to producing furniture (Figure 14.14).

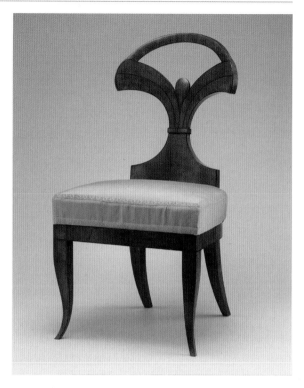

Figure 14.14
Josef Dunhauser, Biedermeier side chair, Vienna, Austria, 1815–1820. Beech, pine, cherry, and mahogany.

Sweden

Swedish art historian Johan Cederlund relates that neoclassicism was late in arriving at the Scandinavian country, and that the preference for rococo designs was enduring (Cederlund 2006, p. 170). There was also considerable overlap between the two periods, with many Swedish projects that exhibit both rococo and neoclassical characteristics.

When neoclassicism did arrive, it was largely due to the interests of King Gustav III. Gustav III's favorite architect was Jean Eric Rehn, and Rehn traveled to Italy. While there, he saw firsthand classical, Renaissance, and neoclassical works. "Rehn's travels initiated a new period in Swedish art history. His exposure to the ancient world and to its echoes in contemporary work definitely shaped not only his own personal artistic development but also that of Sweden" (Cederlund 2006, p. 172).

Swedish neoclassicism is so inextricably intertwined with Gustav III that the style is also referred to as Gustavian. The architect Erik Palmstedt designed the Court Theater at

Gripsholm in 1781, a project that skillfully adapts a rotunda that looks like the Roman Pantheon to be a theater, complete with a generous backstage. The Swedish king's passion for neoclassicism is evidence that France dominated the world in design matters. Gustav III imitated XVI's bedroom stylistically and also initiated the practice of the levée, the publicly viewed awakening of the monarch. Cederlund writes that "more than a few of his foreign guests found this outdated practice strange" (Cederlund 2006, p. 177).

The French-Swedish connection continued into the nineteenth century. The childless King Karl XIII adopted French field marshal Jean Baptiste Berndadotte, who ruled Sweden as Karl Johan. Empire design in Sweden is known as Karl Johan (Cederlund 2006, p. 228). The Swedish interest in neoclassicism was far-reaching, and included architecture and the decorative arts, including furnishings.

Neoclassicism and Romanticism

There is little scholarly consensus on the relationship between neoclassicism and Romanticism. One school of thought considers them as opposed artistic movements and neatly chronologically distinct, with Romanticism following neoclassicism. Another school of thought considers them as contemporary and alike, in sentiment if not in form. In the imagined battle of classicists over Romantics, the former are beholden to a state-sponsored institutionalized art. Their academic art is elite, emotionally cold, and flat. The latter are a group of individualists, and their works are colorful, emotional, and visually bold.

Hugh Honour belongs to the older school of thought, yet his work is more nuanced than is commonly thought, as he notes the connections that bind Romanticism to neoclassicism. He argues that neoclassicism has more in common with Romanticism than neoclassicism does to rococo. He writes that the stylistic change from neoclassicism to Romanticism (which he sees as successive, and not contemporary, movements) was not "the result of a reaction comparable with that which led to the rejection of the Rococo fifty years earlier. The Neoclassical movement contained within itself the seeds of most of the

Romantic forms that were to destroy it" (Honour 1977, p. 186).

The rococo-neoclassicism divide was often reduced to an opposition between a curve and a straight line. Another strand of scholars presents neoclassicism-Romantic schism in terms of the contrast between line and color. Art historian Andrew Carrington Shelton, writing about the painter Ingres, sees the supposed divide in a different way. He writes: "What was at stake in the great debates over line versus color and classicism versus Romanticism in the 1830s and 1840s was not so much a theoretical position as the personal power and prestige of those who came to embody each cause" (Shelton 2001, p. 719).

The Biedermeier furniture exhibit held at the Milwaukee Art Museum in 2006 emphasized the connections between Romanticism and classicism, or at least the German vernacular version of it, Biedermeier (Ottomeyer, Schroder, and Winters 2006). It included many examples of works by known classicists, such as Schinkel, who produced decidedly Romantic works, with Gothic ruins set within foreboding Romantic landscapes.

Conclusion

Even though Romanticism and neoclassicism are often presented as contrary movements, some projects combined aspects of each, a complexity that was a harbinger of the multiple modes of stylistic expression that was to dominate the second half of the nineteenth century.

Neoclassicism, in its various forms, can be seen as the end of a series of stylistic traditions that date back to antiquity. Its effects were found across the design spectrum, from designed objects, to dresses, paintings, and buildings. Neoclassicism provided a resolute answer to the question, what should the world be? Its proponents displayed a sincerity and aesthetic surety that the world would not quickly find again. Neoclassical architects and designers were responding to a political call to arms that was local (Paris, Washington, or Berlin), yet their projects also stressed that classicism was a universal design language, based on simple massing and symmetry, and opposed to changing tastes and fashion.

Neoclassicism is the last of a series of big artistic movements in which each seems a reaction against the previous generation. Stylistically there is a linear progression from Renaissance, to baroque, to regency, to rococo, to neoclassicism. This trajectory, however, was at an end. Instead of seeing neoclassicism as the end of a progression, Gerald Ward sees it as the harbinger of what was to come: "Neoclassicism was the first of many successive yet overlapping revival styles that would come to typify the eclecticism of the nineteenth century. While many of the later revivals were similarly linked to moralistic leanings or social movements, none captured the imagination and profoundly influenced the shape and look of the entire country to the extent of Neoclassicism" (2006, p. 92). From that perspective, neoclassicism was to be usurped into a nineteenth-century mélange of historical revivals.

Sources

Bergdoll, Barry, ed. (2018). *The Complete Works of Percier and Fontaine*. New York: Princeton Architectural Press.

Bordes, Philippe (2005). *Jacques-Louis David: Empire to Exile*. New Haven, CT: Yale University Press.

Brookner, Anita (2000). *Romanticism and Its Discontents*. New York: Farrar, Straus and Giroux.

Cederlund, Johan (2006). *Classical Swedish Architecture and Interiors, 1650–1840*. New York: Norton.

Clouston, R.S. (1906). *English Furniture and Furniture Makers*. London: Hurst & Blackett.

Fastnedge, Ralph (1962). *Sheraton Furniture*. London: Faber and Faber.

Honour, Hugh (1977). *Neo-classicism*. London: Penguin.

Levey, Michael (1966). *Rococo to Revolution: Major Trends in Eighteenth-Century Painting*. London: Thames and Hudson.

Linley, David (1993). *Classical Furniture*. New York: Abrams.

Nanteuil, Luc de (1985). *Jacques-Louis David*. New York: Abrams.

Ottomeyer, Hans, Klaus Albrecht Schroder, and Laurie Winters (2006). *Biedermeier: The Invention of Simplicity*, exhibition catalog. Milwaukee, WI: Milwaukee Art Museum.

Philipp, Klaus Jan (2014). *Karl Friedrich Schinkel: Late Projects*. Fellbach: Edition Axel Menges.

Pile, John (2000). *A History of Interior Design*. New York: Wiley.

Praz, Mario (1964). *An Illustrated History of Furnishing*. New York: George Braziller.

Shelton, Andrew Carrington (2001). "Art, Politics, and the Politics of Art: Ingres's Saint Symphorien at the 1834 Salon." *Art Bulletin* 83, no. 4 (December): 711–39.

Ward, Gerald (2006). "Neoclassicism and the New Nation: The Late Eighteenth and Early Nineteenth Centuries." In *American Decorative Arts and Sculpture*, edited by Nonie Gadsden, Kelly H. L'Ecuyer, Gerald W.R. Ward, and Melinda Talbot Nasardinov, p. 97. Boston: Museum of Fine Arts.

Discussion and Review Questions

1. What are some neoclassical buildings in your area?

2. List some of the many alternate names for styles or movements related to neoclassicism.

3. In its approach to antiquity, how does neoclassicism compare with the Renaissance?

4. What were some of the national strains of neoclassicism and some of each country's unique characteristics?

5. How did early neoclassical works in France retain some rococo elements?

6. When designing, what was important to neoclassical designers? What was unimportant? Chiswick House was an exception; there weren't many neoclassical houses built. Any idea why?

7. Discuss elements of neoclassicism from across the arts—painting, fashion, furniture design, and architecture. What were the common interests?

8. What is the name for middle-class neoclassical furniture from Germany and surrounding countries?

Victorian and Historical Revivals

15

1837–1901	1820–1929	1750–1939	1842–1914	1850–1905	1825–1900
Victorian	Egyptian Revival	Gothic Revival	Greek Revival	Renaissance Revival	Romanesque Revival

In the Victorian period, the universal standards of taste were collapsing in the phenomenon known as the battle of styles. The nineteenth century ushered in the modernist movement, yet it did so in a complex and contradictory way. The era that gave us modernism was also known for a myriad of historical revivals. Often the styles were precisely that—styles divorced from the cultural contexts that originally produced them. The nineteenth century began with neoclassicism, the last universally accepted style, and then proceeded into an à-la-carte menu of styles in the middle of the century. Deep-seated antipathies pitted the proponents of neoclassicism against the champions of Gothic Revival. The plurality of design choices gave little indication that modernism was to arrive at the end of the century.

"Victorian" literally refers to anything in the decorative arts and architecture produced during the reign of Queen Victoria (1837–1901). The profusion of styles was particularly strong, and strongly fought, in England. While the prominent English Victorian style was Gothic Revival, no one style was universally accepted. The artist Frederic Leighton's luxurious home and studio employed a number of styles, from Moorish Revival to Byzantine (Figure 15.0).

Throughout history, technology has significantly impacted the arts and furniture making, from the development of the arch, to paper, to planed lumber. Yet the nineteenth century

Figure 15.0
(*Facing page*)
George Aitchison and Frederic Leighton, Leighton House, Kensington, United Kingdom, 1866–1895.

was besot with technological innovations, any one of which had the potential to significantly alter the way people lived and did business; collectively, these inventions wrenched the world from what we now view as history into the modern era.

Many of the innovations involved communications and media. The nineteenth century started out with sailing ships, relying on the same means of propulsion that had been used for millennia, not essentially different from the feluccas that had been sailing the Nile since time immemorial. The century ended with steam-powered ships, no longer dependent on weather conditions and made from steel, not wood. The dramatic change in the design environment was also due to the explosive population growth and urbanization that accompanied industrialization.

Iron had also been around for centuries, but sophisticated manufacturing techniques greatly increased its use; it became an important architectural material and made an appearance in furniture. Steel was similarly used in greater quantities. Running water, flushing toilets, central heating, first gas then electric lighting, whale oil then kerosene, milled lumber—all affected the world of design. Glass was made in factories in large sheets, just one of the many factors that made a new building type possible—the skyscraper.

With the considerable wisdom of hindsight when looking at nineteenth-century architecture and design, one finds the seeds of modernism all over the place, from Schinkel's Bauakademie in Berlin, 1831, to Henry Hobson Richardson's Glesner House in Chicago, 1885. At first it seems curious that an era greatly impacted by technological achievement was, in the realm of design, defined by historicity and a multitude of competing styles. All artistic movements owe something to the period that preceded them, even if by contrast. There were early indications of the revolution to come. When the nineteenth century is carefully examined, the specter of modernism raises its head in the most unlikely places.

One explanation for the persistence of historical styles in the nineteenth century involves the education and training of designers. Nineteenth-century architects and designers were trained in their respective disciplines and traditions, and like most artists and craftspeople, they knew of no way to respond to world conditions and change except, initially, from within those traditions. Thus, we have the phenomena of Romanesque skyscrapers and Turkish baths in steamships.

A rationale for the historic look of designed objects is that the new technologies implicitly promised to improve the lives of the lower and middle classes. Evidence of this prophecy's fulfillment is the existence of decorated objects that previously were handcrafted, expensive, and available only to the wealthiest. Some new machine-made objects were affordable. Inventions were supposed to provide luxury, or at least the appearance of it, for people for whom expensive-looking baubles were previously out of reach.

Queen Victoria

The nineteenth century and Queen Victoria (1819–1901) are essentially synonymous. The monarch, whose given name connotes etiquette and decorum, lived her years almost perfectly within the 1800s. She was born when the world was in the throes of neoclassicism, and she came of age and to the throne when that period was nearing its end. She lived to see only one year of the twentieth century. As "Victorian era" refers to anything made during her long reign, one frequently finds objects referred to as Victorian that do not stylistically look Victorian. Generally speaking, regarding style, "Victorian" refers to articles that are elaborate in their decoration, utilize a dark and sometimes somber color palette, and freely make use of historical precedents, often in combination. Regarding the configuration of interiors, Victorian design is characterized by an increase in the overall number of objects, and their complexity, that figured in the decorative schemes of lower-, middle-, and upper-class homes. These material attributes are frequently superimposed with an idea of sexual and moral propriety that largely stemmed from the Queen herself (notwithstanding the notoriety surrounding her likely affair with her personal servant, John Brown). Despite its considerable popularity, to many (a big group, including all the modernists) "Victorian" connoted the depths of bad taste, allegedly playing into the desire of unsophisticated people for efflorescent decoration, and a frenzy of decorative excess.

Historic Revivals

The nineteenth century started out with neoclassicism, which was also an artistic movement inspired by the past, but the height of the era of competing historic styles started in earnest in 1830.

Gothic Revival

Gothic Revival was the most important of the mid-century historic revivals. This is largely due to its prominent place in England and France and the English colonies, including Australia, South Africa, and the United States. For proponents of Gothic Revival, it was not one of an array of choices but the way that architecture, interiors, and designed objects should be done.

In England, Gothic Revival was a means of announcing Englishness. Michael McCarthy (1987) dates the beginning of the Gothic Revival in England to the late eighteenth century and the figure Horace Walpole. Walpole created a series of Gothic-inspired **follies**, pavilions with little purpose other than to act as eye-catching accents in picturesque English gardens. For his own home, Strawberry Hill in Twickenham, Walpole created an important set of Gothic Revival interiors. They garnered a lot of attention in his day and also served as inspiration for nineteenth-century Gothic Revivalists.

High Victorian Gothic began with two publications by John Ruskin, *The Seven Lamps of Architecture* (1849) and *The Stones of Venice* (1851). Ruskin promoted medieval European architecture, especially that of northern Italy. His writings connect design to moralistic theories and consider buildings as shells awaiting agglomerations of ornament. In *The Seven Lamps*, Ruskin outlined his belief that ornament is the vital component that distinguishes architecture from mere building. Ornament was central to Ruskin's thought.

Gothic Revival had the advantage that it was related to Christianity from its beginnings, unlike pagan classicism and Egyptian design. Mid-nineteenth-century England built large numbers of churches, which created the need for large numbers of architects, designers, and craftsmen familiar with medieval detailing. Ruskin fostered the idea that good design was moral and related to piety and rectitude, all of which, to his mind, was best expressed in Gothic forms.

Augustus Welby Northmore Pugin (1812–1852) was, like Ruskin, a writer, but as an accomplished furniture designer and sometime architect, he was able to see his ideas translated into forms. He attacked classicism as being inappropriate, meaning too foreign (meaning too Italian), for England. Pugin is the figure at the center of nineteenth-century English Gothic Revival. For Pugin and his followers, Gothic Revival became the symbol of Protestant Christianity, England, and its empire. He came to prominence when he successfully furnished George IV's apartments in Windsor castle. He designed built-ins and freestanding pieces of furniture. Astonishingly, he started his work for the king when he was fifteen years old.

Pugin's signature project was his work on the Houses of Parliament. He collaborated with the architect Charles Barry (1795–1860) on the prominent project, focusing on the interiors. His designs for furniture, ceramics, textiles, stained glass, and wallpaper reveal that he was an accomplished artist, devoted to various phases of medieval architecture and design. The Houses of Parliament, while in the Gothic Revival style, was a building with an incredibly complex program that included extended administrative functions and audience rooms, and also acted as an architectural symbol of the nation. The complex building contains the House of Commons and the Chamber of the Lords.

It is sometimes difficult to reconcile Pugin's rhetoric with his artistic production. For example, he often calls for simplicity, and his complex designs seem at odds with that. An X-frame side chair by Pugin has elaborate carving and is structurally expressive (Figure 15.1). No replica of a medieval piece, its complicated forms and decoration came from Pugin's imagination. Such pieces appear exceedingly elaborate to modern eyes, but one must understand the context in which they were created.

In 1836, Pugin published *Contrasts*, in which he compares the medieval period to the nineteenth century; invariably, the nineteenth century pales in comparison. In 1841, he published *The True Principles of Pointed or Christian Architecture*. This impassioned manifesto was a culmination of his design thought. While Pugin,

his projects, and his publications were influential, they often had the result of influencing people to copy his decorations without understanding the theoretical underpinnings. Pugin was one of many philosophically opposed to revivalism, and he was particularly harsh in his criticism of Egyptian revival. Gothic held such a hallowed place in the English psyche that it was, according to Ruskin's and Pugin's logic, above the stylistic fray.

Pugin's sometime business and design partner, Barry, was first instrumental in introducing a restrained form of Italianate architecture to nineteenth-century London, sometimes referred to as Renaissance Revival. Open-minded regarding styles, he was in part responsible for introducing eclecticism and making it semi-respectable. An accomplished artist, he also worked within the Greek revival realm. Barry and Pugin worked together on several occasions. Barry focused on the architecture, letting Pugin turn his talents to the interiors and furnishings. The most famous of the Barry/Pugin collaborations was the New Palace of Westminster, now the Houses of Parliament (Figure 15.2). A feature of its interiors was extensive use of **polychromy**, the natural result of using many materials. In compositions that featured multiple materials, each retained its inherent color.

Germany

The promotion of Gothic in England reverberated across Europe and around the world. Neuschwanstein, Ludwig II of Bavaria's fairy-tale-looking castle, is just one of many projects constructed in a late Gothic Revival. Work on the castle started in 1869. And while Karl Friedrich Schinkel and Leo von Klenze are mostly known as neoclassical architects, they also did Gothic buildings and paintings.

France

In France, also mid-century, Eugène Viollet-le-Duc (1814–1879) played a similar role as Ruskin and Pugin, writing the publications that supported the adoption of Gothic architecture and that remained the central texts for the movement. Viollet-le-Duc published the *Dictionnaire raisonné de l'architecture française* in 1854, and *Entretiens sur l'architecture* in 1863. An important distinction between the French and English approaches to Gothic stems from their initial defenders. Whereas Ruskin saw architecture as ornament, Viollet-le-Duc saw it as structure.

Figure 15.1
Augustus Welby Northmore Pugin, Carved oak and leather chair, Westminster, London, England, 1859.

Figure 15.2
Charles Barry
and A.W.N.
Pugin, Houses
of Parliament,
Westminster,
England,
1840–1860.

Eugène Viollet-le-Duc was a French architect and preservationist. His knowledge of Gothic was learned on the job while working on the restoration of several cathedrals in the 1840s and 1850s; he oversaw the restoration work on Abbaye Sainte-Marie-Madeleine, in Vezelay, and Saint Denis, Sainte-Chapelle, and Notre Dame in Paris. He vehemently excoriated eclecticism and sought to establish the basis of a modern Gothic architecture, although his own works occasionally combined Gothic shapes with details that are distinctly Byzantine or Early Christian. Interested in prefabrication, he enthusiastically promoted the use of iron, although he himself used it sparingly. His publications were central to relating Gothic Revival in France to French nationalism. The French version of Gothic Revival did not spread to France's colonies to the extent that English Gothic Revival did.

South Africa

In English colonies, the use of Gothic Revival was a way to connect with the homeland and affirm English heritage. For Anglophone South

Africans, it simultaneously differentiated them as a group distinct from the Dutch-influenced Afrikaans population. It also provided an architectural vocabulary that served as a racial divider. Eighteenth- and nineteenth-century European travel accounts regularly, and erroneously, commented on the superiority of European architecture over the indigenous varieties. A Gothic Revival house in Durban relies heavily on forms associated with churches in its salon, down to the inclusion of a stained-glass window.

The United States

Across the pond in the United States, employing Gothic Revival also served as a means to affirm the new country's English traditions (the sore feelings left by the American Revolution having been largely forgotten). American Gothic Revival was also related to several key tendencies of **Romanticism**. Romanticism started out as a literary movement that emphasized emotion and intuition, while relying less on the appeal to reason. It was important in poetry and fiction, with Lord Byron's poetry as the prime example.

A number of painters created landscapes that resonated with Romantic poetry and placed them firmly in the American fold. The relationship of Romantic landscape painting and Gothic Revival architecture had a strong European precedent in the paintings of Caspar David Friedrich and Karl Friedrich Schinkel.

Landscape paintings relate obviously to gardening, and particularly to the informal English garden that was usurping the primacy of the French formal garden. Reinforcing the connection between informal gardens and Gothic Revival, many English country gardens included either real Gothic ruins or constructed Gothic follies.

The Hudson River school was a loosely organized group of mid-nineteenth-century American landscape painters. Their paintings provided a visual affirmation of Edmund Burke's (1729–1797) *A Philosophical Enquiry into the Origin of our Ideas of the Sublime and the Beautiful*, published in 1756. Many of the paintings are views of the Hudson River Valley, although also of other American landscapes featuring rugged mountains, steep cliffs, and the occasional waterfall. In these paintings, the skies often appear as if on the verge of a thunderstorm. The height of the Hudson River school activity came in the 1850s and 1860s, and Thomas Cole (1801–1848) was the key figure. Their pastoral paintings sometimes looked sentimental and nostalgic, and by the 1870s they were considered old-fashioned. Yet a closer look reveals that their naturalistic landscapes included factories with billowing smokestacks and railroads cutting across otherwise pristine landscapes (Wallach 2002). They were not as out of touch with the times as their contemporaries suspected and, within the discrete conventions of landscape paintings, made explicit the tension between nature and industrialization.

Romantic landscape painting connects to American Gothic architecture and furniture design in two ways: in the manner in which architects represented their buildings, sited in natural settings reminiscent of landscape paintings, and in the buildings' designs themselves. A leading figure in American Gothic Revival was Richard Upjohn (1802–1878). A feature of Gothic Revival is a picturesque asymmetry, which can be evident in plan, elevation, or in the rendering technique.

Upjohn started out as an English cabinetmaker in 1819, later emigrating to the United States, where he began his career as an architect. He combined his knowledge of English Gothic with the New England vernacular, thereby creating a strand of American Gothic. His publication *Rural Architecture* made his standardized church designs available across the country. Gothic Revival was deemed appropriate for churches, and it also made its mark in the realm of domestic architecture. Residential projects became the center of his large and successful practice. Looking at the totality of Upjohn's career, house, church, and office all figure equally, related to honor, rectitude, and the visual vocabulary of Gothic Revival.

Alexander Jackson Davis (1803–1892) dabbled in Egyptian Revival, Italianate, and Tudor Revival, but he is mostly known for turning his design talents to creating modest yet picturesque Gothic houses in the United States. Davis rendered some of his buildings within Romantic-looking landscapes. This connected American architecture to European artistic developments, yet with a distinct American slant. Prior to Davis, most architectural views were hard-edged, more a result of drafting and engraving than rendering and painting. Davis's houses were irregular in plan and elevation, and featured a judicious use of towers, turrets, pinnacles, finials, and gables. His only book, *Rural Residences*, was published in 1838.

Andrew Jackson Downing (1815–1852) also worked with the Gothic Revival architectural vocabulary in his efforts at fashioning well-designed, modest American houses. He and Davis collaborated on pattern books, the success of which contributed to the spread of Victorian Gothic throughout the United States.

A response to a positive economic climate, growing urban populations, and a desire to create a public infrastructure that improved the mind as well as the body resulted in a wave of museum building across much of the globe. Many of these buildings were in Gothic Revival, such as Thomas Deane and Benjamin Woodward's Oxford Museum, Oxford, England, 1855. Frank Furness's Pennsylvania Academy of Fine Arts, in Philadelphia, is a particularly inventive take on Gothic architecture. Furness incorporated glass, stone, and metals, and responded to the program of an art museum, a building type for which European churches provided no obvious solution.

Crawford Riddell was an American furniture maker, active in the years 1837 to 1849 in Philadelphia. He created a huge 13-foot-tall (4-meter-tall) Gothic Revival bed, commissioned by Henry Clay, the favorite to win the presidential election that year (Kotz 1997, p. 224). Clay lost, and the giant bed found another client. Gothic Revival frequently had religious and moral associations, and in Riddell's design, Gothic became presidential. A Gothic Revival side chair is unlike the boxy chairs of the Gothic era (Figure 15.3). With turned legs, it cleverly utilizes a Gothic pointed arch as its back, which in turn is composed of three Gothic arches. Eclecticism sneaks in the piece by way of the textile used for the upholstery. It features a laurel wreath, which was a classical motif that Napoleon Bonaparte adopted as his personal insignia. This Gothic Revival chair is upholstered with a neoclassical textile.

Egyptian Revival

Egyptian Revival was one of the more prominent of the exotic revivals. It was less highly theorized than Gothic Revival and proved to be a remarkably persistent if minor trend. The fashion, also known lightheartedly as Egyptomania, received a boost with Napoleon's campaign to Egypt of 1798. Egyptian Revival was never a serious movement like neoclassicism or Greek Revival. Twentieth-century historian James Curl gives the subject a weightiness that many Victorians never did: "Probably no culture (even those of Central America) has produced such mighty works of architecture that are so stark, so basic, so grand,

Figure 15.3
Gothic Revival side chair, United States, mid-nineteenth century.

so instantly memorable, as did ancient Egypt. The pyramid, the obelisk, the pylon, and the symmetrical temple are pure shapes that are best seen within a luminously clear landscape" (1982, p. 232).

British designer Christopher Dresser (1834–1904) was a prolific artist. Multitalented, he designed ceramics, glass, metalwork, furniture, carpets, fabrics, and wallpapers. He was internationally successful, as his designs sold in Europe, America, and Japan. Dresser's primary design affiliation is with English Arts and Crafts. Accordingly, many of his designs refer to English medieval art, but he also belongs to the significant subgroup of those in the reform movement who expressed a serious interest in Japanese art.

Unlike some who contributed to the English cult of **Japonisme**, Dresser traveled to Japan. He freely mixed historical sources, and he was known to draw upon Islamic, Greek, and Egyptian motifs. He was a writer and theorist, although less well known than William Morris. His writings promote honesty, regularity, and angularity. A theorist in tune with the times, Dresser sought to improve popular taste by refining it, not overturning its underlying premises.

One effect of the plurality of styles available to architects and designers is that many experimented. While Pugin is irrevocably linked to Gothic, and Richardson to Romanesque, some designers made a career out of switching stylistic alliances. And many well-regarded designers, at least occasionally, drifted into foreign design milieus.

Thus, avowed neoclassicists Schinkel and von Klenze experimented with Gothic, Egyptian, and Byzantine forms. Tiffany, usually associated with art nouveau, also has Egyptian Revival pieces to his name. Little opprobrium was associated with crossing stylistic borders, as when Christopher Dresser, usually considered as belonging to English Arts and Crafts, created an Egyptian stool (Figure 15.4).

Byzantine Revival and Turkish Revival

John Nash (1752–1835) was a prolific English architect and urban designer, and his works are associated with the glamour of the regency era. Working with the landscape designer Humphry Repton, he designed a series of country houses whose exteriors were consistent with the desire for picturesque landscapes. Nash made use of several different styles throughout his career. He did work in Tudor, Gothic, Renaissance, and Greek

Figure 15.4
Christopher
Dresser, Thebes
stool, 1884.

Figure 15.5
Chinese-style armchair, England, early nineteenth century.

Revival, and his country houses include castle-like forms and detailing.

Regency is a term that relates to the political structure in which a regent stands in for an under-age heir to the throne. Theoretically, it can pertain to any regency. There are two significant furniture styles known as Regency: French Regency (1715–1723) and English Regency (1811–1830). French Regency is a transitional style related to rococo. English Regency is a branch of neoclassicism, although, as John Pile points out, "the most curious aspect of Regency design is its seemingly inconsistent vacillation between the restraint of classicism and the exuberance of fancy" (2004, p. 229). Nash's work represents both ends of the Regency design spectrum.

Park Crescent, Nash's project of 1812, proved him to be an accomplished urban designer. It was a circular band of classically detailed attached houses. It is a confident work of architecture, urban design, landscape design, and was also a successful real estate venture. When he was in his sixties, Nash's career took off in a new direction when he started working for the crown and stopped taking on private clients. His show piece was his transformation of the Royal Pavilion at Brighton. It demonstrates the true spirit of eclecticism, with interior furnishings that include Chinoiserie (Figure 15.5). It had a **cast-iron** structural system, and some of the metal columns sprouted palm fronds at the ceiling. The Brighton Pavilion is a tour de force of exotic decoration in its exteriors, which combine Moorish revival with Byzantine and Gothic elements (Figure 15.6).

Critics of historic revivals decried the superficial emphasis on style and inclusion of exotic elements. The superficiality was sometimes true, but the designers were often interested in exploiting specific qualities of the culture in reference. Turkish Revival often overlapped with Byzantine or Islamic and was sometimes referred to as **Saracenic**.

Turkish revival exteriors, interiors, and furnishings existed within a popular culture milieu in which Turkey (and more generally the Middle East and the Islamic world) was considered a highly sensual environment, full of mystery and intrigue, comforts and pleasures, and a freedom from (Western) cultural restraints.

Part of the nineteenth-century fascination was fueled by the continuation of eighteenth-century interests, such as a Mozart opera and the writings of Mary Wortley Montagu (1689–1762). Many composers were interested in **janissary**, or Turkish, music and incorporated snippets into European opera. There were several prominent productions of Mozart's "The Abduction from the Seraglio."

Montagu was the wife of the British ambassador to Constantinople. She published a popular memoir based on fifty-two letters, written from the Turkish capital, that described a world in which she, as a woman, was able to enter the harem and circulate freely. The veil, in Montagu's telling, allowed her to hide her smallpox scars, freely associate with Turkish women and eunuchs, and, if momentarily, hide her ethnicity as a non-Arab.

Figure 15.6
John Nash,
Royal Pavilion
at Brighton,
England, 1815.

Another British ambassador, the explorer Richard Burton (1821–1890) and his wife, Isabel Burton (1831–1896), spent extensive periods of time abroad, and their writings satiated the desire for scintillating tales from the Middle East. Burton was a respected translator of *The Arabian Nights* and many ethnographic studies, in which he unflinchingly described the sexual practices of North Africans and Arabs. He and his wife traveled widely, and he had an astonishing talent for languages (Kennedy 2005). They traveled to North Africa, the Middle East, India, and Pakistan. For Burton, as for Montagu, the veil was an opportunity to hide his identity most famously when he, in disguise, was one of the few Europeans to make the pilgrimage to Mecca, an account of which he published, his *Pilgrimage to El-Medinah and Mecca*, in 1855. Not many Britons could afford to travel to Turkey, but they could vicariously enjoy its pleasures by going to the opera, reading memoirs, and lounging on extravagantly upholstered pieces of Turkish furniture. Isabel Burton also wrote her memoirs and translated several texts.

To twenty-first-century Westerners, the nineteenth-century representation of the Middle East is nearly the exact opposite of how the Middle East is evoked in today's popular media. Victorian

Britons developed their concepts of the Middle East from sources that highlighted the sensual side of life. What is consistent in the popular references to Turkey and the Middle East is that the harem, veils, and generally Arabic dress were emphasized for their ability to allow Westerners to move freely in the Middle East, unrecognized as foreigners.

The popularity of so-called Turkish daybeds and occasional chairs played into the associations of Turkey with luxury and comfort. They were upholstered and tufted and outfitted with fringe and tassels (Figure 15.7). Freestanding pieces of furniture were not standard features of Turkish

Figure 15.7
Lawrence Alma-Tadema, Turkish revival settee, London, England, 1885. Ebony, sandalwood, cedar, ivory, mother-of-pearl, and brass.

interiors, so the European "Turkish" pieces are hybrids between the desire for pieces of furniture and a fanciful and idealized image of people lolling about in a harem or bath house.

Stage design

The varieties of nineteenth-century historic revivals were endless. There were Venetian Gothic, Pisan Romanesque, and Pompeian Revivals. Egyptian Revival and Turkish Revival were two of the more prominent of the minor trends. Others were Assyrian Revival, Ottoman Revival, and Aztec Revival; they are typically grouped together under the catchall phrase "exoticism." Polymath Karl Friedrich Schinkel showed himself to be an accomplished stage designer. He did a series of well-received Egyptian Revival stage sets for an 1816 production of Mozart's *The Magic Flute* (Figure 15.8). He also designed four sets for an opera that is rarely produced today, Gaspare Spontini's *Fernand Cortez*, in 1818. The style of Schinkel's designs can only be referred to as Aztec Revival. The title of the set from the first act, "Temple of the Peruvians," does not make much historical or geographic sense, as Cortés

was in Mexico. One feature of exoticism was the tendency to combine elements, especially when the artist was not familiar with the cultures being portrayed.

The Industrial Revolution

A brief look at the population changes of three cities, from South America, Africa, and Asia, makes clear that the convergence of population growth, urbanization, and industrialization was a worldwide phenomenon that affected all aspects of life, including design.

In 1810, Buenos Aires declared itself independent from Spain. A modest growth in population followed the split, and the number of inhabitants of the city reached 60,000 in 1826 and 90,000 in 1854 (Pendergast 2002). The city established itself as the social and economic center of Argentina over the next few decades. In 1862,

Figure 15.8
Karl Friedrich Schinkel, Palace of the Queen of the Night, Stage design for the *Magic Flute*, Berlin, Germany, 1847–1849.

DECORATION ZU DER OPER DIE ZAUBERFLÖTE ACT I SCENE VI.

Buenos Aires became Argentina's capital, and the transformation of the city thereafter was phenomenal. Argentina became integral in the world economy, exporting wheat, wool, beef, and other agricultural products that fueled its economic boom. Because of the increase in trade, Buenos Aires grew rapidly as hundreds of thousands of immigrants migrated to the city from Europe from the 1880s to the 1930s. By 1930, 3 million people lived in the city, almost a third of Argentina's total population.

In 1860, Cairo was home to 295,000 people. Less than 40 years later, its population had almost doubled; the ancient city had an estimated 590,000 inhabitants in 1897 (Mitchell 1998, p. 38). The period between the two world wars saw a steady increase in the large cities of northern Africa. By the time of the 1927 census, Cairo became the first African city with a population that exceeded one million (Hance 1970, pp. 212–17).

Shanghai had a population of 149,000 in 1860. A scant 40 years later, its population quadrupled to 651,000 (Mitchell 1998, p. 42). The British were influential in Shanghai, but they were even more influential in another Chinese city, Hong Kong. In the 1860s, Hong Kong's population grew significantly as a result of migration from mainland China and its economy continued to flourish (Domschke 1986, pp. 621–22). As with many world cities, the period of population growth coincided with an emergent infrastructure, including telegraph systems and street lighting (Pendergast 2002, pp. 95–112).

Different regions of the globe industrialized at different rates and at different times, but the specter of technologically driven change was worldwide. Victorian design, in its many manifestations, was an attempt to mediate, hide, or glorify those changes.

The Industrial Revolution is most often presented in an urban context, with visions of London and endless smokestacks, rows of textile workers in steel-framed buildings, and giant stockyards in Chicago, Omaha, and St. Louis. Yet it had an equally profound effect on small towns and villages. African coastal cities had been cosmopolitan for centuries, yet it took the arrival of railroads to connect cities of the interior with global economic and cultural trends. Smaller cities were about a day's train ride away from a major metropolitan center.

The relationship between industrial processes and design is evident in several projects. Joseph Paxton (1803–1865) created the iron-and-glass Crystal Palace, London, in 1851. It was important for its materials—nothing could be more modern than iron and glass—and for its contents, the displays of decorative art objects from around the world. India was represented by the East India Company. In Paris, Henri Labrouste (1801–1875) created Sainte-Geneviève Library and also the Bibliothèque Nationale, both of which relied on an innovative metal structural system. Those who felt that the reliance on historical revivals was leading architecture down the wrong path often saw better results, to their minds, when they turned to engineering projects and industrial buildings. The Eiffel Tower is the prime example of the triumph of engineering. Some thirty years after the Crystal Palace in London, a Crystal Palace was built in Petrópolis, Brazil. Built in France in 1879, it was then erected in Brazil in 1884, part of a horticulture exhibit. Like its English predecessor, it had the desired effect of dazzling visitors with its form, materials, and contents.

A single designed object has all the contradictions, for better and for worse of Victorian art and industry. It was also used by the woman for whom the century is named. Queen Victoria's railroad car features a surprising mixture of industrial technology and hyperdecorated materials. Her private railway carriage was padded and tufted, with heavy draperies and no shortage of fringe and tassels (Figure 15.9). The white silk ceiling was designed with acoustics in mind. Her carriage is scarcely recognizable as a railway car.

Ships

A historian of Victorian decorative arts, John Gloag (1973), posits that the Victorian age outlived Queen Victoria, lasting until the First World War. There is no better example of the contradictory impulses of the Victorian approach to design than the outfitting of ocean liners. Technologically, the ships of the first decades of the twentieth century were highly advanced; they were the largest and the fastest. Their engineering was complicated, as they featured running water, electricity, elevators, and swimming pools. Yet their interiors, based on hotel designs of the period, were a riot of historical styles.

The shipping industry was an economic powerhouse at the center of the world economy. Prime economic statistics involve the movement of goods and people, and shipping was the venue for both. Shipping was also connected to immigration. For both strategic and symbolic reasons, passenger ships had military ties, as in wartime

Figure 15.9
Queen Victoria's
railway carriage,
1869.

they transported troops. Although not planned for these purposes, the ships became tools in international relations. Because of their extreme visibility, many details about their form received the input of national leaders, such as Edward VII, Edward VIII, and Kaiser Wilhelm II (Wealleans 2006). Important symbols of national pride, the press followed their every move, and hundreds of thousands of people lined beaches and quays to get a glimpse of them when they steamed by.

Mewès and Davis, the London architecture and interiors firm headed by Charles Mewès and Arthur Davis, was one of the most successful firms of its day. They had two prominent shipping companies as clients: the German Hamburg-America Line and the English Cunard Line. Ship interiors were true interiors projects, as they were not intended to be permanent. The most optimistic projections by their owners and designers were that they might serve for forty years; they were expected to turn a profit in less than ten years.

Mewès and Davis both studied in France and their designs are based on eighteenth-century French architecture. Yet it is not true that the shipbuilders and designers made no contribution to innovative design. They were at the center of the reconciliation between design and technology. Fierce promoters of traditional styles, they created workplaces with incredibly complex programs, spaces carefully crafted to respond to specific business functions, and they embraced new technologies and materials. In fact, the message that their ship designs communicated to potential passengers was comfort, and this meant electric lighting, elevators, and indoor plumbing. Their designs also incorporated modern materials such as metal, glass, linoleum, and plastic laminate.

Traditional architecture, interiors, and furnishings played a robust part in the world economy. The aspect of ship design that has received considerable attention is how their designs and layouts reflect class and gender models of the time. While it is now ubiquitous that French furnishings of the Louis XV and Louis XVI periods connote luxury, particularly in the hospitality industry, this was not predestined. This came about because of the popularity of the late nineteenth-century hotel and ship interiors.

The designers of the ship interiors worked independently, yet they inadvertently created a system that utilized the entirety of historically inspired designs at their disposal. The most important public rooms, the first-class lounges and dining rooms, were in Louis XV and Louis XVI styles sometimes combined. Often the men's smoking room, particularly on English ships, was Tudor, Elizabethan, or Jacobean. The English ship *Titanic* featured a Turkish bath. Mewès and Davis designed a Pompeian swimming pool for the Royal Automobile Club in 1907, and re-created it in 1913 on the German liner *Imperator* (see Chapter 22).

Furniture

The general features of Victorian furniture include its elaborate surface decoration and a myriad of stylistic references, sometimes combining details from several epochs in a single piece. New materials and manufacturing techniques also figured in the designs. Neoclassicism was a global style of the early nineteenth century, but classicism lived on in numerous revivals for the rest of the century, such as a classical sidechair with a splat that resembles a Greek urn (Figure 15.10).

Figure 15.10
Classical Revival side chair, mid-nineteenth century.

Rococo Revival

John Henry Belter (1804–1863) was a furniture designer and manufacturer. Born in Germany, he immigrated to New York City, where he spent his entire professional career. From 1845 on, he worked almost exclusively in a mode that was referred to as rococo revival. Now his works are considered the essence of Victorian design. The pieces at which he excelled do not constitute a faithful revival of the rococo (Figure 15.11). This style originated in England in the 1820s and spread to Germany and France in the 1830s. Belter had a knack for responding to popular taste. His designs were visually compelling, well built, relatively lightweight, and surprisingly sturdy. He worked in a combination of solid and laminated wood. His three-stage manufacturing process included a combination of contoured shaping, punched decoration, and carving. He created dynamic pieces that curved in several planes. He embellished already-curved shapes with arabesques, scrolls, foliage, flowers, fruit, and vegetables. Mostly using machines, he was able to create pieces that looked hand carved. The rear elevations of his pieces were equally well attended to. The pieces were sculptural in that they were meant to be walked around. Furnished with wheels in the Victorian fashion, they could be moved about within a parlor and pulled up for a conversation grouping. They were not visually related to a specific and fixed architectural location. During Belter's time, Americans started the habit of purchasing furniture *en suite*, a set of sofa and armchairs for parlors, a bed with matching chest and dressing table for bedrooms. Belter's parlor and boudoir suites, with their expressive ornamentation, appealed to a well-to-do clientele.

Figure 15.11
John Henry Belter, rosewood rococo revival sofa, New York, New York, 1850–1860. Rosewood.

Some of the pieces made by his many imitators were more affordable.

Victorian horned furniture

The Victorian approach to design was eclectic, and people appreciated novelty items known as conversation pieces. This resulted in some odd pieces of furniture, such as the minor but nonetheless significant trend in Texas of horned furniture. The most prominent German designer of the genre was H.F.C. Rampendahl whose pieces show an appreciation of unusual materials and forms (Figure 15.12).

Cast-iron furniture

Industrial manufacturing techniques made **cast-iron** furniture possible. For a while cast iron was immensely popular, seen as a wondrous modern material. Some buildings were built entirely out of cast iron, although eventually a series of fires proved its weakness as an architectural material and its popularity declined.

Cast-iron garden furniture also had a sustained period of popularity. The iron itself could be formed into endless shapes and patterns, such as Gothic arches or classical detailing. Cast iron was frequently molded to imitate bamboo.

Figure 15.12 H.F.C. Rampendahl, Victorian horned armchair, Hamburg, Germany, 1850.

Victorian decorating

A feature of Victorian interiors is the juxtaposition of bizarre things that have no logical relationship, and it is precisely that quality that makes them memorable. These include curios, the oddly shaped figurine, and other miscellaneous bric-a-brac. A popular open shelving unit for mementos was called a **whatnot**. The jarring juxtapositions prompt reflection and new trains of thought. Objects in a Victorian interior also acted as repositories of memories.

Victorian design was related to personal memory, collective knowledge, and the importance of new materials and media. The overall quantity of stuff that people owned and that houses contained increased greatly. The Victorian decorating approach was well poised to handle large quantities of objects (this in contrast to modernism, which was an aesthetic at odds with dealing with large personal inventories).

The hallway and stairwell of a house by Church, Vaux, and Withers amazingly holds together as a work of design, given the disparate elements it combines. They include Assyrian stencils, a Buddha statue, Gothic arches, Moorish claustra work, African spears, Chinese vases, and Turkish carpets. The Victorian salon was the focus of design attention, and it managed to be simultaneously formal and comfortable.

Regarding the affordability of decorative arts objects and their distribution across class lines, the collaboration of new industrial manufacturing processes and designers largely succeeded. This was the beginning of a consumer culture, and Victorian parlors accommodated the increasing number of objects. Several economists, most notably Thorsten Veblen, anointed the second half of the nineteenth century as the age of conspicuous consumption. Up until the nineteenth century, design had been the purview of the elite. The Industrial Revolution promised to increase the standard of living of the lower and middle classes. While the Industrial Revolution created as many problems as solutions, objects became affordable to people who in previous centuries would have led lives deprived of shiny bibelots. Complaints about the degraded quality of Victorian design notwithstanding, it was the beginning of the democratization of design. And the effects of Victorian design are still being felt. To many, John Belter pieces were the pinnacle of beauty, luxury, and refinement. To purchase a Belter furniture suite was not merely a response to the functional need for seating, it was an announcement that socially one had arrived. A circular upholstered piece was the **borne**, which was a feature of many hotel lobbies and homes large enough to accommodate them (Figure 15.13).

Reactions against Victorian design

Robert Kerr (1823–1904), a Victorian architect, gained greater renown as a critic. In 1860, he read aloud a paper, "The Battle of the Styles," whose title became the catchphrase for Victorian architecture and design. Regarding design, there was little consensus, and fierce criticism of Victorian approaches began in the Victorian era.

The debate surrounding the appropriateness of Victorian design abated little in one hundred years, for in the 1960s, American architectural historian John Summerson felt the need to address the issue and put it to rest once and for all (he did not). Four lectures he gave in March of 1968 at Columbia University prominently tackled the question of the validity of Victorian design. These famous lectures became the basis of a book (Summerson 1970). Summerson provocatively asked if "early and mid-Victorian architecture was, in its own time and in the eyes of its own best-informed critics, horribly unsuccessful" (Summerson 1970). Summerson's *Victorian Architecture* does not make for a suspenseful read; early on, he answers his rhetorical question about the value of Victorian aesthetics: "Where the Victorians are concerned it would be very much safer to begin, at least, on the assumption that it was wrong." Summerson was writing in the late 1960s, when modernism was still going strong, a movement

antithetical to Victorian design principles. Summerson was not alone; critics of Victorian design were and are many. Perhaps the reason Summerson felt the need to address Victorian architecture is that it remains popular among non-academics, those for whom modernism is a tough sell. Some of the words used to describe Victorian design are *unintelligible*, *garish*, *deplorable*, *monstrous*, *ambiguous*, and *vulgar*. The revulsion that many critics feel about Victorian design exceeds in intensity that of critics of previous epochs when discussing the styles that preceded their own.

Other twentieth-century writers felt the same. Summerson dismissed all Victorian architecture up to 1870 as a failure. Humphrey House in 1948 pinpointed Victorian design's underlying premise that, he felt, doomed it to failure. Victorian architects and designers, he regretted, were trying to combine, in form and detail, elements that were simply incompatible. All Victorian architects, according to House—and he lamented the fact—had to position their work in relationship to style. They either had to announce their belief in the superiority of one style (e.g., Pugin) or affirm the validity of mixing styles, known as eclecticism (e.g., Nash).

Professional organizations and design schools

Until a Cornell architectural historian wrote her book, the story of the rise of professional organizations in the nineteenth century was mostly untold (Woods 1999). Eighteenth-century guilds were forerunners to two important developments of the nineteenth century: the establishment of professional organizations and design education programs.

The organization that became the American Institute of Architects was started in 1857, and its initial members included Andrew Jackson Davis, Richard Morris Hunt, Richard Upjohn, and Calvert Vaux. An important responsibility of a professional organization was to establish the standards for the profession.

Of equal importance was the opening of architecture and design schools. Tuskegee Institute was founded in 1881, with Booker T. Washington as its first teacher. The Rhode Island School of Design opened in 1877. The development of professional organizations and schools and academies was important for architecture and interior design, and this two-pronged development occurred worldwide.

Figure 15.13
Gustav Herter, borne, United States, *c.* 1860.

Romanesque Revival and modernism

The importance of the work of Henry Hobson Richardson is underscored by the fact that a style bears his name, **Richardsonian Romanesque**. He made a significant contribution to modernism, but some twentieth-century historians of modernism felt that his work was in need of redemption. They offered lengthy explanations, clarifying that Richardson's work should not be lumped together with other historical revivals. Richardson's masonry buildings look to French Romanesque architecture, with occasional Byzantine flourishes. He used Romanesque forms, most notably semi-spherical arches, but he unified them in compositions that were commensurate with their modern functions. He was more interested in functional planning and shaping volumes than in historical details.

The J.J. Glesner House was built in 1885 to 1887 (Figure 15.14). Startling severe elevations line two streets; it sits on a corner lot. There are few openings. The garden side is invisible to the street and much different in character. The house's interior spaces intrude into the garden, with several protuberances that have large windows. The asymmetrical plan and the arched entryway—the most obviously Romanesque feature—were among the elements that Louis Sullivan and Frank Lloyd Wright admired.

Paul Clifford Larson stresses that Richardson's buildings are not easy to pigeonhole: "Some of Richardson Marshall Field Warehouse admirers pursued his archeological interests and others his search for distinctively American form; some championed his picturesque compositional schemes and others his penchant for simplification; some enlarged on the exuberance of his detailing and others on his respect for primal volumes" (1988, p. 19).

The underlying rationale for the adoption of Romanesque forms by the early skyscraper designers is not immediately apparent. In architecture circles, Richardson's Marshall Field Warehouse, 1885–1887, in Chicago, was widely admired and became an architectural pilgrimage site. It had an abbreviated cornice and rows and columns of segmental arches. The windows were arranged logically to express the structure's steel frame. The façade, of rough-cut American stone, was no longer hiding or dressing up the structure, but was integral to it. Working within a historical idiom, Richardson found a solution that avoided the fripperies of Victorian design. Cass Gilbert, Burnham and Root, and Louis Sullivan were influenced by Richardson and specifically the Marshall Field Warehouse. This building has a central position in the history of American architecture and interiors. It has open floors supported by a regular grid of columns. Sullivan considered it a monument to trade, noting that a new kind of commerce required a new kind of structure.

It is curious that Louis Sullivan is known for the saying "form follows function." When compared to other great building types of the late nineteenth century, opera houses, newspaper offices, and train stations, skyscrapers were essentially functionless. They provided wide-open leased spaces that, once leased, were outfitted in tune with the renters' needs. Skyscrapers were important because they changed the world's cityscapes, and they made possible the twentieth-century field of corporate interior design, which, in turn, exponentially increased the demand for office furniture. Tenants leased empty floor plates that had to be

Figure 15.14
Henry Hobson Richardson, Glesner House, Chicago, Illinois, 1885.

designed and built. Because tenants changed over time, especially in the United States, a building's interiors had to be periodically reconfigured.

Conclusion

Robert Kerr, not a well-known figure today, was not only prescient with his perceptions about nineteenth-century design, he was wise about what was to come. He placed the blur of nine-teenth-century styles into three categories: the eclectic, the followers of Pugin and other Gothic Revivalists, and the early modernists. This is an astute and productive way of making sense of an era that defies categorization. On the one hand, designers of the Victorian era were buried in the past, yet on the other, they were marching triumphantly toward the future.

Sources

Brooks, Chris (1999). *The Gothic Revival*. London: Phaidon.

Curl, James (1982). *The Egyptian Revival*. London: George Allen and Unwin.

Domschke, Eliane and Doreen Goyer (1986). *The Handbook of National Population Censuses*. Westport, CT: Greenwood Press.

Edwards, Clive (1993). *Victorian Furniture: Technology and Design*. New York: St. Martin's Press.

Fergusson, James and Robert Kerr (1891). *History of the Modern Styles of Architecture*. New York: Dodd, Mead, and Company.

Gloag, John (1973). *Victorian Comfort: A Social History of Design from 1830–1900*. Newton Abbot: David and Charles.

Hance, William (1970). *Population, Migration, and Urbanization in Africa*. New York: Columbia University Press.

Kennedy, Dane (2005). *The Highly Civilized World: Richard Burton and the Victorian World*. Cambridge, MA: Harvard University Press.

Kotz, Suzanne (1997). *Dallas Museum of Art: A Guide to the Collection*. Seattle: Marquand Books.

Larson, Paul Clifford, ed. (1988). *The Spirit of H.H. Richardson*. Ames: Iowa State University Press.

McCarthy, Michael (1987). *The Origins of the Gothic Revival*. New Haven, CT: Yale University Press.

Mitchell, Brian (1998). *International Historical Statistics Africa, Asia and Oceania, 1750–1993*. New York: Stockton Press.

O'Gorman, James (1973). *The Architecture of Frank Furness*. Philadelphia: Philadelphia Museum of Art.

Peck, Amelia, ed. (1992). *Alexander Jackson Davis: American Architect 1803–1892*. New York: Rizzoli.

Pendergast, Sara and Tom Pendergast (2002). *Worldmark Encyclopedia of National Economies*. Farmington Hills, MA: Gale Group.

Pile, John (2004). *A History of Interior Design*. New York: Wiley.

Shenton, Caroline (2018). *Mr. Barry's War: Rebuilding the Houses of Parliament*. Oxford: Oxford University Press.

Snodin, Michael and John Styles (2004). *Design and the Decorative Arts in Victorian Britain*. London: Victoria and Albert Museum.

Summerson, John (1970). *Victorian Architecture: Four Studies in Evaluation*. New York: Columbia University Press.

Veblen, Thorstein (1934). *The Theory of the Leisure Class*. New York: Modern Library.

Wallach, Alan (2002). "Thomas Cole's Rivers in the Catskills as Antipastoral." *Art Bulletin* 84 (June): 334–50.

Wealleans, Anne (2006). *Designing Liners: A History of Interior Design Afloat*. Abingdon: Routledge.

Woods, Mary (1999). *From Craft to Profession: The Practice of Architecture in Nineteenth-Century America*. Berkeley: University of California Press.

Discussion and Review Questions

1. What are some examples of design developments directly related to technological improvements? What were some of the nineteenth-century inventions?

2. What are some examples of design developments that seem to ignore technological developments?

3. What is an example of a historic revival where a specific quality or historical reference is being explored?

4. What is an example of a historic revival that seems superficial, more related to an appreciation of the form rather than a deep understanding of history?

5. How can nationalism be related to design?

6. The Victorians sometimes used a name for a particular historical revival, yet today we normally use a different term. What is an example?

7. What were some of the major historical revivals?

8. What were some of the minor historical revivals?

9. Describe the major trends in Victorian decorating. What specifically did critics dislike about Victorian design?

Reform Movements: Arts and Crafts

16

1860–1910

1910–1930

British Arts and Crafts

American Arts and Crafts

Arts and Crafts was an influential English movement of the second half of the nineteenth century that had worldwide implications and a lasting effect on design. Artists, architects, furniture designers, and patrons were related to the school of painting the **pre-Raphaelites**. Arts and Crafts designers sought to counter two prevailing trends, one economic and technological, the other cultural and moral, that dominated the nineteenth century. The first was the Industrial Revolution and its effects, the second was Victorian design. Arts and Crafts designers sought to renew design by looking at an idealized pre-industrial world.

Although Victorian pieces were popular with the general public, among artists and designers there was a backlash against (what they perceived to be) ostentation, display, and mindless historicism. This artistic revolt took several forms, which are the subject of this and following chapters. In England, the anti-Victorian revolt was generally referred to as the reform movement, as a broad category, with Arts and Crafts as a specific subgroup of the larger trend.

Figure 16.0
(*Facing page*)
Philip Webb, refectory table, 1856, and Sussex chair, 1860; Dante Gabriel Rossetti, Rossetti chair, 1870.

Arts and Crafts

Criticism of Victorian design and all it stood for came about almost immediately. One of the strongest reactions to it was Arts and Crafts. Even the longstanding work of the American Shakers was an aesthetic rebuff to all things Victorian. Art nouveau and the Secessionists, covered later, were also reactions against Victorian design.

It is occasionally difficult to reconcile all the tenets of the Arts and Crafts designers regarding the use of historical forms. On the one hand, they decried historicism; on the other, they extolled the virtues of the medieval era. Understanding the historical context of nineteenth-century Britain aids this effort. The writers William Morris, John Ruskin, and Augustus Welby Northmore Pugin objected to trends in which historic forms were grafted onto new structures with little thought given to their history and meaning. They disliked anything that fell under the broad rubric of Victorian design and the "recent" continental periods baroque and rococo. The English reformists and their followers cherished the medieval side of the Italian Renaissance, hence the name of the painting movement, the pre-Raphaelites (before Raphael).

The leaders and followers of the Arts and Crafts movement felt that two of the biggest scourges of the day, the Industrial Revolution and Victorian design, could be remedied by a return to what they considered good design. They sought to counteract the ugly side of industrialization—the degradation of modern (nineteenth-century) life. In addition to looking favorably at the medieval period, they admired humble objects and those with the knowledge of how to craft them.

These reformists were critical of industrial techniques and their ability to cheaply produce vapid ornament. Their aesthetically minded activities can also be seen in the context of the **muckrakers**, the journalists who were investigating dubious business practices by factories and their owners. Other sympathetically aligned movements were Romanticism (in painting and literature), the garden city movement, the **Chicago school**, and **Prairie style**.

A major focus of their efforts was the unity of the arts, in contrast to the hierarchy that dominated previous periods. This represented a major shift in how those involved with high art—painting, sculpture, architecture—viewed the "lower" arts—furniture and other designed objects. They sought to elevate the status of craftsmanship. This would lead to a reintegration of art, artifacts, and life, only on a higher plane.

For inspiration, they turned to German tribes, Icelandic sagas, Celtic tales, and the story of King Arthur. Although Arts and Crafts enthusiasts objected to the indiscriminate use of historical forms, they objected to history less emphatically than those affiliated with art nouveau and the Vienna Secession. There was frequent overlap between Arts and Crafts and Gothic Revival, both found common ground in the writings of theorist John Ruskin. The 1850s, 1860s, and 1870s were the prime years of the Gothic Revival.

Both movements admired simplicity, although defined in a nineteenth-century way. The exhortation of directness extended to moral virtues, social organization, and methods of fabrication—in other words, an integrated approach to life. Yet there were differences between Arts and Crafts and Gothic Revival. The latter was an explicit return to medieval forms; Arts and Crafts was contemporary design loosely based on the principles and production methods of the medieval period.

An achievement of the Arts and Crafts movement was that it managed to be intellectual and populist at the same time. There was an urban, sophisticated side to it, and it also had a down-to-earth, rural side to it.

The pre-Raphaelites were the English artists interested in medieval subject matter. Usually the term refers to those whose principal activity was painting, in contrast to those involved with decorative objects. Dante Gabriel Rossetti is the most famous of the group. The pre-Raphaelites felt an affinity for the decorative arts, and they collaborated with furniture makers. One product of these joint ventures, Morris and Company's hand-painted chests and bureaus, sold extremely well.

John Ruskin

John Ruskin (1819–1900) was an artist and collector, but he is mostly known as the author of *The Seven Lamps of Architecture* (1849) and *The Stones of Venice* (1851–1853). These two publications constituted the theoretical backbone of Arts and Crafts. Ruskin's Christian faith was a foundation of all his writings. He was important as a philosopher and as an aesthetic advisor. He strongly objected to industrially produced objects. He did not proclaim that all ornament was bad; he objected to meaningless ornament, and his writings provided a way to instill ornament with meaning. Arts and Crafts also showed the way for designers to imbue their projects with meaning. One of the principal strategies involved ornament, specifically ornament that made local references, incorporating motifs based on native flora. The inspiration could lie in the English countryside, the Midwestern prairie, the Hudson River Valley, California, or New Zealand.

Arts and Crafts architects, a distinguished group including Edwin Lutyens, Philip Webb, and C.F.A. Voysey, discussed in this chapter, approached design in a way that resulted in buildings with irregular and strong geometric profiles. Their buildings were characterized by a seemingly ad hoc agglomeration of gables, windows, and chimneys. Houses were designed from the inside out. This was the opposite of the Renaissance and Palladian approach to design, in which the architect developed a pleasing overall form—in plan and elevation—and assigned functions to rooms. The Arts and Crafts approach was simultaneously modern, a forerunner to functionalism, and vernacular, the straightforward method of designing agricultural buildings based on need. At the level of a building's details, Arts and Crafts supporters called for a return to handcrafted pieces.

William Morris

Unquestionably, the central figure in English Arts and Crafts was William Morris (1834–1896). He was important as a designer, as a spokesman for the movement, and as a successful businessman; many of his designs are still in production. Morris was a designer, writer, reformer, and poet. At the start of his career, he worked for Gothic Revival architect George Edmund Street (1824–1881); one of Morris's coworkers was Philip Webb. In 1861, Morris founded a firm with Webb. In 1875, it became Morris and Company, which specialized in a broad array of designed products, including stained glass, furniture, wallpapers, and textiles.

The members of the coterie of reformists took different paths. Morris's friend Edward Burne-Jones became a painter. Although Morris studied architecture and started his career in that profession, he devoted his energies to poetry and two-dimensional designs. Ruskin's writings influenced Morris and Webb alike.

People who admired Victorian decoration liked Morris's designs, and they also appealed to designers. Designers, aesthetes, and the public alike responded to Morris and Company's products.

William Morris made designs for fabrics, wallpapers, and graphics based on nature

Figure 16.1
William Morris, "Honeysuckle," London, England, 1876–1877. Printed linen.

(Figure 16.1). Seeking to recuperate the degraded state of design, the company started producing wallpapers in 1862. Their greatest long-lasting success was as a source of well-conceived flat patterns for textiles and wallpapers. Van der Post explains the lasting appeal of the firm's designs: "The development of Morris' patterns, from early medieval-inspired wallpapers to subtle repeating designs of English garden flowers drawn ten years later for wallpapers and printed textiles, shows his increasing preoccupation with nature and a growing confidence in his own intuitive powers as a pattern designer and botanical draughtsman" (2003, p. 6). Morris's accomplished designs remained popular throughout the career of the firm's founder.

Morris was talented at designing and energetically marshaled the talents of others. The Morris Chair is a sturdy wooden armchair, probably designed by others in the employ of Morris and Company (Figure 16.2). It is a logical piece of furniture, based on traditional inexpensive chairs and made comfortable with unattached cushions. A reworking of a common chair type, it was itself endlessly copied. It was found to be useful as porch furniture, for summer resorts, and for those who wanted to incorporate unpretentious pieces of furniture into their living rooms.

Morris's company also produced an adjustable armchair (Figure 16.3). Webb designed this popular piece for the company based on an original bought in the countryside. The back moves and is secured

Figure 16.2
William Morris
and Co., Morris
chair, London,
England 1866.

Figure 16.3
Philip Webb,
Morris adjustable
chair, London,
England, 1883.

on a metal ratchet. The ebonized finish relates to **Anglo-Japanese** pieces. The bobbin turning on the legs, spindles, and stretchers is a traditional form that dates to the Jacobean period. The wheels are a Victorian touch. The cushions are made of stamped woolen plush velvet. This piece shows how Morris and Company designers synthesized influences from several sources into a cohesive "new" whole. It was sold by catalog, and several American furniture companies copied it. It is from a suite of furniture for a family in Bath, England, and it was designed for the guest bedroom.

Morris had an intellectual side that he pursued in addition to designing. He studied at Oxford, and he and his wife were great readers. In addition to his other areas of success, Morris was a successful poet. The enterprising Morris could apply his energies to reading, writing, managing, and designing.

His firm benefited from the popularity of Gothic Revival, especially in church architecture. Huge numbers of Gothic Revival churches were built in England in the nineteenth century, and they required stained-glass windows. Stained glass became one of Morris and Company's specialties. Morris's stained-glass designs were similar to his textile designs; they looked appropriate but were actually contemporary versions of traditional motifs. Morris was also concerned with preserving historic buildings (Donovan 2008).

Morris promoted in words and deeds the close relationship between art and craft. His writings articulated the advantages to this approach, and his firm put the idea into action. He collaborated with painters and craftsmen. The reason that graphics, typeface, printing, and books play an important role in Arts and Crafts stems from the unity of the high arts and craftwork. The underlying rationale was that if artists (mostly painters) were encouraged to apply their talents to ordinary objects, everything improved.

With their use of complicated patterns in textiles, wallpapers, and title pages, Arts and Crafts designs today seem both traditional and visually complex, but a keen eye discerns how they significantly departed from the Victorian love of clutter. Morris demonstrated his commitment to graphics and publishing with his last project, Kelmscott Press, established in 1888.

Philip Webb

Philip Webb (1831–1915) was an English architect and designer and one of the reformists concerned about the effects of manufacturing. He met William Morris in Street's office and they both became involved with the pre-Raphaelites.

Webb started his own practice in 1859, and his first commission was Morris's house, Red House in Kent. As Webb often did, he developed most of the detailing himself. Red House is so named because of its redbrick walls and tiles (Figure 16.4). It has little ornamentation and is designed from the inside out, meaning that the exterior elements are the result of internal function, a process the modernists admired. Windows correspondingly relate to rooms behind them and are not subordinate to a symmetrical façade.

Figure 16.4
Philip Webb and
William Morris,
Red House,
Bexleyheath,
England, 1859.

The living room of Red House looks like a barn, with a loft (not for hay), exposed rafters, and ladder (Figure 16.5). Yet careful scrutiny reveals that it is scrupulously designed and displays several surprising hints of modernism. The artworks and shelves coalesce into a horizontal band above the chair rail. The paintings are not framed and hung on a wall, but form a continuous horizontal zone. They extend to the corners and nestle directly against the built-in storage unit. The walls are white, and the built-in bookshelves are structural. Furniture was upholstered with Morris fabric.

The principles that govern the house's designs are evident in details, such as the cabinet doors. They are functionally simple, with a straightforward emphasis on visible hardware and clean white paint. This house, and others like it, reflect vernacular structures from agricultural environments.

Webb did many tasteful country houses. He was more of an architect and furniture designer than a designer of textile patterns. A signature move in his houses was the use of paneling painted white.

Figure 16.5
Philip Webb and William Morris, Red House, Bexleyheath, England, 1859. Drawing room.

Webb was a natural fit for Morris's business, as he was anti–Industrial Revolution and anti-commercialism. Influenced by Ruskin's writings, Webb idealized the medieval period. Like the other reformists, he opposed the Victorian parade of styles—Egyptian Revival, Turkish Revival, Venetian Gothic Revival, and so forth. He rejected historicism and purist forms of Greek and Gothic Revival. He favored tradition, not history. By looking to the medieval past, relating to the landscape, and seeking inspiration in vernacular architecture, one could, according to Webb's way of thinking, rediscover the essence of English character. The revival of art was related to social change, and Webb became a socialist. Unlike Morris, he was not a writer.

Webb made a number of sideboards, sometimes collaborating with painters (Figure 16.6). A sometime collaborator was the artist Edward Burne-Jones. Webb used ebonized wood, gilding, stamped leather, and brass and copper hardware. The joints remain visible and the hardware is prominent. A signature detail is the use of metal strap hinges; they are obvious, functional, and medieval. Sheila Kirk delineates the fine line of Webb's design, which is not a strict revival yet is related to history: "Webb's early pieces have no overtly Gothic ornament yet they do call to mind the Middle Ages" (2005, p. 50).

Webb's sideboards rely on a grid for their well-proportioned composition. Subsidiary elements come in threes and twos. An almost perfect square is divided into two, a base and a top. They are simple in their overall visual effect, yet painstakingly hand-painted. Now found in museums, they were initially sold by catalog.

Kirk also articulates how Webb, when designing furniture or architecture, demanded a high level of precision that was more modern than medieval: "Webb never aimed for a primitive, rustic effect. He insisted on good workmanship, and on a smooth but not highly polished finish" (2005, p. 51). When modernists arrived on the scene, they frequently praised the finishes achieved by Arts and Crafts designers such as Philip Webb.

Morris and Company

One of the most popular pieces of Morris and Company was the Sussex chair, named after a country chair from Sussex. Like the adjustable chair, a Morris associate found a chair in the country and thought it suitable for the Morris line. One chair was purchased, and Morris designers set about redesigning it. Simple, detailed turned elements constitute the frame, and it features a simple rush seat. William and his wife Jane Morris used Sussex chairs in Red House and Kelmscott House, and Edward Burne-Jones likewise owned Sussex chairs. It was a modest chair, also used at English colleges. In homes, it found use in dining rooms and living rooms.

Jane Morris

Jane Morris, née Burden (1839–1914), was a muse for the pre-Raphaelites. As students, Rossetti, Burne-Jones, and Morris had all been struck by her beauty.

Prolific interior design author Elizabeth Wilhide wrote: "Her particular type of beauty was so strongly associated with the pre-Raphaelite vision that it was difficult to tell which came first" (1991, p. 15). Morris painted Jane, using her to model as Guinevere. She fell in love with and married William Morris. Jane Morris was not formally well educated, but she was intelligent and a voracious reader. She naturally came by the timeless beauty many of the pre-Raphaelite painters sought in a model.

Initially, the Morrises lived full-time at Red House, but in 1865 they moved back to London to be closer to their booming business. Kelmscott Manor was a sixteenth-century house redecorated by William Morris in 1871. Morris's decorating

Figure 16.6
Philip Webb, sideboard, Bexleyheath, England, 1862.

scheme left the medieval structure intact, yet he simplified the visual effect of the old house with his selection of furnishings and finishes. He decorated the place with simple pieces of furniture—upholstered in Morris textiles and painted the walls. Interior draperies hang at a consistent height and bring order to a group of otherwise disparate elements that includes Sussex chairs, a Wainscot chair, and a hearth with a Gothic arch.

Jane Morris posed for Rossetti (1828–1882) several times, and at some point their relationship became intimate. What was once an illicit affair became public knowledge (Wilhide 1991, pp. 15–26). William and Jane Morris remained married, and just how incensed he was over his wife's affair remains a mystery. Amazingly, he later commissioned Rossetti to paint his wife's portrait, the very same scenario that prompted their initial indiscretion (Figure 16.7).

Rossetti, of Italian background, never visited Italy. When the pre-Raphaelites formed as a group in 1848, Rossetti was friends with William Morris and Edward Burne-Jones. Rossetti later was employed by Morris, primarily working on stained-glass windows for churches. The popularity of Gothic Revival resulted in commissions for stained glass, in houses and churches.

The Rossetti chair was named for the artist, and he is listed as its designer. It is possible that other Morris designers assisted in its creation.

In the case of Arts and Crafts, while their rhetoric praised a return to a simple life and the necessity of designing well for humble households, their own lives were unconventional, with the triangular relationship of William Morris, Jane Morris, and Rossetti as the prime example.

May Morris

Morris and Company offered a three-paneled screen with embroidered canvas panels (Figure 16.8). It relies upon a simple frame-and-panel system. The screens were sold as kits or already completed by catalog. John Henry Dearle was Morris's assistant, and he later became artistic director. May Morris (1862–1938), William and Jane Morris's youngest daughter, directed the embroidery shop from 1885 to 1896. The inclusion

Figure 16.7
Dante Gabriel Rossetti, *The Day Dream*, 1880. Portrait of Jane Morris.

Figure 16.8
May Morris, Honeysuckle fire screen, 1880–1885. Sold as a kit.

of the humble pastime of embroidery as part of the Arts and Crafts aesthetic sphere added to its popularity, particularly among women.

Other Arts and Crafts designers

Edwin Godwin (1833–1886) was an English architect, designer, and writer (Soros 1999, p. 15)—a major figure in the Arts and Crafts movement. The breadth of his stylistic interests resulted in a lack of consistency in his overall body of work, which, depending on one's viewpoint, was a point for or against him. Susan Soros, the editor of an exhibition catalog on his work, writes: "Domestic interior decoration played a significant role in Godwin's career. He was responsible for many highly original interior designs, ranging from an elaborate Gothic Revival scheme of decoration for an Irish castle to a severe minimally furnished, Japanese-inspired interior for an artist's house-studio in London" (1999, p. 185).

Although he expressed his allegiance to Ruskin, his attraction to Japanese art made him an unusual voice in the English reform movements. His pieces were a fusion of Arts and Crafts and Japanese motifs and themes. Gridlike and modular, his Anglo-Japanese furniture was more imaginative than ethnographic (see Chapter 18).

Charles Eastlake (1836–1906) was a British architect, historian, and theorist. He did not build furniture himself, but had furniture made to his specifications that were sold under his name. Through his publications, he was as successful in the United States as in his native country.

As was expected of a knowledgeable person in design, he was influenced by Pugin and Ruskin. Eastlake himself wrote a book that covered Pugin's area of expertise, *History of the Gothic Revival* (1877). He had previously written a book that ensured his ongoing relevance, *Hints on Household Taste* (1868).

Eastlake's furniture was severe-looking. In many respects, his pieces look Victorian, which is how they are often described, only with less decoration. He achieved the severe look by utilizing flat decorative planes. One of his concerns was the ease of cleaning; hence his predilection for flat patterns. Eastlake's use of the word "taste" in his title is telling: he did not overturn trends and stylistic preferences, but assisted people in decorating their homes simply and tastefully. Eastlake's designs were received as the opposite of John Henry Belter's, yet there is a resemblance.

The second generation of Arts and Crafts

Morris, Webb, Rossetti, and Godwin represent the first generation of English Arts and Crafts. A second generation of English Arts and Crafts includes several talented architects and furniture designers whose careers take them into the twentieth century.

Voysey

Charles Francis Annesley Voysey (1875–1910) was an English architect who designed and built a number of beautifully designed country houses in the period 1890–1910. His work was traditional, **vernacular**, and subtly revolutionary. Familiar with Pugin's publications, Voysey later produced work that mostly eliminated any lingering Gothic traces.

He had an architectural practice, and his career was an example of the cross-disciplinary nature of those involved in Arts and Crafts. Hitchmough writes that "Voysey's versatility as a designer went beyond that of any of his contemporaries, in both range and duration" (1995, p. 141). Voysey was successful as a designer of furniture and wallpapers. When the opportunity arose, he designed houses, interiors, details, furniture, carpets, draperies, and wall coverings.

Like his colleagues in Arts and Crafts, Voysey lamented the state of design: "The intemperate indulgence in display and elaboration, in gilding and veneer, and the feverish thirst for artificial excitement, are all part and parcel of our proverbial restlessness. Too much luxury is death to the artistic soul" (1894, pp. 415–18).

The residence he designed for himself, called the Orchard, finished in 1899, is remarkably simple in its façade (Figure 16.9). It fits into the local vernacular of farm buildings, yet there is a clarity in its composition that is the result of careful design work. Similarly, little clutter detracts from the simplicity of the Voysey interior (Figure 16.10). The stairway is framed by a built-in screen formed by vertical slats, a detail also found in the works of Wright, Sullivan, and Mackintosh. The room has white walls and a continuous dado line, the line that delineates the horizontal zones of the wall.

There are subtle historical references in Voysey's work. Some Gothic details are apparent in the detailing, such as the strap hinges that many Arts and Crafts designers used. Yet Voysey considered himself on the periphery of Arts and Crafts. He did not vociferously oppose the machine as did most Arts and Crafts designers.

Figure 16.9
Charles F.A. Voysey, the Orchard, Chorley Wood, England, 1899. Façade.

Figure 16.10
Charles F.A. Voysey, the Orchard, Chorley Wood, England, 1899.

The clarity of his plans, the relative lack of decoration, the simplicity of his elevations, and the liberal use of white paint are collectively the features that made him one of the most forward-looking of those associated with Arts and Crafts. Hitchmough writes: "Voysey's architectural language was deliberately restrained. Where his designs were innovative they were also founded on reason rather than on a contrived attempt to be different" (1995, p. 171). A source of his simplicity was his fondness for indigenous materials such as acorns and oak leaves. His considerable success with elaborate wallpapers was not anticipated by the sparse exteriors of his buildings. Arts and Crafts designers created textile patterns that incorporated humble elements of nature, from corncobs to acorns (Figure 16.11).

Figure 16.11
Textile or
wallpaper design
with acorns,
late nineteenth
century.

Lutyens

Edwin Lutyens (1894–1944) had a career that lasted so long that he outlived Arts and Crafts. He started out doing country houses, skillfully set within gardens. He was a traditionalist, more interested in vernacular country forms than were his contemporaries. For the gardens of his projects, he designed furniture that is still manufactured.

The end of his career took him in a different direction. Always a critic of modernism, when he received the commission for the English Viceroy's House in New Delhi, India, he combined European baroque planning with Mughal decoration. Because of his output in the 1930s and 1940s, he is also covered in Chapter 22.

C.R. Ashbee (1863–1942) was a mainstream Arts and Crafts designer, architect, and theorist. He was a well-known figure in the Arts and Crafts circle in London. He made many types of furniture, known for their simplicity, literal and figural weight, and reliance on the simple panel-and-frame system. He also designed houses, many of which reveal his admiration for Voysey's projects. After Morris died, Ashbee started his own printing press in 1896.

M.H. Baillie Scott (1865–1945) was a British architect, and a designer of interiors and furniture. A major figure in British Arts and Crafts, he belonged to the second generation of designers, and the role he saw for himself is suggested by the house he designed for his family. He named it Red House, after Philip Webb's house for William Morris. Baillie Scott wrote articles espousing his design philosophy. As a consequence of these articles, he was well known in Germany. As with

the work of Mackmurdo, some see his projects as aligned with art nouveau.

Arthur Heygate Mackmurdo (1851–1942) had one foot in Arts and Crafts, one foot in art nouveau. Mostly a furniture designer, he was a strong proponent of the effectiveness of a total environment—meaning that one designer did the architectural envelope and all the objects within it. His Arts and Crafts work was more delicate than Ashbee's, and his output reveals an increasing interest in natural forms. He explored natural motifs in his silhouettes, carving, tracery, and textiles. He is mentioned in Chapter 19.

Mackintosh

Charles Rennie Mackintosh is mostly discussed in another chapter, but it is worth mentioning him here, as he is often found in works on Arts and Crafts. Some of his pieces have a distinct reference to Arts and Crafts projects. He was sympathetic to the reformists, and they admired his work.

Hill House, begun in 1902, is an example of his collaboration with his wife, the artist Margaret MacDonald. The exterior form was innovatively austere, while the interior was a carefully orchestrated assemblage of interior architecture, furnishings, and textile designs (Figure 16.12).

Figure 16.12
Charles Rennie Mackintosh and Margaret Macdonald Mackintosh, Hill House chairs, Helensburgh, Scotland, 1902–1904.

Germany

In Germany, Arts and Crafts was initially related to nationalism and German unification in 1871. While nothing of the pervasiveness of English Arts and Crafts emerged, the work of English architects in designing logical and comfortable houses was greatly admired, foremost by Hermann Muthesius (1861–1927). His book *Das Englische Haus* (1904–1905) is a testament to the virtues of the English house. The book discusses favorably many of the Arts and Crafts designers mentioned in this chapter. The desire to present alternatives to Victorian design was strongly felt in Germany.

One of the most significant figures was Bruno Paul (1874–1968), a German architect and furniture designer. He studied at the Kunstgewerbeschule in Dresden. His early career was involved with promoting finely crafted pieces of furniture and decorative arts. His name is associated with Jugendstil, although as he avoided the exaggerated art nouveau effects, he is also associated with Arts and Crafts. German Arts and Crafts was more integrated with other movements, as its adherents less stridently separated themselves from industrial manufacturing processes. Paul's work later developed into a neo-Biedermeier phase, and eventually he was considered a modernist. Austrian Arts and Crafts, similarly, blurred the lines with those involved with other movements, and the nascent Arts and Crafts movement was quietly superseded by Jugendstil (Chapter 19) adherents and the Secessionists (Chapter 20). Other German design activities took on the onus of design reform, an effort that ultimately paved the way for modernism.

Elsewhere around the world, there were varying degrees of dissatisfaction with Victorian design, and everyone had to cope with the bevy of new inventions and industrialization, urbanization, and population growth. It was mostly in the British Isles and former English colonies, such as the United States, Australia, Canada, and New Zealand, that these impulses consolidated into forms that can rightly be referred to as Arts and Crafts.

United States

The Arts and Crafts movement in the United States had a more direct relationship to the people of rural areas. In England, William Morris and Philip Webb looked to the medieval period for the kind of craftsmanship he wanted to emulate. In the English colonies, such as Australia, New Zealand, and the United States, the time when hardy people fought for survival was recent, scarcely one hundred years in the past. In many cases, American craft traditions were ongoing.

Greene and Greene

The Californians Charles Sumner Greene (1868–1957) and Henry Mather Greene (1870–1954) started a firm they called Greene and Greene. It was the preeminent firm of the American Arts and Crafts movement, and their most prominent project the Gamble House, 1908–1909. The Gamble House was made of wood, low to the ground, bungalow-inspired, with long overhangs. As was often the case with Greene and Greene houses, it was modified as it was being built. One notable feature was the lack of metal fasteners and the ingenious reliance on wood-to-wood connections (Figure 16.13).

American Arts and Crafts related to a literary movement that similarly extolled the virtues of simple living, self-reliance, and the importance of the individual. The works of Henry David Thoreau, Ralph Waldo Emerson, and Walt Whitman also see the heart of American individualism as residing in the countryside. Another connection to Arts and Crafts was the work of reformists such as Jane Addams, whose Hull House was a home for the poor. To the extent that she also sought to counter the negative effects of the Industrial Revolution, her work was related to what the Arts and Crafts designers did in the design realm. Another distinction between the British and American strains of Arts and Crafts is that American design, in general, was less influenced by art nouveau for the simple reason that art nouveau, with the notable exception of the works of Tiffany, was less important stateside.

Figure 16.13
Example of wood-to-wood joint with no fasteners.

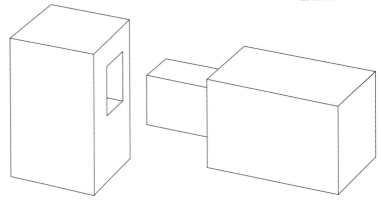

New Zealand

Ann Calhoun writes that the Arts and Crafts movement in New Zealand "was always linked to its British parent but also had a legitimate personality of its own" (2000, p. 9). In addition to expressing a cultural and political allegiance to Great Britain, three features individuate New Zealand Arts and Crafts. Women had a significant role in the British Arts and Crafts movement, and they played an even more prominent role in New Zealand, where the majority of students attending design schools were women. The New Zealand designs made reference to local flora and fauna, and significantly, some pieces incorporated Maori design motifs.

Many design schools were established in New Zealand in the 1870s, 1880s, and 1890s. An aspect of Arts and Crafts that broadened its appeal was its recognition and encouragement of amateur artists. William Morris's daughter May Morris designed embroidery, wallpaper, and jewelry and led the embroidery workshop. Her prominence in the field in England was one of the factors that encouraged women to attend design schools in New Zealand.

A dining room in New Zealand shows how fully the Arts and Crafts aesthetic traveled (Figure 16.14). It has a medieval looking table and ladderback chairs. Elsewhere in the room one sees metal work, and Arts and Crafts draperies and floor coverings. Other works incorporate Maori design motifs, an activity not at the center of English Arts and Crafts, although certainly sympathetic to its respect for premodern cultures.

Conclusion

Despite occasional points of convergence, the Gothic Revival movement and Arts and Crafts were distinct entities. Arts and Crafts was not a historic revival and, in fact, its supporters opposed historicism. A useful way of conceptualizing Arts and Crafts is to consider that tradition and modernity were two sides of the same coin.

The unity of the arts was not just theorized, it was realized, with graphics and book publishing

Figure 16.14
Arts and Crafts dining room with ladderback chairs, New Zealand, late nineteenth century.

playing major roles. In Arts and Crafts graphics, the graphic simplicity responded to a moral and religious appreciation of restraint. This concern for the common good, often with a religious basis, resulted in many progressive elements of Arts and Crafts, such as a concern with countering the effects of industrialization. The Arts and Crafts movements around the world skillfully blended politics, poetry, socialism, and the design of finely crafted objects.

The comparison is anachronistic, but Arts and Crafts played a role in the nineteenth century similar to that played by sustainability in the twenty-first. Both movements were prompted by a concern about the environment and the ill-planned effects of technology and industry. Seeking a solution, designers looked to nature.

By 1910, Arts and Crafts in Europe had started going out of fashion, with its last remnants expiring in the 1930s.

Sources

Calhoun, Ann (2000). *The Arts and Crafts Movement in New Zealand, 1870–1940: Women Make Their Mark*. Auckland: Auckland University Press.

Donovan, Andrea (2008). *William Morris and the Society for the Protection of Ancient Buildings*. New York: Routledge.

Durant, Stuart (1992). *CFA Voysey*. New York: St. Martin's Press.

Eisenman, Stephen (2008). *Design in the Age of Darwin: From William Morris to Frank Lloyd Wright*. Evanston, IL: Mary and Leigh Block Museum.

Gebhard, David (1975). *Charles F. A. Voysey Architect*. Los Angeles: Hennessey and Ingalls.

Haigh, Diane (1995). *Baillie Scott: the Artistic House*. London: Academy Editions.

Hitchmough, Wendy (1995). *CFA Voysey*. London: Phaidon.

Kirk, Sheila (2005). *Philip Webb: Pioneer of Arts and Crafts Architecture*. Hoboken, NJ: Wiley.

Mason, Anna (2021). *William Morris*. London: Thames and Hudson.

Orr, Lynn Federle (2011). *The Cult of Beauty: The Victorian Avant Garde*. London: Victoria and Albert Museum.

Soros, Susan, ed. (1999). *E. W. Godwin: Aesthetic Movement Architect and Designer*. New Haven, CT: Yale University Press.

Todd, Pamela (2004). *The Arts and Crafts Companion*. New York: Bulfinch.

Van der Post, Lucia (2003). *William Morris and Morris and Co*. New York: Abrams.

Voysey, Charles F.A. (1894). "Domestic Furniture." *Journal of the Royal Institute of British Architects* 1: 415–16.

Wilhide, Elizabeth (1991). *William Morris: Décor and Design*. New York: Abrams.

Discussion and Review Questions

1. How did the reformists feel about history?

2. What was the relationship between Arts and Crafts and Gothic Revival?

3. What were some of the distinguishing characteristics of Arts and Crafts in Britain, New Zealand, and the United States?

4. What were some aligned interests in other professional areas?

5. Who were some of the figures whose works crossed over into art nouveau?

6. What was modern about Arts and Crafts?

7. What was elitist about Arts and Crafts? What was populist about Arts and Crafts?

8. What was the role of women in Arts and Crafts?

9. How would you relate Arts and Crafts in terms of today's environmental problems and the involvement of the design community?

Africa

17

This chapter focuses on African traditional furniture pieces as a microcosm of understanding "African design," alongside some examples of architecture, famous and vernacular. This is not this book's first African chapter. There have been several. Neolithic Africa is well represented in the historical record. Egypt is in Africa. And Nubia is also covered in Chapter 2. Many of the other chapters have African connections. The second-largest continent, almost all styles and time periods are represented in Africa. There is African French provincial, art nouveau, art deco, modernism, and postmodernism.

There is no clean dividing line between African traditional and other artistic genres. "Traditional" forms also responded to the vagaries of capitalist production and supply and demand. They were created in the countryside and in urban centers alike. Even if stylistically conservative—not always the case—their creators responded to and embraced technological innovations. These are not timeless pieces removed from chronology, but the category "traditional" does adequately refer to works that cannot easily and reasonably be identified by other stylistic terms, such as "art deco" or "modern."

The artists involved with creating modest pieces were curiously freed from many constrictions. Because their work received less scrutiny, they largely operated outside of aristocratic and religious control. While they did not enjoy the use of

Figure 17.0
(*Facing page*)
Great Mosque of Djenné, Mali, thirteenth century–1907.

expensive materials and produced their products quickly, those involved with crafting simple objects experienced the emancipation of artists who participate in the marketplace. More important for the artisans was functioning within a capitalist framework, and an economy that was embroiled in colonialism for much of its early history.

The nineteenth century plays a big role in this chapter. The nineteenth century saw tremendous changes of a mind-boggling degree in many parts of the world, all the more so for Africa. It was also the period in which the horror of the slave trade was to thankfully wind down, although the specter of colonialism was on the horizon. As historians of culture, we are in the awkward position of decrying the injustice of colonialism yet marveling at the brilliance and creativity of many caught up in it—the presence of English, Dutch, French, German, and Portuguese colonials prompted the creation of many wonderful objects.

A note on chronology. Most African furniture pieces, with some exceptions, can only be dated back to the mid-nineteenth century. Why? For one, Africans and Europeans started collecting African furniture pieces in earnest in the twentieth century. Because many of these pieces were modest, they were not, until recently, deemed worthy of being collected, cataloged, and preserved. Also, many pieces were removed from their initial cultural contexts, and little documentation exists to confirm the dates of their creation and purchase. In the absence of corroborating data, most pieces that are obviously old can only be dated with certainty back to the mid-nineteenth century. Descriptions of objects in European travel accounts suggest that the forms of many utilitarian objects go back centuries. For most of the pieces in this chapter, the type of precise dating found in other chapters is not possible. What is known is that the rate of stylistic change in the twentieth century sped up as new technologies and new materials were available.

Jared Diamond points out that Africa is the most diverse continent on earth ethnically and linguistically (in contrast to China, for which the Chinese language acts as a source of common identity). One-quarter of the world's languages are spoken in Africa, the continent that stretches almost from Antarctica to Mediterranean temperate zones and includes deserts, jungles, and snow-covered mountains (Diamond 1997, p. 377). Africa has fifty-four countries, each one having from two to a hundred or more ethnic groups, often with dissimilar languages. Most of Africa was colonized by the Dutch, English, French, German, Italian, and Portuguese, and several places were colonized by multiple European countries. Senegal, for example, was initially explored by the Portuguese and the Dutch. In the colonial era, they were followed by the English and finally the French; Senegal became independent in the 1960s. Germany lost its African colonies in the First World War. Cameroon, to give one example, was turned over to the British and the French. Overlying the category of domestic and foreign ethnicity is religion, where the main players are Christian, Islamic, and indigenous.

This chapter is not a comprehensive look at African furniture pieces but a representative sampling of some fine pieces, some typical pieces, and some pieces that display the unique qualities of African designed objects, those that render them different from Western and Asian pieces.

The Classic African House

African architecture can be round, ovoid, square, or rectangular; made of stones, brick, mud, wood, or straw; and it can incorporate a myriad of different patterns by which ethnic groups distinguish themselves. The kind of architecture that Africa is most known for is a modest structure made of reeds or rush.

A round house

The classic African round house, to many, is not only the essence of African architecture, it has iconic status; it means Africa (Figure 17.1). There are countless regional variations, but several ethnic groups from across the continent have something formally similar to this standard straw structure. The Wolof and Lebu ethnic groups of Senegal, West Africa, are related and both have a tradition of round houses. It is difficult although not impossible to trace this important building type in its various permutations throughout history. The difficulty arises because it is made of impermanent materials and these structures were never intended to last decades, let alone hundreds of years. But visual evidence for this type of structure, as suggested by the d'Hastrel engraving, gives some idea of what a Lebu/Wolof dwelling looked like in the mid-nineteenth century.

In ancient Africa, Egyptian and Roman artists who created mosaics represented their permanent architecture as different from the autochthonous

Figure 17.1
Adolphe d'Hastrel, *The Village of Dakar, Senegal*, 1851.

varieties. The artists were apparently fascinated by the latter's organic materials and curvilinear geometries. There is a similarity between how workers constructed dwellings in the past and in the present, although it is unlikely that the processes are exactly the same. Yet, some knowledge of ancient practices can be inferred by contemporary building methods that produce similar-looking buildings.

Roy Sieber, an American curator and scholar, wrote:

For Africans, as for us, the house is the center of the world. However, to the African the sense of space at that center is not necessarily interior space, for most African houses are not lived in in the sense we usually use that phrase. An African "home" is not the semi-sealed, closed container for a nuclear family that the West has come to consider it. Rather it often sprawls, housing an extended family and domestic animals: hunting dogs; goats and chickens as scavengers and food; goats, cattle or horses as wealth. There are no pets. Spread over a sizable area, often fenced in and at times with a gateway, the home/compound is at the same time a unit in the larger village.

(1980, p. 15)

d'Hastrel's early view of the village that became the capital of Senegal, Dakar, correspondingly shows a collection of individual dwellings that a palisade of reed connects.

Another d'Hastrel drawing is a rare historical view of the inside of a Wolof straw dwelling (Figure 17.2). The walls and domed roof are made of straw, enlivened with a simple pattern. A single opening acts as the means of egress and lets in light. There are no windows. Some structures of this type have a threshold over which one must step to enter, although this one does not.

This engraving shows the interior of an African dwelling, yet the single piece of furniture is a European **bedstead**, with a reed mat laid over it. Mats such as these also served for sitting outside. This is the home of a chief, who may be demonstrating his social prominence with a European piece of furniture. On the far right, the artist himself sits on a stool, close to the ground, no doubt a modest piece of furniture. A few objects hang on the wall.

A square house

Mid-twentieth-century photographs documented that Wolof houses continued to be built some one hundred years later than the d'Hastrel view, albeit

Figure 17.2
Adolphe d'Hastrel, *Interior of a Chief's House, Dakar, Senegal*, mid-nineteenth century.

with their form changed. The fishing village of N'dar Toute lies across the Senegal River from the city of Saint-Louis, Senegal's second-largest city. The town plan is gridded, which in part explains why its houses are rectilinear. The differences are subtle but significant. The footprint of an individual house in the fishing village is square, not round; the walls, still of straw, are part of a framed construction method, and the door was milled. When making Wolof houses, the straw roof is constructed as a separate element that is later placed on top of the walls. Square houses are also traditionally African, and there is no clean break between historic architectural styles and modern ones. Traditional African dwellings are often written about as if they have undergone no stylistic changes from time immemorial, but Africans were quick to adopt new materials when they became available, such as milled lumber, corrugated metal, concrete, and glass blocks.

Designed Objects Before Industrialization

A nineteenth-century engraving shows a weaver weaving (Figure 17.3). The artist's composition captures a beguiling combination of a mode of sitting, a human figure, a modification to the

Figure 17.3
A weaver
(Tisserand Negre),
Senegal, 1821.

landscape, and two pieces of equipment, a loom and sun shade. Responding to the functional needs of a weaver, this is a complex if forthright designed object. These looms produce long narrow strips of cloth that can then be sewn together to make blankets and other cloths. Many African ethnic groups weave this way; the most famous variety is the **Kente cloth** of Ghana, which, like the round house, has become virtually synonymous with Africa.

A hole has been dug in the ground, over which stands the loom. The male weaver sits with his legs in the hole, operating the poles that raise the warp strings. A separate structure, a woven mat on stilts, shields him from the sun. Mats, made of grass, straw, or reeds, are a common feature in Africa, and they exist continent-wide. Sieber dates their appearance prior to sustained European contact, to at least the ninth century CE (Sieber 1980, p. 5). Mats can be used for sleeping at night and sitting during the day. They act as covers and rugs, as wall hangings and space dividers. Because of their usefulness, many Africans travel with one rolled up. They are a common article that nomads such as the Tuaregs use, after pitching a tent, to furnish the interior. Across Africa, it is common to entertain guests outside by unrolling a mat

on the ground. The deceptively simple designed object of a weaver's apparatus uses a mat as a sunshade, as part of an ensemble that incorporates man-made and found objects.

Industrialization in Africa

Nineteenth-century Africa got a crash course in industrialization, as did much of the world. Many regions experienced a shift toward market agriculture. Imported cast iron found its place on a continent that had been forging iron, in smaller quantities, for centuries. Railroads transformed the African landscape as they did everywhere. People in inland towns and villages, which had been days if not weeks away from urban areas and coastal trading centers, suddenly found that travel to a major city was only a day away and relatively inexpensive. Colonialism had many effects on African populations, one of them being access to European transportation and communication technologies, such as railroads, airplanes, the telegraph, and photography.

The railroad

Towns along railroad lines thrived from the traffic in people, goods, and therefore new forms and ideas. Railway stations in Dakar, Rufisque, and Saint-Louis du Sénégal, are buildings made of a combination of local and imported building products. These were three important trading centers for eighteenth-century North Atlantic seagoing trade, and the railroad continued that tradition.

At the Eastern extent of the continent, the Gare Soarano from 1902 served Madagascar's city Antananarivo. A richly detailed building, it exhibits art nouveau influences, while also showing its industrial influenced structure (Figure 17.4).

Railways, iron manufacturing, steamships, airplanes, electricity, and telegraphs often arrived due to governmental support, yet one art form needed no prompting to ensure its success. Shortly after its invention in France in 1839, Daguerre's photographic process appeared in Africa, and Africans quickly took to it as both producers and consumers.

Photography

Africans initially embraced the pictorial revolution for private portraiture. In the coastal trading city of Saint-Louis du Sénégal, Amadi Coumba responded to the event of having his photographic portrait taken by dressing in his best clothes and jewelry (Figure 17.5). In his case, it meant pairing a **bou-bou**, the flowing African gown, with a French jacket, and a ring and a bracelet. His head was freshly shaved, and his beard combed.

Coumba enters the historic record simply because he had his portrait taken, and the photograph entered the collections of the Institute Fondamental d'Afrique Noire, the research institute affiliated with the University of Dakar. A postmodern interpretation of the photograph is that it mediates Coumba's identity, in which he seeks to reconcile his African heritage (the bou-bou) with the French cultural influences (the jacket) that connected him to international trade. Coumba probably viewed the event of having his portrait taken in a personal way. The interaction with a photographer left him with a two-dimensional likeness that he could, in turn, give to a loved one. No direct evidence documents Coumba's reaction to having his portrait taken. The suppositions offered here are to stress that when photography entered Africa, it became a new player in a society that had complicated familial and social relationships. Even in previous centuries, Africa was connected to the world's economy with trade in consumer items and the circulation of images.

Figure 17.4
Soarano
Railway Station,
Antananarivo,
Madagascar,
1908–1910.

and shows how an American architectural form was locally built (Figure 17.6).

Furniture

African furniture exists in great variety and relates to hundreds of ethnic groups more so than to national divisions, although African furniture can be classified by type or by country. The intent here is not a comprehensive survey of African furniture and designed objects, but a representative sample.

Stools and chairs

African seating is a broad category, with the most ubiquitous piece being the stool. There are numerous types, from simple to grand, but one characteristic, across the board, is that they are low to the ground compared to Western objects designed for sitting.

Ethiopia and Mali

From Ethiopia, in the horn of Africa, comes a type of seating made of two planks. The top one fits into a slot in the bottom one, forming the backrest. The chair is therefore demountable and transportable. A person sits in this chair leaning against the backrest with legs extended. The bottom piece, if well constructed, has the feet integral to the bottom plank, a feat achieved only with a great deal of reduction carving. If the feet are attached, they are likely to shear off.

Laure Meyer (1995), writing about simple African objects, probes the relationship between function and form. She writes that an aesthetic sensibility "shows itself first in the elegance or fitness of the forms, which, in and of themselves, provide simple visual pleasure without recourse to ornamentation. This elegance, however, is never an end in itself, but emphasizes the functionality of the object by subordinating and adapting itself to it. Simple, pure forms are designed with an unerring sense of line" (Meyer 1995, p. 9). Meyer's comment is an ode to the aesthetic of some African pieces, but there are other approaches and methods for understanding these pieces.

The largest group of African seats are stools, and the most prominent type of stools are round.

In many stools, the seats retain their round shape from the tree log from which it is created. A stool becomes a "chair" when it has a back, yet it retains much of the original form.

Figure 17.5
Portrait of Amadi Coumba, Saint-Louis du Sénégal, early twentieth century.

Corrugated metal

Ethnically and historically, Liberia is an unusual country, as it was mostly populated with repatriated African American slaves. Its modern history began in 1821 with the first arrival of African Americans. The United States did not officially have any African colonies, but Liberia comes close. The capital city, Monrovia, was named for the American president James Monroe. In 1847, Liberia declared itself a sovereign state.

Historical photographs show construction workers using the American balloon-framing system, over which they often attach corrugated metal sheeting. The African Americans who moved to Liberia took with them their familiarity with and knowledge of Southern American houses and agricultural buildings. Author Bernard Herman writes: "The most powerful architectural concept behind the mansion houses of Liberia is authority" (Belcher and Herman 1988, p. 129). When given the opportunity to build houses in Africa, they built the type that responded to their notions of utility, comfort, and status. The United States legation building in Monrovia dates to 1900

Figure 17.6
United States
legation,
Monrovia, Liberia,
c. 1900.

One of the types of stools made by the Dogon cliff-dwelling people of Mali employs male-female carved twins to support the seat (Figure 17.7). Although made of a single piece of wood, there are two horizontal planes, representing the Earth and the sky, connected metaphorically by the paired caryatid/telamon figures who represent founding ancestors.

Another Dogon artwork of a female figure shows the blurry line that separates the human figure from sculpture and furniture, further discussed below (Figure 17.8). The seated figure is represented as though sitting on a stool, although her legs and hips form the stool's legs. It dates from between the sixteenth and nineteenth centuries. A neighboring ethnic group to the Dogon, the Senufo, have similar artworks in which a figure and a piece of furniture are literally intertwined.

While numerically small, the Dogon play an outsized role in African arts. In addition to furniture, and sculpture, they craft architectural elements of the highest quality, including carved columns and granary doors (Figure 17.9). The carved figures include the humble but venerated mudfish.

Figure 17.7
Dogon stool, Mali, twentieth century.

Figure 17.8
Seated female figure,
Dogon, Mali, sixteenth
to nineteenth centuries.
Senufo.

Figure 17.9
Dogon granary door, Mali, twentieth century.

Cameroon

The Bamileke of Cameroon produced a variety
of wooden stool types, which are in the middle
in two respects. Graphically they are between
geometric abstraction and natural representation,
for some look like spiders or baskets, while some
are pure geometry (Figure 17.10). The subset
that show idealized spiders are intermediaries
between the living and the ancestral. Arachnids
can burrow into the ground, so they are both in
the company of the departed and are of this world.

Côte d'Ivoire, Nigeria, and Congo

The countries of the center of Africa have
produced multitudes of seating pieces of infinite
variety. What ties many of them together is that
they are made from a single section of a tree
log. The laborious process of reduction carving
ensures an individual piece's stability. These
pieces belong to the category of works that Philip
Ravenhill (1991) wrote about when he proposed a
distinction between utilitarian pieces and those
with a clear aesthetic intent. He wrote about a
work that "combines a response to a need for
functional usefulness with a response to an additional need—the need to surpass mere function

Figure 17.10
Stool, Cameroon, twentieth century. Bamileke.

by inventing form and seeking further refinement" (Ravenhill 1991, p. 4). The Senufo are a subset of an ethnic group known as Voltaic. Senufo come from the Savannah regions in the north of the country of Côte d'Ivoire. A Senufo stool is unornamented, yet its carefully crafted form exceeds the most straightforward means of crafting a modest, low-to-the-ground seat.

Nigeria is the most populous country in Africa, and the Nupe are one of Nigeria's smaller ethnic groups. They are associated with the Nupe River. A Nupe stool also derives its overall form from a log's cross section (Figure 17.11). The leg of a stool is typically one of its functional pieces, but the legs of a Nupe stool exceed what is needed for the purpose of support, they have become the chief decorative item of the stool. The carved top, in low-relief carving, displays a common Islamic motif. The decoration is geometric and not representational. Stools similar to this one are not limited to Nigeria, but are made in several central African countries. The process of chip carving gives Nupe furniture feet a distinctive faceted surface. The Nupe also created beds, painstakingly crafting a platform from a large piece of wood, the contiguous feet similarly taper inward toward the ground.

Across Africa, countless varieties of carved stools are created from a single piece of wood. The round base and seat are consistent, yet the forms and patterns that enliven the space between the seat and the ground is left to the creativity of the artist. These cylindrical stools range from spool-shaped ones that are relatively simple, to elaborate ones in which caryatids support the seat. Carefully ornamented stools are a part of the regalia of nobles and chiefs. Elaborate stools are associated with leadership. A further sign of a person's status occurs when someone travels with a stool bearer, a person designated to carry the stool and set it up. This practice is also recognition that not all houses will have a sufficient number of seats for guests.

Furniture and seated figures in sculpture

A popular type of Senufo-Baule sculpture comes from Ivory Coast and take as their subject a mother and child seated on a round stool. Numerous examples exist in museums across the globe, and they are a delight to behold. A female figure has a crested hairstyle and bare breasts. These mother/child sculptures are common in Senufo art, and found in the Ivory Coast, Mali, and Burkina Faso. They have much in common with the Dogon figure previously examined. The meanings vary, but in a general way, this sculptural grouping relates maternity to fertility and abundance. Such stools typically have but two rear legs. What is interesting is that the mother's legs take the place of the stool's front legs. Many African artworks, including furniture, are anthropomorphic, with human figures or body parts taking the functional role of furniture pieces. Nowhere is this so obvious as when human legs literally stand in for furniture legs. Human figure and piece of furniture work together in this tandem piece. Yet the substitution of the human legs for the stool legs makes this sculpture visually precarious. The mother is solidly placed yet appears as if about to rise.

Backrests and thrones

The Kuba are another one of some three hundred ethnic groups in Congo, and the descendants of the former African kingdom of Kuba. An enigmatic Kuba backrest is covered in its entirety with upholstery tacks. It is meant for reclining, close to the ground, with the sitter in repose with legs extended. The decorative surface treatment also makes the backrest tactile. A backrest is a furniture type virtually unknown in the West. In Africa, it is typically made from a piece of wood, braced to sit at a 45-degree angle with the ground. The Ngombe, also from Congo, make chairs with legs that utilize the same gentle curve of the backrest and are similarly covered with tacks, sometimes in contrasting colors.

The most famous of Kuba artworks are not pieces of furniture but textiles with geometric patterns. The lack of representation and the resolutely abstract patterning give the historic textiles a contemporary air (Figure 17.12). Kuba textiles

Figure 17.11
Nupe stool, Nigeria.

Figure 17.12
Kuba cloth,
Democratic
Republic of
Congo, late
nineteenth
century or
twentieth century.
Woven raffia.

do not belong in the modern category of abstract expressionism, but they have many attributes in common.

Any chair, even when void of an occupant, is related to the human figure, more so than tables and chests, which have a purpose removed from humanity, to support or store things. The formula chair = person is of special importance in the case of Ghanaian thrones. Among the Ashanti, a stool can be related to the soul of an individual, an important leader, or even to all the Ashanti people.

Ghanaian thrones

An example of the richness of forms found within one ethnic group, the Ashanti are responsible for multiple art forms. They are one of the largest of Ghana's fifty ethnic groups, and they are a subdivision of the larger Akan group. The modern country of Ghana is the southernmost remnant of one of Africa's historical polities, the Empire of Ghana, which was dominant in the region from the eighth to thirteenth century.

The simplest type of Ashanti wood stool is transportable. One end gently tapers into a handle so that it can be slung over one's shoulder. In some situations, a man who goes visiting friends, to work, or to a village meeting, takes his chair with him.

There are two principal methods for understanding African household objects. One involves appreciating them for their aesthetic qualities. The other seeks to understand them in their own terms, by delving into the ethnological details of their cultural context. Books about African

furniture are few, but in 1971, a Ghanaian Catholic bishop, Peter Sarpong, devoted an entire book to one type of seating, *The Sacred Stool of the Akan*. In most societies, death does not end a person's participation in the world of the living. Yet unique to the Akan of Ghana is that ancestor worship centers around a piece of furniture, a stool.

Most Ghanaian houses have a stool and more stools than chairs. A Ghanaian stool is formed by two horizontal planes, a base and a top, with a decorated support between them (Figure 17.13). The base is stepped in two or three layers. The top, or seat, exceeds the base in length and is curved. This crescent shape symbolizes a mother's embrace. The depth of the stool is one-quarter its width. The curved seat makes it comfortable to carry the stool on the back; it is never meant to be carried on the head. The name of the piece is alternately translated as "stool" or "throne," and as with most translations, neither is perfect. The word "stool" relates to its form: it is low to the ground and there is no back or armrest. "Throne" is more appropriate to its function, as the literal and symbolic seat of a chief in a public setting that is an artistic achievement of a craftsman. A great deal of time is spent crafting a Ghanaian stool, which is a work of art, a religious object, and a functioning piece of furniture.

Innumerable forms and decorations bridge the space between the top and the base (Sarpong 1971, p. 7). Upon reaching agreement with a client, the craftsman shows his expertise by how he designs and carves the middle portion.

Figure 17.13
Ashanti stool,
nineteenth
century.

The symbolism of this decorative field is vast and prone to differing opinions and multiple interpretations.

The stool's undercarriage functionally needs to support the seat, which it sometimes does with a single trunk, sometimes with three. A common configuration of the middle part is a sphere with a hole in it, sometimes placed in front of a stout support. There are anthropomorphic seats and zoomorphic seats. Of the latter, elephants, leopards, and porcupines are considered most appropriate for this dignified and prized piece.

Men craft these stools, and they should be exemplary citizens, having peaceful relations with wife and parents. The relationship between client and craftsman was important, as it repeated the relationship between the founder of the Ashanti kingdom and his priest. In no other group's foundation myth does a piece of furniture play such an important role. The foundation myth of the Ashanti kingdom is also the foundation myth of the Golden Stool, the first and most important of all Ghanaian stools.

The chief in the foundation myth is Osei-Tutu. He assumes leadership in Kumasi, and his military successes involve his consolidating power, vanquishing enemies, and exerting authority over a region that bears a geographic and cultural relationship with contemporary Ghana. Through the intervention of his priest, Anokye, at a summit of leaders, a stool falls from the sky accompanied by darkness and thunder. This wooden stool is covered with gold. It lands on Osei-Tutu's knee. This stool is the center of the national consciousness and the institution of the Golden Stool. A common stool in its form, with its gilding and exceptional provenance, it became the symbol of the unified nation.

The tradition of these stools became widespread over time, with many variations. Every Akan can have a stool. There are white stools, silver stools, golden stools, and blackened stools.

White stools are left unfinished save for being washed and whitewashed. Silver stools are plated. Golden stools are covered with gold leaf. There are men's stools, women's stools, and children's stools. A groom frequently gives his bride a stool, as does a host his or her guest. There are stools for poor men, priests, attendants, and stool carriers.

Outside of functional use, the most important use a stool has is the role it plays after death, after going through the process of being blackened. The stool selected for blackening is typically a stool that was frequently and repeatedly used by the deceased, such as the stool in the bathroom used for bathing or the stool sat upon while eating.

The blackening of the stool is a ritual of conservation and symbolic consecration. There are several explanations for the choice of the black finish. As the color white is related to happier times, black as the symbolic color of death is appropriate. Black is also frightening, and therefore commands respect. A functional explanation is that as part of the veneration, libations are poured on the stool, including eggs and blood. They would stain a white stool, but they add to the patina of a soot-blackened stool.

The centrality of this stool to the Ashanti reveals itself in many ways. The stool, related to the foundation myth, is a symbol of the nation. It is the symbol of a chief. Chiefs, appropriately enough, can be *enstooled* or *destooled*. But the stool will ultimately serve as the resting place for its owner's soul. While published information on African furniture is scarce, the exception is the Ghanaian throne.

Sarpong admits that Ghanaians are not so strict about a stool's uses today. The scenario outlined here about the use of the throne was true in historic periods and remains true. Yet the rules and practices of use are, no doubt, more flexible and less stringently applied today. The Ghanaian stool is second only to the Kente cloth as an artwork associated with Ghana. A great number of the stools produced today are made explicitly for the tourist market.

Yet for a book that looks at designed objects, the majority of which are pieces of furniture, it is appropriate to expend much textual space on a common furniture type that becomes a symbol of the nation and the final resting place of the soul.

On a traditional Ghanaian throne, the occupant sits perpendicular to its mass. The grandeur comes from the extent of the carving and its overall form. There is little concern for support or comfort in the way of cushions or upholstery, although a mat, a hide, or a textile is frequently placed on top of the throne. This throne is meant for sitting upright, in a public arena, and not for lounging in private. While the base and seat resemble planks, these thrones are traditionally carved from a single piece of wood. These stools are related to political and spiritual functions.

Ghanaian thrones can be appreciated for their artistry, but Michèle Coquet (1998) provided an interpretation that is possible only with an in-depth knowledge of their political and spiritual purposes. She wrote:

The personal seat is conceived as the site where one of the spiritual principles of its user dwells. This principle is called *sunsum* by the Ashanti. Each time he sits on it, the owner transmits a little of this principle to the object. In this respect, the Akan chief's stool is doubly vested with **sunsum:** that of the owner and that of the founder of the lineage the chief represents.

(Coquet 1998, p. 132)

When a throne was not being used by the chief, it was typically laid on its side. The throne operates as a stand-in for royalty, in an individual way but also in a collective way.

A chief's stool was the repository of his soul. After his death, his stool was preserved in a shrine. An enshrined stool commemorated the deceased, provided refuge for his soul, and functioned as ancestor figures did in other cultures.

Ghana and Morocco

Another type of Ashanti chair from Ghana has a European precedent. Its occupant sits high off the ground, with a backrest and curved arms. Thumbtacks cover its surface, a sign of wealth that also affects the visual and tactile experience of the chair. Sieber surmises that the Portuguese first introduced the European armchair to the Gold Coast (Ghana) in 1481 (Sieber 1980, p. 159). This is a typical example of the chronological information that is available, and not available, about historic African furniture (Coquet 1998, p. 98). While it is likely that some European furniture accompanied the early explorers in the fifteenth and sixteenth centuries, this information comes from textual references.

A tall armchair in Africa is sometimes referred to as an **elbow chair** in recognition that, unlike a stool, the chair provides a place for users to rest their arms. The elbow chair easily found a place in a culture in which seats related to status. The form of one Ghanaian chair indicates that it was initially based on a folding European chair. In Ghana, these chairs were known as *akonkromfi* or praying mantis chairs because of the crossed configuration of the legs. It is not an exact copy of a European chair, but a reinterpretation made by an African craftsman.

The elaborate carving and crossing of a stretcher is also a feature of a nineteenth-century chair from Morocco (Figure 17.14). Historically, North African indigenous groups had traditions of sitting on the ground. The presence of such chairs, from Morocco to Ghana to Angola, indicates a circuit of influences between European, African indigenous, and Islamic art forms.

Beds, baskets, gourds, and buckets

There are several categories of items that in Africa take on functions that in other places are accomplished by furniture. Baskets are used for storing clothes, and historically gourds, or calabashes, also served as storage items; these were largely replaced in the twentieth century with plastic buckets. Particularly in the Islamic parts of Africa, many Africans sit and sleep on foam cushions placed directly on the ground.

Figure 17.14
High back armchair, Morocco, late nineteenth century. Hardwood, bone, and ivory.

Beds

Traditional African beds existed in great variety; they are all essentially raised platforms whose chief purpose is to raise the sleeping figure off the ground. In warm climates, the air circulation underneath the bed is desirable; in cool climates, a bed separates the body from the damp. Bedposts or testers, and prominent head- and footboards, were typically not features of indigenous African beds. Most African furniture pieces were freestanding and movable, with an exception for built-in sleeping platforms in cultures that construct with bricks. Mats, mattresses, and blankets rendered these earthen platforms more comfortable. There were also a variety of wooden beds. Some are carved from a single piece of wood, including the legs, while others employ a wooden frame. A companion object to the bed is the headrest, found in several African ethnic groups. Headrests were also used in ancient Egypt for the same purpose: to maintain elaborate hairstyles.

Suakin is a port city on an island off the coast of Sudan. It was a thriving center of trade in the time of ancient Egypt. Today its importance is much diminished. A bed of wood and reed shows how modest utilitarian pieces have served similar functions for millennia (Figure 17.15). The essential function of a bed is to separate the platform from the earth, to avoid damp and to allow for air circulation.

Sieber also reports that among the Senufo, beds are occasionally used as biers or catafalques, for the display of the remains of a loved one during a formal mourning period (Sieber 1980, p. 105). This is an important symbolic and ritual use that takes on a different meaning from its daily use as a piece of furniture. Historic African beds are rarely made today, and the traditional means of creating mattresses has been replaced with foam.

Baskets

For many African groups, baskets fulfill a role elsewhere taken by pieces of furniture. Baskets are durable, lightweight, and inexpensive. Large baskets are used to store clothes, and smaller baskets are used to contain cooking utensils and foodstuffs. Prior to the introduction of mass-produced items, handmade baskets were extremely useful. Across Africa, different ethnic

Figure 17.15
Woven bed, Suakin, Sudan, twentieth century.

groups have different traditions regarding the gender association of certain arts. Among the Tutsi, women are associated with the art of basket making. Baskets figure among the objects exchanged as a part of marriage rituals. Large and small Tutsi baskets from Rwanda and Burundi are created with a spiral technique. Coiled baskets are made from a spiral of fibers or bundled grasses. Subsequent coils are sewn to the previous ones. This spiral method lends itself to the iconic profile of the tapering tops. It also provides a framework for incorporating geometric patterns. Spiral weaving or coiling exists in other parts of the continent, particularly in central and southern Africa.

Crossed or checkered weaving predominates in West Africa (Figure 17.16). The baskets can be decorated with black zigzag forms, and colors are occasionally used as well. Natural materials are often interspersed with plastic.

European furniture

This chapter is mostly concerned with indigenous African furniture traditions. The topic of European forms in Africa, which are many, is covered in Chapter 13, "In the Colonies." Two examples from Cape County, South Africa, give an idea of the variety of European examples in Africa. One chair employs a framing system seen in both Dutch and English vernacular furniture.

This formal relationship between a South African chair and English and Dutch furniture is logical, as England and the Netherlands are the European countries whose presence has dominated South Africa since the seventeenth century. The seat is made from a frame, and stretchers connect the legs at nearly ground level (Figure 17.17). The system of stretchers securely ties the legs together, making this a sturdy piece of furniture. The seat is caned. Other than the local materials, there is little indigenous influence in this chair.

Other Cape County pieces are particularly elegant and intended for those who led a comfortable life. Lifestyles among the Europeans varied greatly, with the distinctions due to class and wealth, which were directly reflected in furniture. This also reflects the difference between the lifestyles of Afro-Europeans in South African cities and those who lived in the countryside. There were accurate renditions of neoclassical chairs, in which giant scrolls constitute the arms (Figure 17.18). The existence of an extremely elegant neoclassical chair in South Africa indicates that many Europeans were no longer merely surviving but enjoying a comfortable if not luxurious life. This suggests an Afro-European desire to participate in the early nineteenth-century international craze for neoclassical pieces.

Figure 17.16
Baskets, Burkina Faso, twentieth century.

Figure 17.17
Cape Coast box-stretcher chair, South Africa, nineteenth century.

Figure 17.18
Sabre-leg
stinkwood
armchair,
Grahamstown,
Cape County,
South Africa,
nineteenth
century.

Figure 17.19
Saharan mud-
architecture,
thirteenth to
twenty-first
century.

The effects of the European presence in South Africa were extensive, more so than elsewhere on the continent. African indigenous traditions were greatly impacted; for example, the classic round house no longer exists in South Africa, although it exists elsewhere on the continent.

Conclusion

A furnished African home and its contents are important to relate the political role that designed objects can play. As a point of comparison, Louis XIV marshaled all the arts—architecture, interiors, furnishings, painting, and costume—to serve his political goal: to embolden France and present himself as its embodiment. Cultural productions in baroque France were at his command, to represent, constitute, and implement his power.

Most of history suggests that it takes state support and great wealth to produce art (Egypt, Rome, Cambodia). Many of the pieces in this chapter suggest that while that is often true, it is not always true. Designed objects can be tools of repression, but they can also be agents of resistance. Making, purchasing, and collecting objects can also be a means of empowerment.

An out-and-out falsehood about African architecture is that indigenous Africa produced no monuments. Chapter 5's examination of Saharan mud-architecture puts that canard to rest. The Great Mosque of Djenné is an impressive structure with a detail that exists nowhere else: protruding scaffolds called toron that become a permanent part of the building (Figures 17.0 and 17.19). It is a detail that gives the building a prickly tactility that is unique.

Sources

Baraitser, Michael and Anton Obholzer (1978). *Cape County Furniture*. Capetown: C. Struik Publishers.

Belcher, Max and Bernard Herman (1988). *A Land and Life Remembered: Americo-Liberian Folk Architecture*. Athens: University of Georgia Press.

Blier, Suzanne (2004). *Butabu: Adobe Architecture of West Africa*. New York: Princeton Architectural Press.

Bradley, Melissa Biggs and Guido Taroni (2021). *Safari Style*. New York: Vendome Press.

Clarke, Duncan, et al. (2022). *African Textiles*. New York: Abbeville Press.

Coquet, Michèle (1998). *African Royal Court Art*. Chicago: University of Chicago Press.

Diamond, Jared (1997). *Guns, Germs, and Steel*. New York: Norton.

Floré, Fredie and Cammie McAtee (2017). *The Politics of Furniture*. New York: Routledge.

Garlake, Peter (2002). *Early Art and Architecture of Africa*. Oxford: Oxford University Press.

Ginzberg, Marc (2000). *African Forms*. New York: Abbeville.

Mazrui, Ali (1986). *The Africans: A Triple Heritage*. Boston: Little, Brown.

Meyer, Laure (1995). *Art and Craft in Africa: Everyday Life Ritual Court Art*. Paris: Terrail.

Nelson, Steven (2007). *From Cameroon to Paris: Mousgoum Architecture in and out of Africa*. Chicago: University of Chicago Press.

Phillips, Tom (1996). *Africa: The Art of a Continent*. New York: Guggenheim Museum.

Ravenhill, Philip (1991). *The Art of the Personal Object*. Seattle: Washington University Press.

Sarpong, Peter (1971). *Sacred Stools of the Akan*. Accra: Ghana Publishing.

Sieber, Roy (1980). *African Furniture and Household Objects*. Bloomington: Indiana University Press.

van Wyk, Gary N. (1998). *African Painted Houses: Basotho Dwellings of Southern Africa*. New York: Abrams.

Discussion and Study Questions

1. How are African furniture pieces different from Western and Asian pieces?

2. Has looking at African pieces prompted you to consider pieces from your own ethnic group in a different manner? Think of examples where the formula seat = person applies.

3. What do you know about Africa?

4. When you hear about Africa in the news, how do you characterize it?

5. What are your ways of defining if something is authentic?

6. As a general group, in what ways do pieces of African furniture differ from Western or Asian pieces? Are there any general characteristics that many pieces share?

7. What designs from other chapters can also be considered African?

8. How did the artists and designers involved in African artistic production respond to technological change?

Japan and Japonisme

18

1603–1867   1853   1868–1912

Edo period   Matthew Perry's negotiations with Japan   Meiji period

Approaching the topic of Japan and its art, Mimi Hall
Yiengpruksawan cautions against conjuring a romantic notion
of a Japanese spirit and to see it expressed in artworks and
objects (Yiengpruksawan 2001, pp. 105–22). Such interpretations, she fears, too often include generalizations and vague
ruminations about Zen Buddhism. In a similar vein, John
Dower warns against considering Japan as having a "unique,
unchanging cultural essence" (1986, pp. 2–3). His admoni-
tion could pertain to any non-Western culture viewed by the
West, yet particularly with Japan, there is a widespread and
persistent temptation to attribute to its designed forms some
intangible quality that renders it fundamentally different from
Western art.

Yiengpruksawan and Dower make an important point:
there is not a unitary essence to Japanese design. Looking at
the totality of Japanese arts across centuries, the variables
are many. Although this chapter on Japan starts with the
Imperial Villa at Katsura—a great example of Japanese
historic architecture—that iconic structure does not define
the nature of Japanese architecture and design, as it is often
purported to do.

Japonisme usually refers to the cult of Japan and Japanese
art in the second half of the nineteenth century. This chapter
considers the wider context of Japanese items that traversed
the globe in many centuries, and their role as inspiration and
model for Western art forms and objects.

Figure 18.0
(*Facing page*)
Inn at Kannawa
Onsen hot springs,
Beppu, Japan,
late nineteenth
century.

Architecture

The building types of historic Japanese architecture include **Shinto** shrines and Buddhist temples, castles, palaces, other governmental buildings, vernacular domestic architecture, and the homes of nobles. An idea of the variety of Japanese architecture, in terms of size, material, and decorative effect, is presented by three different structures. The Castle of Edo is a huge structure built on massive stone foundations, with stone walls and wide moats. North of Edo is the Toshogu Shrine, known for its sumptuous decoration. And the Great Buddha Hall of Todaiji, in Nara, is one of the central buildings of Japanese Buddhism and the largest timber-frame building in the world.

The Imperial Villa at Katsura

A monumental structure, the Imperial Palace at Kyoto, 804 CE, focuses on a great hall that is part of a grand symmetrical complex. A contrasting design approach is represented by a structure that lies on the edge of Kyoto, in Katsura. The detached villa, begun in 1620, with its informal tea houses, presents another side of historic Japanese architecture, one that is asymmetrical, informal, and introspective. It has a rustic and reflective quality to its design that larger structures lack. Constructed over a period of approximately fifty years, it was largely completed by 1663.

Sited on the Katsura River, the villa is a country pleasure house with tea pavilions, all connected by a meandering path made of stepping-stones. Views are carefully controlled, as is the general construction of the plantings and site work that extends into the interiors (Figure 18.1). The studied manipulation of sight lines, and nature itself, is not immediately apparent. One interpretation of its gardens and their various features is that they relate to passages from the *Tale of Genji*, the classic eleventh-century work of Japanese literature. Melissa McCormick discusses the "culture of Genji" in her 2003 article. She writes: "The Tale of Genji for the first time in history, came to embody a kind of timeless aristocratic social body in the capital" (McCormick 2003, pp. 54–85). In its plan and in its details, Katsura is an unassuming study in serenity. The buildings relied upon construction techniques that have stood the test of time. In many respects, some of its pavilions are elaborations of a vestigial hut. Posts sit directly on stone foundations, and the wood is mostly unpolished and unfinished.

Its design is attributed to Kobori Enshu (1579–1647), a tea master and garden designer, although this is under dispute. The building part of the principal complex is made of three sections, or *shoins*. The original structure is now known as the Old Shoin.

Old Shoin

Modernist architects and designers cherish Katsura, sometimes to the detriment of

Figure 18.1
Katsura Imperial Villa, Kyoto, Japan, 1590. Informal tea house.

understanding its historical context. The Japanese architect Arata Isozaki, writing in 1983, notes:

The many layers of design realized in the Katsura palace have made it an almost constant object of study, especially for the members of the modernist movement in Japan. In their attempts to read the design of the Katsura palace along functionalist lines, they base their analysis on its growth in terms of specific responses to material needs. In so doing, they have developed a unified position which transforms the real Katsura, lifting it out of its actual existence into the realm of myth.

(1983, p. 2)

Bruno Taut, Walter Gropius, Kenzo Tange, and countless others visited Katsura and wrote about it in rapturous terms.

The modernists saw in Katsura support for their own design concepts. The publications by Taut, Gropius, and later Tange, although spanning a time period of thirty years, are at similar pains to make the building look cubist. The books feature high-contrast black-and-white photographs that frequently cut off the pitched roofs, a traditional element at odds with a modernist vision. In the Old Shoin, their preferred part of the complex, they saw the **shoji** paper screens and **tatami** mats as harbingers of one of the most important modernist attributes: transparency (Figures 18.1 and 18.2).

Kenzo Tange is one of the most successful Japanese architects of the post-Second World War period. He opines: "The Katsura Palace reveals a simple, straightforward spirit of freedom, never blatantly insistent, but nonetheless tenacious and compelling. There is a marvelous balance between stillness and movement, between the aristocratic and the common, between perfection of form and sheer invention" (Ishimoto, Gropius, and Tange 1960, p. 32). Although he wrote in the 1960s, the qualities he emphasizes—simplicity, perfection of form, and the spirit of freedom—are the very qualities that the Bauhaus apologists, such as Gropius and van der Rohe, emphasized when discussing the German work of the 1920s and 1930s.

At Katsura, simplicity relates to form and materials. Most of the materials are left plain and undressed, and this includes bamboo, rough-cut stones, and loose gravel.

It can be said that each artistic movement has its own Katsura, that designers of any epoch will find what they are looking for: modernists will

Figure 18.2
Shoji screens, domestic architecture, nineteenth century.

see the geometric simplicity, transparency, and honest use of materials; postmodernists will see the historic references, the complexity, and the delightful incongruity of certain details. Looking at the same architectural complex, Isozaki (twenty years after Tange) sees ambivalence. In describing the structure, he writes that "there is no single governing style or design principle to be found in the Katsura. Both the buildings and the garden contain a mixture of styles and construction techniques. This is the source of the ambiguity of the Katsura" (1983, p. 12). Isozaki is also a product of his time. He is often classified as a postmodernist, a movement known for eclecticism, among other attributes.

New Goten

The New Goten Pavilion, the third shoin of Katsura's main structure, features a tea- and food-preparation area that is on a dais. The dais is raised and proportioned to have three mats, trimmed with edging. Where the dais steps up, the gridded ceiling steps down. Built-in cabinets and shelves are a part of this complex portion of the structure. The type of staggered or displaced shelves at Katsura is known simply as the Katsura shelf; similar shelves are found elsewhere in the complex. Yokobori Yoichi writes that "the term

tansu is primarily applicable to cabinetry created during the post-fire Edo period (1657–1868), which became a time of frenetic rebuilding and innovation" (Yoichi in Moss, 2007). Yoichi is referring to the great fire in Edo (later Tokyo) that nearly leveled the city in 1657; a positive outcome of the conflagration was that it prompted a new wave of building.

Shōkintei Pavilion

The Shōkintei Pavilion is separate from the Shoin complex and lies across the pond, ideally reached by rowing in a small boat. The pavilion comprises several rooms, and each section, in turn, is composed of a variety of modular elements, the floors based on the dimensions of the tatami mat, a straw mat of approximately 3 feet (91 centimeters) by 6 feet (182 centimeters) (Figure 18.3). Tatami matting introduced a system of modularity into Japanese architecture. Standard dimensions and modular units are features of furniture, mats, and building components. This systemization of design into modular units occurred earlier in Japan than elsewhere. Kazuko Koizumi is a pioneer in the field of the study of traditional Japanese furniture. On the subject of walls in historic Japanese architecture, he wrote: "partitions had nothing of the solidity of Western or Chinese walls" (Koizumi 1986, p. 11). At Katsura, many of the walls are formed by sliding screens, shoji panels of wood and paper. Some panels are fixed, others are movable. Sliding screens separate the rooms, and several partitions of the Shōkintei Pavilion are decorated with a white-and-indigo checkerboard.

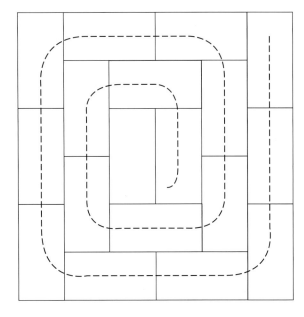

Figure 18.3 Tatami mats, proportional dimensional system, nineteenth century.

Foreigners

The first known European in Japan was Francis Xavier (1506–1552), who arrived in 1549. A Spanish monk, he traveled to Japan after a stop in Goa, India, with the goal of finding converts in both places.

The Japanese in Mexico

Rokuemon Hasekura (1571–1622) was the first Japanese ambassador to New Spain (Mexico). No long-lasting political initiatives are attributed to his tenure, but his presence in North America did start a new trend in furniture design. He initiated a fashion among the elite, Spanish, Mexicans, and foreigners of importing folding Japanese screens. This had the predictable effect that innovative local furniture workshops started producing their own "Japanese" screens. A screen was called a **biombo**; in Japanese, *byo* means protection and *bu* means wind. These culturally hybrid items were made by Mexican furniture makers and incorporated motifs that referenced Japanese design. They were particularly popular with the noble class, including viceroys, the Spanish king's representative.

Art historian Michael Schreffler discusses three different biombos, baroque Mexican folding screens inspired by Japanese imports (Schreffler 2007). One screen displays a view of the vice-regal palace on the Main Plaza of Mexico City. Another Mexican biombo is a panoramic view of the city. Collectively, the images underscore the Spanish presence in New Spain. Furniture traveled from one place to another and acquired new meanings in the process, a part of the global transmission of forms, images, and the ideas associated with them. They impacted what Mexican carpenters made, as folding screens became a part of their vocabulary of products.

The Dutch in Japan

The situation changed after Francis Xavier and Rokuemon Hasekura. The Tokugawa **Shogunate**, also known as the Edo period (1603–1867), is known for its central authority, stability, and sustained economic growth. Culturally, it is known for its fear of foreigners and considerable efforts to restrict their movement in Japan. Simply put, Japan shut itself off from the outside world. The Tokugawa Shogunate expelled the Christian missionaries that they did not execute, and traders' movements were circumscribed. The Shogunate tightly controlled commerce, trading only with the Chinese and the Dutch, whom they further controlled by limiting their access to the southern port of Nagasaki. Trade with Koreans was also carefully controlled.

The Dutch were the only Europeans allowed to trade with Japan, and they were confined to a foreigner's compound. A print from 1800 shows the living conditions of seventeenth-century Dutch captain and officers in Japan. A view of the upper floor of their quarters in Nagasaki is one of a series, from a scroll painted by a Japanese artist and meant for a shogunal official. The subject matter is the Dutch amusing themselves in a variety of ways; this was meant to interest Japanese viewers by highlighting foreigners and their strange ways. The artist employed a compositional strategy, seen in several Japanese media, in which there is a rigid framework, here provided by the house, the bays of its openings, and the tatami mats, visible in the interior. Arrayed across the framework, a variety of human figures mill about in an informal way. Using these and other sources, the officers' quarters have been reconstructed on site (Figure 18.4).

Javanese servants in the prints play subsidiary roles; and the Dutch dine sitting in high chairs. They are contrasted with courtly Japanese men who sit on mats. The prints are representations of otherness from a nineteenth-century Japanese perspective. The island of Dejima, Nagasaki, was a third space, a liminal area between "authentic" Japan and "foreign" Netherlands.

Urban and Urbane Living–Furnishings in Prints

Edo (modern-day Tokyo) was founded in the seventeenth century. Osaka was a center of commerce and Kyoto was the imperial capital. By 1750, Edo had a population of more than 1 million. To escape from the pressures of living in a crowded city, people engaged in pleasurable activities that included walks in the countryside and promenades along the river. Houses of prostitution and kabuki theaters also served as sources of entertainment. Many prints took as their subject matter professional dancers, actors, and geishas.

Figure 18.4
First ship captain's quarters, Dejima, trading post, Nagasaki, Japan, nineteenth century.

The figures wear flowing kimonos and have ovoid faces—they are all curves.

A related genre are the **ukiyo-e** paintings that similarly took as their subject matter secular pleasures. Many were paintings on silk or paper fixed to screens. Oil paintings with these subjects were rare; prints of these subjects were common.

Prints from the mid-century relied on the compositional strategy of the framework provided by architecture, which is set against a casual grouping of human figures involved in various activities. A popular print meant for sale, it is also informative about furnishings and items of material culture. The timber house is delineated with a series of vertical lines that represent columns and balustrades. The human figures include ladies-in-waiting. Props they use include lanterns, fans, and baskets. Some figures kneel on cushions; there is not a lick of formal furniture in sight, showing that it was possible to be engaged in a variety of casual activities, without any furniture.

Furniture

As in all of Asia, the imprint of China was felt in monumental architecture and furnishings. Although Chinese furniture was imported into Japan during the Chinese Sui and Tang periods, prior to the twentieth century, the use of chairs never really took hold. Before chairs, the most important furniture types were platforms, mats, beds, and storage chests with no legs. There were some low chairs.

Traditionally, Japanese lived at the floor level and chairs were not a part of most Japanese households. Additionally, many of the living and social functions that require pieces of furniture in other cultures were taken care of by built-in cabinetry in Japan. And finally, the Japanese household was austere in its overall size and the quantity of objects it contained. Certain pieces, which in the Japanese context are considered furniture, would not be considered furniture in the West, such as trays, pots, and kettles. Often, the line between architecture and furniture is blurred. There were also lanterns, floor mats, and curtains.

To the extent that Japanese furniture existed, it was part of an overall system in which there was a continuity from building to interiors to furnishings. A feature of Japanese carpentry is finely crafted joints.

Among the earliest Japanese pieces were shelving units, either built-in or freestanding (Figure 18.5). The standard layout of a shelving unit was to have a staggered mid-level shelf, either in the food-preparation area as at Katsura, or on a freestanding piece designed for display. The staggered shelf emphasized the piece's asymmetry. Shelving units sat close to the ground. Built-in recessed spaces for objects of aesthetic interest, **tokonoma**, could also feature a staggered shelf (Figure 18.6)

Many Japanese furniture pieces are asymmetrical, in contrast to Chinese design. A desirable feature of asymmetry is that it provides a sense of dynamism, especially when contrasted with the fixity of a symmetrical design. Koizumi writes: "A sensitivity to just such subtleties lies at the heart of the Japanese genius for design" (Koizumi 1986, p. 12). The staggered mid-level shelf became a signifying feature of Japanese furniture, both by Japanese artisans and by those who emulated them. The staggered shelf became a regular feature of European Arts and Crafts and art nouveau furniture.

When homes did have furniture, such as tables, they were low to the ground and often used without chairs. One nineteenth-century print shows a courtesan working at a table. She's painting and has her supplies spread out in front of her on a low table at which she kneels. While most tables were used for practical purposes—eating or painting, for example—a limited number were used exclusively for display. Tall five-legged tables were meant to hold a vase or artwork and are similar to Chinese pieces. Lower tables for writing

Figure 18.5
Four-tiered shelving unit for cosmetics (kurodana), Japan, early seventeenth century. Lacquered wood.

Figure 18.6
Tokonoma, Japan, nineteenth century.

resemble the kang table (Figure 18.7). Because most pieces of furniture were experienced by a person seated at floor level and not far away, the fronts of the pieces were prominent; often there was little attention to the sides and back. Koizumi writes that there was "little stirring after complicated effects" (1986, p. 12).

Boxes and chests

One of the largest categories of early Japanese furniture was space-containing items, such as chests. In the seventeenth century, the repositioning of wealth from a samurai-based economy to a merchant-based economy also added to the growing usefulness and demand for a variety of chests. Oceangoing trade required chests for

general storage and also the storage of personal items such as clothes.

This category is directly related in its details and construction to built-in cabinetry. In fact, the word for chests, *tansu*, also refers to Japanese wooden cabinetry. The range of chest types is extensive, with both functional and regional variations. Chests and boxes were often stacked one on top of the other. Some pieces had metal fittings and hardware.

Chests were made to hold kitchen utensils, spices, sewing equipment, tea services, and money (Koizumi 1986, pp. 75–80). Captains, barbers, and eyeglass salesmen all had personalized commercial chests, often with small drawers. A box for storing writing instruments in effect functioned like a briefcase. A cash box was effectively a cash register. Elaborate **sutra boxes** held Sanscrit inscriptions (Figure 18.8).

Figure 18.8
Sutra box with lotus pond, Japan, early seventeenth century.

Figure 18.7
Writing table with melons and squirrels, Japan, early seventeenth century.

Figure 18.9
Stair storage,
Trading House,
Nara, Japan,
nineteenth
century.

A prime example of the close relationship between carpentry and furniture making is the existence of the Japanese stairway chest (Figure 18.9). With a combination of drawers, sliding doors, and hinged doors, these pieces economically served multiple functions.

Screens

Lacquer screens were a means of defining space and providing temporary privacy without resorting to weighty permanent partitions. Europeans were fond of collecting these items, whose surface treatments they admired, and transporting them back to their home countries (Figure 18.10). At first glance, it appears that a screen's six vertically oriented panels bear no relationship to the scene painted on them (Koizumi 1986, pp. 91–4). Close inspection reveals that each panel was carefully considered.

There are several cases of Europeans who bought lacquered screens and had them reconstituted into pieces of European furniture. Japanese lacquer techniques impressed European buyers. Europeans also bought the highly complex, carefully crafted chests, and sometimes the chests too were incorporated into the design of new ensemble pieces. A Japanese lacquer chest

Figure 18.10
James Forsyth and William Eden Nesfield, screen, England and Japan, late eighteenth and nineteenth centuries. Ebony, paper, and gilding.

Figure 18.11
Cabinet on stand, Japan and the Netherlands, late seventeenth century. On Dutch base.

with a Dutch stand underscores the extent of the Dutch–Japanese cultural interactions (Figure 18.11). It also makes clear the difference between a mat-level mode of living in Japan and the chair-level mode in the Netherlands. Europeans affected furniture production with their tastes. Because they sought exotic oddities, they bought the most elaborate pieces and eschewed simple pieces— which Japanese furniture makers made in great quantity. Furniture makers responded to market forces and increasingly crafted highly decorated pieces specifically to be sold to Europeans.

Chairs

When chairs started to make inroads into Japanese households, they were often modeled on Chinese chairs, such as a Japanese chair that is a fairly faithful reproduction of a Chinese folding chair (Figure 18.12). Koizumi writes that bentwood folding chairs were first introduced into Japan by the Chinese, and later by Western traders operating out of Macao (Koizumi 1986, p. 170). The full integration of the chair into the Japanese way of living did not come until the twentieth century.

Figure 18.12
Bentwood horseshoe-back folding chair, 1868–1912. With leather seat.

The Opening of Old Japan

The ban on foreigners continued up to the mid-nineteenth century. The year the Utagawa woodblock was printed, 1825, was also the year that an edict was issued that stipulated that foreigners who landed in Japan illegally were to be arrested or killed and their ships destroyed. The purpose was not only to keep out foreigners but to keep the Japanese from having knowledge of the outside. Japanese ships were unstable on long oceangoing trips and hence precluded international contact. Despite attempts to limit foreign contact with Japan, and Japanese contact with foreigners, some adventuresome Japanese gained firsthand knowledge of the West, specifically the United States, by traveling with the *Kuroshio* current. *Kuroshio*, in Japanese, literally means "black tide"; it is analogous to the North Atlantic gulf stream and flows north-eastward from Japan to North America. Some Japanese sailors drifted to the East (the United States). Japanese sailors who traveled to foreign countries were barred from reentry to Japan. Yet sailors are typically a rebellious lot, and some discovered ways to sneak back by way of Russian and Chinese ships.

Manjiro

The evocative story of a shipwrecked Japanese sailor has no direct relationship to design, although it is a story of cultural transmission that captivated both sides of the Pacific. Manjiro (1827–1898) was from Shikoku, and when he was fourteen, he was on a 24-foot (7.3-meter) boat that got caught in a strong current and a storm; the boat capsized and he was stranded on Bird Island, Torishima, where he endured six months of depri-vation. An American captain, William Whitfield, rescued him and took him to Hawaii. After they sailed around South America, Manjiro arrived in Massachusetts. In the United States, he was known alternately as John Mung or John Manjiro. On board a whaling vessel, he worked as a cook and navigator. He displayed a facility with learn-ing English and navigation. Author Christopher Benfey writes about Manjiro and other examples of Japanese-American cultural migration in his highly readable book *The Great Wave* (2003).

In 1851, Manjiro returned to Japan, and Benfey reports that he carried with him a camera

and a sewing machine, bought in the United States, to give to his mother. This simple act of gift giving illustrates the technological divide between Japan and the United States. Back in Japan, Manjiro started his career as a naval instructor and interpreter. He acted as a conduit for Japanese eager to hear about the United States, and for Americans curious to observe him firsthand. From 1854 onward, he worked as an interpreter and negotiator. He was part of the team who negotiated with Matthew Perry (Benfey 2003, p. 39).

Commodore Perry

The seminal date of Japan's contact with the West occurred when the American commodore Matthew Perry sailed to Japan in 1853. His voyage and the ensuing treaty marks the end of Japan's isolation, its opening to the world, and the beginning of the modern era. Benfey writes:

The irony was that just as Bostonians were falling in love with Old Japan, Japan was rein-venting herself as a modern state, evolving in the space of 25 years from a feudal backwater to an international power. This is the period known as the Meiji Era (1868–1912), which corresponds almost year for year to America's Gilded Age. The parallel rise of the two young nations, the United States and the "New" Japan, initiated some of the major power struggles—both military and economic—of the twentieth century.

(2003, pp. xii–xiv)

Commodore Perry's arrival in 1853 signaled that Japan had decided to join the world commu-nity and embrace the technological advancements of the nineteenth century. There was no turning back. Japan entered the industrial age.

The year 1868 is when the Emperor Meiji was restored to the throne. The opening that began with Commodore Perry's delegation was complete, and from that time forward, there was a ratcheting up of the efforts to modernize Japan. The restoration of imperial rule signified the emer-gence of a modern state. Yiengpruksawan writes:

Since the political and cultural base of Japan in the middle of the nineteenth century derived from a worldview—a cognitive order—that was not European at a time when Europe and the United States in effect controlled the world, it is not surprising that the policy among modernizers initially was to borrow from Europe what Japan was seen to lack.

(Yiengpruksawan 2001, p. 11)

One way to achieve this was modernization through emulation. The buying practices of foreigners influenced Japanese design.

International exhibitions and museums

The nineteenth century is known as the great age of international exhibitions and museums, inter-twined endeavors related to the official promotion of the decorative arts. The seminal moment was the 1851 Great Exhibition in the Crystal Palace, London. The central structure of the exhibition was Joseph Paxton's glass-and-steel building. The temporary building resulted in the perma-nent South Kensington Museum. Among all the exhibits, national displays of the decorative arts were particularly popular. The South Kensington Museum was renamed the Victoria and Albert Museum in 1899, and many of the images in this book come from its collections.

Countries around the world saw that partic-ipating in international exhibitions was a way to promote their products and arts, and to instill a sense of national pride for both visiting and home audiences. The exhibitions often resulted in museums; the development of exhibitions and permanent museums often went hand in hand.

Japan began to export wares in 1859, and part of the reason for Japan's interest in interna-tional exhibitions was to maintain a competitive advantage against her trading partners—and sometime enemies—China and Russia. Japanese products were shown in the following inter-national venues: Exhibition of Industrial Art, Dublin, 1853; International Exhibition, London, 1862; the Vienna World Exhibition of 1873; the Centennial Exhibition, Philadelphia, 1876; the World's Columbian Exposition, Chicago, 1893; the Paris World Exposition of 1900; and the Louisiana Purchase Exhibition, St. Louis, 1904.

The Japanese government also sponsored exhibitions in Japan with the home audience in mind: the First Industrial Exhibition, Tokyo, 1877; the Second National Industrial Exhibition, Tokyo, 1881; the Third National Industrial Exhibition, Tokyo, 1890; the Fourth National Industrial Exhibition, Kyoto, 1895; and the Fifth National Industrial Exhibition, Osaka, 1903.

The list of prominent museums built in the nineteenth century include the Oxford University Museum, Oxford; the Natural History Museum, London; the Metropolitan Museum of Art, New York, 1874–1880; the Museum of Fine Arts, Boston, 1909; and the Smithsonian, Washington, DC, 1855.

Japanese participation in several prominent exhibitions, or world's fairs, was part of a program to promote Japanese decorative arts, ceram-ics, furniture, smaller lacquer ware, and also prints, especially woodblocks. Not surprisingly, American and European audiences who saw these objects considered them as representative of Japanese art.

Japonisme

French critic Philippe Burty (1830–1890) coined the phrase "Japonisme" in 1872. *Japonisme* refers to European art influenced by Japan. It was part of a general interest in "exotic" cultures, and in that respect, it is related to Chinoiserie. The cult of Japan and Japanese art was most prominent in Britain, although it became a cultural force worldwide.

Tackling Japonisme as the subject of her book, Ayako Ono writes:

Japonisme is considered a phenomenon whose influence spread widely throughout western pictorial art, sculpture, craft, fashion, design, architecture, photographs, theatre and music in the second half of the nineteenth century. It is quite hard to make a clear defi-nition of Japonisme because of the breadth of the phenomenon, but it could be generally agreed upon that is an attempt to understand and adapt the essential qualities of Japanese art.

(2003, p. 1)

Benfey enlarges the list to include more popular subjects, such as judo, geishas, and samurai.

Many American and European designers and artists collected artworks and were influenced by them. Louis Comfort Tiffany collected Japanese ceramics. Aubrey Beardsley (1872–1898) created pen-and-ink drawings that display a thorough knowledge of Japanese woodcuts. Neither C.F.A. Voysey's writings nor those of others about him emphasize Japan's influence on his work, although the visual evidence for this is consider-able. Many of his colleagues associated with the Arts and Crafts or art nouveau movements were known collectors of Japanese art. Edward William Godwin was familiar with Japanese art, and this is evident in his designs of furniture and textiles (Figures 18.13 and 14).

Figure 18.13
Edward William
Godwin, woven
silk brocatelle,
Spitalfields,
England,
1875. Based
on Japanese
crest motif
with magnolia
blossoms.

Figure 18.14
Edward William
Godwin,
Anglo-Japanese
sideboard,
London, England,
1867.

design because of its accomplished construction methods, reliance on simple geometries, and restrained decoration. Japanese artists also incorporated motifs based on local flora into their designs, a design practice in step with the Arts and Crafts belief that art should relate to its local context, be it England, New Zealand, or the United States.

Anglo-Japanese pieces were not accurate representations of actual Japanese furniture pieces. They resemble more closely Chippendale's versions of Chinese pieces. The creation of Anglo-Japanese pieces in India was in response to the British in India who, knowledgeable about changing patterns of taste, were less enamored of Victorian design, and especially Bombay blackwood design. To trace the trajectory of stylistic influences: Indian Anglo-Japanese design is Japanese-inspired design, in India, by way of the British Arts and Crafts movement (Jaffer 2001, p. 359). About the variety of Asian furniture styles, Peter Moss writes: "Furniture has led almost as peripatetic an existence as any other aspect of social dispersion. It has traveled far and wide, influenced whole cultures, cross-pollinated others and evolved unique geographic styles as a result of its exposure to outside influence" (2007, p. 6).

Artists and designers

Among those who can be considered in the Japonisme fold are the Americans Mary Cassatt (1845–1926) and James McNeill Whistler (1834–1903); and the French Edgar Degas (1834–1917), Edouard Manet (1832–1883), Claude Monet (1840–1926), Henri de Toulouse-Lautrec (1864–1901), and Vincent van Gogh (1853–1890). In England, the major figures included Christopher Dresser (1834–1904) and Edward Godwin (1833–1886). Dresser, who actually traveled to Japan, wrote several books, including *Japan, Its Architecture, Art and Art-Manufactures* (1882).

Conder (discussed below) was a good friend of Godwin, who collected Japanese prints. It seems odd that so many figures associated with English Arts and Crafts made references to Japanese motifs in their work. One of the creeds of the Arts and Crafts movement was against the vapid use of historical forms (with the prime example being Nash's Royal Pavilion at Brighton). Arts and Crafts aficionados were interested in restoring medieval woodworking techniques, so they were appreciative of Japanese woodworking techniques and judicious use of decoration.

The Japanese exhibit at the World's Columbian Exposition of 1893 in Chicago was

Anglo-Japanese furniture

The Anglo-Japanese style is an offshoot of the English Arts and Crafts movement. English reformers, including William Morris, felt that the general state of design needed to be rehabilitated, although there was little consensus on how this goal was to be achieved. A significant although modest number of Arts and Crafts designers had an expressed interest in Japanese design and created works known as Anglo-Japanese. English Arts and Crafts artists appreciated Japanese a popular destination. The foreign interest in Japanese art affected the kind of art that was produced, and what was exhibited, both in Japan and abroad. The types of artworks that foreign connoisseurs were interested in also shaped the general knowledge about Japanese arts. Foreigners collected and preferred prints. This fixation gave Japanese prints a prominence abroad that they did not enjoy at home. American designer Louis Comfort Tiffany, like many others, additionally preferred historical Japanese works to contemporary ones—a preference that irked many contemporary (nineteenth-century) Japanese artists. One result of this is that Japanese paintings, especially contemporary paintings, did not sell well abroad although they were popular in exhibitions in Japan. For over a century, Japanese artists and craftsmen have grappled with a foreign preference for historic or traditional Japanese art forms and a dismissal of contemporary works.

Josiah Conder and modern Japanese architecture

Alice Tseng wrote an accomplished article on Josiah Conder and the Museum at Ueno, and most of the information presented here is drawn from her article. Ueno was Japan's first public park. An international exhibition took place in the park, and it ultimately resulted in a museum. Exhibitions whose subject was Japan, abroad and at home, showed lacquers, bronzes, porcelain, Western-style oil paintings, and traditional Japanese prints and ink paintings. Japan had a tradition of timber architecture. Once the building program of the Japanese government included major projects, like railway stations and world-class museums, it was unclear how to design large-scale Japanese buildings in brick, concrete, stone, metal, and glass, the materials of the new (nineteenth-century) age. To help in this endeavor, the Japanese government hired the young English architect Josiah Conder, who arrived in Japan in 1877. Conder's entire career was connected to Japan, and he is widely referred to as the father of modern Japanese architecture.

Conder's building was designed for the Second National Industrial Exhibition in Tokyo in 1881. It reopened in 1882 as a museum. He collaborated with students who had studied with him, and it was built by Japanese workmen. Tseng writes:

The building was in many ways the embodiment of the complex power relations between a nonWestern nation that struggled to maintain its independence and a host of Western nations encroaching on this right. A product of the alliance between a foreign expert and his Japanese host, the museum in Ueno engaged the idea of nation-building and its architectural expression from both sides.

(2004, p. 472)

Many aspects of the design are absolutely foreign to the Japanese architecture tradition. Conder was influenced, in part, by the British architecture of the Raj, and some of these Saracenic motifs made their way into his designs. Saracenic motifs originated with Islamic design, yet in the period of historic revivals they were generically associated with Asia. Conder's own museum was destroyed by an earthquake in 1923. Many of Conder's students became architects and constitute the second generation of Japanese modern students.

While the Japanese architects Tōkuma Katayama (1854–1917) and Kingo Tatsuno challenged the primacy of Western architects active in late nineteenth-century Japan, they continued to design in an international **Beaux-Arts** style, sometimes with gestures to Japanese design in the decoration. Katayama was a student of Conder's at the College of Technology (Tseng 2004, pp. 490–91). A prolific architect, his career was cemented with prominent commissions for three national museums: the Hyōkeikan Museum in Tokyo, 1901–1908 (Figure 18.15); the Kyoto National Museum in Kyoto, 1892–1895; and the Nara National Museum in Nara, 1892–1894.

Several critics noted that Western-trained Japanese architects had no magical formula for making reference to the history of Japanese architecture when doing large modern buildings. Chuta Ito (1868–1954) was an architect, architectural critic, and architectural historian. He was critical of the West-leaning work of Katayama and Tatsuno, although some of his projects were seen by others as reflecting international art nouveau trends.

Prairie style

Frank Lloyd Wright belongs in the ranks of those enamored of Japanese art. He collected Japanese prints and is responsible for the most famous work of architecture by an American in Japan, the Imperial Hotel, 1913–1923. The imprint of Japanese design is evident in many of those whose works are known as Prairie style. This is

Figure 18.15
Tōkuma
Katayama,
Hyōkei-kan
Museum, Tokyo,
Japan, 1908.

especially evident in their exterior renderings of buildings. Many of the perspective renderings of Wright's houses were actually done by Marion Mahoney Griffin (1871–1961). Marion Mahoney was the first licensed female architect in Illinois. Her distinctive style of rendering derived from her familiarity with Japanese woodblock prints. In 1895, she started working for Wright. In her lush renderings, Mahoney surrounded Wright's buildings with flowing vegetation, using a compositional technique that resembled the use of nature in the Japanese prints (Kruty 2007). Her technique asserted that Wright's designs, although in the Midwestern prairie, were inextricably connected to nature. Many of the drawings published in the *Wasmuth Portfolio*, the 1910 German publication that helped establish Wright's international reputation, were done by Mahoney.

She married Walter Burley Griffin (1876–1937) and her career was to remain connected to Asia, although not specifically Japan. The effectiveness of her renderings was proven again when her husband won the prestigious international competition to design a new Australian city, Canberra. It is widely thought that the jury's decision was largely based on the appeal of her renderings. The

Griffins moved to Australia and later to Lucknow, India, where they did several projects.

Conclusion

Akira Kurosawa, the foremost Japanese film-maker, released a film in 1951, *Rashômon*, a crime drama set in twelfth-century Japan. In the film, a samurai is killed and his wife raped. Four witnesses then proceed to give their account of the crime, and each version is different and contradicts the others. This masterful film, a high point of Japanese cinema, also made a wider contribution to twentieth-century intellectual thought. It contributed to a philosophical debate about the nature of truth and the meaning of history. The film suggests that historical reality is not something that can be accessed, but only approached obliquely through tellings and retellings. The film questions objectivity and focuses on the constructed nature of narrative, including historical narratives.

Kurosawa's film relates to this historical project and, in fact, any history, because it suggests that twenty-first-century inhabitants can experience history only through certain venues. It is a fruitful endeavor to understand the past by looking at designed objects, but they are only a part of the story. Different viewers of Katsura see different things in it. Most of the antique Japanese pieces available today are from the more recent past, even when they repeat and reiterate forms that had existed for centuries.

While modernity is too often posited as a Western construct exported from the West, this chapter demonstrates that Japan constructed its own modernity. Furthermore, part of what is globally considered as modernity was achieved because of Japanese contributions. For centuries, Japanese designers have been grappling with a classic problem of the modern age: how to deal with national identity in a time of change and in an increasingly global world.

Sources

Benfey, Christopher (2003). *The Great Wave: Gilded Age Misfits, Japanese Eccentrics, and the Opening of Old Japan*. New York: Random House.

Black, Alexandra and Noboru Murata (2000). *The Japanese House: Architecture and Interiors*. Boston: Tuttle.

Clarke, Rosy (1983). *Japanese Antique Furniture*. New York: Weatherhill.

Dower, John (1986). *Japanese History and Culture*. Manchester: Manchester University Press.

Hashimoto, Fumio (1981). *Architecture in the Shoin Style: Japanese Feudal Residences*. Tokyo: Kodansha.

Iida, Mihoko and Danielle Demetriou (2022). *Japanese Interiors*. New York: Phaidon.

Ishimoto, Yasuhiro, Walter Gropius, and Kenzo Tange (1960). *Katsura: Tradition and Creation*. Minneapolis: University of Minnesota Press.

Isozaki, Arata (1983). *Katsura Villa: Space and Form*. New York: Rizzoli.

Jaffer, Amin (2001). *Furniture from British India and Ceylon*. Salem, MA: Peabody Essex Museum.

Koizumi, Kazuko (1986). *Traditional Japanese Furniture*. Tokyo: Kodansha.

Kruty, Paul (2007). *Marion Mahony and Millikin Place*. St. Louis, MO: Walter Burley Griffin Society of America.

Lerski, Hanna (1979). "Josiah Conder's Bank of Japan, Tokyo." *Journal of the Society of Architectural Historians* 38 (October): 271–74.

McCormick, Melissa (2003). "Genji Goes West: The 1510 Genji Album and the Visualization of Court and Capital." *Art Bulletin* 85, no. 1 (March): 54–85.

Moss, Peter (2007). *Asian Furniture: A Directory and Sourcebook*. London: Thames and Hudson.

Mueller, Laura (2007). *Competition and Collaboration: Japanese Prints of the Utagawa School*. Boston: Brill.

Ono, Ayako (2003). *Japonisme in Britain*. London: Routledge.

Schreffler, Michael (2007). *The Art of Allegiance: Visual Culture and Power in Baroque New Spain*. University Park: Pennsylvania State University Press.

Tange, Kenzo (1971). *Katsura: Tradition and Creation in Japanese Architecture*. New Haven, CT: Yale University Press.

Tensley, Sarah and Chiharu Watabe (2005). *20th Century Design History*. Tokyo: Petit Grand Publishing.

Tseng, Alice (2004). "Styling Japan: The Case of Josiah Conder and the Museum at Ueno, Tokyo." *Journal of the Society of Architectural Historians* 63, no. 4 (December): 472–97.

Waithall, Anne (1998). *Weak Body of a Useless Woman: Matsuo Taseko*. Chicago: University of Chicago Press.

Yiengpruksawan, Mimi Hall (2001). "Japanese Art History 2001: The State and Stakes of Research." *Art Bulletin* 83 (March): 105–22.

Discussion and Study Questions

1. As a group, how do Japanese designs differ from Chinese designs?

2. As a group, how do Japanese designs differ from European designs?

3. What are some of the varieties within the realm of Japanese design?

4. Considering furniture and houses, what are the general characteristics that many ascribe to Japanese designs?

5. What are the two architectural features of traditional Japanese designs that modernists were fond of?

6. What household objects take the role of furniture in Japan, yet would not be considered furniture in other countries?

7. What are the significant Japanese vocabulary words that relate to domestic architecture that are used in the West?

Art Nouveau

19

1880–1914		1900–1920	
Art nouveau (Europe)		**Art nouveau (Latin America)**	

1888–1911	1890–1914	1896–1914
Modernisme (Spain)	**Stile Liberty (Italy)**	**Jugendstil (Germany and Austria)**

Art nouveau literally means "new art." A decorative style that flourished in the late nineteenth century, its prominent artworks were in architecture, interiors, graphics, and the decorative arts, including furniture. The single most important principle motivating art nouveau artists was the belief that artistic forms should take their inspiration from nature; flowers, vines, birds, and insects all served as source materials. Compositionally, this meant that art nouveau works followed a sinuous asymmetrical line. The promotion of art nouveau was part of a general reaction against nineteenth-century historicism (Aubry 1996, p. 13). To reinforce the dramatic break with the past, art nouveau artists rejected classical design and, in fact, most all historical precedent. The corollary to rejecting the past was that art nouveau artists embraced new materials. Using them, they successfully fashioned a new decorative system. Art nouveau pieces were highly ornamented, yet the elaborate forms quietly nurtured the seeds of modernism.

In the beginning, the philosophical underpinnings of the new art came from three principal figures: William Morris, John Ruskin, and Eugène Viollet-le-Duc. From Morris came the commitment to the unity of the arts. That unity was to be achieved by abolishing the distinction between major and minor arts. Art nouveau is one of the few periods whose

Figure 19.0
(*Facing page*)
Giuseppe Mongoni, Vittorio Emanuele II Gallery, Milan, Italy, 1865–1876.

greatest achievements are found in interiors and designed objects. The European architects associated with art nouveau were all accomplished furniture designers.

The lack of specific recognizable historic references made it an ideal candidate to become the first international style. Variants of it grew in Asia, Africa, and Latin America. **Jugendstil** is the German variant, and the word **Modernisme**, in Catalan Spain, refers to art nouveau artworks (Permanyer 1999, p. 9). In Italy, the style is referred to as **Stile Liberty** (Figure 19.0).

Samuel Bing opened a gallery in Paris called "L'Art Nouveau" in 1895 (Borsi 1996, p. 36). This auspicious moment is considered the formal beginning of the movement, yet hints of art nouveau, in a variety of art forms and especially graphics, came as early as 1884. Henri Toulouse-Lautrec's posters played an important role in the dissemination of art nouveau into the French graphic sphere. Following the lead of the Arts and Crafts movement, art nouveau artists rejected Victorian design, its troops of souvenirs, its eclecticism, and its promiscuous combination of historical styles. Those active in many fields—furniture design, jewelry, and advertising—revealed the influence of the new style whose rallying point was nature and her luminescent botanicals. Nature became a cleansing device, sweeping buildings, interiors, paintings, and books of superficial historical references.

English Beginnings

Many of the artistic themes held dear by art nouveau artists came from the polemical writings of Morris and Ruskin. A rallying cry for both Arts and Crafts and art nouveau was the need to counteract nineteenth-century historicism. Compositionally, the design strategy of artists in both movements was two-pronged, in which a rigorous structure was offset with fields of ornamental decoration inspired by local flora and fauna. Both movements frequently required a high level of craftsmanship and promoted a unified approach to design, allowing for no distinctions between major and minor arts. In theory, a pendant necklace was as worthy of attention as a painting.

The painter and poet William Blake (1757–1827) inspired artists in both movements. His illustrated book of poetry *Songs of Innocence* combines image and text. A border creates a field within it, a blank space through which the artist can let meander an asymmetrical composition. Rococo designs did not consistently unite form and text the way Blake did, so his work served as a link between rococo and art nouveau.

The pre-Raphaelite painters, including Dante Gabriel Rossetti, were on good terms with the Arts and Crafts designers and collaborated with them. The languid human figures that populate their paintings anticipate the highly stylized human forms of art nouveau. The actual physical frames of the pre-Raphaelites continue the look and details of the paintings within them, underscoring the unity between the art of painting and the craftsmanship of building a wooden frame. Art nouveau two-dimensional works were often put in art nouveau frames.

The color palette of the American painter James McNeill Whistler's (1834–1903) Peacock Room of 1876–1877 includes purples, greens, and dark woods. These colors, and the featured animal, the peacock, were favorites of art nouveau artists. Charles Voysey (1857–1941) took Arts and Crafts in a modern direction by reducing his buildings to recognizable geometric shapes. His rooms flowed together, and his plans were rationally and simply organized. Yet he juxtaposed the rigor of his architecture with exuberant fields of two-dimensional decoration. His numerous wallpapers and textile designs reveal his training under the watchful eye of Arthur Heygate Mackmurdo (1851–1942). Voysey frequently included lilies, tulips, and egrets in his compositions, revealing his familiarity with Japanese prints. In fact, it was likely due to the ongoing success of English Arts and Crafts members such as Voysey that art nouveau, despite its English beginnings, never really took hold in Britain.

There were two principal English art nouveau artists: Arthur Heygate Mackmurdo and Aubrey Beardsley. Mackmurdo designed most of his furniture with right angles and relied on standard chair profiles. His famous chair of 1881 is unexceptional except for the appearance of art nouveau tracery in the back panel. This chair appears some ten years before the date normally given for the start of art nouveau. Two years later, in 1883, Mackmurdo used the same flaming flowers to embellish the title page he created for the book *Wren's City Churches*.

Aubrey Beardsley (1872–1898) is known for his pen-and-ink drawings. Beardsley, along with Whistler and Oscar Wilde, formed a trio of fashionable dandies, elite men who were wittily risqué and connected art nouveau to a world of drama, literature, and art. Beardsley's drawings, like Blake's, recognize the page's limit, but they also deny it with billowing asymmetric forms that are rendered dramatic by relying on large areas filled with pure black ink. He continued a tradition that started with medieval woodcuts, and he made something new from it. Sharp lines delineate Beardsley's stylized figures. These expressive silhouettes were well suited for mechanical reproduction.

Art nouveau differs from the earlier aesthetic movements in two important respects. Arts and Crafts looked to medieval history, while art nouveau artists, theoretically, eschewed all traditional forms. Arts and Crafts was a knee-jerk reaction against the Industrial Revolution and the manufacturing processes that art nouveau artists embraced.

Belgium

Victor Horta (1861–1947), from Belgium, was an architect, designer, and teacher. Most of his buildings are in Brussels, the place where art nouveau left the pages of books and started turning into buildings. Particularly during the period 1893–1903, he worked in what came to be known as the art nouveau style. His designs revolutionized the design world, and their impact was felt all around the world. He is widely recognized as the single most important person in the development of art nouveau. His interiors are remarkable for their stylistic unity.

The Hôtel van Eetvelde is stylistically his most modern project (Figure 19.1). In the stairway hall, structure, railings, walls, ceilings, and hardware all contribute to an integrated design. The goal of a unified interior is achieved.

The purview of Horta's design focus included wall paneling, ceilings, window details, light fixtures, furniture, and hardware (Aubry 1996, p. 56). His designs are the opposite of eclecticism. No assemblage of disparate items, everything in sight adheres to the same clean aesthetic. In plan, his designs are early explorations of the open plan. Horta's interest in the publications of Viollet-le-Duc reveals itself in his use of both cast and wrought iron. His metal forms are sinuous. Many of his projects treat iron as a ductile material, combining it with glass (Borsi 1996, p. 36).

Although he was born in Ghent, most all of Horta's design explorations were played out in several town house designs in Brussels. His major projects include the private residences the Hôtel Tassel, 1892–1893, and the Hôtel Solvay, 1895–1900 ("Hôtel" in these cases indicates a private home). Horta was interested in the possibilities presented by metal, and he combined metal with wood and glass in his organically inspired compositions. For the balustrade of the Hôtel Solvay, wood and metal swirl together, only to be bolted to the marble stair tread. A ceiling fixture by Horta for the same project displays an aspect of art nouveau designs that the more florid compositions overshadow: its reliance on a strictly controlled system as a backdrop to the flourishes (Borsi 1996, pp. 61–4). The ceiling is divided into rectangular panels of equal measure and regularly placed. A similar composition enlivens the ceiling plane of the Hôtel Max Hallet (Figure 19.1). At the juncture between panels, a light fixture hangs, its lengthy support a bundle of parallel metal tubes of equal diameter. At the bottom, the tubes bend and curl like a bouquet of lilies—only, instead of flowers, the stems sprout glass shades and electric lamps.

Horta's house designs served an elite clientele. The Maison du Peuple (1896–1899), in

Figure 19.1
Victor Horta, Hôtel
van Eetvelde,
Brussels, Belgium,
1897.

contrast, was the headquarters of the Belgian Socialist Party. Also known as the House of the People, it was an early sign of modern architects' interest in the masses and the ability of design to affect the social good (Borsi 1996, pp. 67–74). The Maison du Peuple also shows how art nouveau, with its prescient use of glass and metal, was an early sign of modernism that spread across late nineteenth-century developments. Horta essentially developed a **curtain-wall** structure of metal and glass. The central portion of the curved façade sports a broad expanse of glass held together by a nonstructural metal framing system (Aubry 1996, p. 15). This transparent exterior wall also indicates a separation of structure from wall, and it was accompanied by the use of interior metal columns, visible in the auditorium's interior (Puttemans 1974, p. 64–5). Even though the skyscraper had its debut in Chicago, Horta's unusual building shows that European designers were working with the same elements—metal, glass, and the separation of structure from wall.

Henry Van de Velde (1863–1957) trained as a painter, and his early paintings are vaguely reminiscent of the French Impressionists. Influenced by the written works of William Morris, he explored the relationship between aesthetics and moral qualities by looking at nature and common materials.

The design philosophy he articulated relied on a crucial distinction between **ornamentation** and **ornament**. Ornamentation was attached, a flat composition on flat planes. Ornament was inherent, a logical outcome of a form or material and revealing of its inner structure. A suite of furniture by Van de Velde becomes a sculptural presence in a room; the curves are extensions of the volumes that house various functions—closed and open storage, writing and transaction surfaces (Figure 19.2). The curves also respond anthropomorphically to the seated human figure; the storage and writing areas are within arm's reach of the user. This desk and chair set is a notable work of art nouveau design and an advancement in the history of office furniture. It recognizes the need for storage areas. Function aside, the desk is ornament, according to Van de Velde's thinking, because its decorative qualities derive from its forms and materials.

Ornamentation, according to Van de Velde's mind, was applied and flat, an application of the two-dimensional graphic traditions of Blake and Beardsley to the world of materials. Van de Velde did many designs for wall tiles, evidence of his interest in industrial manufacturing processes and producing well-designed, moderately priced materials. The glaze on ceramic wall tiles is not inherent to the ceramic material but is clearly applied.

Van de Velde's work for the Nietzsche Archive in Weimar resulted in a total designed environment (Figure 19.3). Furniture pieces employ the same easy segmented curves yet stand on their own as well-designed pieces.

One of the major figures in developing Belgian art nouveau, Van de Velde had a significant second act in his career. He played a role in developing modernism as an educator and administrator. In Weimar, Germany, he reorganized the Kunstgewerbeschule (Arts and Crafts School), thus setting the foundations for its reorganization, and radical refashioning, into the Bauhaus. When most designers considered art nouveau artists passé, Walter Gropius continued to admire him (Sembach 1989, pp. 28–30).

In Belgium, the new forms constituted a nationalist design anthem that was decidedly anti-French. This aspect of art nouveau was lost when the style migrated to other countries. Initiated by Horta and a small cadre of Belgian designers, art nouveau forms multiplied and spread across the globe.

Figure 19.2
Henry Van de
Velde, desk,
armchair, and
sidechair,
Brussels, Belgium,
1898.

Figure 19.3
Henry Van de
Velde, Nietzsche
Archive, Weimar,
Germany, 1903.

France

Art historian Domenico Quaranta, in an anthology on twentieth-century art (2006), points out that France had consolidated its position as the arts center of Europe, with Paris its focal point. Paris captivated artists from around the globe with its museums and the support it lent artists with an ambitious exhibition schedule (Quaranta 2006, pp. 112–13). In the opening years of the twentieth century, while the legacy of Impressionists remained strong in the capital, a tendency of many French artists was to seek locations where they could work in France's provinces. France was a major center of European art nouveau, primarily in two cities: Paris and Nancy.

Nancy

The city of Nancy was the artistic and intellectual center of the province of Lorraine, the state that has passed several times back and forth between French and German control in its long history. It had been a consolation prize for the deposed Polish king Stanislas Leszczynski in the mid-eighteenth century, who made it a center of rococo art and design. This fostered a climate that appreciated the arts, and in the late twentieth century Nancy became one of two French centers for art nouveau. Formally established in 1901, the School of Nancy was an association of artists, artisans, and manufacturers.

Emile Gallé (1846–1904), one of the founders, became Nancy's foremost glassmaker, potter, and furniture designer. For his glass work, he worked with acid-resistant materials, metal foils, colored oxides, and a studied use of air bubbles. In all his designs, Gallé made use of the academic training he undertook in botany and mineralogy in Weimar, Germany. Visiting London's museums and private galleries, he saw firsthand collections of Chinese, Japanese, and Islamic ceramics.

He was fond of incorporating water lilies into his designs, and several pieces gave the impression that a dragonfly had just alighted. He first exhibited at the Exposition Universelle of 1878. In 1884, he exhibited at the Union Centrale des Arts Décoratifs in Paris. He brought his interest in unusual materials and organic forms to his furniture designs, in which he employed complex marquetry using exotic woods and mother-of-pearl inlays. A cabinet displays the complex geometry, the feeling of balance that is achieved despite a lack of symmetry, and the ever-present

vines, cattails, and tendrils (Figure 19.4). The complexity of the overall shape was apparent when creating working drawings for art nouveau shapes. To mathematically describe a sinuous profile and give instructions of how to construct it with compasses, was a complicated mathematical exercise. Thus, the effortless appearance of an art nouveau piece belies the difficulty of constructing it.

Gallé's designs create a sense of movement, even though they are static pieces. Things are growing, and the passage of time is represented, long term, with one vine growing around another. Time is also frozen; a picture in marquetry depicts a branch bending in the wind—a transient act of nature is captured for eternity. Françoise Aubry refers to this temporal quality: "The essence of Art Nouveau is ultimately encapsulated in the image of a frozen, enchanted, winter garden" (1996, p. 21).

As the head of a successful company that by 1894 had more than three hundred employees, Gallé was the artist behind his company's

Figure 19.4
Emile Gallé, cabinet, Nancy, France, 1900. Rosewood.

art nouveau products and the businessman who oversaw their production and distribution. Gallé's exhibit at the Exposition Universelle of 1900 was a triumphant retrospective of his career. French author Philippe Jullian wrote an entire book devoted to the Exposition, which he describes as an ephemeral city that "may be considered an important stage in the history of art, for it was the capital of Art Nouveau, a movement of which it marked both the apotheosis and the decline" (1974, p. 17). Lawyer turned furniture maker Eugène Gaillard (1862–1933) was one of many talented designers who contributed to the Exposition (Figure 19.5).

Also from Nancy was Louis Majorelle (1859–1926), a French cabinetmaker who was the son of a cabinetmaker. His father specialized in making reproductions of eighteenth-century pieces. Late eighteenth-century French furniture was a highlight of French decorative arts, and the Majorelle family brought that expertise in craftsmanship to the early twentieth century.

Majorelle studied painting at the École des Beaux-Arts, returning to Nancy to work in the family business. Under Gallé's influence, he started producing pieces in the art nouveau style, with the period 1898–1908 being his most productive years. His armchair is made from carved walnut stained dark (Figure 19.6). Also exhibited

at the Exposition Universelle of 1900 in Paris, it is an iconic piece of French art nouveau. Majorelle incorporated naturalistic forms, yet his compositions are more abstract than Gallé's. His works were sumptuous, made of expensive materials, and featured the meticulous craftsmanship he learned from his father. A master craftsman in wood, his designs took the French expertise in marquetry and carving into the art nouveau fold.

After 1908 he started mass-producing furniture and the quality of his pieces declined. The year 1914 finds Majorelle in Paris working as a decorator. He abandoned art nouveau and started producing more restrained work. The relationship between art nouveau and the 1920s style art deco is under dispute (Aubry 1996, p. 209). Some consider art deco as an artistic reaction against art nouveau. The totality of Majorelle's career suggests an overlap between the two. His later work is more rectilinear and includes many vaguely art deco-looking pieces. The last decades of Majorelle's career are symptomatic of the plight of most artists connected to art nouveau. They were once themselves leaders of the artistic vanguard and fiercely critical of the design

Figure 19.5
Eugène Gaillard, cabinet, Nancy, France, 1899.

Figure 19.6
Louis Majorelle, armchair, Nancy, France, 1899–1900.

status quo and popular taste. By the ends of their careers, they were in turn the object of scorn in a design world that had moved in other artistic directions.

Paris

Hector Guimard (1867–1942) was a French architect, furniture designer, and writer. He attended the École Nationale des Arts Décoratifs, and also later the École des Beaux-Arts, where he did not finish his studies. He was influenced by Viollet-le-Duc, particularly his studies of exposed cast-iron columns. Guimard traveled to Brussels, where he met Victor Horta. During the period 1899–1914, his works developed into full-blown art nouveau. In 1896, he entered a competition to design the Paris Métro stations; he did not win, but the head of the Métro, a fan of art nouveau, gave Guimard the commission anyway, a propitious decision. This extensive project included hundreds of small projects throughout Paris. Some of the designs were just steps and railings, some were decorated shields, and some featured glass roofs shaped like butterfly wings (Figure 19.7). Art nouveau features of his designs include stalks that blossom into lamps. Although based on vegetal forms, his lamps were metal, modern, and made for a sophisticated transportation system. They

were also modular and mass-produced. For the Métro, he designed standardized cast-iron fittings. Guimard's work for the Paris Métro is a wonderful expression of art nouveau in France that would have a lasting impact on the face Paris presents to the world. One of the features of art nouveau was the synthesis of furnishings and décor. Guimard was an accomplished designer of residential furniture and street furniture.

Professionally active in the beginning of the twentieth century, Guimard was no fan of modernism. Guimard, like many others, was interested in Viollet-le-Duc, minus the interest in history.

Art nouveau works look so decorative that it is not immediately obvious that they were technologically advanced. Art nouveau artists married industrial processes with the desire to look to nature to create beauty. Guimard's designs look handcrafted, if not organically grown but they were produced in factories.

Style, artists, and art nouveau

When looking at a body of work that comes to be known as a style—and there is no better example of a style than art nouveau—an issue is the historical status of the individuals who contributed to crafting that style. Many serious art historians dismiss outright the notion of style.

Figure 19.7
Hector Guimard, Paris Métropolitain, Paris, France, 1900.

Their point, and it is a good one, is that style is a convention of historians looking at the past. Artists of a specific time period rarely feel they are fulfilling the requirements of a style. For, obviously, a style cannot predate the artists whose works gave rise to that style. Some artists are so thoroughly associated with art nouveau that they seem to be its essence, to embody it, as though the style could not have existed without them. The notion of style is useful when looking at the careers of Victor Horta, Emile Gallé, and Hector Guimard.

Spain

Artists work and produce artworks that respond to their clients' needs, realize their own goals, and resonate with trends and concerns of their day. Certain artists—Horta, Gallé, Guimard—were astonishingly in step with the precepts that came to be known as art nouveau.

Another category concerns individuals who make important artistic contributions, yet their talent is so deep, complex, and contradictory that their relationship to a single style is tenuous.

A discussion of art nouveau is incomplete without mention of Antoni Gaudí and Louis Sullivan. Yet to present their creative processes and works as derivative of a movement established by others is to grossly underestimate their talent.

Antoni Gaudí

Antoni Gaudí (1852–1926) was a Spanish Catalan architect. He was knowledgeable of medieval history and craftsmanship. His early works indicate that he was interested in ornamental motifs, systems of ornament, and experimentation—like so many others, he read Ruskin and Viollet-le-Duc. He was up front about his inspiration from historic forms, including medieval and Gothic, although in transforming them he sought to create a Catalan regional style.

Gaudí imaginatively experimented with ornament, construction, and prefabrication. He used glazed tiles (**azulejos**). In designs for a factory and stables, he developed a roofing system that relied on parabolic arches. He worked in wrought iron and investigated steel frames.

A criticism of Gaudí's brilliant compositions is that he could not be imitated easily. There was something deeply personal and subjective about his compositions that is sometimes downright bizarre. William Curtis calls Gaudí "one of the

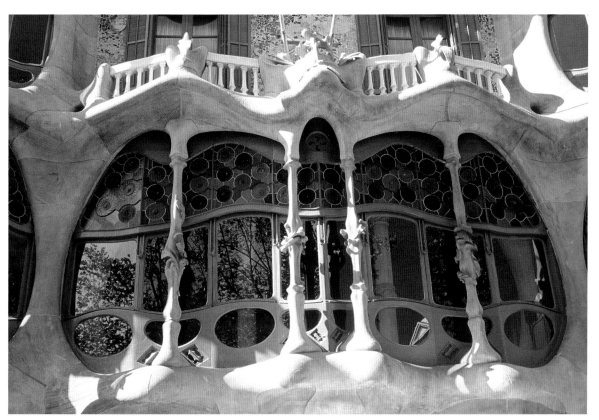

Figure 19.8
Antoni Gaudí,
Casa Batlló,
Barcelona, Spain,
1904–1906.
Façade detail.

most curious and original architects of the past two hundred years" (1996, p. 60).

Gaudí's work has moments of fantasy and represents an early connection to the artistic movement of surrealism; his built forms appear to melt, bend, and sway, as objects do in dreams. Gaudí designed a wavelike façade for an apartment house, the Casa Batlló (Figure 19.8). Glass, masonry, ceramic tile, wood, and metal all appear to effortlessly flow together, yet achieving this required a high level of skill and attention from the construction workers (Permanyer 1999, pp. 60–1). Fellow Catalan Salvador Dalí felt a connection to Gaudí's work, admiring the occasional use of nightmarish elements.

The development of Gaudí's interior spaces became increasingly fluid. The plan of the Casa Batlló demonstrates that for Gaudí, the possibilities offered by flowing forms inspired his design work in elevation and in plan. Shimomura writes: "For Gaudí, interior design was first and foremost the construction of space. The transitions between rooms and staircases weave together freely in both fast and slow motion, and his expressive use of light makes those transitions visual. In short, the main theme of Casa Batlló is the functional continuity of space" (1992, p. 52).

His early projects include two commissions by the Güell family, the Palau Güell, 1886–1891, and the Parque Güell, 1900–1914. These were followed by two apartment houses, the Casa Batlló, 1904–1906, and the Casa Milá, Barcelona, 1906–1910. Gaudí's long-gestating masterwork, the Basilica of the Sagrada Familia, started in 1883 and continued into the twenty-first century. Many of its forms derive from Gothic architecture, although with a twist. The art nouveau interest in stairways reveals itself in screw stairs (Figure 19.9) and a related masonry detail, the skew arch (Figure 19.10).

Gaudí did furniture designs for interiors and also street furniture. His work ranges from eclectic to modern. Although he represented an old-fashioned approach to decoration, he pushed the boundaries of what was structurally possible. His talent exceeds any attempt to define it.

Figure 19.9
Screw stair.

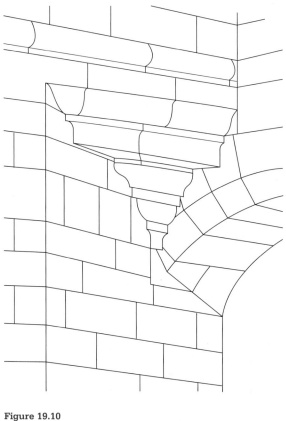

Figure 19.10
Skew arch.

United States

Art nouveau did not exist in the United States as a full-blown movement, the way it did in Belgium and France. But the works of Louis Sullivan, and even more so Louis Comfort Tiffany, reflect its worldwide influence. Louis Henri Sullivan (1856–1924) was an architect and writer. Before opening up his own office, Sullivan worked for Frank Furness in Philadelphia and William Le Baron Jenney in Chicago.

The most important phase of his architecture was when he created a series of early skyscrapers in the 1890s. He was an incredibly gifted designer, architect, and drawer, and his partnership with Dankmar Adler allowed him to focus on his architecture. The organization of their office presents a typical scenario for architectural partnerships: one partner focuses on design (Sullivan) and one on business (Adler). Sullivan recounted the story of his youth and design inspiration in a book, *The Autobiography of an Idea*. He went to Paris and studied at the École des Beaux-Arts; his work is more of a reaction against Beaux-Arts planning than an iteration of it. But he was something of a snob, proud of the French spelling of his first and middle names. His architecture expresses Sullivan's ambitious goals: to create an architecture appropriate to the new age, to create an American, if not Midwestern, strain of architecture, and in the process, to derive an entirely new system of ornamental decoration. Sullivan's accomplished ornament was based on American, not European, flora and was decidedly unclassical.

Sullivan was one of the founding fathers of modernism, with his vociferous disavowal of historically imitative buildings, his desire to express the structural frame and emphasize verticality, and his creation of an American architectural idiom. Yet any review of his work that denies his system of ornament is omitting a major part of his design. His expressive buildings were highly decorative.

His major buildings include the Auditorium, 1889, an opera house and hotel ingeniously contained within a steel-framed office building. Of his high-rises, two of the most significant structures are the Wainwright Building in St. Louis, 1890–1891, and the Guaranty Building in Buffalo, 1894–1896. Because of their height, they are technological achievements, but their façades are also expressive explorations of verticality. His last major project was the Carson Pirie Scott Store, 1898–1904. It is one of his most poetic projects, in which a cellular superstructure grows out of an elaborately decorated two-story base with sumptuous details (Figure 19.11).

Louis Comfort Tiffany came from a family of jewelers, merchants, and designers. Tiffany traveled to Nancy, where he visited Gallé's factory. His father's firm opened a Paris branch that sold jewelry, lamps, and small art objects. Tiffany traveled in Europe and North Africa. During his travels, he focused on Romanesque art and Islamic and Japanese ceramics, using them as points of departure for his experiments with stained glass. He created many lamps (Figure 19.12). His multiple lily lamps fit squarely in the art nouveau fold with their use of a favored flower. They were made of metal and glass.

Initially creating interior designs that were heavily influenced by the aesthetic movement, over time Tiffany's work turned in the direction of art nouveau. He is the most art nouveau of any American artist. Tiffany had a prominent exhibit at the World's Columbian Exposition of 1893.

Figure 19.11
George Grant Elmslie and Louis Sullivan, Schlesinger and Mayer Company store balusters, Chicago, Illinois, USA, 1898–1899. Cast iron.

Figure 19.12
Louis Comfort
Tiffany, lily lamp,
Corona, Queens,
New York, USA,
1902–1917.

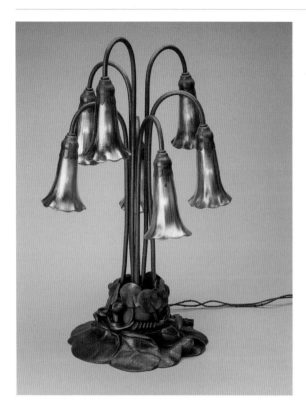

He contributed a glass curtain to the Palacio de Bellas Artes in Mexico City in 1915. As with many art nouveau artists, he found himself at odds with cubism and modernism. Although mostly known for his works in glass, lamps, vases, and windows, Tiffany also worked as an interior decorator, designing rooms in which all the elements adhered to a central scheme, and this included furniture.

Global

Belgium and France are the countries most frequently associated with art nouveau, but also Germany, England, the Czech Republic, and, in a limited way, the United States. In Belgium, the new style expressed a political and nationalist agenda. In Spain, it was given a Catalan regional twist. When it became an international artistic phenomenon, it was often evoked straightforwardly as the most up-to-date style of the times. This is ironic, because its effects were felt later in other regions of the world. When most Europeans were no longer building in the art nouveau style, art nouveau buildings were still being erected in South America, Africa, and Asia. It could

be considered the first international style, as it flourished in Turkey, Argentina, Brazil, and Japan. Brazilian Eliseu Visconti (1867–1944) was an accomplished art nouveau designer. He studied in Paris and completed numerous art nouveau projects in Rio de Janeiro. In the best tradition of the new style, he sought to eliminate the distance between architecture and elements of the decorative arts.

Czech Republic

Prague was Eastern Europe's major center of art nouveau, although the Czech version of the international style followed a different path. For art nouveau artists in Belgium and France, historic styles were anathema. In Prague, the earliest leanings toward an art nouveau outlook came from architects who worked within identifiable period styles. Art nouveau contributed to the creation of modern Czech art. It was followed by a more progressive architectural style that bore the same name as the movement in painting, cubism. In the works of Antonin Balsanek (1865–1921), the divisions between historic styles, Secession, and art nouveau were not pronounced. Jaroslav Benedikt's Imperial Café, in Prague, 1914, is similarly a beguiling composition with elements of art nouveau and neo-Renaissance (Figure 19.13).

This reveals Benedikt's familiarity with a number of contemporary and historical design idioms. The color palette of deep blues, purples, and sepias was decidedly art nouveau. Several of the painted human figures are dressed in patterned robes and offset with gold, a strategy perfected by Secessionist painter Gustav Klimt. One of the rounded arches frames a classically detailed **aedicule** that features a mirror and an air grille. Art nouveau, Secession, and classicism are distinct artistic traditions with differing design philosophies. Yet multiple Czech interior designs deftly blend them together.

Turkey

The last quarter of the nineteenth century saw an enormous amount of new construction in Istanbul. The historic eclecticism of the nineteenth century followed its own path along the banks of the Bosporus, in which Ottoman Revival buildings competed with other historically based styles. The building pace continued unabated, and the opening of the Istanbul Academy of Fine Arts in 1901 gave the design world an additional boost. In the first decades of the twentieth century, Istanbul

Figure 19.13
Jaroslav Benedikt,
Imperial
Café, Prague,
Czechlands, 1914.

became its own center of art nouveau. Turkish art nouveau was enriched by the international mix of the architects, which included Turks, Greeks, Italians, and others; this fascinating subject is the focus of a book by architectural historian Diana Barillari, upon which this section is based. Italian architect Raimondo D'Aronco (1857–1932) spent twenty years of his long career designing in Istanbul. Turkey inherited not the Belgian and French variety of art nouveau but the Italian permutation of it known as "Stile Liberty." Many of the forms of *Stile Liberty* in Italy and Turkey are recognizable as art nouveau, yet many of the meanings that were so important in Belgium and France, notably the antipathy toward historicism, lost their currency when moved to Europe's eastern border. A style created to replace historicism, in Turkey and Italy, happily blended with it.

The hundreds of art nouveau buildings in Istanbul range from superficial facsimiles to inspired meditations. Much of the construction was due to speculative development of rental buildings in which art nouveau was a cheap cosmetic finish to distinguish one landlord's buildings from those of competitors. Art nouveau decoration fulfilled the capitalist intention of attracting customers or, in the case of apartment buildings, tenants.

The art nouveau features of buildings in Istanbul are generally limited to the façades, with little change in plan, or in the buildings behind the façades. This lends the façades a sculptural quality created from the abutment of projecting volumes and recessed volumes. Bay windows and prominently jutting cornices were popular features that furthered the plastic quality of the façades. Yet the building materials were conventional, and the fenestration was achieved using standard rectangular casement windows. The metal structure was hidden, not expressed, nor was metal combined with glass to produce broad areas of transparency; the use of metal was limited to balcony railings. Curved façades were rare.

The Gümüssu Palas is one such example. It bears strong stylistic traces of Italian neo-baroque façades, with its cornice, classical proportioning, and exaggerated (and fake) rustication. Art nouveau sculptures have been grafted onto a baroque-style façade, a process Barillari (1996) calls "decorative and sculptural overkill." Art nouveau buildings in Istanbul, some inspired, some pedestrian, underscore that art nouveau truly became a style, a recognizable grouping of features that could be imitated. In some cases, the new results were divorced from the style's original ideological underpinnings. Even if superficial, art nouveau designs were successful in creating a fresh look, popular with the public, landlords, and tenants alike.

Japan

Chuta Ito (1868–1954) first studied architecture, then studied architectural history, eventually becoming one of Japan's first and foremost architectural historians. A tireless promoter of Asian and Japanese architecture, he opposed the neo-baroque designs proposed for many prominent sites, including the design for the new parliament building, the Diet. These buildings were not only the work of expatriate architects but also that of Japanese followers of Josiah Condor (refer to Chapter 18).

Knowing that Ito supported creating a new urban Japanese architecture, we must consider his own designs from a different perspective. European art nouveau artists counted among their inspirations Japanese art. Many of the art nouveau artists, as well as the English Arts and Crafts artists they admired, collected Japanese prints and glassware. So art nouveau was in part a modern style based on Japanese decorative traditions. The common description of the Aritomo House as art nouveau is recognition of the "foreignness" of the style that was known by a French word. But art nouveau in Japan was simultaneously a homegrown approach that transformed Japanese visual themes appropriate for the modern period.

Peru

The major Latin American cities that were greatly affected by art nouveau were Rio de Janeiro, Mexico City, Havana, and Buenos Aires. The presence of an art nouveau structure in Lima, Peru, is evidence of the style's quick spread around the world, even to those places not typically associated with it. Peru is home to South America's oldest traditions of large-scale urbanism and architecture, its major sites including the Nazca Plains, Machu Picchu, and Cuzco. The capital, Lima, on the western seaboard, was founded in 1535. Peru achieved her independence from Spain in 1822, so by 1890 the Spanish colonial legacy was neither an immediate concern nor long forgotten. In the late nineteenth and early twentieth centuries, many Peruvian artists received travel grants to Europe, which lent them firsthand knowledge of European artistic movements, from impressionism to art nouveau. Familiarity with European capital cities also aided in the project of constructing historically inspired buildings.

In the 1910s, art nouveau in Peru existed mostly in furniture and the decorative arts (García Bryce 1973). There were only a handful of art nouveau buildings, and often the occurrence of art nouveau was limited to doors, windows, balconies, and gates. A major art nouveau structure was built in 1915 by two brothers who worked as builders, the Hermanos Maspero. Their Casa Barragán was a popular hotel.

The new technology of photography was enormously popular and quickly spread all around the world, needing little governmental support. In many places, the art and business of photography linked up with art nouveau. The paper mats that framed photographs were often decorated with borders of tendrils and swirls. Photographic studios were outfitted with art nouveau interiors or, as in Lima, were situated in a building whose exterior was confidently decorated in the latest style, art nouveau (Figure 19.14). Casa Courret is a direct example of the kind of art nouveau structure built in Paris, usually private houses, such as the one owned by Toulouse-Lautrec's favored subject, Yvette Guilbert.

It was customary to paint advertisements directly onto buildings, but art nouveau precepts facilitated the process of combining building and text. Art nouveau graphic layouts promoted the integration of text, border, and figural elements. The Fotografía Courret is a prime example of art

Figure 19.14
Enrique Ronderas, Casa Courret, Lima Peru, 1905.

nouveau in its massing, details, materials, and typography. It does not mix much with traditional architectural detailing (as in Turkey). The column capitals appear as traditional capitals from a distance, yet close inspection reveals them as twisting swirls of foliage. Local carpenters made the interior display cases.

The metal balcony railings and wooden door panels also have a clear art nouveau heritage. The deeply cut swirls of the plaster decoration owe some debt to the neo-baroque style, yet studiously avoid classical elements. Not all buildings reveal the history of their locales. Fotografia Courret announces that one client, operating out of the capital city of a country with a long and rich architectural tradition, linked his fortunes to the new technology of photography and felt that the best architectural expression for his business was art nouveau.

Conclusion

In a design history, the presence of a major stylistic revolution prompts a basic question: is the revolution due to new technologies, materials, or aesthetic expression? As an aesthetic statement, art nouveau shared with other avant-garde movements a distaste for a superficial use of the past. Henry-Russell Hitchcock wrote: "Art Nouveau was actually the first stage of modern architecture in Europe, if modern architecture be understood as implying primarily the total rejection of historicism" (Hitchcock 1963 quoted in Curtis 1982, p. 21). Art nouveau artists switched allegiances from history to nature.

Art nouveau, as a style, was well poised to become the first international style. Art nouveau was not aloof, was not elite, and was immensely popular. Its motifs avoided any direct historical connection, and its two-dimensional variety guaranteed its quick dispersal as a new graphic device. It resonated with a wide audience and had both commercial appeal and domestic success.

The most creative years for art nouveau in Europe was the period 1893–1905. It appeared later in other places around the globe, but by the 1920s its creative energies were spent.

To the extent that artists focused on nature, art nouveau bears similarity to Arts and Crafts, Prairie school, the detailing of Chicago school skyscrapers, and Japanese woodcuts. Unlike Arts and Crafts followers, art nouveau supporters embraced new technologies, new materials such as glass and metal, and industrial production. Many art nouveau objects were electrified. Yet, quick as a wink, the movement heralded as fresh and new was itself criticized as superficial and elitist, qualities all too often associated with decoration. Alastair Duncan, who has written books on both art deco and art nouveau, described the sense of relief many felt when interest in art nouveau dissipated, noting that many considered it "a grave and mercifully brief transgression against good taste" (Duncan 1984, p. 102). The reign of art nouveau was not long, some twenty-five years split before and after the turn of the twentieth century.

Sources

Aubry, Françoise and Jos Vandenbreeden (1996). *Horta: Art Nouveau to Modernism*. Ghent: Ludion.

Barillari, Diana (1996). *Istanbul 1900: Art-Nouveau Architecture and Interiors*. New York: Rizzoli.

Borsi, Franco and Paolo Portoghesi (1996). *Victor Horta*. Braine-l'Allend: J.M. Collet.

Curtis, William (1982). *Modern Architecture since 1900*. London: Phaidon.

Curtis, William (1996). *Modern Architecture since 1900*. New York: Wiley.

Dernie, David and Alastair Carew-Cox (2018). *Victor Horta: The Architect of Art Nouveau*. London: Thames and Hudson.

Duncan, Alastair (1982). *Art Nouveau Furniture*. Minneapolis: University of Minnesota Press.

Duncan, Alastair (1984). *Art Nouveau Furniture*. New York: Clarkson N. Potter.

García Bryce, José (1973). *Art Nouveau en Lima: Galería del Banco Continental*. Lima: La Galería.

Hitchcock, Henry-Russell (1963). *Architecture: Nineteenth and Twentieth Centuries*. Baltimore: Penguin.

Jullian, Philippe (1974). *The Triumph of Art Nouveau: Paris Exhibition 1900*. London: Phaidon.

Permanyer, Lluís (1999). *Barcelona Art Nouveau*. New York: Rizzoli.

Puttemans, Pierre (1974). *Architecture Moderne en Belgique*. Brussels: Marc Vokaer.

Quaranta, Domenico (2006). "Art Nouveau and the Parisian Crucible of the Avant-gardes/Paris 1900–1910," from *Art of the Twentieth Century: 1900–1919*. Milan: Skira.

Robinson, Michael and Rosalind Ormiston (2023). *Art Nouveau: Posters, Illustration and Fine Art*. London: Flame Tree Illustrated.

Sembach, Klaus-Jürgen (1989). *Henry Van De Velde*. New York: Rizzoli.

Shimomura, Junichi (1992). *Art Nouveau Architecture: Residential Masterpieces 1892–1911*. San Francisco: Cadence Books.

Wittlich, Petr and Petra Key (2020). *Art Nouveau Prague*. Prague: Karolinum Press.

Discussion and Review Questions

1. What are the general characteristics of art nouveau?

2. How were art nouveau works modern?

3. Art nouveau is often described as a decorative style. Why?

4. What are some of the regional variations of art nouveau?

5. What were some of the favored flora and fauna used by art nouveau artists?

6. How is art nouveau a repudiation of Victorian design?

7. Who was the American designer whose work is closely related to art nouveau?

8. Who were the Belgian art nouveau designers? Who were the major French art nouveau designers?

9. How did art nouveau artists respond to technology?

Protomodernism

20

1897–1935	1917–1932	1914–1935	1868–1928	1867–1959
Vienna Secession	De Stijl	Russian Constructivism	Charles Rennie Mackintosh	Frank Lloyd Wright

Modernism had many roots, causes, and influences. What binds the various projects in this chapter together is that they aesthetically straddle the nineteenth and twentieth centuries. These transitional projects contain the seeds of modernism. That is, some of these works are predictive of the modernism to come, but it is a mistake to view their forms as introductory exercises, for the ongoing popularity of Hoffmann, Klimt, and Wright suggests that these designers, artists, and architects achieved something significant in their works, a new sensibility and timelessness. Equally important is their shared belief that decorative motifs are carriers of meaning and not necessarily antithetical to artistic expression. In the correct hands, decoration did not mask meaning but enhanced it. Equally important for their popularity is that it was not necessary to be an enlightened member of the **avant-garde** to appreciate their works. "Avant-garde" refers to any group of artists who are experimental or unorthodox. In the case of the early modernists, it means those who experimented with forms and ideas—and their clients—before they were widely accepted.

These are the artists, architects, and painters whose projects gave rise to modernism. Yet to label these merely transitional works would be a mistake, as this group includes some real masterpieces, all discussed below, including the Palais Stoclet, the Postparkasse, and the Glasgow School of Art.

Figure 20.0
(*Facing page*)
Charles Rennie
Mackintosh
and Margaret
Macdonald
Mackintosh,
House for an Art
Lover, Glasgow,
Scotland,
designed 1901,
built 1989.

The works of the Vienna Secession movement are the most formally predictive of the modernism to come. For such a diverse cast of characters, it is surprising that when citing their influences, the artists of the Secession mention time and time again the writings of Arts and Crafts theorists Morris and Ruskin.

Vienna Secession

The design revolution known as the Vienna Secession came about in a period in which there were significant achievements in many fields, including art history, psychology, and philosophy. In many respects, the works of Sigmund Freud, Alois Riegl, and Ludwig Wittgenstein provide the intellectual context in which the aesthetically oriented **Secessionists** thrived.

"Secession" is the noun of the verb "to secede, to leave." It has an aggressive and negative connotation. In art, it refers to a group of artists who withdrew from an academic institution or artistic movement. Members of the artistic community were fed up with Victorian historicism, an eclectic synthesis of styles. Secession groups sprouted up all over Europe, the most important ones in Berlin, Munich, and Vienna. In Vienna, the Secession movement comprised nineteen artists who favored an experimental approach in the arts. The Vienna group included Klimt, Hoffmann, Olbrich, and Kolomon Moser. They favored developing new forms that related to modern life with no ties to traditional design or historic styles.

Riegl (1858–1905) is an important art historian, responsible for establishing the modern parameters of the discipline. Even though he lived only five years in the twentieth century, his thought places him more in the camp of the twentieth century than in the nineteenth. Riegl believed that an artist's individual works are part of a historical development. When stylistic changes occur within that development, they are not, according to Riegl, a response to outside pressures. Rather, Riegl's writings stress that what is important when looking at art is the internal urgency, dynamics, and formal ordering of a movement or period. In architecture, this means that buildings should be self-contained entities. The term associated with Riegl's line of thought is **Kunstwollen**, usually translated as will-to-form, or artistic volition.

Philosopher Ludwig Wittgenstein (1889–1951) was a young man in Vienna when the Secessionists were at their height. He published his only book, the *Tractatus*, in 1922. His thought, a repudiation of traditional philosophy, is one of the beginnings of the twentieth-century push to understand cultural phenomena in terms of language and linguistics. There is no one-to-one correlation between his philosophy and Secessionist design, but he was an integral part of the art world.

Of those active in the arts, the writings of two, Otto Wagner and Adolf Loos, were most significant in defining the ethos of their era. With his theory of architecture, Wagner was the intellectual father of the Secessionist group. He represented a consensus—most of the Secessionists were looking for a modern (and Austrian) national style that was also appropriate for the masses. Loos espoused a provocative theory of culture and design, discussed below, that was extreme in its pronouncements.

For those active in the arts, there were two poles, one the decorative Secessionist pole, represented by three institutions, and the other the austere dogmatism of Loos. Three institutions provided the infrastructure that supported the Secessionists: the Kunstgewerbeschule (School of Arts and Crafts), the Vienna Secession, and the **Wiener Werkstätte**. The prominence of the School of Arts and Crafts underscores the Secessionist support for **Gesamtkunstwerk**, or unity of the arts. A core belief of this approach to the arts is that household objects were worthy of design attention. The Vienna Secession literally was an exhibition building, and the public face of their philosophy. The Wiener Werkstätte was a commercial organization allied with the Secessionists. These three entities supported the Secessionists in their desire to prompt a regeneration of the arts.

The Secession Building: An exhibition hall

The Secessionists were idealistic, sometimes to the extreme. The artistic positions that the Secessionists tried to maintain were sometimes tenuous. Their reasons for protesting against historicism are clear, but understanding their antipathy toward art nouveau is tricky. Historicism, for them, meant the grand nineteenth-century buildings of the **Ringstrasse**, Vienna's major urban design that relied heavily on historical revival architecture. The project was Austria's answer to Haussmann's refashioning of Paris, which similarly provided modern civic infrastructure (roads, sewers, and lights) in traditional garb.

With encouragement from Klimt, Olbrich received the commission to design the Secession Building, a work that established Olbrich as a major force in Austrian design and a progressive architect (Figure 20.1). The Secession Building was an exhibition building; one of the complaints of the artists had been a lack of exposure through exhibitions. The city of Vienna donated the site. The building, solemn but festive, relies upon simple forms and is a prime example of a proto-modern building. The Secession Building acted as a built design manifesto. The phrase "Ver Sacrum" (The Rite of Spring), emblazoned on its façade, was a clear call for a new approach. "Ver Sacrum" was also the name of the monthly design journal that the Secessionists published from 1898 to 1903. On the building, gilded leaves cover an open dome; the use of vegetal motifs is something that the Secessionists shared with Arts and Crafts, art nouveau, and Prairie style.

The Secession Building was formed from pure geometries: it had glistening white walls, and several flat planes that were turned over to artists for decoration. The signature building of the movement, it was home to art exhibits for years. Celebratory and exuberant, its cornices hint of classicism.

The Wiener Werkstätte, the Viennese workshops, was a commercial confederation that existed from 1903 to 1932. The Werkstätte was a business proposition, seeking to find commissions for those associated with the Secession movement. A cooperative group of painters, sculptors, architects, and designers sought to counter the aesthetic devaluation that they saw everywhere. Part of the Secessionist creed was that everyday objects were worthy of consideration by artists as aesthetic objects. They felt that art could touch, revive, and improve all aspects of life. This line of thinking combines the worlds of high art and daily

Figure 20.1
Josef Maria Olbrich, Secession Building, Vienna, Austria, 1897–1898.

life and is clearly based on the writings of William
Morris. The cooperative believed in simplicity,
and good design for the masses. The workshops
functioned as a guild with the practical virtue of
putting artists in touch with clients.

Joseph Maria Olbrich (1867–1908) had a
career that lasted only a decade, but while
professionally active he was an ardent contributor
to the antihistoricist movement. An accomplished artist as well as an architect, he worked
for Otto Wagner. At first, Olbrich's works display
the influence of the Jugendstil designs that were
becoming popular. He was on friendly terms
with Josef Hoffmann, Gustav Klimt, and Kolomon
Moser, his cofounder of the anti-academic
Secession. One of Olbrich's most prominent
commissions involved designing a number of
houses at the Mathildenhöhe artists' colony in
Darmstadt, Germany.

Unity of the arts

Sometimes there are epochs in which art and
architecture appear as if in tandem—neoclassicism comes to mind. The paintings by the
neoclassical artist David are perfectly in concert
with the buildings of the neoclassical architect
Leo von Klenze. With the Secessionists, there is a
connection between visual artists and designers,
yet it is less obvious. Members of both disciplines
were concerned with the same issues. Yet the
paintings of Gustav Klimt, the most well-known
painter associated with the movement, are visual
expressions that are emotional, psychological, and
sexual.

Gustav Klimt (1862–1918) came from a
humble background and became an accomplished
academic painter. He was first a leading figure in
Austrian Jugendstil. He was the first president of
the Vienna Secession movement, founded in 1897.
He studied in Vienna and did interior decorations for several buildings. His foreign influences
include the English artist Aubrey Beardsley. The
imprint of many historical styles is evident in his
work, specifically Mycenaean, Byzantine, and
Egyptian, and recent artistic movements, including impressionism, realism, and abstraction.

Klimt felt that architectural decorations,
such as mosaics and friezes, constituted a highly
valued art form and his paintings were often
part of an ensemble. He designed a frieze with
mosaics for the dining room of the Palais Stoclet
in Brussels. With his *in situ* projects, he demonstrated the publicly stated Secessionist support for
a symbiosis between art and design. (As a point
of contrast, while Renaissance artists painted

panels destined to decorate cassoni, they did not
consider cabinetmakers their equals.)

He supported himself mostly as a portraitist. His
paintings of Adele Bloch-Bauer came from a period
in which he used gold encrustation. As Beardsley
used black ink to dramatic effect, Klimt used gold.
His paintings reveal his experience as a designer
of jewelry and textiles. Spare lines form his figures,
often contrasted by richly patterned robes, and
Klimt himself was fond of wearing caftans. Klimt's
over-the-top decoration presents another aspect
of Secessionist style, one explanation of which is
Freudian psychology—and Freud was from Vienna.

Klimt's paintings have more to do with the
subconscious than questions of how to make twentieth-century buildings. The tectonic explorations of
Olbrich and Hoffmann do little to prepare one for the
visual profusion of decorative themes that dominate
Klimt's paintings. *The Kiss* (1907–1908), includes
enamel, gold inlay, and colored glass (Figure 20.2).
For a painting that reveals relatively little flesh, it
is surprisingly erotic. Were his paintings sexist?
By all accounts, Klimt was a womanizer. He never
married. His frank portrayal of nudes was shocking
to many, and his works are often explicitly sexual.

Artists are often controversial figures with both
supporters and detractors. While some saw Klimt
as the hope of a new age, others saw his paintings
as scandalous images. To many he was an early
modernist; to others he was an example of fin-de-siè-
cle decadence. Rumors about his private life were
abundant and included uncountable girlfriends, ille-
gitimate children, and syphilis. This affirmed some

Figure 20.2
Gustav Klimt, *The Kiss*, 1907.

people's suspicions that his paintings, despite their technical virtuosity and gorgeous surfaces, were a harbinger of the breakdown of the moral order in the waning days of the Hapsburg Empire.

The Secessionist group started to splinter, and Klimt and a group of painters left because of their desire to support the linkages between art and commerce. Although the Secession Building survived, the 1930s and the rise of the Nazis in Austria put an end to the movement as a force for positive change. Klimt is one of the major twentieth-century modern painters. Although he was a rebellious figure, his paintings met with strong public approval.

Otto Wagner

Otto Wagner (1841–1918) was an architect, urban planner, designer, teacher, and writer. A key figure in the development of twentieth-century modernism, his career lasted for over half a century. He studied at the Bauakademie in Berlin, where he admired Schinkel's buildings. He explored the integration of decoration with underlying forms and considered these in relationship to programmatic function. He worked with Olbrich on an ambitious unified urban transportation system, completed in 1901. This involved local train stations, entrances and exits, and bridges

and viaducts. One of Wagner and Obrich's most impressive designs is the entrance to Karlsplatz Station. The projects of urban infrastructure were made of iron, stone, and brickwork.

Wagner disseminated his thoughts about modern architecture as a teacher and a writer. He taught at the Akademie der Bildenden Künste in Vienna. In 1895, he published a book titled *Moderne Architektur* in which he makes clear his disdain for the division of architecture into styles. A subsequent publication, *Baukunst unserer Zeit* (1914), reinforced his commitment to reforming design.

The Postsparkasse, or Post Office Savings Bank, Vienna, 1904, is made of glass and aluminum and is one of the monuments of the early modern movement (Figure 20.3). John Pile calls its banking hall the first truly modern interior. The Post Office Savings Bank resembles a church with a double-height central nave, complete with clerestory, and side aisles. Unlike Paxton's Crystal Palace (mentioned in Chapter 15), which combined technology with Victorian detailing, Wagner's banking hall was a frank, straightforward solution to a program.

Some of the public institution's monumentality derives from its symmetry. Wagner took a form the public was familiar with, train sheds, and applied it to another equally important public institution. The use of glass in the Savings Bank

Figure 20.3
Otto Wagner, Post Office Savings Bank, Vienna, Austria, 1904–1906.

is a literal comment about financial transparency. The floor is made of translucent glass bricks. Restrained decoration enlivens the floor.

Wagner was not formally a member of the Secession. He thought design should display an understanding of purpose and good choices in materials. Materials should be available, workable, durable, and economical. This would result in good, simple detailing. For Wagner, the form that arises from following these principles would be pleasing and understandable.

There is an industrial and engineering side to his work, not always evident in the designs of the Secessionists. Even when he worked with wood—for example, his chairs—his work has an industrial aesthetic. Bolt heads, in his architecture and in his furniture, are visible.

Josef Hoffmann

Josef Hoffmann (1870–1956), another Austrian architect and designer, enjoyed a career that spanned fifty years. His long life allowed him to realize a potential that escaped Olbrich. Hoffmann is one of the most important furniture and interior designers of the twentieth century.

He started studying in Brno, worked in Würzburg, and then studied again in Vienna,

under Wagner. He was a fan of English Arts and Crafts, and admired the work of Charles Rennie Mackintosh. While in Wagner's office, Hoffmann joined the newly founded Vienna Secession. He became a professor at the Kunstgewerbeschule. A multitalented designer, his creations include furniture, jewelry, dresses, book bindings, posters, textiles, and wallpapers. The year 1900 saw a dramatic shift in Hoffmann's work: he moved away from the curvilinear forms that make some early Secessionist pieces nearly indistinguishable from art nouveau, and his work became restrained and sober. Among his many successes in this period were the Puckersdorf Sanatorium of 1903–1906 and the Fledermaus Cabaret of 1908. The Fledermaus table and chairs set became a staple of café design worldwide.

The Palais Stoclet in Brussels, Belgium (1905–1911), with its sumptuous interiors, is a highlight in Hoffmann's career. Adolphe Stoclet was a Belgian financier who had seen Hoffmann's work in Vienna. A wealthy and sophisticated art collector, Stoclet commissioned Hoffmann to build him a house. It has a stunning sequence of public rooms, including a dining room with mosaics by Klimt (Figure 20.4). For the Palais Stoclet,

Figure 20.4
Josef Hoffmann and Gustav Klimt, Palais Stoclet, Brussels, Belgium, 1905–1911. Dining room.

Hoffmann specified the furniture, carpets, fittings, lamps, tableware, and linens. Many of the furnishings were made by Hoffmann and his colleagues at the Werkstätte. The building proves that those working within the Vienna Secessionist style were capable of producing an exclusive and cosmopolitan house. The Palais Stoclet was formal, informal, sophisticated, and modern. One of the most significant residential interiors projects of the twentieth century, it appealed to an international audience of those in the know.

Hoffmann's early work relied on the clarity of classical composition. The Palais Stoclet is a forward-looking design whose music room particularly anticipates art deco. Planes, in Hoffmann's designs, are not just the result of volumes and forms, but flat entities that delimit a two-dimensional space that can and should be emphasized. The exterior relies on gilt bronze moldings to frame and emphasize the square masses. The most important rooms protrude and thereby express themselves in the façades and the overall volume. Hoffmann's design process, from the inside out, lent the house its notable asymmetrical massing.

He made the cube and the square the trademark of his design. Hoffmann liked drawing on graph paper. He explored rectilinear ordering

Figure 20.6
Josef Hoffmann, Sitzmachine armchairs, 1908.

systems, and he was interested in the possibilities presented by permutations of simple forms, particularly squares (Figure 20.5). The square was a favored motif for him, and he used it to great effect in fabrics, carpets, and furniture. One of Hoffmann's significant institutional projects was the Puckersdorf Sanatorium. An armchair from the project was called "Sitzmachine," or "Sitting Machine" (Figure 20.6). It was later mass-produced.

Hoffmann's works often show an understated interest in classical composition. He was in tune with artistic advances, aware of **De Stijl** and Le Corbusier, whose designs he promoted. He was most interested in design and visual treatment, and less interested in structural innovations. For Hoffmann, the process of artistic creativity was important (in contrast to Loos, discussed next).

He was influenced by the writings of John Ruskin, William Morris, and Otto Wagner. Although the Second World War put an end to his career, many of Hoffmann's textiles and furniture pieces remain in production.

Adolf Loos

If Olbrich, Hoffmann, Klimt, and Wagner constitute one strand of early Viennese modernism, an opposing force is represented by the formidable figure of Adolf Loos. Loos (1870–1933) was an Austrian architect and theorist. As a theorist, his writings had a lasting impact few designers

Figure 20.5
Balcony, Austria, early twentieth century.

achieve. A fierce critic of the Secessionist movement, he instead promoted the functionalist
approach. He was argumentative and one of
the most important figures of the early modern
movement. **Functionalism** is a design method
in which the overriding concern is the building,
or object, in use. It is generally associated with
European modernists of the 1920s and 1930s.

Loos came to his pragmatic design philosophy
from the family profession. His father worked as a
mason, and Loos was certified to work as a bricklayer. He studied in Brünn (now Brno), Reichenberg,
and Vienna. In 1893, he traveled to Chicago where
he visited the Columbian Exposition. During his
three years in the United States, he visited New
York, Philadelphia, and St. Louis.

For the American Bar in Vienna's Kärntner
passageway, done in 1908, Loos favored rich
materials (Figure 20.7), reddish-brown coralwood,
translucent yellow onyx panels, and leather
(Bock 2007, p. 45). The bar has a coffered ceiling
of veined marble. It also uses electric lights and
mirrors to expand the space, but the mirrors start
above the level of eye sight, so patrons cannot see
their personal reflections. He usually paneled his
rooms up to the dado level. This small, cozy bar
had a clublike elegance.

Figure 20.7
Adolf Loos,
American Bar,
Vienna, Austria,
1908.

Loos designed few pieces of furniture. He was
usually happy to specify simple pieces designed by
others; he was fond of Thonet's bentwood chairs.
Part of a general project to redecorate a Viennese
apartment in 1900, he designed a bedroom armoire
for Gustav Turnowsky. Loos admired the frame-
and-panel system because, he noted, centuries of
use had perfected the form (Gravagnuolo 1982, p.
99). Loos opposed decoration and also the idea of
a personal intuitive style, anything approaching
kitsch, or that which could not be rationalized. He
strongly expressed his opinions in a lecture that
was later widely published. In "Ornament and
Crime" he equates the superfluous use of decoration with a lower state of human development. In
her *Dictionary of Art* (1996) entry on Loos, Yehuda
Safran states that Loos first presented his materials in a talk in 1910, which he then published in
1913 (Safran 1996, p. 652).

The furniture and interiors of Loos often
emphasized comfort and leaned more in the
direction of decoration than did his austere architecture; such is the case with his Knieschwimmer
upholstered armchair (Figure 20.8).

Adolf Loos fought for truth in design and
sought that which was genuine. He was against
the prestigious buildings on the Ringstrasse. Loos
was an adversary of Hoffmann and Van de Velde,
the latter because Loos disapproved of the fact
that he designed women's clothes to match his
interiors—taking the idea of Gesamtkunstwerk
too far, to Loos's mind. In contrast to the
Secessionists, Loos opposed the idea of style. He
limited his own design activity. He promoted the
idea that designs should look anonymous and that
design should be reserved. For the bedroom Loos
designed for his wife, the closets were concealed,
and he specified white fur for the flooring material.

During Loos's stay in Paris, he designed a
house for the American entertainer Josephine
Baker. Loos's house for Baker provides a
restrained backdrop for a spectacular person
(Figure 20.9). He believed that house exteriors
should be discreet and the functions of interior
spaces should dictate a building's exterior form.
Modernists believed that the internal and the
exterior manifestation became out of whack in
the nineteenth century. The alternating black
and white marble bands obliquely refer to African
decorative motifs.

The entry sequence of Loos's Baker House is
important. The rectangle in the upper portion of
the exploded axonometric is a swimming pool with
underwater windows. Surrounded by a walkway,
Baker could swim while her guests gazed at her
body, shimmering in the water like an exotic fish.

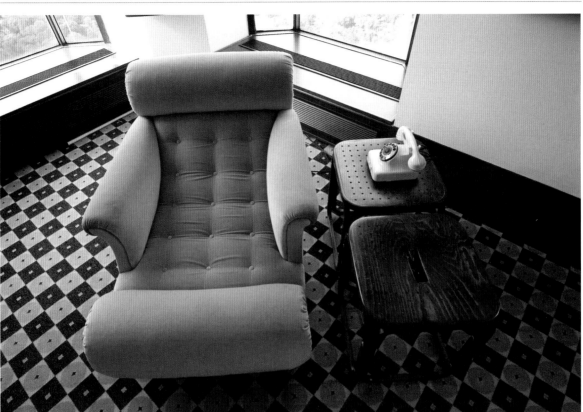

Figure 20.8
Adolf Loos,
Knieschwimmer
upholstered
armchair, Vienna,
Austria, 1906. In
Ronald Lauder's
office.

Figure 20.9
Adolf Loos, Josephine Baker House, Paris, France, 1927. Unbuilt.

It is no surprise that Loos was critical of art nouveau. That he was a severe critic of the Vienna Secessionists requires explanation. This seems odd as, especially in his early works such as the American Bar, his projects bear a strong resemblance to Secessionist works. He loathed the projects of Klimt, Hoffmann, and Olbrich. He sought beauty in form, not ornament. His buildings and interiors display a sense of rectangular control. The sense of control resulted from a design process that subordinated creativity to function.

Despite his impassioned rhetoric, he did sometimes use a restricted, stripped-down classicism. In full command of a simplified aesthetic, his buildings anticipated Bauhaus designs by nearly a decade.

De Stijl

The argument over the role of ornament was sidestepped by proponents of De Stijl and **Russian Constructivism**. The approach of the designers of these two movements had no real place for ornament. "De Stijl" literally means "the Style" in Dutch. It was a movement of avant-garde Dutch artists, designers, architects, urban designers, graphic artists, industrial designers, musicians, and writers. It was also the name of a periodical founded by Theo van Doesburg in 1917. Across disciplinary divides, De Stijl artists explored their fascination with elementary components—circles, triangles, and squares; primary colors; and flat surfaces. They sought to reduce compositions to horizontal and vertical lines. In many respects, this movement was related to, and aware of, **Expressionism**, **cubism**, **futurism**, and **Dada**. The major artist of the period was Piet Mondrian; the major architect and designer was Gerrit Rietveld (1888–1964).

Rietveld's output as an architect was limited. His masterpiece was the Schroeder House. It took the ideas of his Red and Blue chair of 1919 in a three-dimensional direction. With its cleans lines and reliance on primary colors, it was the embodiment of the movement's artistic ideals. More of a polemical statement than a work to be copied, it nonetheless remains one of the major modern monuments of the twentieth century.

Russian Constructivism

Postrevolutionary Russia was a work in progress in all respects, so while the new social, political, and economic system was loosely related to architectural modernism, there was no easy correlation. The 1920s is an interlude—after the Revolution but before the rise of Joseph Stalin's totalitarian regime. What would the architecture be that represented a dramatic break with the past? During this hopeful period, several highly experimental forms of modernism briefly thrived. Significant achievements occurred in graphics, posters, flyers, and pamphlets. Built buildings were few.

Vladimir Tatlin (1885–1953) started out as a painter and attended the Moscow School of Painting, Sculpture, and Architecture. Initially he painted icons, displaying his skill with Russian traditional painting techniques. He worked for a while as a stage designer. He grew increasingly aware of the avant-garde developments of Western European art. Influenced by the October

Revolution of 1917; he joined the cadre of architects who sought to express the spirit of the revolution in architecture. Tatlin's Monument to the Third International, 1919–1920, was a spiral tower with technologically derived forms (Figure 20.10). The movement associated with Tatlin, Constructivism (or Russian Constructivism), involved artists who pursued a program of rational design based on functional processes, the tectonics of reinforced concrete, the possibilities of metal, and the utopian ideals appropriate to a socialist society.

Konstantin Melnikov (1890–1974) was a Russian modernist architect, mostly active in the 1920s. He built six workers' clubs in the period 1927–1929 in the Moscow area. His own house in Krivoarbatskiy Lane was built in 1927–1929 (Figure 20.11). He sought a new way of designing buildings that was to emerge from Russian traditions and Russian mysticism, rather than relying on importing Western European technologies and styles. Initially, his work was in step with the dramatic break from tsarist society to the Soviet socialist society. After a short period of time, mass taste and official doctrine meant that the officially

Figure 20.10
Vladimir Tatlin, Monument to the Third International, Petrograd, Soviet Union, 1920. Model.

Figure 20.11
Konstantin
Melnikov,
Melnikov House,
Moscow, Soviet
Union, 1929.

sanctioned Soviet architecture became a bombastic version of classicism. From 1938, Melnikov was not allowed to practice because his design aesthetic was at odds with the new Soviet realist style.

Le Corbusier built a building in Moscow, 1928–1936. The problems he had seeing his building built were a harbinger of the difficulties that modernism was to have in the Soviet Union.

Mackintosh

Charles Rennie Mackintosh (1868–1928) resists easy categorization, and in fact, Mackintosh's works are frequently found in books on Arts and Crafts, art nouveau, or even Prairie style. (Junichi Shimomura includes Mackintosh in a book on art nouveau residential architecture; Shinomura 1992.) Mackintosh's graphic work shows the connections between his work and both Arts and Crafts and art nouveau two-dimensional works. Graphics done by Mackintosh and his wife, the artist Margaret Macdonald, bear comparison to Beardsley, Klimt, and Rossetti, and blur the line

between commercial and fine art (Kaplan 1996, p. 301).

His early design work includes a series of tearooms. A later project, the Willow Tea Rooms, was in a fashionable area of Glasgow. Roger Billcliffe calls the Room de Luxe, or Ladies Room "one of the most precious interiors that Mackintosh ever designed" (1984, p. 108).

In 1897, he won a competition to design a new building for the School of Art in Glasgow. Unquestionably Mackintosh's masterwork, it is known for its façade, its details, its interiors, and its furnishings. But it is also a building superbly suited to its site, largely due to its design in section.

A pedestrian walking along Renfrew Street first notices the contrast between the massive stone framework and the broad expanses of industrial-looking glass. The system of broad windows indicates an independent invention from Horta's metal-and-glass exploration for the Maison du Peuple in Brussels. Mackintosh's façade is yet another European example of developments related to the Chicago school's exploration of frame and glass. This building is one step toward the creation of all-glass structures. The massing and the glass relate this to warehouses and factories, yet they are nowhere else designed with such care.

The aspects of the project that most resemble art nouveau are the ironwork, railings, and window details. They are loosely based on natural forms. Structurally, the masonry is compression, and the glass and ironwork are tension. This is also figuratively expressed with the contrast of the massive stone piers and the attenuated metalwork.

One of the projects in which Mackintosh collaborated with his wife, Margaret Macdonald is the House for an Art Lover (Figure 20.0). They collaborated on the interiors, the furnishings, and the graphics. It was designed in 1901, but not built until 1996. Mackintosh is one of the designers whose posthumous reputation exceeds anything he enjoyed in his lifetime. Many of his furniture designs are still in production. His designs are personal, and they also relate to contemporary developments. His Argyle chair was shown at the 1900 Vienna Secession Exhibition (Figure 20.12). It shows Mackintosh's ability to negotiate between pure geometries and the scale and shape of a seated human figure.

Figure 20.12
Charles Rennie Mackintosh, Argyle chair, Glasgow, Scotland, 1898–1899. For the Argyle Street Tearooms.

Thailand

European modernism in the first decades of the twentieth century operated in specific contexts—Paris, Vienna, Weimar, and Amsterdam. When modernism started appearing around the world, the forms functioned as a clarion call for something new and forward-looking. Due to the specifics of the political and cultural context changes were unique to each country. In Thailand, modernism was related to the monarchy and its aftermath, a royal gloss that it lacked in France and Germany.

King Rama V (1853–1910) of Thailand was an innovative leader known for his ambitious political and economic reforms. He successfully avoided the colonization attempts of England and France. The King hired a German architect, Karl Döhring, to build a palace for him. Döhring's palace, a modern structure, gestures to the future and affirmed Thailand's place as part of a global culture. So Thailand's brand of vaguely Secessionist-looking architecture derives from the German variant of it. In Vienna, the collective identity of the self-proclaimed Secessionists depended on differentiating themselves from historical styles and pitting themselves against art nouveau. This argument lost some of its currency in this corner of Southeast Asia, where modernism had a different role to play.

The King, who owned several palaces, wanted one to be in a modern European style. Where other parts of the palace incorporate baroque and Romanesque elements, and the exterior is mostly Jugendstil, a few of the most innovative rooms, such as the stairwell, are clearly moving in the direction of the Secessionist style that German architects knew because of the buildings in Darmstadt (Figure 20.13). Overall, the building is one in which modernism is not antithetical to historicism, but capable of coexisting with it. The Palace was started in 1910 and finished by the King's equally progressive son, King Rama VI (1881–1925). Thailand thwarted the imperialist policies of England and France, and when members of the royal family looked to hire European architects, they preferred Germans and Italians.

Figure 20.13
Karl Döhring, Phra
Ram Ratchaniwet,
Phetchaburi,
Thailand, 1909.
Royal palace.

Frank Lloyd Wright

Frank Lloyd Wright (1867–1959) had a long career.
He was prolific, universally acclaimed, and beloved
by the masses. Yet his impact on modernism is
curiously less than that of Le Corbusier and Mies
van der Rohe, even though their austere projects
were less likable to most. Wright is important
for two reasons: for his early contribution to
modernism and for his unique contribution to the
development of a regional, almost vernacular,
American architecture. He is a rare example of an
architect, in the top echelon of important architects, who made his career largely by designing
houses, and modest ones at that. Wright started
out his career working for Adler and Sullivan, and
for a time there was stylistic overlap in their work.
Particularly with respect to the use of ornament, his
early projects bore a similarity to Sullivan's designs.

Houses

Wright left Sullivan and established his own
office, out of his house, in the Chicago suburb of
Oak Park, in 1893. Wright's earliest commissions
show the influence of Victorian design, Arts and
Crafts, and Queen Anne. The Winslow House is at
once an inventive house by a prominent architect
and one that grows out of the vernacular traditions of American suburbia (Figure 20.14). The
Winslow House, River Forest, Illinois, is also one of
a few Wright projects that bear a resemblance to
Austrian Secessionist works.

The hipped roof is a common feature of
American houses, but Wright gives it a strong
horizontal profile, so that it reflects the horizontality of the American prairie. He does this by
cantilevering the cornice over the façade. By then
recessing the second-story windows within a
continuous dark band, he further emphasizes the
horizon. On later projects, the glazing would be

Figure 20.14
Frank Lloyd
Wright, Winslow
House, River
Forest, Illinois,
United States,
1893.

continuous, an American domestic version of Le Corbusier's ribbon window.

The front façade is symmetrical, axial, and grandly formal. A hint of the developments to come is seen in the rear elevation of the Winslow House, in which the internal features push out to the exterior. Wright, like Sullivan, sought to develop a uniquely American, if not Midwestern, type of architecture. Prairie style, in the realm of residential architecture, had a significant impact. His color palettes derived from indigenous plants.

The so-called Prairie style is typically dated from 1900 to the First World War. Unlike Arts and Crafts designers, Wright had no instinctual dislike of industry. The family is the cornerstone of American life, and this is symbolically represented in his houses with scrupulous attention to the design of the fireplace, the front door, and the dining room table. These features, in Wright's houses, become icons of the family. The single-family detached house itself became a symbol of the American family. Prairie houses were appealing to clients; appreciating them did not require that one be a member of the avant-garde.

Wright was a believer in crafting a totally designed environment, a belief akin to the Secessionist Gesamtkunstwerk, down to furniture,

custom built-ins, and stained-glass windows. Tales abound about his post-occupancy dealings with clients in which Wright visited completed jobs and set about removing pictures and rearranging furniture.

The *Wasmuth Portfolio*, a 1911 German publication, presented his work to a European audience. The European avant-garde, including Mies van der Rohe, Le Corbusier, and Walter Gropius, embraced Wright. The high-contrast black-and-white photographs of the publication made his works look more progressive than they were, as though they were cubist designs by Rietveld. Initially, European audiences knew of his work only through the medium of published photographs. This and subsequent publications, ensured Wright an international prominence that started at an early stage in his career and remained throughout the twentieth century.

Wright's later work was organic, asymmetrical, and grew out of his thinking first about interior volumes. The features that came to be known as the Prairie style are more pronounced in the Ward Willets House of 1902. The dining assemble of the Husser House, 1899, is an early version of what became a central feature of Wright's subsequent projects (Figure 20.15).

Figure 20.15
Frank Lloyd Wright, Joseph W. Husser House, Chicago, Illinois,
United States, 1899. Dining room table and chairs, armchair.

The Winslow House and the Ward Willets
House hint at what was to come; with the Robie
House, Chicago, Illinois, we see Wright in the
middle of producing his Prairie style houses and in
confidant command of his powers.

The defining characteristics of his architecture are also present in his furniture design. The
vertical lines of the chairs are formed by a series
of simple millwork slats, a detail that Arts and
Crafts designer Voysey also employed. The iconic
dining room table and chairs of the Robie House
make the dining room and its furniture, like the
centrally located hearth, a symbol of the family.
The exaggerated height of the chairs forms an
implied space in which the chairs themselves
become the boundaries of a transparent "room."
While a little unstable for an imbibing diner, the
ensemble is visually stunning and at one with its
context.

His architectural reification of the nuclear
family was perhaps a compensation for his own
failings in that direction. His marriage spectacularly fell apart and he left his wife to marry
Olgivanna Hinzenberg in 1928. He defaulted on
the mortgage of his Wisconsin home and studio,
Taliesen. Although often fraught with financial
problems himself, Wright was a capitalist, with

few of the socialist leanings of his European
counterparts.

His primary contribution to modernism is
not always visible in his interiors but is best
seen in plan. The Martin House has generous
living spaces and servants' quarters that wealthy
clients demanded. It appeared during the period
in which Wright's projects focused heavily on
ornamentation.

Cross axes dominated his more expansive
floor plans, as they do with the Martin House.
The public rooms of the interiors are formed by
interconnected but overlapping spaces. Rooms
were no longer discrete entities separated by
walls and doors but overlapping areas without
boundaries; Colin Rowe described this innovation
as "transparency" (Rowe 1978). For the Martin
House, Wright designed bookcases, tables, upholstered furniture, armchairs and sofas, lamps, rugs,
textiles, and stained-glass windows.

In 1905, Wright went to Japan. He admired
Japanese architecture and collected Japanese
prints. The decorative period includes one of
his largest works, the Imperial Hotel in Tokyo,
1912–1913, for which he also designed the furniture (Meech 2001).

The Museum of Modern Art in New York
(MoMA) invited Wright to participate in an exhibition of modern architecture in 1932 (Wojtowicz
2005). The co-curators, Henry-Russell Hitchcock
and Philip Johnson, insisted that the design of
the exhibition reflect the forward-looking tenor of
the projects. Because of the book's title, authored
by Johnson and Hitchcock, the exhibition came
to be known as "The International Style." The
exhibition, the book, and Wright's participation in
it are significant moments in the twentieth-
century exploration of new ways of designing
space. Wright exhibited a large model for an
unbuilt house, the House on the Mesa, a project
that expressed Wright's belief in the organic
expression of nature, landscape, and materials.

In Wright's oeuvre, the relationship between
house, material, and landscape achieved its ultimate expression in Falling Water, 1934–1937. This
project also illustrates that over the course of his
career, his use of glass increased.

Wright visited Rio de Janeiro in the fall of
1931. People around the world did not necessarily
copy his forms in Africa, Asia, and Latin America,
but his approach to landscape and materials
suggested a path for creating a local architecture
and not simply importing forms. His midcareer
projects display an interest in modularity and grids.

Although known as the preeminent American architect, there is a universalizing aspect to his work. Like other progressive architects of his time, he abhorred the nineteenth-century parade of historical styles, which is not to say that he was categorically opposed to all historical influences, just European ones. He occasionally incorporated elements whose inspiration lay in Aztec, Turkish, or Japanese design history.

In the 1920s, Wright started experimenting with concrete blocks for walls, floors, and ceilings on projects in California, Arizona, and Mexico. He called his use of concrete blocks the "textile-block" system. He experimented with patterns and also used steel reinforcing bars. His work with concrete blocks drew upon pre-Columbian design for inspiration.

Gradually, his work became less decorative, and he investigated the possibilities presented by permutations of simple geometries, such as triangular "grids" and round houses. This is evident in the architecture and design of Taliesen West (Figure 20.16).

Wright managed to be modern, local, and universal. He is a key but ambiguous figure in the critical debate surrounding the introduction of European modernism to the United States. Neil

Levine says that Wright worked in the European International Style yet refocused its energies and made it American. The last structure he completed during his long career affirmed him as a significant modernist, the Solomon Guggenheim Museum in New York.

Conclusion

Chapter 16 examined the reform movements; in Chapters 17 and 18, Africa and Japan faced the technological innovations of the nineteenth century; Chapter 19 presented art nouveau. Those chapters and this one, are all answers to the question, where did modernism come from? The rallying point for artists of different movements spread across the globe was their opposition to Victorian historicism, the use of styles, and what they considered to be the degraded state of design. Committed to leaving the nineteenth century behind, artists showed little consensus for how to greet the twentieth, despite more than occasional common interests and points of

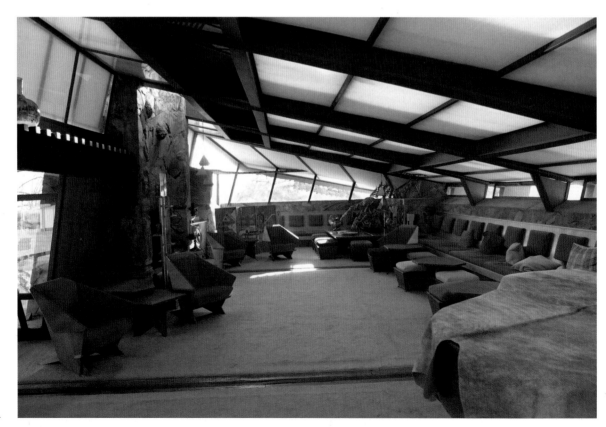

Figure 20.16
Frank Lloyd Wright, Taliesen West, Scottsdale, Arizona, United States, 1937–1959.

agreement. Designers were grappling with how to use new materials, like glass and metal, and reconsidering the relationship between decoration and form, and form and function.

With hindsight we see that modernism was percolating across Europe with movements including the Vienna Secession, De Stijl, and Russian Constructivism. In the United States, Frank Lloyd Wright had a different motive for decrying historicism; he sought to create an American architectural vocabulary. Across the globe, pockets of art nouveau flourished where the design principles had a different weight—and sometimes were less vigorously maintained. In Thailand and Turkey, an architect could combine forward-looking forms associated with both art nouveau and the Secessionists. The proliferation of forerunners to modernism was becoming a global design event.

Even within one design sphere, turn-of-the-century Vienna, there were differing opinions. Loos—the person, his writings, and his designs—were difficult, extreme, and experimental, if truthful. Hoffmann, Klimt, and their artworks, in contrast, were likable, popular, exuberant, if occasionally decadent. Relying on intuition often resulted in designs that appealed to the masses; designing for the masses often resulted in designs that attracted the elite.

The precursors to the modernists were not in lockstep. Yet it would be intellectually lazy to dismiss their collective efforts at change as irreducibly different. The grid and planes had arrived, and with them an industrial aesthetic. Buildings were designed from the inside out, which usually resulted in asymmetry. The status of ornament, history, tradition, and style were all tenuous. This chapter presented the projects, designers, and movements that straddled two centuries, yet there is no doubt that their look was to the future.

Sources

Billcliffe, Roger (1984). *Mackintosh Furniture*. Cambridge: Lutterworth Press.

Bock, Ralf (2007). *Adolf Loos: Works and Projects*. New York: Rizzoli.

Boyd, Virginia (2007). *Frank Lloyd Wright and the House Beautiful: Designing an American Way of Living*. Washington, DC: International Arts and Artists.

Carter, Brian (1998). *Johnson Wax Administration Building and Research Tower*. London: Phaidon.

Gravagnuolo, Benedetto (1982). *Adolf Loos: Theory and Works*. New York: Rizzoli.

Haste, Cate (2019). *Passionate Spirit: The Life of Alma Mahler*. New York: Basic Books.

Kaplan, Wendy, ed. (1996). *Charles Rennie Mackintosh*. New York: Abbeville.

Loos, Claire Beck ([1936] 2020). *The Private Adolf Loos*. Los Angeles: DoppelHouse.

Meech, Julia (2001). *Frank Lloyd Wright and the Art of Japan: The Architect's Other Passion*. New York: Abrams.

Pare, Richard and Jean-Louis Cohen (2007). *Lost Vanguard: Soviet Modernist Architecture, 1922–1932*. New York: Monacelli Press.

Reed, Peter, ed. (2004). *The Show to End All Shows: Frank Lloyd Wright and the Museum of Modern Art, 1940*. New York: Museum of Modern Art.

Rowe, Colin and Fred Koetter (1978). *Collage City*. Cambridge, MA: MIT Press.

Safran, Yehuda (1996). "Adolf Loos." In *The Dictionary of Art*, vol. 19, p. 652. New York: Macmillan.

Sarnitz, August (2003). *Adolf Loos, 1870–1933: Architect, Cultural Critic, Dandy*. Cologne: Taschen.

Shimomura, Junichi (1992). *Art Nouveau Architecture: Residential Masterpieces 1892–1911*. San Francisco: Cadence Books.

Thun-Hohenstein, Christoph, et al. (2020). *Women Artists of the Wiener Werkstätte*. Basel: Birkhäuser.

Topp, Leslie (2005). "Otto Wagner and the Steinhof Psychiatric Hospital: Architecture as Misunderstanding." *Art Bulletin* 87, no. 1 (March): 130–56.

Witt-Dörring, Christian, ed. (2006). *Josef Hoffmann: Interiors 1902–1913*. New York: Neue Galerie.

Wojtowicz, Robert (2005). "A Model House and a House's Model: Reexamining Frank Lloyd Wright's House on the Mesa Project." *Journal of the Society of Architectural Historians* 64, no. 4 (December): 522–51.

Discussion and Review Questions

1. How did the Vienna Secessionists formally predict modern trends?

2. How were the forerunners to modernism reacting against Victorian design?

3. In what ways did the Secessionists not live up to their own antidecorative stance?

4. What were some of the materials that the Secessionists favored, and what does this say about their art?

5. What is meant by transparency in plan?

6. What made Prairie style local? Why did people around the world admire it?

7. Loos equated the use of ornament to a lower level of societal development. Give evidence for and against this position.

8. What did the Secessionists have in common with art nouveau proponents, and how did they differ?

Heroic Modernism

21

Myths and Realities

1919–1931	1929	1938–1941	1939–1940	1939–1945
Bauhaus	Barcelona Chair	Breuer in Britain	Aalto's Finnish Pavilion	Second World War

This chapter is subtitled "Myths and Realities" because the self-proclaimed modernists were bent on creating a myth of their endeavors. They were not merely designing but purposely forging a movement. More so than the leaders of other artistic movements, modernist designers succeeded in constructing a myth, a story complete with gods, lesser gods and goddesses, and shining temples on the hill. Despite decades of scholars who have examined the premises and products of **modernism**, and debunked many of the myths (that modernist architecture was white, that it developed only in France and Germany), it is astonishing that as our knowledge of modernism as a pluralistic phenomenon grows, its status as a simplified iconic entity remains. It is almost as though the more challenges to it, the more resolute it becomes. The hold of modernism on the contemporary consciousness is so strong that the movements and submovements that followed it, such as postmodernism and deconstruction, are defined in relation to it. Many architects and designers today describe what they do in relationship to modernism.

Modernism is a slippery term, something French sociologist Bruno Latour addresses in his book *We Have Never Been Modern* (1993). Latour's paradoxical point is that people of most epochs have sought to be current. Many people confuse modern and contemporary because the words are

Figure 21.0
(*Facing page*)
Mies van der Rohe and Lilly Reich, Barcelona Pavilion, Barcelona, Spain, 1929.

335

used indiscriminately. Here, "modern" refers to the grand period of the avant-garde, associated first with Germany and France, and later other parts of the globe, of the 1920s and 1930s, and the style associated with it, leaving the word "contemporary" to refer to the current state of affairs.

Early Modernism

It often seems as though modernism arrived out of nowhere, yet with the wisdom of hindsight we see that many nineteenth-century artistic endeavors—art nouveau, the aesthetic movements, and Prairie style—were exploring specific issues that contributed to the modern movement. In addition, there was the development of skyscrapers, railroad stations, elevators, moving pictures, automobiles, and photography. While many roads led to modernism, in the early 1920s two countries, Germany and France, were particularly important, and especially the individual contributions of three men: Walter Gropius (1883–1969), Mies van der Rohe (1886–1969), and Le Corbusier (1887–1965).

Modernism is a term used by many professions, although their views of modernism are not the same. When considering modernism in art, music, literature, dance, and theater, certain similarities bridge the disciplinary divides. Proponents of modernism shared several premises, most important the break with the past and the embrace of the present and future. The machine was a source of aesthetic inspiration, taking the central place once held by nature. *Functionalism* was a term used in many professions to describe the new way of designing.

Most of the modernists presented themselves and their work as a break from the past, and in many respects this was true. They were openly critical of designs that incorporated historic references. An attitude that united the modernist designers was the belief that nineteenth-century Victorian designers, distracted by the battle of styles, had it wrong. George Kates, a collector of Chinese furniture, is one of those who, writing about his experiences in the 1930s, made clear that he was no less than contemptuous of "the general level of taste in our stupid nineteenth century" (Kates 1952).

A corollary to rejecting the past was embracing the present and looking toward the future. Largely because of technological innovations, the modernists felt that the twentieth century was uniquely different from other time periods and required a new approach to design. Interior design historian John Pile writes: "The most important development in early twentieth-century design was the emergence of a design vocabulary appropriate to the modern world of advanced technology and the new patterns of life" (2000, p. 323). Modernism was finally an expression of interior design, architecture, and furniture design that embraced the achievements of the previous century's Industrial Revolution.

The Bauhaus

The **Bauhaus** is a building, and it was a design school, a movement, a revolution to some, and, arguably, a style. From their base in Dessau, Germany, students and instructors created works that are virtually synonymous with classical modernism. In 1911, the architect Walter Gropius had achieved great success with his innovative design for the Fagus Shoe Factory in Alfeld an der Leine, Germany. Gropius was fresh from working in the Berlin office of Peter Behrens where, astonishingly, for a brief period in 1910 his coworkers included Charles Edouard Jeanneret, later known as Le Corbusier, and Mies van der Rohe.

The famed city of Weimar, home to Goethe, Schiller, Nietzsche, and Liszt, had two schools related to the arts, a school of fine art and a school of applied art. When Gropius became director, he merged them and bestowed upon the single entity the name "Staatliches Bauhaus," thus indicating the close relationship between art and craft. Simply referred to as "the Bauhaus," the name signaled Gropius's intention to take the school in a new direction, and with it the future of architecture and design. The mantra of the school was to espouse all the principles we now know as modernism, and Gropius and his colleagues had specific pedagogic methods in mind for how an academic institution could achieve them.

In 1925, the Bauhaus relocated to Dessau, Germany. For that propitious move, Gropius designed several buildings, including, most famously, the Bauhaus (Figure 21.1). Since the time of Gothic cathedrals, architects have sought to create what seemed impossible: a wall of glass. Glass is not a structural material; it can barely support its own weight, and the slightest tensile force causes it to shatter. One of the significant modern achievements is the separation of structure from wall, which has several implications. With the signature building of the Bauhaus, the glass sheathing surrounding the design studios is effectively hung from the floor slabs; hence the term "curtain wall." This is the technology that rendered skyscraper façades, or "skins," possible. It also signified new spatial developments on the interior, which was no longer a suite of individual rooms but an open-plan space flooded with natural light. An added benefit is that the Bauhaus building positively glows at night.

Those working inside the Bauhaus forged a new approach to design pedagogy, as well as promoting modern design. Its educational philosophy was an alternative to the Beaux-Arts approach. The Bauhaus curriculum was interdisciplinary and considered the knowledge of craftwork essential to being a designer. It was egalitarian in theory, with a large number of women and foreign students. It promoted functionalism, which was a code word for modernism. The trajectory of a student's education included a year of general instruction, followed by hands-on experience in a workshop, with a final project.

The interdisciplinarity of the Bauhaus exhibited itself over the years in a variety of specializations. Many workshops devoted to one discipline were taught by artists and professionals who practiced in another. The areas of specialization included architecture, town planning, interior design, furniture design, advertising, exhibition design, stage design, photography, film, dance, textiles, fashion, and the creation of objects in wood, metal, or ceramics. The roster of teachers recruited by Gropius included Paul Klee, Wassily Kandinsky, Josef Albers, László Moholy-Nagy, and Marcel Breuer. Another central tenet of the Bauhaus was that designers, if properly trained, knew how to design in an abstract sense and, with the correct outlook, could design anything. They could put their talents to use on objects of any scale and type, including such diverse objects as cigarette packages, buses, and bus stops.

Walter Gropius and Marcel Breuer

Gropius designed a suite of furniture for the Feder department stores in 1927, an important year for the modern movement. Gropius's furniture designs are important in the history of office furniture because of their materials, method of fabrication and installation, design, and function. The pieces were made of plastic laminate, metal

Figure 21.1
Walter Gropius, Bauhaus, Dessau, Germany, 1925–1926.

tubing, and plywood—all straightforward materials. Because of their modularity and standardized parts, they could be prefabricated and manufactured on an assembly line, which eased their eventual installation. Their rectilinear design was straightforward, there were no superfluous details, and they responded to the need for storage and the actual process of working in an office.

Gropius was responsible for the Masters' Houses on the Bauhaus campus, three semi-detached dwellings that housed Bauhaus faculty. Bauhaus student Marcel Breuer worked on the interiors and furniture designs (Figure 21.2). Breuer later taught at the Bauhaus.

Mies van der Rohe and Lilly Reich

In 1927, Mies, who would be the final director of the Bauhaus, oversaw a project that was a who's who of European modernist architects, the Weissenhofsiedlung in Stuttgart (Joedicke 1990). Mies was responsible for the site plan and one of the buildings of the combination building exhibition and housing project. Other buildings were done by Le Corbusier, Mart Stam, and Walter

Gropius. Mies hired a young designer, Lilly Reich, to oversee the exhibition halls in Stuttgart. Lilly Reich was born in Berlin in 1885. Mies was born in Aachen in 1886 and had moved to Berlin in 1905. After working for Behrens he became vice president of the **Deutscher Werkbund**, a showcase for German design in Frankfurt.

Reich assumed command of the artistic direction of the exhibition halls of the Weissenhofsiedlung, and she personally designed the clean, modern layouts. Reich's career involved a variety of design activities, including store windows, exhibition displays, and fashion design. A talented designer, her contributions have only recently achieved attention, decades after her death. Prior to meeting Mies, Reich had directed the exhibitions at the Werkbund. The entire period of Mies's involvement with furniture is coincident with his personal relationship with Lilly Reich, approximately 1924–1927 (McQuaid 1996).

Gropius resigned as director of the Bauhaus in 1928 and Hannes Meyer took his place, a tenure fraught with tension. In 1930, Mies became director, a position he held until the Nazis shuttered the Bauhaus.

During the time of the van der Rohe/Reich collaborations, Mies designed and completed a sumptuous villa in Brno, Czechoslovakia. One of the most important innovations of the modern movement figured into the house's design: the separation of building from structure. In a view of the dining area of van der Rohe's Tugendhat House (1929), columns stand separate from a curved wooden partition that is crisp and thin (Figure 21.3). The building's structural elements are different entities from those that define spatial regions. The semicircle provides an elegant backdrop for dinner, a modern and open rendition of a formal dining room. Curves are not normally associated with Mies's work, but he occasionally uses them to great effect. The shiny X-shaped stainless-steel columns support the flat plane of the roof. The simple sled-based cantilevered chairs, used as dining chairs, came to be known as Brno chairs. They proved extremely successful in post-Second World War office buildings. The furniture included two types of armchairs, the luxurious big Tugendhat chairs and the Barcelona chair (Figure 21.4).

The jewel of Mies's early efforts came in 1928 when he received, on short notice, the commission to design the German Pavilion at the International Exhibition at Barcelona, commonly known as the Barcelona Pavilion (Figure 21.0). Other parts of the exhibition featured cavernous

Figure 21.2
Walter Gropius and Marcel Breuer, Moholy-Nagy/Feinenger Haus, Dessau, Germany, 1925–1926. Desk set.

Figure 21.3
Mies van der
Rohe and Lilly
Reich, Villa
Tugendhat, Brno,
Czech Republic,
1929–1930.

Figure 21.4
Mies van der Rohe and Lilly Reich, Barcelona chair, Barcelona,
Spain, 1929.

halls that contained all sorts of items on display, including furniture, some by Reich, some by Mies, and some collaborations. The Barcelona Pavilion, the highlight of their design efforts, was practically designed overnight and served a specific purpose. A modest-size pavilion, its function was to provide the setting for an inaugural ceremony with the Spanish king and queen, Alfonso XII and Victoria Eugénie, to sign their names in a golden book.

In the Barcelona Pavilion, X-shaped columns similar to those of the Tugendhat house support the flat roof. A series of vertical planes slip and slide, denoting the various areas where separate functions were to take place. With a clear debt to Frank Lloyd Wright, there are no individual rooms but a series of spaces that are transparent and overlap.

Mies, more so than anyone, employed luxurious materials in his designs, as evidenced by the Barcelona Pavilion, in which expensive wood, marble, and white leather dominate. The initial building was a temporary structure for an exhibition; it was rebuilt in 1986 at great expense. Le Corbusier criticized the use of luxurious materials in his publication on decoration.

The pavilion featured two copies of a chair designed for the opening ceremony: the Barcelona chair. It is therefore no less than a modest version of a royal throne. The matching ottoman was also influential, as the detailing of its legs became the basis for a bench and a coffee table (Glaeser 1977, p. 12). One of the most successful chairs of all time, the Barcelona chair had a particularly grand debut. The chair and the building whose name it bears are milestones of twentieth-century design. The deceptively simple piece of furniture is made of stainless-steel bar-stock, with horsehair cushions covered in pigskin and delineated with welts and buttons.

The original chairs were chrome-plated. Mies came to prefer using stainless steel, as the chrome plating tended to flake. An exquisite piece, it was not initially meant for mass production nor to be particularly comfortable. The original cushions were made out of white kid leather and fastened with straps and buckles. The Barcelona chair came after a period in which Mies and Reich developed a series of utilitarian chairs made of tubular metal. In the nuanced vocabulary of modern furniture, bar-stock is a more elite material than tubing.

The Barcelona chair was designed in 1928 and has been in continuous production since then. George Nelson, an accomplished postwar furniture designer, included Mies's Barcelona chair in his publication of 1953. He wrote: "The chair, like all of his buildings and furniture, has been designed with the most painstaking attention to detail and demands perfect execution" (Nelson 1953, p. 133). The signature work of Mies and Reich, the Barcelona line is successful because of its creators' unwavering attention to detail and quality. Nelson also notes that the Barcelona chair is "One of the most costly pieces in production, it has no substitute where the height of elegance is the aim of the interior designer" (p. 133).

The Barcelona chair looks reasonably comfortable, with its raked back, and has pleasing lines. It sits close to the ground, yet it is really not meant for relaxing. It is well suited for the use it usually finds itself in—in the lobbies of contemporary apartment buildings and waiting rooms of corporations.

In the 1930s, after the Barcelona Pavilion and chair, Mies did studies for several chaise longue designs, although they were never built. For the Villa Tugendhat he designed a chair that is similar to the Barcelona chair, although it is slightly larger and more comfortable (Blaser 1982, pp. 66–72). The Tugendhat chair (1930) seems

an improvement over the Barcelona chair, yet it ultimately proved less successful. Several variations of another successful Mies/Reich design, the MR chair, exist, with and without arms, and with a variety of seating materials (Figure 21.5). Steel tubing is not used in a minimalist way but to form elegant curves that are just short of being extravagant. It is another example of the artistic and commercial success of the furniture that resulted from the collaboration of Mies and Reich.

Women and German modernism

The year 1931 saw Mies and Reich collaborate in the Berlin Building Exhibition, which more or less marks the end of his involvement in furniture. Gunta Stölzl (1897–1983), a former student, had been director of the Bauhaus weaving workshop, and the creator, throughout her long career, of many successful textile designs, but she left in 1931 for Switzerland. In 1932, Mies hired Lilly Reich to teach at the Bauhaus in Dessau, taking over for Stölzl as director of its weaving and interiors workshops.

The appointments of first Stölzl and then Reich as directors of a workshop highlight the prominence of women in the modern movement, and specifically at the Bauhaus, as both students and instructors. Although in theory the Bauhaus did not treat women differently, revealing the school's aims for social equality, they tended to

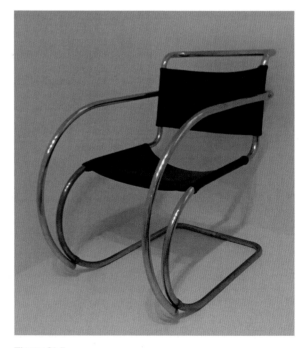

Figure 21.5
Mies van der Rohe and Lilly Reich, MR chair, Stuttgart, Germany, 1927.

specialize in "women's crafts," textiles, furniture, ceramics, and industrial design. The 1920s in the United States saw the rise of women as professional decorators. In the same period in Germany, women associated with the Bauhaus made serious inroads toward equality in the design world.

Reich's design for an exhibit promoting German textiles is indicative of the simple layouts she created for a variety of exhibition halls, known for their clarity and straightforward organization.

The word most often connected to the early designs of the avant-garde was *functionalism*. This is the word the modernist designers used to describe their work. Their works did not constitute a style, they constantly stressed, but were simple expressions of a logical and rational approach to design. The Frankfurt kitchen is a case of a professional female designer employing her talents on a project to help the plight of women homemakers. A central tenet of the Bauhaus philosophy is that well-trained designers could apply their talents to any task. Grete Schütte-Lihotzky's Frankfurt kitchen is incredibly complex, designed down to the level of detail of where to store salt (Figure 21.6). It had a tremendous impact. It impressed many with its hygienic and efficient appearance.

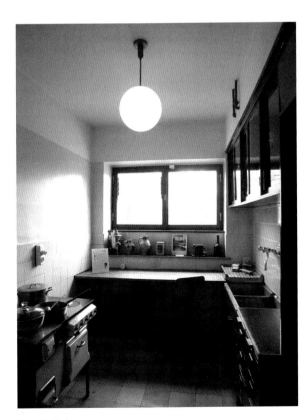

Figure 21.6
Grete Schütte-Lihotzky, Frankfurt Kitchen, Frankfurt am-Main, Germany, 1926.

Occasionally, there were conflicting attitudes toward design and method of creation among the Bauhaus leaders. One example involves the faculty and their approach to craftsmanship. They officially espoused an anti-elitist position and respected the knowledge of those who crafted objects and were familiar with construction techniques. The division of the school into workshops underscores the belief that knowledge of design could only grow out of the experience of making things.

The Weimar Bauhaus had a metal workshop, and students produced a variety of cooking and serving pieces, pots and pans, coffee and tea services, and household items such as electrical lamps. Exhibiting the influence of the cubist movement on their designs, most products stayed as close to pure geometries as possible, departing only for functional reasons. The most talented student in the workshop was Marianne Brandt, who excelled at making light fixtures. Brandt stayed with the workshop in its move to Dessau, eventually becoming its director. The metal workshop reflected a gradual shift in the school's allegiance to craftsmanship, a shift encouraged by Gropius. To extol the virtues of craft is one thing; to put it into practice is another, especially for a school and a movement committed to industrial production. Bauhaus instructors were ideologically committed to a machine aesthetic, and many of their writings express antipathy for what they saw as the retrograde Arts and Crafts movement. An uneasy truce was realized by a shift in their philosophy. Bauhaus students and teachers were to create models, crafted by hand, that were destined for industrial assembly line production. Brandt excelled under these guidelines; many of her metal and glass lamps were mass-produced, and some still are.

Marianne Brandt's deceptively simple design for ceiling fixtures and table lamps are some of the many examples of Bauhaus-designed products that have become ubiquitous (Figure 21.7).

Graphics, theater, dance, and film

The debate over the role of craftsmanship, meaning work by human hands, and industrial production, meaning work by machine, also occurred when considering the construction of buildings. Even though buildings such as the Villa Tugendhat displayed a machine aesthetic, smooth lines, alternating shiny and honed materials, and planar surfaces, the method of construction remained, as it always had been, accomplished by

Figure 21.7
Marianne Brandt,
Lamp, Leipzig,
East Germany,
1951. Based on a
design by Brandt,
1930s.

graphic designs, including paintings. In his graphics he often used vertical type, and a contrast of horizontal and vertical that creates a visual flow on the diagonal.

In the Bauhaus tradition of exhibiting competency in several artistic realms, Oscar Schlemmer (1883–1943), polymath to the core, is credited as a painter, sculptor, teacher, choreographer, costume designer, and dancer (Gropius 1960). He taught the introductory course in design at the Bauhaus.

Considering the hard edges and pure forms of Bauhaus buildings, interiors, and furnishings, it is not immediately apparent how that approach would resonate with artists, such as Schlemmer, whose primary subject was the human figure. In Schlemmer's metal sculptures, one sees the connection between his work and that of other cubist artists. Schlemmer reduced the human anatomy to basic forms, and he then formed the human figure as a series of connected geometric shapes. This is evident in his most famous painting, "Bauhaus Stairway" (Figure 21.8).

Cubism as an artistic movement predated the Bauhaus designers. Colin Rowe, among others, feels that the modernist impulse appeared in

hand. Mies himself had worked as a bricklayer, a skill he was always proud to demonstrate.

The Bauhaus revolution touched all areas of the arts, including painting, graphics, photography, furniture design, and collages. The modern era that was being forged in the Bauhaus workshops required an adequate graphic representation and found it under the leadership of Moholy-Nagy. In his workshop, students worked in a variety of graphic activities, including wood blocks, lithographs, and typography, a department that would today be considered graphic design and advertising. Moholy-Nagy and others were interested in developing a modern typeface (Kostelanetz 1970, p. 77).

Moholy-Nagy arrived at the Bauhaus in 1923. His work was informed by his knowledge of the work of El Lissitzky, Man Ray, and De Stijl artists Rietveld, Mondrian, and van Doesburg. He believed that the photograph would eventually triumph over painting (Staatliches Bauhaus Weimar 1923, p. 141). He sought to improve the visual effectiveness of graphic layouts, relying on simplicity, legibility, and also a dynamic placement of text and image. He created a multitude of

Figure 21.8
Oskar Schlemmer, Bauhaus stairway, 1932.

art before it did in architecture, especially in the paintings of Ozenfant, Le Corbusier, Juan Gris, and Pablo Picasso.

Schlemmer was anxious to carry his novel approach to the human figure to the world of theater, in which he was also active. He conceived and choreographed a ballet, *The Triadic Ballet*, for which he created innovative costumes. The French phrase *"success d'estime"* is perfect to describe Schlemmer's ballets that, by all accounts, were more interesting than entertaining. The Bauhaus performances explored Schlemmer's unusual approach to the human figure, an approach opposite the direction of portraiture: there is a disavowal of any features in the direction of particularity or sentiment; he was neither interested in a naturalistic portrayal of the body in displaying any anecdote, narrative, or emotion, nor in overtly pleasing a viewer of an artwork or a member of the audience. His works explore movement, color, the relationship of the human body to pure geometries, and the position of geometries in three-dimensional space. His sculpture is similar to the costumes he developed for the ballet. Howard Dearstyne, one of the few American Bauhaus students, saw the mechanical ballet and commented:

I encountered something new when I saw Schlemmer's players on the stage. From one to three persons participated. No word was spoken, no story suggested by sign or gesture, no human emotion communicated to the audience. It was unrelated to any drama I had enjoyed in New York City. The performances consisted solely of bodily movements synchronized with music, a form of dance. The movements were abrupt, staccato, angular—more like mobile geometry than fluid arabesques. The performers appeared only remotely human, as did the mannequins in Schlemmer's paintings.

(Dearstyne 1986, pp. 174–75)

Schlemmer's interest in mechanical-looking movements and figures, and his mixture of puppets, marionettes, and heavily costumed human figures, all worked together to deemphasize the flesh of the humans.

Bauhaus furniture

Marcel Breuer (1902–1981), born in Hungary, taught at the Bauhaus in the 1920s and eventually became the head of the school's cabinetmaking shop. He expressed an interest in crafting modern furniture from the start (Hyman 2001). In Breuer's postwar career, his most famous commission was the UNESCO building in Paris. Less well-known as an architect than Mies and Gropius, he was extremely productive and successful with his furniture designs.

Many of the early modernists sought the holy grail of modern furniture design: to make the first modern inexpensive chair out of tubular metal. Mart Stam (1899–1986), a Dutch architect who moved to Berlin in the 1920s, is credited with designing the first cantilevered steel tubular chair, a milestone in furniture design. Stam married Lotte Beese, a former Bauhaus student. His chair attracted the attention of Mies van der Rohe and Marcel Breuer, who followed suit by adopting Stam's ideas in their own designs. This simple idea achieved its most elegant and financially successful iteration with Marcel Breuer's Cesca chair of 1925 (Wilk 1981). The same year he produced his Wassily chair, an ideological statement about the relationship between geometry and furniture (Figure 21.9).

In the 1930s, due to growing pressure and interference from the Nazis, Breuer relocated to London. There, he created several pieces of furniture for the Isokon Company, one of the early producers of modern design in the United Kingdom. His work in London is known for expanding the initially limited palette of modernist building materials. He designed a building that incorporated large expanses of roughly cut stone. His Long Chair was one of many experiments with plywood. Breuer's stay in England was short-lived, and he soon ended up in the United States.

In 1933, the Bauhaus closed.

A position that several designers took up—notably Charlotte Perriand (1903–1999), Le Corbusier, Mies van der Rohe, and Alvar Aalto—was an appreciation of types, the idea that certain industries had produced exquisite examples of design (possibly unknowingly), and that the role of the designer was to pick them out and use them, or, in other words, to be an industrial connoisseur. Sinks, radiators, and Thonet chairs fall into this category.

Michael Thonet (1796–1871) started a company that produced a broad line of products, yet it is famous for two: a bentwood rocking chair and an inexpensive café chair. The firm, Gebrüder Thonet, was successful with their innovative method of bending wood with steam. Millions of their inexpensive chairs were sold, and they

Figure 21.9
Marcel Breuer,
Wassily chair,
1925. Tubular
steel with chrome,
cowhide.

are still seen in restaurants and coffeehouses around the world. Reich used Thonet chairs in the Weissenhofsiedlung project.

Franco Modernism

Outside of Germany and Holland, the other major center of early modernist design activity was France. Le Corbusier dominated the scene, although, the so-called School of Paris was diverse in its members and their work.

Le Corbusier

Born in Switzerland, he headed to Berlin and worked for Peter Behrens in 1910 and 1911. In 1917, Le Corbusier decamped to Paris and set up an office with his cousin, Pierre Jeanneret (1896–1967).

At an exhibition of decorative arts in Paris in 1925, Le Corbusier presented his vision for the domestic interior with his furnished Esprit Nouveau Pavilion. The prototype for a residence was a modular design in several respects. It

featured modular storage units and standard pieces of furniture (Marcus 2000). Using pieces that were typical, cheap, and obvious, it was possible to craft a comfortable and sophisticated interior that was an emancipation from Victorian design. The design centers on a double-height living space, a strategy that Le Corbusier used to great effect later in the Unité d'Habitation, Marseilles, his solution for large-scale public housing. (Curiously, although the Unité became the paradigm for public housing worldwide, it was a privately owned building.) The unit was also an exploration of modularity on a larger scale, because it was his intention that it could be repeated to constitute an entire apartment building. Cubist art decorated the walls in both projects. The Esprit Nouveau Pavilion was a prototype, the Unité a realized housing project based on it. While multiple versions appeared, a common element was a built-in storage unit that acted as a space divider.

Le Corbusier was not fond of the term "decorative art," because "decorative art can no longer be considered compatible with the framework of contemporary thought" (Le Corbusier 1925, p. 115). Although he felt that the word "design" was too broad, he preferred it, as it validated the modernist insistence on functionalism: "It seems to incorporate all the theory of rationalism: the use of new techniques, weightlessness combined with solidity, the juxtaposition of different kinds of materials, and above all the concept of maximum functionalism" (De Fusco 1977, p. 36).

The project Le Corbusier designed for his friend, the artist Amédée Ozenfant, also prominently features a double-height space. It includes many details that came to be associated with Le Corbusier and modernism itself. It incorporates ribbon windows, curved ramps and stairways, metal railings, Thonet chairs, and a corner made of glass. In traditional architecture, corners are structurally important because they hold up the roof. So to have glass meet glass at a corner (Frank Lloyd Wright was fond of this) is a bravura move, to proclaim that the rules have changed.

Charlotte Perriand and furniture

Charlotte Perriand, an associate of Le Corbusier, was born in Paris and studied at the École de l'Union Centrale des Art Décoratifs. After having finished her studies, she contributed to the Salon d'Automne of 1927 (McLeod 2003, p. 15). She intended her project, *le bar sous le toit*, to garner attention and it did (Perriand 2003, p. 13). The dining room of her small apartment on the Place Saint-Sulpice featured many of the elements

that she was later known for (Figure 21.10). Le Corbusier and his coworkers were impressed, and Perriand started working in his office; Perriand worked for him from 1927 to 1937. Hired to concentrate on the studio's furniture design and production, she was responsible for their interiors work and promoting their designs in a series of prominent exhibitions (Musée des Arts Décoratifs 1985, p. 18).

Le Corbusier was already a major force in architecture, having published widely, although his greatest commissions were still to come. When he met Perriand, he was smarting from not receiving the commission for his innovative League of Nations Project (Perriand 2003, p. 55). While working for Le Corbusier, Perriand organized showing their furniture designs at the Salons d'Automne of 1928 and 1929. Perriand's design emphasizes the horizontal, with a modular storage unit on the right literally reflecting the ribbon window on the left. Lounge seating, a chaise longue, and arm chairs from the Le Corbusier/Perriand/Jeanneret collaboration furnish the space.

Perriand and Le Corbusier were well aware of Thonet's bentwood chairs, and their chaise is reminiscent of Thonet's rocking chair of 1860. They frequently used Thonet chairs in their projects, such as the Salvation Army hostel, the Swiss Pavilion resident hall at the Cité Universitaire in Paris, the Esprit Nouveau Pavilion,

Figure 21.10
Charlotte Perriand, dining area with fauteuil pivotant, 1927–1933. Manufactured by Thonet.

and Ozenfant's Studio. Many of the pieces designed by Le Corbusier and Perriand shown at the salons were subsequently produced by Thonet. They collaborated with the Swiss architect Alfred Roth in Stuttgart, and their furnished model apartment contained the Corbusier bed that was in fact designed by Roth (Figure 21.11).

Their lounge chair made its debut at the Salon d'Automne of 1928 (Figure 21.12). It has double tubing at the sides and an integral prolongation of the chaise acts as the footrest. Despite its formal similarity to Thonet's bentwood rocker, the chaise longue is not a rocking chair. The position is decided upon by the sitter before climbing aboard; once sat upon, it remains in a fixed position.

While working together on the chaise, they agonized over the base, eventually deciding on lacquered sheet metal, inspired by products in an aviation catalog. While not intentional, the legs resemble horse hooves. Perriand tracked down pony skin and calfskin from Parisian furriers. The chaise longue, with its use of pony skin, evokes the modernist interest in "the primitive." This is parallel to Picasso's interest in African art, as exemplified by his painting *Les Demoiselles*

d'Avignon. Their use of animal hides suggests a desire to find simple materials, a search for the vestigial.

Perriand reiterated Le Corbusier's three-pronged philosophy about furniture, thereby indicating her total agreement with it: a modern furniture piece should strive to be a "standard unit"; it should act as an artificial limb; and it should embrace new technology. Le Corbusier and Perriand reveled in finding common manufactured objects, such as radiators, sinks, and telephones, that they considered "standard units" in which industrial processes responded perfectly to human needs. Le Corbusier and Perriand sought to do the same for the human activities of sitting and reclining, creating pieces that operated in a clearly logical and functional way.

Another consistent design goal of their furniture is "that household objects can be regarded as artificial limbs, or decorative art turned orthopedic" (De Fusco 1977, p. 36). In her memoirs, Charlotte Perriand wrote: "While our chair designs were directly related to the position of the human body … they were also determined by the requirements of architecture, setting, and prestige" (2003,

Figure 21.11
Le Corbusier, Charlotte Perriand, and Alfred Roth, Weissenhofsiedlung, Haus Le Corbusier, Stuttgart, Germany, 1927.

Figure 21.12
Charlotte
Perriand, Pierre
Jeanneret, and Le
Corbusier, chaise
longue, 1928.
Tubular metal and
pony skin.

p. 29). With the chaise they were successful. When viewed in profile, it copies the form of the human body, with its round cushion taking the place of the human head. Many have noted that it acts as an armature not only of the body but of the mind. It seems perfectly suited to serve as a Freudian couch, something on many people's minds in those days.

By its appearance, the chaise seems to operate in a functional mode and eschew decoration. Made of tubular metal, it has no extraneous decoration but its decorative aspects, as they may be, derive from and are contiguous with the structure.

Of the many women active in the early days of modernism, our knowledge of Charlotte Perriand's contribution is precise, because her relationship with Le Corbusier was strictly professional, so history is not complicated by the specter of love and marriage. Her career garnered considerable attention later in life when she was able to document her work. Perriand published her memoirs in 1998 (and published them in English in 2003). Unlike the uncertainty that surrounds the contributions of Lilly Reich (and Aino Aalto), Perriand's role is clear: "I worked with Pierre Jeanneret at the atelier on full-scale designs during the day, fine tuning them with Corbu in the evenings" (Perriand 2003, p. 30).

The Le Corbusier/Jeanneret/Perriand chaise longue was not initially successful. Because of its formal severity, for years it was one of the least popular pieces of contemporary design. Germany and France were, initially, the leaders of modernism, and it is curious how the biography of Charlotte Perriand repeats many of the details of the life of Lilly Reich. A woman is born in a European metropolis, studies decorative arts, and forms an alliance with a talented member of the avant-garde who hails from elsewhere. The primary difference is that Reich and Mies were intimately involved, whereas the relationship between Perriand and Le Corbusier was strictly professional.

Le Corbusier and Perriand's chair, the Gran Confort chair, is a frame of steel tubing filled with several removable leather-upholstered cushions. It also came in a two-seater and was one of their most successful designs.

Pierre Jeanneret

In 1950, Indian prime minister hired Le Corbusier to design a new capital for the Punjab, Chandigarh. Le Corbusier's cousin Pierre Jeanneret relocated to India where he stayed until his death in 1967. He oversaw Le Corbusier's projects, and embarked on collaborative work at scales large and small with Indian architects, developers, and designers. Multiple furniture designs stem from this period, taking the modern aesthetic into the world of Indian teak, rosewood, and caning (Figure 21.13).

Housing

Le Corbusier's Maison Domino diagram relates to his interiors work and his urban design (Figure 21.14). Often compared to the Abbé Laugier's eighteenth-century primitive hut, it reduces a building to its barest elements. Colin Rowe, ever the jokester, compared it to a club sandwich complete with toothpicks; he more seriously added that "by returning to origins and first principles, we recover purity" (1994, pp. 56–7). This minimal icon of building-as-shelter consists of the structural support of columns, the horizontal planes of the floor slabs, and the stair that vertically connects them. The implication is that space-defining pieces, conspicuously absent, constitute a fourth element. So the architectural features that define space are not structurally operative. This diagram is significant for the development of the modern field of corporate interior design, for essentially what interior designers do when designing a space for a company in a skyscraper is work within the column grid and between the floor slabs, an activity predicted by the Maison Domino.

Although the modernist era was influential for interiors, furnishings, and kitchens, the key modernist figures, in their writings, reserved their most persuasive and fervent language for urban design. An area of concern was social improvement of societal ills and the belief that modern architecture could solve serious urban problems. The modern movement had a significant impact on the global landscape at the urban scale. Many of the modernist impulses—the rupture from tradition, the idealistic utopianism, the pragmatic desire to solve problems, a fetishization of the machine—were mixed up with a naïve but sincere desire to do good on a large scale. This led to a series of planning developments and social engineering initiatives that changed forever the look of cities across the globe.

Urban planners and architects of the 1920s were grappling with the legacy of the nineteenth-century Industrial Revolution and its impact on cities. Cities were crowded, dark, and smelly. Regarding infrastructure, the challenges were enormous. Cities designed for horse-drawn

Figure 21.13
Pierre Jeanneret, furniture set, Chandigarh, India, 1955. Teak and cane.

Figure 21.14
Le Corbusier, Maison Domino, 1914–1915.

carriages had to be revamped for planes, trains, and automobiles.

Le Corbusier submitted a series of drawings of his urban proposals, a Contemporary City (Ville Contemporaine), at the Salon d'Automne in Paris in 1922. It was the first in a series of urban design proposals that he worked on throughout his career. A pencil drawing shows an al fresco dining area, with Le Corbusier's proposal dominating the background. It is a dramatic alternative to the historic urban center. The crux of the proposal is a series of twenty-four skyscrapers in a park; this combination was to replace the dense urban fabric of most world cities. By lifting the buildings up on **pilotis**, the verdant ground-plane continued unencumbered, under and through apartment block and office alike. Pilotis are cylindrical columns or piers, but the word was essentially appropriated by Le Corbusier to refer to his projects.

These towers in the park were configured to maximize light and air. The lack of air and light in crowded urban centers had been a big problem for cities. This is an architectural move that, decades later, would be decried for being anti-street, as the buildings no longer line, and therefore define, the street. No traditional streets figure in Le Corbusier's urban design, in the sense of shops lining a street, separated by sidewalks filled with sauntering pedestrians. This building type was influential for the planning of public housing (which exploded in the postwar period) and hospitals, apartments, and universities, especially dormitories.

The Contemporary City proposal addresses infrastructure problems by placing automobiles on one level and airplanes on another. In the sketch, an airplane lingers in the sky, a surprisingly benign element; it languidly hangs there, like a gentle firefly, a little out of place but not really a menace.

All is seen from the perspective of an outdoor dining terrace whose diners have just briefly fled the scene. The departed left their glasses and a water carafe. This being a project for public housing, best not to show wine bottles, a favored motif for Le Corbusier elsewhere. The only historical references are provided by the furniture on the terrace, simple metal chairs and tables.

The challenges facing urban centers before the Second World War were different from those they would face after the war. The scourge of abandoned urban centers had not yet arrived. The plans for the Contemporary City show another feature of the new way to design cities: to have them grow linearly instead of concentrically. The new city plans developed for Abuja, Nigeria, and Brasília, Brazil, were designed with an eye to Le Corbusier's urban vision.

In 1925, Le Corbusier proposed just such a plan for Paris, his Ville Voisin, which proposed to replace block after block of Paris's historic center with an immense field of skyscrapers in the park, a direct result of his Ville Contemporaine. William Curtis writes: "Instead of the grimy industrial city, a brave new world of light, greenery, air, cleanliness, and efficiency was to arise" (1996, p. 247). Architects of the modern period were particularly interested in housing, with the belief that they could provide comfort, shelter, education, and empowerment through new democratic cultures and mechanization processes that were not available in traditional societies.

Mechanical lyricism

Historian of modernism Kenneth Frampton referred to Eileen Gray's work as possessing a "mechanical lyricism" (Frampton in Riley 1990, p. 15). Expanding the term's usage, it can also refer to other modernist designers whose works do not easily fit into the category of canonical modernism.

Eileen Gray

Eileen Gray (1878–1976) was an architect, interior designer, and furniture designer, several of whose pieces have entered the pantheon of modern furniture classics. Of Scottish and Irish heritage, she saw the Universal Exhibition in Paris in 1900, a visual experience that prompted her to move to Paris in 1902. In 1907, she started learning painstaking finishing techniques from Japanese lacquer artist Seizo Sugawara, a collaboration that lasted forty years. A friend of Gertrude Stein and Natalie Clifford Barney, with fashionably short hair, and dressed in coats and dresses by fashion designer Paul Poiret, she struck a cutting figure on the Parisian scene.

She worked from her apartment and sold her furniture designs from a trendy decorator's shop that she held on to until the 1970s (Constant 2000). Eileen Gray's work presents the opportunity to see what happens when a female decorator takes the reins of modernism. In 1919, she designed apartment interiors for the milliner Suzanne Talbot. The Talbot apartment was unofficially a showroom for Gray, for the client, and for modernism itself. At this early date, it was by no means a foregone conclusion that modernism would prevail, that it would not become an intriguing item on the sidelines of design, like Egyptian Revival.

Gray had to be aware that modern architecture was largely a male-dominated profession, so her projects seem intent on proving her commitment to modernism. The Talbot apartment is unabashedly modern, with white walls, a gridded glass floor, and frameless pivot doors with invisible hardware (Baudot 1998). Gray's own armchair, the Bibendum, is formed from three leather tubes; some ninety years later, it still looks futuristic. The project leaves no doubt that Gray was a committed member of the avant-garde.

But she was also a decorator who catered to wealthy, sophisticated clients. Her project operated successfully within the visual idiom of an elite, in-the-know clientele. The Talbot apartment achieves its glamorous air largely through the materials Gray selected: lacquer, leather, and fur. But if the project was really going to be successful, it had to do more, and this is where things get interesting. Part of the allure of the fashion industry, of which both Talbot and Gray, in different capacities, were a part, was to play upon people's values, to tap into the notions that they hold dear. But at the very top rung of the design professions, the strategy is to slightly shift the comfort level of the consumers, to make them covet items they did not know existed. Gray's Talbot apartment does this brilliantly with its series of African objects, obscure yet erudite items, which were the epitome of taste.

Pointing out the obvious, Talbot's apartment is hardly an ethnographic study of African art and, in fact, part of how it functions, in the middle of Paris, is by decontextualizing the pieces, setting them within a readily understandable context. There is nothing frightening or demanding about the design. It features a very convincing African-looking throne by Pierre Legrain (1889–1929) that

looks as though it could be pulled up to a dressing table. Many modernists played this game. The exotic objects or materials add a quality of texture, pattern, and mood to a room that would otherwise be too stark, too white, and too plain.

Gray's fondness for black lacquer was coincident with the current rage for "otherness." This manifested itself in the popularity of African artworks, and especially the popularity of African American singer Josephine Baker in Paris. Baker had herself photographed, her hair slick and her skin glowing, deliberately looking like an art deco object. Le Corbusier wrote that "it is an excellent thing to keep an element of the savage alive in us" (1925, p. 85). Philip Johnson had a boyfriend in Harlem, jazz was everywhere, and the fondness for polished black surfaces was something that modernist designers co-opted from art deco.

Gray's architectural projects were few, but one of them, her own house at Roquebrune, was built on the Mediterranean in the period 1926–1929. She lived in the house known as E-1027 for several years with Jean Badovici (1893–1956), a Romanian architect with whom she had a six-year collaboration.

It is now considered one of the landmarks of the modern movement, as are many pieces of furniture she designed for it (Figure 21.15). While her work for Talbot was appropriately luxurious for a fashion designer, her own home was comparatively simple and restrained.

Pierre Chareau

Pierre Chareau is another of the French modernists who had a limited architectural career. His modest body of work is so exquisite that his reputation has grown posthumously, largely due to a single project: his remodeling of a doctor's house and office.

Born in 1883, Pierre Chareau first worked as a furniture maker, and his subsequent professional activity doing interiors for elite clients shows in the attention to detail that is a hallmark of his projects. His most famous project, the Maison de Verre (House of Glass), is a remodeling of an eighteenth-century hotel (Figure 21.16). Commissioned in the 1920s, it is a doctor's office and residential apartment; an existing residential apartment, untouched by Chareau, sits on top. A double-height grand salon is the dominant space. It is a place dedicated to art, with a piano and beautifully designed bookcases along with a rolling ladder made of steel and wood. The face

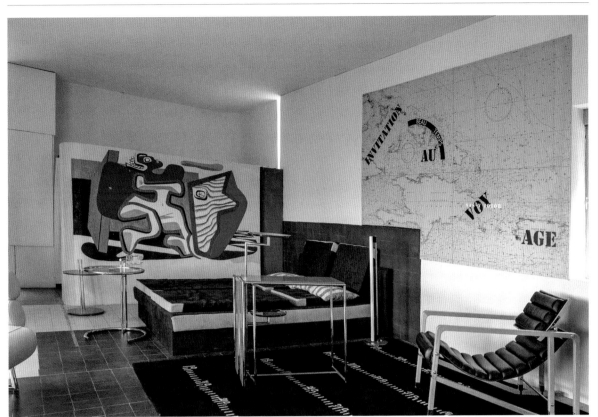

Figure 21.15
Eileen Gray,
E-1027,
Roquebrune-Cap-
Martin, France,
1926–1927.
With tables
and Transillat
armchair.

Figure 21.16
Pierre Chareau, Maison de Verre, Paris, France, 1932.

the apartment presents to the courtyard is a giant glass block façade that lets in diffused light during the day. Shiny brass-framed windows illuminate the rooms at the rear of the house. The residence features a juxtaposition of scales, the dramatic double-height space offset with a single-story dining room and bedrooms. Ironworker Louis Dalbet collaborated with Chareau on perforated metal screens that rotate and provide privacy.

Likened to a finely crafted piece of furniture or musical instrument, the house has been called a gorgeous machine. Its lyricism represents a different strain of French modernism. The Maison de Verre always seemed an alternative to rigid modernism. Critic Nicolai Ouroussoff refers to the Maison de Verre as "the high point of classical Modernism" (2007, p. 1). Chareau's contemporary and friend Paul Nelson wrote: "This house approaches Surrealist sculpture. The pivoting door suspended in front of the metal staircase is a Surrealist sculpture of absolute beauty" (Riley 1990, p. 12).

The furnishings from the interior show the confident hand of Chareau. They, like the house, are simultaneously delicate and robust. With broad expanses of metal, ridiculously delicate metal rods, smooth edges and woods the effect is one of contemporary warmth.

The talented Chareau was not destined for a long career. He fled France when the Nazis arrived, and he died in the United States, in 1950, in New York, with little money earned from his scant commissions.

Emilio Terry, Salvador Dalí, and surrealism

Emilio Terry (1890–1969), a Cuban who emigrated to Paris, is included here to purposely upset the apple cart and to underscore that not all modernists followed a strict formula. Surrealist painter Salvador Dalí admired Terry's work and painted Terry with a house model in the background. Terry's "maison en colimaçon," or Spiral House of 1933, is a proposal for a house that follows the curves of a seashell (Figure 21.17). Terry made the model of cardboard and painted wood. In an age when the major designers were singing the praises of the machine, both as inspiration and as a means of manufacture, Terry was making a gesture to nature, a provocative move to publicly differentiate his approach to design from that of other designers. Terry's work is related to Dada and **surrealism**. The other provocation evident in Terry's work is simply the fact that the house's form represents anything at all. Hard-core functionalists were disinclined to express narrative and subject. Form was to result from a functionalist design process and not be chosen from the outset.

Nordic Modernism

In looking at the furniture designs from the prewar careers of Mies van der Rohe, Le Corbusier, and Alvar Aalto, it is astonishing that so many

Figure 21.17
Emilio Terry,
Spiral House,
1933.

similarities in the historical circumstances led to their creation, some significant, some merely oddly coincidental. For all three men, despite long careers, their greatest successes with furniture came early, not late. All three overtly expressed an admiration for the work of Michael Thonet. When considering the furniture of Le Corbusier, Mies van der Rohe, and Alvar Aalto, one runs into three women: Charlotte Perriand, Lilly Reich, and Aino Aalto. These women played crucial and parallel roles in collaborating with them on interiors and furniture design. A comment made about Aino Aalto is typical; one source claims that Alvar Aalto often named her as his codesigner even when she was not, and that she was more of a critic than an architect.

Alvar Aalto

Alvar Aalto (1898–1976) represents another strand of modernism, one related to his geographical location, Scandinavia; his favored materials, wood and stone; and to his general approach, which can be considered the softer side of modernism.

He shared many of the central beliefs of the modernists and kept himself abreast of their developments. He visited their buildings, attended their exhibitions, and collected their furniture. He similarly saw the modern movement as a break from the past and saw the importance of responding to the present and thinking about the future. He wrote regularly about functionalism, and several of his projects have a distinctly utopian thrust. His approach to hygiene was wrapped up in providing adequate air and light, and ease of maintenance. Where he follows a different path is that he was less obsessed with furthering a machine aesthetic, and his projects relate to nature and their locality in a way that others do not, stances that render his version of modernism more palatable to a wider public. His works avoided the opprobrium that Gropius and Mies and Le Corbusier sometimes garnered.

Purists scoff at the term "Scandinavian design," which smacks of commercialism and IKEA, but admittedly Aalto's work avoided being labeled as cold and austere. Aalto's modernism distinguished itself because he "left the barebones of doctrinaire functionalism behind him" (Shand in Museum of Finnish Architecture 1985, p. 72). The popularization of Aalto's approach is a feature of Scandinavian design, which lacks the subtlety and depth of Aalto's works but nonetheless owes something to him for providing a broadly appealing brand of modernism.

Scandinavia was ripe for modernism because of the pioneering work of people such as Erik Gunnar Asplund. And Aalto was not alone; another early modernist was Arne Jacobsen, whose staggered low-rise Bellavista housing complex near Copenhagen in 1934 was an early example of modernism. Jacobsen was to go on to become an accomplished designer of furniture, industrial arts, interiors, and architecture.

Alvar Aalto and Aino Aalto, interiors and furniture

Alvar Aalto started making furniture in 1919 when he started doing interiors projects. Prior to his success as an architect, he and his wife Aino (1894–1949) enjoyed a lengthy career as furniture designers. Their earlier furniture designs were inspired by historical styles, including the German iteration of art nouveau (Jugendstil), Vienna Secession, and several neoclassical traditions, including Biedermeier. Several of the historical styles they brought to life are clearly influenced by American versions of European furniture pieces, such as their simplified Windsor chairs. These early Aaltos' chairs have a complicated genealogy: they are streamlined Scandinavian versions of American translations of the English eighteenth-century classic. Igor Herler refers to Aalto's early work as "light classicism," an apt term. The Aaltos applied their modernist aesthetic across the historic styles, simplifying line and form and minimizing decoration. Thomas Kellein, who wrote a book about their furniture designs, notes that "prior to 1929 Aalto's furniture was anything but modernist" (2005, p. 13).

Aino and Alvar Aalto married in 1924 and moved to Turku, Finland's Baltic port. The circumstances that led to the development of the Aaltos' modernist aesthetic have been well documented and include their travels, which focused on attending modernist conferences and exhibitions. They took a trip in 1928 to Holland and France, and another in 1929 to attend the Congrès International d'Architecture Moderne (CIAM) in Germany. They looked at avant-garde buildings and cultivated professional relationships and friendships with like-minded progressive designers. They collected modern furniture pieces themselves, such as Breuer's Cesca and Wassily chairs. Their travels, their friendships, and the pieces they collected were all activities that consolidated their commitment to modernism.

After collaborating with his wife on a variety of interiors projects and furniture designs, Aalto established his modernist credentials in 1929 with a six-story office block for a newspaper company, the Turun Sanomat in Turku, Finland, his first large-scale modern building. With its ribbon windows, tapered pilotis, white walls, and functional layout, the Turun building gave him a reputation to rival those of other European modernists. It was successful at establishing Alvar Aalto's ability to design large-scale buildings.

If he burst onto the European architectural scene with the Turun Sanomat building, his reputation was cemented with the Paimio Sanatorium, 1930–1933, a health and recovery facility for which he and his wife also provided the furnishings.

The Paimio armchair, also known as Armchair 41, made its debut as part of the furnishings of the sanatorium by Aalto that opened in 1932 (Figure 21.18). It is a functionalist piece of furniture that is sculptural, with a frame in bent laminated birchwood that makes a continuous loop. The loop is the primary supporting mechanism; three solid wooden bars attach to it, act as stabilizers, and support an L-shaped plywood seat that is lacquered. The loop takes the place of legs. The most significant feature of the chair is that all parts are made of wood. As he further developed the Paimio armchair, he revised its width, making it slightly narrower.

Considered one of Aalto's greatest works, the Paimio Sanatorium reinforces modernism's connection to health (Figure 21.19). It also marks a significant moment, not only for his architecture but for his furniture design, and the relationship of building to furniture. From this point onward, Aalto firmly eschewed historical styles. Only once he had firmly embraced modernism would he state that his furniture designs were inextricably linked to the architectural projects they were designed for. The chair was not a part of the original 1929 project but was developed when the Sanatorium was completed in 1932.

The most obvious difference between this chair and the Bauhaus chairs is that it was made of wood. Kellein stresses the essential difference between the Aaltos' work and that of other modernists: "Surrounded as they were by Breuer's tubular steel tables and Thonet's bentwood chairs, a love of simple forms and a preponderance of wood had evidently become the chosen style for the Aalto's home by 1929" (2005, p. 123). Initially, the Aaltos mimicked the modern pieces in their personal collection and worked with metal tubing. Over time, they turned increasingly to wood.

Figure 21.18
Alvar Aalto and
Aino Aalto, Paimio
armchair, Paimio,
Finland, 1932.
Birch plywood.
Photographed
at Finlandia
Hall, Helsinki,
1962–1971.

Figure 21.18
Alvar Aalto and
Aino Aalto, Paimio
armchair, Paimio,
Finland, 1932.
Birch plywood.
Photographed
at Finlandia
Hall, Helsinki,
1962–1971.

Figure 21.19
Alvar Aalton,
Paimio
Sanitorium,
1929–1933. Lobby.

A project that Aalto won in 1927 led to a work of public infrastructure that was completed in 1933: the Viipuri Library. It included a work of furniture design that remains ubiquitous today, the Aalto stool (Figure 21.20). The library's auditorium was famed for its undulating roof, and it contained hundreds of the exceeding simple wooden stools.

The Villa Mairea at Noormarkku, Finland, 1938–1941, is a residence for a wealthy couple, with a Nordic romantic use of local materials and clever detailing. John McAndrew, in a MoMA catalog, writes, "The national character, closely allied, can be seen in the general Scandinavian trimness, and above all in the use of wood" (McAndrew 1938, p. 3). The personal character of the house reveals itself in the inventiveness of the forms and the use of materials, many of them local, and the witty resolution of details and connections. In Aalto's project, the national character stems from his use of wood and stone. It is not only a change of material, but the new materials affected the form. And part of the local character is that the birch plywood came from Finland. This is what gave his designs a regional touch.

From 1934, Aalto's furniture was exhibited and sold in England, Italy, and the Netherlands.

Figure 21.20
Alvar Aalto, Stool, Vyborg, Russia, 1933. Designed for the Viipuri Library.

His modern achievements with the Turun building and the Paimio Sanatorium might seem like the opening act of a brilliant career designing furniture. Yet within a year of the Paimio opening he turned away from furniture design. Aalto turned to large-scale architecture and urban design. His greatest achievements with the intimate scale of furniture ended in 1933.

British Modernism

The springtime of modern architecture, the early 1920s, was not initially an era of significant developments on the British Isles. Scottish-born Eileen Gray was in Paris, and Mackintosh decamped to southern France where, with little else to do, he painted. The artistic movements of cubism, De Stijl, and futurism had less of an impact in Britain. In contrast, the Beaux-Arts-inspired firm of Mewès & Davis thrived. Lutyens, a friend of architect Arthur Davis, produced projects that resonated with certain contemporary trends but that were nonetheless related to the vernacular tradition of the British countryside.

By the 1930s, a small but committed coterie of modernists started to produce significant work in Britain, their leading figure being Berthold Lubetkin (1901–1990). Lubetkin, born in Russia, brought with him to Britain a familiarity with the Russian modernist movement, Russian Constructivism, and no sentimental ties to the traditions of British architecture. He had studied with Auguste Perret; during his stay in France, he saw Le Corbusier's Esprit Nouveau pavilion first-hand (Allan 1992). He moved to England in 1930, where he married Margaret Church, a radical architecture student.

For his Penguin Pool at the London Zoo, he collaborated with Ove Arup. (Ove Arup was the prominent engineering firm that later had a contentious working relationship with Danish architect Jorn Utzon while working on the Sydney Opera House.) The Penguin Pool represents another kind of modernism, with its free-flowing curves, reinforced concrete ramps in a double-helix formation, imaginative jumps in scale, and nary a grid in sight (Figure 21.21). Certainly one of the beguiling peculiarities of the modern movement is the temporal coexistence of projects such as Mies van der Rohe's Reichsbank (1933), an exercise in rationality, and imaginative flights of fancy such as Lubetkin's Penguin Pool. Henry-Russell Hitchcock touched upon precisely this aspect of modernism's twin impulses in his article "The Architecture of Bureaucracy and the Architecture of Genius" (1947). Following Hitchcock's lead, van der Rohe's work would be an example of the "Architecture of Bureaucracy," while Lubetkin's pool is a prime example of the "Architecture of Genius."

Other modern projects in Britain include Lubetkin and Tecton's High Point Flats at Highgate, and Wells Coates's Isokon Flats in Hampstead. Wells Coates, an understudied figure of British modernism, was a talented furniture designer. Erich Mendelsohn arrived in 1933 and partnered with Serge Chermayeff in the De La Warr Seaside Pavilion. Walter Gropius worked with Maxwell Fry, who after Gropius's departure would embark on a distinguished career with his wife, Jane Drew, in West Africa.

The Lighter Side of Modernism

Just as Frampton's phrase "mechanical lyricism" described those with an unusual place in the modernist fold, Gray, Chareau, and Terry, another phrase by Frampton is appropriate to end the

Figure 21.21
Berthold Lubetkin,
Penguin Pool,
London, United
Kingdom.

chapter. This chapter began by looking at Walter Gropius, Mies van der Rohe, and Le Corbusier—mainstream figures in any history of modernism. But a brief look at someone on the fringes of the design world will deepen and complicate our understanding of modernism. Frampton described Paul Nelson as belonging to the lighter side of modernism.

Paul Nelson

Nelson (1895–1979) worked for Auguste Perret for three years, and one of the notable features of his career is that he repeatedly crossed the Atlantic, traveling between the United States, where he was born, and France, where he became a citizen. He acted as a conduit of architectural information between continents and sectors of the arts. He was well connected in the art world, counting Georges Bracque, Alexander Calder, and Joan Miró as his friends. He was similarly connected to literati: F. Scott Fitzgerald, Ernest Hemingway, and Ezra Pound.

Writing about the School of Paris, the modernists whose activities centered on the Île-de-France, Kenneth Frampton coined the categories of light and heavy to describe two strains of modernist design. About modernism, he emphasized that "far from being monolithic,

it was a product of intense cross-fertilization" (Frampton in Riley 1990, p. 10). Le Corbusier, according to Frampton, was a heavy, not because of the ponderousness of his pronouncements (one presumes) but because of the weighty nature of his works in concrete. Looking at Chareau, Gray, and Nelson, in contrast, their works are "light" because of their deft **tectonic** expression and also in their explorations of material translucency.

Frampton made popular the use of the word "tectonic" to describe architecture, particularly modern architecture (Frampton 1995). Tectonic emphasizes construction and materials, and the relationship of a building to its constitutive parts. But it is also an aesthetic and expressive term whose catchphrase is "the poetics of construction." The tectonic approach sees meaning in materials, their texture, and the architectural details that connect them. This allows for variety within the modernist fold, with some emphasizing weighty rough materials (Le Corbusier, late in his career), and others lighter machined materials (Nelson). The importance to the concept of lightness is evident in the name of one of Nelson's projects: the Maison Suspendue, or Suspended House, of 1936.

The connection between modernism and health was explicit in Nelson's oeuvre. He designed and built hospitals and other medical facilities throughout his career, and focused on unique ways of configuring surgeries and surgery pavilions.

Nelson had an interesting interlude during one of his visits to the United States (1929–1930). His orbit overlapped with that of the actress Gloria Swanson, and at her insistence he was hired as the artistic director of her next film, *What a Widow!* (Figure 21.22). For her he designed a modern backdrop, cubist and pure, that presented her in the *au courant* realm she desired, and thereby exposed American audiences to European modernism, a good three years before its official debut at the Museum of Modern Art's exhibition of 1932. Photographic stills from the film look decidedly Corbusian, with horizontal windows, visible columns, and rounded stairways, like an imagined version of his Villa Savoye. Nelson also relied on the repeated modernist strategy of punctuating his modernist backdrop with recognizable types, but Nelson's types are different from Le Corbusier's radiators. Items from another arena lend qualities of elegance when plunked down intact into a new world—in this case, martini glasses, waistcoats, and Swanson herself.

Conclusion

This chapter introduces modernism as a force to be reckoned with. The chapters that follow grapple with the consequences of modernism.

In twentieth-century architecture and design, many male architects' wives were accomplished and professionally trained designers and architects. This appears a mixed blessing. Many women, certainly, thrived in partnership with their husbands because they were in a personal and professional relationship that respected their abilities and gave them an outlet for their work. Yet it also means that many women had a difficult time making a career in the design field outside of the supportive framework of marriage.

In 1938, Mies emigrated to the United States; Lilly Reich stayed in Berlin and managed his interests (Lambert 2001). After the Second World War, the Barcelona chair and many of his other pieces were made and sold by Knoll. Walter Gropius taught at Harvard University. Marcel Breuer taught there for a while before he established his own firm in New York. Philip Johnson, Paul

Figure 21.22
Paul Nelson, Set Design for *What a Widow!*, 1930.

Rudolph, and Anne Tyng were just three of the students who were a part of the Bauhaus-inspired design milieu at Harvard.

The 1920s and 1930s saw several buildings created that changed the course of twentieth-century architecture. This august group includes the Villa Savoye, the Barcelona Pavilion, and the Paimio Sanatorium. Just as these are landmarks in the history of architecture, the furniture they introduced are landmarks for the history of design. Ironically, those who most clearly sought to make standard pieces, Le Corbusier and Aalto, fashioned handmade luxury pieces that became collector's items. Mies van der Rohe made a chair for a king and achieved the greatest popular success of his furniture career. Likely the two biggest names in twentieth-century architecture, Le Corbusier and Mies van der Rohe, both designed furniture prolifically in the 1920s and 1930s. Despite successful careers that lasted for decades, they were not to repeat that success within the realm of furniture design. After the Second World War, they turned to large-scale architectural projects and urban design.

In the postwar period, twentieth-century design moved on from classical modernism to more popular references and an increased interest in technology. A shining example whose success equals that of the Aalto stool was the plywood dining room chair created by yet another married couple of talented designers, Charles and Ray Eames (Figure 21.23). Their works belong in the category of the dissemination of modernism in the 1950s, the subject of the following chapters.

Modernism would blossom around the world with new forms and meanings. It would have unintended consequences. Some would recoil from it. Some would superficially latch on to its revolutionary shapes, uninterested in the thoughts that led to them. In the 1970s, subsequent movements expanded the repertory of themes. In the 1980s, modernism would be condemned. In the 1990s, modernism would rise, like a Phoenix from the ashes, in a new form.

Sources

Allan, John (1992). *Berthold Lubetkin: Architecture and the Tradition of Progress*. London: RIBA.

Baudot, François (1998). *Eileen Gray*. London: Thames and Hudson.

Blaser, Werner (1982). *Mies van der Rohe: Furniture and Interiors*. Hauppauge: Barron's.

Constant, Caroline (2000). *Eileen Gray*. London: Phaidon.

Curtis, William (1996). *Modern Architecture since 1900*. London: Phaidon.

Dearstyne, Howard (1986). *Inside the Bauhaus*. New York: Rizzoli.

De Fusco, Renato (1977). *Le Corbusier, Designer: Furniture*. Hauppauge: Barron's.

de Muga, Patricia, ed. (2023). *Eileen Gray: Objects and Furniture Design*. Barcelona: Polígrafa.

Di Puolo, Maurizio (1976). *Le Corbusier, Charlotte Perriand, Pierre Jeanneret*. Rome: De Luca Editore.

Drexler, Arthur (1960). *Ludwig Mies van der Rohe*. New York: G. Braziller.

Eidelberg, Martin, Thomas Hine, Pat Kirkham, David Hanks, and C. Ford Peatross (2006). *The Eames Lounge Chair: An Icon of Modern Design*. London: Merrell.

Feiersinger, Martin and Werner Feiersinger, eds. (2015). Chandigarh Redux: *Le Corbusier, Pierre Jeanneret, Jane B. Drew and C. Maxwell Fry*. Zurich: Scheidegger and Spiess.

Frampton, Kenneth (1992). *Harry Seidler: Four Decades of Architecture*. London: Thames and Hudson.

Frampton, Kenneth (1995). *Studies in Tectonic Culture: the Poetics of Construction in Nineteenth- and Twentieth-Century Architecture*. Cambridge, MA: MIT Press.

Giedion, Sigfried (1982). *Space, Time, and Architecture*. Cambridge, MA: Harvard University Press.

Glaeser, Ludwig (1977). *Ludwig Mies van der Rohe: Furniture and Furniture Drawings from the Design Collection and the Mies van der Rohe Archive*. New York: Museum of Modern Art.

Gropius, Walter, ed. (1960). *The Theatre of the Bauhaus*. Middletown, CT: Wesleyan University Press.

Hyman, Isabelle (2001). *Marcel Breuer, Architect: The Career and the Buildings*. New York: Abrams.

Joedicke, Jürgen (1990). *Weissenhofsiedlung*. Stuttgart: K. Kramer.

Figure 21.23
Charles and Ray Eames, DCW chair, 1946.

Kates, George (1952). *The Years That Were Fat*. Cambridge, MA: MIT Press.

Kellein, Thomas (2005). *Alvar and Aino Aalto: Design*. Ostfildern-Ruit: Hatje Cantz.

Kostelanetz, Richard, ed. (1970). *Moholy-Nagy*. New York: Praeger.

Lambert, Phyllis (2001). *Mies in America*. New York: Abrams.

Latour, Bruno (1993). *We Have Never Been Modern*. Cambridge, MA: Harvard University Press.

Le Corbusier (1925). *L'Art décoratif d'aujourd'hui*. Paris: G. Crès et cie.

Lupton, Ellen and J. Abbott Miller, eds. (1991). *The ABCs of Triangle, Square, Circle: The Bauhaus and Design Theory*. Princeton, NJ: Princeton Architectural Press.

Marcus, George (2000). *Le Corbusier: Inside the Machine for Living: Furniture and Interiors*. New York: Monacelli.

McAndrew, John (1938). *Aalto: Architecture and Furniture*. New York: Museum of Modern Art.

McLeod, Mary, ed. (2003). *Charlotte Perriand: An Art of Living*. New York: Abrams.

McQuaid, Matilda (1996). *Lilly Reich, Designer and Architect*. New York: Abrams.

Musée des Arts Décoratifs (1985). *Charlotte Perriand: un art de vivre*. Paris: Flammarion.

Museum of Finnish Architecture (1985). *Alvar Aalto Furniture*. Cambridge, MA: MIT University Press.

Nelson, George (1953). *Chairs*. New York: Whitney Publications.

Otto, Elizabeth and Patrick Rôssler (2019). *Bauhaus Women: A Global Perspective*. London: Herbert Press.

Ouroussoff, Nicolai (2007). "The Best House in Paris." *The New York Times*, August 26: p. 1.

Pallasmaa, Juhani, ed. (2007). *Alvar Aalto through the Eyes of Shigeru Ban*. London: Black Dog Publishing.

Perriand, Charlotte (2003). *A Life of Creation: An Autobiography*. New York: Monacelli Press.

Pile, John (2000). *A History of Interior Design*. New York: Wiley.

Riley, Terence (1990). *The Filter of Reason: Paul Nelson*. New York: Columbia University.

Riley, Terence and Joseph Abram, eds. (1990). *The Filter of Reason: Work of Paul Nelson*. New York: Rizzoli.

Riley, Terence and Barry Bergdoll, eds. (2001). *Mies in Berlin*. New York: Abrams.

Rowe, Colin (1994). *The Architecture of Good Intentions: Towards a Possible Retrospect*. London: Academy Editions.

Safran, Yehuda (2000). *Mies van der Rohe*. Lisbon: Blau.

Schlemmer, Tut, ed. (1972). *The Letters and Diaries of Oskar Schlemmer*. Middletown, CT: Wesleyan University Press.

Staatliches Bauhaus Weimar ([1923] 1980). *Staatliches Bauhaus Weimar 1919–1923*. Munich: Kraus.

Whitford, Frank, ed. (1992). *The Bauhaus: Masters and Students by Themselves*. London: Conran Octopus.

Wilk, Christopher (1981). *Marcel Breuer, Furniture, and Interiors*. New York: Museum of Modern Art.

Discussion and Review Questions

1. Art nouveau artists clearly were inspired by nature. What inspired or motivated the modernists in their design process?

2. The modernists claimed to be antihistory; when did they ignore their own rule?

3. What role did women play in modernism? Who were some of the major female designers?

4. What does functionalism mean?

5. What specifically did the modernists dislike about Victorian design?

6. Who were the major figures and where did they practice?

7. Specifically in the furniture realm, what were some of the modernist goals?

Art Deco, Tradition Continues, and Decorators

1920s	1925		1925–1939
Art deco	L'Exposition Internationale des Arts Décoratifs et Industriels Modernes		Art Moderne

In 1925, a world's fair opened in Paris, L'Exposition Internationale des Arts Décoratifs et Industriels Modernes. The French government sponsored it to support the French decorative arts; there was fear that she was losing ground in this vital arena to Germany. Planners of the exposition intended to show the world that France excelled at making well-designed and well-crafted objects and interiors. The contributors were ostensibly unified in their collaborative mission to tout the superiority of French design. Yet in the planning stages, a rift became apparent, a division into two camps: decorators and functionalists. The decorators included figures such as André Mare, Émile-Jacques Ruhlmann, and Louis Süe. The functionalists included Le Corbusier and Charlotte Perriand. Chapter 21 handled the functionalist stream. This chapter covers those who did not feel so strongly modernism's pull, or who felt it but expressed it differently.

What connects the three strands of design considered in this chapter is that they are responses to a similar economic and artistic climate, yet they are responses in three distinct directions.

Figure 22.0
(*Facing page*)
Émile-Jacques Ruhlmann, interior design illustration, 1925.

361

Art Deco

The terms we now use to describe the two groups that emerged in Paris are problematic, as they were not in use at the time. "Art deco" is an abbreviation of "Arts Décoratifs," and while commonly used to describe the design trend that emerged from the exposition, the term has only been in use since the 1960s. As Christopher Long writes, the term "is unusually elastic and imprecise" (Long 2007, p. ix). Most of the exhibitors referred to their designs as "moderne," and if they were to ascribe to a stylistic moniker, they used "style moderne."

"Art deco" is a frequently used phrase that has currency in the design field. Even if imprecise, it does generally indicate a differing attitude between two groups. The functionalists and the decorators were both responding to their time period, the 1920s, but they did so differently. The designs of the functionalists were aimed toward mass production, a wide swath of the marketplace, and considered the social good that design can achieve. They emphasized the value of engineering and assembly line construction. The decorators crafted exquisite objects that were labor intensive, aimed at an elite market, and not burdened by a belief in the redemptive obligations of art.

Art deco designs are intricately related to a decade, the 1920s. The 1920s are also known as the Roaring Twenties, for good reason. In the United States, the aftermath of the First World War was a period of economic prosperity, whose end would come with the market crash of October 1929 and the start of The Depression. Technologically, it is related to the increased presence of automobiles, movies, and radio. Culturally, it included such varied manifestations as the Charleston dance, jazz, bobbed haircuts, and short skirts. F. Scott Fitzgerald's novel *The Great Gatsby* (1925) perfectly captured the tenor of this period as it played out among the social elite.

The speed with which art deco traveled from France to the United States, and elsewhere, indicates that it quickly became an international phenomenon. The forms associated with twentieth-century optimism in France and the United States resonated with other groups of people who looked to the future for different reasons. To name two: In Mexico, the Mexican Revolution of 1910–1921 ended, so the 1920s heralded a new postcolonial age. And 1923 was the year that Atatürk founded the modern nation of Turkey,

announcing that the smoldering ashes of the Ottoman Empire had gone out and that those living in Anatolia could look forward to a bright, secular, and democratic future. Art deco forms in both these countries reflected this optimism.

Part of the reason scholars and antiquarians have difficulty with the term art deco is that it is used indiscriminately in several ways. This chapter takes its cues from how it is generally used and also recognizes the limits of its usefulness. First, it refers to the period of design immediately following the 1925 Exposition, indicating the French decorative arts aimed at an elite clientele. Then it considers the effect that these forms had in the United States, and specifically their interaction with skyscrapers. Finally, it considers the iteration of art deco forms around the world.

France

The major figures on the decorative side of the divide, typically classified as the pioneers of French art deco, include Paul Follot (1877–1941), Jean-Michel Frank (1895–1951), André Mare (1887–1932), Émile-Jacques Ruhlmann (1879–1933), Michel Roux-Spitz (1888–1957), and Louis Süe (1875–1968). A significant feature of art deco (along with rococo and art nouveau) is that it is one of the few styles whose finest works are in interiors, furniture design, and designed objects. There are art deco buildings, to be sure, but art deco is primarily known for objects, pieces of furniture, lamps, textiles, and jewelry. The ranks of art deco artists include Louis Cartier (1875–1942), a jeweler, and Paul Poiret (1879–1944), a fashion designer who himself created interior designs. Jean Dupas (1882–1964) is one of the few painters whose work belongs exclusively to the realm of art deco.

Art deco is related to commercialism and, by extension, capitalism. French department stores supported the designers who exhibited at the Exposition and hired them to do window displays. The major Parisian department stores—Au Printemps, Galeries Lafayette, Au Bon Marché, and Grand Magasins du Louvre—all supported art deco. The explicit support by the retail industry is again in contrast with the modernists whose works bear more than a whiff of socialism. Art deco was more commercial and less highly theorized.

Some works, particularly graphic works, predate the 1920s and clearly indicate tendencies that look forward to what would later be called art deco. Many pieces also postdate the 1920s. As with all styles and epochs, the general maxims by which the era is known are sometimes at odds with specific artistic utterances. Looking across the spectrum of art deco pieces, one encounters a delightful complexity and occasional incongruity; this is what makes it such an appealing area of study.

The understanding of artistic movements changes over time. Art deco, once seen as the antithesis of art nouveau, is now seen by some as an emanation from it. And although modernists and art deco artists were once seen in opposition, there are considerable areas of overlap, including common interests, materials, and finishes. Like modernism, art deco has affinities to cubism, Russian Constructivism, and Italian futurism.

There is always the case of figures so individually talented that it is difficult to pigeonhole their work. Eileen Gray, often considered an art deco decorator, is now more frequently placed in the modernist camp. She's art deco because of her fine finishes and rich clients, and she worked as a decorator. She's a modernist because of the absence of historical detail in her projects, her adherence to functionalism and cubism, and no less than Le Corbusier admired her work. Yet other designers seem to perfectly belong to a style, in no small part because our definition of it comes from their work. Ruhlmann and Frank (discussed below) are art deco to the core.

One of the most succinct definitions of art deco comes from a writer who spent his career studying it. Alastair Duncan writes: "The term 'Art Deco,' coined in the late 1960s, remains an appropriate way to describe the distinctive decorative arts style which evolved in Europe immediately prior to the First World War, and which remained in fashion in some countries of its adoption until the late 1930s" (Duncan 1988, p. 17).

Ensembliers

The First World War was a tragedy for the Frank family, although it was a tragedy that started the design career of Jean-Michel Frank (1895–1941). Jean-Michel's two brothers were killed in the war and his father, of German-Jewish descent, committed suicide; his mother died in a mental institution. Because of his family's losses, he inherited a sum of money that allowed him to pursue his career of choice, decorator. He participated in the 1925 Exposition as one of the high style decorators.

The French might refer to a decorator as a "décorateur"; they more frequently use the word "**ensemblier**." The denotation refers to one who creates an ensemble, chooses objects, combines them, and in so doing, makes aesthetic choices. There is an undercurrent of taste in the usage of this word, whereas the staunch functionalists grounded their design (or so they said) in abstract principles.

Frank's projects after the exhibition include decorating the Parisian townhouse of the Vicomte de Noailles, a project that included **vellum**-clad walls, bronze doors, white lacquer, and sharkskin. His all-white apartment for the fashion designer Elsa Schiaparelli in 1927 was sparsely furnished and made with inexpensive materials and garnered significant attention.

Frank was also involved in the design business as a patron, hiring Alberto and Diego Giacometti, Salvador Dalí, and Emilio Terry. In 1939, he fled Europe for Argentina, where he worked briefly, fulfilling the desire of wealthy Argentines for the latest trends in Parisian design. (Buenos Aires itself because a vibrant center of art deco.) The year 1941 saw Frank in New York, despondent, and he jumped to his death from a New York high-rise. A distant relative of his, Anne Frank, also gained renown posthumously for her moving Holocaust diary.

A chair and a desk from the height of Frank's career display several key aspects of his attitude toward design (Figure 22.1). Their decoration is limited to the use of an extravagantly exotic material, **shagreen**, the skin of the small spotted dogfish. Shagreen is also called sharkskin. The use of this material on chairs and desks indicates that decoration should be integral to the material and applied flat, not as an extraneous form.

Émile-Jacques Ruhlmann (1879–1933) was a French furniture designer known for fine craftsmanship. He started exhibiting his designs in 1910.

With his contribution to the 1925 Exposition, he cemented his reputation as a major figure in design (Figure 22.0). He had his own pavilion, which also exhibited the works of other designers. The foremost twentieth-century cabinetmaker, he sought to raise French furniture-making to the level it had enjoyed in the eighteenth century.

He specialized in unusual materials, such as ebony, zebrawood, tropical veneers, sharkskin, and ivory, or he employed traditional veneers used in contrasting patterns. He sold several pieces to a famous collector, the Maharaja of Indore. Ruhlmann's work is usually noted for its strict geometries and geometric stylization, yet with his elephant chairs—he did several versions—he

Figure 22.1
Jean-Michel
Frank, desk and
chair, France,
1920–1930.
Shagreen veneer.

Figure 22.2
Émile-Jacques
Ruhlmann,
armchair, France,
1930.

explored geometric forms to great effect (Figure 22.2). The chairs were exhibited at the Exposition Coloniale and he used them in subsequent projects.

Britain

Edward Maufe (1883–1974) was an architect who formed part of the English delegation to the 1925 Exposition. His works had stylistic ties to English Arts and Crafts, and he also worked in the English Gothic style. The stylishness of his work, evident in a desk he sent to Paris, contrasted with the functionalist strain of modernism. He perfected a technique of making silver-lacquered furniture.

His Paris bound writing desk was made of mahogany. Its appearance at the 1925 Exposition garnered praise. It uses silk tassels for drawer pulls, a feature usually associated with French designs. Art deco pieces make occasional references to traditional architectural vocabularies, such as classicism, and some innovatively give life to Egyptian and Aztec forms. This is one of the features that set their work apart from that of the strict modernists. The Maufe desk makes discreet historical references, with fluted pilasters adorned with subtle bases and capitals. Maufe made less expensive versions of this piece, one of which he used as his personal desk.

Owen Williams (1890–1969) was an engineer and architect and was Britain's leading expert on reinforced concrete. Although he moved increasingly toward a functionalist/modernist position, he had little interaction with the major figures of the British modern movement (Maxwell Fry, Jane

Drew, Wells Coates, etc.). The lobby of the Daily Express Building in London is an unusual work for Williams (who is more known for his knowledge of straightforward concrete construction, utilized in factories), yet it is one of the seminal works of English art deco. The exterior nudges art deco in the direction of streamlined forms, and it is made of glass, vitrolite, and chrome (Figure 22.3). The design incorporates a variety of metallic finishes, and it is mostly lit by recessed cove lighting, tucked into a series of stepped planes that dramatically finish in zigzags. Metallic reveals offset one expensive material after another, including black glass. A showpiece of its time, it was designed to demonstrate that its client, a newspaper company, was up-to-date (Yeomans and Cottam 2001, pp. 67–79).

Denham Maclaren created multiple pieces that were striking, most notably a chair made of glass and zebra skin. Some British furniture designers were interested not in working within boundaries set by others, but in exploring new territory. Glass is a difficult material to use structurally, a feat Maclaren managed successfully.

Figure 22.3
Owen Williams, Daily Express Building, London, England, 1932.

Betty Joel (1894–1985) started working with her husband in the business of manufacturing furniture with Betty Joel Ltd in 1921. With no training, she increasingly focused on design, and it was soon clear that her talents outshone those of her husband. She started out in a historicist vein but became increasingly interested in forms and materials that aligned her with French art deco. Her work, in furniture and interior design, brought the aesthetics of American movie sets into British homes. She disavowed functionalism but moved away from pricey veneers to plywood and plastic laminate. Although less famous, she was a British version of Ruhlmann.

Ironies abound in the artistic productions of this period. It is certainly curious that a group of objects that were designed to appeal to an elite appealed to the masses, whereas the modernist projects, which sought to raise the plight of all, were actually very elite.

The United States

Art deco appeared in the United States in ways similar to its use in France—as an appealing design vocabulary with which to outfit a store window or the splashy lobby of an apartment building. Yet it also became associated with the skyscraper, a development not foreseen by the organizers of the Paris exposition. The careers of Raymond Hood (1881–1934) and William Van Alen (1883–1954) were devoted to explorations of how art deco forms could be adapted to tall buildings. Donald Deskey (1894–1989) and Paul Frankl (1878–1958) were active in the realm of interiors and furnishings.

Urban design and architecture

The Chicago school skyscrapers of the 1890s were examples of a logical and inspired response to the economic and technological environment. They expressed the building's structure, which they used as a starting point for a straightforward artistic statement. Yet the glory was short-lived, and many architects turned to historic forms to inspire their skyscraper designs, covering steel frames with Greek columns or Gothic arches. Modernists, including Louis Sullivan and Walter Gropius, did not hesitate to point out how ludicrous this was. With the advent of art deco, another architectural vocabulary was at hand, appropriate and appealing for the cladding of high-rise buildings. The marriage of art deco to skyscrapers seemed preordained. The City of New York also lent its assistance. Many were concerned about the possibility of massive office blocks turning streets into dark, airless canyons, so a 1916 zoning ordinance required that as buildings rose, they had to progressively step back, with the uppermost floors occupying no more than 25 percent of the lot size. This lent a distinctive profile to New York skyscrapers, many of which were tapered by a series of setbacks, often capped off with a spire. This profile was in touch with other aspects of 1920s art deco design, including the use of metal, the vertical emphasis, and the favored zigzag motif.

While art deco is rightfully considered a decorative style, one of the finest twentieth-century urban designs comes under its tenure, Rockefeller Center (Figure 22.4). Despite Le Corbusier's passionate attention to city planning, the legacy and efficacy of his urban vision remains contentious. Rockefeller Center, born of the grid of New York, is an urban design that incorporates skyscrapers and involves public amenities, statuary, fountains, rooftop gardens, all miraculously

Rockefeller Center at Night

Figure 22.4
Raymond Hood, Rockefeller Center, New York, NY, USA, 1931–1933. Postcard, 1942.

nestled into the center of one of the world's most vibrant metropolises. Rockefeller Center unfolds onto three New York City blocks, between Fifth and Sixth Avenues (Stern 1982, pp. 13–15). At its center is a T-shaped plaza, with a sunken court and the famous ice-skating rink.

The defining feature of an art deco skyscraper is its emphasis on verticality. Vertical piers are continuous, while the horizontal bands, the spandrels above and below windows, are intercepted by the vertical piers. Raymond Hood perfected the design of the middle portion of a skyscraper with his projects for countless tall buildings, including the Chicago Tribune Tower and the Daily News Building.

Yet the epitome of art deco skyscraper design came from the hand of William Van Alen (1883–1954). The name of the Chrysler Building, 1929, reflects the ties of architecture to industry. It has setbacks and the standard emphasis on verticality in its shaft. Yet the design of the spire and the lobby renders it an icon of American art deco (Gray 2001, p. 67). At its top, the vertical massing morphs into a series of overlapping curves, sheathed in metal and punctuated with triangle-shaped windows that glow at night.

The lobby and elevator doors hint at the form of the spire. A fan shape is part of a similar design of overlapping curves, emphasized with alternating bands of color and separated by bronze. A triangular light functions as the elevator call light, also a hint of the windows that grace the top of the building (Figure 22.5).

Interiors, stage design, and furniture

Two of the leaders of American art deco, Paul Frankl and Joseph Urban, were born in Austria. Joseph Urban (1872–1933) was one of a group of Austrian architects who brought to American art deco their personal knowledge of the Secessionist movement, and specifically the works of Otto Wagner, Adolph Loos, and Josef Hoffmann. Trained as an architect, Urban was active in Vienna as an architect, interior designer, stage designer, and book illustrator. He first visited the United States as designer of the Austrian pavilion at the St. Louis Exposition in 1904. In 1911, he moved to the United States. Over the course of his career, he created sets for the Boston Opera Company, the Metropolitan Opera, and the Ziegfeld Follies. His work as artistic director of William Randolph Hearst's movie studio led to his commission to design the Hearst Building in New York. Another project, the New School of Social Research, is considered

Figure 22.5
William Van Alen, Chrysler Building, New York, NY, USA, 1928–1930. Lobby and elevators.

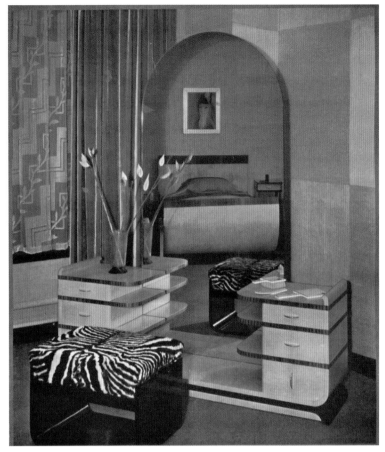

Figure 22.6
Paul Frankl, dressing table and stool, New York, NY, USA, 1933. Maple and Bakelite.

New York's first international-style building (Carter 1992, p. 169). Some of his works still stand, including the most extravagant, Mar-a-Lago, the house of Marjorie Merriweather Post. Urban's professional activity in theater and film underscores an oft-noted quality about art deco interior design: even when designed for real buildings, they look theatrical.

Paul Frankl is known for his skyscraper furniture, in which he sought to create a uniquely American style of design by relating to skyscrapers (Long 2007). He created a number of bookshelves, writing desks, and dressing tables whose forms are inspired by art deco buildings (Figure 22.6). He was aware of the commercial nature of many of his designs. He opened the Frankl Galleries in New York, where he saw firsthand that modern design could be a selling point yet could also turn people away. He thought the United States lagged behind Europe in terms of modern design, and he aligned himself with modernists such as Marcel Duchamp, Francis Picabia, and Man Ray.

Donald Deskey (1894–1989) was an American interior and industrial designer. He studied in Paris, where he was exposed to and learned to appreciate the work of French designers. In New York, he developed window displays for Saks Fifth Avenue (Hanks 1987, p. 10). He designed interiors, furniture, lamps, and textiles.

In a period known for the use of novel materials, Deskey's work still manages to stand out: He favored cork, copper, pigskin, **linoleum**, **Bakelite**, Formica, brushed aluminum, and macassar ebony. His interiors for Radio City include aluminum wallpaper and dramatic use of geometric forms (Figure 22.7).

Tropical art deco

Art deco undeniably had an international appeal and, like art nouveau, an international success. While generally thought of as French, French art deco was chronologically followed by American art deco, which was, in turn, followed by art deco across the globe. Art deco buildings and designed objects appeared everywhere—in Africa, the Americas, Asia, and Australia.

Figure 22.7
Donald Deskey,
Radio City
Music Hall, New
York, NY, USA,
1932. Stage and
proscenium.

In the 1930s, another kind of art deco arrives on the world stage, lightheartedly known as tropical art deco. This represents a third phrase of art deco, at the furthest remove from Paris. Places with warm climates, including Miami, Florida, and Havana, Cuba, were two of the centers of this kind of art deco. Purists scoff at the inclusion of such buildings in the art deco realm, as they stray too far, they feel, from the French originals. The debate pits 1930s Miami against 1920s Paris and takes us unto the murky area of stylistic names and definitions.

Tropical art deco is less reliant on expensive materials and more reliant on silhouette and paint. Miami architects used a variety of pastel hues. Art deco was popular, and an art deco exterior announced to passersby that the company housed within was current (Figure 22.8). This was particularly the case with business ventures that relied on bringing in customers—movie theaters, stores, bars, and hotels—or, as with the *Daily Express*, for businesses that simply wanted the architectural image to present them as modern. Suzanne Tise writes: "A highly exaggerated and commercialized version of Art Deco was popular

in cinemas and theatres during the late 1920s" (1996, p. 522).

This popularized version of art deco spread remarkably fast, to all corners of the globe, and its diffusion was based on its commercial success and not ponderous theorizing. The term "**art moderne**" is sometimes used to refer to this kind of art deco, later in time and divorced in spirit from the Parisian sort. It relies more heavily on mechanical iconography, looking at automobiles and steamships, items not part of the original French repertory of themes.

The existence of art deco buildings all over the world—in the United States, in South Africa, in Brazil, in China—is a sign of each country's wealth. An elevator door, a tall building that emphasizes the vertical, a lobby with cove lighting—all are proof that many places economically prospered in the 1920s.

Paul Veysseyre and Alexandre Léonard were just two of the architects who helped make Shanghai an art deco center to rival New York and Paris. One of their finest buildings was the Cercle Sportif of 1926, designed by the two Frenchmen and built by Chinese workers and contractors. A prominent building in Mexico City, the Palacio

Figure 22.8
Art deco buildings
in South Beach,
Florida, USA,
1930s.

de Bellas Artes, started in 1904 under the design direction of Adamo Boari, and was redesigned in 1932 by Federico Mariscal in the fashionable art deco stylings of the period.

Eritrea, in the Horn of Africa, was a local center of African modernism. The Fiat Tagliero gas station relies on a judicious use of stone, an expensive material, offset with fields of plaster, a less expensive material. Art deco arrived in Ethiopia, Somalia, and Eritrea due to Italian colonists, yet it was not received as an Italian tool of repression but as part of an international modern movement that Africans were anxious to join. A recent publication is rare among books in that it addresses African twentieth-century architecture. The editor, Edward Denison, notes: "Far from the motherland, Eritrea provided a perfect environment for innovation and experimentation" (2003, p. 63). Fred Glennie's Mutual Building in Cape Town, South Africa, 1939, was the tallest building on the continent outside of the pyramids, and cemented Africa's position as a home for art deco. Charles Wulffleff's Governor's Palace in Dakar, on the West coast, makes clear that art deco forms were popular continent-wide (Figure 22.9).

First silent, then talking films were associated with art deco, as were many cinemas built across Southeast Asia. Scores of them came from the hand of the Danish architect B.M. Iversen. Iversen stared out in the art deco fold and increasingly became more modern in his approach. The Ruby Cinema, in Ipoh, Malaysia, was a transitional work (Figure 22.10).

Graphics and fashion

An example of the commercial success of art deco is its prevalence in advertising. Typeface and forms associated with art deco were perceived by viewers as modern and new. In a period in which photographic printing techniques were increasingly available, Ludwig Hohlwein (1874–1919) was a successful commercial artist in Munich who produced handmade lithography work. This flatter stencil-style of posterwork avoided photographic processes. Although trained as an architect, he is considered a master of modern poster art. Even in a less exalted art form such as an advertisement, art deco characteristics are noticeable. The streamlined human form is coupled with a high contrast use of colors (Figure 22.11). This belongs to a strain of art deco graphic work that invokes classical sculpture. Hohlwein's male figure was almost absurdly heroic for the purpose at hand: selling plane tickets.

Scholars such as Judith Butler promote the idea that the human body is a social construction,

Figure 22.9
Charles Wulffleff,
Governor's Palace,
Dakar, Senegal,
1930.

Figure 22.10
B.M. Iversen, Ruby
Cinema, Ipoh,
Malaysia, 1940.

Figure 22.11
Ludwig Hohlwein, Lufthansa Airlines poster, 1936. On the occasion of the Berlin Olympics.

a sign of its time. At first this claim bewilders: surely the human form cannot biologically change itself every decade to respond to fashion's latest whim. Her theories succeed to the extent that each period has its favored body type, favored body parts, or a "constructed gender" (Butler 1999, p. 48). Certain human figures seem to exemplify an era's aesthetic vision. Nancy Cunard, tall and reed-thin, is one such person, and the knowledge that she was active in the art world, as a publisher, author, and patron, confirms that she was in all respects a woman of the 1920s. Dresses from the period are also evidence of the bodies they so beautifully wrapped.

Voisin of Paris made dresses in the 1920s that used expensive materials that looked luxurious—such as silk velvet. His designs carried few of the encumbrances of the history of the dress, in fact, most traditional evening dress elements were eliminated. They also pushed the social mores of their day. The wearer of a Voisin dress had bare arms and embraced a short skirt that was meant to fly about when subjected to the sideways kick of the Charleston. Voisin's contemporary was

Coco Chanel, who by the mid-1920s was well established. Her dresses promoted an attitude toward the ideal female figure that was a dramatic change from what it had been in the late nineteenth century (Figure 22.12). Then bustles, corsets, and large hats all conspired to render the female figure as curvaceous as possible. The ideal female figure of the Roaring Twenties had a flat chest. Women not so naturally endowed were known to bind themselves. The profile of Chanel's dresses are similar to the simple lines of art deco pilasters and low-relief sculpture.

A study of the silhouettes of Coke bottles reveals that the bottles change over time, corresponding to changing ideals of an idealized female figure. Chanel's dress is completely modern, while Hohlwein's poster draws upon popular representational techniques. Art deco pieces were new but designed in a heavily stylized fashion that made historical forms current.

All eras have their ideal body types, and favored body parts, and animals. The art deco artists were fond of chevron shapes, zigzags, stepped profiles, straight hair, bangs, greyhounds, and deer. Some art deco themes and interests cross stylistic divides.

Figure 22.12
Coco Chanel, evening dress and shawl, Paris, France, 1925. Silk.

Both avowed modernists and the designers now classified as art deco had many similar interests. For example, many were fascinated by African art and materials. Yet sometimes the interests of modernists and their more decoratively inclined comrades diverged. Egyptian motifs were evidently too historical and too decorative to be of use to modernists, yet they were important source materials for art deco designs.

Tradition: A Continuity with the Past

The 1920s produced a large class of wealthy people who desired homes that reflected their status. This includes the "**robber barons**," a term usually used pejoratively to describe industrialists and businessmen who dominated their industries and amassed great wealth in the late nineteenth and early twentieth centuries. There is more than a hint of questionable business practices among business leaders such as John D. Rockefeller, Cornelius Vanderbilt, John Jacob Astor, Henry Ford, and Andrew Carnegie. Some economists counter that these business leaders were essential to transforming the United States into a world power, and that they, for the most part, operated through fair business practices in the free market. Questions about their complicity aside, there is no doubt that they had great cultural impact. They were patrons of the arts with the houses they commissioned and the artworks and furnishings they bought to fill them. For this endeavor, they needed assistance in selecting traditional furnishings and finishes, and then arranging them.

The posthumous reputations of traditional architects and designers have flowed and ebbed, in opposite relationship to the ascendancy and fall of modernism. As the tenets of modernism took hold in the 1950s and 1960s, the reputations of Julia Morgan, Arthur Davis, and Addison Mizner crashed, while those of Louis Sullivan, Charles Rennie Mackintosh, and Adolf Loos soared. Only in the late 1970s and 1980s, with the coincident rise of postmodernism, were the careers of some historicist architects reevaluated. They were rediscovered by scholars, but for the general public they had never lost their appeal. A review of their buildings, interiors, and drawings reveals that many of them were talented architects, artists, and designers. Operating as a traditionally rooted architect or designer involved two areas of skill: a thorough knowledge of architectural history and an accomplished ability to draw and paint.

Britain

Edwin Lutyens (1869–1944) was England's preeminent architect for half a century. His career provides an alternative trajectory to the development of English modernism, as his work presents a successful integration of traditional architectural languages and the romantic or vernacular. He was raised in the English countryside, in Surrey, and he was familiar with historic agricultural buildings. His early works have much in common with the English Arts and Crafts movements, specifically the houses of Philip Webb and C.F.A. Voysey, in which, despite a romantic assemblage of features associated with agricultural buildings, a clarity in plan and façade emerges that is distinctly modern. Lutyens used traditional building materials and probed the relationship between house and garden. He, along with landscape architect Gertrude Jekyll, combined the formal and the picturesque.

His work exhibited a growing interest in geometry. A feature of his work was an occasional ambiguity and willingness to build in whatever style his clients wanted. He developed a castle style, and some buildings make clear references to Romanesque, Tudor, neoclassical, Georgian, and Gothic styles. He wanted to land a big, prestigious commission, which he eventually did. He designed some government buildings in South Africa, where he met Herbert Baker. His most prominent commission was to design a scheme of buildings for the new capital in New Delhi, India, an example of monumental classical planning. For this he brought along Baker. In India, Lutyens's most prominent project was the Viceroy's House (Figure 22.13).

He is less well known for his furniture designs, but they exhibit the qualities evident in his buildings. There is an appreciation of traditional detailing and references to specific styles, but at the same time there is an unmistakable air of inventiveness.

Like his friend Arthur Davis, when working on urban buildings, he designed classical stone façades for steel-framed buildings. Knighted in 1918, he was always suspicious of the modern movement. About Lutyens, Pevsner wrote: "The paradox of the revivalist in whose work geometry is more insistent than in any living architect bar Corbusier" (Pevsner 1951, p. 217).

The Alsatian Charles Mewès (1858–1914) and the Briton Arthur Davis (1878–1951) studied at the École des Beaux-Arts. From their London office, Mewès and Davis designed Ritz hotels in London, Paris, and Madrid (Binney 1999). The Ritz Piccadilly, in London, 1903–1906, was the first steel-framed building in London, not that this was evident from the inside. This successful partnership developed many of the interiors for early twentieth-century ocean liners, using an interesting office arrangement: Charles Mewès did the designs for the German Hapag-Lloyd Line, including the *Imperator*, and Davis did the designs for the Cunard Line, including the *Aquitania* (Zerbe 1999, pp. 106–10). Their projects responded to modern programs, relying on their deep knowledge of eighteenth-century French architecture and furniture, acquired at the Beaux-Arts.

The swimming pool of the Royal Automobile Club repeats a design that the firm used multiple times in their ocean liner interiors (Figure 22.14).

David Watkin sensed the discomfort that Davis felt about the direction that British architecture was taking: "Distressed by the insistence of the directors of the Cunard Line that his interiors

for the Queen Mary should be in an art deco style of which he disapproved, Davis suffered a nervous breakdown" (Watkin 2004 quoted in Allinson 2008, p. 292). The twentieth-century version of the battle of styles was keenly felt by many.

The United States

McKim, Mead, and White was the preeminent American architectural firm of the nineteenth and twentieth centuries. It was modern as a business entity, though committed to a renewal of past forms; over the course of its long practice, the firm created some nine hundred designs. At one time, McKim, Mead, and White had more than seventy employees (Roth 1983, p. 57). Their architecture was widely accepted and understood by the public, who held the architects in considerable esteem.

Stanford White (1853–1906), the most flamboyant of the firm's three partners, served members of the new wealthy class. White's shooting because of his affair with Evelyn Nesbitt has guaranteed him a dubious place in history that has little to do with the quality of his firm's work. With the houses they lived in, the buildings they designed for clients, and the public institutions to which they gave large sums of money, they

Figure 22.14
Charles Mewès
and Arthur Davis,
Royal Automobile
Club, London,
United Kingdom,
1911.

impacted architecture and interior design. The success of McKim, Mead, and White, and firms like it across the globe, leaves no doubt that creating traditional architecture was big business.

If McKim, Mead, and White is a large-scale example of a thriving firm that specialized in traditional architecture, David Adler is an example of a small firm, in the same stylistic vein, known for accomplished residential work. Most cities around the world had an accomplished architect who met the needs of clients who wanted traditional houses. David Adler (1882–1949) studied at Princeton, the Polytechnikum in Munich, and the École des Beaux-Arts in Paris. In Chicago, he worked for the architect Howard Van Doren Shaw. Important in many of his houses is symmetry, typically focused on a prominent entry sequence. He gave equal attention to both the front and rear elevations of his houses. He often collaborated with his sister on interior designs, mentioned below.

Adler worked skillfully and academically within the rules of a particular historic period. He was not one for upending traditions. Of note with the Armour house is that it has the grandeur and

presence that the client desired. The symmetrical façade, surprisingly flat and theatrical, looks like a crisp sheet of white paper. The building is Georgian in its massing and Federal in its detailing. Adler further emphasizes the flatness with a lawn that strikes the house's rear elevation with little intermediation of extensive terraces, lawn furniture, and plantings. With Adler, American historical architectural styles are up to the task of creating grand country houses for the mid-twentieth century.

California and Florida

Julia Morgan (1872–1957) was born in San Francisco. She pursued an engineering degree before deciding to study architecture. She also studied in Paris, at the École des Beaux-Arts. The imprint of her traditional French training is visible throughout her career.

After returning to San Francisco, Morgan opened her own office in 1904. She designed hundreds of buildings over the course of her career—houses, primary and secondary schools, and a number of college buildings. The Julia

Morgan School for Girls in Oakland is named after her. In 1919, William Randolph Hearst hired her to design a main building and guesthouses for his property at San Simeon (Kastner 2000, pp. 84–7). Twenty-five years of construction bound Hearst and Morgan together as collaborators on several Hearst projects in California, Arizona, and Mexico. Known as Hearst Castle, the property had thirty-eight bedrooms, most of them designed by Morgan with considerable input from the client (Figure 22.15).

Early in her career, she was working within the stylistic parameters of the American Arts and Crafts movement. By the late 1920s, she was confidently designing in the Spanish-Moorish-Gothic idiom that became her hallmark and that became synonymous with California. For the Berkeley City Women's Club, 1929–1930, her pool is more straightforward than her flights of fancy for Hearst. Her work was often lavish and theatrical, although on the drafting board of Julia Morgan, the architectural vocabulary of Spanish colonial was absolutely appropriate for a variety of modern functions, such as an up-to-date athletic facility. In the lounge, Venetian Gothic windows, vaulted ceilings, tiled floors, and Spanish Renaissance chairs contribute to creating an atmosphere grounded in centuries-old tradition—although built in the 1920s.

The southeast coast also saw a sustained interest in traditional architecture. The romantic vernacular of many Spanish-inspired buildings in Florida is often quite informal. Yet in designing a home for the industrialist James Deering, F. Burrall Hoffman turned to nothing less than the Italian Renaissance, and any comparison between the Deering family and a Florentine papal family such as the Medicis is purely intentional. Colombian landscape architect Diego Suarez planned the extensive gardens that spread out over ten acres, and Paul Chalfin was the general artistic supervisor for the project, which included furniture, light fixtures, doors, fireplaces, and artwork (Rybczynski 2007, pp. 231–32). Many pieces were purchased by Deering and Chalfin on shopping trips in Europe. The elaborate house took two years to build. At the height of construction, some 1,000 workers toiled away at the Villa Vizcaya.

With its combination of Renaissance planning and Spanish and Moorish detailing, the building was once derided as kitsch, the home of a man with too much money to burn. Its reputation, and consequently that of its designers, has been rehabilitated in recent years. A significant moment

Figure 22.15
Julia Morgan, Hearst Castle, San Simeon, CA, USA, 1919–1947. Guest bedroom.

in that process was when historian Colin Rowe started talking about the house favorably, stating that it could withstand comparison to actual Renaissance palazzi.

The association of Florida with the architectural tradition of the Spanish Renaissance is largely an invention of men like Hoffman and Addison Mizner. The Spanish left Florida in 1821, and left little in the way of an architectural legacy. Addison Mizner (1872–1933) was a world traveler, a connoisseur of antiques, art, and furnishings. He collaborated in several types of business ventures with his brother, Wilson. His is an American rags-to-riches-to-rags story, as he became a society architect despite having no formal academic training. He apprenticed with Willis Polk in San Francisco, learning architecture on the job, in the period 1893–1897. Like Morgan, he learned by traveling, especially in Central and South America (Curl 1984, pp. 12–15). Fluent in Spanish, he studied briefly at the University of Salamanca, Spain.

The existence of many architects who created buildings in historical styles was driven not just by clients but by the education and experiences of the architects as well. Mizner loved traveling, and purchasing antiques and reproductions, and selling them to clients or using them in the

houses he designed for them. He described his trips to Europe, in which he bought furnishings to be resold in the United States, as "raids" (Mizner 1932).

He traveled to China with his brothers. He was fond of Japanese gardens, documented by his many sketches and watercolors. In Hawaii, he befriended ex-Queen Liliuokalani and supported himself painting ivory miniatures. He entered a boxing match in Australia, which he won. He imported Guatemalan coffee and Guatemalan woodworking, which he resold. He traveled to Samoa, Italy, and Morocco.

His town planning for Boca Raton, Florida, reveals his keen eye for business. For example, he innovatively developed the idea of selling houses on the fairways of a golf course. Stanford White also helped him obtain commissions.

Mizner was adept at creating houses for moderately wealthy clients, whose more modest riches placed them lower on the social and economic scale than Astors and Vanderbilts (Figure 22.16). His houses typically focus on a central dramatic feature. In George Rasmussen's house, a circular stair tower contains the double-height entry hall. He effortlessly drew upon and combined Gothic, Romanesque, Spanish, and Moorish traditions.

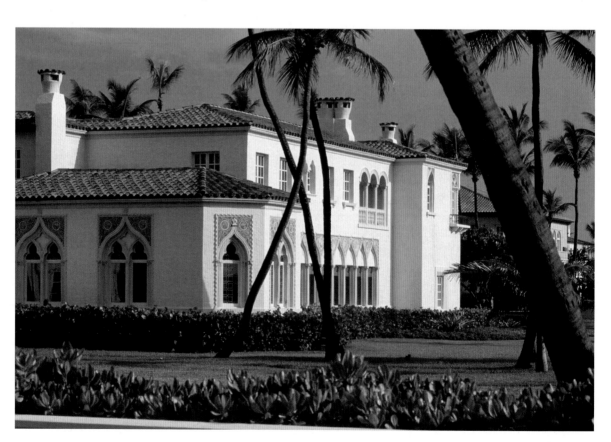

Figure 22.16
Addison Mizner, House on Dunbar Road, Palm Beach, FL, USA, 1923.

Paul Chalfin's masterwork, Vizcaya, Miami, Florida, was built for the industrialist James Deering between 1914 and 1916. Chalfin worked as both architect and interior decorator. There were highly accomplished regionally successful architects who did historicist projects. Lewis Ketcham Davis was active in Indiana, and his masterwork, Lilly House, 1909–1913, resembles a French chateau. George A. Berlinghof did courthouses, libraries, and a number of large houses in a variety of Renaissance Revival styles in Nebraska.

The Rise of the Decorator

Just as architects David Adler and Julia Morgan responded to the need of a wealthy class of people for houses that reflected tried-and-true notions of status, there was a growing need for professionals to help with outfitting the interiors of these houses. Interiors historian John Pile refers to the phenomenon as "The Rise of the Decorator" (Pile 2000). Interior decorating, as a profession, interestingly proceeded in different directions from that predicted by the work of architects also involved in producing traditionally styled houses.

The story of the early days of decorating as a serious business played out with numerous connections that crossed the Atlantic. Many of those who became interior designers, or decorators as they were known then, were people of modest means who had or developed a refined sense of taste. Many of them knew each other. West Coast, East Coast or in England, a knowledge of retailing, including but not limited to antiques was central to their practice. Initially their practices focused on the domestic environment.

The design activities of Candace Wheeler (1827–1923) plants her firmly in the middle of nineteenth-century design interests. She was a prominent figure in multiple arenas, including the aesthetic movements, art nouveau, and American Colonial Revival. One of her greatest successes was showing the American middle class how to lead a tasteful life in ways that were previously associated only with the upper class. She was an early figure who advocated the professionalization of design work, establishing the Society of Decorative Art in New York in 1877. She was

familiar with the work of William Morris across the Atlantic, and he inspired her both aesthetically and professionally. In 1878, she established the New York Exchange for Women's Work. She started a business, Tiffany and Wheeler, in 1879. She opened her own firm, Associated Artists in 1883 that employed only women. While not often credited as such, Wheeler was essentially the first American interior decorator. Although her businesses were successful, they were not large-scale operations; the organizations she founded were important for being the first steps of establishing interior design as a professional entity in the United States.

Wheeler's one time business partner is one of the many people who became an accomplished interior designer after a foundational experience in retail. Louis Comfort Tiffany (1848–1933) was the son of Charles Lewis Tiffany, the retailer. For Tiffany and Wheeler, the design of objects, furniture, and interiors were always considered in light of their commercial possibilities.

A seminal figure for the nineteenth-century United States, Wheeler, with her partner and on her own, was no longer at the center of design by the 1920s. She had been supplanted by a number of designers who, for one, saw the importance of self-promotion. In her nineties, Wheeler wrote her autobiography, *Yesterdays in a Busy Life*, which provides a record of the woman who made it fashionable for wealthy and middle-class homes to be decorated with American antiques and reproductions. Elsie de Wolfe, discussed below, is often erroneously called America's first decorator. If any single person is deserving of the term, it is Candace Wheeler.

In the wake of Candace Wheeler was Nancy McClelland (1877–1959). She was a design journalist and she did window displays before turning to residential interiors. She served as president of the American Institute of Interior Decorators. Her contribution to the professionalization of the field, in addition to organizations, was in fostering design education. Her specific interest was that designers needed to have an extensive, if not encyclopedia knowledge of European antiques and styles. A thorough understanding of the history of decorative arts was central to McClelland's views on design education, a position about teaching designers that remained throughout much of the twentieth century.

A foundational figure for the English side of the decorating business was Sibyl Colfax (1874–1950). A facet of her background that she shared with several of the interior designers who became well known in the late nineteenth and early twentieth centuries is that she had an aristocratic background although little money. Needing income and professional fulfillment, she turned to interior design because it was her most accomplished skill. What she did well was decorating and remodeling houses and relying on her social connections. In 1938 she started a partnership with John Fowler: Colefax and Fowler. The firm they built became an example for others in the design field; it specialized in high-end residential work, specifically country and town houses. While they also did hospitality projects, hotels and country clubs, the design of workplaces was not a significant portion of their output. While they advocated for the profession, they did not promote interior design as a force for societal change. A notable feature of their work is that they favored large-scale textiles. This made their work seem more updated than their Victorian predecessors.

Many of the global figures of the nascent interior design business were in Anglophone countries. Rose Cumming (1887–1968) was born in Australia and later she was professionally active in the United States. Candace Wheeler, Sibyl Colfax, and John Fowler emphasized that they enjoyed the mannerisms and taste of their elite clients. Cumming carved out a niche for herself professionally by becoming another archetype of the professional interior designer: the character. She was considered *outré*, extravagant, and theatrical. Her over-the-top designs, and her personal demeanor, were forerunners of Madeleine Castaing and Tony Duquette.

This group of early designers started their careers in the gilded age, 1870–1900, experienced the First World War, and worked throughout the Roaring Twenties. This was an age of economic growth and social change. The wealthy of the era desired houses that took residential design out of the nineteenth century and into the twentieth, although paradoxically, much of the decorating was historicist including tried-and-true pieces such as wing chairs (Figure 22.17).

There were not, initially, interior design firms the size of the largest architectural firms, such as D.H. Burnham and Company, or McKim, Mead & White. Designers were often sole proprietors, or partners. One partnership that served wealthy clients of the gilded age was the brother-sister duo of David Adler and Frances Elkins (1888–1953).

Francis Elkins (1888–1953) was David Adler's sister. After she married and moved to California in 1918, she ran her own interior design business.

Figure 22.17
Dorothy Draper, wing chairs, mid-twentieth century.

She collaborated with her brother on many projects and also worked independently. They worked on houses on Chicago's North Shore and also in the San Francisco Bay Area. She and Adler traveled together to Europe many times. On one trip, she met Jean-Michel Frank. At first it might seem odd that the modernist Frank should have befriended historically rooted designers such as Adler and Elkins, but he did. Both brother and sister incorporated some of his furniture into their designs. Elkins was, in fact, responsible for introducing Frank's work to the United States. She also used a palm frond table by Emilio Terry to great effect. Her friendship with French designers was important for her career. Elkins's work, more so than her brother's, blends historicist design with avant-garde elements.

Francis Elkins's personal and professional relationship with Frank had parallels. Colefax's business partner, John Fowler (1906–1977) was called "the prince of decorators," and he was part of two of the most prominent design partnerships of the twentieth century. Once Colefax tired of the business, she sold out her interests to the American Nancy Lancaster in 1944, cementing the extent of the cross-Atlantic fertilization of design ideas and products. His specialties included elaborated draperies, large-scale patterns, and the use of antiques with a lighter touch in both color and profile.

Lancaster (1877–1994) was his second business partner. She came from a noble but poor family of the American South. In 1917 she married into the retailing family whose flagship was Marshall Field and Company. She married two of Field's grandsons in succession, both of whom died. She had updated their houses to great acclaim, which started her career. Her third marriage was to an Englishman. Her purchase of Sibyl Colfax's firm brought the experienced John Fowler into her orbit.

In the United States, Parish-Hadley was another male-female firm. Its founder, Sister Parish (1910–1994) had status if not the finances that ideally accompanies it. Not a nun, her name was a childhood nickname that stayed with her. Like many of her contemporaries, she worked with English and French antiques and favored matching color schemes. In her personal demeanor, she was known for her impeccable manners, her taste and erudition. She was not an arch or dismissive personality and was proud of her patrician heritage. Her eventual business partner was Albert Hadley (1920–2012). He joined forces with Parish in 1962. One of his design strategies was using the same pattern on wallpaper, upholstery, and draperies.

Hadley completed the architectural side of their collaborative projects. He showed a great respect for the intricacies and possibilities that stemmed from working drawings and details. The New York Times referred to Parish as "the Queen of Interior Decorating." In a project for the Kennedy White House, Parish developed a color scheme of olive green, and dark peach on white. Their firm grew to twenty-five employees. It was one of the larger residential design firms. John Fowler and Albert Hadley were two of the men, adjuncts to the Great Lady Decorators, sometimes referred to as the Gentlemen Decorators. Many others followed.

Syrie Maugham (1879–1955) started in the antiques department of the retailer Fortnum & Mason. She was married to the writer Somerset Maugham, whose novels and plays frequently made reference to design issues and modernist themes of societal change that were sometimes related to aesthetic changes. As with the other women decorators, she worked within a historicist vein, but she shifted design in a contemporary direction. She was famous for an all-white room, a scenario she repeated several times, in which everything—floors, furniture, walls, textiles—was white. Even while using antiques, which she had painted or pickled, the monochromatic strategy made her design contemporary, of the moment, as it combined old-world elegance with the contemporary gloss of Hollywood.

Elsie de Wolfe (1865–1950) is well known as the pioneer professional interior decorator. She was one of the early women in the European-North American realm to make a career in design. Educated privately in New York and Edinburgh, she started her career as an actress. After redecorating her home to acclaim, she turned her attention to interior decoration and formed her own company in 1901 (she retired entirely from the theater in 1905). She updated historicist decorating, distancing herself from anything that could be called Victorian trends.

In 1903 de Wolfe, together with Elizabeth Marbury, her manager and companion, bought and restored the Villa Trianon in France (Sparke 2005, p. 301). Known for her social connections, the architect Stanford White helped de Wolfe obtain the project that started her career: the interior of the Colony Club in New York. In 1913, she published her first book, The House in Good Taste, likely written with the assistance of a ghostwriter. Her social connections included wealthy people on both sides of the Atlantic. Some of her connections involved Charles Parson, president of the New York School of Fine and Applied Arts. When de Wolfe moved to France, she closely associated with many of the elite, including the American Van Day Truex, head of the Paris campus of Parson's. In Paris, de Wolfe acted as an art dealer and collector. In 1926, she married Sir Charles Mendl, a British diplomat to France.

Elsie de Wolfe did not share the academic approach of Arthur Davis and Stanford White, whose knowledge of French architectural styles was extensive. De Wolfe was committed to eighteenth-century French furnishings, but she used them inventively. She lived in a time when there was a general disdain for Victorian design (an attitude she shared with the modernists), yet it was not immediately apparent how the vocabulary of eighteenth-century French interiors and furnishings could be adapted for the twentieth century. De Wolfe, and others after her, showed the way. She was respectful but not fearful of the periods she used. She relied heavily on white paint and did not hesitate to recommend having wood paneling painted. In the dining room of the New York house she shared with Marbury, she brought about a "dramatic transformation" employing Louis XVI chairs, white paint, and mirrors (Sparke 2005, p. 31).

De Wolfe was a professional woman who helped interior design become a separate entity from the architectural profession. Stanford White's support suggests that he saw her not as a competitor for his core business activities but as a valued consultant. The purview of interior design was not an area of work that most architects were either interested in or capable of doing. This had not always been the case. In eighteenth-century England, France, and Germany, most interior design work, meaning wood paneling and ordering furnishings, was done by men. Another important benchmark for the professionalization of interior design was the development of academic programs. The field of interior design would soon have its own schools.

De Wolfe was a pioneer in many respects, and several of the parameters of her individual approach to the interior decorating business came to be representative of the entire profession. In no small part because of de Wolfe, interior design became a field open to women. Less discussed, although by no means a secret, is that it became a field in which gays and lesbians operated openly. De Wolfe also played a role here. Songwriter Cole Porter, an erudite man with occasionally bawdy tastes, counted de Wolfe among his friends. This did not keep him from writing thinly veiled verses about Lady Mendl:

> Elsie de Wolfe, old and weary
> Might have lived and died a fairy,
> But Sir Charles Mendl she met and wed,
> And *on dit*, they went to bed.

Porter was a master of double entendre and hinted that the Mendls had a marriage of convenience. Porter was one of the most prominent songwriters of his day, and Mendl's appearance in a Porter song underscores that she had become a figure in American popular culture.

Eleanor Brown McMillen (1890–1991) was a decorator known for her rigorous business practices as much as the quality of her designs. She remained a promotor of the design program at Parsons. Like others of her generation, for her, education entailed a thorough understanding of American and European antiques. But central to her understanding of a design enterprise was to run it like a business. She always worked in an office, not her home. She had an accountant, an office manager, and was meticulous about billing.

Dorothy Draper (1889–1969) belongs to the second generation of decorators. Like de Wolfe, she relied on her social connections, a factor that served her extremely well during the development of her interior decorating business, Dorothy Draper & Company, which she started in 1925.

As with de Wolfe's clients, Draper's clients wanted interiors to include traditional pieces of furniture, but they did not necessarily want to see them used in traditional ways. Draper showed how twentieth-century designers could use traditional pieces of furniture and be contemporary. She did a few stylistically modern projects, and in them she showed people how to incorporate decorative pieces and patterned textiles. Whereas designs by Mies van der Rohe and Charlotte Perriand seemed austere to some, designs by Draper were fun and appealing.

Draper began creating homes for other society members, in a style that was uniquely her own and a complete departure from the perceived gloom of the Victorian style of decorating. The type of design associated with Draper (and her imitators, which were legion) is sometimes referred to as "**modern baroque**." She went international with a hotel in Petrópolis, Brazil, La Quitandinha (Figure 22.18). In that project, she went far afield from strict historicist designs, an approach that was ideal for restaurants, stores, and hotels. While some considered her work gaudy, it is more charitably described as bold. Draper, an innovative American interior decorator

Figure 22.18
Dorothy Draper, La Quitandinha, Petrópolis, Brazil, 1944.

of the early- to mid-twentieth century, was the writer of a syndicated newspaper column and also landed on the covers of *Time* and *Life* magazines, leaving no doubt about the extent of her influence. She was a major societal force, which she demonstrated by tackling the problem of how to house returning servicemen, albeit in her own inimitable fashion (Figure 22.19).

Draper's contribution to design received official recognition in May 2006 when the Museum of the City of New York held an exhibition of her work. Freewheeling in her use of historical styles, she sometimes, famously, disfigured original finishes, of furniture or woodworking, to achieve a new look. Her designs drew on many influences, but she was particularly known for dramatic use of black and white on floors, walls, and upholstered pieces.

A leading figure among the second generation of Gentlemen Decorators includes Billy Baldwin (1903–1983). He designed an entrance

Figure 22.19
Dorothy Draper, residence of Ensign Wood, 1946. The sailor had recently been decommissioned.

hall for Cole and Linda Porter's apartment and included it in a book on his design philosophy. One image caption "Country House on the 33rd Floor" refers to Porter's song "Down in the Depths on the 90th Floor" and is a wry recognition of the incongruity of designing a high-rise apartment to look like a well-appointed French country house.

Baldwin's design for the entrance hall includes the clever design moves he was known for: He upholstered a Louis XV settee in what was clearly a twentieth-century textile. What makes it work as part of an ensemble is that it and the artwork are elements in a consistent brown and eggshell color scheme. Baldwin frequently worked with a restricted color palette.

If Vizcaya was for a fabulously wealthy family, Van Day Truex showed that elegance could shape the lives of people of more modest means. He was not a wealthy person, but he decorated his homes with French antiques, proving that with careful placement, elite-style decorating could be affordable. He was not dogmatic, often combining expensive antiques with inexpensive or modern pieces.

The best school for training interior designers was the New York School of Fine and Applied Arts, later the Parsons School of Design. Led by Van Day Truex, it became the foremost training ground for interior decorators.

The quality of admiring historical styles, while simultaneously treating them offhandedly, was characteristic of de Wolfe, Draper, and Baldwin. This attitude toward historical styles, and antiques, was also characteristic of other designers around the world, one of them an eccentric figure in France, Madeleine Castaing (1894–1992). Castaing was a French interior designer and antiques dealer (Liaut 2008). She owned a shop in Paris where she sold antiques and modern works of art. Her favorite periods were neoclassical—Empire, Second-Empire, and Biedermeier. She combined neoclassical furnishings with contemporary textiles, favoring bold stripes and leopard prints. Her own home sported a leopard-print carpet. Examples of her unorthodox views of decorating and fashion were many; she advocated plastic flowers, and in her later years wore a wig with a clearly visible chin strap. She supported the work of the designer Poiret, the artist Modigliani, and counted Yves Saint Laurent among her clients; he admired her penchant for bamboo furnishings. She was photographed wearing a dress that matched the upholstery of the chair she sat in.

Conclusion

Architects and designers who operated within recognizable historical styles played important roles throughout the twentieth century. The 1920s is the decade associated with art deco, one of the styles, along with rococo and art nouveau, in which the greatest artistic achievements are found in interiors, furnishings, and designed objects. France had been a major center for those artistic periods of the eighteenth and nineteenth centuries, as it was for art deco, one of the most significant design developments of the twentieth century. In many respects, art deco designs had a lot in common with the modern designs coming out of Germany and France. As with many modernist pieces, art deco works display affinities to cubism, Russian Constructivism, and Italian futurism. Further evidence of the modernism/art deco link was the presence of Austrian designers, who were familiar with the Secessionists and who became the big names in American art deco.

A lesson learned from the decorators was that the middle class could successfully emulate the lifestyles of the rich. When looking at art deco, modernism, and the ongoing appeal of traditional design, the irony is that fancy designs appealed to the masses while populist designs made of humble materials often found rich fans.

Comparing this chapter to the preceding chapter, significant differences separate art deco and modernism. Art deco designers were less concerned with functionalism and the ability of their products to affect the social good. Art deco was connected to the fashion world, one example of its ties to elite circles. Stylistic differences were felt deeply by the people involved, and a schism developed between the designers/decorators known as *ensembliers* and the modernists. Some designers overlooked differences and were able to collaborate, such as Frances Elkins and Jean-Michel Frank. For many, the antipathy that they felt toward modernism could not be overcome.

Important sidebars to the story of design include the growing importance of women in shaping the interior design profession, and the increased visibility of gays and lesbians. In addition to their professional achievements, both groups were instrumental in fostering an academic and professional infrastructure to support the design field, another significant development of the twentieth century. European modernism was anointed with the title "The International Style"; the next chapter addresses the topic of modernism and the world. Art deco has just as much right to a global claim, as its spread from France to the United States, and then from both to around the world, demonstrates.

Art deco works are easily identifiable, with their shiny materials and characteristic zigzag forms. The works were unashamedly decorative. This chapter presented three design strands—art deco, traditionalists, and decorators. Looking at all three confirms the ability of designers to offer differing views of what the world should look like and how to go about designing and crafting man-made objects. Differences abound; what all three shared was the activity of contending with how to make history new, adaptable, and relevant.

Sources

Albrecht, Donald, ed. (2008). *Paris/New York: Design Fashion Culture, 1925–1940*. New York: Museum of the City of New York.

Allinson, Kenneth (2008). *The Architects and Architecture of London*. London: Architecture Press.

Alonso, Alejandro, Pedro Contreras, and Martino Fagiuoli (2007). *Havana Deco*. New York: Norton.

Benton, Charlotte, ed. (2003). *Art Deco 1910–1939*. Boston: Bulfinch.

Binney, Marcus (1999). *The Ritz Hotel: London*. London: Thames and Hudson.

Bréon, Emmanuel (2004). *Jacques-Émile Ruhlmann: Interior Design*. Paris: Flammarion.

Butler, A.S.G. (2023). *The Architecture of Sir Edwin Lutyens*. Woodbridge: ACC Art Books.

Butler, Judith (1999). *Gender Trouble: Feminism and the Subversion of Identity*. New York: Routledge.

Carter, Randolph (1992). *Joseph Urban: Architecture, Theatre, Opera*. New York: Abbeville Press.

Curl, Donald (1984). *Mizner's Florida: American Resort Architecture*. Cambridge, MA: MIT Press.

Dehan, Amy, with Christopher Long and Elizabeth McGoey (2022). *Joseph Urban: Unlocking an Art Deco Bedroom*. Lewes: Giles.

Delacroix, Henry (2017). *Art Deco Interiors*. Mineola, NY: Dover.

Denison, Edward (2003). *Asmara: Africa's Secret Modernist City*. London: Merrell.

Duncan, Alastair (1984). *Art Deco Furniture: The French Designs*. New York: Holt, Rinehart, and Winston.

Duncan, Alastair (1988). *Art Deco*. London: Thames and Hudson.

Fisher, Richard (1978). *Syrie Maugham*. Dallas, TX: Duckworth.

Gray, Susan, ed. (2001). *Architects on Architects*. New York: McGraw Hill.

Hanks, David (1987). *Donald Deskey: Decorative Designs and Interiors*. New York: Dutton.

Kastner, Victoria (2000). *Hearst Castle: The Biography of a Country House*. New York: Abrams.

Lewis, Adam (2001). *Van Day Truex: The Man Who Defined Twentieth-Century Taste and Style*. New York: Viking Studio.

Liaut, Jean-Hoël (2008). *Madeleine Castaing*. Paris: Payot.

Long, Christopher (2002). *Josef Frank: Life and Work*. Chicago: University of Chicago Press.

Long, Christopher (2007). *Paul T. Frankl and Modern American Design*. New Haven, CT: Yale University Press.

Mizner, Addison (1932). *The Many Mizners*. New York: Sears Publishing.

Pevsner, Nikolaus (1951). "Building with Wit: The Architecture of Sir Edwin Lutyens." *Architectural Review* 109: 217–25.

Pile, John (2000). *History of Interior Design*. New York: Wiley.

Roth, Leland (1983). *McKim, Mead, and White, Architects*. New York: Harper and Row.

Rybczynski, Witold (2007). *Vizcaya: An American Villa and Its Makers*. Philadelphia: University of Pennsylvania Press.

Salny, Stephen (2005). *Frances Elkins: Interior Design*. New York: Norton.

Schwartzman, Arnold (2019). *Art Deco: The 20ᵗʰ Century's Iconic Decorative Style*. New York: Rizzoli.

Sparke, Penny (2005). *Elsie de Wolfe: The Birth of Modern Interior Decoration*. New York: Acanthus.

Stern, Robert (1982). *Raymond Hood*. New York: Rizzoli.

Thorne, Martha, ed. (2003) *David Adler, Architect: the Elements of Style*. New Haven, CT: Yale University Press.

Tise, Suzanne (1996). "Art Deco." In *The Dictionary of Art*, edited by Jane Turner, pp. 519–22. New York: Grove.

Tise, Suzanne and Yvonne Brunhammer (1990). *The Decorative Arts in France, 1900–1942*. New York: Rizzoli.

Varney, Carleton (1988). *The Draper Touch: The High Life and High Style of Dorothy Draper*. New York: Prentice Hall.

Watkin, David (2004). "Davis, Arthur Joseph (1878–1951)." In *Oxford Dictionary of National Biography*. Oxford: Oxford University Press. http://0-www.oxforddnb.com.library.unl.edu:80/view/article/62902 (accessed April 25, 2008).

Yeomans, David and David Cottam (2001). *Owen Williams*. London: Thomas Telford.

Zerbe, Peter (1999). *Die Grossen Deutschen Passagierschiffe*. Hamburg: Nautik Historie Verlag.

Discussion and Review Questions

1. What are the characteristics of art deco that distinguish it from 1920s German and French modernism?
2. What are some characteristics art deco shares with other movements—where it was tapping into broad interests?
3. How has the reputation of some designers changed posthumously?
4. What did decorators do?
5. What does it mean if design is popular—that is, appeals to the masses? What makes art deco decorative?
6. What makes a design elite? Give specific examples of either designs or materials used.
7. What did art deco designers and modernist designers have in common?
8. How did art deco designers and modernist designers differ in their approach?
9. In what ways did art deco designers relate to and incorporate history?
10. What are the differing characteristics between the French and American versions of art deco?
11. How did architects and designers trained in historicst styles respond to the twentieth-century condition? Why are traditional designs appealing to many people?

Other Modernisms

23

1936	1939–1941	1953–1970	1959
Le Corbusier and Niemeyer, Ministry of Education, Brazil	Charlotte Perriand in Japan	Modern architecture in Cambodia	David Mutiso, KICC, Kenya

Modernism, it is commonly said, started in Germany and France. Then, in a classic case of anthropological diffusion, one scenario explains its spread by the variety of mechanisms that cause cultural trends to traverse the globe. Travel, journals, books, and exhibitions were some of the vehicles that distributed the lessons of modernism. The Second World War compelled many Bauhaus designers to emigrate to Britain, to the United States, Brazil, Argentina, Kenya, and Japan. Who-worked-for-whom was another mechanism of knowledge diffusion and served as a designer's pedigree. Le Corbusier worked for Peter Behrens and thereby learned from him; many burgeoning architects and designers worked in Le Corbusier's office, learned from him, and took with them their newfound knowledge when they returned to their home countries. Le Corbusier was particularly significant in this regard. Josep Luis Sert, Kiyoshi Ikebe, Rogelio Salmona, Emilio Duhart, Robert Matta, and Oscar Niemeier all worked at one time in his office.

And of course there are the buildings the masters did themselves around the world: Le Corbusier in India, Japan, Argentina, the United States, and Tunisia; Louis Khan in Bangladesh and India; and Frank Lloyd Wright in Japan. Despite several attempts, Mies had less of an impact on international building and most of his works grace American soil.

Scholars from William Curtis to Colin Rowe, whose statements on modernism are still considered sacrosanct, write that modernism was initially an avant-garde, European intellectual

Figure 23.0
(*Facing page*)
Geoffrey Bawa, Lunuganga, Bentota, Sri Lanka, 1948. House of the architect.

movement that spread around the world in the 1950s. And there is more than a kernel of truth to this explanation. But another story can explain the rise of modernism across the globe, and that is that it flowered, independently, at multiple locations. That is the subject of this chapter.

European and Western architects and designers play a role here, just as Asian, African, and Latin American designers and architects are present in other chapters. And certain figures, such as Antonin Raymond and Geoffrey Bawa, whose identities and allegiances are complicated, can only be described as early citizens of a global design world.

Modernism developed at different paces in different places, and was received sometimes with measured skepticism, sometimes with unbridled enthusiasm. It was initially slow to raise its head in the United States and Britain yet proved a quick study in Mexico and Brazil. Modernism was never a monolithic entity or style, and its designers were reflexive and responsive to local conditions. Far from the idea that multiple global modernisms were void, many find that the "foreign" versions are equally engaging, perhaps more so than some examples of the European variety, with their sensitivity to materials, history, local traditions, and emotional richness.

It is surprising how early on committed modernists spanned the globe. The standard story for modernism's spread is that it occurred after the Second World War; yet, as this chapter shows, modernism was percolating across the globe as early as the 1920s and 1930s. After the Second World War, those areas that had temporarily lagged behind quickly caught up. When examining the rise of modernism around the world, we see that in Brazil, South Africa, Mexico, and Japan, modern ideas and projects were present as early as the 1920s. Clearly, another narrative of cultural genesis is at play. If one considers that modernity is the nebulous entity by which the world lurches forward, and that modernism is the artistic representation of coming to grips with the present and the future, then all regions of the globe experienced modernity and thereby played a part, albeit unequally, in creating "modernism." No region was immune to the technological effects of automobiles, airplane travel, television, radio, telephones, telegraphs, Technicolor movies (and later computers, jets, the internet, the Walkman, the mobile phone, and the smartphone). These were experienced as innovations, or as devices whose use became increasingly widespread. All areas of the globe were modern and thereby produced their unique form of modernism.

Latin America

In Latin America, one explanation for the multiplicity of forms that modernism took is that different Latin American countries had vastly different histories. Mexico and Peru had ancient cultures. The primarily indigenous groups of Brazil and Argentina were talented in textiles, baskets, and pottery, but did not have monumental architecture. Bolivia was poor; Argentina, befitting its name, was rich.

Mexico

For Mexico, the important contemporary contextual note is that modernism is related to the Mexican Revolution, 1910–1920. The political revolution that ended a thirty-year-long dictatorship was followed by a design revolution. Mexico first built a firm foundation of modernist design with works in the 1920s and 1930s by Luis Barragán, Juan O'Gorman, and others. A constant theme in this chapter is that modernism meant different things in different places. Even in one location, such as Mexico City, it held different meanings for different people. As a broad-brush generalization, early Mexican modernism is viewed in conjunction with the revolution and democracy. Yet the leader of Mexican modernism, Barragán himself, opposed it. The dictatorship had favored the wealthy, and Barragán, something of an elitist, was no fan of the people's revolution.

Known as the first modernist in Mexico, José Villagran Garcia approached new architecture from the perspective of functionalism, architecture's relationship to modern art, and its ability to solve special needs in Mexico, from education to housing. An architect and a teacher, Garcia saw two of his pupils become major figures in the development of Mexican modernism. One was Mario Pani, who counted University City among his achievements; Mexico's flagship university was founded in 1551 but moved to its new campus in 1954. Another architect associated with the university was Juan O'Gorman.

Juan O'Gorman's House and Studio for Diego Rivera and Frida Kahlo (1929–1930) looks to Le Corbusier's Ozenfant studio and also Russian Constructivism. It was built for a compelling couple, two Mexican artists who had strong personalities. It's a modern work with geometric profiles, metal railings, and curved stairways, but its bold use of colors and palisade of cacti foreshadow that Mexican modernism was to be no pale imitation of European modernism.

It is also a beguiling architectural portrait of a couple, two artists each with their own studios on the top floor, his a bit larger, which reflects Rivera's oversized body and ego (Figure 23.1). The connections between the two almost separate structures are tenuous (like their unconventional marriage), a catwalk on the top floor and a discreet path on the ground. It was also an opportunity for O'Gorman to experiment with a design that could be industrialized.

One of the outstanding features of Mexican modernism, inaugurated with O'Gorman's Rivera/Kahlo house, is how thoroughly it became a part of the local architectural vocabulary. Modernism became enmeshed in the domestic realm in a way that did not happen in the United States, where the modern house met resistance. Mexico embraced the modern house. Mexico is doubly important for the history of architecture because the reconsideration of modernism as a global phenomenon largely starts with the rehabilitation of the career of Luis Barragán.

Barragán

Latin American modernism has an appealing champion in the figure of Luis Barragán (1902–1988). Keith Eggener succinctly writes that Barragán "endeavored to reconcile modernism with the indigenous architecture of Mexico, in order to express a distinct sense of place" (2004, pp. 116–17). First among his achievements was his confident relationship to history and tradition; European modernists, in contrast, often seem conflicted about history and uneasy in their approach to tradition. Barragán's projects easily make reference to many traditions, including pre-Columbian, Spanish colonial, and the rural hacienda tradition.

Another successful feature of his architecture is its reliance on a deep understanding of local construction techniques. European modernists developed a crisp aesthetic of white planes that was difficult to achieve and hard to maintain. The problems with Le Corbusier's signature Villa Savoye began shortly after its completion; the roof leaked and the walls grew spotty. Barragán ingeniously worked with local building methods that did not require complicated detailing from outside that tradition.

In the 1940s, one of the projects that display many of the features associated with Barragán's architecture, lightheartedly referred to as

Figure 23.1
Juan O'Gorman,
Diego Rivera
and Frida Kahlo
House-Studio,
Mexico City,
Mexico, 1931.
Rivera's studio.

Barraganismo, can be seen in his Casa Pedregal, Mexico City (1947–1950) (Figure 23.2). The stair-hall has a concrete stair, a painting by Matthias Goeritz, and an inexpensive wood chair with a straw seat. The Galvez House (1955) is another frequently published work. A recurring motif in his buildings is that certain details make a sophisticated commentary on the grid's relationship to modernity. An all-encompassing grid fills some windows, with the result that the landscape beyond is overlain with an ordered system of lines, breaking the view into little segments (Rispa 2003, pp. 28–9). Other windows feature a simple cross, a decidedly light touch with religious overtones. Barragán was deeply religious and prominently featured the cross in his own house. The cross also renders obvious the glass's presence as a transparent plane. Because of its inherent planarity and rectilinearity, Barragán's work is most often compared to Mies's, yet Barragán himself cites Le Corbusier as the greater influence.

Barragán's houses frequently feature a chair that he used on several projects. It was designed in collaboration with Clara Porset, a Cuban designer. Known as the *butaca* or *butaque* chair,

it was based on a traditional Mexican chair, although Porset simplified its lines (Figure 23.3). She created several versions of the chair (Zanco 2001, pp. 86 and 101). Porset was at the center of an exciting design milieu that proved a female-led alternative to the world of male architects. Her circle included the photographer Lola Alvarez Bravo, and the textile designers Anni Albers and Sheila Hicks.

Just as European artists relate to the works of Picasso and Mondrian, Barragán was active in the art scene in Mexico City and knew personally many of the surrealists and minimalists, including Diego Rivera and Mathias Goeritz, the latter of whom was a frequent collaborator. And the colors! An example of the technical simplicity of his architecture are the dramatic effects Barragán achieved with paint. He favored saturated colors, including pinks, blues, yellows, and reds, that give his buildings a character unlike anything built in Europe. This approach to color is also evident in the textile designs of Albers and Hicks.

Barragán's work expresses a confident approach to the landscape. Most architects give lip service to relating to nature, yet Barragán does so in an unusual way, often by not making obvious

Figure 23.2
Luis Barragán,
Casa Pedregal,
Mexico City,
Mexico, 1947–
1950.

overtures to the landscape. While his designs frequently make reference to the landscape, he is confident enough to block it out on occasion, with high walls; a typical Barraganesque detail is to have a wisp of tree visible, like a clip of a photograph of a tree, in the distance, floating above a plane. The relationship of Barragán's houses to nature bears resemblance to Mies van der Rohe's collages. Barragán was clever enough to realize that, correctly done, one way to relate to nature is to seemingly ignore it.

Barragán was not a strict functionalist. His buildings have an emotional quality that arises from his use of materials, color, and natural light. He developed a carefully orchestrated sense of surprise and discovery in his houses. His buildings, and photographs of them, evoke a sense of serenity and peace, even when in urban surroundings. But nowhere is the metaphysical aspect of Barragán's work so evident as with his San Cristobal Riding Stables of 1968, Barragán's magnum opus. It is a work of landscape as much as a work of architecture, with Aztec-inspired massive walls, expansive pools, and red walls. It is incredibly photogenic (Eggener 2001, p. 75).

Barragán's international reputation was a long time in coming, but once people started turning their attention to his pink walls there was no turning back. In 1976, the Museum of Modern Art held a retrospective of his work. In 1980, he won the Pritzker Prize. The inclusion of Luis Barragán into the canon of modern masters has been so instrumental that it has resulted in a reevaluation of just what modernism is.

Figure 23.3
Clara Porset,
butaque chair,
1957. The
designer made
countless
variations of this
chair throughout
her career.

The breadth of Mexican modernism

The project for a new university campus in
Mexico City, University City, was a monumental
collaborative effort that included many architects, including Mario Pani, Juan O'Gorman,
and Teodoro González de León. Eschewing
American and English academic models, it
put Le Corbusier's city-planning principles
into action. The complex includes O'Gorman's
Library (1950), the most prominent building
whose façades are richly covered with mosaics
that link modern scientific achievements with
Aztec graphic representation also designed by
O'Gorman.

Nearby, the sports pavilions designed in 1953
by Espinosa Arai ingeniously echo the massing of
low platforms found in pre-Columbian sites such
as Mitla. Made of stone, these forms contain the
audience seating for the sports venues and the
high-dive platform. Sports venues designed for the
Mexico City Olympics included tens of thousands
of a version of the Robin Day Polypropylene chair,
1964.

In Chapultepec Park, the National Museum
of Anthropology in Mexico City by Pedro Ramírez
Vásquez (1963–1964) is a stunning building that
makes subtle allusions to the pre-Columbian
cultures whose artifacts it houses. It is a modern
structural marvel with a huge roof that covers the
immense courtyard, miraculously supported on a
single column that is also a fountain.

Mexico City entered the informal international race to have a major skyscraper with the
Torrelatinoamerica (1957), competently designed
by Augusto Alvarez, proving that Mexican
modernists were capable of mastering tall-building technology. The building is discussed in
Chapter 24. Feliz Candela experimented with
concrete thin-shell technology to produce a variety of sculptural forms that housed everything
from open-air markets to churches (Faber 1963).
The pool of Mexican designers was deep, talented,
and prolific.

Ricardo Legorreta (1931–2011) is a protégé
of Barragán, which is visible in his work that
employs forms reminiscent of Aztec and Mayan
architecture yet is enlivened with a color palette
derived from Mexican folk art. The Hotel Camino
Réal in Mexico City is sophisticated, pleasing
to the public, and looks modern and Mexican
(Legorreta 2004, p. 290). Its popular cocktail
lounge is filled with modern classic furniture.
Yet Legorreta is not afraid to incorporate Spanish
colonial elements, one of his design strategies

that results in a moving evocation of locality.
Legorreta's firm did a number of hotels for the
Camino Real chain, including the Camino Real
Aeropuerto, 2006 (Figure 23.4). Legorreta and his
son, Victor Legorreta (b. 1966), practiced together
and represent the second and third generations of
Mexican modernists.

Brazil

The other major center of early Latin American
modernism was Brazil. Rio de Janeiro was a South
American center of art nouveau, with some of
the finest projects done by Eliseu Visconti. To the
extent that modernism grew out of the modernizing trends inherent in art nouveau, a lack of a
historically based vocabulary, and the embrace
of new materials, Brazil was well positioned for
modernism to flower.

Rio de Janeiro and Brasília

Albertos Santos Dumont (1873–1932) was one
of the inventors of the airplane. There is contro-
versy over who had the first airplane flight (the
argument stands on how long a plane has to stay
aloft to be considered flying). Americans claim
that the Wright Brothers achieved the first flight;
Brazilians stand by Dumont. The argument over
this pivotal modern achievement also plays out
in the field of design. And, interestingly enough,
Dumont was an innovative creator in many
fields. He designed his own house, the Casa
Encantada in Petrópolis, a city in the mountains
close to Rio, which includes a unique flight of
scalloped stairs.

The formal arrival of modernism in Brazil
is easily traced to one building, the Ministry
of Education in Rio de Janeiro, 1936–1945, in
which no less than Le Corbusier was the consulting architect. Hired to act as his assistant was
a precocious young Brazilian architect, Oscar
Niemeyer (Underwood 1994, p. 20). The Ministry
of Education has, like Corbusier's influential
apartment block the Unité, pilotis, a roofscape,
and **brises-soleil**. The latter is a porous architectural screen that lets in air and shields the
building from direct sunlight. This engaging
façade element was particularly well suited for
tropical climates and became a favored device for
sporting a local decorative motif.

Niemeyer was born in Rio in 1907. In 1930,
he went to the National School for the Fine Arts,
where Lúcio Costa was director. Among the
students was the landscape architect Roberto
Burle Marx, who would be a future collaborator

Figure 23.4
Ricardo Legorreta,
Camino Real
Aeropuerto,
Mexico City,
Mexico, 2006.

with Niemeyer and the designer of Rio's Copacabana sidewalks.

Brazil and Oscar Niemeyer were embarking down their modernist road extraordinarily quickly, starting in the 1930s. Some two decades later, Niemeyer was an established architect in his home country. With the house that Niemeyer designed for himself in the Canoas district of Rio, he established his international reputation as a modernist of note (Figure 23.5). Niemeyer's house promoted a sensuous alternative to mechanistic modernism (Underwood 1994, p. 78).

This small house was built in 1953 and is reminiscent of the lightweight concrete structures in Mexico made by Felix Candela. It challenges several modernist conventions. As an iconic work of domestic architecture, it draws comparison to the Mies's Farnsworth House and Philip Johnson's Glass House. Yet it is a poetic alternative to the hyperrationality of both.

A curvilinear white concrete roof caps the walls, many of which are formed from large panels of plate glass. Its whiplash curves hug the

Figure 23.5
Oscar Niemeyer, Niemeyer House, Canoas, Rio de Janeiro, Brazil, 1953. Plan.

Brazilian landscape, and it opens up to forest, sky, and water. A curvilinear pool perches on top of a large outcropping of rock; Burle Marx did the naturalistic landscaping. It was built, in a timely fashion, just before the organization that Le Corbusier founded, CIAM, met in Brazil in 1954. (The International Congresses of Modern Architecture was a group of like-minded modernists who promoted avant-garde architecture.)

Brazil, like many countries in the 1950s, wanted to present itself to the international audience as progressive, and a quick means to do that was through modern architecture. Niemeyer collaborated with his former teacher, Lúcio Costa, in designing a new capital of Brazil, Brasília. This project, controversial and influential, managed to be monumental with a starkly modern vocabulary. Lúcio Costa created a plan in which the grid was absent. It is a plan destined to grow linearly. Because of its large-scale curves, it is compared to a bird or airplane's wings (a subtle nod to Santos Dumont). Niemeyer did an impressive group of major buildings. The long-lived Niemeyer had a prolific career, equaled by few in terms of longevity or quantity and quality of work, including many buildings that formed the core of the capital city of Brasília, 1957–1958.

São Paulo

The rise of Niemeyer presents the activity in the country's artistic and governmental capital, Rio de Janeiro. But Brazil's business center, São Paulo, was home to a lively modern art scene that had been active since the 1920s. São Paulo held a Modern Art Week, Semana 22, in 1922, a seminal moment for the introduction of artistic modernism into Brazil. The industrial city sought to refashion itself as cosmopolitan, international, and more modern than Rio. The goal was to expose Brazilian artists to significant contemporary art trends, to renew avant-garde artistic activities in Brazil, and to lay claim to the legacy of European modernism, especially geometric abstraction. With assistance from Nelson Rockefeller and the Museum of Modern Art in New York, the Museum of Modern Art of São Paulo was founded in 1951. Brazil's place in the contemporary art world was cemented in 1953 when Picasso's *Guernica* put in an appearance at the Bienal (Leite and Burbridge 1995, pp. 197–217). Abstraction offered an alternative to South American stereotypes that frequently portrayed Brazil as exotic and flamboyant, the prime example being the Hollywood movies of Carmen Miranda.

Flavio de Carvalho was an architect and painter who built seventeen modernist houses in São Paulo in the 1930s. Leite and Burbridge describe the designer's own house: "The unusual atmosphere of the farmhouse was created largely by its interior decoration, where Carvalho combined handcraft and feather art made by Brazilian Indians" (1995, p. 212). Modernism was gaining a stronghold in Brazil in the 1930s, by designers who shared the international sympathies of relating to indigenous cultures.

Into this environment arrived Lina Bo Bardi (1914–1992). Italian-born, she had been the editor of the Italian design magazine *Domus* before moving to Brazil in 1947. In 1949, she founded the Brazilian design journal *Habitat*. She started a company, Studio d'Arte Palma, that produced modern furniture (Ferraz 1994, pp. 64–7). She taught industrial design and built her own house. Her largest building was the Museu de Arte de São Paulo. This was followed by a sports and culture center, the SESC Pompéia. Of Lina Bo Bardi's many furniture designs, the one to achieve the most international attention is her eponymous masterpiece Bardi's Bowl (1951) (Figure 23.6).

Brazil had a significant cadre of imported modernist architects and designers, including Jorge Zalsupin, Michel Arnoult, and Gregori Warchavchik (1896–1972). It also produced a distinguished roster of homegrown modernistas: in addition to Costa and Niemeyer, Paulo Mendes

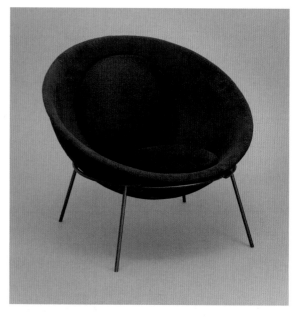

Figure 23.6
Lina Bo Bardi, Bardi's Bowl, São Paulo, Brazil, 1951.

do Rocha, Joâo Batista Villanova Artigas, Rino Levi, Sergio Bernardes, and Joâo Filgueiras Lima all did modern work. Significantly, Brazil became a thriving center for locally produced modern furniture; many pieces did well on the international market.

Some of the other major furniture designers include Joâo Carlos Cauduro, a Brazilian who studied industrial design in Florence and who ended up doing urban furniture (Leon 2005). Délia Beru, from Argentina, arrived in Brazil and started the firm Casa Teperman, which represented Herman Miller. In 1998, she opened Casa 21, which manufactured the designs of Eileen Gray. In the 1970s, Ernesto Hauner (1931–2002) worked for Bo Bardi's firm Mobilinea.

Argentina

Compared to Mexico and Brazil, modernism took root slowly in Argentina, which is curious because it started out the postwar period wealthier and more technologically advanced than either of those countries. Argentina, like Brazil, is a country whose indigenous people were skilled in textiles and pottery yet not active with monumental architecture.

Argentina also had a large immigrant population. Argentina seemed perfectly enamored of concrete, parabolic vaulting, reinforced concrete shells, and they embraced **brutalism** for a while, one of modernism's more extreme offshoots.

Architecture

Amancio Williams (1913–1989) was an architect and urban planner. In 1949, he met Le Corbusier, who hired him to supervise the construction of a house in La Plata, the Currutchet House, not considered one of Le Corbusier's major works.

Williams's own House Over the Brook, 1945, designed for his father, is a distinguished piece of architecture. Boasting a dramatic relationship to nature—a brook flows underneath it—it is related to Frank Lloyd Wright's house Falling Water. Yet it also makes a unique architectural statement. Built like a bridge, a parabolic concrete arch holds the building aloft.

Williams later collaborated with Walter Gropius on an unbuilt project, the West German Embassy. Several of his buildings interface with health and hygiene, but Williams is primarily known for his lyrical forms and an aesthetic that brings architecture in concert with **minimalism**.

Clorindo Testa (b. 1923) was the leader of the rationalist strain of the South American modern movement. Testa freely admitted his ideological debt to Le Corbusier. About the French modernist, he said: "He became my model both in my university years and after graduation" (Glusberg 1984). He is often presented as a textbook example of a brutalist architect. Brutalism, or new brutalism, is related to Le Corbusier's later works. Brutalist works were almost always made in concrete, and a signature detail was showing the impressions made by the wooden formwork. Precise detailing was not a feature of brutalism, the design equivalent of the art brut movement. Testa was a painter, and crisply delineated forms are a feature of both his paintings and buildings. The Bank of London and South America, 1960, was designed as a box within a box. The concrete façade is supported independently from the glazing on the exterior, and the result is a curtain layering effect of glass and large overhanging concrete slabs (Cuadra 2000, pp. 43–51).

Furniture

Jorge Ferrari-Hardoy (1914–1977) belongs to the cadre of architects who turned to furniture design. Born in Buenos Aires, he lived in Paris, where he collaborated with Le Corbusier, and throughout his life he remained active in CIAM. In 1938, he designed a simple chair of canvas stretched over a wooden frame, known as the Hardoy chair. The frame was later made of metal. The chair, used indoors and out, was enormously successful. "The Butterfly Chair," is sometimes known as "The Sling Chair" (Figure 23.7). Knoll and Artek initially manufactured the chair, which John Pile referred to as "handsome, inexpensive, and easy to make" (Pile 1990, p. 114).

Uruguay

Uruguayan engineer Eladio Dieste (1917–2000) studied in Montevideo and later taught structures. He next turned to producing a series of buildings based on light supporting structures, perfect for the series of bus stations and markets that he designed in the 1950s (Anderson 2004). He focused on local technology, materials, and construction methods to ground his designs in their local context. He is another example of a South American architect whose oeuvre expresses a fondness for thin-shelled vaults and ceramic tile.

He designed the Catholic Church of Christ the Worker and Our Lady of Lourdes in Atlántida in 1958 (Figure 23.8). Interested in natural resources, he produced works that show a great deal of respect for and knowledge of a material's properties. He worked in brick, the most humble of

Figure 23.7
Jorge Ferrari-
Hardoy, living
room with Knoll
Butterfly chair,
1938.

vernacular materials, and also in reinforced brick. Dieste's work with steel-reinforced brick allowed him to create flowing curved interiors in brick; he transferred structural innovations originally explored in concrete.

Venezuela

There is not a single Latin American country that did not embrace modernism. In Venezuela, Carlos Raúl Villanueva (1900–1975) is credited with being the father of Venezuelan modern architecture. Paulina Villanueva wrote: "Villanueva placed equal, if not greater priority on the commodious design of interior space—the space where man and architecture meet" (2000, p. 18). Mostly active in the 1950s, he designed his own house in 1952, and the Universidad Central de Venezuela, 1950–1959, for which he designed the campus layout and several buildings.

Lessons from Latin America

Pioneers such as Barragán, O'Gorman, and Niemeyer set the foundation for the second

generation of Latin American architects, including Ricardo Legorreta. In the 1980s, Legorreta took off where Luis Barragán began. One of his projects was his Renault factory in Monterey, Mexico, 1984.

The modernist insistence on a break with the past had a different gloss in Mexico (and Peru). Styles associated with nineteenth-century eclecticism were frowned upon, but forms and materials related to the countries' heritages could be a valued source of inspiration. Louis XVI was out, but Aztec and Inca were in.

One significant aspect of modernism is that it was ripe for incorporating aspects of indigenous cultures, relying upon artistic and cultural traditions. Modernist designers had always enjoyed the bold shot in the arm of the "primitive" culture, vestigial elements, as part of their aesthetic bag of tricks. Amancio Williams took note of what Eileen Gray and Charlotte Perriand did, so he too threw an animal hide on the floor. But in his case, it was a cowhide, which makes a connection with the Argentine pampas tradition of cowboys and ranching.

ni g

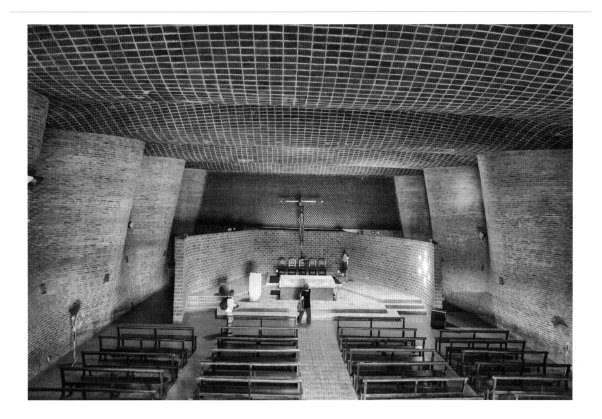

Figure 23.8
Eladio Dieste,
Church of Christ
the Worker
and Our Lady
of Lourdes,
Atlántida,
Uruguay, 1952.

Africa

Kwame Anthony Appiah writes that, throughout history, most Africans have defined themselves in terms of bloodlines and local communities, but the idea of a shared African identity, much less a common culture, is a recent phenomenon, dating to the last one hundred years. Africa has an enormous diversity: "It would take an eye completely insensitive to the particular to reduce this magnificent miscellany to the expression of the spirit of a singular, coherent, African nature" (Appiah in Phillips 1996, p. 7). Only then is the idea of Africa, in which diversity is a central characteristic of what it means to be African, possible.

A few African countries had some experience with modernism before the Second World War, but it was in the late 1940s and 1950s that modernism became widespread in Africa. For many Africans, a modernist building was a symbol of a new way of doing things and an optimistic look to the future. In the 1960s and 1970s, many areas experienced a crash course in modernism.

Modernism was called on for highly visible and prestigious projects, such as airports and football stadiums, which operated as instant status symbols. In many cases, countries went from third world to first world seemingly overnight.

In countries with significant oil reserves, the important chronological benchmark is neither the Second World War nor independence, but before and after the discovery of oil, an example of how dating systems vary from place to place. Many African countries had to deal with changing from a rural and agricultural country to an urban industrialized country—quickly.

If there is a constant thread weaving across modern buildings in Africa, it is that, most important, modern architecture in Africa is related to national liberation movements and colonialism's end, occurring in the 1960s. Even if modernism was first introduced under the colonial regimes, modern architecture was associated with a look to a noncolonial future.

Africans had firsthand knowledge of the European masters through the buildings they designed in Africa. Auguste Perret and Jorn Utzon did buildings in Morocco. Le Corbusier visited Algiers in 1933 and 1938, working on urban designs, and a design for a multistoried building, not realized. There were African architecture schools in Khartoum, Kumasi, Nairobi, Addis Ababa, and Johannesburg, places that all played integral roles in circulating information about modernism.

The genesis of modernism is frequently explained by the legacies bequeathed from previous modernizing movements, such as art nouveau and art deco. It should be noted, therefore, that there are numerous examples of art deco in Africa, in South Africa, Tanzania, Senegal, Eritrea, Ethiopia, and elsewhere.

Egypt

Hassan Fathy (1900–1989) was a philosopher and a teacher as much as an architect. Dissatisfied with the international-style buildings that he saw dotting Cairo's urban landscape in the 1950s, he set about proposing an alternative in both words and bricks. He created a system of building that relied upon traditional construction methods. Because of lower labor costs in Egypt, labor-intensive construction methods were possible. He started in the 1940s with New Gourna, a new town built in the shadow of the ancient Mortuary Temple of Queen Hapshepsut. He ingeniously discovered that concrete-frame housing had a historical connection with Egypt's native Nubian barrel-vaulted structures. These were made out of mud-brick walls, vaults, and low domes.

Fathy was a critic of non-native architects whose designs required the importation of foreign products not locally available. He introduced his ideas in a book, *Architecture for the Poor, an Experiment in Rural Egypt*, published in 1973. He is therefore known not just for his architecture but for giving an ideological approach to a new method that combines old and new and that added a local flavor to the global architecture. Fathy can be considered an Egyptian kindred spirit of Luis Barragán. Yet a limitation of his work is that it really does not explain how indigenous forms can be interpreted to provide high-rise hotels or airports.

He promoted utilizing local building methods, such as the Nubian earthen-dome, that had existed for millennia. Critical of modernization and industrialization, he was the first overt critic of modern architecture, a trend that was to gain steam. An Egyptian, Fathy sought to return his country to methods that predated Egypt's occupations under both the Ottomans and Europeans, and a way of refocusing contemporary Egyptian society on the village. This was a forceful move to counter the push from rural to urban.

At a time when others publicly broke with the past, he connected with history. A drawing for the Abd-al-Razik House deliberately combines plan and elevation, reminiscent of ancient Egyptian art. The Hamid Said House shows the interior of a Nubian barrel vault, a form resolutely applicable to the layout and furnishings of a contemporary Egyptian home. The low built-in seating platform is reminiscent of a diwan, and the resulting composition is Nubian, Egyptian, Islamic, African, and modern. A courtyard from his village of New Baris, 1967, took a traditional form and updated it (Figure 23.9). For those interested in discovering if there were autonomous African modernisms, the starting point for Africa is the life and works of Hassan Fathy.

South Africa

Two architectural schools of thought came head-to-head in South Africa in the late 1920s and 1930s: the remnants of nineteenth-century eclecticism and international modernism. Unlike elsewhere, this clash erases a larger tragedy— namely, the decimation of the local indigenous groups' traditional architectural practices. The impact of Europeans, chiefly Dutch and English, was so far-reaching in South Africa that precontact traditions in most artistic realms were drastically altered or ceased to exist. For example, the traditional round house no longer exists in South Africa.

Modernism's arrival is coincident with the professionalization of architecture. This process involved the establishment of professional organizations and educational programs. As Black and coloured (mixed-race) South Africans were excluded from both, this is a white-on-white story until the end of the twentieth century.

Rex Distin Martienssen (1905–1942) was most responsible for the establishment of modern architecture in South Africa. An architect, theorist, and educator, his position as editor of the *South African Architectural Record* allowed him to publicly advocate for modernist design. This caught the world's attention; Le Corbusier affectionately referred to Martienssen and his like-minded colleagues in South Africa as the Transvaal Group. Martienssen remained friends with Le Corbusier to the end of his life. Highlighting the relationship between modernism and classicism, Martienssen was significantly a respected classicist.

While enthusiasm for the work of Le Corbusier found some supporters, others were not so enamored of the machine-edged purists and felt that Frank Lloyd Wright's brand of modernism, with adjustments, was more adaptable to the exceptional South African landscape. A means to make architecture locally responsive is to interact with the landscape and use locally available materials, qualities that many admired in the work of Wright. This approach conveniently allowed white South African architects to metaphorically hide in the bush, ignore African indigenous traditions, while nonetheless proclaiming their Africanness.

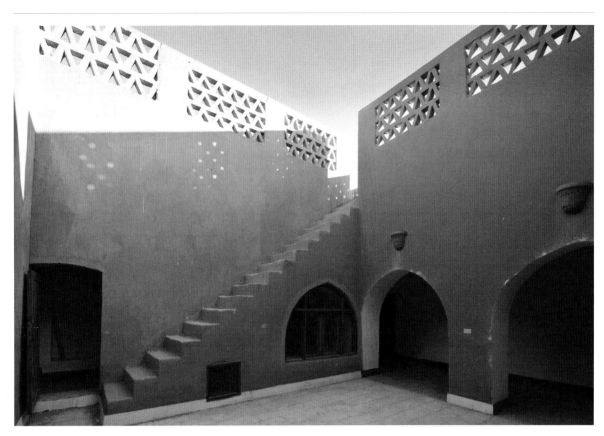

Figure 23.9
Hassan Fathy,
Courtyard from
New Baris,
Kharga, Egypt,
1967.

Modern architecture, it should be pointed out, was not related to the emancipation of locals as it was in other parts of Africa. In South Africa, Black and coloured people found their limited means to express political dissent in contemporary versions of traditional residential dwellings and decoration.

Norman Eaton (1902–1966) was a student in the 1920s, a time when the modern movement was just starting to be recognized and promoted by Martienssen and others. In the trajectory of Norman Eaton's career, some of his buildings, particularly the early ones and the big ones, are clearly modernist. Embracing forms associated with international modernism was not problematic for Eaton. He wanted to be a major architect with large, prestigious projects. He completed several large South African banks in the 1940s. His project for the Ministry of Transport (1944–1948), an unrealized hugely ambitious project, is formally indebted to another unbuilt project, Le Corbusier's League of Nations.

Eaton's sketchbooks indicate that he was eclectic in his tastes and generous in his admiration. A serious traveler, he was fascinated by the Japanese tatami mat as a modular system, and he collected African art. Writing about the kraals of the South African Ndebele people, he admiringly noted that they were "woven out of, and almost wholly dependent upon, the earth and the products of nature from which it drew its material" (Harrop-Allin 1975).

Outside of his large-scale commissions, in his residential projects, Eaton consistently moved away from strict modernism and expressed empathy for the African milieu he grew up in. The houses he designed were mostly in brick, stone, wood, and terra-cotta, and he incorporated rounded forms and patterns based on his studies of local decorative motifs. A door handle of Eaton's Netherlands Bank in Pretoria subtly communicates to visitors entering the bank lobby, lest there be any doubt, that they are, indeed, in Africa.

Anglophone Africa

Ernst May (1886–1970) trained in London and was active in Germany in the 1920s. Not formally a member of the Bauhaus, he worked in the **International Style** and was extremely prolific, operating out of his base in Frankfurt. He coped with the rise of National Socialists by going to the USSR in 1930. This seemed a logical move, as he had specialized in publicly funded housing. Once there, however, he had a difficult time seeing his works realized. In 1933, he made an even more dramatic move and relocated to Africa.

Kenya, Uganda, and Tanzania

May used Kenya as his base. He was "interned" (imprisoned) for two years by the English there, having been classified as an enemy. Upon being let out, he produced modern projects in Kenya, Uganda, and Tanzania. Stylistically, these buildings drew upon his German projects of the 1920s. He did not return to Germany until 1953.

One of the odd consequences of colonialism is that it figured into the responses of Africans who were not part of a colonial regime. May was white, a foreigner, a European, and a talented one at that. The reception his works received was in no small part because he had been imprisoned by the English and, moreover, because he was not English.

Ghana, Nigeria, and Togo

Maxwell Fry and Jane Drew were British modernists, trained in Great Britain, who worked in the realms of both architecture and town planning. A married couple, they were professional collaborators throughout their lives. Over the course of their long and productive careers, they worked with Denys Lasdun, Ove Arup, Walter Gropius, and Le Corbusier. They did projects in Britain and elsewhere, but they are mostly known for their projects in British West Africa during the period 1944–1956. These projects include seventeen schools in Ghana, Nigeria, and Togo.

Rhodri Windsor Liscombe's research brings to light the specifics of how modernism was dispersed to, and grew out of, West Africa (Liscombe 2006). To label the new way of building "the International Style" is one thing; to actually build and furnish buildings in Africa is another.

Fry and Drew were committed modernists, concerned with function, modular planning, bold composition, and new materials like reinforced concrete. Yet they also developed an approach, unique to their West African work, referred to by some, wryly, as tropical modernism. During the period of their African constructions, they operated out of both Ghana and Britain and spent years in West Africa, experiences they looked back on with great affection and that had a deep impact on their designs.

They employed several design strategies to give their buildings a local response. They used bold colors and, because they built in a hot and humid climate, ventilation and solar shading

were paramount concerns. Most of their buildings were interior volumes placed within a larger envelope of breathable screens. These permeable outer-wall systems allowed air to circulate and cast interior walls in a cooling shadow. This also gave Fry and Drew the opportunity to incorporate a variety of patterns in these outer tracery walls that bear a faint resemblance to local patterns found in basket weaving, textiles, and carving. As Jane Drew wrote, their goal was "to design in a way which, without in any sense copying African detail, gives a response which is African" (Drew in Liscombe 2006). A regular feature of their projects was a tracery walls that contrasted the brilliant sun of the exterior with the shade of a perimeter corridor (Figure 23.10). The University of Ibadan in Nigeria is one of their largest projects.

Their work is tied to the transcultural architectural language of modernism, while simultaneously making local reference to topography, climate, and decorative traditions. Their overall body of work was increasingly attentive to the African subject, as client and worker under their employ. Although they first worked mostly with expatriate architects, over the years African architects played a role as part of Fry and Drew's design team. They collaborated with African artists at several junctures, and their buildings were built by African craftsmen.

Kwame Nkrumah, one of the most significant voices of African independence, felt that modernizing by the British colonialist regime, however well intended and aesthetically successful, still underscored the primary goal: the economic exploitation and political domination of Britain's West African colonies.

Ghana achieved independence from Britain in 1957. The African work of Fry and Drew continues to be admired for their deft ability to create modernism within a local context. One of their employees, T.S. Clark, became the first president of the Ghana Society of Architects.

Nigeria

Oluwole Olumuyiwa (b. 1929) was part of the generation of Nigerian architects who rose to prominence in the 1960s. Olumuyiwa studied in London, then worked in London, Rotterdam, and Zurich. Throughout his career, he did multiple projects for the United Africa Company. He helped found the Nigerian Institute of Architects (NIA) in 1958, and in 1981 the African Union of Architects.

His later work included projects such as the Eko Hotel, where a built-up gradient allows for

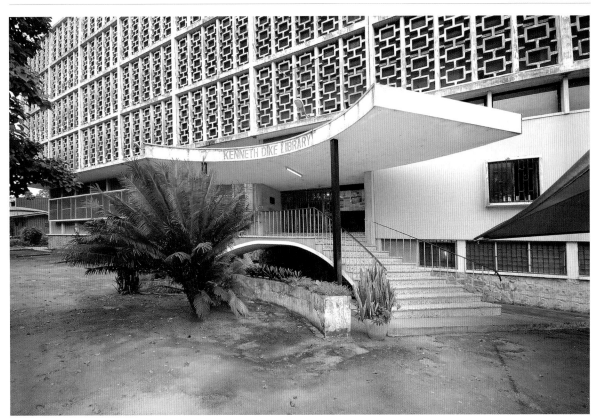

Figure 23.10
Jane Drew and
Maxwell Fry,
University of
Ibadan, Kenneth
Dika Library,
Ibadan, Nigeria,
1953–1959.

breathtaking views of the pool and beach. Lest one presume that an African architect must respect the regionalist approach when designing, Hannah Le Roux noted that Olumuyiwa "represents a transitional figure whose professional background is comparable to that of his colonial predecessors. Somewhat ironically, he stated his resistance to a concept of regionalism in design" (Le Roux 2004, p. 362). He later collaborated with Kenzo Tange on the design of the Central Administrative area of the new Nigerian capital, Abuja.

Francophone Africa

The work of architects in the North African Maghreb represents its own significant strand of African modernism. Because people living in the region were French-speaking, the connections to Le Corbusier were intensified. European architects collaborated with local architects at an early date on projects, and some of these architects went on to have distinguished careers under their own names.

Their works display a familiarity with the French brand of modernism, with adjustments for a hot, dry climate; the influence of Islam is also clear.

Balconies and courtyards contain spaces that are prominent, yet shielded from the public eye.

Morocco

French-trained Moroccan architect Jean-François Zevaco (1916–2003) was prolific. His projects are known for their bold forms and a sharp contrast between brilliant white stucco and cyclopean masonry, the large irregular stones are associated with Neolithic construction. They are not overly concerned with elaborate swaths of decoration. Many of his projects were for the government, including an uncompromisingly modern house for the president.

One way that African modernism is unique is due to the low cost of labor. Correspondingly, the large-scale use of manufactured products in projects was absent. Zevaco's post office lobby incorporated a large amount of custom millwork, including a lounge seating unit whose individual seats echo the curves of ancient Egyptian stools.

The work of Elie Azagury (1922–1979) was closely aligned with De Stijl, foremost his project for the Civic Center at Rabat (1967). Early in his career, Azagury collaborated with George Candilis, an architect known for innovative explorations of multiple-unit housing. The connection might be felicitous, but the Azagury/Candilis collaborations have an affinity with Saharan urban centers such as Timbuktu.

A source of ideological support came from the art scene, where Moroccan artists were similarly dealing with their multiple identities as French-speaking, Arab, African, and Muslim. Moroccan-born Farid Belkahia (1934) was educated at the École des Beaux-Arts in Paris (1954–1959) and then became director of the École des Beaux-Arts in Casablanca. He was a modern painter, at first influenced by George Rouault and Paul Klee. Back in Morocco, he started working with Arabic calligraphy, combining modernism with the ancient art. He also sought to close the gap between art and craft. Ahmed Cherkaoui (1934–1967) and Mohammed Issiakhen were other artists who related the independence struggles of their own countries to the activities of the French avant-garde.

Jean Prouvé's most famous work of architecture was not meant for one country but to be replicated in several. His Maison Tropicale, 1949–1952, was intended for multiple countries, although it failed to reach its potential. One of the countries where it was built was Congo. Prouvé was before his time, for the house was meant to be mass-produced, shipped in a flat-pack, demountable, and naturally ventilated. His favored materials, in architecture and in his many furniture designs, included steel, iron, aluminum, and plywood (Figure 23.11).

Architect Rinaldo Olivieri built a fifteen-story, mixed-use building in Abidjan, Côte d'Ivoire. The project was built in the years 1968 to 1973, and used concrete, marble, and aluminum. Its most notable feature is its arresting shape, as affirmed by its name, La Pyramide. Olivieri sought to create an architecture that was African, paying homage

to the famous structures of Egypt. But he did not stop there, for there is also a prominent triangular shaped atrium, suggesting that a modern African architecture will offer an alternative to Miesian rectilinearity. The project contained offices, restaurants, a supermarket, parking, and a nightclub (Figure 23.12).

Kenyan architect David Mutiso built his own landmark structure in Kenya's capital city, Nairobi. Named for Kenyatta, KICC, a 28-story convention center, it opened in 1973 (Figure 23.13). Mutiso had studied at the University of Sheffield School of Architecture.

Lusophone Africa

Amancio d'Alpoim Miranda Guedes (1925–2015) was an innovative architect in Mozambique whose houses were sculptural, innovative spatially, and related to surrealism. Prolific, he spent most of his career in Mozambique, and over the course of twenty-five years designed nearly five hundred buildings. In addition to his architectural practice, he was an accomplished painter and sculptor.

Figure 23.12
Rinaldo Olivieri, La Pyramide, Abidjan, Côte d'Ivoire, 1970–1973.

Figure 23.11
Jean Prouvé, Antony chair, Nancy, France, 1954. Beech plywood, steel, and aluminum.

Figure 23.13
David Mutiso,
Kenyatta
International
Convention Center
(KICC), Nairobi,
Kenya, 1959.

Lessons from Africa

With his interest in modern architecture around the globe, historian Udo Kultermann was before his time. He published two books on modern architecture in Africa in the 1960s. Nonetheless, the history of modernism in Africa is a story still waiting to be told. Individual monographs on African architects and designers are rare. And there are fewer materials on interiors and modern furnishings.

Architects and designers working in Africa sought a middle ground between European modernism and local regional architectures, seeking to close the gap between Western forms and local traditions. It some cases, it was difficult to find relevant local traditions that related to the needs of the twentieth-century urban center. A frequent solution was the grafting of the indigenous onto the imported, such as the ubiquitous high-rise hotel with a straw-roofed cocktail lounge sitting grandly at its base. Some modern buildings made their local reference by incorporating local artwork. An examination of a few of the many examples of modern architecture from across the continent reveals a rich body of work that are rarely pale imitations of the original and

that indicate the presence of vibrant autonomous African modernisms.

Asia and the Pacific

The canonical narrative of modernism conflates modernism and industrialization, the former being the logical result of the latter. While certainly true in many cases, there remains the necessity of explaining the spread of modernism in the less industrialized parts of the world. Modernism has many sources, and each culture and country had its own methods for interpreting and embracing modernity. Part of "modernism" was the struggle of indigenous cultures to resist domination by their colonizers. There remains the question of how to explain the twentieth-century resurgence of regionalism and vernacular architecture; was it a challenge to the modern movement or evidence that there were always multiple modernisms?

In Asia, Japan and Korea were reeling from the destruction resulting from the Second World

War. Modernism acted as a salve for these countries eager to look forward, and who also had a pragmatic need to build and furnish massive projects. If there is a common impulse in the modernisms that developed around the world, it is the longing to belong to an increasingly global world and also to explore local roots.

Japan

Japan's engagement with modernity in the nineteenth century had been awkward, for while having wonderful traditions of painting, garden design, and building in timber, these art forms didn't provide a vocabulary that easily lent itself to the large-scale building program of railroad stations, opera houses, world-class museums, and government buildings. It was not immediately clear how a timber tradition, however rich, would lend itself to expression in concrete, steel, and glass.

The challenges facing Japan after the Second World War were enormous, foremost among them rebuilding their severely damaged country. With the need for so many buildings, the economy took off in the 1950s.

Japan was not a colonial country, yet the desire to develop a modern Japanese architectural style not based on the West was a constant concern. Modernism's association with the West was, from the Japanese perspective, an unattractive alliance, considering the devastation the country had experienced at the hands of the Allied forces and the still-visible American military presence. But modernism was not solely an import; Japan was quickly modernizing on its own, moving down the path of industrialization and urbanization. Regarding the legacy of traditional Japanese architecture, several factors were favorable regarding the ability of Japanese architects and designers to craft a Japanese modernism. The respect for materiality, the modular tatami tradition, the asymmetrical compositions, the exquisiteness of detailing—all were traditional Japanese design values that were sympathetic to modern developments. Put another way, Mies's geometries needed little tweaking to relate to the Japanese system of shoji screens.

Visiting Japan

Japanese designers had direct knowledge of Western modernism. Frank Lloyd Wright's Imperial Hotel in Tokyo (1916–1922) was filled with inspiring furniture designed especially for it by Wright. Czech-born Antonin Raymond was a figure of growing importance. He arrived in Japan as Wright's assistant and eventually opened his own office.

Charlotte Perriand coped with the threat Second World War posed by moving to Japan, where she stayed from 1939 to 1941; during her time in Japan, Perriand lived in the Imperial Hotel. In Japan, she had the chaise longue that she designed with Le Corbusier and Pierre Jeanneret, and other pieces, translated into wood and bamboo (Figure 23.14). She explored the relationship and synthesis between her modern furniture designs and Japanese craftsmanship. The chaise was a design that grew out of an industrial aesthetic. For this exercise in material translation and exploration of local craftwork, she first graphically reduced her furniture pieces to their iconic profiles; the craftsmen she worked with took these shapes and transformed them using the "new" materials. The transformation of this famous chair, and other pieces, into wood and bamboo demonstrates an underlying confidence in indigenous materials. This process revealed a surprising affinity between bamboo and steel, the connection being tensile strength. Perriand and the Japanese craftsmen she collaborated with linked modern forms with centuries-old traditions.

Postwar modernism

Isamu Noguchi (1904–1988) was foremost an artist, capable of expressing himself in many media, including sculpture, furniture design, stage sets, and gardens. The son of an American mother and a Japanese father, from 1927 to 1928 he worked in Paris for Brancusi. He created stage designs for the dancer Martha Graham. In 1944, he started creating furniture and lamp designs for Herman Miller and Knoll, several of which are still in production. His carefully balanced coffee table is now known simply as the Noguchi table and is one of the masterpieces of classic modern furniture (figure 23.15).

Noguchi collaborated with Isamu Kenmochi, whom he met in Kenzo Tange's office. This underscores that there were a number of Japanese designers who achieved considerable success both in Japan and in the United States. The list includes Toyo Ito, Sou Fujimori, George Nakashima, Katsuhei Toyoguchi, Sori Yanagi, and later Shigeru Ban.

Kunio Mayekawa (1905–1986) worked for Le Corbusier, 1928–1930, in Paris, and then for Antonin Raymond in Tokyo, 1930–1935. His work is known for its integration of international modernism and Japanese traditions based on timber construction. His Harumi Building of 1958, Tokyo, bears the influence of Le Corbusier's Unité d'Habitation, but it is also the building that proved that concrete is a Japanese material.

Figure 23.14
Charlotte Perriand
and Japanese
craftsmen, chaise
longue in bamboo,
Tokyo, Japan,
1940.

Kenzo Tange (b. 1913) worked for Mayekawa and was the most important Japanese architect of the 1950s and 1960s. His Peace Memorial and Museum at Hiroshima, 1949–1950, proves how adept he was at a variety of modernist means of expression. The memorial itself is a sculptural focal point, with an exquisitely detailed rectangular building acting as a backdrop. Raised on pilotis, it evokes European modernism, but the delicacy of its concrete detailing recalls Japanese residential construction in timber. Tange's most important work came in 1964 with his National Gymnasium, built for the Olympics. It is aggressively asymmetrical, curved, and dynamic. It impressed a new generation of Japanese architects, and the roster of architects who studied under Tange includes Arata Isozaki, Kisho Kurokawa, and Fumihiko Maki.

Tange established an office in Tokyo, from which he ran a thriving international practice. In addition to occasional plastic expressions of monumentality such as the Gymnasium, his office produced large numbers of more pedestrian corporate projects. He participated in designing the plan for Abuja, Nigeria, in 1979. He did projects in the United States, Nigeria, Malaysia, Singapore, Saudi Arabia, and Mexico.

Figure 23.15
Isamu Noguchi,
Noguchi table,
1944.

Kiyonori Kikutake (b. 1928) is associated with the utopian movement known as the metabolists. Yet his individual houses have a sensitivity to detail that was often missing in the aggressive urban plans. Kikutake felt that architecture should have two parts—a permanent part and a part that could be rejuvenated during periodic reconstructions. This two-pronged approach to design is evident in his own house, Skyhouse, of 1957 (Figure 23.16). Kikutake related the obviously modern structure to the historical Japanese domestic architecture: "The core of the main space of the Skyhouse is a large space that reflected the 16 tatami mat-parlor of my family house" (Kikutake in Vitta 1997, p. 12). The woodwork is evidence of his appreciation of Japanese timber-frame structures, and the giant concrete piers relate to the metabolists' desire to build in the air.

Lessons from Japan

A pair of American designers made an unlikely contribution to Japanese modernism, and later they were known across Asia. Dale Keller (1929–2016) and Patricia Keller (b. 1926) met at the University of Washington. They studied under Hope Foote, who used Japanese art and design as a way of nudging American students from traditional artistic backgrounds in the direction of modernism. A favored reading assignment of hers was Okakuro Kakuzo's *Book of Tea*. Dale and Patricia relocated to Tokyo, and shortly thereafter started on a series of hotel interiors, including three hotels in Tokyo, the Marunouchi Hotel (1961), the Okura Hotel (1963), and the Tokyo Hilton (1963). Later came their groundbreaking project the Bali Hyatt (1973). A project later still was the Kuantan Hyatt (1980), a collaboration with the Malaysian firm Kumpulan Akitek (Figure 23.17).

The uncertainty that surrounded Japanese architecture in the immediate post-Second World War period seems to have evaporated in the 1970s and 1980s, helped in no small part by Japan's successful economy, but also by a growing confidence in Japan as a distinctive voice that could make a significant contribution to what being modern means. Modernism is the result of the forces of technology, consumerism, capitalism, and urbanism, all of which Japan was experiencing as authentic, not imported, experiences. Japanese designers did not need to look to outsiders for experience with these issues, and could become the model for others, especially with their references to nature, materiality, and spirituality.

India

India became familiar with postwar Le Corbusier when his work was entering a rougher, less pristine phase, embraced by the brutalists. Louis Kahn was a source of inspiration for Indian and Pakistani architects as well, because of buildings he built in both countries. Many Indian people were already familiar with the work of Antonin Raymond. Though modernism had been half-heartedly introduced by the English, it was definitively a symbol of independence and part of a postcolonial order. The sort of crisis that Fathy faced in Egypt was also encountered in India, in which hordes of manual laborers dealt with competition from mass-produced imported products.

Early modernism

India became modern via a variety of circuitous paths, few as interesting as the story of the Maharaja of Indore. The Maharaja's full name was Yeshwant Rao Holkar Bahadur (1905–1956). He studied in England and was a familiar fixture of the Paris art scene. He bought sculptures from Constantin Brancusi and collected avant-garde

Figure 23.16
Kiyonori Kikutake, Skyhouse, Tokyo, Japan, 1958.

Figure 23.17
Dale and Patricia
Keller and
Kumpulan Akitek,
Kuantan Hyatt
Hotel, Kuantan,
Malaysia, 1980.

furnishings from Berlin, London, and Paris, including pieces by Marcel Breuer, Le Corbusier, Charlotte Perriand, Eileen Gray, and Emile-Jacques Ruhlmann.

Man Ray is known as both a Dadaist and a surrealist, two artistic movements that fall under the rubric of "modernism." He took a photographic portrait of the Maharaja in 1930, when the young man was twenty-five. The Maharaja sits in profile in this photograph, which shows how the human body and photography are equal partners in the history of art and design. This portrait is reminiscent of many Bauhaus photographs; an iconic photograph of Eileen Gray similarly captures her in profile. These photographs rely upon the understanding that the human body is also an artistic material and can become a "designed object."

Eckart Muthesius (1904–1989) was also twenty-five when he met the Maharaja. Muthesius had an impeccable modernist pedigree. His father, Hermann Muthesius (1861–1927), founded the Deutscher Werkbund. The Maharaja hired the younger Muthesius to design the family house in India. The enormous house that Muthesius designed, called Manik Bagh (Jewel Gardens), with interiors and furnishings also by Muthesius, was a tour de force of modern design. The house was widely published, revealing the similarities between Muthesius's work and that of his Bauhaus contemporaries. Reto Niggl writes that "modernism as typified by Muthesius and his

client, stands in contrast to the representative, decorative style of the 1920s" (1996, p. 21).

Muthesius worked on many projects for the Maharaja, also designing a railway car, a houseboat (not realized), a meditation temple (not realized), a hotel, a hospital, and airplane interiors.

Antonin Raymond (1888–1976), of Czech birth, became an American citizen and worked in Japan and India. In school in Czech Republic, he had admired the work of Frank Lloyd Wright. It was a dream come true for him when, after he moved to the United States, he ended up working for Wright. Wright sent Raymond to Japan to oversee the construction of the Imperial Hotel in Tokyo. Initially, his work was derivative of Wright's work; then he progressed into a strictly modernist phase, in touch with the 1920s and 1930s. The year 1937 found him working on an ashram, in Pondicherry, India, when his work was less austere. He collaborated with the Japanese-American architecture and furniture designer George Nakashima (1905–1990). The modernist underpinnings are present in Pondicherry, but his explorations of the spiritual qualities possible within a modernist vocabulary are clear (Nakahara 2006, p. 170). Adding to the cosmopolitan character of his life and work is the fact that Pondicherry is a French-speaking enclave in India. So a Czech-born American citizen worked in the French-speaking area of India after a stint in Japan. In 1948, Raymond returned to work in Japan with the Reader's Digest

Building in Tokyo (1950); Isamu Noguchi designed the garden.

Postindependence modernism

Charles Correa (b. 1930) lived and worked in Bombay. He studied in the United States, first at the University of Michigan and then at MIT, where he studied under Buckminster Fuller. He was interested in relating modernism to climate and living patterns, particularly village life. These interests naturally led him to public housing, and he also worked on tourist hotels. One of his highly lauded projects was the Gandhi Memorial Centre in Ahmadabad (1958–1963).

Balkrishna Doshi (b. 1927) studied in Bombay and London. From 1951 to 1955 he worked for Le Corbusier, who hired him to supervise the projects he was building in Chandigarh and Ahmadabad. Doshi then set up his own practice in Ahmadabad. He played a crucial role in arranging for Louis Kahn to build in India. Initially, Doshi's work was similar to the work of Le Corbusier; later in life, he found his own distinctive architectural voice.

Sri Lanka

Contemporary Malaysian architect Ken Yeang (b. 1948) refers to Geoffrey Bawa (1919–2003) as "our first hero and guru" (Yeang in Robson 2002, p. 12). Bawa's ethnic heritage reflects the marvelously complicated heritage of Sri Lanka. (The etymology is complicated, too: In the colonial era, the island was known as Ceylon. The major ethnic group, and their language, is Sinhalese.) He belonged to the ethnic group commonly described as "Eurasian," which, in Bawa's case, meant that he was a combination of Scottish, German, and Sinhalese. Bawa was raised by three women: his mother and his father's two sisters. He worked in Colombo as a lawyer before he turned to architecture.

Bawa traveled extensively. In 1951, he started working as an architect. In 1952, he went to Cambridge, England, where he studied civil engineering and structures. He went to the Architectural Association School. He eventually ended up teaching there, following the path of a classmate of his, the modernist Peter Smithson. There he learned about international modernism.

Bawa's career and his designs relate to two aspects of his identity, both personal and professional. On the one hand he was a trained modernist, familiar with Britain's modern structures, and he knew many of the prominent modernists personally. He returned to Ceylon (as it was then known) and started working for the nation's largest and most prestigious architecture firm, ERB. He outlived the partners and took it over. Under his leadership, the firm proceeded from large-scale traditional buildings to modern corporate offices, tourist hotels, and, ultimately, the firm's and Bawa's most significant commission, the Parliament. Under Bawa's leadership, the firm became internationally known, on a par with the American firm Skidmore, Owings & Merrill of Chicago. The firm was skilled at receiving both governmental and commercial commissions.

As the firm's projects were increasingly reflecting the nation's indigenous character, so too were the ranks of locals sitting at the drafting desks. Initially, the staff was entirely English, but under Bawa's stewardship it became increasingly Ceylonese. Bawa's office included Sinhalese Buddhists, Tamil Hindus, and Muslims, Catholics, and Anglicans. Many of the architects who initially worked for Bawa had successful careers on their own.

There's a parallel story, which author David Robson calls the Brideshead side of Bawa (Robson 2002, p. 19). Robson wrote the most complete book on Bawa to date (Robson 2002). He referred to Evelyn Waugh's story of a gay elite group at Oxford, under the sway of lead character Sebastian Flyte. Bawa, at Cambridge, acted something like Waugh's lead character. Robson wrote: "Handsome and exceptionally tall, Geoffrey would stride around town in a long black cloak with a gold-handled cane. He had always felt something of an outsider in Colombo, but his eccentricities were welcomed in Cambridge" (Robson 2002, p. 20). Bawa belonged to a cosmopolitan group of worldly aesthetes, and he thrived in their company. Throughout his life, he continued to hobnob with wealthy women, designing their houses and gardens, and advising them on antiques and art (Robson 2002, pp. 50–1). He did a house for Minette de Silva, with whom he was close friends. De Silva was the first Asian woman who became a member of the Royal Institute of British Architects (RIBA) and herself was responsible for a small but highly regarded body of work.

At the end of Bawa's life, it was commonly known that he was gay, another aspect of his character that spoke of his ability to operate successfully in several worlds.

Bawa received the most important commission of his life when the Sri Lankan government chose him to design the new Sri Lankan Parliament Building in 1981. He was a good choice, not only because his own family heritage reflected the multi-caste and multi-creed matrix of Sri Lanka. At this point in his career, he was moving away from flat roofs and incorporated pitched roofs into his designs. He was particularly skilled at making the vernacular monumental. Bawa's Parliament looks like an Asian shrine, and it houses a complicated program for a modern government, modeled in part on the Houses of Parliament in London.

Some compare his later work to "tropical modernism." On the one hand, some of his designs look oddly similar to Scandinavian modernism, but as Maxwell Fry and Jane Drew had proven, modernism could be quite applicable to tropical climates. Bawa had worked for a time with Fry and Drew.

Bawa increasingly relied upon and incorporated traditional forms, such as pitched roofs, into his projects. His walls were not crisp white, but achieved a weathered patina. His residential projects drew upon many influences, such as medieval manor houses, Dutch courtyard houses, and Muslim rowhouses. He regularly combined classic modern pieces of furniture with Ceylonese antiques (Figure 23.18).

Thailand and Cambodia

The situation in Thailand is emblematic of how modernism arose in the 1930s in a non-European country, and how it spoke to and responded to a particular political situation. While India and Ceylon experienced colonialism to the hilt, it was a nonissue in Thailand, a country that successfully resisted English and French attempts to colonize it. In Thailand, modernism played a role akin to the role of nineteenth-century neoclassicism in France, in which it was the style of the new post-royal regime and a means by which the new political system stylistically differentiated itself from the ancient regime.

The 1932 revolution in Thailand ended more than a thousand years of royal absolutist rule and signaled the end to royal and state patronage of Western architects. This was a system that promoted the use of historically based styles—essentially guaranteeing that the nineteenth century would continue into the twentieth. Thai architects who had been educated abroad started to replace the old generation, and they increasingly reflected the new era with a prevalence for modern architecture. Noobanjong writes that Thai architects established an architecture school and that several of them started their careers there (Noobanjong 2003). In 1932, the architecture department at Chulalongkorn University started. The year 1934 saw the establishment of the Association of Siamese Architects (ASA). Modern architecture in Thailand became the symbol of the new order, of building a new nation, and an alternative to the ancient royalist regime.

Figure 23.18
Geoffrey Bawa, Lunuganga, Bentota, Sri Lanka, 1948. House of the architect.

Princess Rudivoravan, a granddaughter of Thailand's King Mongkut, thought about her parents in conjunction with their furniture:

My mother's quarters in the palace were attractive. As I remember them, the furnishings were Western, but this touch may have been added after I returned from England. It was customary to provide wives whose children had been educated in Europe with more modern furnishings than the traditional Thai. A few years later my people would be sitting on chairs at desks, but at that time the floor served as desk stool. I can still see my father's low writing bench and table, and the bowls of pens with which he wrote.

(1957, p. 59)

In the Princess' recollection, a chair and (tall) desk have multiple associations. They relate to the West, and to Thais like herself with experience living in the West; she was educated in England as a child. She describes the furniture as modern and of her generation—not her parents. She remembers her father, whom she writes of fondly, as nobly sitting on the floor in front of his writing bench. A parallel development in Thailand, alongside the preference for modern projects, was the career of Jim Thompson, an American heir who developed a successful silk industry in Bangkok. With his own house as an example, he is credited with reviving a fashion for wealthy Thai families to construct lavish houses, filled with Chinese antiques and Khmer sculptures, based on Thai vernacular traditions, and often incorporating actual carpentry from houses dismantled in the countryside and brought to Bangkok by boat. He contributed to the revival of Thai indigenous forms.

The small Southeast Asian nation of Cambodia has one of the world's richest traditions of ancient architecture and sculpture. It was not predestined that Cambodia would experience a second period of architectural achievement in the twentieth century, yet that is what occurred in the period 1953–1970. Helen Grant Ross and Darryl Leon Collins focused on the cadre of talented architects who produced a limited but highly competent body of work (Ross and Collins 2006). Firmly committed to modernism, as a collective corpus their buildings effortlessly achieve what so many non-Western architects sought to achieve, yet which proved so difficult. Their works related to the international movement yet responded to

their own context. They grew out of Cambodia's architectural tradition without being derivative.

Sadly, Cambodia's experience with modernism is more associated with the events that precipitated the end of modernism. Vann Molyvann (b. 1926) studied in Paris, after which he returned to Cambodia. He did a series of projects for Prince Norodom Sihanouk in the 1960s that reveal his French modernist training, but they also refer to Cambodia's grand history of architecture, the monumental temples of Angkor. Sihanouk was a former king turned political leader.

Molyvann's works forged a grand new style of Khmer architecture. The significant characteristic of Cambodian modernism is the evocation of tradition, yet in decidedly modern structures. Some of the buildings are profusely decorated, some feature locally made brick, and many feature steeply pitched roofs. Modernism in many parts of the world was initially dependent on imported talent, but in Cambodia it was mostly a Cambodian affair. The leading figures include Vann Molyvann, Lu Ban Hap, and Mam Sophana. Molyvann's many projects include the Front du Bassac Housing Complex, the Institute of Foreign Languages, and the Chaktomuk Conference Hall (Figure 23.19). His grandest project, the National Sports Complex, was built in 1963–1964.

The painstaking research of Darryl Leon Collins and Helen Grant Ross is invaluable because it recovers the activities of Cambodians in this period, a task made infinitely more difficult with the scourge of the Khmer Rouge. The Cambodian modernists forged a body of work that is remarkably in concert with international modernism yet expressive of a distinct Khmer sensibility. They operated within a modernist idiom on projects large and small.

Australia

Two architects represent two strands of the architectural scene in Australia, Harry Seidler and Glenn Murcutt. Harry Seidler (1923–2006) was born in Austria and studied in England, Canada, and then the United States. At Harvard University, he studied under Walter Gropius, and I.M. Pei was a classmate. His work experience included stints with Marcel Breuer in New York and Oscar Niemeyer in Rio de Janeiro.

International modernism

Seidler is one of the architects who, like Bawa, worked within the modernist framework as a sign of his connection to an international elite. The

Figure 23.19
Vann Molyvann,
Chaktomuk
Conference Hall,
Phnom Penh,
Cambodia, 1961.

sophistication of this style was emphasized in one of his early works, the Rose Seidler House of 1950, which was widely admired and includes a quotation of Perriand's dining area (Figure 23.20).

If architects around the world needed a strategy for incorporating local art into their modern buildings, Henry-Russell Hitchcock and Philip Johnson articulated it for them. Their book, *The International Style,* and the exhibition it accompanied, is one of the many mechanisms, in addition to Le Corbusier's publications, that spread knowledge of modernism around the world. They wrote: how

to decorate contemporary buildings without degenerating into mere applied ornament. Mural painting should not break the wall surface unnecessarily. Yet it should remain an independent entity without the addition of borders or paneling to fuse it with the architecture … there is no reason why painting less abstract should not find its place quite as satisfactorily on the walls of contemporary buildings. It is most important that mural painting should be intrinsically excellent; otherwise a plain wall is better. It need not be related, except in scale and shape, to the wall on which it is placed.

(Hitchcock and Johnson 1932, p. 73)

Sculpture, they wrote, "should retain its own character quite separate from that of its background."

Seidler's primary focus was the integration of geometry with structure, which served him well when his firm started specializing in large-scale complexes that included skyscrapers. These projects included Australia Square, 1961–1967, and Capita Centre, Sydney, 1984–1989 (Frampton and Drew 1992, p. 282).

Some critics thought Seidler's work—and he was a very successful architect—was too foreign. His work, which barely took notice of the Australian landscape, left an opening for an Australian architect who could temper the modern ethos by incorporating elements drawn from the vernacular and the local landscape.

Regional modernism

Glenn Murcutt approached architecture differently than Seidler, in both end results and in office practices. He largely worked by himself, with his wife as his partner, and built mostly single-family houses. He was raised in Papua New Guinea, and his work reflects his knowledge of a rough, if not primitive, landscape. He studied at the Sydney Technical College.

Murcutt's houses draw upon vernacular agricultural buildings, such as toolsheds and

Figure 23.20
Harry Seidler,
Rose Seidler
House, Sydney,
Australia,
1948–1950.

woolsheds. His buildings respond to the rural built environment and the Australian landscape. The Marie Short House is one of his early houses, built in 1975 (Fromonet 2003, p. 96). About a house that mixes the vernacular with modernism, Jim Lewis writes: "It was simple, it was light and nimble, and it seemed autochthonous" (2007). Murcutt is also like Aalto in this respect, as he took modern forms and softened them with his use of materials. He won the Pritzker Prize.

Lessons from Asia

Columbia University architectural historian Kenneth Frampton writes:

> With all the acuteness that is characteristic of the creative mind at its most sensitive, the so-called pioneers of the modern movement began in various ways to qualify the modern project, either by reinterpreting the vernacular in terms of modern technology in order to create an architecture that was socially more accessible and hence capable of embodying local values while still being engaged in modernization or, alternatively, reverting in some measure, to the stereometric regularity of classicism in order to represent the authority of the State.

(2007, p. 87)

Looking at multiple examples of twentieth-century design in Asia makes clear that there were many responses to the challenge of embracing modernism while remaining rooted in tradition.

Conclusion

Modernism was not always imported, but often created locally. The concept of an indigenous modernity that charts its own course is the subject of this chapter. The movement was international, not in the sense proscribed by European theorists, but because it interacted with local cultures from the beginning. Considering the origins of modernism, and specifically its early florescence in Mexico and Brazil, confirms that it was simultaneously imported and it developed in multiple locations.

Mies's professional activities were run from his home base in Chicago. Although he had a number of foreign students at Illinois Institute of Technology (IIT), being in the United States, he was working within a large architectural market. Le Corbusier, based in France, did not have the same wealth of corporate opportunities close at hand. He was, in effect, forced to be more global. Yet it cannot be coincidental that so many African, Asian, and American students worked for Le Corbusier, were inspired by him, and had lifelong professional relationships with him.

The situation of Antonin Raymond is one that was increasingly common as the twentieth century marched toward the twenty-first. A person of one nationality works in another on projects across the globe. The firms of Geoffrey Bawa, Harry Seidler, and Kenzo Tange were the order of the day, as the architecture and design profession extended its global reach.

Regarding the critical reception of modernism, a reassessment of modernism took place. Luis Barragán and Hassan Fathy were the first figures to receive international attention, and it looks as though Vann Molyvann's career is in for a similar reassessment.

Sources

Anderson, Stanford, ed. (2004). *Eladio Dieste: Innovation in Structural Art*. New York: Princeton Architectural Press.

Chang, Jiat-Hwee and Justin Zhuang (2023). *Everyday Modernism: Architecture and Society in Singapore*. Singapore: National University of Singapore Press.

Cuadra, Manuel (2000). *Clorindo Testa, Architect*. Rotterdam: NAI Publishers.

Denison, Edward, Guang Yu Ren, and Naigzy Gebremedhin (2003). *Asmara: Africa's Secret Modernist City*. London: Merrell.

Eggener, Keith (2001). *Luis Barragán's Gardens of El Pedregal*. New York: Princeton Architectural Press.

Eggener, Keith (2004). "Luis Barragán." In *Encyclopedia of 20th-Century Architecture*, edited by Stephen Sennott, pp. 117–18. New York: Fitzroy Dearborn.

Faber, Colin (1963). *Candela: The Shell Builder*. New York: Reinhold.

Ferraz, Marcelo Carvalho (1994). *Lina Bo Bardi*. Milan: Edizioni Charta.

Frampton, Kenneth (2007). *The Evolution of 20th Century Architecture: A Synoptic Account*. Vienna: SpringerVerlag.

Frampton, Kenneth and Philip Drew (1992). *Harry Seidler: Four Decades of Architecture*. New York: Thames and Hudson.

Fromonet, Françoise (2003). *Glenn Murcutt: Buildings and Projects 1962–2003*. New York: Thames and Hudson.

Glusberg, Jorge (1984). *Global Architecture: Sepra y Clorindo Testa*. Tokyo: A.D.A. Edita.

Guillén, Mauro (2004). "Modernism without Modernity: The Rise of Modernist Architecture in Mexico, Brazil, and Argentina, 1890–1940." *Latin American Research Review* 39, no. 2: 6–34.

Harrop-Allin, Clinton (1975). *Norman Eaton: Architect*. Cape Town: C. Struik.

Hess, Alan (2006). *Oscar Niemeyer Houses*. New York: Rizzoli.

Hitchcock, Henry-Russell, and Philip Johnson (1932). *The International Style*. New York: Museum of Modern Art.

Iversen, Ruth Rollitt (2015). *Iversen: Architect of Ipoh and Malaya*. George Town: Areca Books.

Legorreta, Ricardo (2004). *Legorreta + Legorreta*. New York: Rizzoli.

Leite, Rui Moreira and Izabel Murat Burbridge (1995). "Flavio de Carvalho: Modernism and the Avant-garde in São Paulo, 1927–1939." *The Journal of Decorative and Propaganda Arts* 21: 197–217.

Leon, Ethel (2005). *Design Brasileiro: quem fez, quem faz*. Rio de Janeiro: Viana e Mosley.

Le Roux, Hannah (2004). "Modern Architecture in Post Colonial Ghana and Nigeria." *Architectural History* 47: 361–92.

Lewis, Jim (2007). "The Native Builder." *The New York Times Magazine*, May 20. Available online: https://www.nytimes.com/2007/05/20/magazine/20murcutt-t.html (accessed May 2, 2023).

Liscombe, Rhodri Windsor (2006). "Modernism in Late Imperial British West Africa: The Work of Maxwell Fry and Jane Drew, 1946–1956." *Journal of the Society of Architectural Historians* 65, no. 2 (June): 188–215.

Mathur, Saloni (2007). *India by Design: Colonial History and Cultural Display*. Berkeley: University of California Press.

McQuaid, Matilda (2003). *Shigeru Ban*. London: Phaidon.

Nakahara, Mari, et al. (2006) *Crafting a Modern World: The Architecture and Design of Antonin and Noémi Raymond*. Princeton, NJ: Princeton Architectural Press.

Niggl, Reto (1996). *Eckart Muthesius: The Majaraja's Palace in Indore*. Stuttgart: Arnoldsche.

Noobanjong, Koompong (2003). "Power, Identity, and the Rise of Modern Architecture from Siam to Thailand." Dissertation, University of Colorado at Denver.

Paul, Andreas and Ingeborg Flagge, eds. (2003). *Oscar Niemeyer: A Legend of Modernism*. Basel: Birkhäuser.

Phillips, Tom, ed. (1996). *Africa: The Art of a Continent*. New York: Guggenheim Museum.

Pile, John (1990). *Dictionary of 20th-Century Design*. New York: Roundtable.

Posch, Katarina, Bonnie Rycklak, and Tetsu Matsumoto (2008). *Design: Isamu Noguchi and Isamu Kenmochi*. New York: Five Ties Publishing.

Raymond, Antonin (1973). *Antonin Raymond: An Autobiography*. Rutland, VT: Charles E. Tuttle.

Rispa, Raúl (2003). *Barragán: The Complete Works*. New York: Princeton Architectural Press.

Robson, David (2002). *Geoffrey Bawa: The Complete Works*. London: Thames and Hudson.

Ross, Helen Grant and Darryl Leon Collins (2006). *Building Cambodia: New Khmer Architecture: 1953–1970*. Bangkok: The Key Publisher Company.

Rudivoravan, Princess (1957). *The Treasured One*. New York: Dutton.

Schaarschmidt-Richter, Irmstraud (1994). *Kazuo Shinohara: Philosopher of Architecture*. Berlin: Ernst and Sohn.

Taylor, Brian Brace (1986). *Geoffrey Bawa*. Singapore: Mimar.

Underwood, David (1994). *Oscar Niemeyer and the Architecture of Brazil*. New York: Rizzoli.

Villanueva, Paulina (2000). *Carlos Raúl Villanueva*. New York: Princeton Architectural Press.

Vitta, Maurizio (1997). *Kiyonori Kikutake: From Tradition to Utopia*. Milan: l'Arca Edizioni.

Zanco, Federica (2001). *Luis Barragán: The Quiet Revolution*. Milan: Skira.

Discussion and Review Questions

1. What is an example of how knowledge of design circulated to a particular place around the world?

2. What is an example of a certain thread of knowledge being traced from Europe to another country?

3. Give an example of a modern development in Asia, Africa, or the Americas that was an independent development.

4. Identify a characteristic or circumstance of a non-European modernism that has a quality, form, or material that renders it unique.

5. Name some local variants of modernism and mention some of the key features of each.

6. What were some of the design strategies by which modernists around the world made their designs respond to the local context?

Work: Commercial Interiors

24

October 29, 1929	1958	1964	1981
Stock Market Crash	Seagram Building	Herman Miller Action Office	McDonald's Corporate Headquarters opens

People have always worked. Across world history—Akbar in Mughal India, Cleopatra in Egypt, Jayavarman in Cambodia, Louis XIV in baroque France, and the Empress Cixi in Qing dynasty China—leaders have led countries and themselves worked; importantly, legions of people surrounded them working on their behalf. Many of those activities were similar to work today, with something like receptions, meetings, and solo concentration. Those in their service filled the roles of personal assistants, accountants, and managers. There were copious amount of record-keeping, copying, and document storage. But that said, this governmental administrative work was often carried out in buildings and rooms that were built primarily as residences or places of worship. Examples of historical places where work occurred include libraries, bedrooms of state, and monasteries. In the twentieth century, a major strand of interior design came to be devoted to designing spaces for work that were apart from the domestic and religious spheres. The twentieth century saw innumerable projects designed specifically for work, and this chapter examines some famous ones, some typical ones, and some virtual ones—namely, filmed workplaces that made an impact but that were not "real."

People work in hospitals, hotels, and stores, but here the subject is what came to be known as office work. What is

Figure 24.0
(*Facing page*)
Naoum Shebib
Architects,
Maspero Radio
and Television
Building, Cairo,
Egypt, 1959.

unique about the twentieth century for the history of interior architecture is the rise and scale of projects designed for managerial and administrative work, from clerical to executive work. Whereas the beginnings of the interior design industry focused on residential interiors, by the end of the century the situation had changed dramatically. Twentieth-century residential interiors never disappeared, but many commercial design firms focused almost exclusively on commercial or corporate interiors. This chapter tells the story of the confluence of societal, cultural, and economic interests that came about for this to happen and the ensuing developments. By the end of the twentieth century, aggregate interior design fees were the equal of architecture, and half of all interior design was design for the workplace.

Just as the nineteenth century was the age of the industrial revolution, the twentieth century was the age of the **service economy**. And service came to mean offices and workstations. A significant part of this response was the **open plan**. This layout has been a remarkably resilient form from its inception to the current day, and it has proven adaptable at responding to different cultural, commercial, and technological forces. Many of its essential features and components have not changed much over the decades. Jennifer Kaufmann-Buhler is the author of a detailed study of the open plan, and she points out that "The term 'open plan office' flattens and unifies, while in actual practice the open-plan office was never a single or universal idea fixed at a point in time"

(Kaufmann-Buhler 2021, 4). While this typology is occasionally thrilling, it also engenders a great deal of anxiety.

The Service Economy

Frederick Winslow Taylor and Taylorism

Frederick Winslow Taylor (1856–1915) was an American mechanical engineer. He was the most accomplished of what became a global obsession: efficiency experts (much as there are now legions of decluttering experts). Taylor and his ilk looked at work patterns, first in manufacturing, and later they applied their conclusions to offices. An important focus of the drive to improve efficiency included the segmentation of tasks. The belief that efficiency could be improved through management and design was known as **Taylorism**, and a famous and successful example of its implementation was Henry Ford's automobile manufacturing. It was an approach that moved beyond individual craft in which one or a few workers were responsible for an entire assembly. There was attention to workflow: how certain tasks were done and how spatially individual tasks were handed off to the next worker. This came to influence office design, although interior designers were often hesitant to describe offices as assembly lines or paper factories.

Historian Graeme Brooker described how the focus on efficiency impacted the office, for it was evident in "rationalized and efficient structures of clerks, workers and managers, divided into departments and responsible for one section of work before it was passed to the next" (2013–2016, p. 54). While aspects of this indicate surveillance and control, it is important to point out that efficiency and the open plan were also points of comedic relief. A less dour version of Taylorism came in the novel *Cheaper by the Dozen* (1948), which followed two real-life efficiency experts, Frank Bunker Gilbreth and Lillian Moller Gilbreth, the parents of twelve children, who sought to improve household tasks based on Taylorism. Movies and television have combed the assembly line as a source of comedy.

Figure 24.1
Daniel Burnham
and John Wellborn
Root, Offices,
Chicago, 1891.

The office of Burnham and Root

Daniel Burnham and his partner John Wellborn Root were two of the major figures in creating the first skyscrapers. This activity makes them key figures for workplace design because the existence of skyscrapers was paralleled by increasing work for interior designers or architects who crafted tenant space. After Root's death, Burnham went on to become one of the famous architects of the American **gilded age**. His 1891 office plan is an example of a nineteenth-century knowledge-based workplace (Figure 24.1). The central feature is a large work room with drafting tables. This was an **open plan** before the concept. It is noteworthy that the workers, mostly men, were drafting at freestanding individual tables arranged in rows. A few enclosed offices for the partners lined the perimeter. There was considerable attention to the flow of documents, chiefly drawings, from where they were created, where they were printed, and how they were distributed to contractors. Outsiders, such as those who came to pick up drawings or bid packages interacted in the tight reception area. This might have been the only area where women worked. An unusual feature was the gymnasium, a precursor to office amenities. The library was mostly books, not building materials, as they are today, and was also used for client meetings.

Contractors could pick up drawings and calls for proposals without entering the office. Their spatial movement was carefully controlled and surveilled. Burnham and Root was one of the firms of the Chicago school, a group of architects who created the earliest skyscrapers. The open-plan skyscraper is of paramount importance for the history of office design because they created a need for interior design work, which started the ball rolling of workplace design.

This was an office mostly for men. There was a urinal in the printing room, with no privacy, which would have the effect of gendering the print area male, as women would feel awkward if not unwelcome there. If women were present, there was a private lavatory adjacent to the reception area. Looking at the offices of Burnham and Root raises many of the planning issues that are still salient today: the separation of public and private, the hierarchy of general workers and executives, the gendering of spaces, the importance of technology and health, and the dynamics of the architecture business at the time in Chicago, which was mostly male and white.

The skyscrapers Burnham and Root made possible, and the ensuing modern open-plan office, captured the world's attention, and this was reflected in early films. King Vidor's silent film *The Crowd* (1928) is one of the best. Hollywood's approach to the twentieth-century office was twofold. It drew attention to the exciting features of workspaces as up-to-date and glamorous, but also served as a warning that the modern work environment could be foreboding and alienating. This became a standard trope of the filmed office interior. *The Crowd* follows a worker, John Sims, who works for the Atlas Insurance Company. It starts with a thrilling scene in which a camera seems to scale the height of a skyscraper—consistent with the design parameters of the Chicago school—and enters a window, to hover over rows of identical desks, replete with task seating, adding machines, inboxes, and ledgers (Figure 24.2). It establishes features of the modern office that became staples of offices real and filmed. The general work area spread out with a sea of desks and stood in contrast to hierarchical perimeter offices. A favored location for filmed office interiors is the space where vertical circulation becomes horizontal circulation: elevator lobbies. *The Crowd* has thrilling visuals but also presents the downside of this working environment. The lead character Sims becomes frustrated by his lack of advancement in the corporate hierarchy and his salary is woefully insufficient for his growing family. This movie established what became several of the most common visual tropes of the twentieth-century office interior: elevator lobbies, the hierarchical differences between open office area and enclosed offices, and the sea of undifferentiated desks.

A common element in multiple films to show a character's corporate promotion is moving into a private office and having their name painted on glass. In the 1941 movie *Meet John Doe* directed by Frank Capra, the character of Ann Mitchell (Barbara Stanwyck) is an ambitious columnist. There are multiple scenes of the newsroom where she works that are contrasted in other scenes with private offices. Insurance companies and media companies built scores of new office interiors in the twentieth century.

Freestanding Furniture

Initially freestanding pieces of furniture created the open office work area. Many companies that had specialized in residential furniture turned to commercial furniture. The Wooten Patent Cabinet Office Secretary was a late nineteenth-century update of a roll-top desk, replete with hundreds of cubby holes for storing papers. Initially it was thought that this was a logical response to work needs, eventually it was decided to separate work-surfaces from pieces for document storage such as filing cabinets.

A number of furniture companies were adept at creating high-quality furniture for the office environment. The Metal Office Furniture Company was founded in 1912, in Grand Rapids, Michigan, and it later became Steelcase. Many of their early desks remain in use. Sankey-Sheldon was an English manufacturer of freestanding desks

Figure 24.2
King Vidor (Dir.), *The Crowd* (1928). Work area of Atlas Insurance Company, New York.

In your office
use STEEL Desks and Tables

- 70 different types of Sankey-Sheldon steel desks to choose from.

- Fire-resisting, will not warp, easy to clean.

- Alternative drawer arrangements to suit your filing needs.

- Automatic locking for security.

The people to see are DUNCAN ROBERTS of course! Tel. 21058

Sankey Sheldon

Agents: DUNCAN ROBERTS LTD.
Crosby House, Robinson Road, Singapore
Represented throughout the Federation by
The Borneo Co. Ltd.

Figure 24.3
Sankey-Sheldon, "In Your Office Use STEEL desks and tables," 1955.

(Figure 24.3). One of the ways that the open-plan office was to flourish across the globe was that furniture companies sold their products worldwide. English desks made by Sankey-Sheldon were available in Singapore—and thereby much of Southeast Asia—through the retailer Duncan Robert, Ltd.

The Designers and Office Buildings

George Howe, William Lescaze, and the Philadelphia Savings Fund Society

Two art deco buildings worthy of note appeared in the opening years of the twentieth century. They were historicist and predictive of the clean lines of art deco. While technologically innovative, they were not stylistically forward-looking. They played an important role because of their height and the floors of interior offices that they engendered. They were the Woolworth Building by Cass

Gilbert, 1913, and Metropolitan Life by Napoleon LeBrun, 1909. These corporate headquarters created a lot of work for interior designers, through the anchor tenants and those who rented spaces on the speculative floors.

A real-life version of the workplace that Vidor portrayed in *The Crowd* came about in the silent film era. George Howe and William Lescaze were architects, and Lescaze had significant interior design experience having done showrooms, exhibitions, stores, and lobbies. A building they created, replete with its modern interiors, is the subject of a chapter in architectural historian Grace Ong Yan's monograph, *Building Brands* (2020). The Philadelphia Savings Fund Society (PSFS) was a financial institution that sought to provide investment and financial services for the growing middle class. Its leader was the banker James M. Willcox. As with many banks, the PSFS had sought previously to convey stability in their institution through a number of historicist buildings. For their new headquarters, the client and designers envisioned a modern totality, and while the project was in the developmental stages, it moved in a consistently modern direction including the interiors. There was no mixing of period pieces in a modern building, "Both architects clearly placed their faith in the functional tendency of modern architecture" (Yan 2020, p. 34). In 1925, the firm bought property and work began. The building had three principal components: the bank, tenant offices, and retail space.

As an entire entity, PSFS was a speculative project in which offices to let were a means of additional revenue for the bank. Retail space took up the ground floor, and above that, corresponding to the curved glazed element that was a prominent part of the façade, a raised banking floor (Figure 24.4). The features of **streamline modern** and the delineation of the tall building reveals that the architects had knowledge of the works of J.J.P. Oud, Erich Mendelsohn, and Raymond Hood.

Other prominent features that place the project as one of the earliest modern designs in the United States include an entrance canopy and rooftop PSFS sign. The building soon had its imitators, and most buildings of this type were speculative, few were solely owner inhabited. PSFS occupied seven of thirty-three floors. The twenty-six floors of rentable office space were not designed by the architects.

The building was air-conditioned and had multiple open office spaces whose windows bathed them in natural light. This was before the era of fluorescent light, so windows remained a principal means of lighting. Features of the bank's offices include metal partitions, Venetian

Figure 24.4
George Howe and
William Lescaze,
the Philadelphia
Savings
Fund Society,
Philadelphia,
Pennsylvania,
1925.

the interiors. They were part of the interest in open-plan design, which included using metal partitions. As with many designers and architects, their enthusiasm for modernism preceded the products that would support that vision. Yan writes that standardized, contemporary office furniture scarcely existed. This lack—of furniture, interior fittings, and textiles—provided an opportunity for designers who were enthused by modernism. The PSFS architects designed their own modern furniture, heavily influenced by Bauhaus design directions. They were aware of the industrial design work that Norman Bel Geddes and Walter Dorwin Teague (1883–1960) were doing. Lescaze and Howe created a variety of designs, including seating options, benches for the banking hall, upholstered armchairs, and office accessories. Their seating, in the European modernist tradition, included bent chromed tubing. Executive offices contained wood-framed chairs upholstered in leather. Yan documents that although their designs were appealing, they found little purchase outside of the PSFS commission. The term derived from German modernism for a total work of art is Gesamtkunstwerk. Lescaze's had a related theory he termed "entities," in which there was architecture, interiors that related to it, and furniture that were stylistically commensurate with the rooms they inhabited. Yan described this as: "designing all architecture and small-scaled features with a modern ethos and language" (2020, p. 63). Walls, floors, ceilings, furniture designs all part of a designed whole. Yet the effects of imitators of the PSFS were a long time coming, if in the making.

D.J. De Pree, Gilbert Rohde, and Herman Miller

The building of modern skyscrapers acted as a catalyst for modern corporate furniture and furniture systems. This raises the issue of the relationship between architecture, interiors, furniture and textile design. As companies grew and prospered, some of them commissioned modern buildings. Once a company decided to go ahead with a new headquarters, this created a need for interiors, and frequently this created a need for modern interiors and furnishings. Benjamin Thompson wrote about the initial state of availability that faced designers: "once the glorious shell was completed, there was virtually nothing compatible that the pioneering owner or designer could conveniently buy to sit or eat on" (Caplan 1976, p. 6).

Herman Miller's founder was D.J. De Pree, in Zeeland, Michigan, 1891. He had worked for a company, Michigan Star, that created traditional

blinds, and furniture that the architects designed. The banking hall was also modern. It had no full-height metal grilles, but instead low-height partitions with glass. Significant here is that a modern skyscraper created the need for designers to do space planning—before the term came into use—and required modern furniture commensurate with the aesthetics of the building. In many of these early projects, architectural modernism predated modern furniture, but that situation changed quickly.

In 1932, Lescaze and Howe desired to create a whole environment for PSFS, and this included residential furniture, with a focus on bedroom sets. De Pree, like many of his generation, read the work of efficiency experts, such as Frederick Taylor, on time management. He married Nellie Miller, and her father bought Michigan Star for De Pree, which he renamed for his father-in-law, who never worked there.

Many of the designers, even though they were doing residential design, and had origins in traditional furniture, were moving toward modern designs, with standardization, modularity, new materials, and a concern for efficient manufacturing techniques. Their early work with residential pieces set them on the path to creating office furniture and eventually systems furniture (Figure 24.5).

De Pree was ambitious about the company and said that "the only way to take giant steps is to have giants" (Hattwick, Olcese, and Pledge 2014). He includes in the group of giants: Gilbert Rohde, George Nelson, and Charles Eames (he failed to mentioned Ray Eames). In 1930, De Pree met a designer, Gilbert Rohde, who was responsible for shifting the company from residential to commercial and in a modern direction. Rohde pointed the company first to Art Moderne, then to even more modern pieces. Initially Herman Miller still created bedroom sets, but as an interim step, he deleted turned feet on dressers. In their designs, volumes were mostly unadorned, and new manufacturing techniques created cleaner connections that did not need decoration to hide sloppy workmanship. The firm turned to modern storage pieces and sectional sofas, and in the process reduced the number of components across similar lines.

This new direction drew on the work of the Miller designer Frieda Diamond, who had created a Shaker line. Rohde also started Herman Miller down the path of office seating. Their products had been initially sold through Wanamaker's department store. Rohde decided to henceforth sell them in showrooms.

Rohde died in 1944. Herman Miller's first era of prominence in the commercial interiors sector came to a close with his death, but its greatest days were yet to come.

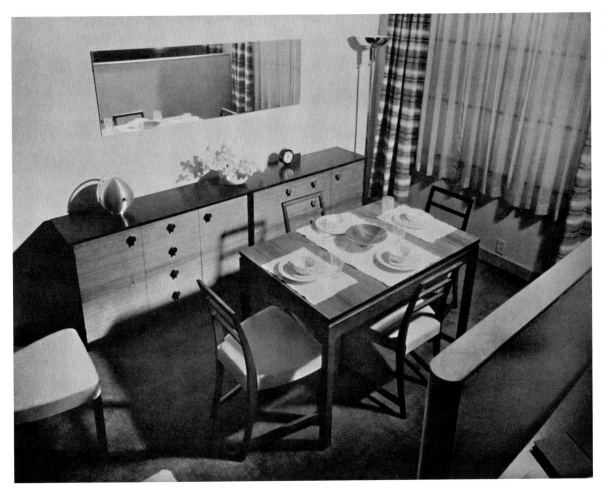

Figure 24.5
Gilbert Rohde, living room, Zeeland, Michigan, 1936.

Frank Lloyd Wright, the Larkin Administration Building, and Johnson Wax

Frank Lloyd Wright had created a significant office interior with the Larkin Building, 1902–1906. Graeme Brooker writes: "It was considered the first purpose-designed environment for a larger organization" (2013–2016, p. 54). It had an atrium that was glazed at the top. This area was filled with freestanding desks that were primarily lit with natural light.

Many of Wright's ideas about workplace design came to their fullest fruition in a later project, the Johnson Wax Building of 1936 (Figure 24.6). It was a company that sold moderately priced consumer goods. The company sought to build relationships with its customers and its employees. It deployed "a counterstrategy by creating a tight-knit, family-like relationship with its employees" (Yan 2020, p. 83). Advertising played an important role in the company's branding and Yan argues that the building that Wright eventually designed

for them and its interiors became part of the corporate brand. Herbert F. Johnson Jr., grandson to the founder, was known as "Hib."

He hired Frank Lloyd Wright, whose Larkin building he admired. The centerpiece was a workroom, which had a 20 foot (6 meter) column grid, surrounded with a 17 foot (5 meter) deep U-shaped mezzanine. There was a carefully crafted relationship between interior space and external form. Columns became part of the ceiling. They resembled Minoan columns in that they flared at the top and were narrow at the bottom. Executives and mid-level managers had semi-enclosed offices that overlooked the light-filled workroom. The famed cantilevered tower came seven years later.

The project took up a generous 54,000 square foot (5,000 square meters), many of whose amenities were devoted to employees' wellbeing. Yan writes that it was an "egalitarian space, which amounted to an architectural equivalent of welfare capitalism" (2020, p. 97). It

Figure 24.6
Frank Lloyd Wright, Johnson Wax Administration Building, Racine, Wisconsin, 1936.

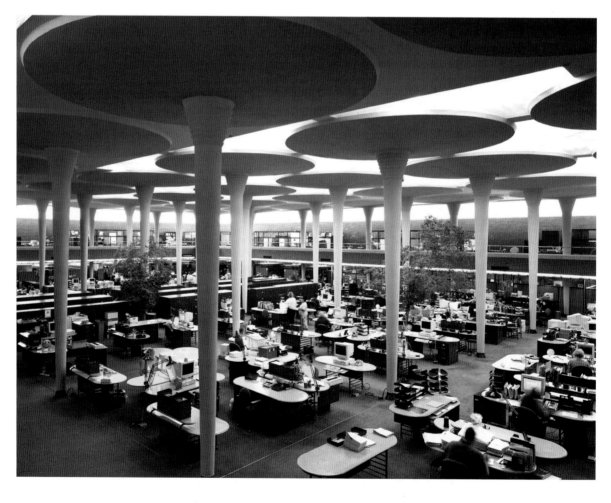

was a symmetrically organized space. The lighting scheme was significant because light came from above, ostensibly emulating the effect of a forest.

Wright felt that the resulting administration building was "as inspiring a place to work in as any cathedral ever was" (Lipman and Wright 2003, p. 93). Important to his design process is that even in conceptualizing the office interiors, he considered the urban context. Because he didn't think highly of the building's neighborhood, his was a space turned inward.

Wright's Great Workroom was uplifting but also exhibited corporate control. The architecture, interiors, freestanding furniture, textiles, and other designed objects were all designed following a similar artistic vision. Attention was also paid to the lobby and advertising offices.

Movies

The 1936 movie *Modern Times* by Charlie Chaplin was released the same year as the Johnson Wax tower and has an iconic scene of an assembly line (Figure 24.7). This shows how the impact of Taylorism was felt in popular culture. More than twenty years later, two films came out that represented the workplace as centered on a giant workspace, a clear development from Johnson Wax. *The Best of Everything* (1959) and *The Apartment* (1960) built on the heritage of the twentieth-century workplace, real and filmed. Jean Negulesco directed *The Best of Everything*, a high-profile movie that follows the travails of three women in New York. It centers on an open-plan publishing house, the fictional Fabian Publishing Company, with perimeter offices and an open area, with primary colors similar to those used by Charlotte Perriand and George Nelson (Figure 24.8). Stuart A. Reis and Walter M. Scott created the sets. Multiple modern offices were built in the postwar era for media companies, including publishing, newspapers, and radio and television. This was an international phenomenon. The chapter opener shows Naoum Shabib's Maspero Radio and Television Building, which took the business and design model of the British

Figure 24.7
Charlie Chaplin (Dir.), *Modern Times* (1936).

Figure 24.8
Jean Negulesco
(Dir.), *The Best of
Everything* (1960).

Broadcasting Corporation (BBC) to the banks of the Nile.

Billy Wilder's *The Apartment* followed *The Best of Everything* and is considered one of the best movies of the twentieth century (Figure 24.9). Regarding its portrayal of women in the workplace, it presents a retrograde workplace environment that has more in common, visually and regarding plot, with *The Crowd*. Its central work area mixed the genders, although the plot focuses on men and one female character. Freestanding desks, filing cabinets, adding machines, elevators, and perimeter offices all figure into the plot.

For French director Jacques Tati, a favorite motif was the alienation of the modern world, as filtered through modern architecture. His is a lighthearted look, in several of his films, but especially *Playtime* (1967). Playtime finds much to criticize about modern architecture and its offices: its central character Monsieur Hulot is confused by the modern designs he encounters, often cannot find the door, fails to see glass partitions, gets lost in a maze of workstations, and has to interact with disembodied voices on speakers (Figure 24.10). The multiple scenes in movies underscores the ambivalence that society on

both sides of the Atlantic felt about the new type of working spaces, and that despite appealing aesthetics, the lives led within them were often fraught with the worries of the age.

Lever House

A major monument in the history of the modern open office interior was Lever House, New York, 1951. It is a 24-story building, built by the architecture firm Skidmore, Owing & Merrill (SOM), with architects Gordon Bunshaft and Nathalie de Blois. Raymond Loewy designed the Interiors. It became an exemplar of corporate architecture. SOM was known for bureaucracy, both in the projects they designed and in their own corporate structure. Lever House was, Yan writes, an example of "a large corporate architecture firm, designing for an even larger corporate client" (2020, p. 132). They ran their own offices in ways commensurate with the business practices of their clients. Prior to Lever House, international style architecture had yet to arrive in New York, although there were multiple examples of accomplished art deco buildings.

The client was Lever Brothers, whose central product was soap. The client catered to a modest clientele, and advertising was all important to

Figure 24.9
Billy Wilder (Dir.),
The Apartment,
1959.

Figure 24.10
Jacques Tati (Dir.),
Playtime (1967).

their business model. Not coincidentally, at the time, there were three major home products companies, and all three created new headquarters: Proctor and Gamble, Colgate and Palmolive, and Lever Brothers.

Lever House became the American headquarters of the English company. The client was Charles Luckman, the company president and an architect. He wanted the American building to take the firm in a different direction than its European real estate. Promotional materials of the time, including coverage in the architectural press, referred to office buildings as the cathedrals of the modern age. Lever House was called "Tomorrow's Office Building."

At the time, some corporations were looking to consolidate their real estate holdings by moving out to the suburbs. Lever House was the opposite of the that trend. Important materials in its design included aluminum, stainless steel, glass, and a variety of plastics. Work started in 1948, and the project had many of the features of international-style buildings worldwide: a slab composition, exposed columns or pilotis, prefabricated windows, spandrel units, and the requisite window-washing system (Figure 24.11). Advertising and branding was important to Lever Brothers and their American headquarters was part of their corporate image-making process.

Bunshaft had himself worked briefly for Raymond Loewy and was not happy about his former boss being in charge of the interiors. After working on Lever House, Bunshaft was to later design other office buildings with modern interiors: Manufacturers Trust Company in New York, 1954, and Connecticut General Life, 1953–1954.

Henry-Russell Hitchcock wrote an article that addresses the totality of modernism and attempts to reconcile two different types of modern architecture, one of which was exemplified by Lever House, "The Architecture of Bureaucracy and the Architecture of Genius" (1947). It is difficult to reconcile that Eero Saarinen's TWA terminal and SOM's Lever House are both examples of modernism. Hitchcock provided a way to differentiate between the hyper-rationalized approach to the design of Lever House and the poetic flights of fancy of the TWA terminal.

With Lever House, unlike PSFS, the company did not seek revenue by renting out stores or extra office space. The entirety of the project was devoted to 1,000 Lever employees spread over eighteen floors. The base was 2,000 square feet (186 square meters). Lever House was able to follow the Corbusian goal of lifting the building

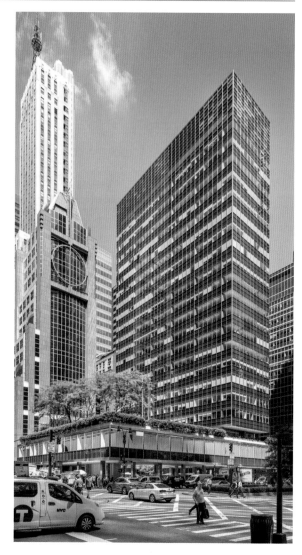

Figure 24.11
SOM, Lever House, New York, NY, 1951. Gordon Bunshaft and Nathalie de Blois were the architects; Raymond Loewy did the interiors.

up. Yan notes that this contrasts with Renaissance palaces in which the ground floor was devoted to retail space.

Loewy, interdisciplinary to his core, had done package design for Lever Brothers' Pepsodent toothpaste carton. In his industrial design work, he balanced a user's desire for the new with their comfort that derived from the familiar. He explained that too much of the new, and the consumer's desire for novelty reached the "shock-zone" (Marcus 2019, p. 138). In his Lever House interiors, this resulted in their not being as cutting-edge modern as the building, which in part explains Bunshaft's displeasure with them. Loewy relied on an all-over background color, Lever House beige, and went so far as to specify that the elevator operators wore uniforms of dark beige. This was not a total work of art, as Loewy contrasted the beige backdrop with a variety of colors specific to departments, from brisk yellow to boudoir pink. Architecture and interiors came from different hands and that was obvious.

Mies van der Rohe's Seagram Building of 1958 has many features in common with Lever House. It has a beautifully detailed curtain wall and was Mies van der Rohe's entry into the world of bureaucratic architecture. There was also considerable variety in the interiors, as the public interiors were by Philip Johnson and the offices by William Pahlmann.

Not all corporations consolidated their various operations in downtown high-rises. There was a parallel move by many companies to move to suburban campuses, which some authors have called "Industrial Versailles" or "Pastoral Capitalism." In 1954, General Foods moved to White Plains, New York, consolidating their offices from three buildings they had inhabited in Manhattan. AT&T moved to Summit, New Jersey. In 1956, Edward Durrell Stone created a suburban office for Pepsi-Cola in Purchase, New York. One of the finest of the genre drew on the talents of Bunshaft and de Blois.

Connecticut General Life

The new headquarters for Connecticut General Life Insurance Company, 1953–1954, were spread out on 280 acres in Bloomfield, near Hartford, Connecticut. Frazar B. Wilde was at the helm of the Insurance Company.

Among corporate histories, Connecticut General Life stands out for the recognition of women as a significant part of the workface, as creators, clients, and customers. In creating their new complex, Connecticut General Life recognized that the work of an insurance company involved clerical work that was mostly done by women. The insurance business was document intensive and involved proposals, policies, claims, and payouts (Wit 2017, 68). This was white-collar work, and the flow of information and corresponding pieces of paper might be influenced by knowledge of how factories worked spatially. The new office space was not to be factory-like aesthetically. Wilde was a naturalist, which explains the attention to the rural setting. He turned to the architecture firm with a proven track record for this type of project, Skidmore, Owings & Merrill, and Gordon Bunshaft. Like Lever House and the Seagram Building, the dominant building materials were steel and glass. The headquarters was essentially a big rectangle punctuated with four interior courtyards. It was three stories tall,

with long open spans. Top talent was used in all aspects of the project. The landscape design was by Joanna Diman and the sculpture by Isamu Noguchi. Official photographs were by famed corporate photographer Ezra Stoller. The project was pastoral in its setting, which workers could enjoy by looking out from floor to ceiling glass. Not intended was the extent to which the project engendered a great deal of new roadway construction and subsequent parking.

One of the architects working under Bunshaft's direction was herself an architect of note, Nathalie de Blois. She had worked on Lever House and was aware of the amount of attention needed on the glass wall. Since the time of Mies's Friedrichstrasse skyscraper unbuilt project of 1921, architects had been intrigued by the idea of all-glass buildings, and Lever House, the Seagram Building, and Connecticut General Life were projects that realized that vision.

The interiors were under the direction of Florence Knoll and the Knoll Planning Unit (Figure 24.12). While Knoll's resolutely modern work was in sympathy with the direction set by Bunshaft, he still rankled at not being in charge, and resented Knoll's influence with the client. Curator Betty J. Blum conducted an oral history with de Blois and attempted to emphasize the schism between interior and exterior. In doing so, she used the term "schizophrenic," which de Blois denied. An unfortunate term, but it does make the point that generally interiors have the potential to extend the architecture, or to depart from it. In the case of Raymond Loewy, the interiors contrasted in multiple ways with Bunshaft's direction in Lever House. This was less so in the work of Florence Knoll and Connecticut General Life. The differences between the working procedures of designing Lever House and Connecticut General Life underscore the difference when the architecture is done by one designer or design team, and the interiors another. At the time of Lever House, SOM did not have an interiors department.

For Connecticut General Life, SOM set up a task force of those on the project which focused on the interiors, and de Blois, although an architect, was a part of that team. Women on various aspects of the project worked on the landscape, architecture, interiors, and ultimately were the users of a space. This group includes Margaret McCurry, who was at the beginning of her career. In the wake of Connecticut General Life, and with Bunshaft's prompting, SOM allocated resources to making its own interiors department capable of handling large projects.

Figure 24.12
SOM and the
Knoll Planning
Unit, Connecticut
General Life
Insurance
Company,
Bloomfield,
Connecticut, 1954.
Gordon Bunshaft
and Nathalie
de Blois were
the architects;
Florence Knoll did
the interiors.

Figure 24.12
SOM and the Knoll Planning Unit, Connecticut General Life Insurance Company, Bloomfield, Connecticut, 1954. Gordon Bunshaft and Nathalie de Blois were the architects; Florence Knoll did the interiors.

Connecticut General Life marks a phase in which the architecture and interiors were designed simultaneously, with each affecting the other in the preliminary planning stages. The all-important distance between the building core and the perimeter curtain wall was designed obsessively in conjunction with the development of workstations and their dimensions, so that any employee's distance to natural light was taken into consideration, and that the spatial sequence "core-circulation-workstations-circulation-perimeter" was optimized. No desks at Connecticut General Life stood more than 30 feet (9 meters) from a window wall.

The bulk of the building was the large area of workstations. Executive offices were in an adjacent office building and on the top floor of the main buildings. Art Institute of Chicago writer and historian Blum said that the space was, "designed with women employees of the insurance company in mind" (2004, p. 59). Although SOM had an extensive team, Florence Knoll of the Knoll Planning Unit played an essential role. The amenities to which the designers paid attention included toilets, coatrooms, recreation facilities, such as billiard tables, a library, a selected shopping area, and a medical department.

The client had requested Knoll's participation on the project. Bunshaft had already established in his discussions with the client the principal features: the project would be open plan. This was established before Knoll joined the project. It was a classic modern project, with a focus on nonstructural partitions, concern with natural light and a field of artificial lighting, and systems furniture. While Bunshaft bristled at not having control over the interiors, there was an aspect of the client relations he was happy to forego.

Florence Knoll and other interiors designers had to deal with some of the executives' penchant for traditional antiques. Some of the offices included Georgian and colonial antiques and reproductions.

In her oral history, De Blois was asked how she balanced having a husband and four children with an acclaimed career in architecture and design. She answered "I didn't really keep it in balance. I had continual problems" (Blum 2004, p. 65). In this too, she was before her time, outlining a situation from the 1950s that decades later would be called "work-life balance."

SOM followed with similar projects for Kimberley-Clark, Neenah-Menasha, Wisconsin, 1957; Reynolds Metal, Richmond, Virginia, 1957; General Mills, Golden Valley, Minnesota, 1959; and Upjohn Corporation, Kalamazoo, Michigan. Many of these projects promoted the use of automobiles, as few employees used the shuttles, and parking

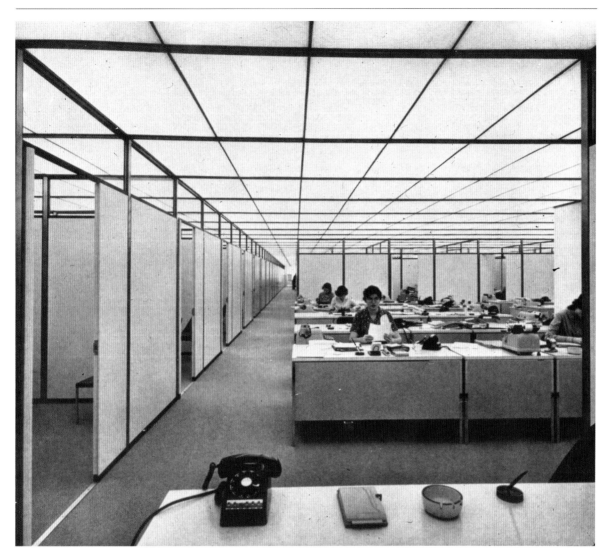

Figure 24.13
SOM, Union
Carbide, New
York, NY, 1957.
The architects
were Gordon
Bunshaft and
Nathalie de Blois.

quickly proved to be inadequate. Two sides of the Connecticut General Life office building were dominated by parking lots. Union Carbide, also known as 270 Park Avenue, saw Gordon Bunshaft and Nathalie de Blois again working together. The project which debuted in 1957 featured a continuous luminous ceiling under which stood freestanding desks (Figure 24.13).

A prominent corporate headquarters for John Deere arose in Moline, Illinois, in 1965. William Hewitt was the client, Eero Saarinen the architect. After the architect's untimely death, Kevin Roche finished the project. Hewitt wanted modern but "down to earth and rugged" (Beemer and Peterson, 1999, p. 24).

The new office environment of workstations in an open area, as represented by Connecticut General Life, Union Carbide, and John Deere, did not go unquestioned. There were two arenas of questioning: How did the new building type of the modern office building, and its accompanying open office interiors, play out across the globe? And, more specifically to the type, what were the concerns about the nature of working in this new type of environment?

The International Turn

Brazil, Mexico, Singapore, Sri Lanka, Turkey

The historian Kenneth Frampton coined the phrase "**critical regionalism**" in 1984 to describe buildings that defied the universality, and sameness, of much modern architecture. He outlined ways that this could be done and brought attention to architects who he thought were talented at inflecting the local in the global. It remains a useful term to address the work of many architects and designers who predated his term although not his sympathies.

In Turkey, Sedad Eldem (1908–1988) sought to nationalize modern architecture, that is, to create a modern architecture grounded in the architectural tradition of Turkey. Yet looking at his life works, there are examples that are inflected with tradition and those that are resolutely modern. He worked on the Istanbul Hilton, 1952–1955, which brought him into contact with SOM architects Jane Kidder and Nathalie de Blois, and SOM's corporate structure in general. The Istanbul Hilton was a standout in the field of luxury hotels for its unrelenting, pure modernism. Eldem was known for bringing the traditions of the Turkish house into contemporary residential designs, he was also capable of being a full-blown modernist. His Social Security Complex, 1962–1964, was particularly deft in its attention to urban context. But his Akbank Headquarters, 1965, and Alarko Office Blocks, 1976, were strikingly modern examples. Across multiple projects, Eldem's interiors were characterized by open offices instead of suites of distinct rooms. His modern office buildings promoted modern open office interiors when his firm did them and when the spaces were let to other clients who hired their own designers.

In Korea, the architect Kimm Jong-Soung studied at the Illinois Institute of Technology in 1956. He later worked in the office of his instructor Mies van der Rohe. He returned to Korea in 1978. A Korean architecture journal notes that "He came closer to the essence of modern architecture than any other Korean architect" (Park 1985, p. 90). With an experience that echoes the trajectory of Eldem, he worked on the Seoul Hilton, 1977–1980, a building that established him as a bona fide modernist capable of thrilling interiors. He did a number of high-rise office buildings after his return to Korea. Daewoo Securities Co. Office Building is just one of the corporate office buildings he created. Throughout his career he has been a vocal proponent who argues that Miesian international-style modernism was not antithetical to a Korean context. He does not really fall into the critical regionalist camp because he studied and worked closely with Mies and resisted the notion of regional differences as a counterweight to internationalism.

The Great Eastern Life Building, 1959, in Singapore is one of the earlier high-rises in Southeast Asia (Figure 24.14). It was designed by the Singaporean architects Wong and Karmakar. The air-conditioned building has seven floors with

Figure 24.14
Wong and Karmakar, the Great Eastern Life Building, Singapore, 1959.

6,000 square feet (557 square meters) of space. The exterior looks like a curtain wall but is actually an ingenious way of aesthetically making reference to a curtain wall using concrete and other materials, including white and black marble. Steel and glass were not available in the quantities necessary for an entire Lever House style curtain wall.

Geoffrey Bawa (1919–2003) is one of the major figures known for his contribution to tropical modernism and critical regionalism. He also made a significant contribution to the development of corporate interiors. His Mahaweli Tower, 1976, housed the State Mortgage Bank (Figure 24.15). Malaysian architect Ken Yeang praised the structure by calling it the first Asian bioclimatic skyscraper. It utilized cross-ventilation and minimized solar gain. It had a connection to and adaptation of the climate. The exterior is load-bearing, so there are only three interior columns, which greatly facilitated the interior layout. Other features include a curtain wall, deep concrete spandrels, and operable windows. Eventually air conditioning was installed. Mahaweli is an unusual building that stands out from Bawa's practice. Bawa was otherwise known for incorporating antiques and locally made textiles into his interiors. He admired the classic modern pieces of furniture by Saarinen, among others, and when he had trouble sourcing

Figure 24.15
Geoffrey Bawa,
Mahaweli Tower,
Colombo, Sri
Lanka, 1976.

the originals, he had copies made. His modernism was rooted in Sri Lanka's history. Although he is mostly known for his residential and hospitality interiors, this one building of his oeuvre brought international-style corporate interiors to Southeast Asia.

Two skyscrapers arose across the streets from each other in Mexico City. The Torre Latinoamericano, 1956, housed an insurance company, La Latinoamericano, Seguros (Figure 24.16). The architect was Augusto Alvarez. There were forty-floor floors, of which the insurance company inhabited floors four to eight. Across the street was the Edificio Miguel E. Abed, 1952. The construction of the two buildings had the effect of making it clear to the world that Mexican architects were in command of tall-building technology and proved a boon to local interior designers.

When local architects created modern buildings, they often turned to local furniture retailers who either created their own versions of the international classics, or who licensed their distribution and manufacture. Brazilian Milly Teperman had graduated from the Escola Politecnica. She did postgraduate studies in the United States, where she became familiar with Herman Miller. She was the daughter of Isaac Teperman, who

Figure 24.16
Augusto
Alvarez, Torre
Latinoamericano,
Mexico City,
Mexico, 1956.

had inherited a furniture company. They licensed Herman Miller products in the 1960s, in time to benefit from the golden age of Brazilian modernism. They made a significant contribution by bringing corporate interiors to Brazil, using Herman Miller products in spaces that were open and modular. This scenario played out worldwide, and Herman Miller was licensed to thirty-five countries. Knoll also had licenses in Brazil.

The Modern Office

Herman Miller: George Nelson, Charles and Ray Eames, Eero Saarinen, and Robert Probst

A number of projects appeared in the wake of Connecticut General Life, including Pepsi-Cola, 1956, and Union Carbide, 1957. These projects made clear that the open plan was an increasingly important part of the twentieth-century workplace interior. More projects were to follow, and they required a design infrastructure of available furniture to support them. In Rohde's wake, George Nelson (1908–1986) became design director at Herman Miller. His mission was to take the approaches of European modernism and apply them to the field of American industrial design. With his focus on function and rationality, he helped establish Herman Miller as a rival to the Knoll Planning Unit, in terms of individual products and overall design services.

Herman Miller President P.J. De Pree hired Nelson as design director. As a designer Nelson had developed two significant modern furniture systems, the Basic Storage Components, 1950, and Comprehensive Storage Systems, 1959–1973. He was also influential in promoting another line of modular office furniture, Action Office, which appeared in 1964.

He was not only concerned with furnishings but oversaw a general marketing strategy. He sought to standardize components and dimensions across lines (Caplan 1976, p. 31). In 1938, Herman Miller opened a showroom in the Merchandise Mart, Chicago. In 1948, the firm produced its final period reproductions. Nelson was to serve as design director for twenty years. Just as Rohde had done the Executive Office Group, Nelson did a Middle Management Group, which competed with successful Steelcase products.

Charles and Ray Eames created a successful case goods line for Herman Miller, the Eames Storage Units. They also collaborated with Eero Saarinen on molded plywood seating, and plastic chairs made by Zenith Plastics. These products affected both the residential and corporate sides of the marketplace that Miller attended to.

The history of these individual companies, and the designers who worked for them is often confusing. George Nelson worked outside of Herman Miller, and although Charles and Ray Eames did a lot of work for Herman Miller, they also worked outside of Herman Miller, and over the years, certain products were licensed to other companies. And licensing abroad differed from American licensing. George Nelson oversaw the work of multiple designers, while also creating individual pieces himself. The new direction of the company came when one of their designers turned his attention to workplace design. The new center of the business was systems furniture for workstations.

Robert Probst's masterwork, Action Office, was the result of extensive research (Figure 24.17). Action Office marked Herman Miller moving into systems furniture, and the world took note. It was a panel system and included wall-hung pieces and accessories. It intentionally had a straightforward design that eschewed the visual excesses of the 1960s. It included stand-up desks, vertical surfaces, shelves, tackboards, and open and closed storage. It was followed by a product line that was oriented to health care, a healthcare system named Co/Struc.

The Aluminum Group of Charles and Ray Eames is one of the many products that rounded out Herman Miller's offerings. Not a furniture system per se, it worked well for private offices, receptions areas, and contemporary residential projects (Figure 24.18).

Davis Allen, Nathalie De Blois, and Margaret Mccurry

Davis Allen (1916–1999) was a modernist who spent the bulk of his career at SOM. His immediate supervisor at SOM was Gordon Bunshaft. He had previously worked for Hans and Florence Knoll in the Knoll Planning Unit, and he worked briefly for Raymond Loewy. There is strong evidence of his flexible approach to design and deft reading of character in his interactions with clients and supervisors. As a designer, he is known for broadening the palette of what could be included in a modern SOM project.

Figure 24.17
Robert Probst for
Herman Miller,
Action Office II,
1968.

For Mauna Kea Beach Hotel, he scoured
Asia purchasing antiques, crafts, and textiles.
This is one of the projects that set the standard
for international hotels. A feature of Allen's work
was his flexibility in culture and in chronology.
Yet when working with the notoriously prickly
Bunshaft, he towed the modernist line. Interiors
for Allen was a mediator, between geographies,
between the international style and local cultures,
and between architecture and end users who had
individual tastes. He was one of the modernists
who catered to the American business community
in macro ways—crafting headquarters—and in
micro ways—helping executives pick pieces for
their individual offices.

Davis oversaw multiple projects for IBM and
Chase Manhattan. A piece of furniture that he
designed with Margaret McCurry for Stendig is
the Andover chair, a contemporary version of the
Windsor chair. It thus met the needs of clients
who wanted traditional furniture and an architecture based on Miesian modernism. In a scenario
that played out multiple times in his career, he
designed the famous office of one executive, David
Rockefeller, 1961, of Chase Manhattan. He was

mentor to many, including McCurry and Margo
Grant Walsh. He joined SOM in 1950 and in 1965
became Associate Partner.

Author Maeve Slavin wrote a book on Allen
and had a firm grasp of how projects of the 1940s
and 1950s differed from what came later: "The
opening of the 1960s produced a sense that strict
Bauhausian discipline had run its course and would
require refocusing" (Slavin 1990, p. 42). Allen was
well poised for the challenge of shifting design
direction. Another change that arose is that in the
1950s firms doing modern interiors often created
their own furniture designs, but commercially
available furniture was in abundance in the 1970s.
With furniture available, such as Action Office and
its competitors, the interior corporate environment
became one where a comprehensively planned
space could be achieved that addressed interior
spatial moves, furniture, art, and accessories.

Art Gensler and Margo Grant Walsh

Art Gensler (1935–2021) founded Gensler in 1965.
It expanded exponentially and came to represent
for the field of interiors what SOM was to architecture. The firm created corporate interiors for

major corporations, and its own business model
was like that of its clients. Eventually it branched
out of interiors and became a commercial architecture firm of note. For years it was the world's
largest corporate interiors firm, then it became the
world's largest architecture firm.

Art Gensler, in 1969, hired Margo Grant
Walsh, when his eponymous firm had only three
employees. By the time of her retirement, the
firm had 2,000 employees. Her significance as
one of the most influential interior designers of
the twentieth century was not tied to a specific
aesthetic contribution as much as it was to business practices. She was interested in the shape
and dimensions of floor plates, so that buildings
were designed with dimensions that made sense
once interior designers laid out offices and work
areas. As with the Bunshaft/Knoll collaboration, a
particular focus on hers was the dimension from
the building core to the window wall.

She worked on maintaining corporate clients
for multiple projects. One part of her focus on
client relations was being adamant that clients
understood what they were getting. She worked
on the San Francisco headquarters of Bank of
America. When they moved their New York

operations into a refurbished Biltmore Hotel, her
project dealt with unusual column placement
but had the signature Gensler combination of
freestanding furniture, panels, storage systems,
and private offices (Figure 24.19). An atrium
brought natural light to interior workstations, a
regular focus in the designs that resulted from her
management. Most of the open office spaces were
created with freestanding furniture.

Textiles

The history of modern (twentieth-century) textiles
is a rich subject in itself that will only be touched
on here as it relates to the development of the
commercial interior design business. As with
many other aspects of twentieth-century design,
the Bauhaus had a tremendous impact on textile
design. Textiles were an important adjunct to
interiors and furnishings, for the modern corporate interior was not possible without appropriate
textiles to support it. A glorious start came from
women associated with the Bauhaus: Gunta Stölzl

Figure 24.19
Margo Grant Walsh for Gensler, Bank of America, New York, NY, 1986.

(1887–1983), Anni Albers (1899–1994), and their students and followers. Albers studied under Stölzl. Along with her husband Josef, she was one of the guiding forces behind the establishment of Black Mountain College in North Carolina, one of the schools that laid claim to continuing the design principles of the Bauhaus. She collaborated with Knoll for thirty years. She took thirteen trips to Mexico, which resulted in multiple projects, including a wall hanging for the Camino Real Hotel in Mexico City, 1968. Many aspects of her life's work are indicative of the development of twentieth-century commercial textiles. Other designers distanced themselves from historical European fabrics, such as toiles and brocades. They experimented with new materials, such as rayon, cellophane, and metallics. Traveling became part of their professional development, especially with their interest in indigenous textiles from around the world.

Lucienne Day (1917–2010) repeated a scenario that many of the textile designers described: because of the unmet need for contemporary textiles, success came relatively easy to her. She considered herself an artist and brought the perspectives of Alexander Calder, Paul Klee, and Joan Miró into the world of textiles. Her designs eschewed obvious historical influences and were at once inspired by nature but looked scientific if not atomic. A major monument of twentieth-century textiles was her Calyx design, which had its debut at the 1951 Festival of Britain.

Alexander Girard (1907–1993) collaborated with Herman Miller on Action Office, as head of the textile division in 1952. Many fabrics used in office interiors at the time were bland and Girard used saturated colors, including famously magenta and pink. He also embraced Mexican and Indian folk arts.

Esther Haraszty (1920–1994) had a Bauhaus pedigree and became director of Knoll Textiles during the period 1949–1955. Her career was championed by fellow Hungarian Marcel Breuer. Another figure who contributed to Knoll's preeminence in corporate textiles was Marianne Strengell (1909–1998), a Finnish designer with success on both sides of the Atlantic. She studied and in turn taught at Cranbrook, where her students included Jack Lenor Larsen. She became director of Knoll Textiles. Like many of the modern textile designers, she was an accomplished colorist whose influence spread beyond fabrics. She led Knoll, and therefore corporate design, in a different color direction than that started by founder Florence Knoll. She made the combination of pink and orange a Knoll signature.

Dorothy Liebes (1897–1972) was an American textile designer and weaver who created textiles used for upholstery, vertical surfaces, and draperies. A University of California graduate, she married a department store heir. Her designs look handwoven but were created with the power loom in mind. She was intrigued by the possibilities afforded by synthetic fibers. She was inspired by the colors and motifs of pre-Columbian textiles.

Jack Lenor Larsen (1927–2020) was a textile designer who opened his office in 1952. He collaborated with a number of designers and architects, including Louis Kahn. He created curtains for Lever House, and from his earliest days he saw the possibilities in the commercial market. He designed for power looms and brought **ikat** and **batik** into the twentieth-century commercial realm.

In the generation following those with Bauhaus or Cranbrook connections, Jhane Barnes (b. 1954) stands out and takes us into the twenty-first century. Barnes is a rare figure in an age of increasing specialization to be active across multiple design disciplines. Her first success came as a fashion designer, specifically menswear in the 1980s. Celebrity clients including John Travolta, John Lennon, and Paul Simon clamored after her sweaters. Although she ceased work as a fashion designer in 2013, her pieces continue to sell in high-end, vintage clothing outlets. She had the wisdom in the 1980s to eye the corporate textiles market, and she created designs on an Atari computer. She worked with patterns, repeats, and long runs, which computer drafting made possible. She specifically created textiles for panel systems and tile carpets.

Bürolandshaft

The response to the new type of office environment came in equal measures of fascination and concern, as exemplified by the Knoll Planning Unit and Action Office. While there was no quibbling with Knoll's aesthetic choices, researchers increasingly turned their attention to what it was like to work and live in such a space. In 1972, the *Journal of Building Research* devoted two issues to what it called "open space" (April/June 1972, and July/September 1972). The articles were remarkably prescient in their exploration of a number of concerns that workplace designers and researchers still ponder. These concerns included acoustic privacy, visual sensitivity, environmental conditions, conflict resolution, corporate branding, ratios of openness or enclosure, the importance of concentration, and the effect of disruption, supervision, and teamwork versus individual work. Geoff Shuttleworth wrote specifically about open-plan projects: "These can be enormous. Their overriding characteristic is visual monotony, endless rows of desks. Sometimes offices planning in this manner contained partitioned cubicles for selected supervisors. Such arrangements are extremely economical in the use of space, but there can be little doubt that few people enjoy working in such an environment" (Shuttleworth 1972, p. 13). These were all themes that were addressed by the various filmed versions of office spaces.

The various authors in the *Journal of Building Research* articles addressed what had come to be the canonical open-plan workplace, perfected by Knoll, Herman Miller, and others, and the various reactions to it. A major response to the geometric open-plan office was **Bürolandschaft**. The German term and the designs it refers to was a significant event in corporate office planning. It arrived in the 1960s with a pair of German space consultants who were not designers per se, but who had an impact on workplace design. Eberhard and Wolfgang Schnelle were organizational consultants and brothers, and they became

known as the Quickborner team. Their influence in the 1960s and 1970s was far-reaching.

Bürolandschaft, or office landscape, was an open-plan concept, but light-years away from Florence Knoll's approach. Their consultancy, in fact, can be seen as a reaction against the crisp grid of the Knoll Planning Unit with its "visually loose, even chaotic arrangement of furniture." The designs that resulted from their consulting were noted for their flexibility. They promoted a flat hierarchy and embraced in the designs the contradictory nature of a corporate environment as a constituent part of society. The designs that resulted from their consultancy were more reliant on freestanding furniture than panel systems. They sought to incorporate employee dissent into their designs. Breakrooms and other amenities were the result of their work. This new type of office environment spread out underneath a continuous ceiling of lighting that was a consistent source of light, not related to specific work areas. Their plan for OSRAM, 1963, in Munich demonstrates the lack of hierarchy that comes with an open space, freestanding furniture, and a lack of full-height walls (Figure 24.20).

Francis Duffy is credited with bringing the ideas of Bürolandshaft into the Anglophone world, specifically the United Kingdom and the United States. He founded the DEGW partnership in 1974. He sought to help businesses use space more efficiently as both a designer and as a consultant. He was interested in organization theory and aware of the growing importance of information technology. His clients came to include the accountancy and consulting firm Arthur Anderson, the Australia New Zealand Bank, CIGNA insurance, and IBM. Duffy wrote two books, *The Changing Workplace* (1992) and *The New Office* (1997).

Historian and administrator Graeme Brooker writes that "The typical plan of a Bürolandschaft office involved free and open planned space with furniture arranged in large, seemingly unstructured, arrangements. The planning could be moulded into a variety of forms but essentially these arrangements were intended to propagate the free flow of people and hence information" (2013–2016, p. 61). While Action Office was not designed specifically with Bürolandschaft in mind, it was utilized multiple times in projects that were indebted to this free, nonhierarchical version of the open plan.

Walter Henn was the architect of the Osram Headquarters Building, Munich, West Germany, 1965. It was Europe's first open-plan building. The

Figure 24.20
Walter Henn, OSRAM,
Munich, Germany, 1963.

six-story building used mostly freestanding furniture, accompanied with some freestanding and partial-height partitions. Significantly, it follows the ethos of Bürolandschaft in that instead of regulating workstations according to a grid, they are organically placed in a manner whose organization is not immediately apparent (Figure 24.20).

William Pulgram and the 1970s

William Pulgram (1921–2020), was one of the foremost experts in workplace design in the final decades of the twentieth century. From Vienna, Austria, he narrowly escaped being sent to a concentration camp. His career was in the United States and his home base was Atlanta. He believed that interiors and architecture were intertwined, even though he often was in charge of the interiors in buildings designed by others. He thought the composite architecture/interiors project should be holistic, and the term he used that described the situation to be avoided was "stylistic dissonance." In 1961, he did the Citizens & Southern Bank of Atlanta. In 1963 he formed his own design firm, Associated Space Design.

In many respects, from the perspective of the twenty-first century, his projects do not appear timeless but embedded in the aesthetics of the 1970s, which explains their popularity then, and the difficulty people now have in appreciating them. He was aware of dissatisfaction with rectilinear open workstation layouts and sought to provide alternatives that users found more to their liking. One way that he contrived to do that was by making more references to nature, such as using plants, and colors that were considered, in the 1970s, to be more natural, such as rust, gold, orange, and brown. In his various projects, he used furniture systems designed by others, including Knoll, Steelcase, and Herman Miller.

He advised the US government on their interiors across the globe. He understood, and supported, the idea of standardization of projects. He thought that for a large organization, be it private or public, a lack of standardization in interiors would lead to chaos, yet he sought to mitigate the effects of standardization by being attentive to users' needs.

Three projects of his are worthy of mention, Haas and Dodd Insurance, Atlanta; Franklin Brothers Insurance Agency, Charlotte; and McDonald's headquarters, Oak Brook, Illinois, 1972. Two insurance company projects of his were published in 1974. In the plan of Haas and Dodd, the dominant elements are plants, freestanding furniture, some partitions, and only a few doors, a layout that lets light shine through to the interior reaches of the floor.

Franklin Brothers shows a particular 1970s bent in its design (Figure 24.21). To the ever-present topic of how do the interiors relate to the architecture, Pulgram provided a then revolutionary approach. He was a proponent of consistency between architecture and interiors, yet for Franklin Brothers he slanted the interiors formed by walls and furniture at a 45-degree angle to the base building. This has the result that the interiors stand out from the building and gives the spaces some of the qualities of Bürolandschaft, but also allows for them to be organized and avoids the purposely chaotic environment of Bürolandschaft. Many architects and designers in the 1970s took out their 45-degree triangles to show that they were moving on from the Miesian international

style box, such as Philip Johnson's Pennzoil Place to I.M. Pei's National Gallery. Pulgram did this with his interiors.

In 1972, he designed the McDonald's headquarters in which all the employees, including the CEO, were in workstations, although of different dimensions and materials.

Conclusion

If skyscrapers are the cathedrals of the modern age, then the twentieth-century office interior is the sanctuary. Where the analogy fails is that it is almost impossible for significant office interiors to be preserved. Very few examples are extent, with Johnson Wax and John Deere being two of the exceptions. Most were subject to almost continual change, and many, base building and interior, have been demolished, including Paul Rudolph's Burroughs Wellcome Laboratories and the SOM/Knoll collaboration, Connecticut General Life.

The Pandemic of 2020, co-working, and work from home have all upended the corporate interior. Many have noted that although the social and economic environment has dramatically changed at the beginning of the third decade of the third millennium, the open office plan is thus far proving remarkably resilient.

Figure 24.21
William Pulgram, Franklin Brown Insurance Agency, Charlotte, North Carolina, 1974.

Sources

Abrahamson, Michael (2018). "Actual Center of Detroit: Albert Kahn's General Motors Building." *Journal of the Society of Architectural Historians* 77, no. 1 (March): 56–76.

Araujo, Ana (2021). *No Compromise: The Work of Florence Knoll*. New York: Princeton Architectural Press.

Auscherman, Amy (2019). *Herman Miller: A Way of Living*. New York: Phaidon.

Beemer, Rod, and Chester Peterson (1999). *Inside John Deere*. Osceola, WI: MBI Publishing.

Blum, Betty J. (2004). *Oral History of Nathalie de Blois*. Chicago: Art Institute of Chicago.

Brooker, Graeme (2013). *Key Interiors since 1900*. Credo Reference.

Caplan, Ralph (1976). *The Design of Herman Miller*. New York: Watson-Guptill Publications.

Gillen, Nicola (2019). *Future Office: Next Generation Workplace Design*. London: RIBA.

Hattwick, Richard, Robert Olcese, and Michael Pledge (2014). "D.J. De Pree: Herman Miller." American National Business Hall of Fame, October 24. Available online: https://anbhf.org/laureates/d-j-depree/ (accessed May 1, 2023).

Kaufmann-Buhler, Jennifer (2021). *Open Plan: A Design History of the American Office*. London: Bloomsbury.

Lipman, Jonathan, and Frank Lloyd Wright (2003). *Frank Lloyd Wright and the Johnson Wax Buildings*. Mineola, NY: Dover.

Marcus, George H. (2019). *Introduction to Modern Design*. London: Bloomsbury.

Park, Junghyin (1985). "The Legacy of Kim Jong-Soung." *SPACE*, no. 216 (June): 90–128.

Shuttleworth, Geoffrey, and Gerald Davis (1972). "Convertible Space." *Building Research* 9, no. 2: 9–15.

Slavin, Maeve (1990). *Davis Allen: Forty Years of Interior Design at Skidmore, Owings & Merrill*. New York: Rizzoli.

Wit, Wim de (2017). *Design for the Corporate World*. London: Lund Humphries.

Yan, Grace Ong (2020). *Building Brands: Corporations and Modern Architecture*. London: Lund Humphries.

Discussion and Review Questions

1. What are some examples of filmed office environments, from either the movies or televisions? What characteristics of the workplaces do they portray?

2. What various roles did women play in the twentieth-century workplace, as clients, designers, and end-users?

3. What are some of the differences between a panel system of workspaces, and one formed by free-standing pieces of furniture?

4. What pieces of designs were found in both residential and corporate spheres?

5. How did Bürolandshaft projects differ from those of the Knoll Planning Unit?

6. What are some major workplace design projects outside of North America?

After Modernism

Modernism Continues, the 1960s and 1970s

1950s	1960s	1960s	1970s
Modernism continued— Festival of Britain, 1951	Commercialization of Design—Terence Conran opens Habitat Store, 1964	Countercultural revolution—Woodstock Music and Art Festival, 1969	Formal end of modernism— Demolition of Pruitt-Igoe housing project, 1972

The Second World War left no one untouched. The rise of National Socialism in Germany led to the closing of the Bauhaus and was the mechanism that drove many designers and architects to the United States and elsewhere. Mies van der Rohe moved to Chicago, where he built a new campus for the Illinois Institute of Technology (IIT). After a stint in Britain, where he produced several distinguished furniture pieces, Marcel Breuer emigrated to the United States. Walter Gropius headed to Massachusetts to direct the Department of Architecture at Harvard University. Born in Finland, the young Eero Saarinen had moved to the United States in the 1920s when his father, Eliel Saarinen, was developing the design academy Cranbrook, in Michigan. Eero eventually taught there as well.

Those who remained in Europe initially experienced a fallow period. For Le Corbusier, Pierre Jeanneret, and Aino and Alvar Aalto, the exciting period of prewar modernism was over, and they scrambled for commissions. Charlotte Perriand coped with the war by traveling to Japan and Indonesia where she became mentor to many aspiring designers. A Berliner all her life, Lilly Reich stayed in Berlin until war's end. Her career evaporated and she was destitute.

Figure 25.0
(*Facing page*)
Carlo Mollino,
Teatro Regio,
Turin, Italy, 1963.

Anne Tyng went to school with Philip Johnson and was a part of the Bauhaus-inspired design milieu at Harvard. Tyng also knew the architect Edward Durrell Stone.

Along with others who fled Nazi Germany, Hans Knoll moved to New York and started a furniture company. Hans's father, Walter Knoll, had produced Bauhaus furniture. Once in the United States, Hans Knoll founded his eponymous company in 1938.

Florence Schust studied at Cranbrook and then started working at Knoll. Eventually, Florence married Hans. As we have seen, the company they built together played a significant role in continuing to manufacture and market the Bauhaus furniture designs that came to be known as classic modern pieces. Knoll, along with Herman Miller, produced the iconic works of Mies, Reich, Perriand, Le Corbusier, and the Aaltos. These companies developed new modern office products and promoted new designers. All these developments made clear that modernism was to have a robust post-Second World War life, but other directions were on the horizons.

Modernism Continued

The 1950s constitutes a second phase of modernism. If prewar modernism was utopian and theoretical, postwar modernism was practical and applied. The avant-garde movement had progressed from scarcely hidden socialism to full-blown capitalism. The 1950s saw a continuation and exploration of modernist principles and forms, and technological innovations played an important role. Increasingly, the furniture and design business became international. Advertising, retailing, and branding were important as never before.

Architects and Furniture

The major architectural players of the prewar period created many of the classics of modern furniture, including Le Corbusier, Mies van der Rohe, Marcel Breuer, Walter Gropius, and Alvar Aalto. Yet after the war, they focused on architecture, and created few to no new furniture designs. Yet the pieces they previously designed, many of them in the 1920s, continued to sell well and played a significant part of the postwar design marketplace. A number of designers were at the ready to take their place.

Mies van der Rohe

Mies van der Rohe moved to the United States in 1937 to escape the Nazis. From 1938 to 1958, he was head of the architecture department at the Illinois Institute of Technology, for whom he would later design a new campus. The central structure of the campus was Crown Hall, built in 1952. One of the most important buildings of the post–Second World War period, it was based on the idea of a factory with vast, uninterrupted space. Mies later realized his dream of glass skyscrapers with the Lake Shore Drive apartments in Chicago, 1950, and the Seagram Building in New York, 1957.

One of his most famous buildings is the Farnsworth House, outside of Chicago. Built in 1944, it is a transparent box framed by eight steel columns and is one of the most fundamentally minimalist houses ever designed. Mies no longer designed furniture, but the pieces he designed in the 1920s and 1930s in collaboration with Lilly Reich continued to sell well. Several of their pieces were specified for the Farnsworth House including the Mies couch and Tugendhat chairs. His office buildings and their imitations created a demand for furniture appropriate to their austere spaces delineated with steel and glass (Figure 25.1).

Le Corbusier

The postwar projects of Le Corbusier (1887–1965) signaled a new direction. Three projects—the Maison Jaoul, 1951–1954; Chapel of Notre Dame du Haut, Ronchamp, 1950–1954; and the Dominican Monastery of La Tourette, 1953–1957—displayed a new means of dealing with concrete that a new generation of architects admired.

Brutalism describes a group of like-minded architects of the 1950s and 1960s. The movement started in Britain and soon spread around the world. It was related to the art brut movement, whose chief figure was the artist Jean Dubuffet. The brutalists built in concrete and idolized the postwar projects of Le Corbusier.

His projects for a new capital city at Chandigarh gave him the opportunity to complete a large-scale governmental complex. For Chandigarh, he designed the Governor's Palace. His swan song was built at Harvard University, the Carpenter Center for the Visual Arts, 1959–1963. Although his prewar furniture designed

with Charlotte Perriand continued to sell well, he completed no new furniture designs. It was the designs of his cousin Pierre Jeanneret, many of them in India, that seem more in touch with the spirit of the age.

Brutalism became a global phenomenon. Paul Rudolph enjoyed a great deal of success in Singapore. Architects such as Keit Jiwakul in Thailand moved away from white painted plaster and explored the materiality of concrete (Figure 25.2).

Louis Kahn and Anne Tyng

Louis Kahn, one of the most influential architects of the twentieth century, infused the International Style of architecture with a poetic use of light and sensitive approach to materials. Although he did few projects, he was renowned for his massive concrete buildings that responded to the human scale and their sites. Kahn and his collaborator Anne Tyng maintained a personal relationship for seven years. In 1953, she traveled to Rome, where their daughter was born. During this time, Kahn and Tyng wrote fifty-three letters whose subjects range from their intense relationship to their individual projects.

Tyng designed a chair that was a modern take on the Arts and Crafts classic the Morris chair. She also specialized in **tensegrity**, an approach to design related to the work of Buckminster Fuller that used complicated mathematical formulations and that resulted in long-span structures. She was responsible for the ceiling of the Yale University Art Gallery, 1953, a plane of tetrahedrons (Figure 25.3).

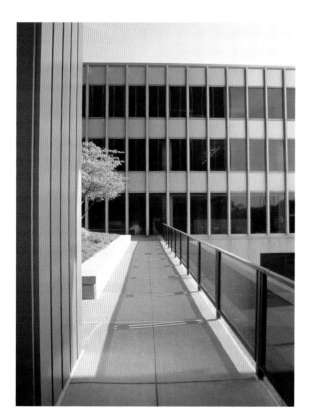

Figure 25.1
Mies van der Rohe and Fujikawa Johnson, Mutual Benefit Life Building, Kansas City, Missouri, 1975.

Figure 25.2
Keit Jiwakul, DOB Hualamphong Gallery, Bangkok, Thailand, 1971.

Figure 25.4
Eero Saarinen, Tulip Chair, 1957.

1950s furniture design

Eero Saarinen, the son of Eliel Saarinen, was born in 1910. He studied in Paris and at Yale University. After a year in art school, he decided to become an architect. He became a US citizen in 1940, and shortly thereafter he embarked on designing furniture with Charles and Ray Eames. They produced an array of furniture products that centered on organic shapes and modern materials. Two of his most famous furniture designs are the Womb Chair and the Tulip Chair (Figure 25.4). Saarinen and his wife named their son Eames, after his collaborator Charles Eames. Eero's first major work was a project completed with his father, the General Motors Technical Center in Warren, Michigan.

In the 1950s, he received commissions from American universities for campus designs and individual buildings; these include the Noyes dormitory at Vassar College, and dormitories, an ice rink, and an auditorium at Yale University. His firm was located in Bloomfield Hills, Michigan, until 1961, when he moved the practice to Connecticut.

Although he's famous for his furniture designs, Eero Saarinen's postwar architecture included some iconic modern masterpieces, such as the TWA terminal in New York. Made out of reinforced steel covered in concrete, it consists of four vaulted domes supported on Y-shaped columns. The domes form an umbrella-like shell that curves 50 feet (15.2 meters) high and 315 feet (96 meters) long, and which is inspired by the excitement of flight.

The designs of many of the early twentieth-century designers continued to sell in the postwar period and, in fact, well into the twenty-first century. Josef Albers designed a set of nested tables, made of oak, beech, and lacquered glass in 1926 (Figure 25.5). Similar versions were made by Thonet and Josef Hoffmann. They were widely copied in the 1950s, and originals and copies sold well. Another piece that became ubiquitous in the 1960s, the Parsons table, owes it origins to Parson's School of Design having a Paris branch, developed by its director Van Day Truex in the 1930s. Jean-Michel Frank, Marcel Breuer, Edward Wormley, and Milo Baughman all produced their own versions (Figure 25.6). Nesting tables and Parsons tables of all sizes made their way into many projects in the 1960s and 1970s.

Figure 25.5
Josef Albers, nesting tables, Berlin, Germany, 1926. Oak, beech, and lacquered glass. For the Moellenhoff-Haus.

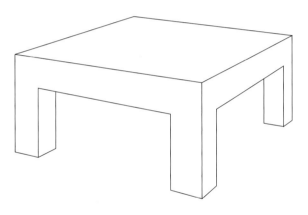

Figure 25.6
Jean-Michel Frank, Parsons table, Paris, France, 1930s.

Philip Johnson active in multiple styles

Philip Johnson's career remarkably reflects all the major phases of post-Second World War architecture and design. A quick look at the stages in his career is a trip through twentieth-century design. The best example of Philip Johnson's modern phase is his own residence, the Glass House, 1949. It is one of eleven buildings on his 47-acre estate. It employs his masterful knowledge of geometry, proportion, minimal structure, and the effects of reflection and transparency. Mies's Farnsworth house inspired Johnson. In this instance, Mies did not consider imitation as the sincerest form of flattery and was publicly displeased with Johnson's homage.

The Seagram Building was designed by Mies van der Rohe in New York City in 1954. It is known for its elegant proportions and use of luxurious materials. Bronze I-beams were applied from bottom to top, making it the first bronze skyscraper and one of the best examples of the International Style. Johnson was commissioned for the public interior of the skyscraper and designed the Four Seasons restaurant. A less well-known part of the Seagram story is that self-described interior decorator William Pahlmann did most of the office interiors, and writers Eggler, Morawski, and Reed argue that his erasure from design history is largely due to the modernist "bias against ornament and decoration and its relationship to gender and sexuality" (2019, p. 8). Considered in its totality, one of the icons of postwar modernism, the Seagram Building was more complex than its presentation in architectural history books would suggest.

Johnson designed the Sheldon Art Gallery, Lincoln, Nebraska, in 1963. It is an example of a group of modernist structures that achieved monumentality with their resemblance to the classical proportions of Greek temples (Figure 25.7). Another famous example of this type of architecture was Lincoln Center in New York City, a civic arena for the performing arts modeled on Michelangelo's Campidoglio.

Johnson's addition to the Boston Public Library opened in 1973. Two important stipulations were that the roofline be maintained with that of the original structure and that a complementary material be used for the exterior. A number of American university libraries were built in the 1960s and 1970s, and many of them, like Johnson's library, belong in the brutalist canon.

1960s

The 1960s was significant politically and culturally. While this societal sea-change made its imprint on the arts, it happened more slowly, or not at all, in architecture, at least at first glance. But there is no doubt that the 1960s was a force in graphics, fashion, and furniture design. Because of the scale and cost of architecture, it is logical that when new movements appear on the horizon, they are visible more quickly in ephemeral arts, such as graphics and textiles. It takes longer for them to make the effects in interiors, architecture, and urban design. Brutalism, and modern architecture as it developed across the globe in a number of regional variations, can all be seen as reactions to the 1950s International Style.

Historically, many places experienced global movements, such as Arts and Crafts, art nouveau, and then art deco, through graphics, textiles, and small-scale designed objects. So it was in the 1960s. There is virtually no 1960s-style architecture, yet there were many arts, including album covers, super graphics, fashion, and movie and television credits.

1970s

Johnson designed Pennzoil Place with his business partner, John Burgee, in 1976. The complex in Houston, Texas, consists of two 36-story, trapezoid-shaped towers covered in bronze-tinted glass. It has the detailing of the Seagram Building, but the forms, with dramatic angles in plan and elevation, are unlike anything Mies would have designed. Gensler and Associates did the interiors. Interior and exterior alike were widely praised and presented new directions for corporate modernism.

Designers and furniture

Scandinavian design

Not all regional variations across the globe were intended as criticism of Miesian modernism, although what happened in Scandinavia, Japan, and Italy affirmed that there were alternative ways of designing outside of European modernism as it developed in the 1930s. There were a number of designers in the Scandinavian countries who

had their beginnings before the war, and the economic environment of the 1950s was favorable for their type of design. Business historian Per H. Hansen suggests that **Scandinavian design**, his subject is Danish modern, be considered not only by its forms, but also by how consumers made sense of it and used modern furnishings in their homes. As a collective endeavor, Scandinavian design has many of the qualities that came to be known as branding. The forms were no doubt beautiful and emphasized simplicity and function. This design was the opposite of the fetishization of the machine, as with the Museum of Modern Art's exhibit that included steel turbines. The ideological godfather of the group was Kaare Klint (1888–1954), who voiced the principles behind the designs. He considered furniture design as a scientific discipline and opposed imitating past forms. He promoted a focus on materiality and detailing. Yet as with any group of artists, there was variety in their approaches and how much they embraced and departed from Klint's mission.

Arne Jacobsen, Finn Juhl, Jens Risom, Hans Wegner, and Eero Aarnio

Arne Jacobsen (1902–1971) was born in Copenhagen, Denmark. He graduated from the Academy of Arts having studied architecture in 1928. Jacobsen was interested in the idea of total design, designing furniture for the majority of his architectural projects. In 1930, he started his own design office, which he headed until his death in

1971. He worked independently as an architect and as an interior, furniture, textile, and ceramics designer.

His architecture includes a considerable number of buildings in Denmark, Germany, and Great Britain. The SAS Royal Hotel, 1956–1961, situated in Copenhagen, is his architecturally most accomplished structure. It is credited with having introduced modern architecture to Denmark. He designed the furniture for the SAS Royal Hotel, and these include the Egg Chair, the Swan Chair, and the Drop Chair. His other furniture designs include the Ant Chair, 1952 (Figure 25.8). The Ant Chair was made of plywood and manufactured in large numbers. It was one of the stacking chairs of the era. Of those in the Danish modern camp, his work resonates most strongly with the international faction. His work is more futuristic, he used metal, and he was generally less beholden to natural wood.

Finn Juhl (1912–1989) was softer in his approach than Jacobsen, and his favored materials include teak, rosewood, and leather. He resisted the move toward over-scaled furniture, and a feature of his chairs and settees is that they had floating backs and seats–the pieces were not

contiguous. His approachable work is resonant with the work of Hans Wegner and Julian Wabbes. His most famous interior is the Trustee Council Chamber of the United Nations.

Jens Risom (1916–2016) studied at the School for Arts and Crafts, then worked for Hans Knoll in the United States. He responded to wartime restrictions on materials by creating his most famous pieces that relied on parachute webbing on a wooden frame. Two of the pieces, the Risom lounge chair and the Risom side chair, are still in production.

Over the course of his life, Hans Wegner (1914–2007) designed some five hundred chairs. His output epitomizes what consumers found likeable about Scandinavian design. If people had trouble picturing Mart Stam's or Marcel Breuer's stainless-steel tubed chairs in their homes, Wegner's pieces seemed at home in residential environments. Among his pieces are contemporary versions of a Chinese horseshoe-back chair, a modernized Windsor chair, and his most famous chair, with a rounded continuous back and arm rail, typically known as the Kennedy or Wegner chair (Figure 25.9).

An outlier among the Scandinavian modern designers is Eero Aarnio (b. 1932). His work was forward-looking and sometimes futuristic. He had more in common with Verner Panton, Joe Colombo, and Quasar Khanh. His colorful plastic

Figure 25.8
Arne Jacobsen, Swan Chairs, Copenhagen, Denmark, 1958.

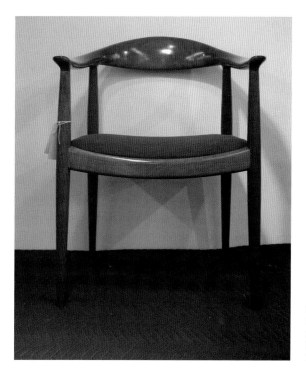

Figure 25.9
Hans Wegner, the Chair or the Kennedy Chair, Denmark, 1949.

furniture resonated with the space age and the era of atomic energy. His Globe chair, 1966, was a **fiberglass** ball on a pivoting metal base. Its follow-up, the Bubble chair, 1968, was the same although hung from the ceiling or a stand (Figure 25.10). His plastic Gyro chair rounded out his collection of contemporary seating.

Italy: Looking to history and the future

Osvaldo Borsani, Mario Bellini, Piero Fornasetti, Carlo Mollino, Joe Colombo, and Ettore Sottsass were Italian designers who dealt with their country's artistic legacy, which includes ancient Rome and the Renaissance. In the 1920s, Italy was not immediately a center of modernism. For the Italian artists who followed, a question with which they had to grapple was how to represent Italy's past, and how much to look toward the future.

Osvaldo Borsani (1911–1985) was the son of a craftsman, and an artistic streak ran in the family. His father ran a furniture company that he had started in the 1930s. Borsani trained as an architect and eventually took over the family business. With his brother, he founded the design firm Tecno in 1953. Tecno creates high-end furniture for offices. *Abitare*, the Italian architecture and interior design magazine, referred to the extraordinary mechanical inventiveness of his work.

Borsani had a distinguished career and was widely lauded as one of the masters of Italian postwar modernism, although his reputation was greater in Italy than abroad. He was proficient in both the corporate and the residential world. Tecno's furniture pieces focused on the high end of the office furniture market. He was known for tasteful interiors that often combined his own pieces with the works of others, setting them, cheek by jowl, next to antiques and other pieces produced by Tecno.

Mario Bellini (b. 1935) was an industrial and furniture designer. For Olivetti, he created calculators, typewriters, and other industrial designs. He was different than his fellow designer, Joe Colombo, for Bellini was less shocking, although he too favored bright colors. His Cab chair for Cassina, 1977, had a steel frame, leather, and zippers, and critics noticed how it pushed the boundaries of industrial design yet with restraint and attention to detailing. He is one of the Italian designers associated with the business machines company, Olivetti. His output includes designs for typewriters and televisions (Figure 25.11)

Harry Bertoia (1915–1978) was born in San Lorenzo, Pordenone, Italy. He came to the United

Figure 25.10
Eero Aarnio,
Bubble chair,
Denmark, 1968.

Figure 25.11
Mario Bellini, Brionvega broadcast television, 1968.

States at the age of fifteen to visit his brother and decided to stay. He too studied at Cranbrook. He began his career as a jewelry maker and later worked with Charles and Ray Eames, Florence Knoll, and Eero Saarinen. His initial interest in jewelry design had a lifelong impact on his work, for he was always interested in working with metal. In 1950, he opened his own studio and designed a collection for Knoll, eventually called the Bertoia Collection. The Bertoia seating collection was famous for its sculptural forms and molded latticework of welded steel. Individual pieces include the Diamond chair, Bird Chair, and Side Chair. They are still in production, available with leather and fabric pads.

Unusual for a modernist, Piero Fornasetti (1913–1988) was known for his trompe l'oeil imagery, often done in collaboration with the architect Gio Ponti. Some of his work relates to the **surrealist** movement. Fornasetti's output raises the question of how could one be a contemporary designer in the age of modernism when interested in decoration, objects, and ornament? He was the opposite of an **abstract expressionist**. He managed to be contemporary and stylish, yet he intuitively recognized that people liked smiley suns, the Mona Lisa, and ceramic cats. He created plastic laminate that looks like newspaper clippings and a wallpaper that looks like library books, in addition to legions of decorative accessories.

Even though Joe Colombo (1930–1971) lived only one year into the 1970s, it is the decade with which he is identified. Contemporary to the core, he was a painter and sculptor in the abstract expressionist movement. In 1962, he opened his own office. Colombo came to design furniture, lamps, glassware, doorknobs, pipes, and alarm clock and wristwatches. His work was futuristic. Like other designers, certain of his objects explore the possibility of crafting something from a single material. He worked with new materials, including fiberglass, **PVC**, and **polyethylene**. His works are not weighty or intellectually self-important. One of his designs solved the problem of how to hold a cocktail glass and a cigarette in one hand. In his later years, he became interested in **all-in-one systems** (Figure 25.12). This meant that a single manufactured unit, such as a kitchen or bathroom, could arrive on site, ready to go. A year after his death, one of his designs made its debut: the Total Furnishing Unit, 1972, which was a combination kitchen, bath, bed, and storage unit. Two of his famous designs are the Roll armchair,

Figure 25.12
Joe Colombo, Visiona 1, Cologne Furniture Fair, Cologne, Germany, 1969.

1962, and the Boby trolley, 1969. His furniture designs appeared in the cult film *The Towering Inferno*, 1974.

Design histories, such as this project, often focus on game-changers, projects that appear to change everything. But life on the ground is often more nuanced. Many changes are not revolutionary but incremental, discussed below. The work of Knoll designer Ettore Sottsass accordingly has one foot planted in the 1970s, and one foot planted in the postmodern era of the 1980s (Figure 25.13). His typewriter is not purely functionalist but related to **pop art**.

Japan and the Japanese Diaspora: Isamu Noguchi, George Nakashima, Isamu Kenmochi, and Sori Yanagi

A group of designers from Japan present a different direction than the pop inspiration that fueled Bellini, Colombo, and Sottsass. It is not solely because of geography but as much a different view of materiality and a designer's place in the world.

Two of the biggest names are Isamu Noguchi and George Nakashima, who took their work in slightly different directions. Noguchi (1904–1988) was a sculptor and furniture designer. He worked in Brancusi's studio, and his works show that some works belonged to global modernism yet took design into the realm of emotion and spirituality. He explored form and material more than functionality. As with many of Japanese descent in the United States, he spent time in a Japanese internment camp. His eponymous coffee table, 1947, is one of the stalwarts of the Herman Miller design group that was examined

in Chapter 23. George Nakashima (1905–1990), was American born of Japanese descent, and he honed his woodworking skills while imprisoned at an internment camp. An aficionado of trees, he used large pieces of wood, portions of which are undressed although finished. Each of his designs is a one-off, and maintains some of the shape and edges of the tree trunks. He exhibited an appreciation of Shaker furniture and Arts and Crafts (Figure 25.14). He built his own house in New Hope, Pennsylvania, 1952, singlehandedly, which is a modern house albeit influenced by Japanese tradition. Yet he can confound expectations, for he was not opposed to industrial materials such as corrugated metal.

Isamu Kenmochi (1912–1971) was a multiple time collaborator of Noguchi. He traveled and met with the important designers of the day, including Walter Gropius, Mies van der Rohe, and Charles and Ray Eames. He worked in bamboo and rattan, and his famous chair was the Bamboo Basket Chair, designed with Noguchi.

Two designers who were deeply imbedded in Japanese artistic traditions were Katsuhei Toyoguchi and Sori Yanagi. Toyoguchi's (1905–1991) most famous piece was the Spoke chair, made of oak with splayed dowels. This is the design of his that was well known in the West. He was a major figure in Japan, and he was focused on the Japanese domestic market. He was a leading figure for decades of a Japanese art movement that was modeled on the Bauhaus.

Sori Yanagi (1915–2011) was deeply embedded in Japanese design foundation. His father Sōetsu Yanagi was an art critic, a leader of the

Figure 25.13
Ettore Sottsass, Valentine portable typewriter for Olivetti, 1969.

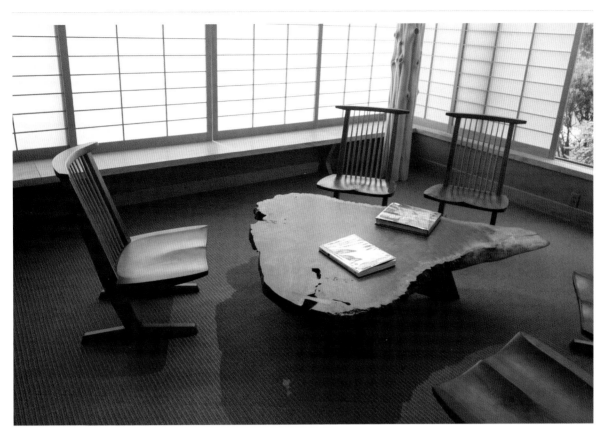

Figure 25.14
George Nakashima, Mira Nakashima, and Lynn Taylor, Reading Room, James A. Mitchner Art Museum, Doylestown, Pennsylvania, 1993. Conoid chairs designed in 1971.

Mingei folk craft movement. The younger Yanagi worked with Charlotte Perriand's Japan studio in the 1940s. His two most famous pieces are the fiberglass Elephant stool, 1954, and the Butterfly stool, 1956 (Figure 25.15). Part of his modernizing efforts is that he was focused on seating, which was not traditionally a part of the Japanese home. The pieces are sometimes used as tables.

Charles and Ray Eames

Charles and Ray Eames dedicated their careers to the need for high-quality and affordable furniture for home and office. One of their ideas was to create a shell that would be comfortable without padding and could be easily mass-produced. Made alternately of molded plywood, wire mesh, cast aluminum, and fiberglass, many of their designs are still being reproduced. The plywood Eames chair was a long time in production, and the result was successful and widely copied. The ESU 400 Series was a line of modular storage units made from metal and plywood that were destined for home, hotel, and as examined in Chapter 24, the office. Their upscale lounge chair and ottoman were conceived similarly to be appropriate for home and office.

Figure 25.15
Sori Yanagi, Butterfly stool, 1954.

There has been much thoughtful work on the careers of Charles and Ray Eames, yet one aspect of their work and careers is still understudied: their decades-long interest in India (Mathur 2011). From 1958 onward, the Eameses had commissions in India, traveled there for months at a time, and bought souvenirs that they took back to their iconic case study house in Los Angeles; India was never far from their minds. The Eameses are the Americans par excellence, but looking at their two decades of involvement with the Indian subcontinent casts modernism in a new light. The Eameses work in India suggests that our understanding of modernism should be recast as part of a global design culture.

They also believed that design as a discipline could address many issues, including those related to health care. With their experience in working with plywood, they created a splint (Figure 25.16). Previously splints had been made in metal and were uncomfortable. One hundred and fifty thousand of the Eameses' splints were made.

There is more of a whiff of truth to the frequent statement that Robin and Lucienne Day were the English Eameses. They were partners in life and professionally. Lucienne created a number of textiles, and later in her career turned to wall hangings. Robin created one of the most successful pieces of furniture of all time, the Polyprop chair, in 1963, which sold in the millions. He also designed the 4-4000 Armchair, made of ABS **injection-molded plastic**, in 1970 (Figure 25.17).

Revolution: The 1960s

The 1960s was nothing less than a revolution, and although it made its mark upon politics, the military, and economics, its most powerful weapons were cultural. Anne Bony writes: "The decade from 1960 to 1970 was a turbulent one: nothing was certain, everything was called into question. Through the mass media, television in particular, new ideas and new aspirations reached a wide audience. Consumer society was in the ascendant" (2004, p. 9).

At the dawn of the third millennium, the 1960s is temporally distant enough to achieve mythic status, and despite the anxiety it once engendered, it is now mostly viewed through

Figure 25.16
Charles and Ray Eames, splint, 1943.

Figure 25.17
Robin Day, injection-molded plastic armchair for Hille, 1970. With wool upholstery.

Janis Joplin's rose-tinted glasses. To see the 1960s as a stint of halcyon days requires considerable mental editing, overlooking the Vietnam War and the inequities that led to the civil rights movement. Looking across the artistic spectrum of the 1960s, what is consistent was a sense of a new spirit, a sense of naïveté, and a broad-based anti-establishment position.

The most vivid expression of change was rock music, and the defining moment in the history of popular music was the Woodstock Festival of 1969. Jean-Luc Goddard ushered in the decade with a film whose plotline evoked irreverence and informality, and whose choppy and fragmented editing heralded a new era in filmmaking. *Breathless* was released in 1960 and featured two attractive leading actors in its story of criminals on the run. Other films of the 1960s include *Barbarella* (1967) and *2001: A Space Odyssey* (1968). One popular kitsch, the other a classic, both looked to the future and came to define the 1960s. The decade had a reasonably strong economy, and what is historically significant is that advertising and consumerism moved to center stage of the cultural arena.

Designers

Of the design professions, the most ephemeral arenas, fashion and advertising, were at the center of the 1960s cultural revolution; while the architecture profession was slow to respond, interiors, furnishings, textiles, and wallpapers were not. Their creators were more keenly tuned to nuance, and admittedly not fearful of being inconsistent, they could reflect major cultural shifts. Terence Conran's success with his Habitat store marked an era in which high-quality design was aimed squarely at the middle class (Figure 25.18). Yet this frenetic vitality barely made a mark, at first, on the field of architecture. While many aspects of life were being turned upside down in the 1960s, Skidmore, Owings & Merrill was consolidating its status as the go-to firm for the ultimate corporate symbol, a Miesian-inspired office building.

Conran (1931–2020) made his mark by focusing on Britain's middle classes. He participated in the Festival of Britain, 1951, and became a retailer and furniture maker. He opened his first store, Habitat, in 1964. He liked the universality of Arts and Crafts and Bauhaus ideals, and sought to take that approach to design to the masses whom he considered to be intrinsically hip. He is not known as much for single designs as his successful commercialization of design, accomplished through stores and books. He paved the way for his contemporaries such as Marimekko and Crate and Barrel, and later, Martha Stewart and IKEA.

Figure 25.18
Terence Conran,
Conran Store,
1964.

Conran's retail success has a parallel in the Finnish enterprise Marimekko. The couple at the head of the firm was Armi Ratia (1912–1979) and her husband, Viljo Ratia (1911–2007). They first focused on fashion and textiles, later expanding into housewares. They were known for bright colors, and bold printed patterns at a large scale. They brought numerous designers into their fold, and Maija Isola created Unikko, or Poppies, in 1964 (Figure 25.19). A related retail enterprise was Crate and Barrel, whose first store opened in 1962. All these retail/design activities were precursors to Martha Stewart and IKEA.

Marimekko was praised for having commercialized pop art, and brought it into fashion and housewares. Critic Reyner Banham summed up the era when he wrote: "The aesthetics of Pop depend on a massive initial impact and small sustaining power and are therefore at their poppiest in products whose sole object is to be consumed" (1981, p. 96).

Many designers in the 1960s explored the pop sensibility in their works, including Verner Panton and Pierre Paulin. They were interested in creating **polyfoam** furniture for the mass market. Their pieces were informal, inexpensive, and easy to rearrange. In the furniture realm, there was a great deal of experimentation with new materials, such as Plexiglas and plastic, often in bright

Figure 25.20
Verner Panton, Heart Cone Chair, 1959.

colors. Panton is known for individual pieces of furniture, but he also created a number of interior designs that sought to eliminate the need for furniture pieces with extensive built-in elements. His furniture designs moved beyond pure functionalism, and several took recognizable forms, such as the enduring Panton chair, 1959 (Figure 25.20).

Roberto Matta

Roberto Matta (1911–2002) is an unlikely candidate to create an iconic piece of furniture, for while he once collaborated with Le Corbusier, he is widely known as an accomplished surrealist painter. The 1960s, the decade in which Matta's Malitte seating unit arrived, was a time period known for confounding expectations. Matta alternately worked as an architect, painter, sculptor, and furniture designer.

His furniture design is an extension of his sculpture and stems from this period. Chairs of the Malitta unit are simply made of polyurethane foam covered with fabric. The ongoing import of surrealism is another way that some designers and artists sought to distinguish themselves from the functionalist strain of modernism.

Figure 25.19
Maija Isola, Marimekko "Unikko" pattern, 1964.

Olivier Mourgue

Olivier Mourgue (b. 1939), like Panton, was a designer invited to present avant-garde living concepts with his Visiona Exhibition of 1971. It was an undulating platform in green that supported a variety of functions, from sitting to storage. His most famous furniture design is the Djinn chair and Djinn lounge chair, 1963. It looks like a slightly comical piece crafted of one material, but its construction was complicated. It had a tubular steel structure, and used rubber webbing, and polyurethane foam. A stretch wool cover gave the illusion of a single material. The futuristic piece was already six years old when the designers for Stanley Kubrick film *2001* used it as lobby furniture in a space hotel (Figure 25.21).

Quasar Khanh

Quasar Khanh (1934–2016) was born in Vietnam but active in France and the United Kingdom. He was interested in working with new materials, crafting objects out of a single material, and designing packaging at the same time as the object it was to contain. All of these interests came together with his Quasar Khanh Inflations that included numerous inexpensive and eye-popping pieces of furniture (Figure 25.22).

Figure 25.21
Olivier Mourgue, Djinn chair and sofa, 1965. From Stanley Kubrick's movie *2001* (1968).

Figure 25.22
Quasar Khanh, inflatable sofa, 1960s.

Any one of the design pieces associated with the 1970s, from Khanh to Colombo, indicate that a new era had begun, but understanding exactly what that was remained unclear. Yet an unusual event in the history of architecture, the destruction of a building, left no doubt that a change was afoot.

Experimentation: The 1970s

History rarely gives us precise dates for the end of an era, but modernism ended on March 16, 1972, at 3:00 p.m., when the Pruitt-Igoe housing project in St. Louis was demolished (Figure 25.23). Critic Charles Jenks anointed this event as modernism's end. The destruction of Pruitt-Igoe was seen as an iconic blow to the primacy of modern architecture.

For a twenty-first-century observer, if the 1960s has become the distant past, the 1970s is still too close, and designers are uncomfortable with much that was created. Many consider the 1970s to be the nadir of taste. It had neither the gloss of pristine modernism nor the shock of the 1960s, but instead was—to its detractors—a sea of brown vinyl, shag carpet, smoked glass, and shiny brass railings. Plastic Tiffany knockoffs and a jungle of potted ferns were all too common. John Portman, a highly successful architect and developer, remains a divisive figure of ridicule among many architects. Although British interior designer David Hicks was able to pull off upholstering Louis XVI chairs in punchy geometric textiles, the works of his less astute imitators have not stood up well to the test of time.

Architecture

John Portman (1924–2017) was a successful architect and real estate developer who created hotels, many of them for the Hyatt Corporation in the 1960s, 1970s, and 1980s. These include the Embarcadero Center, San Francisco, 1961; the Peacetree Center, Atlanta, 1968; and the Hyatt Regency O'Hare, Chicago, 1969 (Figure 25.24). Portman created exciting hotel lobbies with sparkling lights and glass elevators. Long disdained by critics and the architectural press, his buildings were popular with the public and commercially successful. His use of generally proportioned elements, shiny brass, and smoked glass added to an environment the public viewed as chic and contemporary.

Figure 25.23
Minoru Yamasaki, Pruitt-Igoe housing project, St. Louis, Missouri, 1954. Demolished in 1972.

Figure 25.24
John Portman, Hyatt Regency O'Hare, Chicago, Illinois, 1969.

Portman became wealthy in the process and inspired legions of imitators. One of them was Louis Karol, who was a Lithuanian architect of Jewish descent who relocated to South Africa, where he received his architecture degree from the University of Capetown. His Sandton Sun Hotel, 1982–1983, shows the imprint of Portman's work in hospitality with its atrium, glass elevators, and use of earthtone materials and finishes (Book Cover). The difficulty that historians have in understanding the more recent works of the 1970s and 1980s underscores how unusual these projects were.

Designers

Bruce Hannah and Andrew Morrison

Bruce Hannah (b. 1941) and Andrew Morrison (b. 1939) both studied and later taught at Pratt Institute in New York. A collaborative design of theirs, the Hannah-Morrison chair, was manufactured and sold by Knoll from 1972 to 1977. With a cast aluminum base, aluminum extruded stretchers, and fabric upholstery reinforced with fiberglass vinyl, it won several design awards. Hannah and Morrison collaborated on several pieces for Knoll, and Morrison is known as the chief designers of Knoll's workstation system, Knoll Morrison. Long considered the Cadillac of office furniture systems, it was beautifully detailed. The Hannah-Morrison line was the seating line that included the Lounge Chair 2011. It was designed to fill the need for several types of lounge seating, with and without headrests, and with an upright version for offices. It filled the role of "easy chair."

David Hicks

There are certain designers who perfectly understand the pulse of an era, and much of what we consider the 1970s aesthetics came from David Hicks's (1929–1998) hand: chocolate brown and foil wallpaper; bold dark colors, darker than the 1960s; and patterns in burnt orange and gold.

Ettore Sottsass

Ettore Sottsass (1917–2007) was a leader of the progressive postmodern design collective known as the Memphis Group. He trained and worked as an architect, but he was mostly known for his designs of office furniture, lamps, ice buckets, silverware, and a revolutionary Olivetti typewriter. It was a portable red typewriter with a carrying case and a carriage the same height as the keyboard. Having studied in Turin, he opened his studio in Milan in 1947. He is a transitional figure between the 1970s and the later postmodern period because he shares aesthetic gestures with Joe Colombo, but he also was moving in the direction that came to be known as postmodern.

In contrast to the modern position of functionality, Sottsass forms looked like things; a bookcase took the form of a lightning bolt; his Tahiti lamp resembled a tropical bird with a long yellow neck and red beak.

The rise of the big firm

An economic development of the 1970s ran counter to the general antiestablishment mood: the rise of the big firm. Skidmore, Owings & Merrill (SOM) is the prime example. One of its principal designers, Gordon Bunshaft, discussed in the last chapter, collaborated with a number of interior designers over the course of his career. Firms around the United States modeled themselves on SOM, both regarding their structure and their design position toward Miesian modernism. This includes Hugh Stubbins, Boston; HDR, Omaha; Gantt Huberman, Charlotte; HOK, St. Louis; Smith, Hinchman & Grylls, Detroit; and Gensler, San Francisco. The success of the giant architecture or design firm experienced a global spread, with Kenzo Tange in Tokyo, Norman Foster in London, and Harry Seidler in Sydney.

Conclusion

The 1950s constitutes a second phase of modernism. If prewar modernism was utopian and theoretical, postwar modernism was practical and applied. Many of the pieces were the same, and the furniture designs of Mies van der Rohe, Le Corbusier, Marcel Breuer, and Alvar Aalto continued to be successful without faltering. More in touch with their time were Pierre Jeanneret in India, and Paul Rudolph in Singapore. Eero Saarinen was a transitional figure, with modern credentials, yet the aesthetics of a pink upholstered Tulip chair is consistent with the fashions of the 1960s.

A contrast, at once unlike modernism but different from many 1960s trends, is represented by a regional inflection, especially strong in the work of Scandinavian and Japanese designers. Arne Jacobsen, Finn Juhl, Jens Risom, Hans Wegner, and Eero Aarnio all did well in the postwar period. They were a generation after the Bauhaus, yet there remains a commitment to modern principles and a seriousness in their work.

Earnest and serious are certain qualities attributed to the work of designers in the Japanese diaspora, including Isamu Noguchi, George Nakashima, Isamu Kenmochi, and Sori Yanagi. Yet in the return to materiality, the appreciation of historical attitudes of craft, and an anti-urban direction, their works were appreciated by the global elite and hippies alike.

If Scandinavians and the Japanese had little time for the influence of pop art, a number of Italian designers thought differently. Their work was sometimes lighthearted, sometimes bizarre, and interested in trumpeting technological developments. They were well designed but less obsessive in their attention to detail. The works of Mario Bellini, Piero Fornasetti, Carlo Mollino, Joe Colombo, and Ettore Sottsass are both unlike the modernists who preceded them and many of their contemporaries.

There has been considerable nostalgia for the 1960s, including an ongoing appreciation of rock and roll, supergraphics, miniskirts, and paper dresses, and aspects of those cultural productions is seen in the works of other designers, such as Terence Conran, Marimekko, Verner Panton, Pierre Paulin, Olivier Mourgue, and Quasar Khanh. The 1970s has yet to see a reemergence of its popularity, with an affection for shiny bronze and dark brown foiled wallpapers, but that reassessment might still come. All the design activities presented in this chapter are clear in their differences from modernism but do not really prepare one for what was to come: the 1980s and postmodernism.

Sources

Banham, Reyner (1981). *Design by Choice*. New York: Rizzoli.

Banham, Reyner (1996). *A Critic Writes*. Berkeley: University of California Press.

Bony, Anne (2004). *Furniture and Interiors of the 1960s*. Paris: Flammarion.

Bony, Anne (2005). *Furniture and Interiors of the 1970s*. Paris: Flammarion.

Eggler, Marianne, Erica Morawski, and Sara Reed (2019). "The Case of William Pahlmann." In *Design History: Beyond the Canon*, edited by Jennifer Kaufmann-Buhler, Victoria Rose, and Christopher Wilson, pp. 189–208. London: Bloomsbury.

Ferrari, Napoleone (2022). *Carlo Mollino: Architecture and Storyteller*. Zurich: Park Books.

Irvine, Keith and Chippy Irvine (2005). *Keith Irvine: A Life in Decoration*. New York: Monacelli Press.

Kaufmann-Buhler, Jennifer, Victoria Rose, and Christopher Wilson (2019). *Design History: Beyond the Canon*. London: Bloomsbury.

Mathur, Salami (2011). "Charles and Ray Eames in India." *Art Journal* 70, no. 1: 34–53.

Schaffner, Ingrid, ed. (2012). *Anne Tyng: Inhabiting Geometry*. Philadelphia: Institute of Contemporary Art.

Sparke, Penny (1986). *Twentieth Century Design: Furniture*. London: Bell and Hyman.

Tyng, Anne and Louis Kahn (1997). *Louis Kahn to Anne Tyng: The Rome Letters, 1953–1954*. New York: Rizzoli.

Volner, Ian (2020). *Philip Johnson: A Visual Biography*. New York: Phaidon.

Discussion and Review Questions

1. Prior to reading this chapter, what were your general thoughts about the 1960s and the 1970s? After reading the chapter, how have these thoughts changed?

2. Outside of architecture and interiors, what were some major cultural of political events of the 1960s?

3. Who were some of the prewar modernists who had successful careers after the Second World War?

4. What was appealing about John Portman's hotels?

5. What are the characteristics of design of the 1970s?

6. Do an internet search of 1960s graphics, textiles, fashion, or wallpapers. What are the general characteristics of the period from the results?

7. Show examples of modernists whose work shows little imprint of the countercultural revolution.

Postmodernism

1972	1982	1984	1989
Robert Venturi, Denise Scott Brown, and Steven Izenour publish *Learning from Las Vegas*	Michael Graves, Portland Municipal Services Building	Prince of Wales at RIBA gives "Carbuncle" speech Philip Johnson, AT&T Building	Michael Graves, Teapot for Target

The various countercultural movements of the 1960s and 1970s questioned the principles of modernism writ large. Postmodernism, the preeminent movement associated with the 1980s, was a full-on assault of modern principles. One of modernism's leading figures, Mies van der Rohe, famously said "Less is More." Robert Venturi, one of the leaders of postmodernism aggressively replied, "Less is a bore." This chapter and the next cover two movements that had a philosophical/literary component, **postmodernism** and deconstruction, and that came in modernism's wake. Understanding their formal differences is easy enough but detangling the meanings behind the forms is not an easy task.

Postmodernism refers to developments in art and architecture from the 1960s onward. These activities challenged the precepts of modernism, first in architecture, then everywhere. In architecture, buildings integrated elements of classicism and other historical traditions. In other arenas—such as literary criticism, music, dance, and painting—postmodernism provided a biting critique of cultural values and reinforced a growing pluralism.

The Italian **Memphis Group** did the ground work to relate design to **pop art**, and this connection was strong in early postmodern architecture, particularly in the works of Robert Stern, Charles Moore, and Michael Graves. Architects whose works can be described as postmodern are found across the globe, including Hans Hollein in Austria, Ricardo Bofill in France, and Sumet Jumsai in Thailand.

Figure 26.0
(*Facing page*)
Moore, Ruble, Yudell, Am Tegeler Hafen Apartment Block, Berlin, Germany, 1987.

461

Theoretical Framework

Robert Venturi and Denise Scott Brown, Colin Rowe, Jane Jacobs

Across the globe, many were criticizing modern principles from the perspectives of community planning, architecture, and industrial design. At the center of the battle for words were Robert Venturi, Denise Scott Brown, and Steven Izenour. They provided an intellectual and theoretical base for the critique of modernism that came to be known as postmodernism. Robert Venturi wrote *Complexity and Contradiction in Architecture* (1966) and Venturi, Denise Scott Brown, and Steven Izenour wrote *Learning from Las Vegas* (1972). Jane Jacobs wrote *The Death and Life of Great American Cities* (1961), a biting critique of urban renewal and Corbusian planning principles. Fred Koetter and Colin Rowe's *Collage City* (1979), gave direction for urban designers who wanted to move beyond modernism. In a number of case studies, Rowe looked to historic European cities as twentieth-century role models.

Robert Venturi and Denise Scott Brown were theorists, educators, and architects, their writings are among the most significant pieces of architectural criticism of the twentieth century. *Learning from Las Vegas*, their classes and lectures took the shocking approach that the Las Vegas strip, instead of being an urban feature to be reviled, could be a valid source of design inspiration. The projects of Venturi and his wife and business partner, Denise Scott Brown, include the Vanna Venturi House, 1963, and the Guild House, 1962–1966. Both were modest in scale if widely publicized.

Before there were many postmodern buildings to look at, the design press published many evocative drawings. They were graphically appealing with their recognizable historic and pop references and bright colors. Michael Graves, Leon and Rob Krier, Aldo Rossi, and Helmut Jahn were particularly skilled at creating images that oozed enthusiasm. After years of modern drawings, often in black and white, the shock of color and the free use of historic forms got the world's attention. Initially it was not apparent how the new approach would affect the design world, and if postmodern architects would get major commissions. Three prominent competitions of the late 1970s and early 1980s made clear that postmodern architecture had arrived on the scene in a big way.

Three Competitions: Portland, New York, and Chicago

Three buildings built around the same time signaled the ascendancy of postmodernism in the corporate and administrative world. One was Graves's Portland Office Building, Portland, Oregon, 1980–1983, a commission he received by winning a competition. Others followed that cemented postmodernism as a major cultural and economic force.

Michael Graves

A group called the **New York Five** included Peter Eisenman, Richard Meier, Charles Gwathmey, John Hejduk, and Michael Graves. The five men took different directions but were all indebted to modernism. Of the five, Michael Graves was to become one of the most prominent postmodern designers.

Graves had initially been a modernist. He started doing postmodern drawings, often with colored pencils and markers on yellow trace, which added to the polychrome affect. Helmut Jahn's office similarly created highly colorful drawings using colored markers and pencils on mylar. In 1979, Graves entered a competition to design the Portland Office Building, a government office building in Oregon's largest city (Figure 26.1). His drawings constituted an architectural shock wave. The building they presented could not have been more different than a project with a similar program, Mies's Federal Center in Chicago, 1974. Philip Johnson was a sympathetic member of the jury who supported Graves's entry. Graves had not built much at the time, and his solution relied on colored stucco on the outside and painted drywall on the inside. It impressed the jury because it had maximum impact with a modest budget. It was a classically proportioned building, with a base, body, and top. It was lavishly endowed with symbolism and had an enlarged keystone, rustication, statuary, and swags. A subsequent big

Figure 26.1
Michael Graves, Portland Office Building, Portland, Oregon, 1982.

budget commission for Graves was the for the healthcare-related Humana Building, Louisville, Kentucky, 1985.

Graves conceptualized a variety of showrooms for the Sunar Fabric Company in Chicago, Dallas, and Houston that were widely published (Figure 26.2). The plans looked like they were drawn in the Italian Renaissance. His later projects include large office buildings for Disney, Team Disney, in Burbank, California, 1990, and the Dolphin and Swan Hotels, in Orlando Florida, 1990. He also created several successful furniture designs, including the Oculus Chair.

In the previous chapter, Philip Johnson emerged as one of modernism's luminaries, as a curator and critic, and as a designer and architect of several highly influential buildings. He followed his early work with a string of modern buildings that nodded to classicism, and then some buildings that helped create the aesthetics of the 1970s. At an age when many consider retirement, in the 1980s he was in his seventies, he embraced postmodernism with gusto and became one of its leading figures and enjoyed the greatest commercial success of his life.

Figure 26.2
Michael Graves, Sunar Fabric Showroom, Houston, Texas, 1979.

1 Entrance
2 Reception
3 Passage
4 Furniture
5 Loggia (mural)
6 Office systems display
7 Conference / textiles
8 Kitchen / projectioin
9 Office
10 Storage

0   5   10   20   40

Michael Graves, Philip Johnson, and Thomas Beebe

A second major shock wave soon followed and came from Philip Johnson himself. He was awarded the commission to design the new Manhattan headquarters for AT&T (Figure 26.3). He received the commission in 1979, the year when he graced the cover of *TIME* magazine holding a model of the building. The Portland Office Building proved that postmodernism was making its way in the civic arena; AT&T confirmed that corporate America was ready to ride the postmodern wave. A more somber building than Portland, AT&T was replete with its own set of historic references, including a modified broken pediment at the top (Figure 26.4). *Archdaily* wrote: "it may be the single most important architectural detail of the last fifty years" (Langdon 2019). It is the detail that caused the building to be called the Chippendale Skyscraper, because of its resemblance to a Georgian highboy dresser. The building also had a beautiful, classically designed street level arcade that evoked the austerity of Romanesque churches.

Figure 26.4
Classical broken pediment.

Chicago, in 1987, held a competition for a new public library. Architect Thomas Beebe (b. 1941) was relatively unknown outside of Chicago, but that all changed when he won the competition. None of the five entries were modern, and most all flirted with postmodern stylings. Beebe's was the most consistent in its embrace of historical forms and decorative motifs (Figure 26.5). He triumphed in a competition that featured major North America names, including Murphy/Jahn (successor to Mies's firm), Dirk Lohan (Mies's grandson), Arthur Erickson (the SOM of Canada), and a SOM/Ricardo Legorreta collaboration. Beebe's firm also did the interiors, and as this was the largest library in the world, at 972,000 square feet (90,300 square meters), it included a large amount of custom furniture. For the interiors, postmodern in plan, elevation, and detailing, Beebe's firm combined custom pieces with modified pieces that were available on the market.

The Prince of Wales on the offensive

A group of architects and interior designers were successful in the 1980s, and they were not postmodern but premodern. They created well-designed projects that met the needs of clients who wanted traditionally designed spaces. The Prince of Wales admired the work of Rob and Leon Krier, and also Quinlan Terry, especially his historicist Richmond Riverside Development, 1985–1987.

A known architecture aficionado, the Prince spoke on the occasion of the 150th anniversary of the Royal Institute of British Architects (RIBA) on May 30, 1984. Charles, Prince of Wales, started out his speech typically enough: as a champion of the British Commonwealth, the Prince was a natural to nominate Indian architect Charles Correa to receive the Royal Gold Medal. He also made an impassioned call for more accessibility in cities and buildings. He warmed up by calling for an architecture and urbanism that would

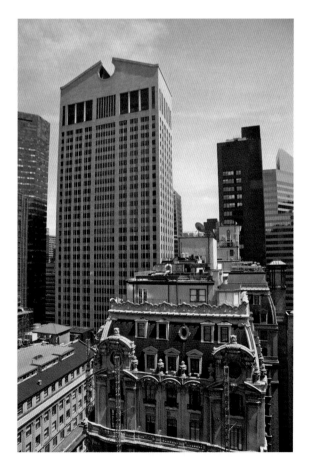

Figure 26.3
Philip Johnson, AT&T Building, New York, New York, 1984.

Figure 26.5
Thomas
Beebe, Harold
Washington
Library Center,
Chicago,
Illinois, 1987.
Wintergarden.

"respect old buildings, street plans and traditional scales and at the same time not to feel guilty about a preference for façades, ornaments and soft materials." Fair enough, this was a position that many who belonged in the postmodern camp would take.

He then shifted the subject to Trafalgar Square, and a recent competition winning entry to design a major addition to the neoclassical National Gallery. The firm of Ahrends, Burton and Koralek won the competition, and their entry was consistent with what they were known for: a contemporary building in the brutalist/high-tech direction. The Prince did not mince words and described their winning entry as "a monstrous carbuncle on the face of a much loved and elegant friend." Audiences were shocked for, as a practice, the royal family did not involve themselves so obviously in policy making. The Prince's speech was a clear-cut repudiation of architectural modernism, and he voiced his support of postmodern alternatives, a call that in no short order was heard around the world.

In no small part because of the Prince's speech, and because many members of the public agreed with him, in 1985, the prominent commission went instead to Robert Venturi and Denise Scott Brown. Their Sainsbury addition to the National Gallery was a high point of their career and demonstrated that they were not only theorists but capable of handling high-profile large commissions (Figure 26.6).

Venturi received the Pritzker Prize in Architecture in 1991 and has held multiple teaching positions. In addition to Venturi and Scott Brown's publications and buildings, they designed a number of pieces of furniture, the most famous of which predated the Sainsbury Wing, and appeared in 1983. Their Queen Anne chair is made of patterned plastic laminate and is a humorous take on a classic chair.

Stanley Tigerman, Margaret McCurry, and Eva Maddox

A major provocateur Stanley Tigerman was a Chicago architect who was a vocal proponent of postmodernism. Margaret McCurry, began her career in the late 1960s working for Davis Allen, and later married Tigerman and became his business partner. A photo collage that he used as a Christmas card in 1978 is another iconic image that signaled the demise of modernism (Figure 26.7). The collage, titled "Titanic," shows Mies's

Figure 26.6
Robert Venturi
and Denise Scott
Brown, Sainsbury
Wing, National
Gallery, London,
United Kingdom,
1991. Gallery
interior.

Figure 26.7
Stanley Tigerman,
"Titanic,"
Chicago, Illinois,
1978.

Crown Hall, the signature building of his modernist campus, the Illinois Institute of Technology, sinking like the doomed ocean liner. Tigerman was a highly entertaining figure who did not hesitate to provoke people. Giving a lecture in which people yelled at him or stormed out energized him. When he presented his drawings for the Daisy House, a beach house in Porter, Indiana, he did not explain its anthropomorphic shape, which in plan has a male and female side. The front elevation clearly resembles a penis, with an ovoid entry. Many members of the architectural establishment were not amused and in Tigerman's work saw the greatest excesses of a postmodern approach.

In 1982, Margaret McCurry merged her firm with her husband's to form Tigerman McCurry Architects. She eventually moved away from the more extreme forms of postmodernism and her later work included many houses for the wealthy. For this body of work, she found a way of drawing from vernacular traditions as a means to imbue the graceful houses with a sense of tradition and calm. In 1994, Tigerman founded a nonprofit organization in Chicago called Archeworks with fellow designer Eva Maddox. It is a multidisciplinary alternative design school that allows students to team up with nonprofit partners. The group focuses on design solutions to contemporary social concerns, which demonstrated Tigerman's serious side. Maddox was a major figure with her own firm that pioneered the idea of branded environments for interiors, which was acquired by Perkins and Will.

Aldo Rossi

Aldo Rossi (1931–1997) was the leading Italian postmodernist. Rossi's book *L'architettura della città* had a similar effect in Europe as Venturi's books did in the United States. His major projects include the Modena Cemetery, 1971; the Elementary School, Fagnano, Italy, 1976; the Teatro del Mondo, Venice Biennale, 1979; and an apartment block on the Rauchstrasse, Berlin, 1985. He started early, in the 1970s, and while it was obvious that he was proposing a different route than the modernists, he predated the arrival of full-blown postmodernism. His drawings were highly colorful and widely published (Figure 26.8). Major commissions followed that were highly influential if small projects.

Figure 26.8
Aldo Rossi, San Cataldo Cemetery, Modena, Italy, 1971.

New Urbanism

Charles Moore, Arquitectonica, and two building exhibitions in Berlin

One of the reasons for modernism's decline, and its spectacular replacement as the leading movement of the day, is that increasingly critics and the public at large viewed it as a failure particularly at the level of urban design. Urban renewal projects decimated many neighborhoods and replaced them with Corbusian towers in the park, which did not always fare so well over time, although some did. The American Interstate Highway system started in 1956 and was in full throttle in the 1960s and 1970s, which added to the assault on the historic centers of American cities. There were some major preservation losses, including Pennsylvania Station in New York, 1963, the Imperial Hotel in Tokyo, 1967, and the Chicago Stock Exchange, 1972.

At the level of furniture, interiors, and designed objects, modernism was not problematic, but the general consensus was that as an urban paradigm it had failed spectacularly. Designers of the 1960s, 1970s, and 1980s held the Bauhaus in esteem, which is not to say that they

wanted to follow its lead. The Memphis Group had provided a pathway for postmodern architects to follow, and many of them turned to furniture and industrial design in addition to architecture.

This new paradigm of postmodern urban design had a splashy debut with Charles Moore's Piazza d'Italia, New Orleans, 1975–1979. It was one of the first built postmodern urban projects and quoted freely from historical sources including Michelangelo's Capitoline Hill in Rome (Figure 26.9). Moore also did a number of postmodern houses, and furniture and industrial designs.

Contemporaries of Moore, Bernardo Fort Brescia, Laurinda Hope Spear, Andrés Duany, Elizabeth Plater-Zyberk, and Hervin Romney founded the firm Arquitectonica in 1977. Based in Miami, it embraced a colorful, Latin-infused type of postmodernism that garnered it a lot of attention. The firm had a commitment to the new type of architecture, and also did urban planning and interiors. The Palm Court Atlantis Condominium, in Miami Florida, is an example of their work that was photogenic, and has received multiple awards (Figure 26.10). Two of the partners, Duany and Plater-Zyberk, soon founded their own firm in 1980. Their work followed more closely historically oriented urban planning. They put their theories into practice with a planned community that took

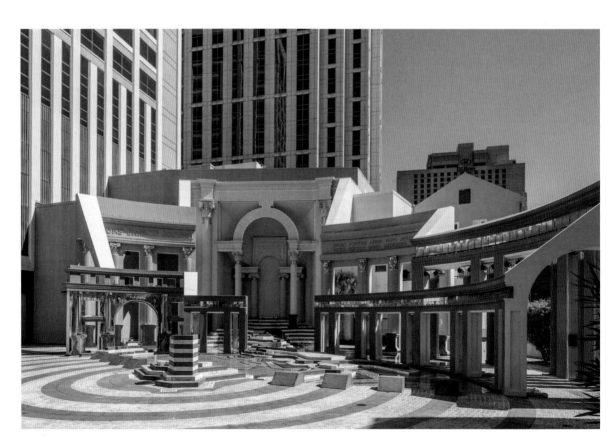

Figure 26.9
Charles Moore, Piazza d'Italia, New Orleans, Louisiana, 1975–1979.

Figure 26.10
Arquitectonica,
Palm Court
Atlantis
Condominium,
Miami, Florida,
1982.

a nostalgic look at traditional American small towns in the South—Seaside, Florida, 1985. The brothers Leon and Robert Krier furthered a similar outlook, operating out of Luxembourg, and both contributed houses to Seaside.

In addition to Duany and Plater-Zyberk, Rob (b. 1938) and Leon Krier (b. 1946) were major figures in the movement known as the **New Urbanism**. They were proponents of classicism for contemporary projects and also drew from a number of vernacular traditions in their work. They were highly influential as architects, urban designers, theorists, and educators.

Interbau 1957 and the International Building Exhibition of 1987

The Sainsbury Wing is a significant building in its own right, and it is a work with an urban design component. It anchors a corner of London's famous Trafalgar Square and does so with considerable dexterity. Berlin exited the Second World War in worse shape than London, and major portions of it had to be rebuilt. There was also a great need for housing. There were two massive building initiatives in the Prussian city, one associated with modernism in the 1950s, and the other associated with postmodernism in the 1980s.

The modern wave of building came in 1957. Some fifty architects from across the globe were awarded commissions, including Walter Gropius, Alvar Aalto, Arne Jacobsen, Oscar Niemeyer, and Hugh Stubbins. The projects are consistent with the principles of modernism, with all their strengths and weaknesses. Several of the architects contributed to a green residential district, the Hansaviertel. In terms of its ongoing success, it is no Pruitt-Igoe, and has been a desirable place to live since its inception.

Yet by the 1980s, the prevailing attitude was that Berlin had been one of Europe's great cities, and that major portions of its urban fabric had been bombed into oblivion. This loss was not made up for with modernism, and a postmodern building exhibition was planned, the International Building Exhibition, 1987, or IBA (Internationale Bauausstellung). Organizers created a strict set of urban planning principles that constituted a European version of the New Urbanism. These parameters included respecting the typology of historic Berlin courtyard apartment houses, following street lines, roof lines, etc. Some projects were overtly historicist, some were clearly contemporary. Many influential architects who had not necessarily built a great deal, such as

Aldo Rossi, Stanley Tigerman, the Krier Brothers, and Charles Moore, built large projects in Berlin (Figure 26.0). The list of architects also included Alvaro Siza, John Hejduk, Peter Eisenman, Arata Isozaki, and James Stirling.

British architect James Stirling (1926–1992) had been a highly admired modernist, whose projects, including the University of Leicester Engineering Building, 1959, showed that he was departing from the strict rules of the International Style, although in ways that drew praise. His subsequent work moved increasingly in a post-modern direction. A building he designed as part of the 1987 IBA exhibition, the Social Science Center (in German, the Wissenschaftzentrum), Berlin, 1988, was highly publicized, largely because of its plan. The Social Science Center is an example of a building that had its drawing circulated around the world before construction began. Before the internet, Stirling's plan went viral. The plan of the center was a shocker. It appears to include a Greek theater, a church, a stoa, and a **baptistery**, yet as an academic building, it actually contains faculty offices, labs, and classrooms. This was a particular postmodern strategy, to use historically recognizable forms, yet to carve out of them their meaning and use them for other purposes. Sometimes this was ironic, for in Stirling's building what looks like a Florentine baptistery, which would have had at its center a fountain, in the IBA building housed toilets. Its lively exterior had bright bands of color, and Stirling, like Venturi and Scott Brown, was interested in exploiting the possibilities of pattern (Figure 26.11). Many postmodern architects showed an interest in reviving the motif of rustication, representing a course of rough masonry associated with buildings of the Italian Renaissance (Figure 26.12).

Early postmodern buildings, such as Portland Office Building, the AT&T Building, and a number of Venturi and Scott Brown's early works, were ironic looks at history. Their designers used pastiche, exaggeration, and quotation in their work. While parts of the Sainsbury Wing are witty visual commentaries on classicism, parts of it are also firmly and without irony in the classical camp. A result of the success of postmodern projects is subsequent buildings were built that really are not postmodern era but historically

Figure 26.11
James Stirling, Social Science Center, Berlin, Germany, 1988.

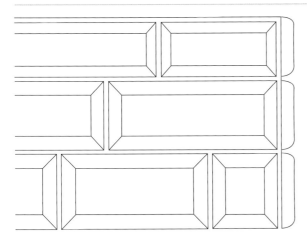

Figure 26.12
Renaissance rustication.

accurate buildings. In 1974, Robert E. Langdon Jr. and Ernest W. Wilson Jr. opened the Getty Villa, which was an accurate re-creation of the ancient Roman Villa dei Papiri at Herculaneum. It is not postmodern, it is ancient.

Alan Greenberg (b. 1938) is a staunch classicist; one of his larger commissions was the News Building in Atlanta, Georgia, 1988–1992. He believes that classicism can respond to the needs of the contemporary world. Mark Hampton was an interior decorator who specializes in historicist residential work. He started out working for David Hicks, and was known for rooms featuring dark mirrored wallpapers, yet he soon moved chronologically in a different direction than his one-time boss. Hampton worked for President and Mrs. Reagan and created a suite of rooms for the US State Department. For the patrician philanthropist Carter Burden's New York apartment, he created a neoclassical room befitting a man active in the arts.

Robert Stern was Dean of the Yale School of Architecture from 1988 to 2017. As an architect he too was a major force in postmodernism, although he was never the polemical equivalent of Venturi, Scott Brown, and Tigerman. His ongoing practice has postmodern, deconstructivism, and strong historicist buildings to his credit. He has designed many apartment buildings in New York, including 15 Central Park West and 520 Park Avenue. *Architectural Record* described his Museum of the American Revolution: "Its massing takes its cues from the neighboring historic buildings' cornice lines, while Pennsylvania red brick, white trim, and keystone-accented arches dutifully reference the neighborhood's aesthetic" (Lind 2017) (Figure 26.13).

Figure 26.13
Robert A.M. Stern, Museum of the American Revolution, Philadelphia, Pennsylvania, 2016.

Stern designed the George Bush Presidential Center. Architectural postmodernism has multiple meanings in its many contexts, but there are multiple projects that express a connection to political conservatism in the United States.

The spectacular success of Johnson and Burgee in crafting multiple postmodern corporate headquarters relied on a pairing that often proves successful: one designer was branded as the visionary (Johnson) and the other one as the practical technocrat (Burgee); clients thus allegedly got the best of both worlds. If there was any doubt that the AT&T building might prove an anomaly, that was quickly put to rest with a number of large corporate clients who clamored for historically themed buildings.

The world's largest architecture firm at the time, SOM, was initially slow to respond, but its partners decided that if they were to compete, they needed to turn in a postmodern direction, which they did with considerable success in numerous projects, such as the art deco NBC Tower, Chicago, 1989.

A new firm, Kohn Pedersen Fox (KPF), arose in New York in 1977, and just as SOM was built on an ideological foundation of modernism, the KPF founders took postmodern historicism to heart. One of the founding partners was Patricia Conway, and the off-shoot company, Kohn Pedersen Fox Conway, did corporate interiors. Florence Knoll, Herman Miller, and William Pulgram answered the question as to how modern interiors were to be done. Once postmodernism was on the scene, it was not clear the direction that postmodern corporate design would take, and Conway was one who provided an answer. Her projects were still open plan, reliant on a combination of closed offices and workstations, freestanding furniture, panel systems, but used more color, had some traditional detailing, and mixed contemporary furnishings with antiques and reproductions. Other interior design firms followed a similar design path, and the commonplace desire of some corporate clients for antiques interspersed with panel system furniture was no longer a problem.

A prominent example of KFP's success in the corporate arena came with the new headquarters for Proctor & Gamble in Cincinnati, 1987. As the firm was known, the massive project makes deft urban moves and was equally compelling for its architecture and interiors. A massive mixed-use development was 900 North Michigan, Chicago, which included a vertical shopping mall anchored by Bloomingdale's, residences, and a hotel (Figure 26.14).

Figure 26.14
Kohn Pedersen Fox, 900 North Michigan Avenue, Chicago, Illinois, 1989.

Arata Isozaki is an interesting figure because he initially was one of the metabolists, the brutalist Japanese urban movement, although he eschewed the label. Throughout his career, he has been active in urban design, architecture, interiors, and furniture. He was one of those invited to build in Berlin as part of the IBA exhibition. He also created Team Disney, Orlando, Florida, 1991, another major entry in the postmodern office interior. Isozaki's activity raised the question of how a style so heavily based on European historical precedents would fare in his hands. He had a strategy, not unlike Stirling's, of reducing historical forms, such as rotundas and barrel vaults, to their purest elements. He managed the nearly impossible with Team Disney, which was to incorporate elements including a giant sundial and mouse ears into a building that was warmly greeted by the press. The interiors were done in conjunction with the local firm of Hunton Brady Pryor Maso.

Isozaki also designed dinnerware, rugs, and jewelry. His Monroe chair, 1973, was designed for the executive areas of a Japanese bank (Figure 26.15). Its playful reference to the American actress is consistent with the interest of those in pop art to make popular cultural references. It also bears similarity to chairs by Frank Lloyd Wright and Charles Rennie Mackintosh.

Reserved furniture designs such as Isozaki's sold well and fit into the market as **transitional** pieces, evoking the history of furniture design while fitting into contemporary settings. Works such as Michael Graves's Oculus Chair were classified as transitional, with historic roots but at home in contemporary settings. Some designs of the period were intended more as ideological statements, such as Ettore Sottsass's Casablanca Bookcase, 1981. It is made of wood and laminate. Because of its imposing size and profile, it serves as a room divider. The angled shelves are intended to hold wine bottles. It makes reference to neoclassical highboys, with its base, body, and cornice, although in a decidedly fresh way. With its multiple references, it is the opposite of functionalism (Figure 26.16).

Postmodernism was global from the start, with strong spheres in France, Germany, Italy, Japan, and the United Kingdom. A lively theater of postmodern design was in Vienna, with Hans Hollein at the helm. He did a number of interiors projects, one a lively travel agency with palm tree columns. His Retti Candleshop of 1964 was an early postmodern project (Figure 26.17). It sold candles and light fixtures, and was later

Figure 26.15
Arata Isozaki, Monroe chair, 1973.

Figure 26.16
Ettore Sottsass, Casablanca Bookcase, 1981.

converted, with few changes, into a jewelry store. A difficulty with postmodern retail projects, such as the Sunar Showrooms and the Retti Candleshop, is that most of them over time were remodeled and few exist in their original state.

Spanish-born French architect Ricardo Bofill did a number of classically styled housing projects in France. As France was the home of the originator of modern public housing, Le Corbusier, Bofill's immense projects, as urban designs based on alternately the Colosseum and the Circus Maximus, and with classical detailing made mostly out of concrete, made clear he presented a different direction. He had four projects in the United States, and his R.R. Donnelley Building, 77 Wacker Drive, in Chicago, was relatively restrained in its detailing compared to his French housing projects (Figure 26.18). It used Greek pediments as its upper most floor and had classical detailing on the ground floor made of marble and granite. Even architects opposed to postmodernism admired the crispness of its detailing and the way it married a curtain wall to classicism. The local partner firm, De Stefano Goettsch, was founded by SOM alumni.

Postmodern buildings were soon seen across the United States and the world. Regional commercially oriented architecture firms in the United States, such as Robinson Green Beretta Architects (RGB), in Providence, Rhode Island, proved their mettle in creating technologically current high-rise office buildings with postmodern stylings. One Citizens Plaza, 1991, sits on the confluence of two rivers, and its thirteen-story height is divided up into base, body, and top; has pronounced corners; and is an accomplished work of architecture with deference to its natural and urban context (Figure 26.19).

Just as every singer of the day was driven to produce a disco album, including no less than The Rolling Stones (1978), Ethel Merman (1979), and David Bowie (1983), so too did many an architect not initially associated with postmodernism produce buildings that at a minimum showed postmodernism's imprint. The highly respected I.M. Pei, with his return to the country of his birth, China, produced the highly anticipated Fragrant Hill

Hotel, outside of Beijing, 1982. Pei was the highly respected architect of a modern addition to the National Gallery in Washington, DC. For his Beijing project, he used traditional motifs and references. The building puzzled critics who were expecting a building more like his other more modern buildings. It left people asking: Is this a postmodern building? Was I.M. Pei a closet postmodernist?

Just as One Citizens Plaza demonstrates corporate postmodernism's regional spread in the United States, another building demonstrates its global reach. The Public Bank Tower, in Kuala Lumpur, Malaysia, 1994, was designed by the Malaysian architecture firm PSP Akitek (Figure 26.20). It was done a few years before its neighbor, the Petronas Tower. This shows that the aesthetics of postmodernism spread quickly and were found across the globe, in buildings grand and vernacular. Grappling with the meanings of this cohort of buildings is a trickier endeavor, including the engagement of Chinese architects with the phenomenon.

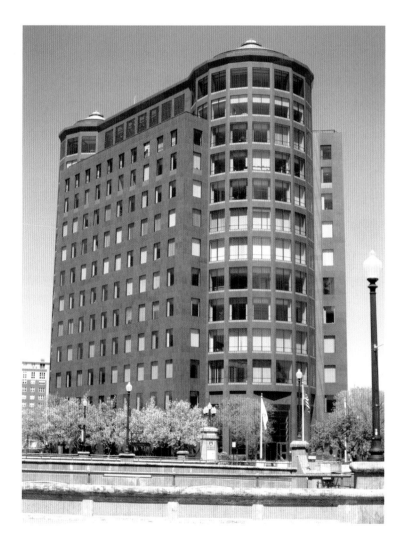

Figure 26.19
Robinson Green Beretta Architects, One Citizens Plaza, Providence, RI, 1991.

Figure 26.20
PSP Akitek, Public
Bank Tower, Kuala
Lumpur, Malaysia,
1994.

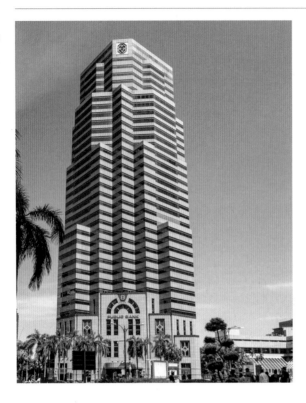

Figure 26.21
Laurie
Beckerman, Ionic
Bench, 2010.

Keystones, broken pediments, arches, and rustication were all forms that postmodern designers employed as favored motifs. Venturi and Scott Brown created a postmodern capitol that they called the Ironic capital. Furniture designer Laurie Beckerman continued the trend with her Ionic Bench, 2010 (Figure 26.21). The form is pure postmodernism, but her construction methods are of the twenty-first century. Made of birch laminated plywood, it is created using CNC technology.

Conclusion

With the benefit of hindsight, we can now see that postmodernism followed a trajectory, from an avant-garde upstart, to a mainstream status quo, to a period of decline in which it was more likely to appear in buildings that belong to a series of not well-crafted revival styles. It did not, as one might expect, lead to a greater appreciation for historic preservation. In fact, in the 2020s, the question arose about the preservation of aging postmodern buildings, such as the Portland Building and the State of Illinois Building.

In its heyday, postmodernism provided a series of prominent competitions and commissions, proved that postmodernism was a serious intellectual force, and was commercially viable.

Deconstruction was like postmodernism in multiple respects. It is also called deconstructivism, shortened to "de-con," and was formally related to Russian Constructivism. As a literary movement, its overt influence started in the 1980s, coincident with architectural postmodernism. By the 1990s, postmodernism as an obvious design form was in decline, and deconstruction entered the mainstream. Once deconstruction entered the mainstream, it was no longer the domain of outsiders. The large corporate architecture and interior design firms, SOM, Kohn Pedersen Fox, Arquitectonica, and everyone else, started producing designs whose ideological origins lay in what had been an obscure French literary theory.

By the 1990s, the creative energies of postmodernism were clearly in decline. While some projects in the postmodern vein continued to be built, it was never the only game in town. There were those who were always obedient to modernism, namely, Richard Meier, Norman Foster, and Richard Rogers. And a new style was on the horizon, similarly, linked to a literary philosophy: deconstruction.

With little fanfare, firms that had been known for postmodern buildings, KPF, SOM, Helmut Jahn, and even Robert Stern, subtlety and decisively moved into a modern/deconstructivism direction. Postmodernism was almost always a point of derision, and architects and designers whose work most considered to be postmodern refused the mantle.

Sources

Adamson, Glenn and Jane Pavitt (2011). *Postmodernism: Style and Subversion, 1970–1990*. London: Victoria and Albert Museum.

Banham, Reyner (1981). *Design by Choice*. New York: Rizzoli.

Boissière, Olivier (1991). *Philippe Starck*. Cologne: Taschen.

Crinson, Mark (2009). *James Stirling: Early Unpublished Writings*. London: Routledge.

Johnson, Eugene (1993). *Charles Moore: Buildings and Projects 1949–1986*. New York: Rizzoli.

Langdon, David (2019). "Architecture Classics: AT&T." *ArchDaily*, January 12. Available online: https://www.archdaily.com/611169/ad-classics-at-and-t-building-philip-johnson-and-john-burgee (accessed May 1, 2023).

Lind, Diane (2017). "Museum of the American Revolution." *Architectural Record*, July 1. Available online: https://www.architecturalrecord.com/articles/12811-museum-of-the-american-revolution-by-robert-am-stern-architects (accessed May 1, 2023).

McHale, Brian (2015). *The Cambridge Introduction to Postmodernism*. Cambridge: Cambridge University Press.

Spangaro, Chiara and Aldo Rossi (2022). *Aldo Rossi Design 1960–1997*. Milan: Silvana.

Sparke, Penny (1986). *Twentieth Century Design: Furniture*. London: Bell and Hyman.

Stern, Robert A.M. (2021). *Between Memory and Invention*. New York: Monacelli Press.

Thadini, Dhiru (2013). *Visions of Seaside*. New York: Rizzoli.

Tigerman, Stanley (2011). *Designing Bridges to BURN*. San Francisco: ORO.

Venturi, Robert ([1966] 1977). *Complexity and Contradiction in Architecture*. New York: Museum of Modern Art.

Venturi, Robert, Steven Izenour, and Denise Scott Brown (1977). *Learning From Las Vegas*. Boston: MIT Press.

Volner, Ian (2017). *Michael Graves: Design for Life*. New York: Princeton Architectural Press.

Discussion and Review Questions

1. The term *postmodernism* appears frequently in the media. What are some examples, from any field, in which you have heard it used? Is there an underlying consistency in its use?

2. How do people in literature departments and other fields use the word?

3. Who were some committed modernists who continued to work during postmodernism's heyday?

4. What is similar across the boards of some of the famous postmodernists, Aldo Rossi, Michael Graves, Philip Johnson, etc.?

5. What is different in the works of some of the postmodernists, such as Arata Isozaki and James Stirling?

6. Were postmodern principals the same at different scales, from industrial design to furniture, interiors, architecture, and urbanism?

7. What is an example of good postmodern design? What is an example of bad postmodern design?

8. How do interior designers who did historically accurate interiors fit into the era?

Deconstruction

27

| 1983 | 1984 | 1988 | 1990 | 1997 |

| Zaha Hadid, Hong Kong Peak competition | Alvaro Siza, Bonjour Tristesse Housing Project, Berlin | MoMA Deconstructivist Architecture exhibit | Issey Miyake, Rhythm Pleats Collection | Frank Gehry, Guggenheim Bilbao |

Deconstruction was a widespread phenomenon that is notoriously difficult to define. Fields outside of design explored several themes, such as multiple identities, multicultural-ism, and the breakdown between high and low or elite and popular culture. Central to all these efforts was an architec-tural metaphor: of a building being built, then being taken apart. A central tenet of most academic fields to derive from the period, after experiencing the work of French philosopher Jacques Derrida, is that meaning of any type is not fixed but contextually created. There is no central agreement as to what deconstruction is or means, but what most proponents in the design disciplines could agree on is that they saw it as a movement that countered the stylistic trappings of post-modernism. Deconstruction was a popular and contentious means of interpreting texts, such as great works of litera-ture, and later, anything and everything. Because a text was "constructed," the author's intentions were not important, nor the literal meaning of words. Critics revealed the deeper under-lying meaning by exposing biases, using a string of metaphors including ripping open seams and applying pressure. According to deconstruction's promotors, no meaning was fixed, and the critic's task was to expose context. Everything was constructed; nothing was essential. At no other point in world history has a philosophy about fundamental truth been so closely related to how one material is visibly designed to

Figure 27.0
(*Facing page*)
Shigeru Ban,
Centre Pompidou-
Metz, Metz,
France, 2010.

join another. Fashion designers literally showed seams, and some pieces looked like they were inside out. Cultural critics referred to tearing open the seam, for example, of a Shakespeare play.

Deconstruction was like postmodernism in multiple respects, and in some quarters it is considered a current of postmodernism. It is also called deconstructivism, shortened to "de-con," and was formally related to the art movement Russian Constructivism. As a literary movement, its overt influence started in the 1980s, coincident with architectural postmodernism. By the 1990s, postmodernism as an observable design form was in decline, and deconstruction entered the mainstream. A string of prominent commissions proved that "de-con" was no longer the domain of outsiders. The large corporate architecture and interior design firms, SOM, Kohn Pedersen Fox, and everyone else, started producing designs whose ideological origins lay in what had been an obscure French literary theory.

Modernism Continues

Just as there were stalwart modernists who stayed true to their calling, and resisted the excesses of the 1960s, 1970s, and above all postmodernism, so a number of accomplished architects and designers in the 1990s and onwards carried forward the mantle of modernism and resisted the most extreme forms of deconstruction. These include Minsuk Cho, Twitee Vajrabhaya Teparkum, Norman Foster, Callum Frase, David Chipperfield, and countless others (Figure 27.1). Yet they were active in the period of deconstruction. And for many of them, their success constitutes an ongoing phase of modernism.

Figure 27.1
David Chipperfield, Amorepacific Headquarters Seoul, South Korea, 2010–2017.

Big firms adapt

Large firms had adopted postmodernism as much of economic necessity as of conviction, but in the 1990s, most had moved toward an aesthetic realm that relates to deconstruction. In the United States, this included the giant firms, such as SOM, Gensler, and KPF; and Woods Bagot in Australia and the United Kingdom. Arquitectonica's Brickell City Centre is an urban shopping mall that demonstrates how their twenty-first-century work has left behind the Latin-inspired postmodernism they initiated.

Several firms were formed initially around the reputation of individual designers, often referred to critically as "Starchitects," and became major corporate entities, including, Zaha Hadid, Norman Foster, and Richard Rogers in the United Kingdom. The French architect Jean Nouvel has projects across the globe, and unlike many architects who are known for a signature look, all his buildings look different, including his theater in Minneapolis (Figure 27.2). Philip Johnson's partnership with John Burgee was dissolved in 1991, and his day of huge corporate clients was over. Johnson was friends with both Frank Gehry and Peter Eisenman. One of Johnson's final projects was

Figure 27.2
Jean Nouvel,
Guthrie Theater,
Minneapolis,
Minnesota,
2001–2006.

a collaboration with the sculptor Frank Stella for a pavilion of the grounds of his house in New Canaan, Connecticut. Built in 1995, it was known as Da Monsta, and showed that in his final years, Johnson moved out of postmodernism and was exploring the aesthetics of deconstruction.

One feature of deconstructivist architecture is that many of its adherents pursued architectural goals that previously had been thought impossible. They tried to make architecture that moved or changed, that was impermanent, that was made of watery materials, that had qualities of light, and that related to media. And above all, architectural geometries became more complicated than had ever been seen before.

Deconstructivist architecture exhibit

The Museum of Modern Art (MoMA) put on an exhibit in 1988 that presented the work of a number of architects, titled "Deconstructivist Architecture." It was curated by no less than Philip Johnson. The galleries featured work by Coop Himmelblau, Peter Eisenman, Frank Gehry, Zaha Hadid, Rem Koolhaas, Daniel Libeskind, and Bernard Tschumi.

On the face of it, the work of these architects was in contrast to the historically oriented designs of postmodern architects. Yet the Deconstructivists were indebted to some previous periods, such as the surrealists, including Marcel Duchamp. They admired some historical artists who were active in the 1910s and 1920s, such as the Russian Constructivists, Vladimir Tatlin, Alexander Rodchenko, and El Lissitzky. They were unanimous in their admiration of the work of Bauhaus artist Wassily Kandinsky. Contemporary artists mentioned in the same breath with deconstruction include Julian Schnabel, Maya Lin, Gordon Matta-Clark, Jean Dubuffet, and Jeff Koons.

When discussing stylistic labels, it is worth pointing out that even though the architects who formed the core of the 1988 exhibition were the most prominent names associated with deconstruction, it does not mean that the artists and designers self-identified that way.

These artists and architects were often quite familiar with the philosophical writings of the day. Peter Eisenman was notable in throwing himself into the theories of deconstruction. The grandfather of theoretical deconstruction was Jacques Derrida, who wrote *Of Grammatology* in 1967. Others who followed him include Michel Foucault (*Discipline and Punish*, 1975); Edward Said (*Orientalism*, 1978); Judith Butler (*Gender Trouble*, 1990); Gilles Deleuze and Feliz Guattari (*What Is Philosophy*, 1991); and Homi Bhabha (*The Location of Culture*, 1994).

Many of the architects also did interiors, furniture, and other industrial design work, but there were a number of industrial designers whose output fits the general characteristics of deconstruction: Ora Ïto, Ron Arad, Karim Rashid, Fernando and Humberto Campana, Ronan and Erwan Bouroullec, Patricia Urquiola, and Hella Jongerius.

SITE

Some of the earliest buildings that are obviously indebted to deconstruction came from the hand of James Wines (b. 1932) and his firm SITE. In the 1970s he unleashed several provocative projects, including the Tilt Showroom and a series of Best Product stores. This roster of provocative projects included some of the most literal examples of what it meant to deconstruct a building. Wines undertook a series of big-box retail outlets that began in 1972, the BEST Product stores. The buildings alternately look as though they are falling apart, have survived an earthquake, have buckled in intense heat, or are reverting to piles of bricks. Their façades peel away, and the corners are disengaging. These eye-catching buildings garnered a lot of publicity. The buildings seemed to be a joke based on the name of the company, BEST when the buildings appeared to be the worst, making an ironic statement about architecture's alleged permanence.

Frank Gehry, Peter Eisenman, Zaha Hadid, and Bernard Tschumi

Because of his inclusion in the MoMA exhibit, and his decades-long friendship with the artist Julian Schnabel, Frank Gehry reigned as the leader of the deconstructivist pack and put forth with a number of provocative projects, foremost his own house in Santa Monica, 1991. It was a modest clapboard house that he stripped down to the studs, and in his expansion of it he used some of the most inexpensive materials, including chain-link fencing, low-grade plywood, and unplastered drywall.

Santa Monica Place, 1980, was a low-budget project in which he used chain-link fencing in a creative way; the Schnabel House for the artist

Julian Schnabel, 1990, enjoyed a higher budget. Other projects included the Fishdance Restaurant, Kobe, Japan, 1986; the American Center in Paris, 1993; and Millennium Park, Chicago, 1999–2005. Frank Gehry's Guggenheim-Bilbao in Spain, 1997, was a watershed moment for deconstruction.

It proved that architects on the extreme edge of conceptual design were capable of large-scale prominent projects. It proved an enormous financial success for its Basque home. Projects such as the Guggenheim and later the Walt Disney Concert Hall confirmed that Gehry had left his avant-garde status behind and had entered the cultural and corporate mainstream (Figure 27.3). He has made several furniture designs for Knoll using cardboard and **Masonite** (Figure 27.4). While initially these pieces were affordably priced, over time they became more and more expensive.

Peter Eisenman is sometimes included in discussions of postmodernism because of his occasional use of historic forms. A prominent project of his, the Wexner Center, Columbus, Ohio, 1989, demonstrates the extent of his involvement with both movements, but especially deconstruction (Figure 27.5). He explored grids as organizing systems, and multiple overlapping grids informed several of his projects. He considered the grid as a human construct overlain on the landscape. He collaborated with Jacques Derrida, who elliptically said of Eisenman's work "I think something should either be missing or … something which should not only prevent you from totalizing but also motivate an infinite desire to start again" (Patrão 2021). As much as anyone, Eisenman interacted with the work of philosophical deconstruction and sought to explain his projects in that light.

Zaha Hadid was born in Baghdad and later studied at the American University of Beirut, where she received a degree in mathematics, and at the Architectural Association School of Architecture in London. Upon graduation she worked for Rem Koolhaas at his Office for Metropolitan Architecture (OMA), where she became a partner in 1977.

She was the first female to win the Pritzker Architecture Prize, and the Guggenheim New York honored her in 2006 with a retrospective of her work. Her well-known projects include the Rosenthal Center for Contemporary Art, Cincinnati, Ohio, 1998, and the Vitra Fire Station, Weil am Rhein, Germany, 1994. Throughout her career, she also developed several furniture lines. After decades of fame, if not large commissions, her status changed with her museum in Cincinnati. An example of the prominent work

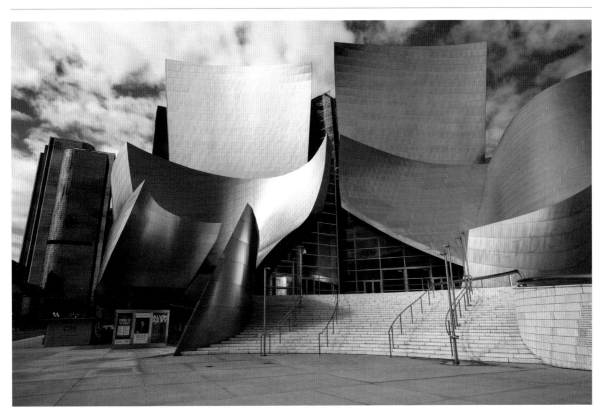

Figure 27.3
Frank Gehry, Walt
Disney Concert
Hall, Los Angeles,
California,
1991–2003.

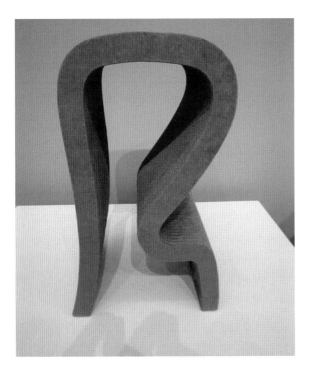

Figure 27.4
Frank Gehry, Easy Edges High Stool, 1971. Cardboard and
Masonite.

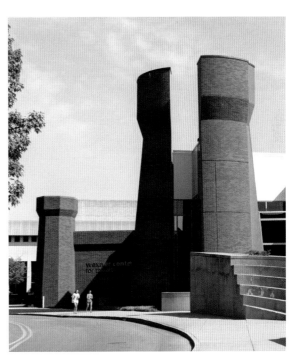

Figure 27.5
Peter Eisenman, the Wexner Center for the Arts, Columbus, OH,
1989.

that followed is the massive Dongdaemun Design
Plaza in Seoul (Figure 27.6).

From the beginning Zaha Hadid was an
avant-garde figure in multiple respects, for one,

in her early adaptation of **computer-aided
design (CAD)**. AutoCad version 1 was released
in 1982, and CAD became increasingly important for how design offices operated. Hadid's

Figure 27.6
Zaha Hadid,
Dongdaemun
Design Plaza,
Seoul, South
Korea, 2014.

work explored how computers fundamentally changed not only how offices produced working drawings but also how architects designed, what architectural drawings represented, and the type of architecture they made possible. Her earliest projects presaged what she became known for in the 2000s: designs that could only be created on computer and whose fabrication was assisted by computers. Her firm was a worldwide leader in the sophisticated software programs that relied on **algorithms** to design and build complicated geometries whose various parts were of different dimensions (Figure 27.7).

There was a competition to build Paris' largest park, and Bernard Tschumi (b. 1944) beat Koolhaas, Hadid, and Nouvel. It was no eighteenth-century landscape; even though designed in the 1980s, it looks to the twenty-first century. It was heavily influenced by the literary theory of deconstruction. *ArchDaily* wrote that Tschumi "envisioned Parc de la Villette as a place of culture where natural and artificial are forced together into a state of constant reconfiguration and discovery" (Souza 2011). Tschumi envisioned it as an overlapping series of points, lines, and surfaces. Most visibly, it has a series of red follies, that look like remnants of an industrial past, but that initially had no function (Figure 27.8).

Figure 27.7
Parametric design.

Designers in the 1990s

The state of design in the 1990s shows that there was still considerable life to be had in modernism, although with a more pronounced futuristic technological twist. Major figures of this period who are active in both the design and architectural arenas include Rem Koolhaas, Philippe Starck, and Andrée Putman. In many ways, their designs show a return to the aesthetics that predated the 1980s, when form was related to function and abstraction, and in which purely historical forms played a less important role.

Ron Arad

Ron Arad is an architect, artist, and industrial designer, and his work demonstrates that deconstruction was impacting design at all scales. Born in Tel Aviv, Israel, in 1951, he studied at the Jerusalem Academy of Art from 1971 to 1973, after which he moved to London. He established Ron Arad Associates with Caroline Thormon in both London and Italy. In addition to his practice, he worked as a professor of industrial and furniture design in London. He has worked for the furniture companies Flos and Vitra. His work is considered as an outgrowth of the high-tech

movement, and he is discussed in the same breath with Peter Cook, Bernard Tschumi, and Zaha Hadid. He created a number of avant-garde furniture pieces that combine contemporary and industrial materials.

Israel's most prominent industrial designer of the twenty-first century was a natural choice to design the country's first museum dedicated to design. The National Design Museum in Holon, Israel, is made of five giant bands of Corten steel that undulate and meander, inside and out, and that reflect the site's rolling topography (Figure 27.9).

Three pairs of brothers

Karim Rashid was born in Cairo, Egypt, in 1960, but has spent significant periods of time in Canada, the United States, the Netherlands, and Italy. He studied under Ettore Sottsass. His work belongs in the categories of high-tech or industrial, and bears some similarity to the work of Ward Bennett, although Rashid, like Arad, explored the less refined side of industrial design, a reason that the *New York Post* calls him the "tattooed bad-boy industrial designer." Hani Rashid is an architect of note who founded the firm Asymptote Architecture in New York City.

A pair of brothers (the Irmãos Campana) that hail from Brazil, Humberto Campana (b. 1953) and Fernando Campana (b. 1961) took the desire to

Figure 27.8
Bernard Tschumi, Parc de la Villette, Paris, France, 1984–1987.

Figure 27.10
Campana Brothers, Vermelha Chair, 1998. Iron, aluminum, and cord.

work with inexpensive materials to an extreme. They have worked with PVC tubing, rope, cardboard, and rubber bands. Their Favela Chair, 1991, is made from wood scrapers. Their Banquete Chair, 2002, is made from what appears to be abandoned stuffed animals. In a series of one-off pieces, they added armatures onto the ubiquitous **Monobloc** plastic chair. Their Vermelha Chair, 1998, is made of what appears to be scraps of thread (Figure 27.10). Their work is considered radical, although like Gehry's furniture, quite expensive.

Modernists from the Bauhaus forward had investigated modest materials, but designers associated with deconstruction took this interest to new levels. They worked with the most common, if not debased, materials, such as chain-link fencing, cardboard, particle board, and corrugated metal.

The French Bouroullec brothers are Ronan (b. 1971) and Erwan (b. 1976). Their work steers clear of the shock value of the Campana Brothers, although their designs are often surprising, if not quirky. They explore micro-architecture, designs that are larger than furniture, smaller than architecture, and they explore the spatial possibilities of furniture and other space-defining elements, such as dividers. They developed a modular furniture system, Joyn. Clouds made its debut in Chicago, 2012, as part of a retrospective of their

work at the Museum of Contemporary Art and is a modular textile system made of fabric tiles. Their Vegetal chair, 2008, is sustainable in its material, dyed polyamide, and in its imagery for it looks like it grew instead of being manufactured (Figure 27.11).

Patricia Urquiola (b. 1961) is Spanish born and active in Italy where she studied. Her mentors include Vico Magistrelli and Piero Lissoni. She founded Studio Urquiola in 2001. Her famous Husk chair looks like the offspring of a wing chair and a sleeping bag. She is not as symbolically overt as the previous generation of Italian designers, the Memphis Group, with their allegiance to pop art, or postmodernism.

Hella Jongerius (b. 1963) is a Dutch furniture and textile designer. She opened Jongeriuslab, Rotterdam, and her projects include updating the United Nations North Delegates' Lounge, 2013. She explores materiality and has worked with felt, porcelain, glass, polyurethane, latex, and foam. Her work can be seen as an adjunct to fellow countryman Rem Koolhaas, although she works at a smaller scale.

Two boutique hotels: Philippe Starck and Andrée Putman

With the designers that this book will close out with, the point is not to describe how they adhere to principles of deconstruction, but to show some

Figure 27.11
Bouroullec Brothers, Vegetal chair, 2008. The stackable chair is made of dyed polyamide.

of the overall directions that design is taking. The first two became establishment figures of French design, Philippe Starck and Andrée Putman. They reigned for years as France's preeminent designers. Starck was born in France in 1949, he started his first design firm in 1968 after dropping out of school. His career soared after he designed the interiors of two nightclubs that won the attention of the French president François Mitterand, who asked Starck to refurbish his private apartments in the Elysée Palace. Two years later, in 1984, Starck designed the interior of the Café Costas, Paris, and was on his way to becoming a design celebrity. His edgy redesign of the Paramount Hotel in New York set a new direction for hotel design. He collaborated with the hotelier Ian Schrager. Prior to Starck, most upper-end hotels were traditionally furnished, with a few classically modern exceptions. He initiated the phenomenon of modern "boutique" hotel design, that drew upon the strengths of both traditional and modern design. His work is more modern and less traditional than postmodernists, yet many of his designs can

only be explained with a knowledge of formal meaning, and a sense of humor. His Bubble Club furniture can be used outdoors, but the pieces of the line clearly resemble upholstered furniture (Figure 27.12). He has also designed lamps, motorbikes, boats, and a line of housewares.

Andrée Putman (1925–2013) was a French designer known for her hotel interiors and minimalist, avant-garde furnishings. She was born and schooled in Paris. She studied piano at the Paris Conservatory before she turned to interior design. She is often mentioned in the same breath with Starck, and the pairing has its logic but also its limitations. Her work avoids the more shocking directions of Starck's work. She was a more committed modernist than Starck, and less likely to make overt historic references. While her work is visually arresting, she avoided being funny or irreverent. Her escalators for the famed Parisian department store Le Bon Marché, 1989, are an example of how she can work contemporary elements into a historic structure. She did the updating of the Air France Concorde interiors, and she oversaw the restoration of two buildings by Le Corbusier in Switzerland.

Her contribution to the boutique hotel category is the Morgans Hotel in New York, 1984. A one-point perspective of its typical bathroom became iconic: she used inexpensive black and white tiles in an arresting checkerboard pattern. Into that gridded room she inserted an industrial steel sink. Two of her former employees represent the next generation of design in France: Rodolphe Parente and Elliott Barnes.

Two other architects were born in the 1940s, yet in the opening years of the twenty-first century they had built relatively little, although that changed. Rem Koolhaas (b. 1944) won the competition to build the Seattle Central Library in 1987. The partner in charge of design was Joshua Prince-Ramus (b. 1969). The award-winning building is a large faceted greenhouse that houses five platforms that are separated by four in-between planes (Figure 27.13). Light-years away from the Harold Washington Library in Chicago, it opened in 2004 to widespread acclaim for its reinvention of the large public library.

Another competition for a cultural institution took place in the Midwest. The Nelson-Atkins Museum of Art was looking to build an addition to its 1933 classical building. Steven Holl (b. 1947) designed a project for the eastern edge of the museum's property. It is a series of five buildings, and the ensemble is a work of architecture, landscape, and art. The new buildings are sheathed

Figure 27.12
Philippe Starck,
Bubble Club
furniture, 2003.
Polypropylene.

Figure 27.13
Rem Koolhaas and
Joshua Prince-
Ramus, Seattle
Central Library,
Seattle, WA, 2004.

in translucent glass that when lit at night glow. A meandering interior path connects them (Figure 27.14). The *New York Times* called the building "breathtaking" (Ouroussoff 2007).

David Adjaye is one of the leading contemporary architects in the United Kingdom. Born in Dar Es Salaam, Tanzania, in 1966, to Ghanaian parents, he studied architecture at the Royal College of Art; he currently practices in London. Adjaye has won important commissions in the United Kingdom, the United States, and across Europe. His projects are known for his ingenious use of materials and ability to sculpt light.

Adjaye's Sugar Hill Housing project in Harlem, 2014, is a mixed-use project that contains affordable housing, a cultural institution, and facilities for early education. The liveliness of its façade derives from his deft use of textured concrete. In the interiors, he mixes a neutral palette with neon green millwork, which gives the effect of colored light (Figure 27.15). With his multicultural background, Adjaye is not afraid of expressing cultural identity and multiculturalism, but he does so in an abstract way, through detailing and materiality. This came to play an important role in his most significant

structure to date, the Smithsonian National Museum of African American History in 2017.

Tadao Ando was born in Osaka, Japan, in 1941, and has since become an admired and influential architect. His work is clearly in the aftermath of postmodernism but has no formal or theoretical connection to deconstruction. In 1995, he was awarded the Pritzker Prize. Inspired early on by the works of Le Corbusier, Ando's projects consist primarily of reinforced concrete and attempts to define space in ways that allow for changing patterns of light. In his hands, a common material, concrete, becomes an expressive and beautiful material, as with his Church of the Light, in Ibaraki, Japan, 1999. One focus of designers who do not align themselves with modernism, postmodernism, or deconstruction is the spiritual, reflective qualities of design. Ignoring this vital aspect of life, many feel, was a shortcoming of the modernist approach. Spiritual is not meant in a religious sense but rather how it feels to be in a space, and how one interacts with the world through technology, light, and materials. This is something Ando does exceptionally well.

Figure 27.14
Steven Holl, Nelson-Atkins Museum of Art, Bloch Building, Kansas City, Missouri, 2007.

Figure 27.15
David Adjaye,
Sugar Hill mixed-
use development,
Harlem, New York,
NY, 2008.

Figure 27.15
David Adjaye, Sugar Hill mixed-use development, Harlem, New York, NY, 2008.

All of Ando's signature moves are at play in his Art Centre at Château La Coste, France, 2011. He weaves materials, textures, and light into a series of simple geometric spaces, whose result is a feeling of serenity (Figure 27.16).

Shigeru Ban

Shigeru Ban works with paper, paper tubes, and cargo containers. Operating out of Paris, New York, and Tokyo, he has worked on a variety of small-scale but high-profile projects. He studied at Cooper Union and previously worked for Arata Isozaki. His designs are related to Gehry's early furniture designs in that he works with the least exalted materials available, paper and cardboard, yet works with them elegantly. He is also indebted to computers for design, creating complicated geometries, and his projects blur the lines between design and fabrication and installation. Initially he created a number of low-budget projects, a benefit of working with paper and cardboard, but his projects became increasingly bigger, more prominent, and with correspondingly larger budgets, such as the Centre Pompidou-Metz in France (Figure 27.0). He also tackles important issues, such as temporary housing for refugees and people coping in the aftermath of natural disasters.

Figure 27.16
Tadao Ando, Art Centre, Château La Coste, France, 2011.

Ban's countryman, the fashion designer Issey Miyake, is one of those who sought to make clothing that clearly reflected the imprint of deconstruction. His dress from 2014, in the collection of the Victoria and Albert Museum, was designed using software and is composed of a single sheet of material through a complicated series of folds (Figure 27.17). Other designers, including Giorgio Armani with his "unconstructed" jacket, similarly were interested in making visible the process of creating an article of clothing.

This book takes as its topic design in all its forms across millennia, so visuals are all important. What is equally important are the serious issues that designers, from fashion to furniture, have begun to grapple with. From sustainability to wellness, designers of all stripes are tackling issues as diverse as luminescent materials and same-handed hospital rooms (Figure 27.18).

Diller Scofidio + Renfro

The firm Diller Scofidio + Renfro designs architecture and urban design, but it was a group of unusual projects that garnered them considerable attention. Their innovative projects include the Blur Building, a structure on Switzerland's Lake Neuchâtel that is enshrouded in mist. They redeveloped the support areas of Lincoln Center in New York. One of their larger architectural projects

Figure 27.18
Healthcare diagram: same-handed patient rooms.

to date was the Institute of Contemporary Arts, Boston, 2006. What is significant about their work is that their projects are advanced technologically, yet the trio are interested in technology not as an end in itself but as a means to an end (Figure 27.19).

The computer room of the museum hangs precariously underneath the part of the museum that cantilevers over Boston Harbor. Structurally impressive, the poetics of the room are the equal of its physics. The entire front wall is glazed and looks down to the water. With the proportions of a computer screen, it looks like the projected desktop of an idle computer whose screen saver is on. It is also like the missing fourth wall of a theater. Computer users who raise their eyes from their keyboards face water, the primordial sea where life began.

Their work at Lincoln Center is significant because while they are architects, they are also designers who can be called to breathe life into buildings that have problems or limitations. They did for Lincoln Center what British architect Haworth Tompkins did for Denys Lasdun's National Theatre in London, 2015.

Conclusion

It is difficult and impossible to predict where things are headed. One can, however, point out some of the current concerns that strike a serious cord and that rise above the level of fad. An aspect

Figure 27.17
Issey Miyake, Flying Saucer Dress, 1994. Polyester.

Figure 27.19
Diller Scofidio +
Renfro, Institute of
Contemporary Art
(ICA), Boston, MA,
2006.

of twentieth- and twenty-first-century design that differs from that of previous centuries is that the means of its creation and dissemination has changed—that is, broadcasting, computers, and the internet. Most people get their information about interior design and furnishings from television, other popular media, commercial sources, and above all, the internet. Technologies will continue to affect design's creation, fabrication, and reception.

Julia Child and Bob Vila politely pioneered domestic-improvement television on PBS. The respective hosts of *The French Chef* (1962) and *This Old House* (1979) offered informative alternatives to mainstream escapist programming. In 1991, Martha Stewart became the reigning queen of domestic television with *Martha Stewart Living*, offering a range of advice. Stewart, in innumerable ways, has taken the unofficial mantle of popular American interior designer once held by Elsie de Wolfe. Although in different forms, viewers tuned in to these three shows because they could apply the hosts' ideas to their own lives, or at least be inspired by them. Following in Stewart's footsteps, cable television proved itself as the perfect outlet for lifestyle programming, with several channels focusing some or all of their programming on the home, including Home and Garden Television, and the Discovery Channel.

The variety of these shows speaks to practically every aspect of lifestyle.

The home-improvement sphere was shaken up with a show that initially seemed shocking, Bravo's *Queer Eye for the Straight Guy* (2003). Historically speaking, what was novel about *Queer Eye* is that it made explicit what had long been an interior design secret: that a gay designer is somehow in command of the multiple sensitivities and skills necessary to produce a successfully designed and furnished space. Around the same time, TLC's *Trading Spaces* (2000) and *Extreme Makeover: Home Edition* became popular. Some attribute the success of home shows to both post-9/11 cocooning and the rise in popularity of reality shows. *Queer Eye*'s 2017 reboot appeared in a different context in which its premise was no longer shocking.

Critics contend that many shows portray home improvement unrealistically, making it seem as though the process of designing and executing such projects requires only a few days and a modest budget. In addition, on-screen designers often have little formal design training. The entertainment factor is imperative to these shows' success, and they include humor, human interest, aspirational ideals, and elements of surprise.

The 1990s and the opening decades of the twenty-first century were not only concerned with the aesthetics of deconstruction. Two major arenas for many designers, including some of those mentioned here, were sustainability and designing for wellness. The focus on the health-care sector represented a desire of the interior design profession to move beyond the aesthetics of domestic decorating, and to solve societal problems with methods that included evidence-based design.

This chapter has focused on the broad subject of deconstruction with a focus on its aesthetics, but the period from the 1960s to the present day also saw designers exploring a number of interest outside of stylistic consistencies. Many designers explored sustainability, such as Philip Cobonpue.

Looking at the history of design history, and pondering its future, this book presents several subject areas that I hope will continue to be the subjects of individual study. For one, to continue to research and herald the design contributions of women. Secondly, the global reassessment of twentieth-century modernism that began with Luis Barragán and Hassan Fathy is continuing. Contemporary designers Lanzavecchia + Wai in Singapore, and Younes Duret in Morocco, are just two of the designers today who are following in the footsteps of Barragán. All countries produced interesting modern work, and exploring the lives and words of the designers involved—through detailed studies—is greatly needed. With the exception of Europe, North America, and China, books on the furniture of all regions need to be written. While it is clear that television and film are integral to reflecting and shaping design tastes, researching and writing serious books about these subjects proves difficult. Often the work is not fully credited, and the documentation not preserved. In touching on these, and other issues, this book has endeavored to show how design participated in major movements and, just as importantly, design and designed objects suggested alternate paths. My position is that there are multiple characteristics of the field of design (including interior design, designed objects, and furniture) where it differs from art and architecture. One is a lack of ideological purity that ultimately results in more conceptually nuanced compositions. And another, that designers' activities force them to engage with the details of daily life, real and imagined.

In touch with immediate needs and wants, designs of a human scale avoid the single-mindedness of some works of art and architecture. That is their strength, and the subject of this book.

Sources

Adjaye, David (2005). *David Adjaye: Houses, Recycling, Reconfiguring, Rebuilding*. New York: Thames and Hudson.

Ando, Tadao (2003). *Tadao Ando: Light and Water*. New York: Monacelli Press.

Banham, Reyner (1996). *A Critic Writes*. Berkeley: University of California Press.

Boissière, Olivier (1991). *Philippe Starck*. Cologne: Taschen.

Diller, Elizabeth and Ricardo Scofidio (2002). *Blur: The Making of Nothing*. New York: Abrams.

Jodidio, Philip (1997). *New Forms: Architecture in the 1990s*. Cologne: Taschen.

Johnson, Philip (1988). *Deconstructivist Architect*. New York: Museum of Modern Art.

Olshavsky, Peter (2020). "Allure of Water: An Interview with Steven Holl." *Journal of Architecture Education* 74, no. 1: 149–53.

Ouroussoff, Nicolai (2007). "A Translucent and Radiant Partner." *The New York Times*, June 6.

Patrão, André (2021). "Derrida and Eisenman. "*Drawing Matter*, March 22.

Souza, Eduardo (2011). "AD Classics: Parc de la Villette." *ArchDaily*, January 9. Available online: https://www.archdaily.com/92321/ad-classics-parc-de-la-villette-bernard-tschumi (accessed May 1, 2023).

Sparke, Penny (1986). *Twentieth Century Design: Furniture*. London: Bell and Hyman.

Sudjic, Deyan and Ron Arad (1989). *Restless Furniture*. New York: Rizzoli.

Discussion and Review Questions

1. The terms *modernism, postmodernism, deconstruction*, and *contemporary* are often used inconsistently. What are some examples, from any field, in which you have heard these terms used? Are there any underlying consistencies in their use?

2. How do people who sell furniture use these terms?

3. How do people in literature departments and other fields use the term *deconstruction*?

4. How was deconstruction shocking and avant-garde?

5. What were the signs that deconstruction had become mainstream?

6. What are examples of historically rooted projects in the 2000s?

7. What movement is associated with the 1990s?

Glossary

Chapter 1: Prehistory

corbel, or false arch: Masonry technique in which each layer of construction cantilevers over the preceding layer.

dolmen: A megalithic structure consisting of two or more upright stones supporting a horizontal capstone.

henge: Neolithic monument in a circular form, created with banks, ditches, and stone or timber construction.

lintel: A horizontal member that spans an opening, such as a door or window, and supports the load above it.

lithic: Using stone.

megalith: A prehistoric monument comprising large, undressed blocks of stone.

menhir: A large single upright stone.

Neolithic: "New Stone Age" period, from the fourth to sixth centuries BCE, characterized by the use of refined stone implements and extensive use of pottery.

Paleolithic: "Old Stone Age" period, before the eighth century BCE, characterized by the first development of stone implements.

post-and-lintel: The simplest form of construction, in which vertical members (columns) support horizontal members (beams or lintels).

trabeated: A construction method based on the post-and-lintel method.

Chapter 2: Ancient Civilizations

ankh: An ancient Egyptian hieroglyphic symbolizing life and prosperity.

Assyrian: One of the ancient Mesopotamian cultures in the region fed by the Tigris and Euphrates Rivers.

booty: Items seized during warfare.

couch: A long piece of furniture for sitting or reclining, without a back support.

ergonomics: The science of designing furniture pieces to respond to the human form.

hieroglyphs: An ancient Egyptian system of writing that used symbols for words or sounds.

inlay: A method of ornamentation in which precious materials are set into a contrasting ground material.

mastaba: An ancient mud-brick tomb with a flat roof and sloping sides.

mud brick: A building material consisting of wet earth compacted and dried in the sun.

necropolis: A large ancient burial ground.

polychrome: Multicolored.

pylon: A truncated pyramidal tower flanking the entrance to an ancient temple.

pyramid: A building with a square base and sloped sides.

relief: Ornamentation that projects from a flat surface.

spathe: The leafy part of a plant that encloses a flower.

stretcher: A horizontal furniture element that structurally connects the vertical supports.

volute: A spiral scroll, especially of a capital.

ziggurat: A large stepped pyramid temple, common in ancient Mesopotamia.

Chapter 3: Classical Civilizations

agora: The large open public space at the center of a Greek city.

amphora: A tall Greek vase with a narrow neck and two handles.

architrave: The lowest horizontal portion of an entablature or lintel.

atrium: The inner courtyard of a building, open to the sky.

Attic: Made in Athens.

barrel chair: A circular seat made of timber and straw, or of stone that resembles one made of timber or straw.

barrel vault: A continuous semicircular arch.

caldarium: The room with hot water in an ancient Roman bath.

capital: The upper element of a column.

caryatid: A sculptured female figure used in place of a column.

cathedra: An ancient Roman chair with a curved back and flared legs; formally similar to the Greek Klismos chair.

cella: The central enclosed chamber of an ancient Greek temple.

citadel: A hilltop fortress.

coffer: A sunken ornamental panel in a ceiling or dome; a chest used to store valuables.

Corinthian: The third and most elaborate of the Classical Greek and Roman orders of architecture, characterized by carvings of acanthus leaves on the capital.

cornice: The uppermost portion of an entablature; any projecting portion at the top of a wall or building.

cyclopean masonry: An elemental type of construction with large irregular blocks of stone.

domus: An ancient Roman house for a wealthy or middle-class family.

Doric: The earliest and simplest of the three orders of Classical Greek architecture.

dromos: A long passageway leading to an ancient underground chamber.

entasis: In classical architecture, the slight convexity or swelling of the shaft of a column.

forum: The large open public space at the center of an ancient Roman city.

frieze: The decorated middle portion of an entablature, between the architrave and the cornice.

frigidarium: The coldest part of a Roman bathhouse sequence of pools.

fulcrum: A Roman headrest for leaning on.

hydria: A wide-body Greek vase with broad flat shoulders, frequently used for black-figure vase painting.

in antis: The columns between the projecting side walls of a building.

insula: An ancient Roman apartment block, occupied by the lower and middle class.

Ionic: The second of the three orders of Classical Greek architecture, characterized by the use of volutes.

kaolinite: A watery matrix of white clay used as a base for painting.

klismos: A Classical Greek chair with curved legs, splayed at the front and back, and a concave curved back.

megaron: The archaic Greek structure consisting of a single room with a central hearth and four columns; also used for the large central hall of Minoan and Mycenaean palaces.

metope: The square spaces between triglyphs in a classical frieze, often sculpted.

mosaic: Small pieces of glass, stone, or tile composed and set in mortar; either geometric or representational, on floors, walls, or ceilings.

oculus: A circular opening in a wall or top of a dome.

order: One of the established modes of designing a column and entablature in Classical Greek and Roman architecture, the primary three being Doric, Ionic, and Corinthian.

palaestra: In ancient Greece and Rome, a public exercise facility for the training of athletes.

pediment: In Classical architecture, the low-pitched gable above a portico; also found above doors and windows.

peristyle: A colonnade surrounding a building or enclosing a court.

polis: The Greek city-state.

portico: A covered porch, supported by columns, forming the entrance to a building.

rotunda: A circular, domed room or building—for example, the Pantheon.

Satyrs: Human figures with goat legs, ears, horns, and tail.

sella curulis: An ancient Roman x-shaped folding chair used by officials and dignitaries.

stoa: A covered colonnaded porch.

stylobate: A structure's base, the platform that supports columns.

symposium: An all-male dining and drinking social event.

tabernae: An ancient Roman shop within an indoor market, often covered by a barrel vault.

tablinum: The main living area of an ancient Roman house, with one side open to the atrium.

tepidarium: The intermediate pool of a Roman bathhouse, part of a sequence.

tholos: An elongated entryway with retaining walls that increasingly rise in height.

triclinium: The dining room of an ancient Roman house.

triglyph: The rectangular blocks that separate metopes in a frieze, characterized by three vertical elements formed from two grooves.

trompe l'oeil: Literally, to trick the eye; a painting technique that imitates another material or creates the illusion of a three-dimensional scene.

tympanum: The triangular area bounded within a pediment, often carved; also, the semicircular sculpted relief above a door.

wainscot: A panel, applied or integral, of the lower portion of an interior wall.

Chapter 4: Early Christian and Byzantine

aisle: The circulation spaces at the sides or center of a church.

apse: The semicircular or polygonal projection at the end of a church.

arcade: A series of arches supported by piers or columns.

basilica: An ancient Roman colonnaded room for public use; term adapted to describe rectangular early Christian churches.

clerestory: The windows or openings in the upper portion of a wall.

cupola: A small dome crowning a roof.

entablature: The horizontal upper portion of a Classical order, supported by columns and consisting of an architrave, frieze, and cornice.

gallery: An upper story over an aisle, open to the nave.

illumination: An image used to adorn and illustrate a medieval manuscript.

Latin cross: A church plan with three equal arms and one longer one.

monoxylous: Made of one piece of a material.

nave: The central space of a church, usually flanked by side aisles.

pendentive: A triangular element that transitions from the base of a dome to a wall, pier, or column.

pier: A vertical architectural element, structural or applied.

sanctuary: The most sacred area of a church, typically surrounding the high altar.

spandrel: A horizontal architectural element that connects piers or columns.

tesserae: The small cubes of stone, glass, or tile used to create mosaics.

transept: The transverse arms of a cross-shaped church that intersect the nave.

Chapter 5: Romanesque and Islamic

ablaq: Alternating rows of light and dark stone, found in Islamic, Romanesque, and nineteenth-century architecture; can be made with bricks or plaster.

ablutions fountain: A fountain outside of a mosque for ritual cleansing.

ambulatory: The semicircular space on the perimeter of a choir.

aqueduct: An elevated channel (often arcaded) for carrying water.

bahut: A leather envelope for protecting a chest during travel.

Carolingian: The French and German Romanesque style of the eighth to tenth centuries; literally refers to the reign of Charlemagne (768–814).

chevet: The end of a church, opposite the entry, consisting of the choir and ambulatory, often with chapels.

chip carving: A technique in which a knife and hammer remove material from a single piece of wood.

choir: An area of the church reserved for clergy; part of the *chancel* behind the transept.

diwan: An Islamic reception chamber with raised platforms for seating; furnished with carpets and cushions.

hutch: A type of storage chest with upright ends that constitute the legs and the sides; not used for travel.

hypostyle hall: A space with many rows of columns supporting a flat roof.

Islamic arch: A semicircular pointed arch, often expanding further than 180 degrees; also known as a horseshoe arch; in Spain, also known as a Moorish arch.

mihrab: A niche in the qibla wall of a mosque indicating the direction toward Mecca.

minaret: A tower adjacent to a mosque, used for call to prayer.

minbar: A pulpit in a mosque from where the sermon is delivered.

Moorish: Of or related to the Muslim people of African origin in Spain.

mosque: An Islamic place of worship.

Mughal: Islamic dynastic rule of Northern India, sixteenth to nineteenth centuries, known for the splendor of its decoration, and whose finest monument is the Taj Mahal.

narthex: The entry chamber or vestibule of a church, directionally transverse to the nave.

plank construction: Assembly in which the original wooden materials remain visible.

prayer hall: The central space of a mosque, often with many columns.

qibla: The wall in a mosque that points toward Mecca and contains the mihrab.

Romanesque arch: A semicircular structural element, similar to the ancient Roman arch.

roshan: In Islamic domestic architecture, a protruding window with open screens, allowing for air to circulate but preventing visual access.

sillón frailero: A Renaissance chair with a hung leather seat, sometimes hinged.

skeuomorph: An object whose form and decoration once had purpose and that remain after functional changes.

toron: In West African Islamic architecture, the permanent wooden structure that projects from walls, used as scaffolding.

vargueño: A Spanish Renaissance drop-fronted desk.

voussoir: A wedge-shaped stone used to form an arch.

wattle and daub: Construction technique in which interwoven twigs (wattle) are plastered with mud (daub).

X-frame chair: A transportable folding chair.

Chapter 6: Gothic

abbey: A Christian monastery or convent.

buffet: A side or serving table with open shelves and closed storage.

crenellated: Referring to repeated square indentations on the top of a wall.

dais: A raised platform in a room.

finial: A formal ornament at the top of an element.

flying buttress: A structural element, separated from the wall, that counteracts the thrust of an internal vault.

Gothic arch: A semicircular pointed structural element.

High Gothic: Medieval architectural period.

linenfold: Gothic ornamental panel carved to appear as folded textile.

Merovingian: A period of French architecture that predates Romanesque.

Norman: English Romanesque style of the eleventh and twelfth centuries.

quatrefoil: A four-lobed ornament.

rayonnant: French Gothic architecture of the thirteenth century, characterized by complex tracery.

strainer arch: An additional structural element in an opening that resists forces from adjacent members with additional diagonals.

tracery: An ornamental interlacing pattern, typical in Gothic detailing and emphasizing decoration over structure.

trefoil: A three-lobed ornament.

triforium: In a Gothic church, an arcaded gallery above the nave and below the clerestory.

Chapter 7: The Americas

ball court: A pre-Columbian large horizontal masonry structure, flanked with sloped walls at either side, used to play Mesoamerican ball games.

chacmool: Pre-Columbian Mesoamerican stone statue depicting a human figure lying down with a tray or bowl on its stomach.

hacha: The squat element used in Mesoamerican ball games attached to a yoke around the waist.

iconoclasm: The purposeful destruction of art or architecture, often in the name of religion.

Mesoamerican: North American and Central American region.

metates: Stone-grinding platforms, possibly used as seats or sacrificial altars.

palma: The tall thin element used in Mesoamerican ball games, attached to a yoke around the waist.

pre-Columbian: The Americas prior to the arrival of European explorers.

spolia: A synonym for booty, items seized in warfare used to commemorate victory.

tablero: A framed stone panel, typical in pre-Columbian Mesoamerican architecture.

talud: A base, frequently sloped, that supported an upper framed panel.

zoomorphic: Designed elements related to animals or animal parts.

Chapter 8: China, India and Southeast Asia

chattri: A stone parasol or finial that crowns a stupa.

howdah: An ornate carriage used to ride an elephant; also spelled houdah.

jian: The central room of the main hall in a traditional Chinese courtyard house.

kang table: Kang historically meant heated platform; a low table placed on top of the platform, resembling a modern coffee table.

Khmer: An ethnic designation that refers to the ancient Cambodian empire that reached its peak in the ninth to twelfth centuries.

mandala: A Buddhist geometric pattern, diagrammatic of the cosmos.

pagoda: A Buddhist tower-shaped religious building.

palanquin: A boxlike platform attached to horizontal poles, carried on the shoulders of four bearers.

quincunx: A geometric arrangement of five objects, with four at the corners of a square and one in the middle.

sinicize: To make Chinese in character.

spandrel: In architecture or furniture, the horizontal element that spans between vertical risers.

splat: The central part of a chair's backrest, independent of the vertical supports.

stupa: A Buddhist dome-shaped earthen monument.

zhuo table: A rectangular surface with legs at the corners (not inset).

Chapter 9: Renaissance

asceticism: The practice of rigorous self-denial for religious purposes; associated with restraint and simplicity in design.

cabinet: An upright storage unit with shelves and doors or drawers.

cassapanca: An Italian Renaissance chest/bench with arms and a back, used both for storage and seating.

cassone: An Italian Renaissance large, highly ornamented chest, originally used to store the belongings of a bride.

chest: A rectangular volume with a lid, utilized for storage or transport.

credenza: A storage unit used for display, taller than a chest, shorter than a cabinet.

dado: The lower portion of an interior wall of a room, distinguished from the upper portion.

Dante chair: An Italian Renaissance folding seat based on the x-frame chair.

dovetail joint: A strong mortise connection formed by interlocking trapezoidal pieces of wood.

eclectic: Representative of different sources or styles.

fluting: Shallow, concave, vertical grooves found on classical columns.

gilded: Covered in a thin layer of gold leaf.

intarsia: An elaborate composition using multiple wood types, in veneer and inlay, to construct a picture.

joist: A horizontal member that spans a structure's walls.

loggia: A gallery or pillared room open on one side.

mezzanine: An interstitial story between principal stories.

one-point perspective (linear perspective): The mathematical system developed during the Italian Renaissance for representing three-dimensional space on a two-dimensional surface, with all lines converging on a single vanishing point.

palazzo: An Italian large public building or residence in an urban setting.

piano nobile: The principal public floor of an Italian Renaissance palazzo, typically the first floor above the ground floor.

pilaster: A rectangular pier or column engaged in a wall.

putti: Cupids, common decorative figures in Italian Renaissance art.

refectory table: A long, narrow dining surface with upright panel supports at either end.

rusticated: The use of rough-cut masonry, usually on a lower floor, to create a deep texture; also, manipulated stucco that resembles rough masonry.

Savonarola chair: A simple, austere x-frame chair, standardized during the Italian Renaissance.

sedia: An Italian Renaissance armchair with blocky legs and a leather-covered seat and back.

sgabello: An Italian Renaissance side chair or stool, with a small seat.

stanze: In Italian, literally "rooms"; also refers to a suite of rooms or an interiors project—for example, Raphael's *stanze*.

string course: A prominent horizontal element in a façade.

trestle table: A horizontal surface supported by two uprights at either end and a stabilizing cross-piece.

turned construction: Indicating a method of object creation with wood pieces that are carved while being rotated.

Tuscan: A Roman variation of the Doric order, typically without a fluted shaft.

villa: An Italian or Roman large countryside residence.

Chapter 10: Baroque

armoire: A large wardrobe.

Aubusson: Tapestry and textile region of southern France.

baroque: Characteristically extravagant or elaborate in style; seventeenth-century style.

baroque armchair: A seat with a straight back and legs, rests for appendages, and curved stretchers.

bouchon: The cylindrical part of a table or chair that takes the form of a bottle stopper.

Boulle work: The veneered furniture of André-Charles Boulle, his workshop, sons, and imitators, of the late baroque and regency periods, characterized by elaborate marquetry.

canapé: A French sofa, or settee, with back.

chateau: A large French country house.

console: A small table designed to be placed against a wall.

ébéniste: A highly skilled French carpenter who specialized in veneering.

ensemble: A complementary furniture set popular in the baroque period.

Greek cross: A centralized church plan with four equal arms.

japanning: European simulation of the Asian style of lacquering furniture.

marchands merciérs: Sellers not producers of furniture and decorative arts; with their sophisticated aesthetic sense, they were a precursor to decorators.

marquetry: Ornamental veneer work utilizing diverse woods to form scenes or represent objects.

obelisk: A tall rectangular stone pillar tapering to a point at the top.

ormolu: Gilded bronze ornaments and hardware added to furniture.

parquetry: Ornamental veneer work utilizing diverse woods to form geometric shapes and nonrepresentational patterns.

piazza: An Italian open public square.

Regency armchair: A seat with cross-stretchers, a curved back, and slightly curved legs.

salon: A large formal room used for receiving and entertaining guests.

Savonnerie: A French carpet manufacturer supported by Louis XIV and specializing in high-pile wool rugs.

Chapter 11: Rococo

apron: A shaped piece below a seat rail or tabletop.

bergère: A comfortable upholstered armchair with a deep seat, a separate seat cushion, and closed continuous arms.

boiserie: French woodwork of the seventeenth and eighteenth centuries, often painted white.

bureau: A piece of furniture with a writing surface, often hinged and concealed.

bureau à cylinder: A roll-top desk with a concealed writing surface and storage.

cabriole: A leg with a graceful S-curve, used in Ming, rococo, and Queen Anne furniture.

cartouche: A French decorative oval tablet with curled edges.

castrati: Male singers whose soprano voices were achieved through surgery; important cultural figures in France, Germany, and Italy.

chaise longue: A long lounging seat with an extended portion for feet and one raised end.

charpentiers: In the French hierarchy of those who worked wood, the people who did rough carpentry; they mostly worked on architectural interiors and created simple pieces of furniture.

chassis: The framework of a chair or sofa.

Chinoiserie: European art loosely inspired by China.

ciseleur: In the creation of fine French mounts or hardware, the chaser was responsible for filing and finishing, and preparing the object for the next stage of gilding.

commode: A low, upright chest of drawers or shelves.

confidante: An upholstered settée with seats at both ends and vertical divisions.

doreur: In the creation of fine French mounts or hardware, the person responsible for the outer layer of gilding.

duchesse: A chaise longue that resembles two continuous attached armchairs.

duchesse brisée: An upholstered daybed in two or three pieces.

en suite: Matching sets of furniture; also indicates the presence of plumbing within a hotel room in lieu of elsewhere.

fauteuil: An armchair, especially Louis XV and XVI.

gondole: An upholstered armchair with a concave, semicircular arched back; tub chair.

gueridon: A small ornate pedestal table that supported either a candlestick or a candelabra.

hôtel: A French town house, public or private.

levée: A ceremonial ritual in which the monarch publicly wakes up and rises out of bed, signally the official start to the political day.

Louis Quinze: Furniture and decorative arts from the reign of King Louis XV, also known as rococo.

manchette: Upholstered pads on chair arms for resting one's upper limbs.

marquise: A broad chair with an upholstered seat, back, and arms; synonym: causeuse.

menuisiers: In the French hierarchy of those who created furniture, they created refined pieces including tables and chairs.

méridienne: A small French empire sofa, with one end lower than the other.

provincial: Sixteenth-, seventeenth-, and eighteenth-century, French country furniture inspired by formal pieces.

Regency: A transitional style between baroque and rococo.

settée: A seat with back and arms for two or more people.

singerie: A strain of exoticism with monkey motifs or monkeys dressed as humans.

voyeuse: A low armchair with a padded upper back and used as an armrest for a standing figure; in English, a conversation chair.

Chapter 12: England

ball turning: Also known as sausage motif, a twisted-looking stretcher made on a lathe, popular in the Jacobean period; also, a feature of continental baroque design.

bartizan: A small castle-like turrets that protrude from a wall; initially defensive.

bespoke: A commercial transaction predating manufacturing, of individually commissioning furniture.

bow-back: A type of Windsor chair with a continuous bent top rail.

Carolean: An English baroque transitional style between Jacobean, and William and Mary.

chest on chest or chest on stand: A tall dresser with two sections and multiple drawers.

chintz: Printed and glazed cotton cloth.

comb-back: A type of Windsor chair with a straight top rail.

Cromwellian: Related to the tenure of Arthur Cromwell, in design a continuation of Jacobean forms with a subtle nod toward simplification.

cup-and-cover: The signature design motif of the Elizabethan era, a melon-shaped bulbous form on vertical supports.

Elizabethan: Period 1558–1603; one of the great epochs of world history, with design characterized by medieval forms, a profusion of decoration, and the beginnings of the English Renaissance.

fachwerk: German term referring to timber-frame construction, similar to English Tudor.

farthingale chair: A boxy seat with an upholstered pad and back, and no arms, also known as a back chair.

gate-leg table: A horizontal surface with a folding top supported by a swinging framed leg.

Georgian: The classical style of the reigns of the three English King Georges, important for both architecture and furniture, visually heavier than Queen Anne.

great hall: A central feature of English castles and country houses, a rectangular-shaped communal dining area.

half-timber: A construction technique in which horizontal and vertical timbers are exposed and infilled with plaster.

Jacobean: During the reign of James I, both the introduction of continental Renaissance forms and the continuation of Elizabethan trends; lighter in visual weight than Elizabethan.

kneehole: A recessed space in a desk for a user's legs.

Mortlake Tapestry Works: The principal manufacturer of wall hangings and other textiles in Restoration England.

Queen Anne: A distinct period of furniture, if not architecture, of the early eighteenth century. Simple, elegant, curvilinear pieces with light profiles.

Restoration: The reestablishment of the English monarchy after Cromwell, related to continental baroque and the grandeur of Louis XIV.

ribband or ribbon-back: A type of chair decoration in which the wood of the back is carved to resemble curling ribbons; popularized by Chippendale.

screen: A wall with openings, of wood or stone, that provided a passageway through the English great hall.

settle chair: A box-shaped Tudor seat similar to the Italian Renaissance sedia.

sideboard: A table of the medieval period and after, for display or serving, with open or closed storage.

stick-back: Another name for the Windsor chair.

strapwork: An ornament based on interlaced bands and popular in many media, particularly plaster-work in the Elizabethan and Jacobean periods.

tester: A bed's architectural canopy.

Tudor: Period 1500–1558, relating to the Tudor monarchs and the end of English medievalism; architecture characterized by timber-framing, leaded glass, and Gothic arches, in furniture, a continuation of medieval forms.

turned chair: A Jacobean seat based on a medie-val triangular stool yet rendered elaborate with numerous turned vertical supports.

virtuoso: An enlightened collector who seeks to further knowledge through objects such as curios.

wainscot chair: A boxy seat, similar to the Italian Renaissance sedia, with turned vertical legs and a carved back.

William and Mary: Characterized by Dutch, Flemish, and French influences, curvilinear and ornate, a submovement of English baroque, moving in the direction of lighter profiles.

Windsor chair: A rustic seat made during the Queen Anne period and utilizing turned legs, stretchers, and vertical supports, with a continu-ous top rail.

Chapter 13: In the Colonies

Afrikaans: A Dutch-based dialect spoken in South Africa.

banister-back chair: A colonial wooden seat with a backrest formed of vertical rails.

Batavia: Historical Dutch name for Jakarta, Indonesia.

bombé: An eighteenth-century casework with a curved body (in contrast to curved externals, such as feet).

camelback sofa: A Georgian seating unit with a rounded back that resembles a camelid.

Churrigueresque: Late-Spanish baroque design, chronologically following plateresque and charac-terized by elaborate ornamentation.

colonial: Related to a colony or colonies; in the United States, of or related to the thirteen British colonies.

coloured: Mixed-race ethnic group in South Africa.

early American: Furniture from the second half of the seventeenth century, with visible joinery, simple finishes, not painted or veneered; relying on readily available woods including pine, birch, maple, and oak; growing increasingly refined over time and similar to European pieces, especially English; and later revivals.

escutcheons: A metal plate that acts as a base for hardware, such as a doorknob or drawer pull, attached to a door or drawer.

flamboyant: Literally, "flaming"; late Gothic style with elaborate tracery.

habitants: A French word for a West African mixed-race ethnic group.

Hadley chest: A colonial storage unit above a drawer or drawers; from the Hadley area of Massachusetts.

highboy: A tall chest of drawers.

humpback sofa: A Georgian seating unit with a rounded back.

kraal: South African indigenous communal enclo-sure with a stockade at the perimeter.

ladderback chair: A colonial wooden seat with a backrest formed of horizontal rails.

Lemoenhout: South African furniture made from citrus wood.

lowboy: A short chest with one or two drawers; used as a dressing table.

mestiço: Portuguese mixed-race, or Creole, ethnic group; also mestizo.

mudéjar: Spanish medieval style, of the twelfth to fifteenth centuries, incorporating Islamic motifs.

Pennsylvania Dutch: Descendants of German immigrants; from German "Deutsch."

plateresque: In Spanish, plateresco; highly orna-mented Spanish design of the sixteenth century, related to baroque.

Puritans: A persecuted religious group from England and English colonies who sought to simplify the Church of England and free it of outside influences.

Saint-Dominique: French historical name for Haiti.

scalloping: A decorative motif reminiscent of shells and featuring incised curves.

Shakers: Early nineteenth-century New England religious group that related moral piety to aesthetic simplicity.

signares: West African word of Portuguese deriva-tion for mixed-race women of the *habitant* ethnic group.

stinkwood: A material native to South Africa that emits an odor after felling.

transitional Tulbagh chair: A simplified wooden version of the Tulbagh chair.

Tulbagh chair: A caned seat unique to South Africa and based on a Queen Anne chair and a Dutch boxchair, with a vase-shaped splat and box-stretchers.

Yellowwood: A light-colored material native to South Africa.

Chapter 14: Neoclassicism

Biedermeier: Neoclassical vernacular design in Germany.

classical: Authoritative, traditional, of or relating to a form or system felt to be of first significance before modern times, specifically refers to the art and design of ancient Greece and Rome.

Directoire: A French neoclassical style, similar to Empire, related to the government of the Directory.

Directory: The representative French government that followed the revolution, 1795–99.

Empire: The French government of Napoleon, 1804–15, and the neoclassical style associated with it.

Federal: Neoclassicism in the United States.

goût grec: The initial name for the fashion for ancient Greek artifacts, prior to neoclassicism.

Hitchcock chair: Classically inspired wooden seat made by American furniture maker Lambert Hitchcock.

Jeffersonian: Neoclassical and Federal design in the United States that resembles the works of Thomas Jefferson.

laurel wreath: A crown made of aromatic, dark green, glossy leaves, from the classical period, and a popular neoclassical motif.

lyre: A classical musical instrument, a popular neoclassical motif.

Récamier: A settée, named after David's painting of Juliette Récamier.

Regency: The English neoclassical period.

Chapter 15: Victorian and Historical Revivals

borne: A 360-degree upholstered bench with a central upholstered vertical.

cast iron: A metal alloy formed in a mold.

folly: A whimsical picturesque garden pavilion.

janissary: Turkish or Turkish-inspired music.

Japonisme: The European cult of Japanese-inspired artworks.

polychromy: Something of multiple colors.

Richardsonian Romanesque: A revival style associated with Henry Hobson Richardson that was as much forward- as backward-looking.

Romanticism: A nineteenth-century literary and arts movement that emphasized emotion.

Saracenic: Islamic architecture and design; also, Turkish design.

whatnot: Victorian open shelving unit.

Chapter 16: Reform Movements

Anglo-Japanese: Furniture and decorative arts pieces by English designers inspired by Japan; related to Japonisme.

Chicago school: Referring to the late nineteenth-century architects and engineers who pioneered the skyscraper.

Hudson River school: A group of New York landscape painters associated with Romanticism.

muckrakers: Nineteenth-century journalists who investigated harmful business practices.

Prairie style: Midwestern American architecture and design movement whose leader was Frank Lloyd Wright.

Pre-Raphaelites: An art movement, related to Romanticism and Arts and Crafts, whose members sought inspiration in medieval art.

vernacular: A term, derived from linguistics, referring to indigenous or humble architecture or furniture not consciously designed.

Chapter 17: Africa

bedstead: A framework of wood or metal that supports a mattress.

bou-bou: African traditional dress.

elbow chair: The name for a European armchair in Ghana and elsewhere.

Kente cloth: African strip cloth.

sunsum: Ashanti (Ghanaian) spiritual principle of a seat's user.

Chapter 18: Japan and Japonisme

Beaux-Arts: Literally, the fine arts—painting, sculpture, and architecture; also refers to the Parisian school École des Beaux-Arts.

biombo: Baroque Mexican screens based on Japanese prototypes.

Shinto: Indigenous pre-Buddhist religion of Japan.

shogunate: A military political entity.

shoji: Partitions made of wood and paper.

sutra boxes: Small, highly decorated containers designed to hold scriptures, can have semi-precious veneer work.

tansu: Chests and cabinetry.

tatami: Modular straw mats.

tokonoma: Recessed display alcove in Japanese homes for precious objects.

ukiyo-e: Seventeenth- and eighteenth-century Japanese woodblock and other prints, and revived in the nineteenth and twentieth centuries, showing scenes of daily life.

Chapter 19: Art Nouveau

aedicule: A small single-roomed structure used as a shrine.

art nouveau: A nineteenth-century style characterized by stylized natural forms; important for decorative arts.

azulejos: Glazed tiles.

curtain wall: A modern glass façade that is hung from a building's structure and is not self-supporting.

Jugendstil: A German variant of art nouveau.

Modernisme: A Spanish variant of art nouveau.

Stile Liberty: An Italian variant of art nouveau.

Chapter 20: Protomodernism

avant-garde: Culturally progressive, vanguard.

cubism: A modern art movement that emphasized geometric forms.

Dada: A nihilistic art movement committed to form-less expression and nonrepresentational form.

De Stijl: Twentieth-century Dutch art and architecture movement influenced by cubism.

Expressionism: A modern art movement characterized by stylization, related to cubism, and committed to representing inner experience.

functionalism: A modernist design theory based on a building's or object's use.

futurism: An Italian movement inspired by technology and a Utopian urban view.

Gesamtkunstwerk: Unity of the arts—a nonhierarchical philosophy of the arts in which all arenas are equally valid and that supports collaboration across professional lines.

Kunstwollen: "Will to form," art historian Alois Riegl's concept of artistic volition.

ornament: That which adorns or embellishes; an individual part of an overall decorative scheme.

ornamention: A general scheme or larger scale system of adornment of adornment; applied ornament.

Ringstrasse: Vienna's nineteenth-century urban-renewal project.

Russian Constructivism: A post-revolutionary Russian avant-garde movement, a utilitarian and technological form of modernism.

Secessionists: A group of Viennese artists who sought to unite the arts and who were opposed to art nouveau and nineteenth-century historicism.

Wiener Werkstätte: Viennese workshops, a business-oriented confederation whose intent was to foster the business prospects of the Secessionists.

Chapter 21: Heroic Modernism

Bauhaus: The 1920s modern movement in Germany; also, a design school and a building of that school.

Deutscher Werkbund: A German association of architects and designers beholden to functionalism; a harbinger of the Bauhaus.

modernism: Twentieth-century avant-garde movements that embraced functionalism and rejected ornamental and historic styles.

pilotis: Cylindrical freestanding columns associated with modernism and Le Corbusier.

surrealism: An art movement whose inspiration lay in dreams, the subconscious, and that explored altered states of consciousness; an approach at loggerheads with abstract expressionism.

tectonics: An architectural term with multiple meanings but that refers to an honest integration between structure, construction, and material.

Chapter 22: Art Deco, Tradition Continues, and the Rise of the Decorator

Art Moderne: A term that often refers to a later phase of art deco, characterized by mechanical iconography (cars, trains, and buses).

Bakelite: Synthetic rubber.

ensemblier: A French term for one who creates as an aesthetic action.

linoleum: Hard, washable flooring material made from cork and linseed oil on a canvas backing.

modern baroque: A whimsical term for efflorescent modernist designs.

robber barons: A pejorative term for nineteenth- and twentieth-century American industrialists.

shagreen: The rough skin of a shark or dogfish, popular in the art deco period.

vellum: Translucent paper used as wallpaper in the art deco period.

Chapter 23: Other Modernisms

brises-soleil: A porous façade screen that lets in air and casts the building in shadow.

brutalism: Name taken from a French word for raw concrete, "beton brut" and related to the art movement art brut. A strain of modernism that emphasized not perfection but materiality, especially that of concrete.

International Style: A term for modernism that includes early European and American works.

minimalism: Not a defined movement, but an artistic attitude that sought spirituality in the qualities of materials and sparsely designed space.

Chapter 24: Work

batik: Indonesian resist-dyed fabric with complex, multicolored patterns.

Bürolandschaft: A free-form, open-plan workplace design characterized by organic forms, a contrast to the regimented layout of the Knoll Planning Unit.

critical regionalism: A term coined by Kenneth Frampton to indicate place-based approaches in architecture that contrast with the alleged universalism of modernism.

gilded age: Late nineteenth-century American era characterized by rapid economic growth, with a cultural emphasis on luxury and consumption, resulting in opulent historicist design.

ikat: The fabric that results from the resist-dyeing technique done to threads.

open plan: Workplace design lacking full-height walls and with spaces delineated by freestanding elements including furniture and partitions.

service economy: A sector of professional activity conducted within an office space, in contrast to manufacturing, health care, hospitality, etc.

streamline modern: A design activity from the 1930s to the 1950s, an offshoot of art deco inspired by the design of transportation.

Taylorism: Fred W. Taylor's application of scientific processes to how work is conducted resulting in increased efficiency.

Chapter 25: After Modernism

abstract expressionism: Nonrepresentational artistic movement with two subfields: action painting and color-field painting.

all-in-one-systems: A goal of multiple industrial and furniture designers to create designs that were prefabricated and that combined multiple functions such as sleeping and storage.

injection-molded plastic: A means of manufacture involving a mold or form; often used for low-volume production, testing or prototyping; it involves a material force-fed from a hopper.

fiberglass: Materials, including textiles, made from glass filaments.

polyethylene: A common type of plastic; a non-soluble polymer.

polyfoam: A rigid or semi-rigid rubbery polymer prized by designers seeking to create objects, such as seating, from a single material.

pop art: A contemporary movement in multiple arenas that constituted an affront to mainstream artistic traditions: it was considered sensational, irreverent, and drew on common inspiration, from comics to consumer products; one variant is kitsch.

PVC: A chemically resistant synthetic resin.

Scandinavian design: An approach initially associated with Denmark, Finland, Norway, and Sweden; an offshoot of modernism less beholden to functionalism, and reliant on natural materials and a sense of place.

tensegrity: An approach to design heavily reliant on complicated geometries, promoted by Buckminster Fuller, and others, often resulting in space-frame ceilings and long-span construction.

Chapter 26: Postmodernism

baptistery: A room or building for the Christian rite of baptism; often round or octagonal.

Memphis Group: Italian arts movement with no connection to the American city; related to pop art, which embraced the nonsensical, a precursor to postmodernism and including kitsch.

New Urbanism: The urban design strain of post-modernism that rejected modernism and sought to reshape town planning by relying on traditional civic planning.

New York Five: Peter Eisenman, Richard Meier, Charles Gwathmey, John Hejduk, and Michael Graves. Because of their early affinity for neutral models and the buildings that resulted from them, they were also referred to as "the Whites."

pop art: An art movement that recognized commerce and popular culture and the incorporation of found objects.

postmodernism: A rejection of modernism, and a return to historically inspired forms, of the late 1970s and 1980s; related to a philosophy in which truths are not inherent but socially constructed.

transitional: A contemporary category of interior architecture and furniture design that drew upon the characteristics of both modernism and historicism, and whose appeal was its broad adaptability.

Chapter 27: Deconstruction

algorithms: Computer-based design process or instructions for solving a task; a constituent part of parametric design.

computer-aided design (CAD): Computer-aided design or drafting; initially it replicated the process of creating drawings done by hand; increasingly it moved into other arenas, such as design, fabrication, and building information modeling (BIM). It began in the 1950s but became widespread in the 1990s.

deconstruction or deconstructivism: An architectural movement of the late 1980s and 1990s, in tandem with a method of literary interpretation; with frequent references to popular culture, technology, common materials, and revealing structure, with formal similarities to Russian Constructivism.

Masonite: An engineered hardboard created from pressed fibers; it may or may not have a surface-backing.

Monobloc: An injection-molded one-piece plastic chair; inexpensive, ubiquitous, and stackable, it has sold in the billions.

Credits

All photos courtesy of author Mark Hinchman unless otherwise indicated.

All illustrations courtesy Fairchild Books unless otherwise indicated.

9.10	Artokoloro/Alamy Stock Photo
9.14	The Cloisters Collection, 1937/The Metropolitan Museum of Art
9.15	Gift of George Blumenthal, 1941/The Metropolitan Museum of Art
10.0	Petr Svarc/Education Images/Universal Images Group via Getty Images
10.2	ZU_09/iStock.com
10.3	DNY59/iStock.com
10.5	DeAgostini/Getty Images
10.6	Universal History Archive/Getty Images
10.7	Rogers Fund, 1920/The Metropolitan Museum of Art
10.10	Gift of J. Pierpont Morgan, 1906/The Metropolitan Museum of Art
10.12	Fletcher Fund, 1959/The Metropolitan Museum of Art
11.0	Eye Ubiquitous/Universal Images Group via Getty Images
11.1	Fletcher Fund, 1959/The Metropolitan Museum of Art
11.3	Gift of Donato Esposito, 2013/The Metropolitan Museum of Art
11.5	CHICUREL Arnaud/hemis.fr/Alamy Stock Photo
11.6	Purchase, Martha Baird Rockefeller Gift, 1966/The Metropolitan Museum of Art
11.8	Purchase, Mrs. Henry Ford Gift Fund, 1958/The Metropolitan Museum of Art
11.9	Purchase, Mrs. Charles Wrightsman Gift, 1986/The Metropolitan Museum of Art
11.10	frederic REGLAIN/Alamy Stock Photo
11.11	Gift of Mr. and Mrs. Charles Wrightsman, 1979/The Metropolitan Museum of Art
11.12	Gift of Mr. and Mrs. Charles Wrightsman, 1972/The Metropolitan Museum of Art
11.13	The Jack and Belle Linsky Collection, 1982/The Metropolitan Museum of Art
11.14	Gift of Mrs. Russell Sage, 1909/The Metropolitan Museum of Art
11.15	Rogers Fund, 1918/The Metropolitan Museum of Art
12.0	Hugh Rooney/Alamy Stock Photo
12.1	Tim Graham/Getty Images
12.4	Steve Vidler/Alamy Stock Photo
12.5	The Print Collector/Getty Images
12.9	Gift of Gordon D. Meals and Jean F. Meals in memory of Moselle T. Meals 1986.207/The Cleveland Museum of Art
12.10	Gift of Yvette and Thomas Cole, in memory of Louis W. Cole, 1994/The Metropolitan Museum of Art
12.11	Gift of Mr. and Mrs. Benjamin Ginsburg, 1984/The Metropolitan Museum of Art
12.12	Purchase, Friends of European Sculpture and Decorative Arts Gifts, 2015/The Metropolitan Museum of Art
12.15	Purchase, Bequest of John L. Cadwalader, by exchange, and Peek Family Foundation Gift, 2016/The Metropolitan Museum of Art
12.16	Gift of Edwin C. Vogel, 1957/The Metropolitan Museum of Art
12.17	Friends of the American Wing Fund, 1962/The Metropolitan Museum of Art
13.0	Chris Hellier/Alamy Stock Photo
13.2	Gift of Mrs. Russell Sage, 1909/The Metropolitan Museum of Art
13.3	Purchase, Joseph Pulitzer Bequest, 1940/The Metropolitan Museum of Art
13.4	Sage Fund, 1926/The Metropolitan Museum of Art
13.6	Rogers Fund, 1917/The Metropolitan Museum of Art
13.7	Gift of Mrs. Russell Sage, 1909/The Metropolitan Museum of Art
13.8	Purchase, Gift of Mrs. Louis Guerineau Myers, in memory of her husband, by exchange, 1972/The Metropolitan Museum of Art
13.9	John Stewart Kennedy Fund, 1918/The Metropolitan Museum of Art
13.11	Gina Rodgers/Alamy Stock Photo
13.15	National Gallery of Victoria, Melbourne. Purchased through The Art Foundation of Victoria with the assistance of the Jane Williamson Bequest, 1982. This digital record has been made available on NGV Collection Online through the generous support of The Vizard Foundation
13.16	National Gallery of Victoria, Melbourne. Purchased through The Art Foundation of Victoria with the assistance of the Jane Williamson Bequest, 1982. This digital record has been made available on NGV Collection Online through the generous support of The Viza Foundation
13.19	Michael Dunning/The Image Bank/Getty Images
14.0	Reinhard Krull/EyeEm/Getty Images
14.1	Purchase, Gifts of Mr. and Mrs. William Randolph Hearst Jr., Irwin Untermyer, and John D. Rockefeller Jr., by exchange, and Bequest of John L. Cadwalader, by exchange, 1996/The Metropolitan Museum of Art
14.2	Lifestyle pictures/Alamy Stock Photo
14.3	David A. Barnes/Alamy Stock Photo
14.5	Buddy Mays/Alamy Stock Photo
14.6	Purchase, Mrs. Paul Moore Gift, by exchange, 1994/The Metropolitan Museum of Art
14.8	Gift of C. Ruxton Love Jr., 1959/The Metropolitan Museum of Art
14.9	Gift of James Robert Sands and Laurance M. Land, in memory of Margaret Queen Sands, 1970/The Metropolitan Museum of Art
14.11	Christopher Simon Sykes/Hulton Archive/Getty Images
14.14	Purchase, Friends of European Sculpture and Decorative Arts Gifts, 1996/The Metropolitan Museum of Art
15.1	Purchase, Gift of Irwin Untermyer, by exchange, 2015/The Metropolitan Museum of Art
15.2	Vuk Valcic/SOPA Images/LightRocket via Getty Images

15.4	Cooper Hewitt, Smithsonian Design Museum
15.6	Education Images/Universal Images Group via Getty Images
15.7	Bequest of Elizabeth Love Godwin, 1975/The Metropolitan Museum of Art
15.8	The Elisha Whittelsey Collection, The Elisha Whittelsey Fund, 1954/The Metropolitan Museum of Art
15.9	SSPL/Getty Images
15.11	Purchase, Friends of the American Wing Fund and Lila Acheson Wallace Gift, 1999/The Metropolitan Museum of Art
15.12	DeAgostini/Getty Images
16.0	John Hammond/Alamy Stock Photo
16.1	Theodore M. Davis Collection, Bequest of Theodore M. Davis, 1915/The Metropolitan Museum of Art
16.3	V&A Images/Alamy Stock Photo
16.4	lm_photography/Alamy Stock Photo
16.5	lm_photography/Alamy Stock Photo
16.7	VCG Wilson/Corbis via Getty Images
16.8	Gift of Crab Tree Farm Foundation/Art Institute of Chicago
16.10	RIBA Library Photographs Collection
16.12	DeAgostini/Getty Images
16.14	ewastock diningrooms/Alamy Stock Photo
17.0	Bibliothèque Sainte-Geneviève
17.1	Bibliothèque Sainte-Geneviève
17.2	Florilegius/Alamy Stock Photo
17.3	Pierre-Yves Babelon/Moment/Getty Images
17.5	History and Art Collection/Alamy Stock Photo
17.7	The Michael C. Rockefeller Memorial Collection, Gift of Nelson A. Rockefeller, 1969/The Metropolitan Museum of Art
17.10	University of Nebraska-Lincoln Libraries
17.11	Heritage Art/Heritage Images via Getty Images
17.12	Holden History/Alamy Stock Photo
17.13	Robert Lehman Collection, 1975; The Metropolitan Museum of Art
17.14	Eric Lafforgue/Art in All of Us/Corbis via Getty Images
17.19	Joerg Boethling/Alamy Stock Photo
18.0	sot/Getty Images
18.1	Werner Forman/Universal Images Group/Getty Images
18.4	David Parker/Alamy Stock Photo
18.5	Mary Griggs Burke Collection, Gift of the Mary and Jackson Burke Foundation, 2015/The Metropolitan Museum of Art
18.7	Mary Griggs Burke Collection, Gift of the Mary and Jackson Burke Foundation, 2015/The Metropolitan Museum of Art
18.8	Mary Griggs Burke Collection, Gift of the Mary and Jackson Burke Foundation, 2015/The Metropolitan Museum of Art
18.9	Klaus-Werner Friedrich/Alamy Stock Photo
18.10	V&A Images/Alamy Stock Phot
18.11	BTEU/RKMLGE/Alamy Stock Photo
18.13	V&A Images/Alamy Stock Phot
18.14	Historical Views/Alamy Stock Photo

18.15	Prisma by Dukas/Universal Images Group via Getty Images
19.0	Frank Bienewald/Alamy Stock Photo
19.1	DEA PICTURE LIBRARY/De Agostini via Getty Images
19.2	RIEGER Bertrand/hemis.fr/Alamy Stock Photo
19.3	Wenzel-Orf/ullstein bild via Getty Images
19.4	DeAgostini/Getty Images
19.6	V&A Images/Alamy Stock Photo
19.7	Michel RENAUDEAU/Gamma-Rapho via Getty Images
19.8	Daniel Thistlethwaite/Construction Photography/Avalon/Getty Images
19.12	Historical Views/Alamy Stock Photo
19.13	Willy's Pictures/ullstein bild via Getty Images
19.14	SAWASSAKORN MUTTAPRAPRUT/Alamy Stock Photo
20.0	Martin Thomas Photography/Alamy Stock Photo
20.1	Andrew Michael/Education Images/Universal Images Group via Getty Images
20.2	DeAgostini/Getty Images
20.3	Godong/Universal Images Group via Getty Images
20.4	brandstaetter images/Hulton Archive/Getty Images
20.6	DeAgostini/Getty Images
20.7	MAISANT Ludovic/hemis.fr/Alamy Stock Photo
20.8	James Leynse/Corbis via Getty Images
20.10	Sovfoto/Universal Images Group via Getty Images
20.11	Bloomberg/Getty Images
20.12	DeAgostini/Getty Images
20.13	Michael Freeman
20.14	Universal Images Group via Getty Images
20.15	Peter Horree/Alamy Stock Photo
20.16	Jim Steinfeldt/Michael Ochs Archives/Getty Images
21.0	Timo Christ/Alamy Stock Photo
21.1	JOHN MACDOUGALL/AFP via Getty Images
21.2	Alizada Studios/Alamy Stock Photo
21.3	Stillman Rogers/Alamy Stock Photo
21.7	INTERFOTO/History/Alamy Stock Photo
21.8	steeve-x-art/Alamy Stock Photo
21.9	Keystone-France/Gamma-Keystone via Getty Images
21.10	Ernst Wrba/Alamy Stock Photo
21.11	Malcolm Park/Alamy Stock Photo
21.12	Courtesy of Jason Cote
21.13	Steve Speller/Alamy Stock Photo
21.15	Peter Cavanagh/Alamy Stock Photo
21.16	B.O'Kane/Alamy Stock Photo
21.21	Caroline Morley/Alamy Stock Photo
21.22	Bettmann/Getty Images
22.0	Historical Picture Archive/CORBIS/Corbis via Getty Images
22.1	DeAgostini/Getty Images
22.2	DeAgostini/Getty Images
22.3	Grant Smith/View Pictures/Universal Images Group via Getty Images

Index